Workouts & Turnarounds II

Workouts & Turnarounds II

Global Restructuring Strategies for
the Next Century
Insights from
the Leading Authorities in the Field

Edited by Dominic DiNapoli

John Wiley & Sons, Inc.
New York • Chichester • Weinheim • Brisbane • Singapore • Toronto

Library of Congress Cataloging-in-Publication Data:
Workouts & turnarounds II : global restructuring strategies for the
  next century: insights from the leading authorities in the field /
  edited by Dominic DiNapoli.
      p.   cm.
  Includes bibliographical references and index.
  ISBN 0-471-24636-0 (cloth : alk. paper)
  1. Corporate turnarounds—Management.   2. Corporate
reorganizations.   3. Organizational change—Management.
4. Bankruptcy.   I. DiNapoli, Dominic.   II. Title: Workouts and
turnarounds 2.   III. Title: Workouts and turnarounds two.
HD58.8.W682   1999
658.4'063—dc21   99-18780

Printed in the United States of America.

10 9 8 7 6 5 4 3 2 1

Note from the Editor

The need for global restructuring expertise has never been more apparent as evidenced by the economic turmoil experienced in the vast regions from the Pacific Rim to Russia to Eastern Europe to Latin America and Africa. As we reflect on the past decade from a restructuring perspective, one thing is evident: the drive for growth and shareholder value has caused companies and their stakeholders to become globally oriented. As such, companies have embarked upon global corporate restructurings to quell stakeholder unrest and increase value. With complexity comes the need for global awareness and knowledge of the economic conditions in which these companies operate. The term "Cross-Border" may soon be replaced with "Trans-Global" as corporate boundaries dissipate. Stakeholders' demand for knowledge and understanding of the arena in which companies operate will be put to the test in the next century. As such, it is my goal to provide thought leadership on global restructurings and I am pleased to present our new edition of what I hope becomes a useful tool and source of knowledge for the restructuring community at large—*Workouts & Turnarounds II: Global Restructuring Strategies for the Next Century.*

As you explore the chapters in this book and gain insight into various restructuring and bankruptcy topics, I would like to point out that many outstanding firms and prestigious institutions contributed their collective thoughts and ideas to various chapters in this book. I would like to personally acknowledge the contributions of colleagues and senior practitioners from:

Latham & Watkins
New York University
PricewaterhouseCoopers LLP
Sitrick & Company
Skadden, Arps, Slate, Meagher & Flom LLP
Stroock & Stroock & Lavan LLP
The Chase Manhattan Bank, N.A.
Wachtell, Lipton, Rosen & Katz
Weil, Gotshal & Manges LLP
Willamette Management Associates

The partners and staff of PricewaterhouseCoopers LLP, as members of the world's leading accounting and consulting organization, have amassed considerable experience in assisting distressed and under-performing companies in the formulation and execution of corporate recovery plans both at the domestic and international levels. We have been called upon to advise on acquisitions, divestitures, liquidations, turnarounds, workouts, and buyouts in a plethora of industries spanning the globe.

I hope this book, written as a result of our collective experience, provides practical assistance to readers who tackle the problems inherent in insolvency, turnaround, or business recovery situations.

I would like to acknowledge Florence V. Lentini, a director in Pricewaterhouse-Coopers' Business Recovery Services in New York, for her assistance in coordinating and editing this book.

About the Editor

Dominic DiNapoli is the partner-in-charge of PricewaterhouseCoopers LLP's North American Business Recovery Services practice. The Business Recovery Services practice is comprised of Corporate Recovery Services, Business Regeneration Services, Lender Services, and Distressed Corporate Finance. Mr. DiNapoli has participated in a wide variety of workout and insolvency related assignments as lead partner. In addition to client engagement responsibilities in corporate reorganizations and negotiated workouts, his assignments include acting as the Special Trustee in the second largest civil forfeiture in the history of the United States; preparation and dissemination of data on financially distressed corporations and practice guides for providing professional assistance to financially troubled companies; instructional presentations to corporate and financial institutions active on creditors' committees and providing technical assistance to practice offices serving parties-in-interest in bankruptcy proceedings.

Mr. DiNapoli has provided litigation support both to debtors and creditors of financially troubled companies, specifically in the areas of fraudulent and preferential transfers. He assisted in the development and negotiation of plans of reorganization on behalf of debtors and/or creditors' committees of companies in chapter 11. Services provided included valuation and development of appropriate capital structures, creation of financial models, and assessment of key assumptions used to develop financial projections. Mr. DiNapoli has represented creditors in many of the largest chapter 11 cases ever filed, including Drexel Burnham Lambert Group, Inc., Montgomery Ward & Co., Inc., the Loewen Group, and Hechinger Investment Company of Delaware, Inc.

Mr. DiNapoli is a Certified Public Accountant, a Certified Insolvency Reorganization Accountant, and is a member of the American Institute of Certified Public Accountants, the New York and New Jersey State Societies of Certified Public Accountants, the Turnaround Management Association, and the Association of Insolvency Accountants. He is currently the Chairman of the AICPA's Bankruptcy Task Force.

About the Contributors

Mitchel R. Aeder is a tax partner at PricewaterhouseCoopers LLP, where he specializes in the federal income tax aspects of mergers and acquisitions and troubled company reorganizations. He formerly was associated with Weil, Gotshal & Manges. Mr. Aeder has represented numerous chapter 11 debtors, including Marvel Entertainment Group, Drexel Burnham Lambert, Camelot Music, Leslie Fay Companies, and Crystal Brands, as well as many other companies that have (so far) avoided bankruptcy. Mr. Aeder is a graduate of Brown University and received his JD and LLM from New York University School of Law, where he received the American Jurisprudence Award in Bankruptcy and Business Reorganizations.

Edward I. Altman is the Max L. Heine Professor of Finance at the Stern School of Business, New York University. He has an international reputation as an expert on corporate bankruptcy and credit analysis. He was named Laureate 1984 by the Hautes Etudes Commerciales Foundation in Paris for his accumulated works on corporate distress prediction models and procedures for firm financial rehabilitation and was awarded the Graham & Dodd Scroll for 1985 by the Financial Analysts Federation for his work on default rates on high-yield corporate debt. His most recent co-authored book is *Managing Credit Risk: The Next Great Financial Challenge* (John Wiley & Sons, Inc., 1998). Dr. Altman's primary areas of research include bankruptcy analysis and prediction, distressed securities, credit and lending policies, risk management in banking, corporate finance, and capital markets. He serves on the board of directors of the Franklin Mutual Series Funds and is an advisor to numerous financial institutions.

Jack Barthell is a partner in PricewaterhouseCoopers LLP's Financial Advisory Services Group, specializing in real estate capital markets transactions. He specializes in capital formation and transaction structuring from economic and financial accounting perspectives. He has developed new concepts and unique strategies to consummate real estate deals for a broad array of entrepreneur and institutional capital users and providers, including pension plans, developers, opportunity funds, offshore investors, banks, life insurance companies, real estate investment trusts, real estate operating companies, and others. Before joining PricewaterhouseCoopers LLP, Mr. Barthell had been engaged in a number of simultaneous business enterprises, these include a consulting firm, a value-added equity fund, and a real estate development and investment firm. Previously, Jack was a Managing Partner of the Kenneth Leventhal & Co.'s Los Angeles Management Advisory Services consulting practice. During his 10 years at that position, the MAS practice became the largest dedicated to real estate consulting in the United States. While at Kenneth Leventhal & Co., he established the firm's appraisal and valuation practice, the pension consulting group, and he cofounded the Pacific Rim and hospitality practice areas. Jack has been a frequent speaker at various real estate industry gatherings, has written numerous publications, and has appeared on television and radio on topical real estate matters. He has been admitted as an expert on real estate and related matters in various state and federal courts. He is a certified public accountant in California, Illinois, and New York (pending) and a member of the American Institute of Certified Public Accountants as well as respective state CPA societies. He has been a member of numerous industry groups, including the Pension Real Estate Association, N.Y.U. Real Estate Advisory Board, and Institutional Investor's Advisory Board. He received his undergraduate degree with honors from Tulane University and has an MBA from the University of Chicago.

David R. Caro is an associate at Wachtell, Lipton, Rosen & Katz, practicing in the firm's Creditors' Rights group. Mr. Caro's practice focuses on out-of-court reorganizations and restructurings, chapter 11 reorganizations, and leveraged acquisitions and recapitalizations. He has collaborated with other attorneys at Wachtell, Lipton, Rosen & Katz on a number of academic submissions and projects. He received his BA from Stanford University and his JD from New York University School of Law.

Kris Coghlan is a partner in PricewaterhouseCoopers LLP's Business Recovery practice in Chicago. He specializes in Lender Services and is dedicated to assisting lenders, investment banks, and other financing sources with new loan due diligence, collateral evaluations and monitorings, and loan workout investigations. Mr. Coghlan has also assisted the management of troubled companies in devising short- to medium-term financial and operational strategies for use in troubled debt restructurings, and implemented controls over cash expenditures, overheads, and operating costs. Mr. Coghlan has held management positions in financial planning at a $3 billion division of a *Fortune* 20 company and directed operational performance initiatives at a publicly held, high-growth specialty retail company. He is a CPA and has an MBA from the Pennsylvania State University and a BA in Economics from Bucknell University.

Daniel V. Dooley is a partner in the Financial Advisory Services group of Price-waterhouseCoopers LLP and leads its national securities litigation consulting practice. Mr. Dooley has over 24 years of experience in auditing, accounting, and litigation consulting and has served as an expert witness in a number of cases involving issues of forensic accounting, securities litigation, and financial fraud. He has consulted on numerous federal and state class action securities litigation matters and has practiced extensively in every aspect of securities litigation, including investigations, forensic accounting, as a consulting and testifying witness, and in matters before the Securities and Exchange Commission. His audit and accounting experience includes examinations of companies in a wide range of industries, including retail, manufacturing, high technology, electronics, and regulated enterprises. Mr. Dooley is a CPA licensed in Connecticut and New York. He regularly lectures on financial accounting, internal control, and corporate governance issues at, among others: the Federal Judicial Law Center, Stamford University Law School (Directors College), and St. John's University.

Chaim J. Fortgang is a partner at Wachtell, Lipton, Rosen & Katz and an Adjunct Professor of Law at New York University Law School. He is a member of the National Bankruptcy Conference and a participant in the Annual New York University School of Law Workshop on Bankruptcy. He belongs to the New York City and State Bar Associations as well as the American Bar Association Bankruptcy Committee. He is a member of the American College of Bankruptcy. Mr. Fortgang represented many institutional lenders in significant troubled debt situations, including the following: Evans Transportation Company, North American Car Corp., Intel Corporation, United States Lines, Todd Shipyards Corporation, Kaiser Aluminum & Chemical Corporation, Wang Laboratories, G. Hellerman Brewing, Colorado Ute Electric Association, Donald J. Trump, Campeau Corporation, Charter Medical, Host Marriott Corporation, Lone Star Industries, Northwest Airlines, Inc., Leslie Fay Companies, Inc., Crystal Brands, Best Products, Columbia Gas System, Hills Department Stores and R.H. Macy's, Ithaca Industries, Kmart Corporation, Morrison Knudsen Corporation, Montgomery Ward & Co., Inc., and Marvel Entertainment Group, Inc. Mr. Fortgang has represented international clients in significant cross-border transactions, including the Creditor's Committee of Maxwell Communications Corporation, a bank group in Ferruzzi Montedison Group, the Creditors' Committee of Confederation Treasury and Services Ltd., and banks in Metalgesellschaft and Von Roll. Mr. Fortgang has written many articles. He coauthored *The Proposed New Bankruptcy Act in 10 Rev, Sec Reg. 849* 1977; *The 1978 Bankruptcy Code: Some Wrong Policy Decisions in the 56 New York University Law Review 148*, 1982; and *Valuation in Bankruptcy* in 32 UCLA Law Review 1061, August 1985. He is a contributing author of *Collier Bankruptcy Practice Guide* 1981. He is a coauthor of *The Course Materials Journal*, Vol 12, No 4, February 1988; *Trading Claims and Taking Control of Corporations in Chapter 11* in 13 Cardozo Law Review 1,

October 1981; and *Developments in Trading Claims: Participations and Disputed Claims*, in 15 Cardozo Law Review 733, December 1993. He graduated from Brooklyn College in 1968, BA, summa cum laude, and in 1971 he obtained his JD cum laude from New York University School of Law. He was a member of Phi Beta Kappa, Order of the Coif, and won the University Graduation Prize for the best record over six terms.

Elliot Fuhr, a partner in the PricewaterhouseCoopers LLP Business Recovery Services practice, specializes in assisting senior management and boards of directors in the areas of financial and operational restructuring, mergers and acquisitions, divestitures, loan workouts, and business planning. He has broad industry experience, including engagements with apparel, retail, manufacturing, financial institutions, real estate, chemical, and oil and gas companies. Mr. Fuhr was a senior engineer and economist at Exxon Company, U.S.A. for six years. He then joined another "Big Five" firm and a boutique turnaround firm where he developed an expertise in restructuring troubled companies. He has had hands-on involvement in several major bankruptcy and restructuring engagements including: LTV Steel, L.F. Rothschild, Inc., L.J. Hooker, Channel Home Centers, Rickel Home Centers, and Ames Department Stores. Mr. Fuhr was involved in the highly successful sale of National Car Rental Systems on behalf of General Motors. Mr. Fuhr has published articles about troubled company restructuring including: "Diagnosing Distressed Companies: A Practical Example," *ABI Journal* (October 1994); and "Business Aspects of Chapter 11 Reorganization," Advanced Chapter 11 Bankruptcy Seminar, University of Michigan Law School (1995). Mr. Fuhr holds a Bachelors degree in Chemical Engineering from the University of Pennsylvania and an MBA in Finance from the Stern School of Business at New York University. Mr. Fuhr is a member of the Turnaround Management Association, the American Insolvency Association, and the American Bankruptcy Institute.

Seth Gardner is an associate at Wachtell, Lipton, Rosen & Katz. Mr. Gardner concentrates his practice in the areas of out-of-court reorganizations and restructurings, creditors' rights, and insolvency. He is the coauthor of written submissions on an array of bankruptcy-related topics, including debtor-in-possession financing, postpetition interest, trading claims, plan confirmation, break-up fees and lock-up agreements, valuation, prepetition automatic stay waivers, and the treatment of derivatives in insolvency proceedings. He has also been a panelist in the New York University School of Law Workshop on Bankruptcy and Reorganization. Mr. Gardner received his BA (1989), JD (1994), and MBA (1994) degrees from Duke University.

DeLain E. Gray is a partner in PricewaterhouseCoopers LLP. Mr. Gray has served as consultant, advisor, and auditor to companies in numerous industries for over 20 years. Currently, he is the leader of the firm's East Region Business Recovery Services practice and is based in Washington, DC. Mr. Gray also serves as managing partner of the firm's East Region Financial Advisory Services practice. Mr. Gray has extensive experience, representing both creditors and debtors in formal bankruptcy and out-of-court restructurings. This experience encompasses a wide variety of industries, ranging from charter aircraft operations to retail companies, healthcare, textile manufacturing, waste management, high technology, communications, and leasing/financial services concerns, among others. Activities performed in this area include analysis of cash flow projections and operating results; review and development of business plans and cash management programs; operational/strategic consulting; valuation and sale of numerous businesses; and negotiations with parties-in-interest. In addition, Mr. Gray has participated in a number of prelending due diligence reviews on behalf of parties-in-interest. Mr. Gray has also provided extensive litigation consulting services in areas such as preferential and fraudulent transfers, breach of contract, fraud/forensic accounting investigations, and business interruption.

David S. Heller is a partner in the Finance and Real Estate Department of Latham & Watkins. He has represented private and public companies in connection with the restructuring of financial obligations in and out of judicial proceedings. Mr. Heller has spoken to the Commercial Finance Association; United States Bankruptcy Judges' Conference; the Accountants, Bankers, and Credit Managers' Association; the annual PricewaterhouseCoopers Corporate Recovery Symposium; and Robert Morris Associates, as well as other industry associations on subjects ranging from workout and debt restructuring strategies to the purchase and sale of distressed debt securities and debt positions. Mr. Heller is identified in *Leading Illinois Attorneys* and is included in *A Guide to Leading US Insolvency Lawyers* (Euromoney Publication PLC). In 1997, Turnarounds & Workouts named him one of the top ten bankruptcy lawyers in the country.

Robin E. Keller has been a partner in Stroock & Stroock & Lavan LLP's insolvency department since 1988. She is admitted to practice in the state and federal courts of New York. She has expertise in both debtor and creditor representations and in recent years has played a leading role in the reorganizations of Levitz Furniture Corporation (the second largest furniture retailer in the United States), Anchor Glass Container Corporation (the third largest glass manufacturer in the United States), Tiphook Finance Corp. (a U.S. finance subsidiary of one of Europe's largest truck and trailer leasing companies), The Columbia Gas Systems, Inc. and Columbia Gas Transmission Corporation (a public utility holding company engaged in diverse energy investments including natural gas production, transmission, and distribution, and its interstate natural gas pipeline subsidiary), and A Program Planned for

Life Enrichment, Inc. (APPLE), the largest substance abuse treatment facility operator on Long Island. Ms. Keller has advised on bankruptcy and insolvency issues in two of the largest out-of-court restructurings of real estate debt, representing developers of real property throughout the country. In addition, Ms. Keller frequently represents high-yield and distressed debt investment funds in transactions, often as a troubleshooter or intervenor in complex situations in bankruptcy court or in out-of court negotiations. Articles by Ms. Keller on bankruptcy topics have appeared in the *New York Law Journal*; in *International Legal Strategy*, a Japanese legal publication; and in trade publications such as *Bankruptcy Court Decisions*. Ms. Keller has been nominated by her peers for inclusion in Euromoney Legal Publications Group's *Guide to the World's Leading Insolvency and Restructuring Lawyers* for 1999. Ms. Keller is a graduate of Harvard University (BA, cum laude, 1975) and Boston University School of Law (JD, 1978). She completed Federal District Court and United States Bankruptcy Court clerkships before joining Stroock in 1980.

Harvey R. Kelly is a partner in the Financial Advisory Services practice of PricewaterhouseCoopers LLP. Mr. Kelly has provided litigation consulting services in connection with numerous bankruptcy and other court proceedings. As a CPA and a forensic accountant, he has extensive experience in such matters as fraud investigations, solvency analysis, and fraudulent conveyance disputes. Mr. Kelly has served as a court-appointed examiner in bankruptcy proceedings. He has lectured extensively on the subjects of bankruptcy and litigation, including as a member of the faculty of the Federal Judicial Center. Mr. Kelly was a member of the American Bankruptcy Institute's Task Force on Preferences.

Lewis Kruger is co-head of the Insolvency Department of Stroock & Stroock & Lavan LLP and a member of the Executive Committee. He has over 30 years of experience as an insolvency lawyer. Mr. Kruger has played a major role in many of the significant reorganization proceedings in the United States. He had been lead counsel representing banks such as the Chase Manhattan Bank, National Westminster Bank, and Deutsche Bank; and financial institutions including Bear Stearns and Salomon Brothers. Mr. Kruger has represented debtors and creditors' committees in cases including: Leslie Fay, The Icing, Zale Corporation, Southmark Corporation, McCall Pattern Company, Columbia Gas Systems, NuCorp Energy, Victor Technologies, Tosco, Penn-Dixie Steel, Phoenix Steel, Neisner Brothers, Hillsborough Holdings, Western Union, Forstmann, Edgecomb, Charter Medical, Cabot Cabot & Forbes, Daniel M. Galbreath, Harvest Foods, Phar-Mor, Anchor Glass Container Corporation, Tiphook Finance Corporation, and Pinnacle Brands. Mr. Kruger taught corporate reorganization at Columbia Law School from 1972 to 1988, and is a frequent lecturer for the Practicing Law Institute, Bar Association on

Bankruptcy in the United States and overseas, and is a Fellow of the American College of Bankruptcy. Mr. Kruger has acted as special counsel to the U.S. Senate Committee on the Judiciary with respect to reorganizations, and as special counsel to the governor of New York and the Urban Development Corporation. Mr. Kruger's publications include *Bankruptcy: Practice and Procedure* in 1972 and annually thereafter, *Creditor Representation in Bankruptcy and Insolvency Proceedings*; *Current Developments in Bankruptcy, Reorganization & Arrangement Proceedings*, 1972–Present; *Bankruptcy Reform Act of 1978*; *Business Reorganization and Rehabilitation: The New Chapter 11*; and many other monographs for newspapers and journals. Mr. Kruger has been nominated by his peers for inclusion in Euromoney Legal Publications Group's *Guide to the World's Leading Insolvency and Restructuring Lawyers* and in *The Best Lawyers in America*. Mr. Kruger earned his LLB with honors from Columbia Law School in 1959 and his AB with honors from Harvard University in 1956.

David S. Kurtz is a partner at Skadden, Arps, Slate, Meagher & Flom LLP (Illinois) in Corporate Restructuring. Mr. Kurtz concentrates his practice in the areas of bankruptcy, insolvency, and creditors' rights, with particular experience representing debtors, institutional lenders, and creditors' committees in chapter 11 and out-of-court reorganizations and restructurings. His experience also includes representation of secured lenders in acquisitions, refinancings, and other leveraged transactions. Mr. Kurtz' major bankruptcy representations as lead counsel include the debtor in *Montgomery Ward & Co., Inc., Morrison Knudsen Corporation, Trans World Airlines, Inc., Physician's Clinical Laboratories, Inc., Fretter, Inc.*, and *Gantos, Inc.*; the Zell Disney Group, a prospective purchaser in the Rockefeller Center bankruptcy; the bank group in *Levitz Furniture, Inc.*; the bank group in *Venture Stores, Inc.*; the *Grant Geophysical, Inc.* plan sponsor; and the creditors' committees of *Commercial Financial Services, Inc., Mercury Finance Corporation, Edison Brothers Stores, Inc., MobileMedia Communications, Inc., Stratosphere Corporation*, and *First Executive Corporation*. He also has represented numerous debtors and financial institutions on a variety of out-of-court restructurings. Mr. Kurtz received his BA from Case Western Reserve University.

Patrick R. Leardo is chairman of PricewaterhouseCoopers LLP's Real Estate Advisory Services group, which develops real estate strategies and performs evaluation of acquisitions and development activity, real estate appraisals and valuation, portfolio analyses, strategic planning, market studies, financing support, construction project control services, and corporate real estate asset monitoring. Mr. Leardo has led PricewaterhouseCoopers LLP's practice in the workout and restructuring of real estate assets valued in excess of $3 billion. In addition, the Practice has provided due diligence and related services for over $2 billion in real estate securitizations. He has served PricewaterhouseCoopers

LLP clients in a number of reorganization and appraisal consulting engagements which included Olympia & York, Shimizu, Marine Midland Bank, and VMS Public Mortgage Funds, among other restructuring assignments. Prior to joining PricewaterhouseCoopers LLP, Mr. Leardo was chief operating officer for a major real estate development and syndication firm in the Northeast where he was involved in all areas of real estate financing and development. Mr. Leardo has a BS in Civil Engineering from the University of South Carolina, and is a member of the New Jersey Supreme Court District Fee Arbitration Committee. He is a frequent lecturer and authority on real estate bankruptcy and restructuring methods.

Jeffrey W. Linstrom is a Counsel at Skadden, Arps, Slate, Meagher & Flom LLP (Illinois) in Corporate Restructuring. Mr. Linstrom's experience involves representing creditors' committees, debtors, and secured creditors in major chapter 11 cases, representing borrowers and lenders in secured and commercial loan transactions, and representing buyers and sellers of financially troubled companies. Mr. Linstrom received his AB from Miami University (Ohio) in 1984 and his JD from the Ohio State University College of Law in 1987.

Harvey R. Miller is a senior partner in the New York City–based international law firm of Weil, Gotshal & Manges LLP. He is also an Adjunct Professor of Law at New York University Law School. He is a member on the Board of Visitors at Columbia University School of Law, a member of the National Bankruptcy Conference, a Fellow at the American College of Bankruptcy, and a Fellow of the American Bar Foundation. Mr. Miller and his firm have been involved in almost every major bankruptcy reorganization case since the enactment of the Bankruptcy Reform Act of 1978. He has represented debtors, institutional creditors, creditors' committees, and court-appointed fiduciaries. Mr. Miller is and has been active in debt restructurings and chapter 11 cases, including: *Texaco Inc., Bruno's, Inc., Marvel Entertainment Group, Inc., Montgomery Ward & Company, R.H. Macy Co., Inc., Federated Department Stores, Inc., Eastern Airlines, Inc., Continental Airlines Corporation, Pan Am Airways International, Inc., Jamesway Corporation, Edison Brothers Stores, Inc., Best Products Co., Inc., Donald J. Trump, Global Marine, Inc., Storage Corporation, ITEL Corporation, Leslie Fay Companies, Inc., Weiner's, Inc., W. T. Grant, Inc.,* and *Western Company of North America*. Mr. Miller has authored many books and articles and served as a contributing author for *Collier on Bankruptcy*, 15th edition. A frequent lecturer for the American Law Institute/American Bar Association and many other law associations, Mr. Miller was admitted to the bar in 1959 after receiving his AB from Brooklyn College and LLB from Columbia University.

Thomas J. Millon, Jr., is a principal of Willamette Management Associates and director of the McLean, Virginia office. Mr. Millon has substantial experience in the appraisal of business entities and business interests, in the appraisal of fractional business interests, and in the valuation and remaining life analysis of intangible assets. Mr. Millon has performed numerous valuation engagements including those for employee stock ownership plan feasibility and compliance appraisals, security structuring and valuation analyses, merger and acquisition appraisals, post-acquisition purchase price allocation appraisals, business and stock valuations, and litigation support appraisals. He has performed valuation and remaining useful life analyses on many types of intangible assets as well as performing pre- and post-acquisition business and asset appraisals. Mr. Millon is an accredited senior appraiser of the American Society of Appraisers, certified in business valuation. He is also a chartered financial analyst of the Association for Investment Management and Research.

Joel Nitzberg is a partner in the Business Recovery Services practice of PricewaterhouseCoopers LLP. He has 25 years of both public accounting and private industry experience. Mr. Nitzberg has held positions as chief financial officer/treasurer and director of internal audit as well as many interim operating positions on behalf of client companies. During his tenure with PricewaterhouseCoopers, Mr. Nitzberg has assisted companies experiencing financial and operational changes. He specializes in advising companies in all aspects of financial restructurings, cash flow management, and enhancement programs as well as providing interim management services. Mr. Nitzberg is a frequent speaker at seminars and conferences, speaking on a variety of topics involving internal auditing, forensic auditing, and bankruptcy and restructuring issues. Mr. Nitzberg is a Certified Public Accountant, Certified Fraud Examiner, and Certified Internal Auditor. He served as a Regent for the National Association of Certified Fraud Examiners and is a member of The New York State Society of Certified Public Accountants and its Insolvency and Bankruptcy Committee. He has a BS in accounting from the State University of New York, Albany and an MBA in Finance and Management from Fairleigh Dickinson University.

R. Carter Pate is a partner and leader of PricewaterhouseCoopers LLP's Business Regeneration Services. He has acquired extensive experience in operational and financial restructuring in the industries of real estate, retailing, health care, financial services, manufacturing, and service industries. Past clients include Kmart, South African Breweries, DIMON International, Ben Franklin Stores, Braun's Fashions, Fitz & Floyd, HomePlace, Crown Books, and NeoStar Retail Group (Babbages, Software, Etc., and Super Software, Inc.). Mr. Pate served as Advisor, Trustee, CEO, CFO, and Examiner of the Nelson Bunker Hunt bankruptcy ($1.7 billion) and has been featured in articles in the *Wall Street Journal, Forbes, Newsweek, Dallas Morning News, Dallas Business Journal,* and *D Magazine*. He is a National Director of the Turnaround Management Association, a certified turnaround professional, and a certified insolvency reorganization accountant.

Robert S. Paul is a partner and leader of PricewaterhouseCoopers LLP's Lender Services practice. He has worked nationally on behalf of numerous secured lenders in connection with new and troubled loans; debtors, regarding financial and operational turnarounds and refinancings; and as an advisor to unsecured creditors' committees. He has also served as an examiner and has provided testimony on numerous occasions. Mr. Paul is a former special agent with the Federal Bureau of Investigation and was Chief Accountant–Enforcement for the Chicago Regional Office of the United States Securities and Exchange Commission. He has taught in the Commercial Finance Association Wharton School of Finance program and is a member of the CFA's Education Foundation Governing Board. Mr. Paul has authored or coauthored various articles in the Secured Lender NY, NY including "Tax Loss Carryovers: A Lender Perspective," "Troubled Debt Restructuring," "Tax Reform and Inventory—What the Lender Should Know," and "Lenders' Due Diligence— More Than Just Kicking the Tires." He is a CPA and a certified insolvency and reorganization accountant.

Timothy R. Pohl is an associate at Skadden, Arps, Slate, Meagher & Flom LLP (Illinois) in Corporate Restructuring. Mr. Pohl concentrates his practice in the areas of bankruptcy, insolvency, and creditors' rights, with particular experience representing debtors, creditors' committees, institutional lenders, and purchasers in chapter 11 and out-of-court reorganizations and restructurings. Mr. Pohl received his BA from Amherst College in 1988 and his JD from the University of Chicago in 1991.

Shannon P. Pratt is a managing director and founder of Willamette Management Associates, one of the oldest and largest independent valuation consulting, economic analysis, and financial advisory service firms in the country. He is also an outside director of Paulson Capital Corp., an investment banking firm. Over the last 30 years, he has performed valuation engagements for mergers and acquisitions, employee stock ownership plans, fairness opinions, gift and estate taxes, incentive stock options, buy–sell agreements, corporate and partnership dissolutions, dissenting stockholder actions, damages, marital dissolutions, and many other business valuation purposes. He has testified in a wide variety of federal and state courts across the country and frequently participates in arbitration and mediation proceedings. Dr. Pratt received his doctorate in business administration from Indiana University and is a chartered financial analyst, a Fellow of the American Society of Appraisers, past chairman and a life member of the ESOP Association Valuation Advisory Committee, and a life member of the Institute of Business Appraisers. He currently serves as a trustee of the Appraisal Foundation. Dr. Pratt is coauthor of *Valu-*

ing a Business: The Analysis and Appraisal of Closely Held Companies 1996, 3rd edition, *Valuing Small Businesses and Professional Practices* 1998, 3rd edition (McGraw-Hill. Inc.) and *Guide to Business Valuations* 1998, 8th edition (Practitioners Publishing Company). He is also editor-in-chief of *Shannon Pratt's Business Valuation Update*, a monthly newsletter on business valuation, and *Pratt's Stats*, a database of privately held business sale transactions. He is a member of the editorial advisory board and a columnist for *Valuation Strategies*, a bimonthly journal. Dr. Pratt is a course developer and teacher of business valuation courses for the American Society of Appraisers and the American Institute of Certified Public Accountants and a frequent speaker on business valuation at national legal, professional, and trade association meetings.

Kevin Regan is a director in the Business Recovery Services practice at PricewaterhouseCoopers LLP, specializing in the retailing and consumer goods sector. He has worked on such cases as *Montgomery Ward*, *Levitz Furniture*, and *Caldor*. Prior to joining PricewaterhouseCoopers LLP, he was the chief financial officer of such retailers as Jamesway, Seattle Standard, Pay 'n Save, and Linen 'n Things, and was a cofounder of a retail startup in the home medical equipment sector. Mr. Regan graduated from Fairfield University (BA, 1972), New York University (MBA, 1974), and Seton Hall University (JD, 1978).

M. Freddie Reiss is a partner and leader of the Corporate Recovery practice at PricewaterhouseCoopers LLP. He has acquired extensive experience in workouts, turnarounds, and bankruptcy matters in the industries of real estate, retailing, health care, financial services, manufacturing, and service industry, representing debtors, creditors, or equity interests. Mr. Reiss has worked on many complex bankruptcies and restructurings, including America West, American Continental/Lincoln Savings, Circle K, Executive Life, and EuroDisney. Among other assignments, he is currently representing creditors of the Orange County Investment Pool, House of Fabrics, and Baldwin Company, and is acting as assignee in the WestFed Holdings case with the U.S. government and is also crisis manager for various out-of-court restructurings. Mr. Reiss is a Certified Public Accountant, certified insolvency and reorganization accountant, and has a BBA from City University in New York. He was a board member with the Association of Insolvency Accountants, Turnaround Management Association, the Los Angeles Bankruptcy Forum, and was recently inducted as a Fellow of the American College of Bankruptcy. He is currently a board member of the American Bankruptcy Institute. Among numerous articles published, Mr. Reiss coauthored Chapter 1: "Identifying a Troubled Company" in *Workouts and Turnarounds: The Handbook of Restructuring and Investing in Distressed Companies* (Homewood, Illinois: Business One Irwin) in January 1991. Mr. Reiss also coauthored Chapter 34 of *Accountant's Handbook*, entitled "Forensic Accounting and Litigation Consulting Services" in November 1990.

William C. Repko is a managing director in Chase's Global Investment Bank with responsibility for the restructuring and refinance group. Mr. Repko joined the bank in 1973. During the early 1980s, he was responsible for managing the bank's restructurings for International Harvester, Allis-Chalmers, The Charter Company, A.H. Robins, and Zapata Corporation, among others. In 1988, Mr. Repko was appointed to head the bank's Corporate Finance Group in the Emerging Markets, where he was responsible for the conversion of sovereign debt to equity in private sector corporations. In 1992, Mr. Repko assumed his current responsibilities and has led the refinancing efforts for Chrysler, International Business Machines Corporation, Case Corporation, General Motors, Kmart, and Evergreen International Aviation. He has also led the DIP financings for Barney's New York, Bradlees Stores, Inc., The Caldor Corporation, Flagstar (now Advantica Restaurant Group), Mobilemedia Corp., Marvel Entertainment, and Bruno's, Inc. In 1998, Mr. Repko assumed responsibility for Chase's restructuring advisory business in Asia. The group acts as financial advisor to restructuring debtors throughout the Pacific Rim. Mr. Repko earned a BS (Finance) degree from Lehigh University.

Mitch M. Roschelle is a partner in PricewaterhouseCoopers LLP's Real Estate Advisory Services practice. Mitch has more than 15 years of experience in the areas of real estate acquisition, development, and disposition. He is regularly called on to develop solutions in complex real estate restructurings. In recent years, Mitch has dedicated much of his efforts in the securitization of real estate assets and performing due diligence reviews of real estate portfolios on behalf of investors, lenders, and asset managers. The reviews have transcended all property types and domestic markets. Mitch is responsible for leading the firm's efforts in the analysis of sophisticated real estate transactions and capital markets activities for a diverse set of institutional clients.

Robert J. Rosenberg is a member of the law firm of Latham & Watkins, resident in its New York office. He was an Adjunct Professor at New York University School of Law, where he taught Bankruptcy Reorganization and Business Planning. Mr. Rosenberg was also formerly an Adjunct Professor at Rutgers Law School, and an Assistant Professor at Ohio State University School of Law. He served as official American Bar Association Advisor to the National Conference of Commissioners on Uniform State Laws in its project to draft the new Uniform Fraudulent Transfer Act. He is a fellow of the American College of Bankruptcy, has been an Associate Conferee of the National Bankruptcy Conference, a member of the ABA Committee on Business Bankruptcy, and served on the New York City Bar Association Committee on Bankruptcy and Reorganization from 1976 to 1978. A prolific author, Mr. Rosenberg's articles and books include *Intercorporate Guarantees and the Law of Fraudulent Conveyances*; *Lender Beware*, 125 University of Pennsylvania Law Review 235 (1976), and *The Fraudulent Conveyance and Preference Implications of Leveraged Business Acquisitions* (Practicing Law Institute, 1979). He is also a coauthor of Matthew Bender's *Collier Forms Manual* (2nd edition) and *Collier Bankruptcy Practice Guide* and has chaired several Practicing Law Institute Seminars on aspects of bankruptcy law. In addition, he is the author of the single-volume treatise *Collier Lending Institutions and the Bankruptcy Code*. Mr. Rosenberg has served as counsel to the creditors' committees in the *Continental Airlines, Mcorp, First RepublicBank*, and *Harvard Industries* chapter 11 cases, to *Harrah's Entertainment, Inc.*, in the chapter 11 case of Harrah's Jazz Company, and to Musicland in its out-of-court restructuring. He is presently counsel to Cityscape Corp. in its chapter 11 case.

Sudhin N. Roy has worked in numerous restructurings and bankruptcies within the United States, focusing primarily in assisting distressed companies sell assets and raise capital. Over the course of the last year, he has spent a significant amount of time in Southeast Asia, where PricewaterhouseCoopers LLP is involved in serving as financial advisor to a number of major companies in Thailand and Indonesia. Mr. Roy is currently a partner within the Financial Advisory Services group of PricewaterhouseCoopers LLP based in Chicago, and is personally involved in a number of international and domestic restructuring plans. Mr. Roy's major assignments include Reliance Acceptance Group, Fruehauf Trailer Corporation, First Merchants Acceptance Corp., Trans World Airlines, Jamesway Corporation, Ganton Technologies, Inc., ABS Industries, Monon Trailer Corporation, Fretter, Inc., Premier Cruises Limited, and the Oren Benton Estate.

Jeffrey A. Sell is a senior credit executive of Chase Manhattan Bank with responsibility for managing the Special Loan Group. Mr. Sell joined Chase in 1967 and was named a senior vice president in 1985. Prior to assuming responsibility for managing Chase's loan workout group in 1981, Mr. Sell held various marketing assignments in the Mining and Project Finance Divisions. In addition to loan workout, Mr. Sell has had responsibility for several other credit functions including those relating to equity investment and merchant banking. He assumed his current responsibilities coincident with the merger with Chemical Bank in 1996. Mr. Sell holds a BA degree in biology from Gettysburg College and an MBA degree in finance from New York University.

Michael S. Sitrick is chairman and chief executive officer of Sitrick & Company, a public relations firm specializing in corporate, financial, transactional, and crisis communications. A nationally recognized expert in the strategic use of communications, Mr. Sitrick has been the subject of numerous articles and profiles focusing on the results he has achieved for clients. Since founding Sitrick

& Company, he has provided advice and counsel to more than 500 companies, including some of the nation's largest corporations and highest profile individuals—on both routine and extremely sensitive matters. Under his direction, Sitrick & Company grew to the fifteenth largest independent firm in the nation in its first year of business and broke into the top 10 in its second year. Prior to forming the firm, Mr. Sitrick served for seven years as Senior Vice President, Communications, for Wickes Companies, Inc. As one of seven members of the Senior Management group, Mr. Sitrick was the architect of Wickes' chapter 11 communications programs. He also directed the company's communications efforts through a series of takeover attempts and defenses, litigation issues, a major product liability problem, and numerous other critical matters. Mr. Sitrick holds BS degrees in Business Administration and Journalism from the University of Maryland, College Park. He is the author of *Spin*, published in 1998 by Regency Publishing Co.

Deborah M. Smith is a partner responsible for PricewaterhouseCoopers' Business Recovery Services practice in the New York Region and in Latin America. Ms. Smith's 17 years of experience include corporate recovery services, trustee operations, fraud investigations, forensic accounting, internal control, and auditing and litigation consulting engagements for debtors, creditors, financial institutions, foreign, federal, and local governments, healthcare services, real estate concerns, manufacturers, oil and gas corporations, and not-for-profit organizations. Ms. Smith has represented the bank groups in some of the larger restructurings in Latin America, such as Buenos Aires Embotelladora S.A., Corimon S.A.C.A., and Compania Anomina Nacional Telefonos de Venezuela. She is a Certified Public Accountant and a member of the AICPA, International Women's Insolvency & Restructuring Confederation (New York Chapter, founding officer and treasurer), Turnaround Management Association, and the Association of Insolvency Accountants. Ms. Smith recently served on a panel for the National Conference of Bankruptcy Judges addressing valuation in bankruptcy and on a panel speaking on cross-border insolvencies for the NYU Law School alumni. She has a Bachelor of Science degree in accounting from the University of New Orleans.

David R. Williams has considerable consulting experience with numerous corporations, primarily in the retail, financial services, real estate, and distribution industries. Specifically, his background includes advising boards of directors regarding asset sales, securitization of receivables, restructuring of liabilities, raising new secured financing, and negotiating with creditors. Within PricewaterhouseCoopers LLP, he currently maintains responsibilities for the U.S. Financial Advisory Services–Distressed Corporate Finance group in addition to his role as the Global Financial Services Leader. Some of the more recent assignments that Mr. Williams has led include: Bankers Trust Company, Dow Corning Corporation, Fretter, Inc., Fruehauf Trailer Corporation,

Oren Benton Estate, Reliance Acceptance Corporation, US West Communications, Western Pacific Airlines, and Westmoreland Coal Company. Mr. Williams is a trustee and director of the Center for the New West, member of the AICPA, NACVA, Arizona Society of CPAs, Association of Insolvency Accountants, and the American Bankruptcy Institute. Additionally, he coauthored the original version of *Workouts and Turnarounds, the Handbook of Restructuring and Investing in Distressed Companies*, published in 1990.

Contents

Preface

In today's bull market economy, which has seen one of the strongest stock market upturns in history, corporate restructuring and workouts continue to be common occurrences, not only among U.S. corporations, but also in companies throughout the world. With increased investment in emerging markets, increasing pressures to maximize shareholder value, the instability of certain industries and economies, U.S. corporations are calling on today's restructuring and workout professionals for assistance.

According to the Administrative Office of the United States Courts, in Washington, D.C., and *The 1999 Bankruptcy Yearbook and Almanac*, even though the number of bankruptcy filings (for all companies) decreased by 18% in 1998 from the previous year, the number of public companies filing for bankruptcy in 1998 increased by 46% from the previous year and by 71% from the lowest point in this decade, which occurred in 1994. Furthermore, in 1998, the total value of assets of public companies in bankruptcy was approximately $29 billion, representing a 68% increase from the previous year and a 247% increase from the decade low experienced in 1994.

According to Securities Data Company, one potential precursor to corporate bankruptcy filings is high-yield debt issuance (public, non–investment grade, nonconvertible debt issues). If we track high-yield bond issuances over the past decade, the total through 1998 of $568.6 billion is greater than the amount issued during the 1980s ($168.5 billion) by 237%, and the trend is up! In 1998, $156.8 billion was brought to market, an increase of 24% over 1997.

All this points to heightened activity in both U.S. and global restructuring in the next century. As such, I am very pleased to present *Workouts & Turnarounds II: Global Restructuring Strategies for the Next Century—Insights from The Leading Authorities in the Field.*

In editing this book, I have assembled experts in the field of workouts and turnarounds, corporate restructuring, and bankruptcy consulting. This group of experts provides an insightful overview of the restructuring process covering both out-of-court and in-court options.

You will gain insights about key issues involving workouts and turnarounds, including:

- How to identify and decide the appropriate forum to deal with a troubled company
- Techniques in managing distressed situations—the perspective from the company and the creditors
- The legal and practical considerations of international restructuring
- Ways to protect your assets
- Ways to evaluate investing and trading in troubled securities

The first five chapters deal with the *patterns* of a troubled company and the *process* of getting it back to health—how to identify a troubled company and determine the likelihood of a turnaround. What are the key reasons for failure? Have negative trends been accumulating? What should management focus on early before it is too late? Should a crisis manager be brought in to facilitate the turnaround or is current management up to the task? If a company considers filing, chapter 3, Preparing for Bankruptcy, addresses a key variable in the equation—the war chest. Bankruptcy costs money. Does the company have enough cash to get it through a potentially long and arduous bankruptcy? When should management start building the war chest? Why is it important and how big should it be? Filing for bankruptcy takes careful planning and consideration. Chapter 5 addresses the art of managing both internal and external communication—a key component of guaranteeing a successful workout.

Chapter 6 deals with the key role of the lawyer in representing the distressed company. Chapter 7 discusses the advantages of being a secured creditor—at the front of the line and at the head of the pack. The role of the lawyer in representing the unsecured creditor is explored in Chapter 8.

Chapters 9 and 10 deal with both the pitfalls and opportunities for lenders in dealing with distressed companies. Chapter 11 discusses the concepts and methods involved in the valuation of companies within workout and turnaround situations. Chapter 12 focuses on the performance of distressed and defaulted debt securities. Learn about this volatile, yet growing market.

Chapters 13 and 14 provide an international overview in dealing with cross-border situations. How does international restructuring differ? What obstacles do creditors have to overcome? Chapters 15 and 16 address the role of accountants and employee-related issues in the bankruptcy or restructuring situation. These are the facilitators of the turnaround process. Learn what you should expect and why they are essential to a successful workout or bankruptcy.

Chapter 17 investigates the financial aspects of a multitude of financial disputes that may arise in a bankruptcy proceeding. Chapter 18 deals with the tax considerations for out-of-court or bankruptcy reorganizations.

Chapters 19 and 20 provide an overview of two key industries, retail and real estate.

The book concludes with Chapter 21, which focuses on merger and acquisition strategies for distressed companies. The chapter starts by considering short-term financing options for the distressed company and then leads into the longer term merger and acquisition possibilities available.

I believe that this book provides an excellent reference for professionals, including business people, lawyers, accountants, investors, bankers, and other professionals involved in the business world today. It is a compilation of expertise from the leading authorities in the field of workouts and turnarounds.

1

Trouble Spotting: Assessing the Likelihood of a Turnaround

Dominic DiNapoli and Elliot Fuhr

PricewaterhouseCoopers LLP

INTRODUCTION

Can It Be Fixed?

If this is your starting point, then you have probably waited too long. By this point in time, you have already heard from your vendors, shareholders, customers, and employees that the business has a problem. Collectively, these stakeholders are sorting through the wreckage seeking answers to questions ranging from "What's in it for me? to "What are my alternatives?" to "How did this happen and when do I get my money?" Behind these questions is each stakeholder's desire to assess:

- The fundamental causes of the company's distress
- Action steps required to affect a "turnaround"
- Management's ability and related costs to execute a turnaround plan
- Alternatives to a turnaround and the related costs
- Goals of the various stakeholders
- The value that can be realized from a turnaround, a sale or liquidation of the business

In the final analysis, value is the only thing that matters to stakeholders, as well as, of course, some timely cash or potential for capital appreciation. Value means different things to different stakeholders and may include cash repayment and new collateral for lenders and creditors; preservation of jobs and benefits for employees; or, alternatively, the avoidance of the opportunity cost of staying "in the game" for all stakeholders. Regardless of the form of value, each stakeholder must have access to the necessary information to make an informed decision on the appropriate course of action.

1

The Turnaround

For purposes of this chapter, we will define *turnaround* as follows:

> An all-encompassing plan that maximizes an underperforming company's value for the benefit of its stakeholders through a four-step process of stabilization, analysis, repositioning, and strengthening.

Rather than focus on the death spiral leading to a bankruptcy, our view of turnarounds begins much earlier in the business life cycle. It is the ability to detect and spot the signs of trouble early in the cycle that leads to a more rapid and successful turnaround. The business demise curve is graphically illustrated in Exhibit 1.1. In a later chapter, we will explore the early warning signs leading to trouble.

While there are several definitions and attributes one could ascribe to the concept of turnaround and underperformance, this chapter will focus on value as the key element of a turnaround. In almost any turnaround, whether in the context of a bankruptcy case or an out-of-court workout, the value of the company is what all stakeholders and investors wrestle with.

Today's real-time information, supplied to us by the Internet and 24-hour news channels, provide the astute stakeholder with an extraordinary amount of information to digest. Notwithstanding today's technical advantages over yesteryear, our savvy stakeholder must still assess the likelihood of a turnaround in down market conditions, in industries as complex as high technology, to assessing the ramifications of a global economic meltdown on his or her stake.

We will address assessing the likelihood of a turnaround in a high-technology

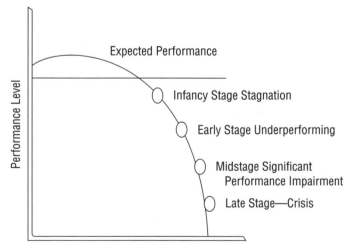

Exhibit 1.1   The Business Demise Curve

company later in this chapter. We will also consider the question of whether the company can be "saved" and what that means, including:

- An analytical approach to shareholder value or destruction
- Fixing the business with tools, a crisis manager, and hard work
- Managing expectations, including assessing what can be done and making it happen

For now, however, we will explore some fundamental concepts in assessing a turnaround.

FUNDAMENTAL CAUSES OF UNDERPERFORMANCE

Did You Hear the One About . . .

The performance excuses of companies in trouble have been repeated too many times to remember, but they usually go something like this:

- "Although our results are disappointing, we are very excited about the new product line that we plan to bring to market."
- "We will have improved results next quarter."
- "Bankruptcy is just a hiccup; we have a fresh start, our future is bright."

If you have visited the insolvency abyss, these statements and their permutations probably sound all too familiar but provide little in the way of useful reference points for future business decisions by the lender or investor.

Why Do Businesses Fail?

Although the onset of a crisis may come as a surprise, the underlying situation has frequently affected the company for a long period of time. Indeed, a well-designed set of metrics focused on important drivers of value could save many businesses.

Management is often unable to discern whether it has a firm grasp on the link between the company's macro goals and the micro shareholder value drivers on a day-to-day basis. Although generic value drivers lack specificity and cannot be used effectively at the grassroots level, a well-designed program to implement drivers can help steer the business.

Poor management information systems typically receive the blame for the inability of management to "see it coming." In reality, most companies do not understand the value drivers that create shareholder value, which we will discuss further shortly.

Another crisis in the making is the product of today's volatile merger and acquisition (M&A) environment and the inappropriate expansions embarked on in search of the fabled synergies. We have all heard the "1 + 1 = 3" boardroom banter as the mantra for acquisitions. With the recent strength of the economies in the United States and continental Europe, chief executive officers (CEOs) may decide to pursue expansion strategies that involve acquisitions at high multiples. Although a deal might look good on paper, postmerger integration of the new acquisition can sometimes fail to go forward with the projected ease of execution, creating enormous problems for management. Such issues may not only place serious demands on senior management time, but there is the good possibility that they will involve additional costs, including debt that could expose the new company to shifts in business climate or interest rates. This does not bode well, since overaggressive financing at the end of a business cycle accounts for many company failures.

On another front, the global impact from the demise of once-thriving emerging markets in Korea, Thailand, and Indonesia is having a significant impact on U.S. companies. Once profitable joint-venture opportunities for U.S. companies may lead to underperforming investments, loss of production, and, in some instances, financial peril. This phenomenon has most notably affected semiconductor companies that rely on the Asian marketplace for its low-cost manufacturing base. We will explore the impact of these events as it affects the likelihood of a turnaround in the high-technology sector.

As Exhibit 1.2[1] indicates, the linkage of growth in highly leveraged transactions and the proportion on bankruptcy assets is quite strong, albeit time lagged. That is, as highly leveraged deals increase as a form of financing for companies, the natural growth in bankruptcies based on historic default rates is fairly evident. In particular, a 24- to 36-month lag from the time of issuance of the highly leveraged debt appears to boost the amount of corporate bankruptcies. Moreover, based on current indications, the amount of highly leveraged transactions appears to be approaching record levels that may in time lead to significant increases in assets experiencing bankruptcy.

There is a recurring pattern in business cycles that somehow manages to lure even the most sophisticated business people time and again.

- As the cycle progresses, money chases deals ever more aggressively. Yes, participants comment on the excessive prices being paid for businesses, and, yes, lenders note that interest rate spreads have vanished.
- By the time the cycle nears its peak, industry/strategic buyers are often outbid by financial buyers, who focus on supposed growth prospects and efficiency gains to justify prices that would exceed the most extravagant synergy gains that an industry player could expect from a merger.
- Cash flows tighten as the business cycle turns down, or markets simply fail to deliver forecasted growth.
- Business decisions become less than optimal as investment in operating plant or new product development is curtailed, and the underlying value of the company is traded in for short-term survival.
- Management and shareholders are put in a position where, if they do not address the situation, performance and value will begin to erode.
- Eventually, businesses in which the situation is allowed to continue, face a funding crisis and potential failure.

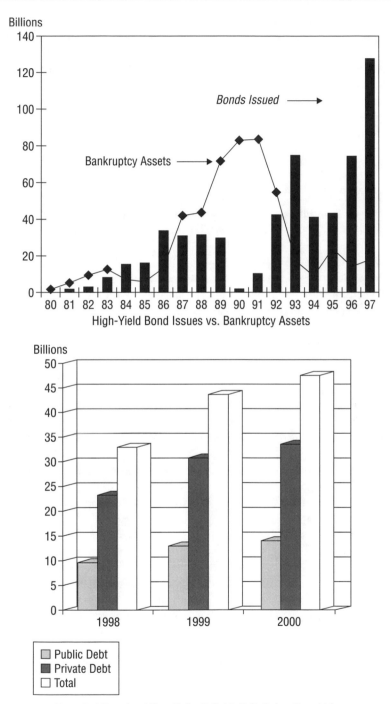

Exhibit 1.2   High-Yield Bond Issues and New Default Debt

Although the symptoms of distress can affect all companies from time to time, management's astute interpretation and diagnosis of these symptoms is critical to taking appropriate actions. In the distressed company, management typically is aware of the problems but unable to formulate and execute a strategic turnaround plan without outside assistance.

Outsiders, lenders, or investors must make their own assessments of the company's performance in order to judge whether current management is capable of determining the corrective actions to be taken, as well as implementing the resulting turnaround plan.

Two Classes of Problem

The company in trouble usually has two types of problems—internal and external—although many would argue that the former are the cause of the latter.

Internal.   In a recent survey on business failures conducted by PricewaterhouseCoopers,[2] at the top of the list of internal woes is *ineffective management*. This is where the proverbial buck stops, because every failing company is theoretically under the control of the CEO, chief financial officer (CFO), and other senior executives. "Management failure" was cited as number 2 among primary causes of business failure, as well as the number 1 secondary factor (see Exhibit 1.3 for a summary of the causes of business failure).

The most common of the internal problems found on the road to bankruptcy—all leading back to ineffective or incompetent management—is excessive leveraging of company assets. The company is trying to do too much with too little. As a measure of a company's ability to stay in business, despite a variety of financial setbacks, capital is critical to offsetting losses without going out of business. Undercapitalization can be deadly, as the company performs a complex and endless balancing act. Who decides the appropriate level of debt and equity? *Management!*

Other internal problems frequently point to a lack of good internal controls, which may range from lack of planning and budgeting to poor management information systems. They may also stem from outmoded ideas about the way to do business today, such as concentrating customers in too narrow an unprotected niche or a failure to penetrate new markets.

A rigid organizational design can create obstacles to effective communication, forcing managers into decisions in a vacuum when important information is readily available within their own organization through a simple phone call. Weak middle management exacerbate organizational design problems as they often lack the creative problem-solving skills required to overcome such obstacles. Notwithstanding middle management, it is senior management that sets the tone, creates the organizational design, and sets the foundation for how effectively the organization communicates.

Whatever part the CEO may play in these potential calamities—and it is assumed to be a large one—he or she no longer takes all the blame for a company's downfall. While in decades past, corporate health was predominantly the charge

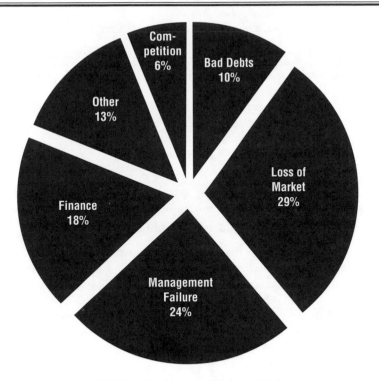

Exhibit 1.3   Causes of Business Failure

In a survey of companies that had serious financial difficulties but subsequently achieved some form of turnaround or change in ownership, management, senior managers, and company advisors all regarded "foresight or planning issues" as the company's major problem.

of management, that is no longer the case. The board of directors today is expected to play an increasingly large role or face the consequences. An increasingly activist shareholder body, particularly among pension funds such as California Public Employees' Retirement System (CALPERS) and other institutional investors, has shown that there is no place to run or hide from the inadequacies of management or its boards.

External.   From the external side, one could argue that the causes of a company's downfall are not always foreseeable. However, it could also be argued that the prescient CEO understands and develops contingency plans for the volatility of a company's environment, whether or not it is actually on the horizon. This would include:

* The cyclical nature of business, including general industry conditions, foreign competition, shifting consumer preferences, declining market for products or services, obsolescent technology, global impacts

- Economics, including labor problems, natural disasters, scarcity of strategic resources
- Politics, including regulatory issues and other legislation relating to business in general or a specific industry

After the stakeholders have identified the root causes of the problem, the next step is to determine the action steps and costs required to affect a turnaround that sufficiently addresses the problems.

THE PLAYERS

Rising from the Ashes: Shareholder Value and the Stakeholders

According to legend, when the mythical phoenix reached the end of its 500-year life, it set itself aflame and was reborn from its ashes. Can a company that has entered bankruptcy do the same? More specifically, can a troubled company's value be recreated once it has been destroyed?

To investigate the concept of recreating value, consider what constitutes value[3] and how the stakeholders of a company perceive it (see Exhibit 1.4).

The Value of Value

Many companies today declare themselves to be on "a relentless quest for value." This might sound good on the cover of an annual report, but what exactly does it mean? From our point of view, the phrase simply means that the company wants its business to create, preserve, and realize value for all its stakeholders, ranging from owners to employees.

The shareholder value of a particular company may not always be clear, even to its principals, and they frequently look to outside consultants to help them conduct what we call *shareholder value analysis*, in order to help them develop a philosophy of value creation and position themselves to thrive in the global financial environment. At a basic level, this involves:

- Understanding where they are (from a value creation perspective)
- Develop strategies for improving their position
- Establish a system of rewards for employees who play a role in these improvements

In today's marketplace, financial value is the key issue, specifically relating to cash that takes the form of:

- The return it gives to shareholders
- The cash flow that is the sign of a healthy company in the eyes of the marketplace

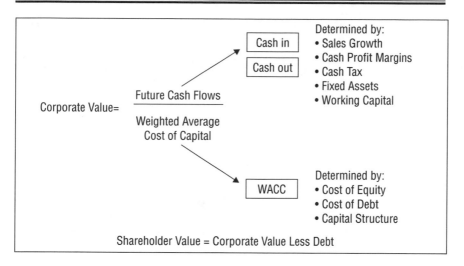

Exhibit 1.4   Corporate Value Formula

Who's Who Among a Company's Stakeholders

Among the factors to consider in determining whether a company can be regenerated into a strong, viable entity is an understanding of the motivational factors of all parties-in-interest and what they expect to receive from the entity.

Stakeholders.   A company's stakeholders can be broken down into four basic categories:

- Shareholders seek total returns in the form of dividends and capital appreciation.
- Debtholders seek prompt repayment of their loans in the form of principal and interest (their profit).
- Employees want higher wages and salaries as well as job satisfaction and security.
- Customers and suppliers want a steady stream of goods and services at prices and terms that provide good value for their "investment."

They each have a stake in the continued health of the company, although certain of them might be happy to "take the money and run."

Shareholders.   A company is owned and operated for the benefit of shareholders, whose liability is limited to the amount of their investment; therefore, their main concern will be total return—a combination of capital appreciation and dividends. Shareholders desire a return at least as great as that obtainable on an investment of similar risk elsewhere in the market, and to achieve these goals they delegate a business's operational authority and power to the management team.

The split between "church and state"—in this case, investors and management—traditionally meant a hands-off attitude on the part of many institutional shareholders. If they did not like the way one investment in their portfolio was performing relative to others, they would sell their shares in the company and perhaps buy those of a competitor.

This quiet disenchantment with the underperforming company's performance gradually gave rise to shareholder activism, with investors such as CALPERS, the California pension organization, and Mercury Asset Management, taking leading roles in questioning management decisions and seeking changes to protect their investments. Despite these efforts, shareholder claims on company assets are generally last in line in an insolvency situation. Therefore, it is investor mobility that serves as an important check on management power. In order to appease shareholders, companies may authorize substantial dividend payments, possibly in excess of what they can afford.

A good example of this approach comes from the U.K. recession of the 1990s, when 60 percent of companies maintained or increased dividends in the face of falling profits. By contrast, 28% cut dividends and only 12% of companies missed a dividend payment. Most evidence suggests that companies have a target payout rate for dividends and seek to maintain this even when business conditions are unfavorable (i.e., they are willing to sacrifice long-term shareholder value creation in favor of the short-term shareholder satisfaction).

Debtholders.   Debtholders provide funds in the form of loans, generally receiving a return on their investment in the form of interest. A lender's primary risk is default—the risk that interest payments will be missed and the face value of the loan will not be repaid when due.

Debtholders have a more limited stake in a company than shareholders, with less upside potential, usually limited to interest margin and their return of principal. If all goes well, the debtholder repeats the process, potentially increasing the amount of principal loaned.

Management finds debt attractive for the very reason that debtholders have limited their upside potential. If the company has a high probability of success, management will seek to raise additional debt, because this will leave more gains for shareholders. If the likelihood of success is not as high, then management may seek equity capital to meet additional financing needs.

Management.   While management is the appointed guardian of the company's assets on behalf of shareholders, some may suggest that a natural conflict exists. Fragmented shareholdings and an institutional hands-off policy can result in considerable power being absorbed by management, which can award itself a substantial part of value created by the company.

It is in reorganization situations that the interests of management can deviate most from those of the shareholders. Presumably, a company in difficulty is one that has already made a series of poor decisions. In a recent survey,[4] "management failure" was cited as number 2 among primary causes of business failure, as well as the number 1 secondary factor, by a wide margin.

Although management can probably look forward to remaining in place during recovery, if the situation demands a turnaround manager, it is highly likely that management will be the first to be sacrificed as new strategies are introduced and implemented.

Employees. Employees represent the core of many businesses and collectively embody the know-how and human capital of the company. Increasingly, it is the company's ability to differentiate itself in this area that will create the conditions for long-term survival. Management has to ensure that crucial employees are retained, because their loss can jeopardize a recovery program.

Customers/Suppliers. In business reorganization situations, it is important that both suppliers and customers are convinced that they have a material interest in the company's continued operation. This is easier to do when the cost to the customers and suppliers of switching is high or when there are a few alternatives.

These relationships can be fortified with long-term contracts. The stake can become so high that the customer or supplier buys the other out. When that happens, a market transaction is replaced by an "insider" transaction and the company becomes more vertically integrated. This phenomenon appears to be weighted to industries that may have a high-technology component (i.e., telecommunications, computers, software, etc.).

VALUE RE-CREATION AND ALTERNATIVE STRATEGIES
FOR A TURNAROUND

In all but the most dire situations, there will be a number of choices available to stakeholders for retrieving their investments in an operation (see Exhibit 1.5).

- *Sell it.* The first option is to dispose of the business as quickly as possible, in order to obtain reasonable fair value.
- *Liquidate it.* A second option is the liquidation of the assets in the form of a "wind down." This course of action may be appropriate where the assets have significantly greater value to potential purchasers than to the current business operator. For example, a factory site with substantial real estate development value may have higher intrinsic value when sold to a mall developer than as an ongoing manufacturing operation. The liquidation option, while unappealing to employees and most business managers, may, in some instances, yield the highest value to its stakeholders.
- *Enhance it.* A third option involves seeking short-term performance enhancements that could enable the business to generate enough cash to mollify creditors without concern for its long-term outlook. In this instance, the focus is typically on making improvements to the business, either by raising the effectiveness of business processes or by eliminating poorly performing operations, products, or customers. This option is not meant to set the busi-

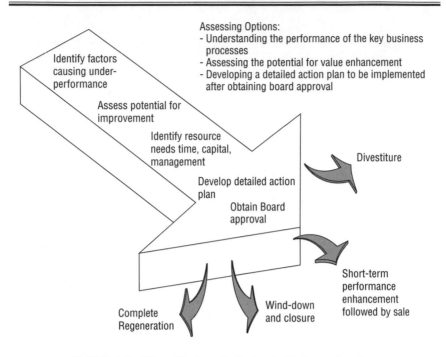

Assessing Options:
- Understanding the performance of the key business processes
- Assessing the potential for value enhancement
- Developing a detailed action plan to be implemented after obtaining board approval

Identify factors causing under-performance

Assess potential for improvement

Identify resource needs time, capital, management

Develop detailed action plan

Obtain Board approval

Divestiture

Complete Regeneration

Wind-down and closure

Short-term performance enhancement followed by sale

Exhibit 1.5   When Business Is Seriously Underperforming, Various Options Must Be Assessed

ness up for sale but to maintain the company's competitiveness through tighter controls, including more judicious spending on capital expenditures.

The Four Phases of the Turnaround

The option of pursuing a full turnaround is clearly the most far-reaching. Although it has the highest level of risk, it also offers the company the greatest opportunity to return to financial health. As depicted in Exhibit 1.6, every phase of the value recovery process, from stabilization to strategic repositioning and strengthening of operations, will be involved.

Phase I: Stabilize.   In general, the first step in helping a troubled company is to assess the situation and take immediate actions to stabilize it. This is not a time of refined analysis; rather, it is a focused effort to stem losses, conserve cash, and take action. The focus of this phase is:

- Increasing cash flow because "cash is king"
- Reducing losses and cash demands of the business

The assessment must take place quickly, generally with the assistance of skilled turnaround professionals, in order to:

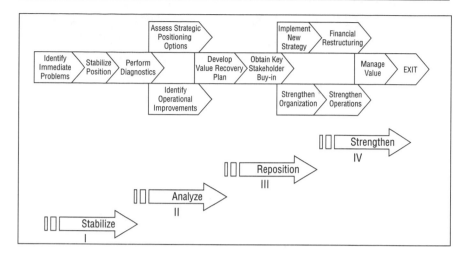

Exhibit 1.6   Value Recovery Process

- Reschedule payments
- Reduce working capital demands
- Renegotiate future commitments

Noncore assets may have to be sold to generate cash, and a sense of urgency must be instilled throughout the organization, from the top down. Foremost in the collective mind of management must be the survival axiom:

OUT OF CASH + OUT OF CREDIT = OUT OF BUSINESS

During this phase, it is critical to build credibility with lenders in order to buy the time necessary to put a long-term value creation plan into place.

Phase II: Analyze.   Once immediate cash needs have been addressed and important stakeholders have bought into a restructuring process, the company needs to analyze its business prospects. A thorough business plan review must be conducted to determine, among other things:

- What business results can be achieved?
- What debt can be supported?
- What unknown hurdles must be overcome?

During the course of this process, other factors may arise that give pause to even a seasoned turnaround professional. The company must nevertheless pursue a strategy to revitalize the company with vigor. The process of recreating value in the business, *business regeneration*, must focus on the strategic position of the company as well as its operational effectiveness. To assess the likelihood of the turnaround, the company must address:

- The core competencies of the business and how they are being exploited
- Which products and customers should be retained and which should be eliminated

This diagnostic phase should give stakeholders a better understanding of the business and choices available—alternatives focused around products or processes offering competitive advantage in selected markets.

In order to regenerate the business and unlock its value potential, the company must determine what resources are required, in terms of time, capital, and management. Generally, the turnaround will call for the addition of outside expertise, because it is unlikely that the current management team will be able to convince stakeholders that they can "do it right this time." After all, they are being called upon to re-create value that their earlier actions may have helped destroy.

Phases III and IV: Reposition and Strengthen.   After the analysis phase, the next and most crucial phase will require the company to create a value recovery plan that needs buy-in from all major stakeholders. There will be a fine line between the resources the company can commit to the program from internal cash flow and additional resources needed from stakeholders. The management team, along with its advisors, must produce the actions necessary to create new growth.

The value plan will have two distinct parts:

> *Financial Restructuring.*   The first part of the value plan involves financial restructuring, that is, taking a look at the company through the eyes of a financier. Management will seek to bring in new funds in the form of debt when a good outcome is reasonably certain, enabling upside potential to be distributed to the shareholders.
>
> A financial restructuring that involves raising more equity sends out contradictory signals to the market. As the most expensive form of financing in the long term, equity is something a company will look for when the outcome of its plans is uncertain.
>
> *Organizational Restructuring.*   Accompanying the financial restructuring package, as the second part of the value recovery plan, must be equally strong measures to strengthen the organization. The options could include:
>
> - A new management structure
> - Installation of a new executive compensation program that is heavily weighted to defined targets in the recovery plan
> - A dedicated effort to manage the key business drivers identified as part of the value chain

By combining new financial structures with new organizational initiatives, the sound basis for recovery and recreation of value can occur. As the recovery process continues, it may be possible to find a buyer who will pay a significant premium for the company reaping the most value to the organization.

ASSESSING A TURNAROUND: FOCUS ON TECHNOLOGY SECTOR

The technology sector is a prime example of some of our concepts relative to turnaround and underperformance. The technology sector poses many interesting situations relative to defining adequate performance. Finding a margin of safety in companies that trade at 40 times book value and 10 times sales does require some creativity, if not antacid tablets. The technology sector of the U.S. economy is a major driving factor of gross national product (GNP) and a place where re-emerging companies tend to trade based on their prospects rather than general market direction.

In assessing a turnaround opportunity, investors tend to shy away from battered technology stocks for a variety of reasons. Growth investors tend to prefer companies with bright prospects and often believe that once a technology stock has fallen, it is very hard for them to regain their position. Value investors tend not to mind taking a chance on a fallen angel, particularly those companies that are not heavily covered on Wall Street (although most are covered closely).

Most value investors tend to favor predictable businesses. This tends to cause enormous problems for value investors in technology as rampant technical innovation creates enormous uncertainty for even comparatively healthy technology companies.

In attempting to assess the likelihood of a turnaround for a technology company, an investor should consider whether the company has enough cash to stay solvent while its managers figure out what is wrong and how to fix it. Consider our example for the assembly and test equipment companies in the integrated circuit manufacturing sector in Exhibit 1.7.

Companies operating in an environment in which the supply-and-demand factors are severely cyclical need enough cash and credit to survive the massive swings in the cycle. This phenomenon is quite curious as a smoothing of book-to-bill indicates that overall demand in this sector has been growing at over a 17% compounded annual growth rate. Interestingly, deep trough periods of 9 to 15 months have been experienced during the same period. This cyclical swing

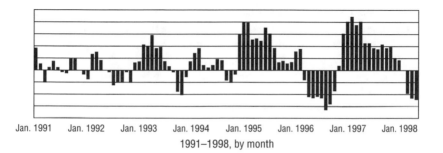

Jan. 1991   Jan. 1992   Jan. 1993   Jan. 1994   Jan. 1995   Jan. 1996   Jan. 1997   Jan. 1998
1991–1998, by month

Exhibit 1.7   Assembly and Test Equipment Book-to-Bill Ratios, 1991–1998
Source: Morgan Stanley Dean Witter Research, Assembly and Test Equipment.

creates havoc for a short-term investor and does create uncertainty among share-holders as to whether the trough is really a cliff.

It is the management of these companies that must make the critical decisions on how best to survive the trough periods. Unlike most industrial companies, high-technology companies must continue to invest heavily in research and development (R&D) despite downturns in demand. Fortunately for most technology companies and unlike manufacturing companies, high-technology companies tend to have low fixed costs. That is, by reducing labor requirements during trough periods (layoffs), technology companies can reduce their variable costs low enough to withstand the down periods and buy the time to turn around the business. Of course, this logic does not help if the technology company has loaded itself up with debt and cannot meet debt service payments.

Fortunately for some technology companies, many have a monetary advantage as they may be flush with cash from a past initial public offering (IPO) or they may have raised additional funds in the form of preferred convertible securities or some other equity instruments when times were better.

Of relative importance in considering the likelihood of a turnaround in the technology sector is whether the company has another form of financial life support that it can rely on when its primary market is weak or under pressure. Things like service agreements, maintenance contracts, and software/hardware upgrades may provide enough revenue to help buy time.

Got Something to Sell?

Of course, as with any business, a key criterion to assess in technology companies is determining whether the company still has something to sell. Cash alone will not drive a technology stock's value up in the marketplace; one must determine whether it has niches and viable products. Unlike manufacturing companies, which tend to generate products that an investor can fundamentally understand, technology companies reinvent themselves on almost a daily basis. Therefore, it is important to assess a company's track record in *bringing out products* to market. If "research and development is the touchstone of a technology business,"[5] then it is important to validate a company's ability to achieve significant returns from its R&D spending. The investment in R&D must be carefully scrutinized much as an investor in a manufacturing company looks at capital expenditures to determine whether management has been reinvesting in the business.

More importantly, when things are not going well for a technology company, consider whether the company has increased its R&D spending (generally in excess of 7% of sales) or whether the company has decreased these initiatives. Naturally, one needs to look at research and development spending relative to industry competitors to benchmark the situation.

Percentages of spending are not everything. You need to consider whether the R&D spending has been spent wisely. To assess this, we like to revisit the annual reports to see whether the company was able to deliver on projects it had under development in the past years. Moreover, one could consider what percentage of a company's revenues has come from products introduced in the past three years (hopefully at least 50%).

The Management Thing

Many high-technology companies faced with poor performance tend to need new management before a turnaround can begin. The boost a new CEO can give a company faced with first-time underperformance should not be underestimated. The return of Steve Jobs helped Apple Computer stock achieve a 118% total gain in the first half of 1998.

The key action a new manager can bring to an underperforming technology company is cost containment. When technology companies are thriving, management's focus tends to be on keeping the engineers happy, and cost control takes a backseat. When the company gets into trouble, management needs to be able to control costs. Many times, a new manager is brought in to do the layoffs and cost containment because prior management either did not recognize the problem or refused to do it.

While the major example is an American company, its ramifications reach much further, not only for U.S. companies considering business relationships with foreign partners, but for foreign businesses as well (despite the differences in their local laws).

Benchmarking Can Be Fun?

Perhaps a critical factor to assess in a high-technology company is whether the company's balance sheet is strong enough to withstand a down period. We like to do a sector chart analysis in which the company's balance sheet and income statement performance can be benchmarked relative to perceived competitors, as indicated in Exhibit 1.8.

The sector charts help one analyze his or her company versus the competition. For instance, in looking at the balance sheet performance, companies operating in the top right region of the Inventory Turns versus Return on Assets (ROA) charts are the strongest performing of the groups in terms of inventory utilization as their investment in inventory is minimized. For most high-technology companies, minimizing the investment in inventory can be a good thing because not only does it require less working capital financing, but the company minimizes an investment in a product which may becoming obsolete as new variants are seemingly created every day.

A company in the top left region of the Days of Sales versus ROA chart is not only yielding strong returns on balance sheet assets, but also is in a good position in terms of keeping customers on a tight leash. The further you yield credit to your customers, the more subject you are to a downturn in the economy. For instance, in the capital equipment sector of the integrated circuit industry, many customers are global and heavily concentrated in the Pacific Rim. Weakness in global economies and specifically in the Pacific Rim not only may make it more difficult for these customers to pay for product, but devaluation of their currency vis-à-vis a U.S. high-technology company exporter can further exacerbate a tenuous situation.

In considering the amount of SG&A (sales, general and administrative) expenses a high-technology company invests in, one has to understand the relative

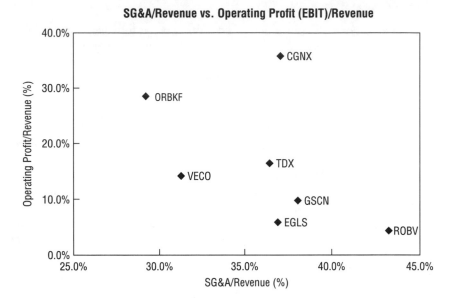

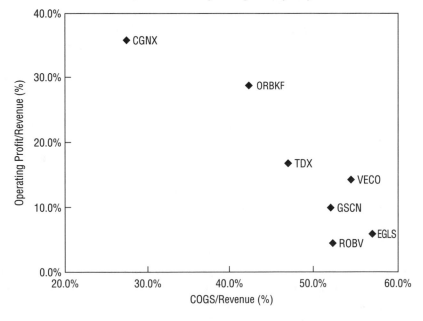

Exhibit 1.8

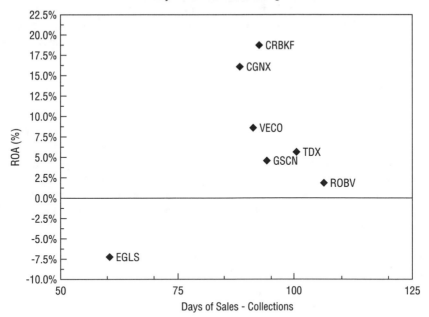

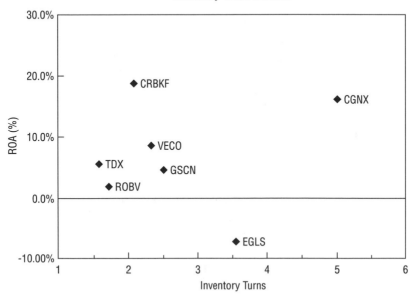

Exhibit 1.8   *(Continued)*

components of sales expense. Is the level of sales expense appropriate for the business? Will the investment in research and development bring immediate results? Therefore, careful scrutiny as to the underlying fundamentals involved in the income statement side of our analysis must be performed. High-technology companies in particular may in fact require incremental R&D spending even though the company is facing a liquidity crisis.

What Do the Analysts Say?

Of course, notwithstanding all the fundamental analysis in the world, when a company is in the technology sector, a successful turnaround must also be played out in the public arena. The CEO/CFO team must direct a successful turnaround not only inside the company but also outside the company. The credibility of the management team should not be underestimated, particularly in technology companies that may not have a long track record. As the darlings of the investment community, technology companies are closely scrutinized and in many instances are valued far in excess of financial performance. With price to earnings ratio (P/Es) in the stratospheric 40x range, it is no wonder that when the technology company announces weak or lower-than-expected results, the stock can plummet more than 50% of its market capitalization.

In assessing these situations, the management team cannot lose sight of what got them to this stage of demise. Rather, a rededication to the fundamental aspects of the business is critical. Typically, the CFO, "guardian of the numbers," must placate the technology community, analysts, and investors to drive a turnaround plan. Moreover, continued investment in R&D, the lifeblood of most technology businesses, must continue to be made. In these times, assessing the likelihood of a turnaround in the technology sector boils down to the key ingredient: Is management credible?

NOTES

1. *Bankruptcy Almanac*. New Generation Research, Boston, MA. 1998.

2. Survey by Business Planning and Research International for PricewaterhouseCoopers LLP.

3. Alfred Rappaport, *Creating Shareholder Value*, Free Press, New York, NY, 1986.

4. See note 2 above.

5. Michael Murphy, *Every Investors Guide to High-Tech Stocks and Mutual Funds*, Broadway Books, New York, NY, 1997.

2

Looming Financial or Business Failure: Fix or File— a Legal Perspective

Harvey R. Miller, Esq.

Weil, Gotshal & Manges LLP

INTRODUCTION

As the availability of credit continues to expand, the opportunities for financial distress and commercial failure increase proportionately. This environment creates multifaceted challenges for debt collection and rehabilitation of distressed businesses. These challenges have resulted in a dynamic evolution of the law of bankruptcy and reorganization. The responses to the challenges implicate the selection of alternatives for rehabilitation of businesses and the recovery of claims against debtors. The particulars of the governing principles of law, the proclivities of individual bankruptcy courts, and the condition of credit markets have all impacted on any decision by a distressed business or its creditors to seek relief under the federal bankruptcy law. The Bankruptcy Act of 1898, as amended, which governed bankruptcy proceedings until November 1, 1979, provided financially distressed businesses with a number of options to deal with financial or operational failure. Most distressed businesses under that Act had a choice of (a) liquidation under chapters I through VII; (b) chapter X (corporate reorganization); or (c) chapter XI (arrangements). None of the choices were particularly palatable to the distressed business debtor that desired to retain a measure of control over its destiny and protect the interests of equityholders.

In addition to the notoriety and perceived stigma of bankruptcy that prevailed during most of the existence of the former Bankruptcy Act, liquidation was not a desired solution, and chapter XI had significant limitations in terms of its scope and the ability to deal with secured and other reorganization needs pursuant to an arrangement. The comprehensive provisions of chapter X that, generally, mandated the appointment of one or more disinterested trustees in any chapter X proceeding, effectively ousting management, and the rigid immutable application of the absolute priority rule, which in most cases eliminated equityholders and sometimes junior creditors, as well as the extended term and expense of a chapter X proceeding, discouraged the use of that chapter.

The 1973 report of the National Bankruptcy Commission that had been appointed in 1970 recognized the limitations of the former Bankruptcy Act and recommended the enactment of a single reorganization chapter in lieu of chapters X, XI, and XII (real property arrangements) of the former Bankruptcy Act.[1] After extensive consideration and numerous hearings over the following four years, Congress enacted the Bankruptcy Reform Act of 1978. Congress adopted the recommendation of the National Bankruptcy Commission and provided for a single business reorganization chapter as part of title 11 of the United States Code (the Bankruptcy Code). The 1978 Bankruptcy Code and chapter 11 were intended to eradicate the perceived barriers to effective bankruptcy reorganization. Many provisions were enacted to encourage distressed business debtors to seek relief under the Bankruptcy Code before the economic erosion precluded effective reorganization, including the retention and expansion of and statutory preference for the debtor in possession concept of former Chapter XI. The Bankruptcy Code was intended to significantly reduce or eliminate the stigma of bankruptcy by recognizing that there must be a remedy for overextension of credit and the vicissitudes of economic cycles. However, from the perspective of many, it appeared that the Bankruptcy Code was debtor friendly.

Nonetheless, it took a number of years subsequent to the effective date of the Bankruptcy Code and the onset of another economic cycle of recession for the aversion to bankruptcy reorganization to dissipate. As the economic conditions of the early 1980s deteriorated and high-profile, publicly owned corporations began to use the provisions of chapter 11, its popularity as a strategic, tactical business option became a reality. The commencement of chapter 11 cases by Johns-Manville Corporation, a *Fortune* 500 corporation, and its affiliates,[2] demonstrated the ability to use chapter 11 reorganization provisions to deal with mass tort litigation that had affected the financial stability of a business. The continuation of Continental Airlines as a functioning commercial airline after the 1983 commencement of its chapter 11 case[3] established that even in a highly sensitive industry, a business could operate and survive in the context of chapter 11. Thus, the Bankruptcy Code did accomplish a lessening of the stigma associated with bankruptcy as it became recognized that the general public would continue to patronize the businesses of chapter 11 debtors. In addition, the enforcement of the debtor protection provisions of the Bankruptcy Code by the bankruptcy court increased the attraction of chapter 11 as a strategic and viable business option for a distressed debtor.

As the size and volume of the chapter 11 cases in the late 1980s and early 1990s mushroomed and the perception of debtor-friendly bankruptcy courts persisted, creditor constituencies joined forces and mounted vigorous efforts to moderate the bankruptcy courts. Legislative lobbying began in earnest and over time, significant and far-reaching amendments were made to the Bankruptcy Code for the purpose of tilting the playing field to a more level or pro-creditor stance. Debtors' powers as to (1) assumption and rejection of executory contracts, particularly as to shopping centers and collective bargaining agreements; (2) retiree benefits; (3) scope and enforcement of the automatic stay; and (4) use of collateral security of secured creditors, among others, were contracted.[4] Significant changes were made in the Federal Rules of Bankruptcy Procedure (the Bankruptcy Rules) to facilitate administration of chapter 11 cases for the benefit of creditors.[5] Consistent and persistent pressure has been exercised to limit a debtor's exclusive right to file a plan of reorganization.

The surge of huge chapter 11 cases as a result of the merger and acquisition mania of the 1980s also resulted in the recognition that the debt of a distressed business constituted a commodity that could be traded by speculators and investors. Financial institutions and other creditors desiring liquidity did not hesitate to sell claims held against a debtor. Trading in distressed debt often resulted in a concentration of debt in major investors, who then assumed a very key and significant role in the chapter 11 case, sharply limiting a debtor's ability to control its destiny through the chapter 11 process. Questions concerning the survival of the new value corollary to the absolute priority rule to retain equity interests by the old equityholders raged in the courts. The debate illuminated the high level of sophistication of distressed debt traders and their use of the absolute priority rule to eliminate or reduce the role of junior creditors and equityholders in the process of bankruptcy reorganization.

As a result, bankruptcy reorganization has become less appealing to a distressed debtor than it may have been in the early 1990s. The pendulum has moved back to a more creditor-oriented process reminiscent of proceedings under the former Bankruptcy Act. The perceived loss of control by virtue of the changes that have occurred in chapter 11 has caused the distressed debtor to defer and delay resorting to chapter 11 reorganization as a means to restructure. Chapter 11 has become the option of last resort.

This chapter briefly reviews restructuring alternatives that may be considered by debtors and creditors confronted by a financially distressed business. Restructuring and reorganization is not a science. It is an art that encompasses negotiation skills, economic analyses of the particular business, the nature of the industry, a reality recognition factor, and a wide range of legal issues. As a result, there may not be any certainty that the restructuring alternative chosen by the distressed business and accepted by its creditors and interest holders will be successful. Due diligence and comprehensive consideration of the material facts are prerequisites to any decision as to restructuring and the need to commence reorganization under the Bankruptcy Code.

ALTERNATIVES TO CHAPTER 11 REORGANIZATION

The onset of financial distress triggers the need on the part of the debtor's management and policy makers to undertake the inquiry necessary to ascertain the causes of such distress. The disappearance of liquidity and the incurrence of operational and financial losses do not occur spontaneously. Before determining an appropriate cure for the problems, the distressed business must ascertain the nature of the problems and their pervasiveness. The distressed business must establish whether the causes of the distress are aberrational or persistent. Once the causes are isolated, the distressed debtor must determine if the problems are curable or terminal. That evaluation will materially influence the ultimate decision as to how to effect a restructuring.

Depending on the conclusions as to the causes and remedial actions that may be necessary to fix the problem, there are a number of informal means to cure illiquidity or excessive debt burdens. Among such options is the infusion of additional equity capital by current equityholders or third persons. To attract equity investors normally means that the causes of the problems of financial distress have been appropriately isolated, cures established to eradicate them, and that the prospects for growth are good. If all of those elements are present, the need to resort to formal restructuring is remote.

In the more common cases, the situation is not as black and white. The lines are less clear, and, usually, the distressed business has overexpanded and is overleveraged by substantial debt obligations. Often, default under various debt instruments is looming. Sometimes, the situation is aggravated by indications or assertions of misconduct or poor executive leadership, pending or potential litigation, and public dismay.

The first objective of any restructuring effort is to stabilize the operation of the business while the restructuring process is pursued. In those cases in which a simple equity infusion is inappropriate, the effort must be made to avoid default and the race to the courthouse with the potential dismemberment of the business's assets and properties. The commencement of debt collection litigation will impair the ability to effect an informal restructuring and may prejudice and destroy the value of all or a part of a debtor's business. Therefore, waivers of defaults and standstill agreements may serve to maintain the status quo while protecting the interests of all affected parties.

The price requested for waivers and standstill agreements may become a major factor in the determination of the appropriate restructuring option. If the cost is too high in terms of fees, charges, and demands for the granting of liens and security interests in favor of the creditors and waivers of potential bankruptcy protections, it may compel the distressed debtor to resort to formal restructuring under the Bankruptcy Code. The debtor's policy makers are subject to fiduciary duties in the context of the insolvency of the debtor or the fact that the debtor may be in the vicinity of insolvency. At that point, the policy makers must consider the interests of all parties and not prefer any one party over another.

Accordingly, in making the decision of whether to fix or file, the distressed business has to consider, among other issues:

- Fiduciary duties to all parties in interest, including, usually, creditors and any potential liability in connection with such duties
- The nature of the problems confronting the distressed debtor and their severity

- The effectiveness of any proposed cure, whether by reason of additional equity infusion, borrowing, disaggregation, sale, or restructuring
- The cost of effecting the cure in terms of the impact on the continuing business or the sale or other disposition of the business and its assets and properties
- The ability to prosecute any claim for the benefit of the debtor, including actions to avoid particular transactions as preferences or fraudulent transfers under the Bankruptcy Code
- The nature or type of liabilities and indebtedness of the distressed business and the probability of resolving pending or proposed litigation that has or might affect the viability of the distressed business
- Compliance with any applicable securities laws
- The costs and expenses of restructuring under the different alternatives

Each element of the decision-making process requires comprehensive examination and evaluation. Distressed businesses should employ the expertise of qualified professionals in reaching conclusions as to any proposed restructuring or reorganization. While a nonbankruptcy restructuring may be preferable, it is extremely important that the distressed debtor, and often its creditors and equity-holders, agree that the restructuring proposed will be a permanent fix and not simply a temporary solution. If the latter occurs, it is probable that the restructuring scenario will be repeated in the very near future in circumstances of heightened tension and more limited opportunities for the distressed business.

In the face of the vagaries that are integral to the restructuring process, notwithstanding the distaste for the uncertainty of chapter 11 cases, the fixing of the ailing debtor may necessitate resorting to relief under the Bankruptcy Code. Because of the desire to avoid contact with the bankruptcy court as much as possible, various bankruptcy-related restructuring options have been developed. The following parts of this chapter describe those developments, as well as the traditional chapter 11 case, and reiterate the considerations that must be evaluated in the circumstances of fixing the problems or filing for relief under the Bankruptcy Code.

OUT-OF-COURT RESTRUCTURING

An out-of-court restructuring, or workout, is a nonjudicial process pursuant to which a distressed debtor and its significant creditors attempt to agree on an adjustment of the debtor's obligations. In the simple case of a nonpublic corporation or business entity that is dealing with a comparatively limited group of creditors of the same class, a composition of the outstanding debt may be accomplished by agreement. In the workout, it generally seeks to exchange or amend its existing debt and, sometimes, to change the composition of its equity interest holders. If the debtor is a publicly owned entity, it may exchange existing publicly traded securities for new securities with different terms through a consensual exchange offer under the Securities Act of 1933, as amended (the

"Securities Act"). Consensual exchange offers, generally, are implemented in one of the following ways:

- *Registered exchange offer.* A registered exchange offer requires the filing of a registration statement, usually on form S-4, with the Securities and Exchange Commission (SEC). The SEC takes 30 to 60 days to comment. The debtor requires additional time to respond to the SEC comments. A registered exchange offer has the benefit of avoiding restrictions on the securities that can be imposed if the exchange offer is premised on certain exemptions to the securities laws.
- *Section 3(a)(9) exchange offer.* Section 3(a)(9) of the Securities Act provides an exemption from the registration requirements of the Securities Act. Such an exchange offer generally must satisfy three requirements: (1) the exchange must involve the "same issuer," (i.e., the exchange must be initiated by the issuer for its own securities); (2) the debtor's old securities holders must not be asked to contribute any consideration other than the exchange of the old securities (with certain exceptions); and (3) the issuer may not compensate any person directly or indirectly for soliciting the exchange. The last requirement means that a debtor cannot compensate an investment banker to assist in the solicitation of the exchange nor may the banker's fee be dependent on the outcome of the exchange offer.
- *Other techniques.* In addition to the foregoing options, an issuer of securities may: (1) implement an exchange offer predicated on the private placement exemption set forth in Section 4(2) of the Securities Act; or (2) implement a settlement exchange under Section 3(a)(10) of the Securities Act, which requires, among other things, that a qualified court or governmental entity (other than a bankruptcy court) approve the exchange.

Apart from exchange offers, a debtor may obtain written consent to the modification of existing securities through a consent solicitation; amend equity securities in accordance with the company's charter, bylaws, and applicable nonbankruptcy (mostly state) law; and/or repurchase existing securities for cash, which is normally not an option for a distressed debtor. Under nonbankruptcy law, most public debt indentures require unanimity to change the payment-related terms of the security, and any dissenters must be bought out in cash or pursuant to the original terms of the debt issue. These "holdouts" can use their bargaining leverage to drag out any out-of-court restructuring process by demanding additional concessions, which may come at the expense of other creditors or interest holders.

COMBINATION EXCHANGE OFFER AND CHAPTER 11 PROPOSAL

An exchange offer or other out-of-court restructuring may simply not be feasible for a debtor, due to the requirement that each and every impaired creditor is required to consent to the proposal. Under chapter 11, a confirmed plan of reorganization will bind minority creditors and equityholders as well as dissenting classes of such persons. Therefore, an exchange offer combined with a proposed chapter 11 plan and a provision notifying holders that the debtor may commence a chapter 11 case and use acceptances of the exchange offer as acceptance of the chapter 11 plan may be very effective to induce the requisite approvals of the exchange offer.

PREPACKAGED CHAPTER 11

A prepackaged chapter 11 case contemplates that the debtor negotiates the terms of its restructuring with its major creditors and then prepares a disclosure statement and solicits acceptances of its chapter 11 plan before it commences its chapter 11 case. Prepackaged chapter 11 cases commonly are referred to as single-track or dual-track cases. A single-track case is the classic case in which the debtor negotiates and proposes a reorganization plan and solicits acceptances of the plan with the specific intent to commence a chapter 11 case on completion of a successful solicitation. In contrast, a dual-track case, as noted above, combines a traditional exchange offer with the solicitation of a prepackaged chapter 11 plan. The exchange offer will govern if the required percentage of acceptances is reached. If such percentage is not obtained, however, then the acceptances of the exchange offer are treated as acceptances of the chapter 11 plan of reorganization.

Although the debtor may have the necessary plan acceptances, it is possible that a prepackaged plan will not be confirmed if dissenting creditors attack the adequacy of the prepetition disclosure, the solicitation process, the classification and treatment of claims, the tabulation of votes, and/or the feasibility of the prepackaged plan.[6] In the event a prepackaged case gets sidetracked by such issues, the total restructuring period and, perhaps, the expenses incurred may correspond to that of the traditional chapter 11 case.

When a prepackaged case is successful, the results are impressive. An example is the case of *Consolidated Hydro, Inc.* (CHI).[7] CHI was a holding company with a significant number of subsidiaries. The subsidiaries operated hydroelectric installations throughout the United States and each had its own debt obligations. The financial restructuring of CHI involved the conversion of $184 million of public bonds into 100% of the common stock of the reorganized company, the conversion of $240 million of preferred stock into warrants, the elimination of all existing equity interests, and the payment of 100 cents on the dollar to creditors holding general unsecured claims. CHI launched a section 3(a)(9) exchange offer on August 9, 1997; the holders of the public bonds and the preferred stock overwhelmingly accepted the plan. On September 15, 1997, CHI commenced its chapter 11 case. The bankruptcy court did not schedule a disclosure statement hearing. Several common stockholders objected to confirmation. After a contested confirmation hearing, the bankruptcy court confirmed the plan. CHI's plan became effective on November 6, 1997, just 52 days after the commencement date. As contemplated by the chapter 11 plan, none of CHI's subsidiaries or their operations were affected by CHI's chapter 11 case.

PREARRANGED CHAPTER 11

If there are too many creditors or classes of creditors or equityholders to effectively solicit, or pending litigation or other factors preclude the lead time necessary for a prepackaged chapter 11 case, the debtor's restructuring may also be effected through a prearranged chapter 11 case. In a prearranged case, as of the commencement date, the debtor will have reached an agreement on the terms of a plan of reorganization with one or more of its major creditor constituencies, but will not yet have solicited acceptances of its plan. Typically, the reorganization plan and disclosure statement are filed together with the chapter 11 petition, putting such cases on a fast track toward confirmation. An example of that technique is the case of *G. Heileman Brewing Company, Inc.* and its affiliates.[8] They commenced chapter 11 cases by filing voluntary petitions together with a joint chapter 11 plan on April 3, 1996. The plan was confirmed on June 26, 1996, fewer than 90 days later.

TRADITIONAL CHAPTER 11

A traditional chapter 11 case is commenced by the debtor's filing of a chapter 11 petition. Within days of the commencement of the case, the United States Trustee appoints an official committee of creditors and, in certain cases, additional committees of creditors or equityholders. Each official committee is entitled to retain professionals at the expense of the debtor's estate.

The duration of a traditional chapter 11 case depends on (1) the extent to which the debtor's operations have to be reorganized, (2) the amenability of the bankruptcy court to granting extensions of the debtor's 120-day exclusive period for filing a plan, and (3) the extent to which creditors resort to litigation to resolve issues among or between them. Reorganization of a large debtor pursuant to a traditional chapter 11 case is rarely concluded in less than one year and typically takes 18 months to two years.

A chapter 11 case was the ideal vehicle for *R.H. Macy & Co.*,[9] the operating revenues of which were insufficient to meet its operating costs, even without debt service, when it commenced its chapter 11 case in 1992. While under the protection of chapter 11, Macy's was able to install new operating standards and systems and turn losing operations into a profitable business. While the process took over three years, the enterprise value of Macy's was increased by over $1.5 billion. Ultimately, pursuant to its chapter plan, Macy's was acquired by Federated Department Stores.

Macy's was an atypical chapter 11 debtor due to its size, which may account for the duration of the case. Moreover, the results obtained in Macy's may not be achievable today; the introduction into the bankruptcy arena of distressed debt traders has changed the dynamics of chapter 11 because, to such traders, time is money. The need for a fast and substantial return colors all judgments and causes demands for a quick finish to any chapter 11 case. From that perspective, as a general matter, distressed debt traders who gain control of the creditor constituencies do not believe that operational problems must be cured during the chapter 11 case administration. Their credo is "more bankruptcy is less good" for the debtor and their investment. Consequently, they are more concerned about rehabilitation of financial statements and a projected capital markets exit for debtholders. It may work in some cases and, in others, may result in the proverbial "chapter 22" case.

IDENTIFICATION OF THE CAUSES OF THE DEBTOR'S DISTRESS

The decision to seek relief under the Bankruptcy Code is not one lightly taken. Ironically, however, the decision is easiest for a debtor that has severe operational problems. A business that is unable to generate enough revenue to pay its operating expenses has fundamental business problems that require aggressive measures. The possible causes of the debtor's problems are many: its expenses are higher than those of its competitors, it sells an obsolete product, it sells a product that has caused personal injury on a massive scale, or it has been mismanaged. Regardless of the specific cause, the need for remedial action usually is immediate, and the extraordinary remedies of chapter 11 become increasingly attractive. Indeed, it may be that commencement of a chapter 11 case is the debtor's only realistic hope for reorganization or even survival.

The decision is much more difficult, however, for a business that appears to have sound operations and projected earnings and is simply unable to satisfy its debt service obligations or a crippling legal judgment.[10] For such a debtor, the decision to enter the bankruptcy arena with the concomitant imposition of bankruptcy court and U.S. Trustee oversight, the intrusion of one or more creditors or equity committees, and the ever-present uncertainty of what may transpire in the process may jeopardize an otherwise potentially viable business. The potential for second-guessing the debtor's policy makers always exists. In those circumstances, a record that demonstrates the debtor's consideration of all relevant factors will be an appropriate defense.

ANALYSIS OF DEBTOR'S NEED FOR THE EXTRAORDINARY REMEDIES AVAILABLE IN CHAPTER 11

Automatic Stay

Upon the filing of a voluntary petition for relief under chapter 11 of the Bankruptcy Code, all persons are enjoined from commencing or continuing any judicial, administrative, or other action or proceeding against the debtor that was or could have been commenced prior to the commencement date.[11] The automatic stay generally enjoins parties from instituting or continuing any lawsuit to obtain property of the debtor's estate, to create or perfect a security interest in property of the estate, or to obtain or enforce a judgment against the debtor in an attempt to collect on a claim against the debtor that arose prior to the commencement date.[12] Filing a chapter 11 petition is often necessary in order for a debtor to stave off a foreclosure action or a creditor's enforcement of a judgment. For example, when Texaco, Inc. was the subject of an $11 billion judgment in favor of Pennzoil Company, Texaco delayed commencing its chapter 11 case until it believed it could no longer preclude Pennzoil Company from enforcing its judgment. Nonetheless, the delay may result in an attack upon the chapter 11 case as not being filed in good faith or on the basis that there is no possibility of reorganization.[13]

Additional Financing

Often, the debtor's crisis is precipitated by a default under its working capital facility that precludes additional advances until a restructuring is completed. If the debtor needs immediate access to additional financing, it may find that it is better able to obtain credit in a chapter 11 case than in the workout context. The Bankruptcy Code enables the trustee or debtor in possession to obtain unsecured credit or incur unsecured debt in the ordinary course of business.[14] The court may also authorize the debtor in possession to obtain credit or incur debt outside of the ordinary course of business on a secured or unsecured basis.[15] The Bankruptcy Code establishes a hierarchy of those permissible credit transactions in which the debtor in possession may engage. Subject to bankruptcy court approval, the debtor in possession may obtain credit or incur indebtedness which: (1) is unsecured or has administrative expense status; (2) has superadministrative expense status or is secured by a lien on unencumbered property or a junior lien on encumbered property; or (3) is secured by a superior or equal lien on encumbered property.[16] The bankruptcy court may not authorize the incurrence of secured credit unless the debtor in possession (DIP) cannot obtain unsecured credit.[17]

An additional or alternative financing vehicle for a chapter 11 debtor is the use of cash collateral, which may be available for a debtor that is able to sustain its operations by utilizing the cash it generates. If the debtor had secured financing prepetition, substantially all of its cash is likely to constitute cash collateral, which may not be used absent consent of the secured creditor or court approval.[18] In order to establish that it is entitled to use cash collateral, the debtor must provide the secured creditor with adequate protection. In the retail or manufacturing industry, in which collections generated by the sale of inventory will often constitute cash collateral, adequate protection may be provided by making periodic interest payments or by providing a replacement lien on postpetition receivables.

Conventional wisdom has generally been that the commencement of a chapter 11 case enables a debtor to obtain unsecured trade credit more easily than would be the case outside of such a proceeding, due to the administrative expense treatment afforded to postpetition claims of suppliers. Historically, the most common form of DIP financing involved unsecured loans coupled with superpriority administrative expense status. The recent trend in DIP financing, however, has been toward DIP financing secured by all unencumbered assets of the debtor, a junior lien on encumbered assets, and, in certain cases, a priming lien. With the increased popularity of secured DIP financing, certain vendors have been unwilling to restore normal delivery of inventory and unsecured credit terms. To continue in business, debtors have been constrained to resort to alternative sources of inventory supplies or to agree to prepayment, payment on delivery (COD), or the granting of a lien in favor of trade vendors.[19] Depending on the protection ultimately granted to the trade, the debtor may not be able to take advantage of the float provided by normal trade terms and the amount of financing required by the debtor is likely to be greater. The debtor and, ultimately, its creditors bear the cost of a larger DIP financing facility through higher commitment and unused line and other fees. In sum, therefore, depending on the debtor's industry, the conventional wisdom that trade credit may be more readily available in chapter 11 may be inapposite.

Rejection of Executory Contracts

Subject to the approval of the bankruptcy court, a chapter 11 debtor may reject any executory contract or unexpired lease.[20] Through rejection under section 365, the Bankruptcy Code provides a mechanism for a debtor that seeks to contract substantially the size or geographic distribution of its operations. The ability to reject leases in the exercise of the debtor's business judgment is particularly useful to a retail debtor that has hundreds of stores located throughout the United States. Although rejection under Section 365 is not cost free,[21] the lease rejection tool has enabled many retail debtors to reposition themselves and to focus their operations on a core group of store locations.

The Bankruptcy Code also enables a debtor in possession to reject a collective bargaining agreement if the court finds that a proposal calling for necessary modifications to the agreement has been rejected by employee representatives without good cause.[22] Section 1113, which sets forth rigorous standards governing whether rejection will be permitted, was enacted in 1984. Even if rejection of the collective bargaining agreement is approved by the bankruptcy court, the union generally remains the authorized representative of the employees, and the employer and the union have the obligations imposed on them under applicable federal labor laws to negotiate in good faith to try to agree on the terms of a new collective bargaining agreement.

Nevertheless, a debtor whose operating expenses are disproportionately high for its industry due to a burdensome collective bargaining agreement may have the ability to obtain some relief in the context of a chapter 11 case. Similarly, the DIP may modify retiree benefits if it can demonstrate that the proposed modifications are necessary to permit the reorganization of the debtor and have been rejected by the authorized representative of the retirees without good cause.[23] The extent to which employees have a claim for lost wages under a rejected collective bargaining agreement depends on whether the agreement includes a guarantee of employment.[24]

In the event that the bankruptcy court authorizes the rejection of an executory contract, or unexpired lease, the nondebtor party will have an unsecured claim for damages arising from the rejection. In most cases, however, such a claim is treated like all other unsecured claims and may receive only the consideration that is proposed in the chapter 11 plan. In order to prevent huge damage claims arising from the rejection of long-term employment contracts or unexpired leases from consuming the assets available for unsecured creditors, the Bankruptcy Code limits the amount of the claims that may be asserted as a result of such rejections.[25]

The ability to reject leases and executory contracts, and the concomitant limit on the magnitude of certain damage claims arising therefrom, are powerful reorganization tools. Although the DIP cannot modify an executory contract, collective bargaining agreement, or lease without the consent of the *contra* party, the leverage afforded to the debtor by the rejection power will often enable a debtor to renegotiate such agreements on more favorable terms.

Relief from Anti-Assignment Clauses and Other Restrictive Provisions

The DIP may assign an executory contract or unexpired lease to a third party notwithstanding a contractual provision that prohibits, restricts, or conditions the assignment thereof.[26] In order to justify such assignment, the DIP is required to provide adequate assurance of future performance of the contract or lease.[27] Unlike the case in the out-of-court context, assignment of a contract or lease relieves the debtor from liability for any breach that occurs subsequent to the assignment.[28] The Bankruptcy Code, therefore, offers a mechanism for the debtor to capitalize on valuable assets that may not fit with the debtor's business plan, but that may be of value to third parties.

Bankruptcy courts have also relieved debtors from complying with "going dark" provisions contained in many shopping center leases. Such provisions preclude tenants from conducting going-out-of-business sales, in order to uphold the image of the center and, where percentage rent is payable, maintain earnings. In cases in which the debtor determines to close stores and conducts liquidation sales, such lease provisions directly conflict with the bankruptcy policy of maximizing the value of the estate. Landlords have been largely unsuccessful in arguing that debtor tenants are required to comply with such lease covenants in cases in which bankruptcy courts have approved liquidation sales.[29]

Despite any contractual provisions to the contrary, the chapter 11 debtor may sell property free and clear of any interest of any other entity, such as a secured party, if one of the following is true: (1) applicable nonbankruptcy law permits a sale free and clear of such interest; (2) the entity consents; (3) the interest is a lien, and the proposed sale price exceeds the aggregate value of all liens on the property; (4) the interest is in bona fide dispute; or (5) such entity could be compelled in a legal or equitable proceeding to accept a money satisfaction of its interest.[30] In addition, under certain circumstances, the DIP may sell its own interest as well as the interest of any co-owner in property in which the debtor had an undivided interest as a tenant in common, joint tenant, or tenant by the entireties.[31]

In order to obtain approval of a request to sell property free and clear, the DIP will still have to satisfy the bankruptcy court that the sale on the terms proposed represents a reasonable business decision. In addition, in most cases, the bankruptcy court will issue an order that provides that the lien of the secured party will attach to the proceeds of the asset sale, to the same extent as it existed on the original asset, without any further action by the secured creditor. The advantage of a sale "free and clear" under Section 363(f) is that it enables the DIP to effect a sale of an asset, the value of which may be diminishing, even though issues regarding the extent and priority of the liens thereon remain to be resolved. In effect, Section 363(f) prevents a secured creditor from using its ability to consent to a sale as unfair leverage in order to extract a distribution to which it might otherwise not be entitled.

Ability to Bind Nonconsenting Creditors

The keystone of an out-of-court restructuring is consensus; no creditor may have its rights adversely affected in an out-of-court restructuring unless it has specifically agreed to less favorable terms.

The Bankruptcy Code defines acceptance of a plan by a class of creditors as acceptance by at least two thirds in amount of claims and more than one half in number of holders that have voted on the plan.[32] Moreover, under the cram-down mechanism,[33] a plan can be confirmed even if it has not been accepted by every class of claims and interests, if it is "fair and equitable" and satisfies other statutory criteria. Commencement of a chapter 11 case may, therefore, be necessary if the debtor is unable to obtain the requisite number of acceptances to its out-of-court restructuring proposal.

Unliquidated or Contingent Claims

If the magnitude of the claims against a debtor cannot be ascertained, formulation of a reorganization plan that fairly allocates the assets available for distribution among the debtor's creditors and stockholders is virtually impossible. The Bankruptcy Code provides a mechanism that debtors may utilize in order to estimate any "contingent or unliquidated claim, the fixing or liquidation of which . . . would unduly delay the administration of the case."[34] Estimation of claims may be solely for purposes of voting, as in the chapter 11 case of *Johns-Manville Corporation*,[35] in which the court estimated thousands of asbestosis claims at $1 each for voting purposes, subject to each claimant's right to establish the actual amount of his claim after confirmation of the plan. Alternatively, estimation may be used to allocate the consideration distributed under the plan, as in the chapter 11 case of *Eagle-Picher Industries, Inc.*, in which consideration was allocated among unsecured creditors and personal injury plaintiffs allegedly injured by asbestos manufactured by Eagle-Picher.[36] Finally, estimation may be for purposes of allowance of a claim under the plan, in which case the creditor is barred from litigating its claim and establishing its entitlement to a greater distribution.

Section 502(c) has been particularly useful to debtors faced with mass tort liability. The estimation procedure enables the debtor in such circumstances to quantify the claims for which it has to provide treatment under its reorganization plan and, therefore, proceed with plan formulation. Moreover, although plaintiffs cannot be deprived of the ability to have their personal injury claims adjudicated in state court proceedings, chapter 11 offers a vehicle for centralizing liquidation of such claims in a claims processing facility such as those used by Manville, Eagle-Picher, and others.

Avoidance Actions

If the debtor has a significant fraudulent conveyance claim under applicable state law, the statute of limitations for which may be near expiration, the commencement of a chapter 11 case may be preferable to an out-of-court restructuring. Pursuant to the Bankruptcy Code, a transfer may be set aside as a fraudulent conveyance only if it occurred within one year before the date of the filing of the petition. However, because a DIP may avoid any transfer of property that may be avoided under applicable state law by a hypothetical creditor holding an unsecured claim against the debtor, in chapter 11, transfers of property may be subject to the generally longer limitations period of state fraudulent transfer law.[37] Under the Bankruptcy Code, the DIP has two years after the commencement of the case to commence an action, the statute of limitations for which had not expired as of the commencement date.[38] The loss of a potentially valuable asset through the expiration of the limitations period may be a critical factor in the debtor's decision as to the appropriate restructuring vehicle. Indeed, the desire to prevent one creditor or group of creditors from "getting a leg up" on the others by escaping any potential liability might prompt creditors to commence an involuntary case against the debtor even during restructuring discussions.

In a similar vein, the 90-day and one-year periods during which preferential transfers to noninsiders and insiders, respectively, may be avoided[39] should be borne in mind by the debtor, both to ensure that a potentially valuable asset is not lost and to anticipate the possible commencement of an involuntary case by creditors allegedly harmed by such transfers.

Tax Advantages

Outside of the bankruptcy context, where debt is canceled, in whole or in part, for less than the full amount owing, a debtor will recognize cancellation of debt (COD) income, which likely will be taxable in whole or in part.[40] When a nonbankrupt debtor is insolvent (under the tax code, when the debtor's liabilities exceed the fair market value of its assets as determined immediately before cancellation of debt), the amount of COD income recognized will be the amount, if any, by which the amount of the debt canceled exceeds the amount of the insolvency; the remaining amount of the cancelled debt will be applied to reduce the debtor's favorable tax attributes (such as net operating losses and other loss and credit carryovers).[41]

For a debtor in bankruptcy, however, no portion of a simple COD will be taxable if the debt is cancelled pursuant to a bankruptcy discharge; instead, only the amount discharged will be applied to reduce the debtor's favorable tax attributes.[42]

If a proposed restructuring of the debtor's operations includes significant as-set sales, the tax treatment of certain transfers under state law may influence whether sales should be conducted pursuant to a plan of reorganization or pur-suant to an out-of-court workout. Under the Bankruptcy Code, "the issuance, transfer, or exchange of a security, or the making or delivery of an instrument of transfer under a plan confirmed under section 1129 . . . may not be taxed under any law imposing a stamp tax or similar tax."[43] Outside the contest of a con-firmed chapter 11 plan, however, the Supreme Court has upheld the general power of a state to impose sales or use taxes on bankruptcy liquidation sales un-der chapter 7 or chapter 11.[44]

Section 1146(c) raises two issues: what kind of taxes are within its scope and when does a transfer occur "under a plan." Transfer taxes on real estate are in-cluded within its scope,[45] although taxes on a transferor's gain are not.[46] With re-spect to sales and use taxes on transfers of personal property, the breadth of the exemption is unclear. Arguably, any tax that is imposed on the transfer itself is within the spirit of the exemption.

Courts have generally held that any sale conducted in order to effectuate a plan is a sale under a plan and therefore within section 1146(c). A significantly higher standard may apply, however, if the sale occurs before confirmation and particularly before the filing of the chapter 11 plan.[47]

Exemptions from Securities Laws

Transactions involving the offer, sale, or exchange of securities in connection with a reorganization under chapter 11 are exempt from the registration requirements of Section 5 of the Securities Act, the proxy solicitation rules under the Securities Ex-change Act of 1934, the "going private" rules, and certain other federal securities regulations.[48] In addition, such transactions are also exempt from registration re-quirements under state securities laws. The rationale for the exemptions is that the oversight generally provided by the SEC in such transactions is provided by the bankruptcy court, which must approve the transactions and the related disclosure, after notice and a hearing. Thus, the chapter 11 debtor is spared the time and ex-pense necessary to comply with overlapping statutory frameworks.

Exclusive Right to File a Plan

A chapter 11 debtor is provided with a 120-day "exclusive period" during which only the debtor may file a reorganization plan.[49] The retention of exclusivity is key to the debtor's ability to control the outcome of its chapter 11 case. During the exclusive period, the debtor is afforded an opportunity to stabilize its opera-tions and formulate a long-range business plan, which is then used as a founda-tion for its reorganization plan, all without the distraction that might result from plans that could otherwise be filed by other parties-in-interest. In addition, the debtor's senior management and employees can focus on the debtor's opera-tions, rather than the implications of any plan proposals on their own futures. As long as exclusivity is maintained, all creditors and other parties-in-interest must negotiate the parameters of a reorganization plan with the debtor.

The "Breathing Spell"

Another benefit of chapter 11 is that it offers a debtor a "breathing spell" within which it may negotiate the restructure or payment of its prepetition indebtedness to creditors while continuing to operate its businesses and thus preserving (or enhancing) the going concern value of its business. Moreover, a chapter 11 debtor is generally not required to make payments in respect of its prepetition debts. Once a debtor files for relief under chapter 11, interest ceases to accrue on its unsecured and undersecured debt. Particularly for operating companies, the opportunity for the debtor, in the first instance, to formulate and test a business plan that will form the basis of its reorganization plan is invaluable.

RISKS ATTENDANT TO THE COMMENCEMENT OF THE TRADITIONAL CHAPTER 11 CASE

Chapter 11 offers a distressed debtor innumerable restructuring options that are simply not available in the out-of-court context. Prior to the decision to seek relief under chapter 11, the distressed debtor must take into account the significant risks attendant to chapter 11.

Loss of Control

One of the radical innovations of American bankruptcy law is that, absent extraordinary circumstances, the debtor's policy makers and management remain in place in a chapter 11 case (i.e., the DIP concept). By rejecting the rule under chapter X of the former Bankruptcy Act, in which a trustee was automatically appointed to run the debtor's affairs, Congress concluded that debtors would be encouraged to seek relief under chapter 11 before their businesses became moribund.[50] Thus, consistent with congressional intent, the debtor is not automatically displaced at the commencement of a chapter 11 case. Since 1978, a number of statutory amendments and the return swing of the pendulum have eroded the DIP concept.[51] As a result, as noted, debtors are more reluctant to make the chapter 11 decision unless there is no other choice.

The Fishbowl Effect

By commencing a chapter 11 case, a debtor commits itself to extensive disclosure concerning how it operates its business, with whom it does business and on what terms, and its financial, operational, and other problems. The debtor is transformed, in part, into a debtor in possession, subject to the oversight of the bankruptcy court and its creditors, acting as one or more creditors' committees. Although a public company may be generally accustomed to the disclosure requirements of federal securities laws, for the privately held debtor, the disclosure requirements may be daunting. Debtor executives must appear for and be examined at the initial meeting of creditors, as well as periodic adjournments thereof, and at creditors' committee meetings.[52] Some protection may be available against disclosure of trade secrets, confidential research, or other valuable proprietary commercial information; however, such information usually will be made available to creditors' committee members, and confidentiality cannot be guaranteed.

Transactions Outside the Ordinary Course of Business

While the chapter 11 debtor is free to operate its business, it must obtain bankruptcy court approval for transactions out of the ordinary course of business.[53] Management is almost always shocked at how this limitation imposes upon its ability to operate its business. When the time needed for educating the creditors' committee, preparing the necessary pleadings, and providing appropriate notice is included, many debtors, especially those that do not have an orderly and well-planned introduction into chapter 11, feel that their ability to operate effectively in a competitive business environment is crippled. Apart from timing issues, management has to learn that its business decisions may be second-guessed, often by persons who may not be familiar with the peculiarities of the debtor's industry.

Retention of Senior Management

The employment contracts of the debtor's senior management (as well as other employees) will be executory contracts subject to assumption or rejection in chapter 11. Absent assumption of their contracts, members of senior management lack the assurance that their claims for bonuses or severance will be entitled to administrative priority and therefore paid in full. In most cases, the thresholds for performance bonuses set forth in existing employment contracts make no sense in the debtor's current condition. Nevertheless, retention of experienced and expert management is critical to the debtor's survival. In order to ensure that key members of management remain with the debtor, soon after the commencement date, the debtor will want to prepare and file motions for the assumption or modification of existing agreements or the execution of new agreements.

From the creditors' perspective, however, such motions are often brought on just as the creditors are realizing the magnitude of the debtor's problems. One natural reaction is for creditors to blame the very management whose contracts are before the bankruptcy court. Creditors may, therefore, be unsympathetic to the debtor's need to retain key management, especially in light of the large administrative claims that may result from assumption. From the perspective of the bankruptcy court, the compensation sought by senior management may seem astronomical, particularly faced with the possibility of a distribution to unsecured creditors that may be a fraction of their respective claims.

Consequently, at a time when the debtor needs great stability, and management needs to know that it can put its own individual interests aside and operate in the best interests of all creditors, it may be exceedingly difficult to obtain bankruptcy court approval of a management compensation and retention program. If it is not possible, the debtor is vulnerable to having key members of management cherry-picked by the competition, further exacerbating the debtor's problems.

Exclusive Right to File a Chapter 11 Plan

In the past, repeated extensions of the debtor's exclusive period for filing a plan have been commonplace. Lengthy extensions have been granted due to the size and complexity of the debtor's estate, the unresolved status of major litigation, and the seasonality of the debtor's business, among other things.[54] More recently, however, lengthy extensions of exclusivity have become less common. Courts commonly note that sheer size alone will not justify extension of a debtor's exclusive period for filing a plan.[55]

Although a large debtor is still likely to obtain at least one extension of exclusivity, it cannot rely on having adequate time within which to effectuate a turnaround. This lack of certainty has made chapter 11 a much more difficult environment, and one in which a debtor has less control over its own fate.

Appointment of a Trustee, Examiner, or Mediator

The Bankruptcy Code provides for the appointment of a trustee for cause or in the best interest of creditors.[56] The Bankruptcy Code also contemplates the appointment of an examiner; an examiner is a person usually charged with certain investigatory powers.[57] Two recent trends have impacted on the debtor's ability to manage the chapter 11 process. The first is the recent tendency of bankruptcy courts to appoint "an examiner with expanded powers." The concept is to appoint someone to perform more than a merely investigatory function, yet not go so far as to appoint a trustee and oust management. The expanded powers are generally enumerated by the bankruptcy court's order. For example, in the *Public Service of New Hampshire* case, an examiner was appointed to mediate negotiations aimed at arriving at a consensual plan of reorganization and to report to the court on the status of negotiations.[58]

The other recent trend, following a trend prevalent in other litigation contexts, is the appointment of a mediator, either to mediate a particular dispute or to broker a deal on a reorganization plan among the debtor and competing groups of creditors. Although there does not at first blush appear to be a downside to nonbinding mediation from the debtor's perspective, the risk for the debtor is that the bankruptcy court will view an impartial mediator as the voice of reason and view the debtor's refusal to accede to the mediator's view as unjustified intransigence.

Dubious Survival of the New Value Corollary

The Bankruptcy Code contemplates the confirmation of a consensual plan of reorganization. Pursuant to a consensual plan, creditors and stockholders may agree among themselves, within certain limits, as to how to share distributions under a reorganization plan. The Bankruptcy Code also provides for the confirmation of a nonconsensual or cram-down plan.[59] In the cram-down context, however, the "absolute priority" rule must be satisfied. Under the absolute priority rule, no junior class may receive any distribution under a reorganization plan until all senior classes have received property having a value equal to the allowed amount of their claims. Consequently, equityholders would ordinarily not be entitled to any distribution unless all creditors have received distributions equal to the full amount of their claims.

The so-called new value corollary was developed by courts under the former Bankruptcy Act. It provided that former equityholders may exchange "new value" for equity in the reorganized debtor, even though some creditors will not be repaid in full under the plan. The judicially established criteria for application of the new value corollary are that the capital to be contributed by old equity must be (1) new, (2) substantial, (3) money or money's worth, (4) necessary for a successful reorganization, and (5) reasonably equivalent to the value of the property that old equity is to retain or receive. Although the Bankruptcy Code incorporates the absolute priority rule, the Bankruptcy Code and its legislative history do not indicate whether the new value corollary continues to be available.

Courts of appeal have split over whether and to what extent the new value corollary survives the enactment of the Bankruptcy Code.[60] The key distinction in the conflicting cases is whether an existing equityholder that provides tangible new value is receiving anything "on account of" its equity interests. Those courts that have upheld application of the corollary have held that the new equity is being distributed on account of the new investment. Conversely, those courts that have strictly interpreted the corollary have held that, unless investments are solicited from third parties, existing equityholders impermissibly would be receiving something on account of their former equity—the exclusive opportunity to invest in the reorganized entity. The split among the courts of appeals should be resolved shortly, inasmuch as the Supreme Court has recently granted certiorari and will review the Seventh Circuit's decision in *In re 203 North LaSalle Partnership*.

If the Supreme Court adopts the position of those courts that have adopted a strict interpretation of the new value corollary, chapter 11 will be fraught with even more uncertainty from the perspective of the debtor's equityholders. In order to obtain confirmation of a new value plan, the debtor may have to demonstrate that third-party investors were solicited. Such solicitation, however, may result in the equity being outbid; that is, a third party may be willing to make a greater investment for the same portion of new equity. Former equityholders may lose any interest in the reorganized debtor or have to increase the amount they are willing to pay therefor.

All of the foregoing demonstrate that actual practice under the Bankruptcy Code has proceeded far afield from what the legislators contemplated when the Bankruptcy Code was enacted. While the norm in chapter 11 often assumes that management is expected to remain in place and run the debtor's operations and its restructuring, there appears to be less likelihood than ever that the DIP will be able to orchestrate its chapter 11 case and shepherd its reorganization plan to confirmation.

Expense of Restructuring in Chapter 11

As is the case with respect to out-of-court restructurings and other remedial proceedings, a chapter 11 case may be expensive to administer. The structure of chapter 11, with the imposition of statutory committees and the U.S. Trustee, necessarily elevates costs. The addition of any significant litigation likewise will materially add to the cost of administration. However, many of the cost items would be incurred despite the chapter 11 case. That factor should not be ignored. In any event, the use of cash to meet the costs of professionals, experts, and the like hired by the debtor and, beyond its control, by statutory committees may be very substantial.

Chapter 11 also extracts a huge toll in soft costs—the amount of time devoted by senior members of management to complying with the chapter 11 process rather than operating the business. Similarly, the delay occasioned by the need for bankruptcy court and statutory committee approvals may preclude the debtor from taking advantage of business opportunities. The debtor's employees are invariably affected by the commencement of a chapter 11 case; many employees will leave the debtor to pursue other opportunities, and those that remain may have poor morale in light of the uncertain futures.

DEVELOPMENT OF A RESTRUCTURING STRATEGY

The optimal restructuring scenario for most debtors is to take advantage of the extraordinary remedies available in chapter 11, but to do so in a controlled process, the outcome of which is all but assured (i.e., a prepackaged or pre-arranged chapter 11 case). Chapter 11 offers debtors a wide panoply of tools with which to effect a restructuring of both their financial status and their operations. On the other hand, a traditional chapter 11 case can be time consuming, expensive, and unpredictable. For some debtors, the incremental benefits available in chapter 11 may be outweighed by the risks attendant thereto. Thus, if the debtor's primary problem is overleveraging, but there are some provisions of chapter 11 that might confer some minimal additional benefit, commencement of a case under chapter 11 may not be appropriate. Conversely, if a debtor can obtain a restructuring of an amount of indebtedness outside of chapter 11 sufficient to allow it to continue its business without impairment, commencement of a chapter 11 case may nevertheless be warranted in order to correct debilitating operational problems. As previously noted, the circumstances require the debtor's business managers to review and evaluate:

- How extensive a restructuring is necessary?
- What is the threshold of debt or other relief the debtor must achieve if it is to avoid chapter 11?
- Regardless of the magnitude of concessions made by its creditors, is the debtor's resort to chapter 11 necessary or appropriate because of pressing litigation, avoidance claims, or other reasons?
- Are the primary creditor constituencies fully secured or undersecured, and does their concern over their potential recoveries in chapter 11 give the debtor negotiating leverage?
- How much can the debtor afford to give up to creditors in the form of additional collateral?
- Will the pledge of additional collateral obviate the possibility of a successful chapter 11 case, should chapter 11 ultimately prove unavoidable?
- How does the seasonal nature of the debtor's business affect the timing of

commencement of restructuring discussions and, if necessary, a chapter 11 case?

- Are there impending debt defaults, required public filings, or other external considerations that affect timing?
- Does the debtor require a freeze of creditor rights to attempt an operational turnaround?
- Is the payment in full of trade claims, a typical feature of prepackaged cases, a feasible option that is likely to be acceptable to the senior creditors?
- What will be the impact on the business if the commencement of restructuring discussions becomes public?
- Can the debtor withstand the possible contraction of trade credit?
- What unilateral measures, if any, can the debtor take during the period of negotiation and documentation to reduce its operating expenses?
- Are there any outstanding obligations for "trust fund taxes" for which "responsible officers" may be personally liable, and what arrangements, if any, have been made for satisfaction of such obligations?
- Has the debtor failed to pay any outstanding corporate or other business taxes that may lead to the commencement of a chapter 11 case?
- If the debtor has one or more pension plans, are they fully funded, overfunded, or underfunded, and what impact does their status have on restructuring discussions?
- Does the debtor face any environmental liabilities that may not be discharged in chapter 11?
- Does the debtor have sufficient cash on hand or projected to be received to support its efforts to negotiate an out-of-court restructuring or a prepackaged or prearranged bankruptcy?

After consideration of all factors and evaluation of the benefits and risks of chapter 11, unless the debtor requires immediate relief under the Bankruptcy Code, the distressed debtor should formulate an initial restructuring proposal and commence negotiations with its major creditors to obtain what relief is necessary. The debtor must maintain its credibility, and it will have to provide financial data to justify the concessions and changes it requests.

Unless the debtor has significant unencumbered assets to offer to creditors in an out-of-court restructuring, the debtor's only leverage in the restructuring negotiations is the commencement of a traditional chapter 11 case. Of course, by virtue of the absolute priority rule, creditors, and particularly distressed debt traders, recognize that the debtor's equityholders are vulnerable to having their equity eliminated if the debtor is insolvent or is in the vicinity of insolvency. Nevertheless, creditors may believe that the bankruptcy court tends to favor debtors, at least initially, and fear the delay and risks attendant to a chapter 11 case thereby extending some leverage to the debtor. Distressed debt traders may fear that in chapter 11 the debtor will be put "in play," increasing the price such traders would have to pay to obtain control of the reorganized entity.

CONCLUSION

Although out-of-court restructuring negotiations may not go as planned, and the debtor should remain flexible, it is essential that the debtor's policy makers and management not allow the momentum of the workout strategy to overtake them. In fact, the ideal course is for the debtor to conduct restructuring negotiations at the same time it prepares for commencement of a chapter 11 case. Two purposes are served by pursuing parallel courses. First, creditors will recognize that the prospect of a chapter 11 filing is not an idle threat by the debtor. Second, the debtor's policy makers and senior management will continue to focus on chapter 11 as a viable option.

There are many different avenues to a successful restructuring. The only approach that is obviously doomed to fail is for the debtor to agree to the terms of an out-of-court restructuring that provides the debtor with only a piecemeal, short-term reprieve from its financial difficulties.

NOTES

1. *See* Commission on the Bankruptcy Laws of The United States Report, H.R. Doc. No. 93-137, 93d Cong., 1st Sess., pt. I, at 237-48 (1978).

2. *In re Johns-Manville Corporation, et al.*, Chapter 11 Case Nos. 82-B-11656 through 82-B-11676 (BRL) (Bankr. S.D.N.Y. 1982).

3. *In re Continental Airlines Corporation, et al.*, Consolidated Chapter 11 Case No. 83-04019-H2-5 (Bankr. S.D. Tex. 1983).

4. *See, e.g.*, Bankruptcy Code §§ 365(b)(3), 1113, 1114, 362(c)(3), 362(e), 363.

5. *See, e.g.*, Bankruptcy Rule 4001.

6. *See, e.g., In re Southland Corporation*, 124 B.R. 211 (Bankr. N.D. Tex. 1991).

7. *In re Consolidated Hydro, Inc.*, Chapter 11 Case No. 97-1924 (SLR) (D. Del. 1997).

8. *In re G. Heileman Brewing Company, Inc., et al.*, Consolidated Chapter 11 Case No. 91B-10326 (FGC) (Bankr. S.D.N.Y. 1991).

9. *In re R.H. Macy & Co., Inc.*, Case No. 92 B 40477 (BRL) (Bankr. S.D.N.Y. 1992).

10. For example, *Texaco, Inc.* and its affiliates, which commenced their chapter 11 cases on April 12, 1987 (Chapter 11 Case Nos. 87 B 20143, et seq. (HS) (Bankr. S.D. N.Y.)).

11. Bankruptcy Code, § 362(a)(1).

12. Bankruptcy Code, § 362(a).

13. *See, e.g., In re Little Creek Development Company*, 779 F.2d 1068 (5th Cir. 1986) (court of appeals remanded case to bankruptcy court for further evidence regarding bankruptcy court's decision to grant secured creditor relief from automatic stay based on statements of debtor's counsel that petition was filed in order to escape the necessity of posting a bond in a state court proceeding).

14. Bankruptcy Code, § 364.

15. Bankruptcy Code, §§ 364(b), (c).

16. Bankruptcy Code, §§ 364(a), (b), (c), (d).

17. *See, e.g., In re Snowshoe Co.*, 789 F.2d 1085 (4th Cir. 1986) (although the debtor is not required to seek credit from every possible source, the debtor must establish that it has made reasonable efforts to seek other sources of credit under sections 364(a), (b) and (c)).

18. Bankruptcy Code, §§ 363(a), 363(c)(2).

19. For example, in *In re Food Barn Stores, Inc.*, Case No. 93-40012-2-11 (Bankr. W.D. Mo.) the

trade vendors requested (and received) a carve-out from the DIP lender's post-petition liens in the amount of $2 million. *See also F&M Distributors, Inc.*, Case No. 94-52115 (Bankr. E.D. Mich.) (trade vendors received a superpriority administrative expense and lien on inventory *pari passu* with lien granted to DIP lenders).

20. Bankruptcy Code, § 365(a).

21. *See* discussion, *infra*.

22. Bankruptcy Code, § 1113.

23. Bankruptcy Code, § 1114 (enacted in 1988).

24. *See, e.g., In re Continental Airlines Corp.*, 901 F.2d 1259 (5th Cir. 1990).

25. Bankruptcy Code, §§ 502(b)(6) (lease rejection) and 502(b)(7) (employment contracts). The ability to reject contracts and unexpired leases will not provide any benefit to a debtor if the debtor's obligations thereunder have been guaranteed by a non-debtor entity; the relief afforded by sections 365 and 502(b) is only available to a debtor under the Bankruptcy Code.

26. Bankruptcy Code, § 365(f).

27. In the case of a shopping center lease, adequate assurance has certain particular requirements as to tenant mix, percentage rent and other matters. Bankruptcy Code, § 365(b)(3).

28. Bankruptcy Code, § 365(k).

29. *See, e.g., In re R.H. Macy & Co., Inc.*, 170 B.R. 69, 76 (Bankr. S.D. N.Y. 1994); *In re Ames Department Stores, Inc.*, 136 B.R. 357 (Bankr. S.D. N.Y. 1992).

30. Bankruptcy Code, § 363(f).

31. Bankruptcy Code, § 363(h).

32. Bankruptcy Code, § 1126(c).

33. Bankruptcy Code, § 1129(b).

34. Bankruptcy Code, § 502(c).

35. *See Kane* v. *Johns-Manville Corp.*, 843 F.2d 636 (2d Cir. 1988) (affirming confirmation order in appeal by asbestos claimant who challenged, *inter alia*, the voting procedures).

36. *In re Eagle-Picher Industries, Inc., et al.*, 189 B.R. 681 (Bankr. S.D. Ohio 1995).

37. Bankruptcy Code, §§ 548, 544(b).

38. Bankruptcy Code, § 108.

39. Bankruptcy Code, § 547.

40. 26 U.S.C. § 108.

41. 26 U.S.C. § 108(a), (b), (d).

42. 26 U.S.C. § 108(a)(1)(A), (a)(2).

43. Bankruptcy Code, § 1146(c).

44. *California State Board of Equalization* v. *Sierra Summit, Inc.*, 490 U.S. 844 (1989).

45. *In re Jacoby-Bender, Inc.* (*City of New York* v. *Jacoby-Bender, Inc.*), 758 F.2d 840 (2d Cir. 1985).

46. *In re Jacoby-Bender, Inc.*, 40 B.R. 10 (Bankr. E.D.N.Y. 1984), *aff'd*, 758 F.2d 840 (2d Cir. 1985).

47. *See, e.g., In re Jacoby-Bender*, 758 F.2d 840 (2d Cir. 1985); *In re Smoss Enterprises Corp.*, 54 B.R. 950 (E.D. N.Y. 1985); *In re Permar Provisions, Inc.*, 79 B.R. 530 (Bankr. E.D. N.Y. 1987).

48. Bankruptcy Code, § 1145(a).

49. Bankruptcy Code, § 1121(b). In addition, if the debtor files a plan within such time period, it is given an additional 60-day period during which to solicit acceptances of its plan. Bankruptcy Code, § 1121(c)(3).

50. *See* H.R. Rep. No. 95-595, 95th Cong., 1st Sess. 233-34 ("[A] standard that led to too frequent appointment [of a trustee] would prevent debtors from seeking relief under the reorganization chapter and would leave the chapter largely unused except in extreme cases. One of the problems that the Bankruptcy Commission recognized . . . is that debtors too often wait too long to seek bankruptcy re-

lief. Too frequent appointment of a trustee would exacerbate that problem, to the detriment of both debtors and their creditors.")(footnotes omitted).

51. *See, e.g.*, Bankruptcy Code, § 1104(b) (providing that within 30 days after the bankruptcy court orders appointment of a trustee, the U.S. Trustee shall convene a meeting of creditors for the purpose of electing a trustee).

52. Bankruptcy Code, §§ 341, 1103(c); Bankruptcy Rule 2003.

53. Bankruptcy Code, § 363(b)(1).

54. *See, e.g.*, *In re Manville Forest Products Corp.*, 31 Bankr. 991, 995 (S.D. N.Y. 1983) (affirming bankruptcy court's order granting the debtor's fifth extension of its exclusive periods even though the debtor was solvent, faced no liability for asbestos claims and had operations which were separate from those of Manville and its other subsidiaries, the court held that "[t]he sheer mass, weight, volume and complication of the Manville filings undoubtedly justify a shakedown period.").

55. *See, e.g.*, *In re Public Service of New Hampshire*, 88 B.R. 521, 537 (Bankr. D.N.H. 1988).

56. Bankruptcy Code, § 1121(a).

57. Bankruptcy Code, § 1121(c).

58. 99 B.R. 177 (Bankr. D.N.H. 1989). *See also In re Ionosphere Clubs, Inc.*, Case Nos. 89 B 10448 and 10449 (Bankr. S.D. N.Y. 1989) (Eastern Airlines, Inc.) (court ordered appointment of examiner with expanded powers and engendered a quasi-official offering of the debtor's business to the world at large).

59. Bankruptcy Code, § 1129(b).

60. *Compare In re 203 N. Lasalle Partnership*, 126 F.3d 955 (7th Cir. 1997), *cert. granted*, 118 S. Ct 1674 (1998) (upholding confirmation of the debtor's new value plan); *Bonner Mall Partnership* v. *U.S. Bancorp Mortgage Co.,* 2 F.3d 899 (9th Cir. 1993), *cert. granted*, 114 S. Ct. 681 (1994), *appeal dismissed as moot*, 512 U.S. 18 (1994)(same), with *Coltex Loop Cent. Three Partners, L.P.* v. *BT/SAP Pool C Assocs., L.P.*, No. 96-5140, 1998 U.S. App. LEXIS 2662 (2d Cir. Feb. 19, 1998), as corrected Mar. 3, 1998 (adopting a very limited interpretation of the corollary and holding that "if old equity's new interest under the plan results in any significant way from its old status, the plan may not be confirmed.") and *Travelers Insurance Co.* v. *Bryson Properties XVIII*, 961 F.2d 496 (4th Cir. 1992) (same).

3

Preparing for Bankruptcy— Building the War Chest

Joel Nitzberg

PricewaterhouseCoopers LLP

INTRODUCTION

Cash is king—no matter how many times you hear it, read it, or say it, it is not often enough when a company is facing the possibility of a bankruptcy filing.

Typically, most business executives and key management personnel are expected to manage for profits. Their compensation quite often is linked to how they manage expenses and how they manage the cash associated with these expenses. They consider cash as a number they see when they look at a balance sheet. Ask a typical executive or middle management personnel the definition of working capital, operating cash flow, or free cash flow, and the odds are you will receive nothing but a quizzical stare. So it should not be too surprising that as a company begins to spin into crisis, one of the most difficult areas to get management to focus on is *cash*—cash that is required to fuel the turnaround, cash that is required to fund the war chest.

THE WAR CHEST

What is the war chest? It is the cash that needs to be set aside to allow the turnaround process to proceed—the cash that is in the bank accounts of the company that is available for use by the company. It is the additional availability that is being created under an asset-based revolving line of credit. It is the cash that is available to the company to send a message, when necessary, that the company has cash to use in key situations. It is the cash necessary to pay vendors for the delivery of merchandise on a cash on delivery (COD) basis, to fund payment of employee payroll and benefits and other first-day orders that are critical to the survival of the company during the early stages of bankruptcy.

45

CASH MANAGEMENT

In the process of building the war chest, one of the most critical determinations is to be able to identify that point in time in the foreseeable future when the war chest has been maximized and vendor payables have been stretched to their limit in terms of time and amount. One of the simplest oversights is to assume that the company has total control of the process. Remember, vendors can shut the company off and, worse yet, move for an involuntary filing.

To maintain control, the cash management process must be given the highest of priorities. Responsibility for the cash management process must be given to a member of the crisis management team. This individual must have oversight responsibility for all aspects of the cash process encompassing both cash receipts and disbursements. The cash management process must include a method wherein cash receipts and disbursements can be forecasted on a rolling 13-week period. The forecast should set forth the significant disbursement items such as payroll, travel, capital expenditures, and so forth. Each week, actual results should be compared to forecast with explanations and corrective actions for material differences presented. The forecast should be updated weekly and rolled forward for the next 13-week period. Mandatory weekly reporting to the crisis management team must occur. Re-evaluation of the cash maximization point must be continued throughout this forecast period.

Each of the critical components of the balance sheet, accounts receivable, accounts payable, inventory, and cash must be rolled forward during the forecast period. For critical vendors, a detailed account balance roll forward should be developed, reflecting anticipated purchases and payments. To the extent possible, the projected balances should be aged to determine the extent to which vendors are being stretched as to time and amount. Trade vendors talk to each other, and one key vendor definitely does not want to be treated worse than any other vendor.

This same analysis process should be applied to significant customers. A company cannot allow cash flow to be negatively impacted by a buildup in accounts receivable. As word begins to filter out within the industry that a company is experiencing financial problems, it is not unusual to experience customers trying to slow down payments or requesting discounts. It is critical to be able to recognize any slowing down in payments as soon as it begins to happen. Having an action plan set out prior to its becoming a significant problem will be extremely beneficial.

Probably the most difficult item to forecast is inventory. Very few companies have the tools or information process necessary to properly forecast the components of inventory. Forecasting inventory involves many individual components that will directly impact the cash flow forecast. Even a company with the simplest of assembly processes will need to understand and forecast not only the material requirements but also direct labor and overhead components.

It is important when developing the cash flow forecast to take the time required to ensure that the individual cash receipts and disbursement line items directly correlate with the amounts used to forecast the change in the corresponding balance sheet accounts. It is not unusual to find, when trying to reconcile differences between actual and forecast, that it is the failure of having a direct correlation between the components of the increases and decreases in the balance sheet accounts and the detail components of the receipts and disbursements forecast that is causing the variances. When forecasting inventory, the calculation for determining the ending inventory is: beginning inventory plus purchases less cost of goods sold equals ending inventory (purchases being materials, labor, and overhead).

In building the war chest, varied cash maximization initiatives must be identified and implemented, with the overall goal being to create as much cash liquidity as possible. Almost all companies have additional sources of cash and liquidity. Even the company that seems to be running out of liquidity that has never undertaken a cash maximization initiative will find ways to increase cash and liquidity.

One additional point to mention involves not forgetting to undertake a detailed analysis of any secured credit agreement that exists. Understanding what type of restrictions exists with regard to the sale of assets outside the normal course of business and the expected disposition of those funds is very important. Determining how and if separate bank accounts can be established for the proceeds generated from the cash maximization initiatives will sometimes impact on how, what, and when some things are done. In some situations, having foreign subsidiaries and intercompany transactions will facilitate the availability of creating a war chest, outside of the dominion of control of creditors, that will not be in violation of the existing credit agreement. Not all credit agreements preclude the paydown of intercompany balances or the movement of cash between subsidiaries.

COMPONENTS OF THE BUSINESS CYCLE

The following sections discuss the various aspects of the process of building the war chest. However, it should be noted that the discussion presumes that enough time exists for the cash maximization initiatives to be implemented and the benefits realized. In terms of time, the thought is that the normal business cycles will have occurred more than once. All companies have business cycles; that is, the time from a vendor's acceptance of a purchase order to the time that the cash is ultimately collected from the customer for the sale of product. Understanding and identifying the individual components within each aspect of the business cycle will help focus the attention of the crisis management team to those aspects where the most benefit will accrue.

Accounts Receivable

The goal here, of course, is to collect as much of the outstanding accounts receivable as possible. To accomplish this, it is strongly recommended that one individual within the credit and collection function be given responsibility for coordinating the overall effort—an effort that will require the interaction of the credit and collection function with other functional areas of the company, such as shipping, sales, and customer service. This individual must have the respect of the other managers within the company and be able to deal effectively with customers while being driven to collect as much as possible. This individual should also be given the authority to resolve disputes and initiate discounts within predetermined limits without having to deal with a time-consuming approval process. Time can be very critical in resolving disputes and differences of opinion.

Begin with the existing outstanding accounts receivable. The first step is to analyze the accounts receivable listing for those accounts that are past due. Once these accounts have been identified, a team of collectors should be assigned to call on these specific accounts, even if they are not the same collectors who would have normally called the account. The goal now is to develop a very focused group of collectors to deal with past due accounts. The collectors should believe they own the accounts and be responsible for ensuring that any issues are resolved quickly and correctly. Some collectors are not as good as others in dealing with contentious customers or problems. In most situations, the reason the account is past due is because something is just not right. If the same collector is responsible for calling on his or her accounts in the normal course of business, the focus and time required in resolving past due amounts might not occur. Consideration should be given to hiring temporary staff to provide administrative support to collectors. Having an experienced collector making copies of invoices or filling out proofs of delivery is not an efficient use of the collector's time. If the company conducts business within different time zones, adjust the working hours of the collectors so that coverage is sufficient and appropriate within each time zone. Finally, an incentive plan should be established to compensate the collectors on their initiative.

Documentation of collection calls, including follow-ups required and customer commitments, should be made in a standardized manner to facilitate easy follow-up and review. There is nothing worse than trying to follow up a call and not being able to understand what has previously transpired. When the customer is contacted, all the pertinent information needed to discuss the situation should be readily available. A customer payment commitment should be obtained if there are no open items. Partial payments can be requested if necessary. A call-back date should be established and the most accessible time determined. This will give the customer the opportunity to be prepared for the call. Without spending too much time, the collector should try and verify that any other outstanding invoices have been received and determine whether there are any other unresolved issues. Identifying and quickly resolving customer issues that can be used as an excuse not to pay is the objective. The collector must find out what they are and who has to do what to correct them. In summary, the objective is to eliminate customer arguments and to persuade the customer to pay all or at least some of the outstanding balance, even if it means offering discounts or adjustments that might not occur in the normal course of business.

Having addressed past due amounts, the next step is to direct attention to the remaining outstanding amounts. Reducing the overall days outstanding and the dollars of accounts receivable subsequently becoming past due in the near term is also very important. Consideration must be given to those accounts with the larger amounts due to ensure that they are being contacted timely and any problems are ferreted out quickly. Developing a customer call profile that specifies who in the customer's accounts payable function handles the account, when is the most convenient time to call, and when invoices are selected for payment is very helpful. Calling about an invoice before it misses the payment cycle if a problem exists and expeditiously resolving any issues could increase cash collections in some situations by more than one week.

One further area of discussion for improving cash flow and therefore creating the war chest involves specific aspects of the revenue cycle. Shipping and invoicing are the key aspects that also need to be addressed. During the period when cash maximization is paramount, it is absolutely imperative that shipments and invoicing occur steadily throughout the month and ratably throughout the week. The classic phenomenon of shipping the majority of customer orders at the end of the month will severely impact the collection of receivables for these shipments. The faster the goods are shipped and invoices mailed, the quicker the cash can be collected. Trying to reduce freight costs by consolidating the shipments is not what is needed. Also, processing and mailing invoices daily can greatly increase cash flow.

Accounts Payable

Dealing with a supplier even during normal times can be a time-consuming and difficult task. Suppliers want and need to be paid on time, to have disputes resolved quickly, and, most importantly, to receive payment by an agreed-upon date. Add the dynamic of a company experiencing financial difficulty and uncertainty, and the problems and concerns magnify and multiply. Almost every supplier wants a payment commitment and up-to-date information. At the same time, the company must conserve cash while still maintaining a steady flow of materials in order to continue to supply customers with product. Attempting to build the cash war chest just to use the cash to pay down suppliers defeats the purpose. Also, it will trouble any lender, particularly a secured lender, who sees a conversion of collateral into cash to reduce the exposure of subordinated creditors.

The following discussion sets forth some thoughts and ideas that have been used to deal with suppliers and the types of issues that arise during a period of uncertainty. However, it is important to remember that there is very little a company can try that suppliers have not heard before and learned not to believe anyway. What it really comes down to is a sense of trust and someone's word. Therefore, in the early stages, failing to live up to promises will virtually eliminate any opportunity of getting help and being believed as times get worse. An experienced accounts payable manager I knew is a good example.When cash began to get tight, instead of telling "tall tales" he told trouble-some suppliers that "the company is not sure that we should continue to do business with you if you do not have the financial strength to take a business risk and continue to supply our company during this temporary period of difficulty" and that he would have to discuss this with the purchasing department. As farfetched as it seems, this worked better than telling the classic "tall tale". The reason was that the supplier's collection person did not want to jeopardize the business relationship and therefore would usually ship one or two more orders.

As previously mentioned, this is a period that requires trust between the company and its suppliers. Therefore, the crisis management team should evaluate whether the existing accounts payable manager should be the company's representative or whether the treasurer or chief financial officer should be more directly involved. My recommendation would be to let the accounts payable manager continue to handle issues, but within a set of established guidelines as to message and promises. As the situation becomes more tenuous, then the involvement of others might become necessary.

The key to managing suppliers and cash disbursements during this period is to ensure that all calls are answered timely and returned when promised. Just letting the phone ring or putting the call on hold does not work. Usually, it results in the suppliers trying to reach others in the company who will only be caught off guard by such calls. Some companies have hired temporaries to answer the phones and ascertain the nature of the calls and inform the caller of when and who will be getting back to them. Finally, when contact occurs with the supplier they should be told the truth. The company must not commit to something that in all likelihood cannot be delivered. The last thing that anyone wants to happen is for the supplier to shut the company off entirely, even to COD shipments. Accepting an offer for the supplier to ship on a cash-in-advance basis is probably not a smart idea, especially if the company has large outstanding balances. Obviously, all they will do is apply the payment to the outstanding balance and not ship. The goal of all this time and effort is to ensure that materials continue to flow and that every time a critical supplier receives a payment, an equal amount of materials is received. Otherwise, it will not be too long before suppliers will realize that they have the upper hand and continue to exert pressure to have their outstanding balance paid down, and other suppliers will find out.

Having discussed the psychology of the process, we will now examine some of the tactics. This process involves deciding which suppliers are critical to the continued operation of the company. As one might suspect, this involves stratifying suppliers into categories. Label them A, B, and C suppliers, with A being the most important. This is a process that should include as much input as possible from all the functional areas of the company. The analysis process and negotiating strategy should include input from purchasing, manufacturing, inventory control, engineering, finance, and so on. It is a process that will help ensure agreement of the facts among all involved. The accounts payable function must be aware of how critical a supplier is. Sole-source suppliers must be dealt with differently than one-time suppliers. In one situation of which I am aware, the accounts payable manager was very concerned with a supplier that was thought to be critical to the manufacturing process. A significant amount of time was spent negotiating a payment method. As it turned out, the part being supplied by this supplier had been redesigned and sourced from another supplier.

As a realist, I recognize that it is just not possible to not pay a supplier anything. Therefore, as cash is generated from the asset side of the balance sheet, some of it will have to be used to satisfy critical suppliers. However, this is when the cash forecast model becomes critical in identifying the maximum cash point.

Another opportunity that sometimes occurs involves identifying overstock and slow-moving inventory in terms of its disposition. In some situations, the supplier will be willing to take back product in lieu of cash payment and continue to ship on some basis. If inventory is to be returned for credit, then it should be considered the same as cash from the company's perspective. One should try to negotiate the receipt of new merchandise for all or part of the value returned. One tactic to be considered is to determine whether there is someone else who will be willing to buy the inventory for cash. This can work as a good negotiating point with the primary supplier. Even if selling the inventory to a third party results in less value, it just might be worth it if it creates more cash.

Other possible areas of generating cash or reducing supplier exposure involve resolving disallowed deductions with the supplier and collecting supplier receivable balances. Another possible initiative that can be considered is to hire a third party to conduct an accounts payable payment audit. These firms work strictly on a contingency fee basis and quite often will be able to identify duplicate amount and payment errors that will reduce the supplier's perceived exposure or real cash. The contingency fee is never paid until the cash is collected or the offset agreed to.

Inventory

The acquisition of material, labor, and overhead, necessary to manufacture products for sale, is probably the single largest process that impacts the company's cash requirements. Therefore, even a slight improvement in inventory levels can significantly improve the company's cash position. Focusing on ways to improve cycle time to reflect a just-in-time approach, evaluating safety stock levels and manufacturing costs will very quickly improve cash flow and create cash available for the war chest. Focusing on reducing indirect costs will have an immediate impact on cash flow. Just make sure that, when considering a reduction in staff, the severance outlay does not offset the cash benefit in the short term. Always pay severance on a continuation basis and not a lump sum. Regardless, when reducing head count, it is not only the compensation aspect that is saved but also all the related and tag-along expenses. Consideration should be given to an unpaid shutdown as times get tough.

Of course, identifying and eliminating the sale of low-margin products, short-run production runs, and special orders will help by reducing the need to purchase new materials. Conversely, creating an incentive for the sales force to sell off the odds and ends, even at a discount, will help. Undertaking a cost-to-complete analysis of noncurrent or slow-moving inventory often will identify opportunities to convert inventory into products that can be sold for cash quite quickly with very little incremental cash outlay. Coordinating this type of initiative should be the responsibility of the crisis management team and involve the sales organization and the manufacturing and inventory-control organizations.

OTHER CONSIDERATIONS

The following list outlines various other approaches and considerations to convert assets into cash.

- *Letters of credit.* Sometimes a company can avail itself of back-to-back letters of credit. When properly structured this approach will allow the supplier to be paid directly by the customer. This method also helps convince the customer that they will receive the product they need.
- *Other receivables.* Try to sell, factor, or discount all other receivables. In each individual situation, the company's financial position will most likely be irrelevant to the acquirer as long as the transaction occurs without recourse. The only real issue is the financial cost of the decision and whether a very negative message will be perceived by third parties.
- *Prepaid expenses and deposits.* It is not unusual to identify deposits and prepaid expenses that can be recovered or applied against outstanding balances. Canceling memberships and recovering deposits is sometimes possible. Converting insurance policies so that they can be financed is also sometimes available.
- *Property plant and equipment.* The first obvious option is to investigate entering into a sale and leaseback transaction. Of course, this assumes that a secured creditor does not have a collateral position that requires a paydown. In a recent situation, a company was able to sell and lease back an entire warehouse and distribution operation, which included all of the racking and shelving equipment involved in the operation. To generate additional cash, the company outsourced its delivery operation to a third party. They received a substantial payment from the third party for the right to provide the outsourcing service and acquiring the fleet and personnel. Of course, identifying how to consolidate space, sublet, or turn back the space will create cash flow.
- *Licensing.* Investigating the possibility of licensing the rights to use trademarks, trade names, or technology can be a successful undertaking. This is

particularly interesting to companies in other parts of the world. It is not unusual to receive a payment representing the minimum guarantee upon execution.

- *Other general considerations.* Elimination of all types of discretionary spending and deferring payroll expenses again serve as ways to conserve cash. Looking to senior management to defer a percentage of their compensation can only help send a positive message. A company should look for alternative suppliers with whom it can establish some terms and lower costs.

4

Business Regeneration: Early Detection— Early Intervention

R. Carter Pate

PricewaterhouseCoopers LLP

INTRODUCTION

It is a tragic fact of business life that many companies fail not because of an irrevocable downward spiral of their financial health, but because of management's inability to face serious problems and take action. In my years as a management turnaround consultant, this simple act of denial has contributed to the demise of a huge number of companies that might otherwise have been saved.

Denial is insidious because it delays important actions that, if taken in the early stages of underperformance, can dramatically improve the chances of survival. One does not have to be a psychologist to understand why company executives fall into the denial trap. They have invested tremendous emotional and intellectual energy into a management strategy that is failing. To change direction means sometimes admitting failure, exposing them to criticism by the company's board of directors, shareholders, and peers within larger corporate structures.

Parent-company management and directors, in turn, find it hard not to trust the chief executive officer (CEO) and admit that the company has developed substantial problems on their watch. Both parties are reluctant to consider outside intervention because of the specter of company upheaval, mass firings, and other unpleasantness that is associated with some turnaround efforts.

How can companies avoid the denial trap? First, clear-eyed, vigilant, and independent oversight by the board of directors in key areas will help detect problems early and allow the company to be positioned for a successful future. Rarely does a single event lead to the eventual demise of a company. Reflecting on one's history and actions helps to ensure that similar mistakes will not be repeated. First, we will examine the big picture of detecting a business that is ripe for failure.

EXTERNAL CAUSES OF BUSINESS FAILURE

A number of external forces will impact the ability of a company to succeed. Some of the most frequently mentioned factors include:[1]

- Economic change
- Competitive change
- Social change
- Technological change
- Governmental actions and regulation

Economic Change

One of the leading culprits of business failure in a free market system is market forces, which require companies to adapt to economic change such as inflationary and interest rate pressures. In fact, the entire economic health of the nation, as well as individual perception of well-being, can have a profound effect on the purchasing habits of consumers and corporate buyers. The balance of trade and the exchange relationship of the U.S. dollar to our foreign trading partners can either benefit or damage the import/export business. Almost imperceptible on a day-to-day basis, the effects of continued and sustained economic pressure may be harmful to a company's liquidity position. Movement of economic forces by more than 10% annually should be discussed at the highest level of the company.

Competitive Changes

Pressure from competitive forces can take many forms and sometimes hold entire management teams captive while ignoring the long-term goals of the company. The free market forces allow the highest-quality/lowest-cost producer to quickly rise above the competition. Often, a company will overemphasize the goal of gaining market share, while ignoring the long-term health of the company and neglecting to take decisive action such as abandoning noncore product lines. Raw materials, high labor cost, union unrest, and transportation cost issues also affect the ability of a company to find its appropriate niche and prosper. These factors notwithstanding, the consumer has the final say, often being the most fickle and demanding constant improvement in quality features and price reductions. The most clandestine competitive factors include targeted pricing and oversaturation of goods. Management can sometimes find itself faced with a choice that can ultimately make or break the company: match balance sheets in order to weather the storm and outlast the competitor or exit the product line. It is better to tactfully withdraw and live to fight another day than to die on the battlefield.

Social Changes

Social changes will come in many forms, including the products sold, means of distribution, methods of production, and many other ways we operate our business. Casualization of the workplace, telecommuting, demands for daycare, women in the workforce, and retirement villages are all examples of social changes affecting our world. These changes impact the way companies operate, including labor management, employee costs, flex-time schedules, and other changes in the way we manage people. As the baby boomers start entering retirement during the next 20 years, we will continue to see major changes continue, such as the inflow/outflow of mutual funds to and from retirement accounts. These social changes often require companies to incur significant capital expenditures in the short term, but with no appreciable payback for 10 to 20 years.

Technological Change

The old saying goes "don't get caught making buggy whips," and that continues to be even more important in the Information Age in which new ideas and technology come and go at the blink of an eye. Just as our great-grandfathers traded in the slow, high-maintenance horse for the automobile, consumers today continue to want it all and will do whatever it takes to improve their quality of life, both at home and at the office. New advances in technology are the leading cause for obsolescence, and management bears full responsibility for ensuring that the company is adequately funding a research and development (R&D) program. In some low-technology industries, the need for the R&D effort may be as simple as attending the leading trade shows to observe the latest breakthroughs. Just as the laptop computer, facsimile machine, and cellular phone revolutionized the business world, technology is changing the way products are made and sold. I believe that history will record the microchip as this century's greatest technological advancement, spawning many new industries as well as affecting the life of nearly every person on the planet. The Internet is another example of how changes in technology can revolutionize business. It is estimated that the amount of goods sold over the Internet is doubling every four months. This is a startling fact in the world of retailing, considering that many industry leaders did not know it even existed just five years ago. Technology will continue to change the world through innovations such as fiber optic cable, genetic enhancement of plant and feed stock animals, and robotic replacement of simple manual labor.

Government Actions and Regulation

Dickens wrote, "It was the best of times, it was the worst of times"; he undoubtedly could have been thinking about our current regulatory environment. Indeed, a curious paradox has emerged over the past 20 years: on the one hand, governmental interference in commerce has reached an all-time low in many areas such as antitrust review and enforcement. On the other hand, government has had a tremendous impact on other areas such as waste disposal cost, asbestos removal, the North American Free Trade Agreement (NAFTA), and environmental impact studies prior to construction, as well as social costs such as required family leave and escalating Social Security cost. Occupational health and safety has become a leading cost issue in companies as they try to stay abreast of the latest rules and use coveted financing dollars to purchase new compliant machinery. In fact, in the retailing industry there are regulations as to how large the type must be on sale signs. There seems to be no end in sight as to what social movement could cause the government to spring into action and write new laws with which business will have to contend. The increasing amount of trade conducted with customers outside the United States only further exacerbates the problem that management will be forced to deal with in an effort to grow the business and compete globally.

INTERNAL CAUSES OF DECLINE

While external causes often contribute to business failure, internal factors tend to be the largest components behind many failures. These are often harder to identify and, as detailed at the beginning of this chapter, are often denied by management until it is too late. Internal factors may include:[2]

- Management issues
- Management ineffectiveness
- Failure to develop and motivate employees
- Poor response to market changes
- Lack of internal controls
- Management's disregard of the planning or budgeting process
- Excessive levels of management
- Poor employee retention programs
- Management's inability to control working capital
- Few suppliers or customers
- Highly leveraged businesses
- Poorly developed management information systems
- Failure to implement a risk management program

Management Issues

The management team is often cited as the main reason for a company's underperformance. Management dictates a company's vision for the future, and when that gets cloudy, the finish line becomes questionable. The "personality of one" is often cited as the most frequent issue for a stalled company when the founder or family member is no longer capable of managing a business that has outgrown his or her ability or style. This factor can sometimes be coupled with the desire of such leaders to build monuments to their rule in an effort to make a statement in their industry. These unusual expenses can manifest themselves in the form of corporate apartments, private planes, country clubs for officers, cars, and customer junkets. The founder or one-person rule is seldom questioned by the internal beneficiaries of these perks and are often justified as necessary to keep management or customers from defecting.

Management Ineffectiveness

Management ineffectiveness is the single biggest factor behind a business' failure. An ineffective management team diminishes any opportunity that a business has of succeeding. Management's responsibility is to provide leadership, direction, and order for the company so that it is able to reach its goals. Failure to do so leads to the downfall of the organization. The fact remains that any function within the organization ultimately falls into the responsibility of management. Therefore, effective implementation of operations is imperative.

Management ineffectiveness comes in many different forms. Failure occurs when management is unable to identify the mistakes it has made, together with the inability to lead the organization through the necessary change to correct these errors. Management's lack of focus on operational issues such as internal controls, the planning and budgeting process, and timely reporting leads to a loss of control over operations and contributes to the company's likelihood of failure.

The management of a company in which the individuals are inexperienced in completing an initial public offering, merger, or acquisition; lack industry experience; or have never been challenged by the major aspects and decisions in operating a business are severely challenged by any critical change. A company that has recently merged with another presents management with numerous strategic and leadership challenges. Management may embrace the challenge and anticipate success. However, the realization of growth may never be achieved as lack of experience causes poor or untimely decisions. Other pitfalls in the process include the failure to plan the overall strategy or a misjudgment in reading the marketplace. Attempts to grow can also strain an already weak management team, leading to losses rather than gains. Rarely does an inexperienced management team admit to these poor decisions or, more importantly, address its mistakes.

Unrealistic expectations of management may also lead to business failure. Management's expectation of rapid growth compels a company to obtain more financing which is used to build operating lines and hire new employees. Growth is the plan, but the plan may backfire as it incurs substantial debt to address the increase in demand, and the demand never evolves. The company is left with idle operating lines, minimal sales growth, higher labor costs, and excessive interest costs.

High turnover is another indication of ineffective management. A management team that continually needs to fill key positions indicates that the team itself is not cooperatively organized or focused on the company's goals. The reasons for the departures might have to do with the personalities of those at the top of the team or team members' lack of abilities to work with or lead others. The incompatibility among management has dire effects on a company's operations. Individuals leave, and leadership and direction suffer. Further, the company incurs significant costs and time in the process of finding, hiring, and training management. The resignations of individuals become costly, as severance packages are common and lawsuits are possible. Besides the distractions, the lack of a full, well-trained management team results in decisions made without all members truly knowing the impacts. The decisions that are made are not fully informed and, as a result, damage the capabilities of the organization.

The board of directors has a responsibility to the owners of the company: it is their job to ensure that management operates in the best interest of the ownership. A good board is one that is critical of management's intentions to ensure that major decisions of the company are made in the best interests of the owners—the shareholders. A board that is too friendly or lax with the management may allow actions or approve of motions that do not truly address the concerns of the organization. Outlandish management spending on items such as travel or gifts is an indication that the board is not truly overseeing management operations. Further, it is management's and the board's responsibility to ensure that the relationships and communications among members are supportive to the company's overall goal. Failure to create such an environment will be detrimental to the company's operations.

Failure to Develop and Motivate Employees

The abilities of its people are the most important assets of a company. Therefore, one of management's greatest responsibilities to the organization is to ensure that its employees receive the proper training and experience. Management must also motivate and lead its employees to overcome all challenges.

A company that is failing due to poor training or lack of motivation in its employees can be identified in many different ways. The workforce performs inefficiently if the incentive to get the job done quickly does not exist. There are many errors in the process or excessive rework must be completed, as the employees do not know how to control the production process. Damaged machinery is an indication that the employees have not received the proper training on how to use the machines. Projects continually run over budget due to management's not providing the leadership or the motivational needs that the employees desire. It may also be an indication that the employees do not have the proper training to be given such responsibilities in the project. Poor motivation creates an environment in which the employees do not show initiative or develop ideas on how the business can improve. Poor training creates employees who are not apt to change and, as a result, the company falls behind the competition. Some incentive plans do not inspire employees; instead, they are encouraged to maintain the status quo. Other incentive plans may provoke employees to manipulate results so that the company may appear to be doing well, but it will be only a matter of time before the actual results catch up.

Poor training or lack of motivation can result in an organization that continues to perform poorly in the marketplace as it fails to meet the demands of its customers. Orders get canceled and sales get lost. Soon, customers develop relationships with the competition, and the company is left out, wondering how it can survive.

Poor Response to Market Changes

Management has the ultimate responsibility of how the company will get its product to the customers. Management decides the pricing strategy, the marketing approach, and the production process. Management's failure to effectively analyze or slowly react to its competition, consumer behavior, or general market trends can lead to significant problems.

Management's failure to attack a market or identify a change in the market is a missed opportunity in the ever-changing world of business. The missed opportunity may arise from a change in demographics that goes unnoticed. A change in the market may arise when competition utilizes new technology or creates a new product that is a better fit with customer needs. A market change may also occur when the customers' preferences change. Failure to react, or even a slowness to react to changes such as these, often leads to the failure of a business.

Poor responses to market change can result in inaccurate pricing or overproduction. As inventory levels escalate, production slows, working capital shrinks, operating lines close, and sales plummet. Further, the company may miss an opportunity for growth and must battle for survival instead. It is a critical error when the company's other products or business strategies are losing out to competition.

Conversely, when management decides to penetrate a market, it risks the chance that the strategy may not succeed. Improper planning, poor market analysis, and inaccurate forecasts may lead to excessive inventory, write-offs of excess or obsolete inventory, and high storage costs. A misjudgment of the market size or the relationship of price and demand may result in a failure to penetrate, ending with disastrous financial results. The company could miss the target market altogether as management fails to identify who its customers really are. The result is high penetration costs that fail to generate the desired revenue. As a result of its failures, the company is required to focus on alternative plans to somehow pay for the costs and obligations incurred.

Management's responsibility includes the need to push the company into new product development or technological enhancements. The inability to implement these changes weakens the company's competitive edge. By anticipating and responding well to market changes, management will have the ability and the resources that it needs to critically assess corporate needs and maintain an advantage over its competitors.

Lack of Internal Controls

Management's disregard to internal controls can cause significant damages to the ongoing operations of an otherwise healthy organization. A company will have no ability to detect errors in reporting, theft in operations, or actual fraud in the business without the proper controls in place and management's belief in enforcing these controls. The consequences of weak internal controls may include the loss of money that is often not recoverable. Poor controls potentially create inaccurate reporting that, when used, may result in poor decision making. Depending on the severity of the controls that are circumvented, it can place a company at a competitive disadvantage. Additionally, the result may be a business that has to face legal battles in addition to the battles it faces in the marketplace.

Management's Disregard of the Planning or Budgeting Process

Poor budgeting and planning arises when the company fails to take the time to stress the value of creating a budget that is critiqued at all levels of the organization. A weak budget occurs when management fails to create a process in which each department scrupulously analyzes its operations to accurately determine future projections. The budget is instead created carelessly without introspection or market analysis. Further, when departments take the care to create a resourceful budget, this budget still needs to be analyzed and adjusted by the department heads and ultimately by upper management itself. Failure to do so creates an incomplete budget. Finally, an important step in the budget process that often gets missed is management's ongoing analysis of current operations against the budget.

Poor budgeting by a company potentially results in improper allocation of resources and the inability to foresee problems that require immediate attention. Without adequate planning, a company may fail to allocate proper resources to a market or product area that has tremendous potential. Alternatively, there may be markets or products that are draining the company and require immediate attention to reverse a downward trend. These issues cannot be properly addressed without placing significant time and effort into the establishment and monitoring of budgets.

An important connection to budgeting and analysis is the need for timely internal reporting. Management must put in place a reporting system that is accurate and prompt. Beyond this, the reports must help management analyze how the company's operations are performing. Accurate reporting provides no value if management cannot identify developing problems or poor results.

Excessive Levels of Management

Unless properly assessed and structured, this increase in the bureaucracy leads to slow or inaccurate management decisions. The long chain of command creates errors in communication from the operating level up to the top level of management. Additionally, too much red tape causes unnecessary delay in the decision process.

Excessive levels of management cause the company to fall behind; as its competitors react quickly to the changes in the market, the company is left battling the bureaucracy from within. The company also significantly reduces its chances of finding the optimal solution to a problem when there are "too many chefs in the kitchen."

Poor Employee Retention Programs

High turnover is expensive, especially when the training is specialized. A company needs to develop a plan to retain key employees, because the quality of its operations deteriorates when these employees leave. In many instances, key employees may depart to competitors, which will further hinder the company's ability to compete in the market.

Management's Inability to Control Working Capital

The presence of capital provides a cushion for times when the company incurs losses or unanticipated expenses. The lack of capital weakens the company's ability to run operations smoothly.

An indication that a company has poor control of its working capital position is when the company's balance sheet has a negative working capital position or its cash flow statement continually presents negative operating cash flow.

Poor management of working capital results in the company's allowing for the slow process of collecting receivables, which leaves needed cash outside the hands of the company. An undisciplined management of inventory creates unnecessarily high inventory levels and less cash available for other parts of the business's operations. Another example of managing working capital accounts poorly is when the company errs by paying vendors promptly but receives cash slowly. Mismanagement results in a company that fails to institute controls in its collection process, creating an opportunity for customers to delay payments. Poor controls allow for the approval of customers who are credit risks and, as a result, the receivable balance grows. Additionally, because of the poor collection process, the company incurs substantial and unnecessary costs of trying to receive payment or writing off accounts due to dispute or inability to pay. Products go out the door, but the money never comes rolling back in. Poor management of the financial positions of working capital accounts forces the company to rely on debt to build capital. When the market is weak, this result forces the company to try and obtain other means of financing to continue operations, because it does not have a line of credit to use in emergencies. A weak working capital position is a sign of management's inability to control and defeat the small battles that forever exist in the ongoing operations.

A company that is performing well can become undercapitalized as it experiences rapid, unplanned growth. Rapid growth limits management's ability to control its capital position, as it may be unable to meet the new levels of demand. Increased growth will heighten inventory and accounts receivable levels, which requires additional means of financing either through borrowing or the use of other current assets. Unexpected increases in demand strain the company in other ways as well. Heavy use of machinery and equipment may require additional costs related to maintenance and repair. These unanticipated costs are funded through already weakened current assets accounts.

Undercapitalization places a company on the edge of failure. A slight slip in operations or misjudgment in strategy results in a company that is foundering and has little to resuscitate itself. The company needs to rely on its lenders. These lenders are only so willing to assist, in circumstances that may really strain what a company would like to do.

Few Suppliers or Customers

Companies that rely on few large customers or suppliers place themselves at a severe risk if one key customer or supplier fails or chooses to do business with a competitor instead.

Many companies today have tried to align themselves with a few select suppliers. The intentions are good in that the two tend to work together in developing a strong business relationship, and terms are set to be fair to each other over the long run. However, a company that has very few suppliers leaves itself susceptible to severe drops in production (and the sale of products) when a supplier has chosen to close its operations, because it is unable to compete in the market or it decides to terminate its relationship. Management's failure to recognize the supplier's weaknesses causes the company to suffer. Late deliveries, incomplete orders, and pressure to pay are indications that the vendor is struggling.

Companies that rely on only a few customers for its main pieces of business also place themselves at great risk. The significant customer may cancel its business, significantly reduce its purchase level, or fail. Indications that the customer is suffering are late payments, requests for extensions, and a general market awareness that the customer is operating poorly.

The failure in management to identify the questionable credit in a customer creates a traumatic impact to the company's financial position. The company is forced to write off significant amounts in its account balances and must address the likelihood that sales will plummet due to the loss of business.

Highly Leveraged Businesses

Over the past two decades, leveraged buyouts have increased tremendously, creating many debt-financed businesses. Leveraged buyouts can place a well-managed business into an operation that is near default due to debt servicing requirements. Highly leveraged companies need to be aware of (and in some cases rely on) the interest rates in the market, as any change could minimize whatever income was expected. Although the business may remain operationally strong, the company may incur losses and potentially fail due to the obligations it must meet in interest and principal payments. A company with a small capital position that is highly leveraged is very susceptible to failure, because any setback in operations has a severe impact on the financial and cash obligations of the company.

As the situation worsens, the company is unable to address the cash demands of the business. In order to survive, the company must go out into the market to look for additional funding, but it does so with a weak financial position that will lead to more interest and fees that further deteriorate the profitability of the company.

Poorly Developed Management Information Systems

It is imperative for a company to have reporting that is timely, accurate, and useful. Data that are generated through the system must provide the organization with the information necessary to make the right decisions. The decisions must be made with the consideration of how they affect other functions in the organization.

Systems that are installed in an organization are often inadequate to the tasks desired. The problems result from poor design, improper implementation, or the lack of skilled users. The result is a reporting system that does not generate the information desired and, in turn, management makes inaccurate or uninformed decisions. The results may be tumultuous, as the company may move in a direction that hinders operations and causes the business to fail.

Failure to Implement a Risk Management Program

Inadequate risk management causes a business to incur unnecessary costs. Management that fails to prepare for product lawsuits arising from use or misuse of a product exposes the company to a variety of risks. Management should take steps to apprise itself of the risks that it faces when customers use its products, because product liability lawsuits can bring an organization to its knees.

Lawsuits may arise internally as well. Management's failure to implement risk management within the organization leaves a company ill prepared in dealing with the lawsuits resulting from employee mishaps or actions made by employees. Injuries on the job are rather common. Failure to place proper insurance policies leaves a company susceptible to any legal recourse that an employee may take. The costs incurred are unnecessary and do not assist the company in any way in its operations.

Other lawsuits against the company may arise because of a lack of controls within the organization. Management must oversee the actions of its employees and place controls within to ensure that business is performed properly. An overabundance of injuries on the job relates to management's neglect in implementing a proper training program or other preventive measures. Failure to implement a well-controlled environment may also result in employees committing abuses against the company or its customers. This is common in service industries in which an employee's actions have destroyed a company. The end result may be a lawsuit from the shareholders or from those who were damaged. Further, the company must live with the stigma of those crimes or abuses that were committed as part of its image forever.

EARLY ANALYSIS OF A PROBLEM

There are a number of quantitative tools of the trade to help diagnose the financial health of a business. The traditional ratios reviewed below are of particular importance when used over a period of time and subjective review is applied to determine whether deterioration rather than a single aberration is indicated. Finally, we will discuss a measure of financial distress and the most widely used bankruptcy prediction model.

Z Scoring and Logit Analysis

The most widely used predictor of bankruptcy is the one proposed by Edward Altman, Professor of Finance at the Stern School of Business, New York University, over 30 years ago. Altman's Z score, or zeta model, combined various measures of profitability or risk. Altman's model initially used 33 chapter 11 or chapter 7 bankrupt manufacturing companies with average assets of $6.4 million and another 33 companies with assets between $1 million and $25 million and achieved 94% success in using historical data to predict their ultimate failure. The calculation is as follows:

$$X1 = \text{Working capital/Total assets}$$
$$X2 = \text{Retained earnings/Total assets}$$
$$X3 = \text{Earnings before interest and taxes/Total assets}$$
$$X4 = \text{Market value of equity/Total liability}$$
$$X5 = \text{Sales/Total assets}$$
$$Z = \text{Overall index}$$
$$Z = 1.2(X1) + 1.4(X2) + 3.3(X3) + 6(X4) + 1(X5)$$

According to Professor Altman's model, if the score is above 2.99, the company is in good shape financially. If the score is below 1.81, the company is in danger of being financially insolvent and the chance of failure is high. Scores falling between 1.81 and 2.99 are in a gray area and warrant further analysis to determine whether the company is in decline or has reason to be considered at risk.

Other individuals, such as Christine Zavgren, have developed other models to correct for variables in the data not normally distributed uniformly. Her model uses logit analysis to predict bankruptcy and provides a probability or percentage of bankruptcy. Application of the logit model requires four steps. First, a series of seven financial ratios are calculated. Second, each ratio is multiplied by a coefficient unique to that ratio. This coefficient can be positive or negative. Third, the resulting values are summed together (y). Finally, the probability of bankruptcy for a firm is calculated as the inverse of $(1+eY)$.

Financial Ratio	Coefficient
Intercept	+0.23883
Average inventories/Sales	−0.108
Average receivables/Average inventories	−1.583
(Cash + marketable securities)/Total assets	−10.78
Quick assets/Current liabilities	+3.074
Income from continuing operations/	
(Total assets − Current liabilities)	+0.486
Long-term debt/(Total assets - Current liabilities)	−4.35
Sales/Net working capital + Fixed assets)	+0.11
Y =	Sum of (Coefficient * Ratio)
Probability of bankruptcy[3]=	**1/(1+eY)**

Other Financial Ratios

There are many individual ratios that are used as tools for monitoring performance and can serve as a basis for financial planning. These ratios are generally grouped into four major categories[4]:

1. Liquidity ratios measure the adequacy of a company's cash resources relative to its near-term cash obligations.
2. Activity ratios evaluate the level of output generated by a company's assets.
3. Debt ratios examine a company's capital structure in terms of the mix of its financing sources, as well as the ability of the company to satisfy its longer-term debt and investment obligations.
4. Profitability ratios measure the net income of a company relative to its revenues and capital.

The following table highlights the individual ratios to be discussed and provides the formula used to calculate each. It is important to note these ratios are most effective when compared with benchmarks and calculated over a period of time, because taken by themselves their predictive value is not clear-cut. When the calculated results are unfavorable vis-à-vis a company's competition or industry, the company's future competitiveness is questionable. Similarly, negative trends observed over several periods are indicative of future financial problems.

	Category	Name Formula
Liquidity ratios	Current ratio	Current assets/Current liabilities
	Quick ratio	(Current assets – Inventory)/
		Current liabilities
Activity ratios	Inventory turnover	Cost of goods sold/Average inventory
	Days' sales outstanding	Accounts receivable/(Net sales/360)
	Fixed-assets turnover	Net sales/Average fixed assets
Debt ratios	Debt to equity	Total debt/Total equity
	Times interest earned	EBIT/Interest expense
Profitability ratios	Return on sales	Net profit/Annual net sales
	Return on assets	Net profit/Total assets
	Return on equity	Net profit/Net worth

Current Ratio.   Current ratio is used to express working capital in terms of a ratio relationship. The term working capital is used to indicate the excess of a company's current assets over its current liabilities; when balance sheets are reviewed, this area is always the most closely scrutinized. Having sufficient working capital is critical to maintaining adequate inventories, meeting current trade payable obligations and taking advantage of discounts offered, and extending adequate terms to customers in order to attract larger-volume sales. The competitive nature of business requires that the current ratio be approximately 2:1 or better, and, historically, lenders and suppliers used this ratio as a benchmark for continued top credit relations. In most workout situations, this area garners my most immediate attention in order to ensure short-term survival. In fact, there are countless cases in which total assets far exceeded liabilities, and yet the company failed due to its inattention to maintaining its current ratio at adequate levels.

Many issues can affect working capital, and often the nature of the company's business will also have significant impact. Capital-intensive industries, such as railroads and utilities, have inventories that are primarily made up of supplies that are used in making repairs. These industries need significantly less working capital than do retailers and manufacturers. Likewise, retailers selling on a cash or third-party credit card basis need less working capital than do manufacturers granting credit. The requirements are different from industry to industry and bear further study. Generally speaking, utilities, railroads, and other similarly situated industries can operate on a ratio as little as 1:1. I have seen some companies fighting a product launch mistake needing a ratio of 3:1 or higher in order to liquidate the error and gain precious time to relaunch the product. The composition of current assets is important, and many managers have fallen due to inaccurate information concerning the quality of the receivables and inventory in their portfolios. The reason is that the cash portion of the current ratio calculation is a forgiving part of the formulation, assuming there is plenty. When cash is low, the managers are under increased stress to turn the receivables and inventory with greater frequency to avoid unforgiving payment dates, such as payroll and principal and interest payments.

Quick Ratio. Quick ratio is a more conservative measure of liquidity than the current ratio. Obviously, a company with large balances of cash and marketable securities is more liquid than a company with large inventories. By eliminating the less liquid inventory category and concentrating on assets more easily converted into cash, the quick ratio determines whether a company could meet its creditor obligations in the case of a real crisis—on the assumption that inventories have no value at all. As drastic tests of the ability to pay in the face of disaster, both the current and quick ratios are helpful.

Inventory Turnover. Inventory turnover is important to a company because inventories are the least liquid form of current assets. Because the company must tie up funds to carry inventories, it is in their best interest to sell inventories quickly and free up cash for other uses. A precise evaluation of inventory would require an actual count, verification, and appraisal of value. However, a more efficient option is to relate recorded inventory to the cost of goods sold to see whether there is a shift in the relationship over time. Before any interpretations are made, inventory ratios should be compared with industry averages, because the ratios can vary widely among industries. For example, a company selling perishable goods will normally have a high inventory turnover rate, whereas a heavy equipment manufacturer's inventory turnover will be much lower. Generally speaking, the higher the turnover number, the better. However, inventory turnover figures that are well above industry averages may signal the potential for inventory shortages resulting from poor planning or control, and a competitive disadvantage.

Days' Sales Outstanding.   Days' sales outstanding measures the effectiveness of a company's credit policies and indicates the level of investment in receivables needed to maintain sales. As with other ratios, days' sales outstanding must be examined against other information. If a company's policy is to extend credit to customers for 30 days, then a period of 45.8 days implies that the company has trouble collecting on time and should review its credit policy. Conversely, if a company sets a 60-day collection period for customers, a 45.8-day average indicates that the company's collection policy is working effectively. When computing receivables turnover, it is important to include only trade receivables, excluding receivables related to financing and investment activities. Adjustments to the calculation may be necessary if a company has sold receivables during the period.

Fixed-Assets Turnover.   Fixed-assets turnover indicates the amount of assets needed to support a particular level of sales. The dollar amount of sales generated by each dollar of assets is another way to look at it. As with other ratios, it is important to look beyond the numbers when evaluating fixed-asset turnover. While sales fluctuations are continuous, fixed-asset changes are discrete, depending on the addition or disposition of factories, equipment, warehouses, and so forth. As a result, individual turnover ratios are somewhat erratic and should be calculated over a period of time. Furthermore, two companies with similar operating efficiencies may show differing ratios, depending on when their assets were acquired. Due to inflation, more recently acquired assets tend to be more expensive, which distorts the comparison with companies using older assets. Simply put, fixed-asset turnover is another of several clues that, in combination, can indicate unfavorable performance.

Debt to Equity.   Debt to equity is a traditional ratio used to measure a company's leverage and provides an indication of how strong its finances are by comparing what the company owes with what it owns. Potential lenders or investors use this ratio to evaluate risk. Obviously, the higher the equity in the business's capital structure, the less risky the company appears to a lender or investor. This ratio measures the extent to which a company has been capitalized by debt or the extent of the leverage. In recent years, companies have seen ratios as high as 90+%, but 33% has been traditionally seen as the standard benchmark. This ratio is often used in conjunction with the interest coverage ratio to determine whether the company has adequate capital resources.

Times Interest Earned.   Times interest earned is often referred to as the "interest coverage ratio." It indicates the degree of protection available to creditors by measuring the extent to which earnings before interest and taxes (EBIT) "cover" required interest payments. The ratio is developed with the expectation that operating earnings can be considered a basic source of funds for debt service, and that a deteriorating relationship might signal difficulties. Low interest coverage indicates that a decline in economic activity could reduce EBIT below the interest a firm must pay, leading to default and ultimately insolvency. Determining a company's ability to meet its debt obligations is most meaningful when a review is made over a long enough time period to indicate the major operational and cyclical fluctuations that are normal for the company and its industry. This may involve financial statements covering several years or several seasonal swings in an attempt to identify high and low points in earnings and funds needs. No hard-and-fast standards for the ratio itself exist. Rather, the specifics are based on judgment, often involving a detailed analysis of a company's past, current, and prospective conditions.

Return on Sales.   Return on sales measures a company's profitability using the relationship between its costs and sales. The greater a company's ability to control costs in relation to its revenues, the more its earnings power is enhanced.

Return on Assets.   Return on assets (ROA) measures the operating efficiency of a company without regard to its financial structure. The issue is the effectiveness with which management has employed total assets as recorded on the balance sheet. Although the relationship is a valuable analytical tool, the nature and timing of the financial statement amounts used in the calculation (e.g., nonrecurring gains and losses, changes in the company's capital structure, significant restructuring and acquisitions, and changes in federal income tax regulations) can distort results. If these conditions are present, adjustments should be made to eliminate their effects from the calculation. Differences in ROA can be traced to both changes in activity and changes in profitability. A low ROA, for example, can reflect either low turnover resulting from poor asset management or low profit margins even when turnover is high. Return on assets will rise if fewer assets are employed or gross margin is improved and expenses are reduced. Minimizing taxes will also improve the return.

Return on Equity.   Return on equity (ROE) focuses on the returns accruing to shareholders—the residual owners of a company. The relationship of net profit to net worth is the most common ratio used for measuring the return on the owners' investment. Return on equity is a widely published statistic. Rankings of companies and industry sectors are compiled by major business magazines as well as rating agencies. The ratio is closely watched by stock market analysts and, in turn, by management and the board of directors. As with ROA, the accuracy of financial statement amounts used in the calculation can be an issue, and adjustments may be necessary if there are major inconsistencies. Return on equity consists of two elements: the net profit on assets and the degree of leverage or debt capital used in the business. As with ROA, improving profitability of sales combined with effective use of assets that generate sales enables management to raise ROE. An added factor is the boosting effect from using debt in the capital structure. The greater the liabilities, the greater the improvement in ROE—

assuming, of course, the business earns more on its investments than the cost of debt.

Qualitative Factors

While quantitative analysis of a company's results is extremely valuable in the early detection of potential financial problems, it is not the only way in which such difficulties can be discovered. Closer observation of the efficiency of the company itself can be very illustrative as well. In fact, there are factors that are actually easier for an outsider to observe and evaluate, because those inside the company can be too close to the situation. In particular, planning, monitoring, and control situations in which management is directly involved are important indicators that are often overlooked. Like quantitative factors, these qualitative characteristics are not necessarily predictive individually. However, seen in combination over a period of time, they raise questions about a company's long-term viability.

Management Problems.   When management is effectively directing a company's operations, they are not only in control of day-to-day activities, but also are anticipating and planning for events that are yet to occur. Particularly in light of the increasing rate of change that exists in the modern business environment, management must do more than simply monitor and react to the current results of operations. A focus on immediate problems is crucial to keep a company running, but short- and long-term planning is equally necessary. If management is not proactive in this regard, a company can easily find itself in trouble. When management starts reacting to problems and implementing short-term solutions, they are essentially losing control of the company. This behavior can become a cycle in which management finds itself being controlled by an endless series of problems requiring immediate and full attention. Eventually, the situation can spiral to a point of near chaos in which it seems no one is in control. At that point, it becomes extremely difficult for management to rectify the situation.

The impacts of management problems can be seen in several different areas. Employees are often the first to notice because they are closest to the business. Like players on a losing sports team, it is difficult for employees to perform at a high level. Managers struggle to maintain the quality of work when employees are aware that the company is underperforming. It is not too long before suppliers and customers also become aware of management problems. It can become difficult to negotiate favorable prices or justify credit terms when suppliers perceive that the company is at risk. Similarly, customers may not be willing to pay high prices or sometimes even do business with a company they believe is lacking management direction.

Information Problems.   When a company has management problems, the root of these problems can often be traced to a lack of timely and accurate information. Without basic financial information, all the quantitative analysis described in this chapter would be impossible. More detailed internal information is also necessary to run a company successfully. For example, a lack of detail concerning both short-term cash requirements and cash resources can quickly lead to trouble, and accurate purchasing and shipping detail is crucial to many short-term decisions. Bad information can be especially problematic when it comes to long-term issues. When flawed numbers are used in assumptions and then extrapolated over a number of years, the results can lead to poor decisions that prove quite costly. The decision to launch a new product or purchase a new plant, for example, if made as a result of faulty information, could seriously damage a company's health. Additionally, it is not hard to imagine how the lack of timely and accurate external information—customer and competitor information, for example—could lead to poor planning.

Like other problems in a troubled company, information problems emerge for a number of different reasons. A big culprit can be the information system on which management relies for important information. A company that is experiencing difficulties will often neglect areas like the information systems department. Without the ongoing maintenance and upgrades required by technology, the eventual impact will be inaccurate output from the information system, which will in turn have a negative impact on management's performance. Often, operational problems cause information to be delayed or inaccurate, as well. When company personnel are trying to get materials from suppliers who have been paid late or not at all, dealing with production delays, or trying to maintain the favor of unsatisfied customers, it is unlikely they can simultaneously focus on the goal of keeping management informed about company operations.

Beyond the potential for unforeseen or inadvertent problems is the unfortunate possibility of company information being intentionally misstated. Some employees may engage in this kind of activity in an attempt to meet goals that have been set for them, or management may want to give the appearance their plans are succeeding to a greater extent than they are. Whatever the motivation, there are obvious negative consequences when intentionally inaccurate information passes among those within a company, but when such information is disseminated externally, the company is at the very least being deceptive and at worst committing fraud. Furthermore, a company providing lenders, investors, and others with intentionally erroneous information is clearly headed for trouble. Intentional misstatements come in various forms. A company's balance sheet can be improved through inventory adjustments, reductions in reserves for doubtful accounts, or the omission of liabilities. Additions to sales before items are actually shipped or failing to record sales returns and credits can give the appearance of greater income than actually exists. Nonfinancial misrepresentations can include anything from inaccurate quality information to exceedingly optimistic estimates about the ability to meet a deadline.

Problems with Lenders. Outside lenders are one group who can be significantly impacted when they receive inaccurate information. Decisions about whether to extend credit and in what amount are based on financial statement amounts that if inflated could cause lenders to offer financing where they otherwise would not or to make undersecured advances. Similarly, if a company with-holds information, the relationship between the two parties will be strained. Lenders do not simply accept details provided by a debtor company, and it is likely to cause greater embarrassment and mistrust when lenders eventually discover hidden problems. Often, lenders seek to verify the veracity of information given by a company through audits performed by their own staff or by someone independent from the company. Using all available information, lenders perform their own analyses to determine whether a company is in a suitable position currently and prospectively to receive funds. These necessary qualifications then often lead to financial covenants written in to loan agreements to help assure the lender that a company will stay on a healthy course and maintain the ability to pay its debts.

Because of the stigma attached to having a lender relationship severed, it is in the best interest of a debtor company to be forthcoming about potential problems.

Production Problems.   Production is the central function of a manufacturing company, so it is not surprising that various production problems almost always precede financial difficulties. It is especially important to be aware of these problems, because there can be a delay before they impact the results of operations at levels that can be detected quantitatively. For example, there are frequently an increasing number of defects detected by either a company's quality control department or its customers. Sometimes, the defects can be the result of the manufacturing process itself, a result of poor design, implementation, or obsolescence. Other times, it is the human component that causes the process to function ineffectively. Workers may simply not be paying attention during production or inspection, due to poor supervision or motivation. Regardless of the cause of defects, the result is rework, which reduces profit margins. Some rework is present in all manufacturing operations, but excessive or increasing amounts will eventually lead to production and shipping delays, dissatisfied customers, and lower revenues and increased costs.

Shipping Problems.   Shipping problems can be the result of different factors. As noted above, production problems can cause shipping delays. Delays can also occur when there are not sufficient production inputs on hand due to either purchasing delays or inadequate monitoring of raw materials inventory. Shipments of the wrong merchandise or the wrong amount of the correct merchandise can be traced to anything from order entry errors to packaging and loading mistakes. No matter what the cause of shipping problems, though, the result is always the same—dissatisfied customers and loss of revenues. Whether customers receive their shipments late or get prompt but incorrect shipments, they will eventually look for another supplier. There are other costs associated with shipping problems even if a company can maintain the favor of its customers. Delayed shipping means slower cash flow, which has a negative impact on the company. Incorrect shipments increase expenses related to restocking and reselling returned items, as well as shipping the order a second time. All of these problems contribute to inaccurate sales data, which can inhibit management's ability to monitor company performance.

CONCLUSION

I have examined several of the early internal and external causes leading to business failures and the issues surrounding these symptoms. The single most important steps are to take control of the cash and immediately engage competent professionals familiar with the company's particular type of issues. This section started with the subject of denial, and rightfully so, because the leading cause is often ignoring the warning signs discussed in this chapter. The sooner detection of the problem can be made, the greater success intervention can make in the life cycle of an underperforming business.

NOTES

1. White Paper, *The Turnaround Management Association*, Chicago, IL, 1998.

2. Ibid.

3. Zavgren, Christine V. "Assessing the Vulnerability to Failure of American Industrial Firms: A Logistic Analysis," *Journal of Business Finance and Accounting* 12 (Spring 1985):19–45.

4 . Gerald I. White, Ashwinpaul C. Sondhi, and Dov Fried, *The Analysis and Use of Financial Statements*, New York, John Wiley & Sons, 1994.

5

Spin Control: Managing Internal and External Communications

Michael S. Sitrick

Sitrick & Company

NEED FOR EFFECTIVE COMMUNICATION IN CRISIS SITUATIONS

"Why would a company operating under chapter 11 need public relations counsel?" The question is a common one, despite the fact that companies filing chapter 11 have been turning to experts in this area for nearly two decades. Our firm alone has worked on more than 100 in- and out-of-court restructurings since 1989, about 70 of which involved chapter 11 filings, and my own personal experience in the area dates back to 1982. Still, for most people, it is a difficult concept to grasp. They think of public relations as being mainly concerned with promotion and publicity, and they think of most public relations firms' expertise as being concentrated in those areas.

As it happens, those impressions are not entirely inaccurate. The fact is, very few public relations professionals understand the intricacies of what has come to be known as bankruptcy communications. Even fewer have any real experience in the field. Indeed, many public relations people who claim to be crisis communications experts actually have only limited hands-on experience. Often, what experience they do have was sandwiched between promoting the biggest hot fudge sundae in the world and touting the latest new fall fashion. It is not that there are no public relations firms that can provide effective support and counsel in major crisis situations. It is just that they are few and far between.

Still, there is no getting around it. Companies do need to practice sound public relations during a chapter 11 if they want to stabilize their workforce and control the information flow—in short, if they want to ensure that perceptions are the same as fact.

As much as we may like to believe that the facts can speak for themselves, the reality is that facts can be presented and reported in a variety of different ways. How an individual situation is presented can significantly influence the way it is reported. This is not to suggest that one should ever stray from the facts or in any way try to mislead. However, one should be aware that there are always a number of ways to look at and present each individual situation. In this context, each fact should be examined and every angle explored.

Companies should not wait until they find themselves in bankruptcy court to begin developing and implementing an effective communications program. After all, the need to seek protection under chapter 11 rarely arises overnight. More often than not, weeks and months of fiscal strain precede the actual filing—along with days, weeks, and months of negotiations with banks and other creditors. It is in this environment that controlling the information flow becomes essential.

Consider the typical prefiling atmosphere. Vendors begin requesting cash on delivery. Customers start questioning whether they can depend on the company for that fall order. Employees put off buying a new house. Calls start coming in from the media asking whether the company is in trouble.

Rumors begin growing, in both frequency and size, faster than Jack's proverbial beanstalk. No matter how preposterous they are, they seem to be given credence by at least some of the company's constituencies.

This is when a company's future hangs in the balance, for if left unattended, rumors of a company's impending demise can become self-fulfilling. In a troubled company, particularly one in a chapter 11 situation, it is not uncommon to find employees departing en masse, motivated by the belief that liquidation and unemployment are imminent. Those who stay begin worrying more about whether they will continue to have a job, rather than about how best to do their job. Productivity suffers; morale sinks.

All too often, the instinctive corporate reaction to this sort of dangerous climate is to do exactly the wrong thing: In a misguided effort to calm things down, executives try to keep a low profile and say as little as possible to anyone about anything. "We really do not have anything we can say" is the common response to questions.

Unfortunately, the grapevine does not remain silent. Rumors spread from vendor to customer, from banker to investor; employees begin wondering when the company will start announcing layoffs. Soon, the media is smelling blood, and stories about the company's shaky condition begin appearing with increasing frequency.

How those calls are handled—even the ones that seem to be innocuous or involve reports that have no basis in fact—can often mean the difference between maintaining control of the company's destiny and having a rumor become a self-fulfilling prophecy. Sound overly dramatic? Consider what happened not too long ago to a major publicly traded retailer.

It was early on a Tuesday morning that an executive at what was then one of the country's largest retail chains received a phone call from a reporter at *The Wall Street Journal*. The reporter wanted the executive's comment on some disturbing rumors he had heard. Apparently, word was going around that the company was experiencing financial difficulties, and as a result, vendors were supposedly no longer willing to ship it goods on credit, but rather were demanding cash up front, or at least on delivery.

Rumors like this can put a retailer out of business, especially if it is well known that the company is experiencing financial troubles. This particular rumor was not only dangerous, it was also false. Although the company did have financial problems, its vendors were all still shipping on normal terms. The executive was thus understandably outraged (not to mention somewhat panicked), and he brusquely dismissed the reporter's inquiry as nonsense. "I will not even dignify that with a response," he snapped, "except to say that it is patently untrue." Then he hung up.

The next day a story appeared in *The Wall Street Journal* recounting the rumors the reporter had heard, backed up by quotes from three of the company's vendors, all of whom said they would no longer ship their merchandise to the chain without payment in advance. The executive's one-sentence denial was also included in the story.

As it happened, the three vendors quoted in the article were completely unrepresentative of the chain's more than 10,000 suppliers. The reason they had stopped shipping merchandise was that they had been "cut off"—the result of a dispute with the chain over the quality and timely delivery of some previously contracted goods. Nonetheless, once reported by the *Journal*, their comments set off what is known in the trade as a vendor stampede.

Suppliers who had been previously shipping goods on normal credit terms suddenly began to get nervous that they were in the minority—so nervous that many of them simply pulled the plug. The chain's headquarters was flooded with calls. "Look, I believe in you guys," company executives were told over and over again, "but I cannot afford to be the only vendor still shipping on terms. After all, if something were to happen to you, I'd be screwed. I'm sorry, but I have to protect my interests. I still want to do business with you, but it will have to be on a COD or cash-up-front basis."

Determined to restore faith in his company, the chain's chief executive officer (CEO) traveled to New York to meet with his bankers and personally reassure his most important suppliers. At the same time, his PR people contacted the *Journal* and convinced the newspaper to report on his efforts to calm vendor fears. The resulting story, however, only made matters worse.

While it noted what the CEO was doing, this second article also surveyed a wider array of the company's vendors. By now, nervousness had turned to panic, and many of them were refusing to ship. In the end, the story wound up exacerbating the situation.

Over the next few weeks, the situation continued to worsen, until finally what the *Journal* had reported became reality. The company's vendors stopped shipping on any terms except cash or COD. Eventually, the company had no choice but to file for chapter 11 bankruptcy protection. Throughout the bankruptcy proceedings, its communication missteps continued. Today, it no longer exists.

Of course, not all crises are launched with a story in the *Wall Street Journal*. A company may not be big enough or prominent enough to warrant attention from a major national publication. Even if it is, the initial stories about the company's troubles may appear only in a local trade publication. Then a major market daily begins writing about the company. Suddenly, stories about the companies troubles—or imminent demise—are appearing on the local television news. If the company is big enough or publicly traded, it may find itself featured on CNN and CNBC.

Then it begins! Customers begin canceling orders. Vendors take the company's cash, but do not ship it goods, instead applying the funds to monies previously owed.

Now the banks will not extend terms, fearing that the additional funds will just be used to pay off trade debt. In a short time, the company has no choice but to seek protection.

The company's lawyers head down to the court, file the papers, and issue a standard news release containing the usual legal boilerplate. That evening, local radio and TV in each of the company's markets tell the world that the company has declared bankruptcy.

The next morning, half the company's stores do not open because its people do not understand what a chapter 11 means. Customers immediately begin making alternative arrangements. The company's workforce is in a state of panic. The business is paralyzed.

Sound farfetched? It is not. The corporate graveyards are littered with the corpses of scores of companies that traveled this route. Just compare what happened at Wickes Companies (where I was senior vice-president of communications) with what happened at Braniff Airlines. Both companies filed for chapter 11 protection back in the 1980s at about the same time. One emerged from bankruptcy; the other did not.

THE BRANIFF WAY VERSUS THE WICKES WAY

The day after Braniff filed, there was pandemonium. Planes were not flying. Reservations desks were not staffed; phones were not being answered. Employees did not know if they should show up for work, so many did not. It took days to get things back to normal, but they never really were the same, and the airline eventually went out of business.

At Wickes, which filed on a Saturday, all 3,200 retail outlets and 100 manufacturing locations were open the following Monday. Every desk and every phone in every one of the company's offices and stores was manned. In what the bankruptcy judge called "a miracle," the company emerged from chapter 11 just two-and-a-half years later. It is still in business today.

Coincidence? I think not. At Wickes, communications was a key part of the reorganization process. Rather than trying to keep a low profile, management made communications a top priority. The results speak for themselves.

The basic aim of Wickes' communications plan was to minimize the impact of the chapter 11 filing on the company's day-to-day business operations. Among other things, that meant making sure all the company's various constituencies understood the fundamentals of what was going on: what a chapter 11 filing meant and what it did not mean, why the filing was necessary, and what everyone concerned could expect.

The day before the company filed, mailgrams were sent to all Wickes retail outlets, offices, and manufacturing facilities, explaining what was about to happen and why. In particular, the mailgrams emphasized the fact that filing chapter 11 did not mean anyone was going to lose his or her job, nor did it mean that there was no longer any chance for advancement at the company. Employees were also told what to do if a bank refused to cash their paychecks or a vendor tried to reclaim goods.

That afternoon, reporters were contacted to determine where they could be reached over the weekend, when the formal announcement would be made. Media briefings were prepared, complete with lists of likely questions and appropriate answers.

That night, Wickes' top managers were flown to the company's headquarters for a meeting with the company's new chairman and CEO. At the meeting, information packets were handed to each manager. The packets contained an agenda; a list of people each manager was to call immediately after the meeting; a suggested script for those phone conversations; a suggested schedule for employee informational briefings, including where and when each briefing should be held; a copy of the news release announcing the chapter 11 filing; a memo from the chairman instructing that all media inquiries be referred to a central office; a copy of a letter from the chairman to each of the company's employees in which he explained what was going on; a copy of the mailgram that had been sent to all company locations; a list of people to call to get more information; and a list of questions employees, vendors, and customers were likely to ask, along with appropriate answers.

Senior members of management as well as the company's bankruptcy lawyers were on hand to answer questions. Immediately following the meeting, the managers were dispatched to their rooms to call their key subordinates to let them know what was going on.

Saturday morning, after the chapter 11 documents were filed, releases were messengered to key publications and one-on-one interviews were scheduled with reporters.

At the same time, teams of managers, accompanied by bankruptcy counsel, were dispatched across the country to hold briefings at critical company locations first thing Monday morning.

When employees arrived at work on Monday, they found on their desks two letters and a copy of the bankruptcy announcement. One letter was from the chairman, explaining what had happened and why; the other was from their local manager, announcing a staff meeting at which he would be able to answer any questions they might have.

By Tuesday morning, employee morale was higher than it had been in months. A new spirit was pumping through the company. A new confidence infused the entire organization. Employees began sporting buttons reading "This Team Wins."

Over the next few weeks, management followed up its initial communications efforts by establishing a variety of new informational pipelines and fo-rums. The company's monthly magazine was replaced with a weekly newslet-ter that reported both the good and the bad news. Weekly letters were sent to vendors, advising them of the company's increasing cash position. Procedures were established to ensure that shareholder and bondholder inquiries were answered promptly, and regular communiques were sent to all the company's investors.

As a result of the company's new openness, the tone of news coverage shifted dramatically. Instead of portraying the company as ailing, troubled, and strug-gling, the media were now reporting management's efforts to resuscitate opera-tions, reduce expenses, increase its cash position, and repair its businesses. Soon vendors were once again shipping on credit. One could feel and see the tide be-gin to turn.

In the first several months after the chapter 11 filing, barely a day went by without the company's having to squelch one rumor or another—a lumberyard was closing in Louisiana, a furniture store was going out of business in Chicago. Often, by the time the company got wind of the rumor, the employees at the lo-cation involved would be in absolute panic.

In such a hothouse atmosphere, it was absolutely essential that the communi-cations group stayed up to date on everything that was happening, including what the current word was on the grapevine. To make sure gossip never got out of control, we made a point of giving reporters and store managers our home phone numbers. "I would rather be awakened in the middle of the night and have a chance to correct a misperception," I once told a reporter, "than wake up in the morning only to find that an incorrect story had been printed, leaving us to try and undo the damage that had been done."

Because Wickes was headquartered in California, this resulted in many 5 A.M. phone calls. Still, it was worth it, as the practice nipped innumerable prob-lems in the bud.

Clearly, it took more than just good public relations to save Wickes. The turn-around would not have been possible without plenty of hard work by a dedicated management team. A well-executed communications strategy was definitely one of the most critical aspects of the reorganization effort. Keeping Wickes' various constituencies informed, controlling the information flow, stemming the rumors, and keeping employees motivated were all elements crucial to the company's re-covery.

DEVELOPING A CRISIS COMMUNICATIONS PROGRAM

In virtually every chapter 11 situation with which I have been involved over the years, the same prescription has worked to enable management to accelerate the recovery process, stem employee exodus, and achieve requisite stability: the de-velopment of a crisis communications program aimed at enhancing the flow of information throughout the organization.

Needless to say, every crisis is different and no two communications plans are alike. Nonetheless, nearly every effective plan involves the same series of timely procedures designed to bolster management's credibility by keeping employees, customers, creditors, investors, and the rest of the company's constituencies fully informed.

With this in mind, we generally recommend that a company facing chapter 11 take the following key actions:

- *Create a crisis team to address communications issues.* In anticipation of the filing, assemble a task force of professionals to prepare a complete package of materials. Include answers to likely questions, copies of press releases, explanations of the chapter 11 process, and letters to employees, customers, bankers, creditors, and vendors. Obviously, the preparation and contents of this package must be kept strictly confidential until the exact hour of disclosure.

- *Make the lawyers part of the communications team.* This may sound strange coming from a public relations professional, but a good bankruptcy lawyer is one of the most important members of the communications team. The fact is, your PR and legal objectives should not be mutually exclusive. Quite the contrary, an effective public relations strategy should advance your legal tactics. To that end, the presence of a lawyer on the PR team can help you avoid taking any actions that, however helpful they may be to your public relations campaign, might hurt you in court or undermine the negotiation of your reorganization plan. Beyond his or her sensitivities to the legal niceties, the bankruptcy attorney's insights into the politics and strategy of the case can prove invaluable in shaping the design and execution of an effective communications program.

- *Restrict who is allowed to speak to the media.* While the uninformed may regard this as "muzzling," the last thing a company needs in a troubled situation, in which rumors often outnumber products produced per hour, is for someone who is not fully informed on an issue to be quoted in the media on behalf of the company. Facts change rapidly in crisis environments. It is important that only the most informed people speak on the company's behalf. Limiting the number of people permitted to speak to reporters is the best way to ensure accuracy and consistency in the dissemination of information.

- *Refer all media inquiries to a central point. Make sure that the people handling the calls are well informed about the company, its people, and its products.* This accomplishes several objectives: It ensures that media calls will be answered accurately, promptly, and responsibly; it helps to ensure that calls will be referred to the right people within the company; and it prevents inquiries from "falling through the cracks."

- *Make sure there are procedures in place specifying precisely how particular shareholder, bondholder, vendor, customer, and other inquiries are to be answered.* In the immediate aftermath of the Wickes chapter 11 filing, the corporate communications department received more than 1,000 calls a week. In such a frenzied atmosphere, you do not want your people "winging it."

- *Decide in advance what you want the story to be.* Never draft a major announcement or press release without first deciding how you want the story to play. What is the message you want to transmit? What is the story you want to tell? These considerations may sound obvious, but you would be surprised how often they are ignored.
- *Prepare for questions.* Do not get caught unprepared. Before you make any public announcements, consider what sorts of questions your news will likely provoke the media to ask. Write them down, then review possible answers with other members of your management team and your lawyers.
- *Schedule a meeting of key managers just before the formal court filing.* Just before the announcement of a chapter 11 filing, crisis team members should summon senior officers and managers for a meeting to (1) explain what is going to happen and why; and (2) hand out assignments. At the meeting, the crisis team should also distribute a special package of informational materials that includes a point-by-point discussion guide for staff briefings and a check-list of actions that will need to be taken in the first critical days immediately following the filing. A vital part of this meeting should be a presentation on emotional issues—how to deal with employee concerns.
- *Follow up every oral presentation with written materials.* To ensure that your message is heard accurately, key points made in live presentations should always be repeated in writing. Distribute a letter to every employee, under the chief executive officer's signature, that reinforces the information employees receive from their managers.
- *Maintain an open-door policy; increase the visibility of senior management.* Virtually every employee survey ever taken shows that employees want more contact with senior officers. This is especially true during a crisis. In the weeks following a chapter 11 filing, it is essential that employees feel that management is accessible. To that end, senior executives should make a point of making themselves available to employees. That means scheduling regular visits to all facilities, especially stores and other key locations, and regularly circulating letters to keep people informed.
- *Replace fear with information.* Even though employees will receive a communications package on the first day after the filing, it is important to recognize that most people can absorb only a small amount of information in one sitting. To reinforce the original messages, as well as to assuage fears of wholesale layoffs or major changes in operations, it is generally a good idea to start producing and distributing a company-wide newsletter within the first two weeks after the filing. In my experience, this sort of publication often becomes the main vehicle through which employees can obtain updates on the reorganization and get authoritative answers to their questions.
- *Disseminate bad news as well as good news.* In order to provide effective leadership, you must have credibility with your people. They must feel you are leveling with them. Among other things, this means you cannot refuse to acknowledge disappointing developments. Tell your people the bad news as well as the good news, and provide explanations and rationales for both.

- *Control the rumor mill.* In the absence of information, the rumor mill runs rampant. You can minimize destructive speculation by establishing hot-lines and feedback programs that help employees separate rumor from truth and allow management to keep track of what the word is on the grapevine.
- *Without diminishing the severity of the situation, emphasize the positive aspects of what is going on.* In the midst of a crisis, there is a tendency to concentrate on the negatives and forget the positives. Without glossing over the challenges faced by a company going through reorganization, managers should remind employees that despite the chapter 11 filing, they can continue to count on what is essentially "business as usual." Specifically, they still have their jobs, their benefits, and their normal prospects for advancement. (Indeed, in some situations, a reorganization actually increases the opportunities for advancement.) Providing such reassurance to employees, while affirming the seriousness of the reorganization process, helps employees to achieve a balanced perspective.
- *Maintain your momentum.* Once the immediate crisis has passed and stability returns to day-to-day operations, it is important not to lose the momentum created by the urgency of the filing. This can be accomplished by implementing new programs designed to build motivation and productivity. These programs can take many forms, ranging from breakfast meetings with management to sales competitions to feedback and recognition programs.
- *Provide a vehicle for employee suggestions.* Whether it is a suggestion box in the stores or an employee hotline at headquarters, provide some way for employees to share their ideas. Some of the smartest and most effective ideas in business arise out of such forums. After all, the people in the field grapple with your company's problems every day. Employees generally know the truth about what is going on and have a good perspective on what went wrong.
- *Acknowledge successes as they occur.* Amid the pressure of reorganization, it is more important than ever that the hard work of employees be recognized throughout the organization. Employees should be kept informed of sales increases, new contracts, and other signs of "recovery." Recognize exceptional performance with meaningful rewards.
- *To the extent possible, avoid holding press conferences. Instead, schedule one-on-one interviews with key reporters.* Because the group format allows lazy reporters to piggyback on the work of their better prepared colleagues, most journalists do not like press conferences. In deciding to hold one, therefore, you run the risk of annoying (if not actually alienating) the sharper members of the press corps. You also run the risk of stumbling over a particularly tough or embarrassing question, or making a statement that you wish you had not made and then having your words reproduced in not just one publication but many.
- *Keep your vendors in the loop.* You cannot stay in business without the support of your vendors, and they will not support you if they do not know

what is going on. Consider sending them a weekly cash statement, perhaps in the form of a letter from your chief financial officer. Depending on how it looks, you might occasionally want to release this statement to the media.

HOW TO HIRE PUBLIC RELATIONS COUNSEL

Back in the 1980s, when I was senior vice-president of communications at Wickes, I met with more than my share of senior-level PR people and listened to more than my share of PR agency pitches. It was not, on the whole, a pleasant experience. However, I did learn what to look for in a PR professional.

- Look for experience in the areas where you need help. The turnaround business, especially restructuring and bankruptcies, is very specialized. Ask the people you are considering to be specific about what similar situations they have worked on in the past and how they handled them. With whom exactly did they work? What exactly did they do? Often, a good way to check people out is to ask for the names of the attorneys with whom they worked. Having spoken with scores of public relations professionals over the years, I must be one of the only ones who is not claiming credit for Johnson & Johnson's Tylenol success or for having worked on the Three Mile Island debacle. Ask for references.
- Look for judgment. When you are speaking in public, you cannot take back mistakes. A misstatement given to a newspaper—or worse, to a wire service or TV network—is out there for the world to see. You should look for people who have the sense to ask when they do not know, people who are not afraid to tell an impatient reporter on deadline they will have to get back to him because they do not have the information he wants. By the same token, you want people who will not wing it under pressure—people who, before they say anything, consider the different ways a given comment may be interpreted.
- You should look for integrity. All you have in business is your reputation. Your reputation and the reputation of your company are directly affected by the integrity of the people who represent you.
- The people you work with must have news sense. They must understand what makes a good story. They must be able to sift through all the details and pull out the pearl. Similarly, they must be able to gauge, when questioned by a reporter, what he or she is looking for and even why.
- Finally, you should look for people who like what they are doing. I have found that people who like what they do are almost always the best at what they do.

The PR people working for your company should exhibit all of those qualities. In a chapter 11 situation, they must have more, for in a crisis there is little if any shoulder to the road. A misstep, even a relatively small one, can be fatal.

Here are three questions you might want to ask relative to your internal staff:

1. Do we have someone on staff who is experienced in chapter 11 public relations and communications?
2. If the answer is yes, does he or she have sufficient backup to get the job done?
3. Do we have the public relations and communications experience necessary to develop an effective strategy?

The following eight questions should be asked of an outside public relations firm.

1. What other chapter 11 situations have you been involved in?
2. Can you give us the name of two bankruptcy attorneys you have worked with in prior cases that we can call?
3. What type of actions do you generally take in a situation like ours?
4. Who at your firm would be directly involved with our management on a day-to-day basis?
5. What sort of experience do you have in dealing with the financial media, the investment community, shareholders, and bondholders?
6. Can we talk to the CEO or some other senior executive of a company with whom you have previously worked in a similar situation?
7. How long has your firm been in business?
8. What other type of work do you do?

To lay people, public relations seems relatively easy and straightforward. That is part of the problem.

Communications in a chapter 11 is not something with which you can gamble. Choose your communications counsel with the same care you would devote to any other critical position on your professional team. Your company's survival could depend on it.

6

The Lawyer's Role in Representing the Distressed Company

Lewis Kruger and Robin E. Keller

Stroock & Stroock & Lavan LLP

THE ROLES OF THE DISTRESSED COMPANY LAWYER

This chapter addresses the multifaceted roles of the lawyer for a distressed company with respect to out-of-court restructuring options and in connection with Title 11 U.S.C. Sections 101 to 1330 (the Bankruptcy Code), particularly chapter 11 reorganizations. Those roles include identifying warning signals, highlighting the strategic use of workout or bankruptcy techniques, and guiding the company through the in- or out-of-court process. The lawyer for the distressed company is not looked to just as an advocate or "mouthpiece," but more frequently as a trusted business advisor, an objective observer and commentator, a facilitator of negotiations with multiple parties-in-interest in and outside of the company, and even the company's lifeline in certain circumstances.

The lawyer for the distressed company must advise on courses of action that have extreme and permanent consequences for management, shareholders, employees, customers, and perhaps the public interest. In addition to providing corporate legal advice, the lawyer may be asked to help facilitate the location of financing, to locate management turnaround consultants, to advise on criminal or securities fraud concerns, and to help management make difficult judgments in an unfamiliar environment in which demands and needs usually exceed the resources available.

In addition, in a bankruptcy proceeding, counsel for the debtor must be formally retained by court order in a case, and is subject to the highest standards of fiduciary responsibility to the court, the estate, and its creditors, including requirements of disclosure, disinterestedness, lack of adverse relations, and stringent billing requirements that add many layers of administrative duty to the role of counsel.

WHO PLAYS THESE ROLES?

In today's environment, any lawyer involved in commercial practice may be called on to identify and quantify problems that exceed the norm. One may be the intellectual property lawyer, or the real estate lawyer, or the international tax lawyer for a company when a matter is brought to his or her attention that goes to the heart of the company's viability. In addition to the usual problems caused by operating losses or liquidity constraints, life-threatening concerns can arise from contract disputes, litigation relating to products liability exposure, sudden changes in technology, the domino effect of company or bank failures in Asia, or a myriad of other sources that exceed the everyday capability of the company to cope.

While retailers and manufacturing companies have frequently availed themselves of bankruptcy restructuring options, it is a less familiar avenue or strategy in certain other industries, and yet insolvent, in-and-out-of court restructuring is accelerating in such industries as telecommunications, energy, financial services, and health care (including for-profit and not-for-profit entities).

Thus, any sophisticated commercial practitioner should be able to identify warning signals and respond in an appropriate manner to help the company address its problem. Such responses may include calling in a more specialized practitioner in corporate restructuring, bringing in specialized accounting expertise, or calling on a bankruptcy law specialist.

In fact, the practice of bankruptcy law, and even its application to out-of-court workouts, is a highly specialized and technical area of the law. More so than most commercial lawyers, bankruptcy lawyers have an awareness of and expertise in both the corporate aspects of restructuring and the litigation strategies applicable to contested court proceedings. There are unique, complex statutes and regulations relating to the treatment in bankruptcy of, for example, employee benefits, union contracts, and tax attributes of a corporate debtor.

The particular provisions of the Bankruptcy Code that affect the rights and remedies of secured creditors, and of lenders generally to a debtor both pre- and postpetition may be subject to different interpretation and application in different jurisdictions. In addition, the willingness of bankruptcy courts to grant various forms of relief and the timetable by which they can be expected to act integrally affect the reorganization process and are recognized to be known best by the specialized bankruptcy bar.

WHAT WARNING SIGNALS SHOULD COUNSEL WATCH FOR?

Regular counsel, accountants, and other advisors to a company should be aware of its financial condition generally. Obviously, those who work for a public company have the constant opportunities provided by public disclosure and reporting to monitor and evaluate a deteriorating financial condition or a troubling lawsuit, to determine when it crosses the line from a contingency to a crisis. However, even when working on regular disclosure documents such as the company's 10-

Q or 10-K, the lawyer may need to ask questions that help the company elicit information that exists but is not normally reviewed, or even information that simply does not exist or does not get formally recorded in the normal course of the company's recordkeeping. Disclosure of such information may help counsel address an unusual problem, or consult with parties not normally in the chain of preparation of such disclosure within an organization in order to appreciate the troubling parameters of a threatening business crisis.

For nonpublic companies, access to such information may be more difficult to come by; however, advisors involved in any unusual or sizable transaction for a company should check on the company's financial condition at the time, the impact of the transaction on its future financial condition, or on other obligations of the company that may be affected by the transaction. Typical warning signs that should trigger close scrutiny of a company's viability can include:

- Excessive trade debt
- Lengthening of payment terms
- Shortage of working capital
- Inability to make interest payments on public or private debt
- Covenant defaults under long-term credit agreements
- Litigation or casualty losses
- Downtrending sales; uptrending competition

There is a natural tendency of management, and advisors to management, to want to accomplish the goals that are set for them, and to gloss over the obstacles or consequences that may result not only from failing to achieve those goals, but also from achieving inappropriate or insufficient goals or targets. The failure to obtain a projected new account, missing a bank covenant, or the loss of a company's best overseas customer are events that obviously resonate with dire consequences. Other events or failures that may simply exacerbate existing weaknesses may not be as fully examined in a business-as-usual environment.

Court decisions that adversely affect a company's business may signal an impending financial crisis. Regulatory changes in a regulated industry or the abolition of regulation may pull the rug out from under business-as-usual techniques and attitudes. Interest rate changes, stock market downturns, overseas instability, management turnover, and increased competition in an industry sector may all signal a potential problem for the survival of a company that require a more comprehensive and intensive examination of the company's financial condition and prospects, including its compliance with loan agreements and other contractual obligations.

Most viable companies grapple with and adapt to significant changes in their operating environments all the time. One of the most frequently encountered exacerbating factors in severely distressed companies is the consequence of delay in recognizing, identifying, and remedying the life-threatening problem. Whether it is the absorption of operating losses rather than taking steps to cut costs or eliminate unprofitable lines, the downplaying of disclosure over troubling developments, or the simple inability of management to respond to an emerging crisis, delay and the failure to recognize and use the techniques available to distressed companies frequently exacerbates the problem.

EVALUATING THE STRATEGIC OPTIONS

The professional workout or bankruptcy practitioner understands and lives with dynamics that are unfamiliar to executives and commercial practitioners involved with solvent companies. These unfamiliar dynamics require, for example, questioning or second-guessing the judgment of the usual experts on a matter within a company by, for example, recommending the appointment of a special board committee to investigate the scope of a problem or the hiring of new outside counsel or other professionals to bring a fresh eye to the issue. In many cases, such unusual scrutiny is not undertaken until embarrassing public disclosure of a problem has already occurred or the magnitude of the problem has accelerated.

Alternatively, a financial crisis may require the perception and admission that the company's problems are also the problems of its bank lenders, suppliers, or customers and the need to bring those third-party entities into the decision-making process.

An additional dynamic brought to a business crisis by special distressed company counsel consists of "thinking outside the box" of normal problem-solving solutions for a company. A professional distressed company lawyer will offer a number of options to a company to address the problem or problems causing the crisis that are beyond the scope of everyday practice; most notably, but not at all exclusively, including the evaluation of the impact of bankruptcy proceedings.

Changes in Corporate Governance Requirements

A significant example of the fundamental shift of thought as well as action that is imposed on the corporate debtor and its managers as a result of insolvency is the expansion of fiduciary obligations to include the creditors as well as the shareholders of a company and the company itself.[1] This concept may be applicable both in and out of a bankruptcy proceeding, but is specifically embodied in the many duties owed by a debtor-in-possession to creditors under the Bankruptcy Code.

A number of cases have addressed issues of corporate governance of insolvent entities, including the rights of shareholders to call meetings and elect directors and officers, and the potential abrogation of those rights in the event that their exercise is detrimental to the reorganization process.[2]

As a general rule, normal corporate governance procedures will apply to management of the distressed company, but such rights can be restricted if their exercise is adverse to the interests of creditors or other parties-in-interest by injunctions against shareholder meetings, replacement of executives by the court at the request of creditors, or the appointment of a trustee.

Thus, management and the board should be advised by counsel to consider their obligations to creditors as well as shareholders, and take appropriate action to protect the interests of all entities with a stake in the survival of an enterprise.

Assuming that management, shareholders, or the board have determined that a crisis is threatening the company's survival, or that unusual steps are required, such as a sale of the company when it is insolvent, a distressed company legal expert will be called on to outline the options. In particular, the lawyer must explore the viability and consequences of an out-of-court workout of the problem versus an in-court proceeding, whether a full-fledged bankruptcy filing or some other court proceeding. The lawyer must evaluate the legal pros and cons; costs and timing; the impact on internal management; employees or shareholders; external credit and competitive position considerations; and other factors that will affect the company's decision.

The lawyer may need to advise the company to hire outside management consultants, accounting experts, investment bankers, brokers or appraisers, or others who can help provide the information necessary to make an informed judgment about the course to pursue.

The Workout

The goal of a successful workout is to achieve a permanent resolution of an acknowledged core business problem that requires the participation of key affected parties in a legally binding agreement. The workout is intended to be effectuated out-of-court, avoiding the costs, uncertainties, and delays of the adversarial process. Obviously, a workout is something less than a full-blown court proceeding with all the requirements of disclosure, without the comprehensive impact on all relationships of the company that a full-fledged bankruptcy proceeding entails.

The lawyer for the distressed company in a workout must help the company identify the nature of its core problems as well as which parties must be brought in to participate in their solution. A legal analysis must be made of the various forms of resolution that are achievable and lawful and how to bind interested parties in that resolution. The distressed company's lawyer must help the company ensure continuity of operations in the interim and manage publicity and the concerns of employees and others during the process.

A significant component of the workout lies in the comparison of out-of-court solutions to a chapter 11 or chapter 7 bankruptcy scenario. The experienced bankruptcy lawyer can address the costs and risks of the in-court process compared to the effectiveness or lack thereof of the out-of-court process. The availability of the automatic stay, of avoidance powers to recover preferential or fraudulent transfers, and other remedies available only under the Bankruptcy Code, such as the power to assume or reject leases and executory contracts or to bind dissenting parties within a class under a bankruptcy plan, may sway the decision of whether to proceed in court or out. The significant complexities that can arise from an adversarial in-court process will be factors to consider and analyze.

Working with management, accountants, and other financial advisors, the lawyer must help the company craft a business plan to address the company's crisis. The lawyer's particular role is to help shape the business plan so as to address the legal aspects of the problem and to address the treatment of the creditors, outside agencies, and the like that need to be part of the workout. The lawyer must then overlay restructuring concepts on the plan.

For example, if what is needed is simply a stretch-out of terms under existing lending documents, a deferral of payments or reduced interest rate, the lawyer will first help the company determine its needs, approach the lender or lenders, and convince them that modifications to the existing loan agreement will solve or at least mitigate the company's difficulty, which is preferable from the lender's perspective to the consequences of calling a default.

The lawyer must then help the company negotiate and draft or comment on drafts of the revised loan documents. Perhaps a new loan agreement will replace the existing debt instruments requiring consents, modifications of leases or other company agreements, regulatory approvals, and board and/or shareholder ratification.

The lawyer's role thus includes structuring the workout plan, advocating its merits to various constituencies in and outside the company, documenting, and closing the transaction. The workout plan is limited only by what consenting third parties will agree to within the confines of contractual, banking, or other applicable law.

While a workout can affect the rights of multiple parties, the lawyer must help the company judge whether a more comprehensive process is needed to fully effectuate the relief required by the distressed company.

The Prepackaged Plan

Increasingly, in companies with large issues of public or private debt, or with multiple layers of debt obligations that do not easily lend themselves to a simple workout, a more formal process for restructuring or satisfying liabilities such as by converting debt to equity, effectuating subordinations, stretch-outs, interest rate reductions, extensions of maturities, waivers of defaults, or effectuating asset sales and binding dissenting or unreachable holders becomes necessary. Section 1126(b) of the Bankruptcy Code contemplates the formulation of a plan outside of a bankruptcy proceeding that meets all of the requirements of an in-court plan and can be confirmed by a filing under the Bankruptcy Code after the acceptances of the requisite creditor majorities have been solicited and obtained. Acceptances of a prepackaged plan can be solicited prior to the filing of a bankruptcy case by compliance with applicable securities laws governing proxy solicitations or pursuant to exemptions from such rules, or can be solicited postfiling pursuant to a bankruptcy court–approved disclosure statement.

It is increasingly common for troubled companies to look to a prepackaged filing as a comprehensive, court-approved solution for serious capital structure or cash flow problems, although generally the process is utilized in situations in which the underlying business is fundamentally sound and an operational restructuring is unnecessary; thus, trade debt and most contractual obligations normally will not be impaired by a prepackaged filing. For a company with widely held public (or private) debt, the vote of the requisite class majority to a restructuring plan can be made binding on nonvoters or dissenters without the frequently encountered problem of holdouts adding extra cost and a perception of unfair treatment to the workout process. The prepackaged plan is perceived as a process that permits the avoidance of prolonged in-court proceedings, which add risk, uncertainty, and cost to the company's restructuring.

Troubled companies are increasingly turning to this prepackaged method of reorganization as a vehicle to speed themselves through the process of reorganization. . . . In these cases, negotiations relating to the alteration of the rights of creditors and equity security holders and the formulation of the plan, which would otherwise begin after the chapter 11 filing, have concluded before the filing occurs. Consequently, the plan is confirmed shortly after the chapter 11 plan is filed and the reorganized entity emerges from bankruptcy soon thereafter.

Many companies, for good reason, prefer to restructure debt without going into chapter 11. For those with bonds, notes and debentures in the hands of public investors, the preferred method to restructure outside of chapter 11 is through an exchange offer. In a conventional exchange offer, the issuer seeks to retire outstanding debt that has high interest cost and near-term maturities by issuing in exchange new equity or debt securities with lower fixed charges and stretched-out maturities. The goal of an out-of-court restructuring is the same as that sought in a traditional chapter 11 reorganization, namely, creation of a capital structure that allows the company to service its debts with cash flow from its operations. . . . Financial viability normally requires a high degree of acceptance by investors . . . There are incentives for holders not to accept the offer, but instead to "hold out." . . .

As a way to overcome this holdout problem, financially troubled companies, particularly those that have previously undergone a leveraged buyout or leveraged recapitalization, have increasingly used a prepackaged plan with an exchange offer as a way to achieve recapitalization. In these instances, a company has included with the exchange offer document a chapter 11 plan of reorganization. The documentation submitted by the bondholder . . . includes a line item to vote yes or no on the chapter 11 plan. If the exchange offer fails but enough "yes" votes for the chapter 11 plan are received, then the company files for reorganization.[3]

Due to the complex interplay of bankruptcy and securities law statutes that govern the typical prepackaged solicitation, the troubled company lawyer's role is again a multifaceted and integral one. Selection of the prepackaged proceeding as a workout option involves the careful evaluation of the nature of the company's problems and method of solution. Does the company have the time and the liquidity to effectuate a sometimes prolonged structuring and negotiation of a prepackaged plan out of court? Will adverse parties stand still, refrain from litigation, toll deadlines, and so forth? Are there organized, effective counterparties representing a sufficiently critical mass of the affected creditors with which the company can negotiate and reach agreement on a plan that can then be voted on and brought to court?

The distressed company lawyer must help the company fully evaluate, in advance, the viability of a prepackaged plan option. This entails an overall assessment of the problem to be addressed, the solutions that a restructuring plan or other bankruptcy remedies will provide, and the impact of a restructuring and filing on the company's relationships and competitive position. The advantage of a presolicited plan is that the company need not file for bankruptcy unless an agreement which effectively resolves the company's problem is reached and accepted by the necessary third parties, and the full panoply of restructuring remedies available to debtors under the Bankruptcy Code can then be utilized to ratify the agreement.

The difficulties, however, include the burden of working through all of the requirements of a full-blown chapter 11 plan and disclosure statement process, the need to disclose the company's problems to significant third parties during that process, the costs and burdens of putting together appropriate documentation that meets the requirements of the Bankruptcy Code and, if applicable, federal and state securities laws. Even in a presolicited, prepackaged plan context in which normal course obligations frequently are left unimpaired or unaffected by the restructuring, the impact of a bankruptcy filing on employees, vendors, and others must be evaluated and addressed.

A variation on the prepackaged plan option again involves the prebankruptcy filing negotiation of a restructuring plan for the company, which will be effectuated in a chapter 11 case, postfiling. In this scenario, the company will seek bankruptcy court approval for a disclosure statement, thereby obviating the need to comply with applicable securities law requirements which may be more onerous than the disclosure requirements of Section 1125 of the Bankruptcy Code, requiring in some cases Securities and Exchange Commission (SEC) approval of the disclosure document. Because more time will be spent in a bankruptcy case under the jurisdiction of the court, much more time and attention will be required to achieve compliance with the procedural requirements of chapter 11, greater costs may be incurred due to more active and broader creditor or other third-party involvement in the case, and, as always, greater risks of loss of control or adverse unexpected consequences due to the adversarial nature of the court proceeding may occur. However, liquidity concerns, intransigence of key third parties, or other legal or business concerns may mandate this approach.

The Free-Fall Filing

Compared to the workout or the prepackaged plan process, it might be said that filing for chapter 11 without a reorganization plan in place represents a "free-fall" approach to addressing a troubled company's business problems. However, it may be that there is no choice in the matter, due to the dire consequences to the company imposed by a liquidity crisis, a sizable adverse judgment, a regulatory change that undermines cash flow and debt service projections, acceleration of key debt obligations, or an involuntary filing or similar devastating event, including the need for court protection during a prolonged operational restructuring. The experienced distressed company lawyer should help the company plan for as controlled and stress-free a transition to chapter 11 as possible.

Debtor in Possession Financing.   Such assistance may include the identification of alternative financing sources, since prefiling lenders are no longer obligated to advance funds postfiling. Under 11 U.S.C. Section 364, the debtor in possession (DIP) is permitted to obtain unsecured credit and incur unsecured debt in the ordinary course of business, payable as an administrative expense of the bankruptcy,[4] to obtain unsecured credit out of the ordinary course after notice and a hearing,[5] or if such unsecured credit is unavailable, to obtain credit or incur debt with a priority over other administrative expenses, or secured by a lien on otherwise unencumbered property of the estate, or secured by a junior lien on otherwise encumbered property.[6]

Finally, 11 U.S.C. Section 364(d) permits the obtaining of credit or the incurring of debt (after notice and a hearing) secured by a senior or equal lien on property of the estate that is already subject to a lien, if the debtor cannot obtain credit otherwise, and there is adequate protection of the interest of the existing lienholder, proof of which is the debtor's burden. The conceptual underpinnings and implementation of the various forms of DIP financing can be complex and esoteric. The standards for adequate protection are unique to the bankruptcy forum and may vary between jurisdictions.

Pleadings must be prepared and lending agreements negotiated in advance of the filing, if possible, to ensure the availability of funds to operate the company. More so than in the normal financing environment, the lawyer for the distressed company will likely play a large role in locating DIP financing, because there is a limited universe of entities familiar with the process and willing to advance new money to a bankrupt company. In addition, the statutory requirements and custom and usage applicable to DIP financing is different from that of normal financing and sufficiently arcane to effectively mandate the input of a specialist in negotiating and drafting DIP financing agreements.

Use of Cash Collateral.   If no DIP lender can be found or if the time constraints are too tight to prenegotiate a DIP financing arrangement, the company may be permitted an appropriate application to the court to utilize the cash collateral of secured lenders. The cash collateral of existing secured lenders can be utilized based on a showing by the debtor of adequate protection, which may consist of one or more cash payments equivalent to any decrease in the value of the creditor's interest in property affected by the bankruptcy case, or the granting of additional or replacement liens to protect against such decrease in value, or other relief constituting the "indubitable equivalent" of the creditor's interest in affected property.[7]

The crafting of appropriate adequate protection remedies will be critical to the company's survival, and requires a highly specialized knowledge of applicable law, custom and usage, and jurisdictional variations in acceptable offers. In addition, there are a wide variety of prefiling motions for relief that can be prepared that allow the payment of employees and other costs critical to the company's survival in chapter 11.

POSTFILING PROCEDURES

More so than in probably any other event in the company's history, management will be inexperienced in evaluating its bankruptcy options, and will rely heavily on the advice of distressed company counsel on the business as well as the legal consequences of the various options available.

Outlining the Debtor's Duties

The Bankruptcy Code contemplates that when a debtor files for chapter 11, it will remain in possession of its business and properties unless replaced, by court order, by an operating trustee, or unless the case is converted to a chapter 7 case, in which event a liquidating trustee will be elected by creditors or appointed by the court. The DIP has most of the rights, powers, and duties of a trustee, and is authorized to operate its business and use its property (subject to restrictions to protect secured interests as described below) in the normal course. Out-of-the-ordinary-course transactions require bankruptcy court approval before they can be undertaken.

It is apparent that the threshold issue of what constitutes an ordinary course or an out-of-the-ordinary-course transaction will be a focus of attention for management and counsel throughout the course of the proceeding, requiring a factual analysis of the nature of the company's business, industry practices, and the specifics of the transaction at issue to be analyzed in light of the applicable case law and the purpose of the bankruptcy statute.

The core duties specified for the DIP include being accountable for all property received; examining and, if necessary, objecting to proofs of claim filed against the estate; furnishing information regarding the estate and its administration as requested by parties-in-interest; filing with the court, the U.S. trustee, and any governmental taxing authorities responsible for collecting taxes arising from the operation of the business periodic reports and summaries of the operation of the business, including a statement of receipts and disbursements, and such other information as the U.S. trustee or the court may require; and making a final report and filing a final account of the administration of the estate with the court and with the U.S. trustee.[8]

In addition, the DIP is required to file a comprehensive list of creditors, a schedule of assets and liabilities, and a statement of the debtor's financial affairs, including a listing of prebankruptcy transfers of money and property (the Schedules). Signed under oath by an officer of the company, the Schedules provide a comprehensive overview of the company's condition as of the filing date, its obligations to creditors, and the assets available to satisfy those obligations.

Creditors will look to their listing on the Schedules to determine whether they need to file proofs of claim, and the creditors' committee and other parties-in-interest will look to the listing of prepetition transactions to determine whether there were improper transfers or voidable transactions that can be attacked to increase the estate for creditors. Again, counsel will need to help guide the company through the compliance obligations contained in both the Schedules and the monthly operating filings to ensure adequacy of disclosure and technical compliance with bankruptcy requirements.

Dealing with the Plan Process

Most pervasively, the company and counsel will focus together on structuring a confirmable plan of reorganization and guiding the process to as prompt a conclusion as possible. The Bankruptcy Code defines who may file a plan,[9] the mandatory and permissive contents of a plan,[10] what constitutes impairment of a claim or interest under a plan thereby requiring the impaired creditor, interest holder or class of creditors or interest holders to vote on the plan,[11] how to classify claims or interests,[12] what constitutes adequate disclosure in connection with a plan,[13] and specifies the requirements for consensual or contested confirmation of a plan.[14]

These core statutory guidelines are elaborated by legislative history, case law, and the practices of courts and counsel throughout the country. While many of the core requirements are standardized, there is a wide range of different local practices, and case law ranging from the bankruptcy court level to circuit courts of appeal that interpret differently the application of fundamental reorganization requirements and concepts.

In addition, the Bankruptcy Code provides many procedures for the protection of creditors' and equityholders' rights, including the appointment of official committees of creditors and in some cases equityholders in the case, and for their retention of counsel, financial advisors and other professionals who will help them monitor the debtor's activities and enforce their views of an appropriate plan.[15] For secured creditors, protection of their interests in property that might otherwise be utilized by the debtor in its reorganization efforts include restrictions on the use of cash collateral,[16] requirements for adequate protection,[17] relief from stay provisions,[18] and protections against priming by postpetition lenders.[19]

While the automatic stay imposed on the recovery by creditors of prepetition claims[20] and the protections for debtors embodied in the exclusivity provisions for filing a reorganization plan[21] permit a wide degree of control over the process, the existence of creditor remedies such as lifting the stay, terminating exclusivity, and the supervisory role of the creditors' committee requires at the least close communication with creditor constituencies. Frequently there will be contested motion practice over a variety of issues affecting creditors' rights, or even major litigation over control of the case, the nature and scope of claims, and the formulation of the plan.

Counsel for the debtor plays a central role in helping the debtor comply with its statutory duties. Counsel must help the debtor map out a strategy both for compliance with statutory requirements and for guiding the bankruptcy process. Communication with the court, the U.S. trustee, the official committees, and other significant parties-in-interest is integral to the success or failure of the chapter 11 process. The debtor's counsel must be an advocate for the debtor's views, but also, as a fiduciary of the court and the estate, must be able to articulate and reconcile competing interests, explain to the debtor the strengths and weaknesses of its own and other parties' positions, and be the proponent of a process that is participatory, open, and focused on the legitimate achievement of appropriate ends.

It is all too easy for the debtor and/or its creditors to become enmeshed in litigation over the calculation of claims or the enforcement of rights to the detriment of the broader goal of an effective and expeditious reorganization. Balancing competing interests is at the core of a debtor's counsel's duties to a greater degree than usual in the legal advocate's relations with its client.

RULES FOR RETENTION OF LAWYERS AND AVOIDANCE OF CONFLICTS

There is an extensive statutory scheme governing the retention and compensation of counsel retained to represent a DIP. Generally, the statutory scheme is intended to eliminate or limit the retention of counsel with conflicts of interest vis-à-vis the debtor and its creditors or shareholders, and to regulate the sensitive area of compensation that is paid out of usually insolvent estates ahead of prepetition creditors. Compliance with the requirements of the Bankruptcy Code is mandatory, and sanctions for failure to comply can be severe, including removal of counsel from the case, denial of all or some of the fees earned, and in the rare instance of willful nondisclosure of conflicts of interest, criminal penalties.

Retention of Debtor's Counsel

The Debtor must make a motion to the Bankruptcy Court for authority to hire counsel.[22] Section 327(a) requires that such counsel "do not hold or represent an interest adverse to the estate, and . . . are disinterested persons." A disinterested person is defined, for this purpose, in 11 U.S.C. Section 101(14), as a person that:

> (A) is not a creditor, an equity security holder, or an insider; (B) is not and was not an investment banker for any outstanding security of the debtor; (C) has not been, within three years before the date of the filing ... an attorney for such an investment banker in connection with the offer, sale, or issuance of a security of the debtor; (D) is not and was not, within two years before the date of the filing . . . a director, officer, or employee of the debtor or of an investment banker specified in subparagraphs (B) or (C) of this paragraph; and (E) does not have an interest materially adverse to the interest of the estate or of any class of creditors or equity security holders by reason of any direct or indirect relationship to, connection with, or in-

terest in, the debtor or an investment banker specified in paragraphs (B) or (C) of this paragraph, or for any other reason.

A distinction is made between counsel retained generally to "represent or assist the trustee in carrying out the trustee's duties under this title"[23] and counsel employed "for a specified purpose, other than to represent the trustee in conducting the case"[24] in terms of whether the "disinterestedness" requirement must be met. Conceptually, counsel hired for a limited specific purpose under 11 U.S.C. Section 327(e) that is not technically disinterested may be retained if it is in the best interests of the estate, and counsel does not hold an adverse interest to the debtor or the estate in the matter on which it is to be employed.

The chapter 11 retention provision, Section 1107, also contains an exception, by providing, in 11 U.S.C. Section 1107(b), that "[n]otwithstanding section 327(a) of this title, a person is not disqualified for employment . . . by a debtor-in-possession solely because of such person's employment by or representation of the debtor before the commencement of the case."

In reality, it is to be hoped that a distressed company has retained counsel prior to filing for bankruptcy to advise it of its options, and to represent it in preparing for filing, and that such counsel will continue to represent the debtor-in-possession postfiling. As a further exception to the disinterestedness requirement, 11 U.S.C. Section 327(c) clarifies that "a person is not disqualified for employment . . . solely because of such person's employment by or representation of a creditor, unless there is an objection by another creditor or the United States trustee, in which case the court shall disapprove such employment if there is an actual conflict of interest."

There is a long-standing judicial and congressional concern with avoidance of conflicts on the part of counsel that are fiduciaries of the court and the estate and charged with representing a company with fiduciary duties to its creditors as well as its shareholders.

The disinterestedness requirement finds its roots in the Bankruptcy Act of 1898 and the Bankruptcy Rules in effect prior to the adoption of the Code. *See In re Philadelphia Athletic Club*, 20 B.R. 328, 333 (E.D. Pa. 1982) (citing 1 Collier Bankruptcy Manual §101.13 (1981)). Under that law, a trustee had to be "independent and disinterested so far as possible. *"In re Ocean City Automobile Bridge Co.*, 184 F.2d 726, 729 (3d Cir. 1950). The courts applied a rather rigid test of disinterestedness. *See Meredith v. Thralls*, 144 F.2d 473, 475 (2d Cir.), cert. denied, 323 U.S. 758, 89 L. Ed. 607, 65 S. Ct. 92 (1944) (noting that the test of disinterestedness could not be waived because of the integrity or ability of the particular individual involved) . . . This disinterestedness requirement applied to counsel for the trustee as well. *See In re Chicago Rapid Transit Co.*, 93 F.2d 832, 835 (7th Cir. 1937) (denying petition for employment of a law firm, and noting that the rule defining those attorneys with adverse interests should be given a 'liberal construction') . . .[25]

The motion or application filed by the debtor with the court to retain its bankruptcy counsel must be transmitted in advance of approval to the U.S. trustee for scrutiny. The U.S. trustee is appointed by the Attorney General for the United States pursuant to 28 U.S.C. Section 581. The duties of the U.S. trustee involve supervision of the administration of bankruptcy cases, including review and comment on requests for compensation by professionals.[26]

In addition, as set forth in Bankruptcy Rule 2014, "[t]he application shall state the specific facts showing the necessity for the employment, the name of the person to be employed, the reasons for the selection, the professional services to be rendered, any proposed arrangement for compensation, and, to the best of the applicant's knowledge, all of the person's connections with the debtor, creditors, any other party in interest, their respective attorneys and accountants, the United States trustee, or any person employed in the office of the United States trustee."[27] An affidavit or verified statement of the person to be employed setting forth such connections must accompany the debtor's application.

Accuracy and completeness of disclosure is a key tenet underlying the retention and compensation of counsel to a debtor in a bankruptcy case, in light of the concerns over avoidance of conflicts of interest and fairness to creditors. Any attorney representing a debtor in a bankruptcy case, whether or not applying for compensation during the case, is required by 11 U.S.C. Section 329(a) to file a statement with the court of compensation paid or agreed to be paid within one year prior to the bankruptcy filing, for services rendered or to be rendered in connection with or contemplation of the case, and the source of such compensation. Under 11 U.S.C. Section 329(b) and Bankruptcy Rule 2017, if such compensation paid prior to the bankruptcy filing exceeds the "reasonable value" of any such services (as determined by the bankruptcy court), then on motion of any party-in-interest or on the court's own initiative, the court may, after notice and a hearing, cancel any such agreement, or order the return of any excessive payment to the estate (if estate property) or to the entity that made the payment, if other than the debtor or its estate. Similarly, the court may determine whether any payment or agreement to pay money or transfer property by a debtor to an attorney after the entry of the order for relief is excessive, whether made directly or indirectly, for services in any way related to the case.[28]

The obligation of counsel to the DIP to disclose connections that may give rise to conflicts or interests adverse to the estate or its creditors continues throughout the case. With certain exceptions previously described, 11 U.S.C. Section 328(c) provides that the court may deny allowance of compensation and reimbursement of expenses to a professional if at any time during such professional's employment it is not a disinterested person, or represents or holds an interest adverse to the interest of the estate with respect to the matter on which such professional person is employed.

Notwithstanding the apparent clarity of the Code's provisions regarding disinterestedness, and the forcefulness with which Congress has emphasized the need for professionals retained by the debtor or trustee to avoid conflicts of interest, there is both intellectual debate over the scope of prohibited conflicts of interest, and surprisingly frequent disagreement between practitioners, the U.S.

trustee offices, and the courts as to the appropriate level of disclosure and what constitutes prohibited relationships or connections.[29]

Even prominent bankruptcy specialists run afoul of the disclosure requirements and face sanctions due apparently to ambiguity over the application of the disclosure requirements to their connections before or after the commencement of the case with other parties, or in some cases willful failure to comply with those requirements.

For example, in *In re Leslie Fay Companies, Inc.,*[30] Judge Brozman wrote at length on the disclosure requirements applicable to debtor's counsel, and imposed sanctions in the form of substantial reductions of fees paid and disqualification of counsel from the performance of certain future services for the debtor. The issue arose in connection with the creditors' committee's objection to the first interim fee request by debtor's counsel, and their request for examination as to the disinterestedness of that counsel. The *Leslie Fay* court appointed an examiner to investigate whether debtor's counsel was disinterested or held or represented interests adverse to the estate, whether it had made adequate disclosure of such connections, and whether services performed had been tainted by improper conflicts.

The *Leslie Fay* bankruptcy filing occurred following disclosure of a reporting fraud by senior financial officers of the company. At the time of the bankruptcy filing, debtor's lead counsel was retained both to commence the chapter 11 case and to complete its prebankruptcy representation of the audit committee of the board of directors charged with investigating the fraud, its source, and possible claims that might be asserted as a result on behalf of the corporation against its professionals, officers, and directors.

The postbankruptcy inquiry by the creditors' committee and the U.S. trustee resulted in the supplementing of debtor's counsel's initial disclosure, to reveal that the firm had a significant client relationship with companies in which certain members of the audit committee were partners, and also a client relationship with an accounting firm, which board members and accounting firm were potential targets of the audit committee's investigation. That subsequent disclosure also revealed a long-standing representation of one of the largest creditors in the case, none of which relationships had been disclosed previously to the court.

The examiner's report concluded that debtor's counsel was not disinterested that the disclosure made had been improper, and that had proper disclosure been made it would have cast substantial doubt on counsel's ability to conduct a fair and impartial investigation. However, the examiner also determined that the actual representation of the audit committee had been appropriate: " '[t]he conflict presented [was] principally one of perception: under all the circumstances, there [was] a fair perception that because of multiple representations and client relationships, [counsel] would be unable to act solely in the debtor's best interests.' According to the examiner, [debtor's counsel] caused the debtors no actual injury, and represented them in an exemplary fashion."[31]

The *Leslie Fay* examiner recommended a sanction consisting of the costs of his investigation, but not a disqualification of counsel or a further disallowance of fees. The U.S. trustee, however, moved to disqualify counsel based on the report and for the imposition of economic sanctions, arguing that the lack of disinterestedness called into question the integrity of the audit, regardless of how thoroughly it was actually performed. The creditors' committee at the time opposed disqualification as detrimental to the debtor's reorganization efforts, and sought an economic sanction.

The court ruled that it had "wide discretion in [its] selection of an appropriate remedy," including imposition of monetary sanctions and disqualification.[32] While disclosure at the outset might have permitted the court to determine the appropriateness of the retention, the report indicated that counsel had properly fulfilled its fiduciary duties to the estate. Weighing the integrity of the judicial process against the potential injury to the estate from disqualification of its counsel at a critical juncture in the reorganization effort, the court permitted counsel to continue to effectuate the reorganization efforts, finding also that since no claims could be brought against the firm's other clients, that conflict had been removed. The court required the retention of new counsel to handle litigation relating to claims arising out of the prepetition accounting irregularities. The court further required disgorgement equal to the costs incurred by the examiner and his professionals, and the committees in dealing with the conflict issues.

The *Leslie Fay* court's legal analysis of the standards applicable to counsel constituted a fair summary of the law. Noting that the disinterestedness requirement prohibits holding an interest materially adverse to the interest of the estate, the court approvingly cited the First Circuit view that "'the twin requirements of disinterestedness and lack of adversity telescope into a single hallmark.'" [33]

The *Leslie Fay* court stated that "[t]he requirements of section 327 cannot be taken lightly, for they 'serve the important policy of ensuring that all professionals appointed pursuant to [the section] tender undivided loyalty and provide untainted advice and assistance in furtherance of their fiduciary responsibilities.' Once counsel is employed, 'a lawyer owes his allegiance to the entity and not to the stockholder, director, officer, employee, representative or other person connected with the entity.' "[34]

Addressing the frequently noted absence of express guidance in the Code on the nature of an adverse interest, the *Leslie Fay* court noted that:

> The Code does not attempt to define what constitutes an adverse interest. However, interests are not considered "adverse" merely because it is possible to conceive a set of circumstances under which they might clash. . . .
> The more difficult area is when a live conflict of interest has not quite emerged, yet the factual scenario is sufficiently susceptible to that possibility so as to make the conflict more than merely "hypothetical or theoretical." The courts have been far from uniform in the way they have formulated tests for dealing with this type of situation.
>
> A handful of courts has held or implied that only "actual," and not "potential," conflicts of interest are disabling. *See In re Stamford Color Photo, Inc.*, 98 B.R. 135, 137-38 (Bankr. D. Conn. 1989); *H&K Developers, Inc. v. Waterfall Village of Atlanta, Ltd. (In re Waterfall Village of Atlanta, Inc.)*, 103 B.R. 340, 344 (Bankr. N.D. Ga. 1989); see also, Comment,

Bankruptcy Code Section 327(a) and Potential Conflicts of Interest-Always or Never Disqualify? 29 Hous. L. Rev. 433 (1992). A greater number of courts . . . have concluded that even "potential" conflicts of interest are disabling. *See In re Codesco, Inc.*, 18 B.R. 997, 999 (Bankr. S.D. N.Y. 1982) ("There should be no *opportunity* for the exercise of conflicting interests...." (emphasis added)); *In re Proof of The Pudding, Inc.*, 3 B.R. 645, 647 (Bankr. S.D. N.Y. 1980); *see also Bohack Corp. v. Gulf & Western Industries, Inc. (In re Bohack)*, 607 F.2d 258, 263 (2d Cir. 1979). Yet other courts have been critical of the very distinction between actual and potential conflicts. *See e.g., In re Kendavis Industries, Inc.*, 91 B.R. 742, 744 755-56 (Bankr. N.D. Tex. 1988). . . .

The debate over this issue may be more semantic than substantive, for a close review of the cited cases indicates that the results were largely driven by the facts of each case. And indeed, in the context of section 327, that is precisely the way it should be. *See Iannotti v. Manufacturers Hanover Trust Co. (In re New York, New Haven & Hartford Railroad Co.)*, 567 F.2d 166, 175 (2d Cir. 1977) (no "mandatory requirement that reorganization courts woodenly must deny compensation in every case of conflict of interest, regardless of the facts."); *Interwest Business Equipment, Ltd. v. United States Trustee (In re Interwest Business Equipment, Ltd.)*, 23 F.3d 311, 315 (10th Cir. 1994) (citing several cases for proposition that bankruptcy court has broad discretion in disqualification cases); *In re Garza*, 1994 WL 282570 *2 (Bankr. E.D. Va. Jan. 19, 1994) ("[C]ourts have generally declined to formulate bright-line rules concerning the criteria for disqualification, favoring instead an approach which evaluates the facts and circumstances of each particular case.") Potential conflicts, no less than actual ones, can provide motives for attorneys to act in ways contrary to the best interests of their clients. Rather than worry about the potential/actual dichotomy it is more productive to ask whether a professional has "either a meaningful incentive to act contrary to the best interests of the estate and its sundry creditors—an incentive sufficient to place those parties at more than acceptable risk—or the reasonable perception of one." *In re Martin*, 817 F.2d at 180-81. In other words, if it is plausible that the representation of another interest may cause the debtor's attorneys to act any differently than they would without that other representation, then they have a conflict and an interest adverse to the estate.[35]

Addressing the requirements of disclosure, the *Leslie Fay* court enunciated the fundamental standards of interpretation: "The purpose of Rule 2014, as expressed by the *Collier* treatise, is to provide the court (and the United States Trustee) with information necessary to determine whether the professional's employment meets the broad test of being in the best interest of the estate. To that end, a failure to disclose any fact which may influence the court's decision may result in a later determination that disclosure was inadequate and sanctions should be imposed on the professional. . . ."[36]

In a test of disclosure obligations that resulted in the imposition of a sanction on debtor's counsel for its failure to bring to the court's attention inadequate disclosure by another professional, the court in *In re CF Holding Corp. and COLT's Mfg. Co., Inc.*,[37]decided objections by the creditors' committee and the U.S. trustee to the final fee applications of the debtor's legal and financial advisors.

Following the bankruptcy filing and the retention of debtor's professionals, the financial advisor to the debtor obtained an undisclosed financial interest in an entity that became a bidder for the debtor's assets. Although no supplemental disclosure was filed with the court or given to the creditors' committee, the financial advisor advised the board of directors of the debtor of its conflict and recused itself from advising the board on the negotiations with the potential purchaser. Counsel to the debtor was aware of the financial advisor's interest and the arrangements with the board, but asserted that it had no obligation to bring the matter to the court's attention.

The court disagreed, imposing a substantial reduction of fees on debtor's counsel, as well as the financial advisor, and articulated the following basis for liability of counsel:

> The Code contains a provision, which, if not directly on point, is sufficiently so as to give the court guidance on the question of [debtor's counsel's] responsibility to the debtors' estates. If a trustee had replaced the debtors in these cases, Code §326(d) would require the court to deny compensation "to the trustee if the trustee failed to make diligent inquiry into facts that would permit denial of allowance under section 328(c) of the title or, with knowledge of such facts, employed a professional person under section 327 of this title." It could have been reasonably anticipated that in light of the duties of an attorney for a debtor in possession, that no lower standard would be applied to such attorney with actual knowledge of another professional's loss of disinterestedness.
>
> . . . The rule of law of no responsibility proposed by [debtor's counsel] . . . cannot be consonant with the fiduciary responsibilities imposed on bankruptcy estate professionals. The general concerns of the Code and the courts to promote public confidence in the integrity of the bankruptcy system are compelling reasons to apply a prophylactic rule in considering the extent of the fiduciary duties of an attorney for a debtor in possession.[38]

However, it is a prevalent view that conflicts must be actual or potential, not hypothetical or imaginable. In the recent acrimonious bankruptcy proceedings of Marvel Entertainment Group, et al., the District Court appointed a chapter 11 trustee to attempt to resolve the apparently irreconcilable differences of the debtor entities and their creditor groups. In seeking to retain his law firm as counsel, the trustee disclosed that his firm had represented one of the lead bank creditors in unrelated matters, which retention was terminated at the time of the application. Various parties urged the court to deny the retention due to the appearance of impropriety allegedly caused by this prior representation. The Third

Circuit Court of Appeals, in *In re Marvel Entertainment Group*,[39] overturned the District Court's disallowance of the retention based solely on the "appearance of conflict." The Third Circuit held that the conflict alleged was neither actual nor potential. "If we were to uphold the district court's order under these circumstances, it is with the utmost difficulty that we could imagine how a law firm with any prior relationship to a secured creditor could ever serve as trustee's counsel."[40]

The Third Circuit court reiterated its prior holding in *In re BH&P Inc.*[41] that: "Section 327(a) presents a per se bar to the appointment of a law firm with an actual conflict, and gives the district court wide discretion in deciding whether to approve the appointment of a law firm with a potential conflict. [However,] the district court erred when it held that it could disqualify as disinterested any person who 'in the slightest degree might have some interest or relationship that would even faintly color the independence and impartial attitude required by the Code and the Bankruptcy Rules.'"[42]

In an unusual and perhaps unique case, prominent bankruptcy counsel for a large corporate debtor faced indictment and ultimately conviction on felony criminal charges of making a false declaration in a bankruptcy proceeding in violation of 18 U.S.C. Section 152 and use of a document containing a false declaration while testifying in a bankruptcy proceeding in violation of 18 U.S.C. Section 1623. In *In re Bucyrus International, Inc.*, in the Eastern District of Wisconsin, counsel failed to disclose close connections between his law firm and the Bucyrus debtor's major secured creditor and its principal, including active representation of that creditor in allegedly unrelated matters prior to and during the course of the Bucyrus bankruptcy. Testimony at trial evidenced that counsel had discussed the conflict internally and determined that it was "not a problem" and did not have to be disclosed to the court.

Aggressive investigation by a creditor resulted in a referral of the conflict disclosure issues to the U.S. trustee and the United States attorney. Following a week-long jury trial before the federal district court in Milwaukee in the summer of 1998, the lead lawyer for the debtor "admitted on the witness stand that he should have disclosed the simultaneous representations so the bankruptcy judge could decide whether he and his law firm had such divided loyalties they could no longer represent Bucyrus-Erie."[43]

The sentencing judge determined that "a tough sentence was needed to send a message about ethics to the legal profession as a whole."[44] The lead lawyer received a 15-month prison term, and was fined $15,000. He has been fired as a partner from his law firm and disbarred from the practice of law as a result of the felony convictions. His law firm returned $1.9 million in legal fees to the estate, representing the entire fee paid. A legal malpractice action is pending, brought by Bucyrus and the avenging creditor against the law firm.

Compensation Requirements

The trustee (or DIP) is permitted by U.S.C. Section 328(a) to retain a professional person "on any reasonable terms and conditions of employment, including

on a retainer, on an hourly basis, or on a contingent fee basis. Notwithstanding
such terms and conditions, the court may allow compensation different from the
compensation provided under such terms and conditions after the conclusion of
such employment, if such terms and conditions prove to have been improvident
in light of developments not capable of being anticipated at the time of the fixing
of such terms and conditions."

As previously stated, 11 U.S.C. Section 328(c) permits denial of compensation if a professional is not disinterested or represents or holds an adverse interest to the estate during the course of its employment.

The filing of interim and final fee applications by professional persons retained under 11 U.S.C. Section 327 or 11 U.S.C. Section 1103 is provided for
under 11 U.S.C. Sections 330 and 331. Section 331 permits interim filings
"not more than once every 120 days after an order for relief in a case . . . or
more often if the court permits .. . . " Notice to creditors and a hearing are required before any allowance of fees may be awarded by the court, and no payments of fees or reimbursements of expenses may be made postfiling without
a court order.

Bankruptcy courts vary in the strictness with which they apply 11 U.S.C. Section 331; some courts permit no filings or fee awards more frequently than every
120 days; other courts will sign an order at the commencement of the case permitting professionals to submit monthly bills and receive an on-account payment
of some percentage of that bill, subject to the filing of quarterly fee applications,
and ultimately allowance of the final fee application. The practice of withholding
a portion of interim fee requests (a hold-back) is widespread in bankruptcy
courts, in light of the court's power to revisit fee awards at the end of the case,
and the uncertainties surrounding the reorganization process including uncertainty as to whether administrative expenses will be paid in full in a case. Thus,
debtor's counsel will frequently encounter a substantial delay in payments of
fees that are ultimately allowed.

The standards for allowance of compensation are set forth in 11 U.S.C. Section 330(a), and extensively interpreted in case law throughout the country. Section 330(a)(1) provides that the court may allow "(A) reasonable compensation
for actual, necessary services rendered by the . . . attorney and by any paraprofessional person employed by any such person; and (B) reimbursement for actual, necessary expenses." In addition, the court may, on its own motion, or the
motion of the U.S. Trustee or other parties in interest award "compensation that
is less than the amount of compensation that is requested."[45]

The standards for reasonable compensation are now codified in 11 U.S.C.
Sections 330(a)(3) and (4) and represent on amalgam of comparability to
charges for similar services in the nonbankruptcy context and special restrictions
that affect the recoverability of otherwise comparable charges for services, such
as the nature, extent, and value of the services, taking into account relevant factors including the time spent on such services, the rates charged for such services, whether the services were necessary to the administration of or beneficial
toward the completion of the bankruptcy case, and whether the services were

performed within a reasonable amount of time commensurate with the complexity, importance, and nature of the problem, issue, or task addressed. The Bankruptcy Code expressly disallows compensation for unnecessary duplication of services or services not reasonably likely to benefit the debtor's estate or not necessary to the administration of the case.

Bankruptcy Rule 2016 details the requirements for applications for compensation, and local court rules frequently supplement these requirements as to both form and substance, in some instances specifying, for example, disbursements that may be allowed or disallowed.

Counsel seeking compensation under the Bankruptcy Code must file an application with the court containing a detailed statement of the services rendered, time expended and expenses incurred, and the amounts requested. In practice, specialized recordkeeping is required, whereby each attorney or paraprofessional performing services must detail the services rendered, broken into time increments of tenths of an hour. In certain jurisdictions, each task must be identified as to time; in other jurisdictions, each case must be broken down into multiple categories with time allocated to the appropriate category and itemized as to the time spent. Failure to properly record time spent may result in disallowance of the fees or disbursements requested, and in fact, in most jurisdictions, time spent preparing these detailed fee reports is compensable by the estate.

In addition to the requirements applicable to all professional persons, Bankruptcy Rule 2016(b) further provides that attorneys for the debtor, whether or not applying for compensation, must file the statement required by 11 U.S.C. Section 329 stating whether the attorney has shared or agreed to share its compensation with any other entity, and to provide the details of any such sharing arrangement, except for the arrangements between members and associates of the same law firm.[46] Again, there is an express continuing obligation to update this disclosure throughout the case.

It is beyond the scope of this article to examine the history of issues relating to fee awards in bankruptcy cases. However, it is apparent that the stringent requirements of disclosure, undivided loyalties, avoidance of actual or potential conflicts, the performance of duties to the court and the estate, and the administrative detail and special payment (or risk of nonpayment) provisions contained in the compensation sections of the Code highlight the special and integral relationship of the debtor's attorney to the reorganization process.

CONCLUSION

The conclusion may be drawn that counsel for the distressed company is much more than a draftsman, a technical advisor, or even an advocate. The distressed company's attorney is in fundamental ways a participant in the process of restructuring the company and shares responsibility for ensuring, to the extent possible, the integrity of that process.

NOTES

1. See *Davis v. Woolf*, 147 F.2d 629 (4th Cir. 1945).

2. *See Lionel Corp. v. Committee of Equity Security Holders (In re Lionel Corp.)*, 30 B.R. 327 (Bankr. S.D.N.Y. 1983); *Manville Corp. v. Equity Security Holders Comm. (In re Johns-Manville Corp.)*, 52 B.R. 879 (Bankr. S.D.N.Y. 1985), aff'd, 60 B.R. 842 (Bankr. S.D.N.Y. 1986), *rev'd,* 801 F.2d 60 (B.A.P. 2d Cir. 1986), *opinion on remand,* 66 B.R. 517 (Bankr. S.D.N.Y. 1986); see generally Anna Y. Chou, *Corporate Governance in Chapter 11: Electing a New Board,* 65 Am. Bankr. L.J. 559 (1991).

3. *Current Issues in Prepackaged Chapter 11 Plans of Reorganization and Using the Federal Declaratory Judgment Act for Instant Reorganization,* C647ALI-ABA 1, 8-9 (1991). *See also Prepackaged Chapter 11 Plans,* 647 PLI/Comm 617 (1993).

4. 11 U.S.C. § 364(a).

5. 11 U.S.C. § 364(b).

6. 11 U.S.C. § 364(c).

7. 11 U.S.C. § 361.

8. 11 U.S.C. §§ 1106-1107.

9. 11 U.S.C. § 1121.

10. 11 U.S.C. § 1123.

11. 11 U.S.C. § 1124.

12. 11 U.S.C. §§ 1122, 1123(a)(1), (4).

13. 11 U.S.C. § 1125.

14. 11 U.S.C. § 1129.

15. 11 U.S.C. §§ 1102–1103.

16. 11 U.S.C. § 363.

17. 11 U.S.C. § 361.

18. 11 U.S.C. § 362.

19. 11 U.S.C. § 364.

20. 11 U.S.C. § 362.

21. 11 U.S.C. § 1121.

22. 11 U.S.C. §§ 327, 1107.

23. 11 U.S.C. § 327(a).

24. 11 U.S.C. § 327(e).

25. *In re Marvel Entertainment Group, Inc.*, No. Civ. A. 97-638 RRM, 1998 WL 181084, 32 Bankr. Ct. Dec. 102 (Bankr. D. Del. Jan. 27, 1998), *rev'd in part*, 140 F.3d 463, 32 Bankr. Ct. Dec. 479 (B.A.P. 3d. Cir. 1998).

26. 28 U.S.C. § 586.

27. Fed. R. Bankr. Proc. 2014(a).

28. Fed. R. Bankr. Proc. 2017(b).

29. *See Employment of Attorneys by Debtors in Possession: A Proposal for Modification of the Existing Attorney Eligibility Provisions of the Bankruptcy Code and the Existing Conflict of Interest Provisions of the Ethical Rules of Professional Responsibility,* 47 Bus. Law. 671(1992).

30. 175 B.R. 525 (Bankr. S.D. N.Y. 1994).

31. *Id.* at 530–531.

32. *Id.* at 538.

33. *Id.* at 532 (quoting *In re Martin,* 817 F.2d 175, 181 (1st Cir. 1987)).

34. *Id.* (citations omitted).

35. *Id.* at 532–533.

36. *Id.* at 533.

37. 164 B.R. 799 (Bankr. D. Conn. 1994).

38. *Id.* at 808.

39. 140 F.3d 463 (3d Cir. 1998).

40. *Id.* at 477.

41. 949 F.2d 1300 (3d Cir. 1991).

42. *Id.* at 477.

43. 1998 Journal Sentinel Inc., Milwaukee Journal Sentinel, July 25, 1998.

44. *Id.*

45. 11 U.S.C. § 330(a)(2).

46. Fed. R. Bankr. Proc. 2016(b).

7

At the Front of the Line: The Secured Creditor

Chaim J. Fortgang
Seth Gardner
David R. Caro

Wachtell, Lipton, Rosen & Katz

INTRODUCTION

The purpose of chapter 11, under the Bankruptcy Reform Act of 1978, as amended (the "Bankruptcy Code," or the "Code"), "is to restructure a business's finances so that it may continue to operate, provide its employees with jobs, pay its creditors, and produce a return for its shareholders."[1] Implicit behind chapter 11 is the belief that there are companies that are unable to operate profitably with their current capital structure or organization but, if given the opportunity, can be restructured into profitable companies. As a secured creditor of a company that is in workout or considering commencing a chapter 11 case, the foremost questions that must be answered are whether the company can be made profitable and at what cost. To a great extent, the answers to these questions will depend on how and why the company ended up in its distressed situation.

Companies end up in distress for innumerable reasons. There are certain kinds of distress that are more amenable to repair than others, and the tools provided to debtors and their creditors by chapter 11 are more adept for dealing with certain problems than with others. One distinction that should be made is between financial distress and operational distress. Filing a chapter 11 case may allow a company that otherwise has competent operations to survive a short-term liquidity crisis, but is far less likely to take a company that does not produce a viable product or is in an outmoded business and turn it into one that has good products or a good business. For example, if a company has competitive products and actual or potential markets for them but is facing default of its obligations simply because it has too much debt or its debt payment schedules are mismatched with its revenue streams, then the temporary relief from interest payments and the ability to restructure its payment obligations may allow this company to survive and potentially prosper, to the benefit of its shareholders, employees, and creditors alike. On the other hand, if the company has demonstrated a consistent inability to create a market for its products or generate profits or is being forced out of its current markets because it is an inefficient competitor, a successful restructuring is far less likely. Nonetheless, chapter 11 can be used advantageously by a debtor to attempt to change its cost structure or renegotiate important contracts. The key issue will be distinguishing between the operations of the company that are worth trying to protect and continue and the ones that are best shut down before further assets are fruitlessly dissipated.

A "realpolitik" mindset, however, is warranted for the secured creditor. While there can be successful restructurings of distressed companies, the majority of chapter 11 reorganizations fail and end in liquidation, almost inevitably at the further expense of the secured creditor.[2] Most companies end up in bankruptcy because they deserve to be there.

In addition to the debtor's condition, the secured creditor must also evaluate the status of its own security interests. The secured creditor must confirm that its liens are valid and enforceable and not subject to avoidance or subordination in bankruptcy. The methods by which a creditor's liens can be attacked by the debtor in a chapter 11 case will be discussed in detail in this chapter. If there are deficiencies in the creditor's security, these should be remedied to the extent possible before the commencement of bankruptcy proceedings by or against the debtor. With respect to many of the avoidance actions available to debtors in chapter 11, the farther removed a transfer is from the filing date, the less susceptible it is to attack.[3]

Beyond the enforceability of its liens, the secured creditor must also evaluate the status and extent of its collateral and the effect that bankruptcy will have on the value of its collateral. As will be discussed, the effects that a chapter 11 case will have on a creditor are significantly determined by the extent that its claim is collateralized. In a chapter 11 case, a creditor is secured only up to the value of its collateral, and the ability of the creditor to recover postpetition interest and fees and costs and charges, as well as the debtor's ability to modify the payment terms of its obligations to the creditor, depend greatly on whether the claim is under- or oversecured. As a starting point, if a secured creditor has a valid and unavoidable security interest in collateral of value substantially in excess of its claims, it should be able to cautiously ride out a chapter 11 case relatively unharmed. Any other secured creditor will have to make a number of difficult decisions about what kind of proposals it is willing to accept from the debtor.

Understanding the options available to a secured creditor in chapter 11 is important even to a creditor faced with a restructuring proposal outside of chapter 11, because the secured creditor's assessment of any restructuring proposal the debtor makes to it must begin with a comparison of that proposal with the secured creditor's analysis of what might happen to its claim and its collateral in a chapter 11 case. In order to properly assess its options and plan a strategy, the secured creditor must have an understanding and expectation of the treatment it is likely to receive in a chapter 11 case. For example, on the one hand, chapter 11 offers many advantages to the debtor, chief among them being the automatic stay, and presents many risks to secured creditors, most threatening being the possible erosion of the value of their collateral during the pendency of the case. On the other hand, chapter 11 provides stability and court control over the debtor's actions that do not exist outside of a bankruptcy case, which often benefit the secured creditor. A comparison with the possible outcomes of a chapter 11 case is the basis for the secured creditor's judgment of whether to agree to restructure its secured claim and, if so, on what terms. This chapter presents an overview of the chapter 11 process with an emphasis on those issues that most affect the secured creditor in order to provide a starting point for making such evaluations.

While chapter 11 is intended to create an environment that allows a debtor to reorganize and avoid liquidation, secured creditors have property rights that were duly bargained for prebankruptcy and that should be respected in bankruptcy. It is a fundamental principle that, at least in theory, secured claims must be paid in full or survive the reorganization process. The goal of promoting reorganization must be tempered by the rights provided to the secured creditor by virtue of its lien on the debtor's property. The legislative history to the Bankruptcy Code recognizes the special circumstances of the secured creditor in a bankruptcy case: "The secured creditor is entitled to realize his claim, and not have his collateral eroded by delay or by use of the estate."[4]

Many of the Code's provisions are specifically designed to protect the secured creditor's interests. For instance, although the creditor is prevented from taking immediate possession of its collateral by operation of the automatic stay, which stays actions against the debtor's property, the creditor may seek to lift the stay, and, in order to retain or use the property, the debtor must provide the secured creditor with adequate protection against erosion in the value of its collateral. Also, the best interests test and the fair and equitable requirement for confirmation of a plan notwithstanding a secured creditor's rejection thereof (each discussed below) ensure that the secured creditor will realize on its claim an amount, in theory, at least equal to the value of its collateral. There are, however, numerous pitfalls that await a secured creditor in a chapter 11 case that can seriously threaten the secured creditor's recovery.

RISKS POSED TO THE SECURED CREDITOR BY CHAPTER 11

While a secured creditor has a protected property interest in the collateral, the collateral is part of the debtor's estate. Until the creditor actually forecloses on or takes control of and sells the collateral to satisfy the debt, it is exposed to the risk that the collateral might depreciate in value or be lost, consumed, or destroyed. At a minimum, the commencement of a bankruptcy case extends the period during which the creditor must bear these risks.

The filing of a bankruptcy petition by the debtor triggers the automatic stay, which acts as a stay against all entities of, among other actions, the commencement or continuation of any action or proceeding against the debtor that was or could have been commenced prior to the commencement of the case or any act to obtain possession of property of the estate or of property from the estate or to exercise control over property of the estate.[5] The automatic stay interrupts the creditor's attempts at collection of its debt through repossession or foreclosure proceedings. This stay of the secured creditor's ability to seize its collateral is potentially detrimental to the creditor's ultimate recovery because the value of the collateral may diminish in excess of any adequate protection received.

Although the secured creditor is entitled to eventually receive the full value of its collateral, it is not entitled to the immediate possession of the collateral.[6] In the typical case, the collateral provided as security to the creditor will consist of property that is necessary for the continuation of the debtor's business. Rightly or wrongly, courts rarely grant a motion to lift the stay to proceed against any significant assets, the foreclosure of which will result in the almost immediate closing of the debtor's business.[7] Instead, if the court allows the debtor to retain the collateral for use in its business, the debtor must provide adequate protection to the creditor (which could consist of cash payments, additional collateral, or replacement liens) to compensate the secured creditor for any loss in value of the collateral resulting from its use or depreciation. In many cases, however, adequate protection will not prove sufficient, and when the creditor is finally allowed to recover the collateral, the loss to its value may be greatly in excess of the adequate protection the creditor has received.

In addition, creditors are generally not entitled to interest accruing during the pendency of the chapter 11 case. Oversecured creditors, however, are allowed postpetition interest and can also recover their fees, costs, or charges, including attorney's fees, to the extent of the excess of the value of their collateral over the amount of their claims.[8]

The commencement of a chapter 11 case also creates remedies and causes of action that are otherwise unavailable under state law. Of primary importance to the secured creditor are certain avoiding powers created by the Code that allow the debtor or a trustee to undo transactions in favor of its creditors that would otherwise be valid under state law. These powers include the "strong arm" provision, which allows the debtor to avoid unperfected liens, and the preferential transfer provision, which allows the avoidance of transfers made while the debtor was insolvent and on account of antecedent debt within 90 days prior to the commencement of the case. The Code also contains its own fraudulent conveyance provisions, which may be more extensive than those provided by applicable state law, and, in addition, the Code allows the debtor to bring state causes of action, for the benefit of the estate, that could otherwise be brought by its individual unsecured creditors.

If a secured creditor's loan was made to the debtor on terms that are advantageous to the debtor, the debtor in chapter 11 can cure any defaults and reinstate the terms of the original loan. Thus, if the creditor is holding a below-market-rate obligation from the debtor, the debtor can nullify the effect of any acceleration clauses and reinstate the debt notwithstanding a prior default. If the current payment terms are unfavorable to the debtor, the debtor may accomplish the reverse of reinstatement; it may revise the payment contract to its benefit. Such a revision may take the form of an extension of the payment terms at a judicially determined market rate of interest, which is often significantly below what a rational creditor would demand to make an equivalent loan in the absence of coercion.

The priority of a secured lender's claim may also suffer as a result of a bankruptcy filing. If adequate protection proves inadequate, the creditor is typically left with a superpriority administrative unsecured claim, which may be valueless against an administratively insolvent estate.[9] Also, under the Code, courts can confirm plans that provide for the substitution of the creditor's collateral as long as the creditor receives the "indubitable equivalent" of its claims.[10] This substitute collateral may prove in hindsight not to have provided the creditor with the indubitable equivalent of its claims. Under certain circumstances, a secured creditor may be subjected to a postpetition lender that is granted liens superior in priority to its own.[11] A court also has the power to equitably subordinate the claims of a secured creditor that has committed wrongdoing.[12]

The filing of a bankruptcy case allows for the creation of committees of unsecured creditors and equityholders, whose expenses, including the fees and expenses of retained professionals, are paid out of the debtor's estate.[13] Often, members of such committees' recoveries will depend on the continuation of the debtor's business, which may place their interests in conflict with those of the secured creditor that wishes to foreclose on its collateral. Unsecured and trade creditors often will be able to better protect their interests once organized in a chapter 11 case than as individual creditors outside of chapter 11.

In addition, once a debtor enters chapter 11, there will be little incentive for it to move the case forward expeditiously. To the contrary, chapter 11 allows the debtor to avoid payment of postpetition interest in respect of its unsecured and undersecured obligations during the pendency of the case (often referred to as *pendency interest*). The average debtor remains in chapter 11 for nearly two years, with some cases lasting for many years as the debtor becomes dependent on bankruptcy protections in order to survive.[14] With the increase in the time spent in bankruptcy comes the inevitable increase in administrative expenses, particularly when a multitude of committees and their financial and legal advisors are involved. The complexity of case administration also increases. Once the debtor is under the supervision of the court, routine issues that could be dealt with informally during an out-of-court workout will often require lengthy court filings and notice and hearing procedures.

Finally, a bankruptcy case is a court proceeding and injects a judicial third party into what is often a volatile commercial negotiation (or as one judge described a recent case, a "rolling commercial rumble"). A creditor or creditor's counsel should never underestimate the impact that a judge's own personality and predilections can have on the outcome of a case.

ADVANTAGES FOR THE SECURED CREDITOR OF A CHAPTER 11 PROCEEDING

Notwithstanding the dangers posed by chapter 11 enumerated earlier, the commencement of a chapter 11 case can offer several significant benefits to the secured creditor. Chapter 11 is a rehabilitative provision, and the protections from creditors provided by chapter 11 may improve a debtor's ability to pay its claimants. Many secured creditors, particularly lending institutions and bondholders, prefer to have their claims paid as opposed to having to take possession of the collateral.[15] The stable environment created by the automatic stay and the relief from having to make current interest payments can free up significant assets of the debtor, which can be used to make payments to the secured lender, for example, as adequate protection.

Perhaps the most significant benefits that a secured creditor derives from chapter 11 is the imposition of court supervision and control over the debtor along with the extension of fiduciary obligations by the debtor to its creditors. The commencement of a chapter 11 case deprives the debtor of the basically unfettered discretion in dealing with its creditors that it enjoys outside of bankruptcy.

A basic distinction drawn in any bankruptcy case is between claims and interests. The Code defines *claim* broadly to include any right to payment, whether such right is liquidated or unliquidated, fixed or contingent, matured or unmatured, disputed or undisputed, legal, equitable, or secured or unsecured.[16] Interest is not defined in the Bankruptcy Code but presumably means equity interests.[17] Debt, a claim, is a specific contractual obligation of the debtor and has a superior right to the assets of the company over equity, which, by definition, is merely that which is left over after the debts have been paid. Equityholders therefore "own" the debtor only to the extent that there is value in the debtor in excess of the claims against it.[18]

As a general matter, state corporation law bestows corporate governance rights exclusively on the equityholders, leaving to creditors only the protections for which they have contracted. When a company defaults on its contractual obligations to its creditors, creditors are entitled to exercise their contractual remedies in order to satisfy their claims. The bankruptcy protections of chapter 11, particularly the automatic stay, prevent creditors from, among other things, exercising their state law rights to foreclose on or take control of the assets of the debtor. However, at least in theory, equityholders no longer retain unrestricted control of the debtor and its assets, particularly if the debtor is insolvent.[19]

When the debtor enters chapter 11, although it retains the ability to make ordinary-course-of-business decisions with respect to the use of its property, it may not dispose of property out of the ordinary course of business without court approval, accomplished through notice and hearing procedures.[20] Also, cash collateral (consisting of cash, bank accounts, negotiable instruments, securities, or cash equivalents) is entitled to special protections under the Code. Without the secured creditor's consent, the debtor may not use the secured creditor's cash collateral without a court order and must provide the secured creditor with adequate protection.[21]

The Code mandates the creation, on commencement of the bankruptcy case, of a legal entity, distinct from the debtor, known as the *bankruptcy estate*. The estate is made up of all of the debtor's legal or equitable interests in property at the commencement of the case and any interests in property that the estate acquires after the commencement of the case.[22] While in chapter 11 cases, the debtor can remain "in possession" of the estate, and operate its business, the debtor in possession (DIP) has the same duties and obligations to the estate and its creditors as would have a chapter 11 trustee.[23] The debtor's corporate governance can no longer be exercised primarily for the benefit of its equityholders because, as custodian of the bankruptcy estate, it owes fiduciary duties to its creditors as well. If the debtor is insolvent, its primary fiduciary obligations are to its creditors.[24] The debtor's failure to properly execute these duties constitutes cause to remove the debtor from possession and appoint a chapter 11 trustee.[25] Significantly, the professionals retained by the debtor's estate, including any attorneys or financial advisors, also have fiduciary obligations to its creditors.[26] Thus, in chapter 11, the debtor must protect the interests of its creditors.

Particularly in cases where there are strong antagonisms between the debtor and its creditors, the duties imposed on the DIP in a chapter 11 case help to protect the creditor's interests. For instance, the debtor has obligations to preserve and maintain any property of the estate for the benefit of its creditors.[27] Unscrupulous or particularly hostile debtors may attempt to create leverage over the secured creditor by allowing the creditor's collateral to depreciate in value or otherwise allowing estate assets to waste. This tactic is particularly threatening when the debtor has no equity in the assets, as the loss in value is shouldered solely by the secured creditor. In a chapter 11 case, if it cannot first convince the court to lift the stay, the secured creditor can seek assistance from the court to force the debtor to maintain or insure the collateral[28] or can seek the appointment of a chapter 11 trustee.

A secured creditor may be able to improve its relative position by extending credit postpetition, sometimes gaining the added protection of a superpriority lien. The proceeds of a postpetition loan can be used to pay adequate protection on the debtor's existing secured debt as well as to provide working capital financing to the debtor. The postpetition or DIP facility has the additional advantage that it may substitute for the debtor's use of the secured creditor's cash collateral pursuant to court order, which typically provides fewer protections for the secured creditor than can be provided for in a new postpetition loan.[29]

In addition, chapter 11 improves a secured creditor's access to information from the debtor. The debtor is compelled to make certain disclosures when it files its petition.[30] It also becomes subject to examination by its creditors and discovery requests.[31] Further, periodic financial reporting is required,[32] and reporting is often made a condition to the use of cash collateral or the extension of postpetition financing.

The bankruptcy case also provides a forum for settling litigation or claims with the debtor. For example, a secured creditor may settle claims that arose prepetition that the debtor has against it through the plan process as these claims constitute property of the estate.[33]

Finally, if the estate wishes to keep the property subject to the secured creditor's liens, chapter 11 provides the secured creditor with recourse against the debtor for the unsecured portion of its secured claim, irrespective of whether the claim was originally nonrecourse.[34]

The remainder of this chapter will summarize and discuss the legal doctrines and elements involved in a chapter 11 case in order to provide some guidance to the secured creditor for determining how the previously discussed advantages and disadvantages of chapter 11 may come into play in any given case.

THE SECURED CLAIM

A secured claim under the Code is an allowed claim secured by a lien on property in which the estate has an interest. It is secured only to the extent of the value of the secured creditor's interest in estate's interest in the property.[35] In basic terms, it is a secured claim only to the extent of the value of the collateral that secures it.

Allowed Claim

Unless a party-in-interest objects to the claim, a claim is deemed allowed on the filing of a proof of claim.[36] If a party objects to the allowance of the claim, the bankruptcy court determines the amount of the allowed claim.[37] In a chapter 11 case, if a claim appears on the various schedules of liabilities, the Code requires the debtor to file at the commencement of a case and it is not scheduled as disputed, contingent, or unliquidated, then a proof of claim for that claim is deemed to have been filed.[38] However, a debtor may later amend its schedules; thus, it is usually the better practice to file a proof of claim and not to rely, possibly to one's detriment, on the debtor's schedules.[39]

Postpetition Interest

For the reasons discussed earlier, typically an issue of great importance to the secured creditor is the allowance of postpetition interest. As a general rule, the Code does not authorize the payment of postpetition interest.[40] Section 506(b) of the Code, however, carves out an exception to this general rule for oversecured creditors to the extent of such creditor's equity cushion (i.e., the amount by which the value of the collateral securing their claims exceeds the amount of their claims).[41] In addition, some courts have allowed postpetition interest that has accrued on unsecured claims when the debtor was solvent.

The allowance of postpetition interest and fees, costs, and charges to unsecured creditors may be significant to the secured creditor to the extent that it has an unsecured deficiency claim or its equity cushion has been exhausted. In brief, courts allowing these claims on behalf of unsecured creditors have based their decisions on both (1) the "best interests test" combined with the unsecured creditor's entitlement, in a chapter 7 case, to any assets in the debtor's estate before the debtor can receive any distribution[42] and/or (2) general equitable principals, reasoning that it would be more equitable to allow claims for postpetition interest than to permit the debtor (and thus, indirectly, the shareholders) to receive, in effect, a windfall to the extent of the value of that postpetition interest.[43]

As mentioned, the Code specifically provides that a secured claim may recover postpetition interest to the extent of any value in the collateral in excess of the principal amount of the claim.[44] Most courts have held that postpetition interest accrues at the contract rate.[45] Further, courts have generally held that oversecured creditors are presumptively entitled to contractual default rates for purposes of calculating pendency interest, subject to rebuttal in light of equitable factors.[46] Postpetition interest is allowed to the secured creditor even in the absence of a contractual provision providing therefor (this is in contrast to the allowance of fees, costs, and charges, which is governed exclusively by the contract). The Supreme Court has determined that Section 506(b) should be read to permit postpetition interest on both consensual liens (e.g., mortgage liens) and nonconsensual liens (e.g., tax liens), thus reversing earlier Code cases that had not allowed postpetition interest to accrue on tax liens.[47]

Subject to the exception for solvent debtors, postpetition interest is allowed only up to the excess value in the collateral.[48] Excess value is determined after deducting the value of any prior liens and without regard to any junior liens there may be on the collateral, and after deduction of certain costs and expenses of the estate that are charged against the collateral.[49]

Oversecured creditors are also entitled to include in the amount of their allowed claim, to the extent of the excess value in their collateral, "any reasonable fees, costs, or charges provided for under the agreement under which such claim arose,"[50] including attorney fees. Note that such fees, cost, or charges must be provided for under the agreement in order to be allowed. Secured creditors can also assert claims for prepayment premiums as part of their secured claims.[51] Finally, secured creditors may be able to assert an unsecured claim for amounts that the court determines are not reasonable if the documents under which such claims arose provide for reimbursement of such amounts.[52]

In certain cases, such as when there exist numerous mortgage bondholders or similar types of secured creditors sharing an interest in the same collateral pool,[53] it may be appropriate for the court to appoint an official committee of secured creditors.[54] If an official committee is appointed, the costs and expenses of secured creditors' advisers acting as professionals retained by the secured creditors' committee may be compensated along with other committee professionals from the debtor's estate without regard to the value of the secured creditors' collateral.[55] Additionally, an undersecured creditor may be able to participate in an unsecured creditors' committee.[56]

Expenses of Preserving or Disposing of the Collateral

The trustee or DIP may offset certain costs and expenses in respect of collateral against the value of such collateral. Expenses that can be charged against the collateral pursuant to Section 506(c) of the code are "the reasonable, necessary costs and expenses of preserving, or disposing of [the collateral] to the extent of any benefit to the holder of such claim."[57] Courts generally agree that expenses incurred in selling collateral (e.g., advertising and auctioneers' expenses) may be deducted from proceeds of collateral.[58] Beyond these direct expenses of liquidating the collateral, courts have not applied a uniform rule specifying other costs and expenses which may be deducted from the secured creditor's collateral.

A few courts have interpreted the Code as permitting the charging of expenses that enabled the debtor to continue as a going concern, reasoning that the preservation of the going concern value of a business can constitute a benefit to the secured creditor for purposes of Section 506(c). Employing this standard, these courts have permitted the administrative expenses of a proceeding to be charged against the collateral.[59] Notably, these courts generally considered the secured creditor to have consented to deduction of costs and expenses from its collateral.[60] Courts differ in their willingness to infer the secured creditor's consent to expenditures from its actions or inaction. While a few courts have deducted costs and expenses when the secured creditor consented to the continued operation of the debtor's business, most have applied a stricter standard, for example, that a secured creditor only consents to those expenses that it caused the debtor to incur.[61]

Other courts have been more protective of secured creditors' interests, requiring that the expenses be incurred primarily for the benefit of the secured creditor and that the creditor be directly benefited. Courts applying this standard are likely to test the benefit to the secured creditor quantitatively: An expenditure should be charged against a secured creditor's collateral only if the creditor would have received less from its collateral had the expenditure not been made.[62]

After-Acquired Property Clauses

As a general rule, the Code precludes the extension of prepetition liens to property acquired by the debtor after the filing.[63] For example, notwithstanding an after-acquired clause in the collateral documentation, a creditor's prepetition lien in all the debtor's accounts receivable will not extend to accounts receivable generated postpetition.[64]

The Code carves out an exception to the general rule with respect to liens on postpetition "proceeds, product, offspring, rents, or profits" of property to the extent the prepetition security agreement so provided and to the extent the agreement is enforceable under applicable nonbankruptcy law.[65] Thus, if such conditions are satisfied, a lien will attach to postpetition proceeds of prepetition accounts receivable.[66] Whether particular property constitutes "proceeds, product, offspring, rents, or profits" of collateral is determined by state law.[67]

The Code also exempts from the general rule liens on postpetition rents and certain fees, charges, accounts, or other payments in respect of property to the extent the prepetition security agreement so provided.[68] In applying this exception, courts have struggled with the allocation of postpetition rental payments between an undersecured creditor's secured and unsecured claims. Some courts have applied what is commonly referred to as a subtraction approach, whereby to the extent that Section 552(b) proceeds are paid to the undersecured creditor during the chapter 11 case, such payments reduce the secured portion of the creditor's claim (hence, the reference to such cases as subtraction cases).[69] In contrast, other courts have applied an "addition" approach, whereby the postpetition rents are treated as the creditor's additional collateral and any payments received by the undersecured creditor on account of such rents are deducted from the creditor's unsecured deficiency claim.[70]

It should be noted that, with respect to either exception, a court can limit or deny altogether the exception permitting a lien on postpetition proceeds if the equities of the case compel that result.[71] In the course of such consideration the court may evaluate expenditures by the estate relating to such proceeds and any related improvement in position of the secured creditor.[72]

Valuation of the Collateral

It should come as no surprise that often the most important issue for a secured creditor in a chapter 11 case is the valuation of the collateral. As discussed above, a secured creditor's entitlement to postpetition interest and fees, costs, and charges depends in large measure on the value attributed to the collateral. Other significant aspects of the chapter 11 case to be discussed further, such as the availability of adequate protection, preference actions, relief from the automatic stay, and confirmation of a plan over the secured creditor's objection by means of the Code's cram down provisions, also depend greatly on collateral valuation.

An allowed claim is secured only to the extent of the value of the secured creditor's interest in the debtor's interest in the collateral. The remainder of the claim, if any, is an unsecured claim.[73] For example, a claim based on a $100 loan secured by collateral worth $60 is a secured claim in the amount of $60 and an unsecured claim for $40. With respect to the holder of a junior lien on collateral, the value of such holder's secured claim will be reduced by the amount of any senior liens on such collateral.

Despite the importance of the issue, the Code does not prescribe a specific method of valuing collateral. Instead, the Code provides generally that "value shall be determined in light of the purpose of the valuation and of the proposed disposition or use of such property."[74] As a result, courts apply a wide range of methodologies, including liquidation, going concern, or otherwise, in valuing collateral and may even apply one methodology when valuing collateral for one purpose (e.g., adequate protection) and another methodology in a different context (e.g., postpetition interest). The timing of the valuation is also critically important since collateral values can fluctuate during a case. For example, even though the Code provides that oversecured creditors are entitled to postpetition interest, the statute is silent as to when in the case it is to be determined that a creditor is over- or undersecured. If a determination is made early in the case that the creditor is undersecured for purposes of postpetition interest, the creditor may be unable to collect postpetition interest even though the collateral subsequently increases in value such that by the plan confirmation date the creditor is

in fact oversecured. Clearly, in this circumstance, the creditor would have preferred a confirmation date valuation for purposes of postpetition interest rather
than the earlier valuation.

Although a determination of value for one purpose (e.g., adequate protection)
is not binding in another context (e.g., postpetition interest),[75] in practice, courts
may be reluctant to revisit valuation issues absent compelling evidence of a valuation change or to make valuation judgments uninfluenced by prior valuation
proceedings. Thus, in many cases, debtors and secured creditors negotiate an
agreement on collateral value rather than leaving such a significant determination to the court's discretion. Importantly, the Code allows senior classes (by
class vote) to allow value to pass through to junior classes over the dissent of individual class members, facilitating the ability of different classes of creditors
and interest holders to reach compromise on valuation issues without resorting to
a judicial valuation.[76]

Valuation issues will be treated in greater detail below.

AVOIDING POWERS

The Code gives the trustee (and the DIP),[77] the power to avoid certain liens or recover certain payments. By virtue of these avoiding powers, a secured creditor
may find that its lien is avoided and its claim is treated as wholly unsecured. The
avoiding powers of the trustee are found primarily in (1) the so-called strong-
arm provisions of the Code, (2) the provisions for avoiding preferential transfers,
and (3) the provisions for avoiding fraudulent transfers.

Strong-Arm Provisions of the Code

Upon commencement of a case, Section 544(a) of the Code grants the rights and
powers of, and allows the trustee to avoid any transfer of property of the debtor
that would be avoidable by, a hypothetical lien creditor, judgment creditor, or
bona fide purchaser of real property on the date the case was commenced.[78] Because Section 9-301 of the Uniform Commercial Code provides that an unperfected security interest is subordinated to the rights of a lien creditor, including a
trustee in bankruptcy, a trustee may avoid any lien that was not perfected at the
time of the filing of the petition.

A trustee will scrutinize the documentation relating to the secured creditor's
collateral to determine whether all legal formalities for perfecting the lien in the
collateral were observed. Generally, state law determines whether the lien was
properly perfected.[79] For example, in a state that requires Form UCC-1 to be
filed in two places, locally and centrally, a lien may not be perfected if the secured creditor filed its Form UCC-1 in only one place. Even minor or technical
defects in the perfection of a security interest may leave the interest unperfected
and thus avoidable. For example, if the signature of the debtor has not been properly acknowledged as required under state law, a mortgage lien will be unperfected even if the mortgage was otherwise correctly filed.[80] Further, except as

specifically provided for in the Code,[81] state law defenses to the subordination of unperfected liens are generally inapplicable in bankruptcy. For example, there may be an exception under applicable state law making the lien enforceable against creditors with actual knowledge, even though it was unperfected. Notwithstanding the existence of such an exception, the trustee may be able to avoid the lien under those circumstances for the benefit of all unsecured creditors, regardless of any actual knowledge it or any other creditor may have had.[82]

The Code also gives the trustee whatever avoiding powers unsecured creditors are given by applicable state law.[83] State law, for example, typically permits unsecured creditors to avoid a lien that constitutes a fraudulent conveyance. In some states, the relevant statute of limitations is as long as six years. Although the Code provides for avoidance of fraudulent conveyances, the statute of limitations provided in the Code is only one year. A trustee could potentially avoid a lien utilizing the applicable state law fraudulent conveyance provisions if the one-year statute of limitations for actions brought under the bankruptcy fraudulent conveyance provisions had expired.

Preferential Transfers

The trustee may avoid certain prepetition transfers, including certain prepetition liens granted to or for the benefit of a secured creditor, as preferences if certain statutory conditions are met.

Under the Code, the basic elements of a preference are a transfer: (1) of an interest of the debtor in property; (2) to or for the benefit of a creditor; (3) for or on account of an antecedent debt owed by the debtor before such transfer was made; (4) made while the debtor was insolvent; (5) made (a) on or within 90 days before the date of the filing of the bankruptcy petition or (b) if the creditor was an insider at the time of such transaction, between 90 days and one year before the date of the filing of the petition; and (6) that enables the creditor to receive more than it would receive if the case were a chapter 7 liquidation case.[84]

Because no transfer on account of a fully secured claim could give the secured creditor more than it would receive in liquidation (since, in liquidation, the fully secured creditor would have received the entire amount of its claim), a payment to a creditor that was fully secured at the time of the petition cannot be recovered as a preference.[85]

Even if all the elements of a preference are present, the transfer will not be avoidable if it was an ordinary-course payment made on debt incurred in the ordinary course of business.[86] Payments on long-term debt, as well as payments on short-term debt, may qualify for the ordinary-course-of-business exception to preference avoidance.[87] In the course of a workout, a creditor may agree to restructure its debt by altering the interest rate, the principal amount, or the payment terms, or forgoing the protection of certain covenants. As part of this workout package, the creditor often receives some consideration in exchange. For example, it may be granted collateral it did not previously have, it may get an increased interest rate, and/or it may get a paydown of a certain portion of its debt. There is a risk that any consideration received by the creditor in the workout may be recovered if the chapter 11 petition followed the consummation of the workout within the applicable preference period.[88]

The Code excludes from the preference avoiding power transfers made in exchange for new value; however, new value is narrowly defined.[89] *New value* means "money or money's worth in goods, services, or new credit, or release . . . of property."[90] The definition specifically excludes the substitution of one obligation for another obligation.[91] Several courts have held that, generally, forbearance in enforcing remedies against the debtor (for example, as part of restructuring an existing obligation) does not by itself constitute new value.[92] Creditors who received payments or collateral within the preference period as part of a workout therefore may find their payments or liens avoided in a preference action.

If a creditor seeks additional collateral or payments as part of its agreement to restructure the debtor's obligations, it is preferable, if possible, that the additional collateral or payments be provided by a solvent third party, rather than by the debtor itself. The Code's provisions for avoiding preferential transfers apply only to "property of the debtor." If the collateral is granted or payments are made to the creditor by a third party, or even if money is loaned by a third party to the debtor in order to satisfy the claim of a designated creditor, the collateral or proceeds never become property of the debtor.[93]

If the recipient of an alleged preference can demonstrate that the debtor was solvent at the time the transfer occurred, one of the basic elements of a preference (that the debtor was insolvent at the time the transfer was made) would not be present and the transfer would not constitute a preference. There is, however, a rebuttable presumption created by the Code that the debtor was insolvent during the 90-day period immediately preceding the filing of the petition.[94]

The preference period is extended to one year for insiders, instead of the 90-day period applicable to noninsiders. The presumption of insolvency, however, is not extended beyond 90 days. In the case of a debtor corporation, the Code defines an insider as including any officers of the corporation, persons "in control" of the corporation, partnerships in which the corporation is a general partner, general partners of the corporation, and relatives of a general partner, director, officer, or person in control of the corporation.[95] Affiliates of the debtor and insiders of affiliates also are deemed to be insiders.[96]

Although most traditional secured creditors fall outside of the definition of insider, a creditor might be classified as an insider if it could be deemed to be in control of the debtor. Cases determining what constitutes the exercise of control sufficient to create insider status have generally required that the secured creditor do more than merely enforce its contractual rights against the debtor. For example, a creditor should not be deemed "a person in control of the debtor" where its loan was an arms-length transaction and the debtor remained in managerial control of its business. Unless the creditor was actually in a position to decide to make the transfer to itself, it should not be considered an insider for preference purposes.[97] An avoidance of a preferential transfer by the trustee results in the recovery by the estate of such a grant or transfer from its transferee for the benefit of the estate and, thus, for the benefit of all general unsecured creditors.[98]

Fraudulent Conveyances

The trustee may also avoid, in whole or in part, the lien of a secured creditor (or recover payments made on account of such a creditor's claim) for the benefit of the estate if such lien was granted (or payment was made) in a transaction that constituted a fraudulent conveyance.[99] Fraudulent conveyance laws protect creditors from transfers of property that are fraudulent to the extent those transfers are intended to impair creditors' ability to enforce their rights to payment (intentional fraud) or have the effect of depleting a debtor's assets at a time when its financial condition is precarious (constructive fraud). The Code contains provisions for the avoidance of fraudulent transfers and obligations. In addition, there are two prevalent uniform state law fraudulent conveyance acts: the Uniform Fraudulent Conveyance Act (UFCA) and the more recent Uniform Fraudulent Transfer Act (UFTA).

The Code's provisions relating to fraudulent conveyances empower the trustee in bankruptcy to avoid any transfer of an interest of the debtor in property or any obligation incurred within one year prior to the date of the filing of the bankruptcy petition in the case of intentional fraud and three instances of constructive fraud. Under the Code and the UFTA, the existence of constructive fraud depends on the lack of adequate consideration for a transfer combined with either insolvency, unreasonably small capital, or an intent by the debtor to incur debts beyond its ability to pay. Specifically, the Code permits the trustee to avoid any transfer of an interest in property, or any obligation incurred by the debtor, that was made or incurred, voluntarily or involuntarily (1) with actual intent to hinder, delay, or defraud its creditors; or (2) if the debtor received less than a reasonably equivalent value in exchange for such transfer or obligation, and (a) was insolvent on the date of such transfer or obligation, or became insolvent as a result of such transfer or obligation, (b) was engaged or about to engage in business for which the property remaining with the debtor was an unreasonably small capital, or (c) intended to incur, or believed that it would incur, debts beyond its ability to pay as they matured.[100]

Note that for purposes of the Code and the UFTA, *value* is defined to include the satisfaction or securing of a present or antecedent debt of the debtor.[101] Thus, the debtor's granting collateral to secure an existing obligation to the creditor does not constitute a constructive fraudulent conveyance to that creditor.[102] Also, except to the extent that a transfer is otherwise voidable under the Code, a transferee who takes for value and in good faith may be granted a lien on or be permitted to retain any interest transferred or may be permitted to enforce any obligation incurred to the extent of value given to the debtor.[103]

As noted above, the Code empowers the trustee to avoid a transfer made (or obligation incurred) by the debtor that is avoidable under state law by an unsecured creditor holding an allowed claim.[104] Consequently, with certain limitations, the trustee can avail itself of the fraudulent conveyance provisions of both the Code and state law, primarily the UFCA or the UFTA. The fraudulent conveyance provisions of the UFTA are substantially the same as those for the Code, discussed above, but the statute of limitations, under most of its provisions, is four years.[105]

The UFCA defines four types of transactions that are fraudulent and, therefore, avoidable by creditors. The first three are variants of constructive fraud, which means that transfers are deemed fraudulent whether or not the transferor actually intended to defraud creditors. Constructive fraud exists in situations in which transfers are made without fair consideration *and*, at the time of the transaction, the transferor (1) is either insolvent or rendered insolvent by the transaction, (2) is in business and is left with unreasonably small capital, or (3) anticipates incurring debts beyond its ability to pay.[106] The fourth type of fraudulent transaction is intentional fraud; the UFCA enables creditors to recover property that was conveyed with an actual intent to hinder, delay, or defraud creditors.[107] The UFCA does not specify a statute of limitations; therefore, the applicable statute of limitations will vary among states in which it has been enacted.

The UFCA contains two exculpatory provisions that protect innocent transferees and recipients of transfers from such transferees. Under the first of those exculpatory provisions, creditors cannot recover from a purchaser who purchased for fair consideration and without knowledge of the fraud.[108] Under the second, a transferee who paid less than fair consideration, but who did so without actual fraudulent intent, may retain the property or obligation as security for repayment of the consideration paid.[109]

The main difference between the Code (and the UFTA) and the UFCA is in the phrasing of the consideration element in the definition of constructive fraud: The UFCA requires "fair consideration," whereas the Code and the UFTA require a "reasonably equivalent value" in exchange.[110] *Fair consideration*, as the term is used in the UFCA, requires that the transferee pay "fair equivalent" value in "good faith." In contrast, the construction used in the Code and UFTA does not require an inquiry into the good faith of the transferee; the inquiry is limited to whether there was reasonably equivalent value given in exchange.

The majority view among courts is that fraudulent conveyance laws are applicable to leveraged buyout transactions.[111] Fraudulent conveyance actions based on leverage buyout transactions are typically brought pursuant to the constructive fraud provisions of the relevant statutes.[112] In determining whether a transfer is avoidable under the constructive fraud provisions of the Code and the UFTA, the first requirement is that the debtor received reasonably equivalent value for the property transferred or the obligation incurred. Similarly, under the UFCA, the debtor must have received fair consideration in return for the property transferred or the obligation incurred. These are factual determinations made on a case-by-case basis.

Several courts that have addressed the issue have determined that the target of the leveraged buyout and its affiliates do not receive reasonably equivalent or fair value as a result of the typical leveraged buyout transaction because the proceeds of the acquisition financing are paid to the target's shareholders in return for their shares, and, thus, the payments confer no direct benefit to either the target or its affiliates.[113] These courts collapse the transactions and treat the proceeds as if they had been transferred directly from the lenders to the recipient shareholders. As a result, any grant of security by the target/debtor to the creditor who finances the transaction may be avoided as having been given in exchange for less than reasonably equivalent or fair value.[114] Similarly, the tender of stock by selling shareholders in connection with the leveraged buyout transaction may not in and of itself constitute fair or reasonably equivalent value.[115] Thus, the target/debtor may be able to avoid any obligations incurred or recover any funds transferred to its shareholders as part of the buyout transaction also on the grounds that the debtor did not receive any value in exchange for the obligations or payments.

The other elements that must be demonstrated in order to establish that a leveraged buyout transaction constitutes a constructive fraudulent conveyance (i.e., whether the transaction rendered the debtor insolvent, left the debtor with unreasonably small capital, or caused the debtor to incur debts beyond its ability to pay) are factual inquiries that will vary from case to case. Nevertheless, a lender who (1) obtained solvency letters, valuation opinions, and asset appraisals showing the debtor was solvent at the time the leveraged transaction occurred; and (2) can demonstrate that the revenue and cash flow projections it used in evaluating the loan were reasonable at the time the loan was extended, should be in a stronger position to rebut the financial elements of the fraudulent conveyance analysis than lenders who did not take such steps.[116] It must be emphasized that, if a court is considering these issues, the solvency letters, valuation opinions, cash flow projections, and the like were probably based on assumptions that turned out to be too optimistic. Having the benefit of "hindsight," the court may be skeptical of the reasonableness of some of these devices and the assumptions on which they were based.

Subordination

The Code also permits a court, after notice and a hearing, to subordinate part or all of an allowed claim, including a secured claim, to part or all of another allowed claim under principles of equitable subordination.[117]

Broadly stated, a claim, whether held by an insider or another party, can be subordinated if the creditor engaged in inequitable conduct that either harmed other creditors or advantaged it. In order to prevail on a claim for equitable subordination, the plaintiff must prove: (1) inequitable conduct; (2) resultant injury to the debtor or unfair advantage to the creditor; and (3) that subordination is not inconsistent with other provisions of the Code.[118]

Courts hold creditors who are insiders to a higher standard of conduct than others, because they are viewed by the courts as fiduciaries of the debtor, if not also to other creditors. Creditors that are not insiders may nevertheless find their conduct judged by this higher standard if they exercised sufficient control of the debtor to be, in effect, deemed an insider.[119] Conduct of a creditor that is not an insider or otherwise a party deemed in control typically must be of an egregious nature to justify subordination.[120] If the requirements for subordination are met, the claim is subordinated only to the extent necessary to offset the harm caused by the inequitable conduct.[121]

The Code also recognizes contractual subordination. If a secured creditor agreed to subordinate part or all of its claim or lien to another creditor, the agreement will be enforceable according to its terms, to the extent permitted under nonbankruptcy law.[122] Of particular interest to the secured creditor is the enforceability of contractual provisions that subordinate junior creditors to accrued postpetition interest owing to the senior lender when interest on such senior lender's claim is not an allowed claim against the debtor. Many courts follow a "rule of explicitness" and enforce subordination to unallowed interest only if the subordination agreement explicitly so provides.[123]

ADEQUATE PROTECTION

Adequate protection is designed to protect the secured creditor from diminution in the value of its collateral during the pendency of the case, whether from erosion of the collateral's value or from the debtor's use of the collateral. This protection is grounded, to a limited extent, in the constitutional protection of property in the due process clause of the Fifth Amendment of the United States Constitution.[124]

Situations in which adequate protection must be provided, to the extent necessary to protect the value of collateral, include (1) when a court denies the motion of a secured creditor seeking to lift the automatic stay in order to foreclose on its collateral[125]; (2) when a trustee is permitted to use, sell, or lease a secured creditor's collateral[126]; and (3) when a trustee is permitted to incur indebtedness secured by a lien that is senior to, or has the same priority as, the lien of another creditor in the same property.[127]

The Code specifies that adequate protection may be in the form of (1) periodic cash payments or a single cash payment, (2) a lien on additional or replacement collateral, or (3) relief providing the secured creditor with the "indubitable equivalent" of its lien.[128] The forms of adequate protection specified are not exclusive. The debtor may fashion other forms of adequate protection subject to agreement of the secured creditor or, if it objects, to approval of the court. The Code explicitly rejects the grant of an administrative claim (one that has priority over all other unsecured claims) as a form of adequate protection.[129] If, however, a secured creditor receives an acceptable form of adequate protection, which, in hindsight, did not adequately protect the secured creditor's interest in its collateral, the secured creditor is entitled to an administrative claim with priority over all other administrative claims.[130]

Valuation of the collateral (as well as valuation of any proposed additional or replacement collateral) is crucial in determining whether adequate protection is necessary and, if so, to what extent. The Supreme Court has made it clear that value (and, therefore, the adequate protection to which a secured creditor may be entitled) does not include the value of immediate possession of the collateral.[131] While a secured creditor is entitled to protection from diminution in the value of its collateral during the case, the time value of the money a creditor may have received, had it not been stayed from foreclosing and realizing on the collateral, is not protected.[132] Note that the time value of an oversecured claim is protected (depending, of course, on the applicable interest rates) by statutory provision, which specifically permits an oversecured claim to accrue interest postpetition to the extent of the excess value in the collateral.

Automatic Stay

The automatic stay is one of the chief procedural protections afforded a debtor by the Code. It is very broad and is designed to give the debtor breathing space in which to reorganize by staying all actions by creditors to recover on their prepetition claims.[133] Thus, the automatic stay prohibits a secured creditor from foreclosing on collateral included in the debtor's estate, irrespective of whether the creditor or the debtor is in possession of the collateral at the time of the bankruptcy filing. The stay also relieves the debtor of the obligation to make current payments on postpetition interest accruing on prepetition obligations. The stay is effective immediately on filing of the petition, whether filed voluntarily or involuntarily.

Effect of the Stay.   The automatic stay protects all property of the estate. Property of the estate is broadly defined to include all interests—legal, equitable, or beneficial—of the debtor in property as of the commencement of the case and any property thereafter acquired by the estate.[134] The jurisdictional statute grants courts worldwide jurisdiction over the estate's property.[135] Thus, even for the secured creditor with collateral in a foreign country, the automatic stay prohibits it from taking any action against that collateral.[136] As a practical matter, when property is located in another country, a United States bankruptcy court may be able to enforce the stay against such property only if it has personal jurisdiction over the secured creditor or any of its property by threatening the creditor with a contempt citation. A foreign court with jurisdiction over the collateral may choose to recognize the automatic stay and also enforce it, effectively on behalf of the bankruptcy court, through principles of comity. It is also possible that the foreign court will choose not to enforce the automatic stay and permit the secured creditor to proceed against the collateral.

Conversely, a secured creditor with collateral in the United States and a debtor that is the subject of a reorganization proceeding under the laws of a foreign country may also find its actions against the collateral stayed by the automatic stay provisions of the Code. The Code permits a foreign trustee to commence an ancillary case in a U.S. bankruptcy court, and it permits the bankruptcy court to stay actions against property of the estate.[137]

There are exceptions to the types of actions blocked by the stay. Most do not have general applicability. To illustrate, one exception allows governmental actions to enforce police powers (e.g., a criminal prosecution) to continue.[138] Other examples are the ability of the Secretary of Transportation to foreclose a mortgage in a vessel[139] or of a creditor with a security interest in certain aircraft and related equipment to foreclose.[140] However, one narrow exception is of general interest to secured creditors: the right to perfect certain liens postpetition.

The Code permits a creditor to perfect its lien postpetition if, under state law, the perfection would be deemed effective at an earlier time and would have given the secured creditor rights in the collateral superior to the hypothetical lien creditor.[141] For example, in some states, a mechanic's lien for services can be perfected after the services were rendered (within a statutorily prescribed time), and the perfection will relate back to such time.[142] Perfection of purchase money security interests also can relate back to a time prior to the filing of the financing statement under the Uniform Commercial Code.[143] In both cases, filing the requisite notice or financing statement under state law after the petition date will not violate the stay, so long as perfection relates back to a prepetition time.

Section 362, creating the automatic stay, applies literally only to actions concerning the debtor or property of or in possession of the estate. Courts can, however, and sometimes have enjoined actions against third parties or their property relying primarily on their broad equitable powers,[144] rather than the automatic stay provisions, but with essentially identical effect to extending the automatic stay. The circumstances in which courts have been willing to enjoin such actions generally are ones in which the interests of the debtor are perceived to be so intertwined with those of the third party that allowing the actions to proceed would impede the debtor's ability to reorganize or diminish the estate.[145] For example, creditors have been enjoined from going against codefendants in products liability actions or against officers or directors of the debtor. Courts have generally let creditors whose claims were secured by letters of credit draw on them, reasoning that letters of credit are not property of the estate.[146]

Lifting the Stay. In the absence of a motion by a creditor to lift the automatic stay, it continues until the chapter 11 case has been dismissed or closed or the debtor's liabilities discharged, whichever is first to occur.[147] Once property leaves the estate, it is no longer protected by the stay. If the trustee abandons (or sells) property subject to the liens of secured creditors, those secured creditors are no longer stayed from foreclosing on their liens.[148]

A creditor may move to have the stay lifted on one of two grounds: (1) for cause, including lack of adequate protection; or (2) if the debtor lacks equity in the collateral and the collateral is not necessary for an effective reorganization.[149] Valuation is obviously a crucial component of either basis for seeking relief from the stay.

As discussed above, adequate protection is a concept designed to protect a secured creditor from diminution in the value of its collateral. If the creditor is prevented from taking possession of or liquidating its collateral by reason of the stay, the debtor must offer the secured creditor some form of adequate protection to compensate it for any loss in the value of its collateral. Although the issue is not closed to debate, several courts have found that if the value of a creditor's collateral significantly exceeds the amount the creditor's claim, such an equity cushion[150] can itself constitute adequate protection.[151] The accrual of postpetition interest and other fees, costs, and charges permitted by Code Section 506(b), and/or a decline in value of the collateral, however, can completely erode an equity cushion. Yet, at least one circuit court has held that a creditor is not entitled to preserve the value of its equity cushion during the pendency of a bankruptcy case.[152] Courts should, however, require some additional form of adequate protection once an equity cushion has eroded substantially.

In some cases, the potential for deterioration in the value of collateral is obvious. Retail merchandise is a classic example of collateral that can rapidly diminish in value. With other collateral, it is more difficult to determine whether there is any loss in value necessitating adequate protection. Further complicating the determination is the issue of which standard for valuation (e.g., liquidation or going concern value) should be used to value collateral for purposes of adequate protection. While Congress did not specify the method of valuation to be used in bankruptcy, Section 506(a) of the Code states that value shall be determined in light of the purpose of the valuation and of the proposed disposition or use of such property, and in conjunction with any hearing on such disposition or use or on a plan affecting such creditor's interest. Thus, whether a secured creditor would be entitled to adequate protection in any situation is within the court's discretion and may, therefore, vary from case to case.

Even if the value of the collateral is not diminishing, the secured creditor is still entitled to relief from the stay if the debtor has no equity in the property (i.e., the value of the collateral is less than the claims secured by it) and the collateral is not necessary for an effective reorganization.[153] To determine whether property is necessary for an effective reorganization, the Supreme Court has made it clear that the reorganization should be more than a theoretical possibility; it must be a reorganization "that is in prospect" (i.e., "there must be 'a reasonable possibility of a successful reorganization within a reasonable time'").[154]

Procedure.   The Code prescribes specific procedures and time constraints for hearing and adjudicating a motion to lift the stay. Once a secured creditor has filed a motion seeking to have the stay lifted, the stay will automatically be lifted 30 days later unless the court has, within that time, either made a final determination denying the creditor's request or has made a preliminary determination that "there is reasonable likelihood that the party opposing relief from [the] stay will prevail."[155] If the court has made only a preliminary finding, the final hearing must be concluded not later than 30 days after the preliminary determination, unless such period is extended with the consent of the parties or by the court for compelling circumstances.[156]

The Code provides for an emergency procedure to lift the stay *ex parte* if necessary to prevent "irreparable damage."[157] The Bankruptcy Rules, however, require that notice be given orally to the trustee and establish a procedure for reinstating the stay.[158] *Ex parte* stay relief is an extraordinary procedure employed in limited circumstances.

The Code also specifies burdens of proof in a motion to lift the stay: The creditor seeking relief from the stay must prove that the debtor has no equity in the property; the trustee has the burden on all other issues.[159] The congressional record indicates that such a hearing is not the appropriate forum for determining counterclaims that the debtor may have against the secured creditor.[160] Assertions of, for example, lender liability will not be permitted to extend interminably the automatic stay hearing. As a consequence, however, the secured creditor should be aware that it could regain its collateral only to find later that it must defend against claims, such as allegations of lender liability, by the debtor.[161]

Disputes over the automatic stay inevitably require balancing the debtor's interest in reorganizing against the secured creditor's protected interest in its collateral. Given the importance of the stay to a reorganization and the discretion courts have to select the applicable valuation methodology and determine what constitutes adequate protection, it is difficult to predict whether a secured creditor will be able to foreclose on its collateral once a petition has been filed; certainly it should not assume so.

Use, Sale, or Lease of Property

A trustee's ability to use, sell, or lease a secured creditor's collateral without the creditor's consent is governed by the Code. A trustee may dispose of collateral *in the ordinary course of business* without notice and a hearing (i.e., without the secured creditor's consent or court approval).[162] It may dispose of property *out of the ordinary course of business* only after notice and a hearing. "[N]otice and hearing" is a defined phrase meaning "after such notice as is appropriate in the particular circumstances, and such opportunity for a hearing as is appropriate in the particular circumstances." A hearing can be conditioned on a party-in-interest requesting it; the secured creditor, therefore, must usually respond quickly to a trustee's motion to dispose of its collateral in order to have its objections heard.[163] Even if the secured creditor opposes the disposition of its collateral, at a hearing, the court may approve the proposed use, sale, or lease over the secured creditor's objections.[164]

A secured creditor's cash collateral is afforded special protection: It may not be used (or sold or leased), even in the ordinary course of business, unless the secured creditor consents or the court authorizes the disposition after notice and a hearing.[165] Thus, on the filing of the petition, the trustee may not use cash collateral absent consent or court approval. As discussed above, cash collateral includes the cash proceeds of collateral generated postpetition to which the prepetition lien is permitted to attach pursuant to the Code.[166] The trustee must segregate and account for all cash collateral.[167]

Property may also be sold free and clear of all liens, with the lien attaching to proceeds of the sale or the secured creditor otherwise receiving adequate protection for its collateral.[168] When collateral is sold over the objection of the secured creditor, the collateral cannot be sold free and clear of liens for less than the aggregate value of all liens against it.[169] The required consent may be implied if a secured creditor fails to object timely to the sale, after it was given adequate notice.[170]

Upon the secured creditor's request, the court must condition the sale, use, or lease of its collateral on the provision of adequate protection.[171] A common form of adequate protection is the grant of a substitute lien in the sale proceeds. Since valuation to determine adequate protection in the context of a motion to sell property will often be determined by reference to the sale price, a lien in the sale proceeds will frequently constitute adequate protection.[172]

It does not follow, however, that adequate protection will always be in the form of a lien on cash. First, the consideration paid for the collateral does not have to be cash, and a lien on proceeds will not, therefore, necessarily mean a lien on cash. Second, the form of adequate protection offered by the trustee does not have to be a lien on the sale proceeds. If, for example, the property is sold for cash needed in the debtor's operations, the trustee may offer another form of substitute collateral as adequate protection.[173]

As further protection, secured creditors are permitted to bid in the full amount of their claims at a sale of their collateral, not just the secured portion of their claim.[174] If, for example, a trustee seeks to sell manufacturing equipment for $75,000 and the equipment secures a claim for $100,000, which was valued earlier in the case as a $50,000 secured claim and a $50,000 unsecured claim, the secured creditor may bid in up to the full $100,000 of its claim to purchase the equipment, leaving it with an unsecured claim for the remainder.

Obtaining Credit

Under certain circumstances, a trustee may obtain financing postpetition, known as *DIP financing* and, if certain conditions are met, may grant the postpetition lender a lien in property equal or senior to other liens in the property. However, a lien that is equal or senior to prepetition liens on collateral (a priming lien) may be granted only after notice and a hearing, at which the trustee must establish that (1) DIP financing cannot be obtained on any other basis, and (2) the prepetition secured creditors can be given adequate protection for the amount by which the value of their collateral will be reduced by the priming lien.[175]

PLAN CONFIRMATION

The code creates two confirmation procedures: One is consensual, the other authorizes the court to confirm a plan over the objection of creditors under its so-called cram down powers. This section considers both of these confirmation procedures.

Before a plan of reorganization may be implemented, it must be voted on by creditors and confirmed by the court. The court must conduct a hearing to consider confirmation of the plan.[176] The purpose of this hearing is to ensure that the plan complies with the statutory requirements of the Code governing confirmation, which are designed, in part, to protect the secured creditor's interest in its collateral.

Treatment of Claims and the Secured Creditor's Response

In preparing a plan, a debtor has a variety of options for treating its secured claims. A plan can propose to leave a secured claim impaired or unimpaired. If the plan impairs a secured claim, that claim is entitled to vote, either for or against the plan. Depending on the outcome of voting, a plan will be dealt with either through the consensual confirmation process or the involuntary cram down procedures. In addition to the treatment provided to the secured creditor discussed in this section, secured creditors are entitled to elect different treatment pursuant to Section 1111(b) of the Code, which is discussed at the end of this chapter.

Leaving a Claim Unimpaired.   If the plan leaves a class of claims unimpaired, it is presumed to have accepted the plan and, thus, is not entitled to vote.[177]

The Code defines impairment broadly. A class of claims or interests is impaired under a plan unless one of the two exceptions set forth by Section 1124 of the Code is satisfied.[178]

The first exception treats a class of claims as unimpaired if the proposed plan "leaves unaltered the legal, equitable, and contractual rights to which such claim or interest entitles the holder of such claim or interest."[179] Creditors can generally expect that if the plan proposes to modify, alter, or eliminate any of a creditor's legal, contractual, or equitable rights, they will be considered impaired under the plan and, thereby, be eligible to vote on the plan.[180]

The second exception, embodied in Section 1124(2), allows the debtor to treat as unimpaired obligations on which it has defaulted by allowing the debtor to cure defaults and decelerate any claims that have been accelerated due to the debtor's default of a contractual term or applicable law.[181] Under this second exception, the debtor may decelerate claims only if the plan: (1) cures any default that occurred before or after the commencement of the case, other than a default that occurred as a result of an *ipso facto* bankruptcy clause (providing for a default solely because of the filing of the chapter 11 petition); (2) reinstates the maturity of the claim or interest, as such maturity existed before any default; (3) compensates the holder of the claim or interest for any damages incurred by such holder in reasonable reliance on its right to accelerate; and (4) leaves the legal, equitable, and contractual rights of the holder of the claim or interest otherwise unaltered.[182]

Although the standard is not fully settled, there seems to be general agreement in the case law that damages, which must be compensated pursuant to Section 1124(2)(c), include, at a minimum, any contract interest and late charges due on the date of the filing of the petition and attorney's fees and expenses incurred by the creditor in pursuit of a foreclosure judgment.[183] Other issues that may arise under the second exception include whether a debtor needs to compensate the creditor for its opportunity costs or pay the postdefault interest rate on the accelerated debt provided for by the contract. At least where the underlying obligation has not matured by its own terms, to affect a cure and reinstatement under the second exception, the debtor generally neither needs to compensate the creditor its opportunity costs (i.e., the difference between the contract rate and the market rate of interest) nor pay interest at the postdefault rate.[184]

A debtor will often choose to leave a creditor unimpaired for one of two principal reasons. First, it may leave a creditor unimpaired in order to prevent that creditor from voting on and rejecting the plan. Second, a debtor may reinstate a claim in order to take advantage of some favorable terms it may contain, such as a below market rate of interest.

Treatment of Claims Impaired by the Plan.   The methods by which a plan may propose to impair a secured creditor's claim are limited only by the protections provided by the Code, although the holder of a secured claim (like the holder of any impaired claim or interest) may consent to any method of treatment under the plan.[185] The holder of an impaired secured claim may vote against the proposed plan and/or object to its confirmability. As will be explained further in connection with the discussion of voting and classification (see below), if such objecting claimant is part of a class that rejects the plan, the plan can be confirmed over the rejection of that class only if the court finds the plan meets the confirmation standards set forth in the cram down provisions. If such objecting claimant is part of an accepting class, the plan may still be confirmed over the claimant's objection, unless such claimant can show that the plan is otherwise defective and not confirmable, including that such creditor is receiving less for its claim under the plan than it would receive under a liquidation under chapter 7.[186] A class of secured claims that is to receive nothing under the plan is deemed to have rejected the plan, and the proponent of the plan would have to demonstrate compliance with the cram down provisions before the court could confirm the plan.[187]

Voting and Classification

Voting.   Voting in respect of a proposed plan is conducted on a class-by-class basis, and a plan can be confirmed as a consensual plan only if all the classes voting for that plan vote to accept the plan. If one or more classes reject a proposed plan, the plan can be confirmed only in accordance with the Code's cram down procedures.

Acceptance of a plan by a class of claims requires the affirmative vote of not less than two thirds in amount and a majority in number of the allowed claims of creditors in that class that actually vote.[188] For a class of interests, acceptance is required by two thirds in amount only of voting interests.[189] Claims held by creditors whose acceptance or rejection of a plan was not in good faith, or whose votes were not solicited or procured in good faith or in accordance with the provisions of the Code, can be "designated" by the court and not counted.[190]

Classification.   In general terms, the provisions of the Code governing the classification of claims provide: (1) subject to certain exceptions, a plan may classify a claim or interest in a particular class only if such claim or interest is substantially similar to the other claims or interests in such class,[191] and (2) a plan must provide the same treatment for each claim or interest in a particular class, unless the holder of a particular claim or interest within a class agrees to less-favorable treatment than the other claims or interests in that class.[192] The phrase *substantially similar* has been construed to mean similar in legal character.[193]

Claims and interests are not substantially similar; therefore, a claim cannot be placed in the same class as an interest. Secured claims also cannot be classified together with unsecured claims, because the secured claims' right to recover from specific collateral renders them significantly distinct from unsecured claims.[194] Ordinarily, each holder of an allowed claim secured by a security interest in different properties of the debtor must be placed in a separate class.[195] If claims are secured by the same property, they may be classified together only if they are of equal priority.[196] The Code does not specifically provide for how the unsecured portion of an undersecured creditor's claim should be classified, but case law indicates that such claims should be classified as unsecured claims.[197]

Significantly, there is no requirement in the Code that all substantially similar claims be included within a particular class.[198] The absence of this requirement (at least explicitly) potentially provides a mechanism for circumventing the requirement that claims or interests in the same class must be treated equally. For example, by classifying similar claims separately, a plan can effect different treatment of similar claims, even though the Code would have required equal treatment for such claims if they had been classified together.

Not surprisingly, the question of the extent to which similar claims can be separately classified, and thus accorded different treatment, has been the subject of dispute. As a general matter, the classification of the claims is within the discretion of the proponent of the plan subject to limitations by the court. [199]

In order to prevent the classification process from being used to cause a circumvention of the class voting process or of the policies underlying the Code, a majority of courts have held that classification cannot be used solely to gerrymander class voting.[200] For example, several courts have concluded that a plan proponent cannot use the classification process in order to confirm a cram down plan by "carving out" an impaired accepting class—typically accomplished by placing the unsecured portion of the secured creditor's claim[201] in its own class and according the remaining unsecured creditors preferential treatment in order to assure their acceptance of the plan.[202]

Other courts have allowed (or even required) plan proponents to separately classify the unsecured portion of the secured creditor's claim based on the reasoning that the unsecured portion of a secured creditor's claim has different legal characteristics than other unsecured claims.[203] However, several of these courts have used the prohibition against unfair discrimination contained in the cram down provisions of the Code (see below) to limit the extent to which a creditor's claim can be subjected to disparate treatment if it is classified apart from similar claims.[204]

Confirmation of Plan

The section of the Code governing confirmation specifies 13 requirements that must be met before a plan may be confirmed.[205] The proponent of a plan carries the burden of proving each element.[206]

Consensual. A proposed plan may only be confirmed as a consensual plan if each of the classes voting on such plan accepts the plan or is left unimpaired by the plan.[207] An important protection provided to creditors by the Code is the so-called best interests test set forth in Section 1129(a)(7)(A)(ii). The best interests test is an individual objection and can by raised by any dissenting creditor regardless of the vote of its class. It essentially provides that each dissenting member of an impaired class of claims or interests must receive or retain under the plan property of a value, as of the effective date of the plan, at least equal to what such member would receive or retain if the debtor were liquidated under chapter 7.[208]

The best interests test, however, provides only limited protection because the value a creditor would receive in a chapter 7 liquidation is generally interpreted by courts to mean the liquidation value of the collateral.[209] Liquidation value of collateral is the amount such asset would bring at a sale less the costs of disposition; it assumes no future or a limited future for an asset's relationship to a going concern. Accordingly, the best interests test provides some protection for dissenting creditors or interest holders by creating an absolute floor with respect to the distribution such creditor or interest holder will receive in respect of its claims.

Cram Down.   If a plan meets all the standards for the confirmation of a consensual plan, other than acceptance by every impaired class,[210] the court still may confirm the plan under its cram down power if: (1) the proponent of the plan requests confirmation, (2) the plan does not discriminate unfairly, and (3) the plan is "fair and equitable" with respect to the dissenting class.[211] Even if the cram down process is employed, at least one class of impaired claims must accept the plan.[212]

Unfair Discrimination.   The requirement that the plan not discriminate unfairly with respect to a dissenting class was initially intended to protect the rights of a dissenting class in a manner consistent with the treatment of other classes whose rights were interrelated with those of the dissenting class.[213] The trend in the case law has been to broaden the concept of unfair discrimination, inquiring into whether the plan separately classifies similar claims or groups of claims and proposes disparate treatment for those classes.[214]

Fair and Equitable.   Under the Code, a plan will generally be considered to be fair and equitable with respect to a dissenting class of secured claims if one of three alternative tests is satisfied:[215]

1. The holders of such claims (1) retain the liens securing such claims, whether the property subject to such liens is retained by the debtor or transferred to another entity, to the extent of the allowed amount of such claims, and (2) each holder of a claim of such class receives on account of such claim deferred cash payments totaling at least the allowed amount of such claim, of a value, as of the effective date of the plan, of at least the value of such holder's interest in the estate's interest in such property.[216]
2. If the collateral is to be sold, subject to the right of such holder to credit bid at such sale,[217] free and clear of such holder's liens, such liens will at-

tach to the proceeds of such sale, and such liens on proceeds will be treated either under the method described in the preceding paragraph or under the method described in the following paragraph.[218]

3. Such holders will realize the indubitable equivalent of such claims.[219]

Under paragraph 1, above, the key issues will be valuation of the collateral and the appropriate rate of interest to be applied (both discussed below).

As for paragraph 3, determining the indubitable equivalent of a claim can be a difficult and unpredictable process. The term *indubitable equivalent* is derived from a decision by Judge Learned Hand in which he analyzed the issue of adequate protection of creditors during the pendency of a debtor's reorganization.[220] The legislative history of the cram down provisions and case law indicate that abandonment of the collateral to the secured creditor or substituting collateral of a similar type and quality may satisfy the indubitable equivalent standard.[221] The legislative history also includes examples that would not satisfy the standard, such as the granting of unsecured notes or equity securities.[222] Beyond those situations, the determination of whether a plan will, in fact, give a creditor the indubitable equivalent of its claim is left to the court's discretion on a case-by-case basis.[223]

It should be noted, however, that technical compliance with the foregoing requirements of Section 1129(b)(2) does not ensure that a plan is fair and equitable.[224] For example, courts have held that, in order for a cram down plan to be fair and equitable, and therefore confirmable, no class of claims or interests senior to the dissenting class can receive distributions in excess of the allowed amount of such senior claims or interests.[225]

Valuation.   Valuation is fundamental to the cram down process. In fact, the legislative history of the Code's confirmation provisions states that a valuation will almost always be required in connection with a confirmation that is to occur pursuant to the cram down power because of the fair and equitable requirement.[226] As previously noted, under the cram down provisions, a secured creditor is entitled to retain the lien securing its claim to the extent of the allowed amount of the claim, and to receive deferred cash payments totaling at least the allowed amount of the claim and having a present value equal to the value of the creditor's interest in the estate's interest in the collateral. Thus, a court will have to (1) value the collateral and (2) with respect to deferred cash payments, determine the appropriate discount rate that provides the secured creditor with the present value of its secured claim. Alternatively, a secured creditor is entitled to receive the indubitable equivalent of its secured claim, which requires the court to value both the original collateral and the proposed indubitable equivalent thereof.[227]

Bankruptcy Code Section 506(a) governs the determination and valuation of secured claims.[228] The Code, however, does not specify the valuation standard to be used other than by prescribing two factors which courts must take into consideration when valuing property subject to a lien: the purpose of the valuation and the proposed disposition or use of the property. The legislative history to Section 506(a) indicates that the provision grants the bankruptcy courts broad discretion in making valuation determinations[229]:

"Value" does not necessarily contemplate forced sale or liquidation value of collateral; nor does it always imply a full going concern value. Courts will have to determine value on a case-by-case basis, taking into account the facts of each case and the competing interests in the case.[230]

Further, by instructing courts to take into account "the purpose of the valuation," Congress expressly precluded that a valuation made for one purpose in a case be *res judicata* with respect to a valuation for a different purpose.[231] A secured creditor should be aware, however, that early valuations may, in practice, influence later valuations in a case.

Section 506(a) valuations are only temporal and, as a consequence, should be made as of or close to the date to which the valuation relates. Accordingly, the majority of courts hold that for purposes of plan confirmation, valuation of the collateral securing a claim should be made as of confirmation and/or the effective date of the plan.[232] Consistent with Section 1129(b)(2)(A)(i)(I), which affords confirmation cram down protection to a secured creditor by allowing the secured creditor to retain its lien on the subject property, a secured creditor should not be deprived of any appreciation in the value of its lien during the course of its case by fixing the value of the property as of the petition date.

An issue of significant consequence for secured creditors is whether a forced sale valuation or a replacement valuation is the appropriate standard to apply under Section 506(a) when a debtor's plan proposes to retain and use the property subject to the lien. In a recent decision, *Associates Commercial Corporation* v. *Rash*, the Supreme Court held that when a debtor seeks to retain and use the creditor's collateral in a plan of reorganization over the objection of a secured creditor, the value of the collateral is to be determined by what the debtor would have to pay for comparable property (its replacement or fair market value) and rejected a foreclosure-value standard.[233] The court defined fair market value as the price a willing buyer in the debtor's trade, business, or situation would pay to obtain like property from a willing seller.[234]

When a plan proposes to substitute a creditor's collateral, the substitute collateral must be valued to ensure that the creditor is receiving the indubitable equivalent of its claim.[235] Where a plan proposes to cram down a class of secured creditors by distributing notes or other instruments representing the right to receive a stream of future payments, the court must value the future cash stream so as to establish the present value of the deferred cash payments provided for by the plan, as of the effective date of the plan. This calculation requires the court to determine whether the discount rate applied to the future cash flows offers the secured creditor the present value of its secured claims.

As a general matter, in determining the present value of a secured claim, the appropriate discount rate is to be determined by the court on a case-by-case basis.[236] Methods applied by courts to arrive at the proper discount rate vary. Exemplary of the majority approach, the Second Circuit has recently held that the postconfirmation interest rate "should be fixed at the rate on a United States Treasury instrument with a maturity equivalent to the repayment schedule under the debtor's reorganization plan" plus "a premium to reflect the risk to the creditor in receiving deferred payments under the reorganization plan."[237] In general, factors that should be considered by a court in establishing the appropriate interest rate are the term of the loan proposed in the debtor's plan, the quality of the collateral securing the indebtedness, the credit standing of the borrower, and the risk of subsequent default.[238]

SECURED CREDITOR'S SECTION 1111(b) ELECTION

Although the Code bifurcates undersecured claims into two claims—a secured claim to the extent of the value of the collateral and an unsecured claim to the extent the debt exceeds the value of the collateral, the Code permits an undersecured creditor to elect to have the entire amount of its allowed claim treated as secured in the chapter 11 case.[239] Absent this right, the debtor could take advantage of a depressed market for the secured creditor's collateral by using the cram down provisions of chapter 11 to reduce the amount of the secured creditor's postconfirmation lien to the value of the collateral at the time of confirmation. The secured creditor's lien, once so reduced, would not extend to any increase in the value of the collateral postconfirmation. Instead, any appreciation in the value of the collateral would benefit the debtor by increasing its equity in the collateral. The secured creditor is entitled to an unsecured claim for the deficiency, but it may recover only a fraction of its unsecured claim under a plan while the debtor retains the collateral.

Prior to the enactment of the Code, nonrecourse creditors (i.e., creditors with a lien on property of the debtor's estate but with no right beyond its collateral for repayment) were subject to extraordinarily inequitable treatment: Not only would their lien be reduced to the depressed market value of their collateral, their entire claim would be reduced. To prevent this outcome, the Code converts a nonrecourse claim automatically to a recourse claim, thus entitling the creditor to an unsecured claim for any deficiency.[240] If, however, the secured creditor believes that the potential for appreciation of the collateral is worth more than its unsecured claim, the secured creditor can make the election to have its entire allowed claim treated as a nonrecourse secured claim.[241]

To expand on an example given in the legislative history of the cram down provisions, suppose the secured creditor loaned the debtor $15 million secured by real estate worth $18 million at the time of the loan. The real estate market subsequently declined and the collateral was now worth only $12 million. Absent election, the secured creditor would have a secured claim for $12 million and an unsecured claim for $3 million. The plan could be confirmed so long as the cram down provisions for the $12 million secured claim and $3 million unsecured claim were satisfied in the plan. As previously discussed, the cram down provisions for the secured $12 million claim would be satisfied if the secured creditor (1) retains its lien and (2) received cash payments over time totaling at least $12 million and having a present value of at least $12 million. The remaining $3 million claim would be treated as an unsecured claim under the plan. If the real estate market recovered after confirmation and the value of the collateral increased to $15 million, the secured creditor's lien would still be capped at $12 million and the debtor would then have $3 million of equity in the collateral.[242]

If the secured creditor had made the election to have its entire allowed claim treated as secured in the foregoing example, the cram down provisions for the secured claim could only be satisfied if (1) all $15 million was secured by a lien postconfirmation and (2) the secured creditor received cash payments over time totaling at least $15 million (not $12 million) but having a present value of $12 million. However, having made the election, the secured creditor would have lost its right to an unsecured claim for $3 million and, with it, the right to vote and participate in any distribution made to the unsecured creditors.

Because, in either scenario, the present value of the cash payments to the secured creditor is capped at $12 million, the benefit to the secured creditor of making the election is not immediately evident, particularly since it will have given up its unsecured claim for the deficiency. However, there are certain strategic advantages of making the election in particular situations. First, as discussed above, making the election entitles the secured creditor to any appreciation in the value of the collateral postconfirmation. Second, if the secured creditor believes the reorganized debtor will default on its postconfirmation payment obligations to it, the secured creditor may be better protected by making the election: The secured creditor who has made the election will have a secured claim of $15 million (less any postconfirmation payments) in any subsequent bankruptcy case or foreclosure proceedings, whereas the secured creditor who has not made the election will have a secured claim of only $12 million (less any postconfirmation payments). Third, making the election can prevent the debtor from cashing out the secured creditor by paying off the secured claim, which otherwise is limited to the value of the collateral, and recovering the collateral.

The election must be made on a class basis. The minimum necessary approvals are the same as for approval of the plan: two thirds of the amount of the claims in the class and one half of the number of allowed claims in the class must choose to make the election.[243] Once the election is made, it is binding on all members of the class.[244] (As noted earlier, the secured creditor will frequently be alone in its class.) Generally, the election may be made any time before the end of the hearing on the disclosure statement.[245] Once made, it is probably irrevocable, at least absent changes in the treatment of creditors under the proposed plan.[246]

There are limitations on the secured creditor's ability to make this election. The election may not be made if either (1) the collateral is to be sold during the case or under the plan or (2) the value of the secured creditor's lien in the collateral is of inconsequential value.[247] If the collateral is to be sold, the secured creditor (both recourse and nonrecourse) will be permitted to bid in the entire amount of its debt, protecting its expectation of either receiving payment in full or its collateral.

In determining whether to make an election, assuming it is available, the secured creditor must compare the treatment of secured claims to that of unsecured claims under the plan. It is possible, particularly if the value of the collateral is a small part of the secured creditor's claim or if the plan proposes a high recovery to unsecured creditors, that the present value of the distributions made to the unsecured portion of the creditor's claim under the plan will be greater, as a percentage of the secured creditor's entire claim, than the present value of the payments made on account of the creditor's secured claim after election.

In addition, the secured creditor should consider the potential strategic impact of an election. It may be easier for a plan to be confirmed without the consent of a class of secured claims than without the consent of the class of unsecured claims, particularly if the value of the collateral is a small portion of the claim. To cram down a secured claim, it must receive cash payments equal to the secured claim with a present value equal to the value of the lien in the collateral. If the value of the lien is small, payments could be stretched over a long time. In contrast, for unsecured claims to be crammed down, either they must receive distributions (which need not be in cash) with a present value equal to the entire allowed unsecured claims or all junior classes of claims and all equity may not receive or retain anything under the plan. Depending on the amount of the secured creditor's deficiencies (i.e., the amount by which the secured creditor's claim exceeds the value of the collateral), the secured creditor may be able to block consensual confirmation of a plan if it retains its unsecured claims. Thus, even if the debtor could cram down the secured portion of its claim and the unsecured creditors were willing to approve the plan, the secured creditor could vote its unsecured claim, which may be controlling, against approval, forcing a cram down of the unsecured creditors as well.

CONCLUSION

As the discussions in this chapter illustrate, the inherent uncertainties in a chapter 11 case generally make precise analysis of the potential treatment of a secured claim in a chapter 11 case extremely difficult. There are certain protections that the Code affords the secured creditor, as identified in this chapter. However, whether these protections will in the end be adequate is very difficult to predict. Chapter 11, however, offers debtors and their secured creditors an enormous amount of room to negotiate the outcome and the treatment of the claims of such creditors. In order to be prepared for these negotiations, either in an out-of-court workout or in a bankruptcy case itself, the secured creditor must understand the effects that the Code provisions can have on its claims and how to use them to its best advantage. Also, the prudent secured creditor should examine the risks that chapter 11 poses for its claim and use this "worst case" scenario as a benchmark before accepting— or rejecting—any restructuring proposal from a troubled company.

NOTES

1.   H. R. Rep. No. 95-595, 95th Cong., 1st Sess. 220 (1977) .

2.   *See* Ed Flynn, *Statistical Analysis of Chapter 11* at 13 (Administrative Office of the United States Courts, October 1989) ("it can be estimated that only about 10 to 12% of chapter 11 cases result in an actual reorganization of the filing entity").

3.   For example, the Code's provisions for avoiding preferential transfers to creditors apply only to transfers made within 90 days (one year for insiders) of the filing date. *See* 11 U.S.C. § 547(b)(4). Also, the Code's fraudulent conveyance provisions apply only to transfers made or obligations incurred within one year of the filing of the petition; however, state fraudulent conveyance statutes generally have longer statutes of limitation. See 11 U.S.C. §§ 548(a), 544(b).

4.   *See House Report, supra* note 1, at 181.

5.   Property of the estate is a very broad concept and includes all legal or equitable interests of the debtor in property as of the commencement of the case or acquired by the estate after the commencement of the case. *See* 11 U.S.C. § 541. Also, the stay applies to property that is not property of the estate but merely property in the possession of the estate, in order to prevent dismemberment of the estate by creditors rushing in to retrieve their property from the debtor's possession. *See House Report, supra* note 2, at 340–342; *n re Zartun*, 30 B.R. 543, 545 (B.A.P. 9th Cir. 1983). However, if the property does not belong to the debtor, the court should require its return to the owner or lift the stay to allow the owner to repossess it. *See In re Dascoli's, Inc.*, 49 B.R. 519, 521—522 (Bankr. E.D. Pa. 1985) ("[I]n the absence of any legal or equitable interest of the debtor in this property, we find that the stay should be lifted for 'cause' [pursuant to Section 362(d)(1)]). There is no controlling reason to keep the stay in effect here, as to do so would only frustrate movant's legitimate aim of recovering his property from a debtor who now occupies the premises and has possession of personal property without any legal or equitable right to do so."); *In re Slater*, No. 095-70848-511, 1996 WL 699719, at *9 (Bankr. E.D. N.Y. Aug. 1, 1996) (where debtor's rights in property had been terminated prepetition, debtor's bare occupancy and possession were not sufficient interests to warrant continued protection of automatic stay); *Grimes* v. *Green Point Sav. Bank*, 147 B.R. 307, 316 (Bankr. E.D. NY. 1992).

6.   *See, generally, United Sav. Ass'n of Tex.* v. *Timbers of Inwood Forest Assocs., Ltd.*, 484 U.S. 365 (1988).

7.   A creditor is most likely to triumph on such a motion if it can demonstrate to the court that the closing of the debtor's business is likely to occur in the near future and that allowing the debtor to retain the collateral merely postpones the inevitable at the exclusive risk of the secured creditor.

8.   11 U.S.C. § 506(b).

9.   *See* 11 U.S.C. § 507(b).

10.   *See* 11 U.S.C. § 1129(b)(2)(A)(iii).

11.   *See* 11 U.S.C. § 364(d).

12.   *See* 11 U.S.C. § 510(c); *In re Mobile Steel Co.*, 563 F.2d 692 (5th Cir. 1977); *see also United States* v. *Noland*, 517 U.S. 535 (1996) (discussing *Mobile Steel*); *United States* v. *Reorganized CF&I Fabricators of Utah, Inc.*, 518 U.S. 213 (1996) (same).

13.   *See* 11 U.S.C. §§ 327, 328, 1102, and 1103.

14.   *See Flynn, supra* note 2; Lynn M. LoPucki, *The Trouble with Chapter 11*, 1993 Wis. L. Rev. 729 (1993).

15.   In contrast, some secondary purchasers of the debtor's obligations may have acquired their claims specifically in order to foreclose on or take control of the collateral. A thorough discussion of trading in claims is beyond the scope of this chapter; however, it is important to note that the composition of a debtor's secured creditors in any large commercial chapter 11 case is not static. Risk-averse creditors often sell their claims to more speculative investors. Tensions between secured creditors can develop if diverse creditors seek conflicting goals. For instance, bank lenders may desire to be cashed out by the debtor, whereas secondary purchasers may seek equity or control of the company in exchange for their claims. A secured creditor should keep itself informed of the identity and strategies of any other secured creditors in order to avoid or manage potential conflicts.

16.   *See* 11 U.S.C. 101(5).

17.   The legislative history indicates that interest should be interpreted to mean "equity security." *See House Report, supra* note 2, at 413—418. As defined by the Code, equity securities include shares in a corporation, limited partnership interests, and certain types of rights and warrants. *See* 11 U.S.C. 101(15).

18.   See *See* 11 U.S.C. 1129(b)(2) (codifying "absolute priority rule"); *Kham & Nate's Shoes No. 2, Inc.* v. *First Bank of Whiting*, 908 F.2d 1351, 1360—1362 (7th Cir. 1990) ("contracts give creditors priority over shareholders"; "Creditors effectively own bankrupt firms.").

19.   *Cf. In re Johns-Manville Corp.*, 801 F.2d 60, 65 n.6 (2d Cir. 1986) ("We note that if Manville were determined to be insolvent, so that the shareholders lacked equity in the corporation, denial of the right to call a meeting would likely be proper, because the shareholders would no longer be real parties-in-interest.").

20.   11 U.S.C. § 363(b).

21.   11 U.S.C. § 363.

22.   11 U.S.C. § 541.

23.   11 U.S.C. § 1107.

24.   *See Commodity Futures Trading Comm'n* v. *Weintraub*, 471 U.S. 343, 355 (1985) ("the debtor's directors bear essentially the same fiduciary obligation to creditors and shareholders as would the trustee for a debtor out of possession"); *id.* at 356 (directors of DIP have an "obligation to treat all parties, not merely the shareholders, fairly"); *Geyer* v. *Ingersoll Publications Co.*, 621 A.2d 784, 787 (Del. Ch. 1992) (directors owe fiduciary duty to creditors on insolvency in fact).

25.   11 U.S.C. § 1104; *Wolf* v. *Weinstein*, 372 U.S. 633, 651 (1963) ("the court's willingness to leave the Debtor in possession is premised on an assurance that the officers and managing employees can be depended on to carry out the fiduciary responsibilities of a trustee. And if they default in this respect, the court may at any time replace them with an appointed trustee."), *cited with approval by Weintraub, supra* note 24, 471 U.S. at 355 (Bankruptcy Code case); *See also In re Marvel Entertainment Group, Inc.*, 140 F.3d 463, 473—475 (3rd Cir. 1998) (affirming appointment of chapter 11 trustee).

26.   §§ 327(a) and (e); *In re Hathaway Ranch Partnership*, 116 B.R. 208, 219 (Bankr. C.D. Cal. 1990) (debtor's attorney is not disinterested and will be disqualified whenever fees or a retainer are paid by a person or entity other than the debtor; attorney cannot be placed in situation where it is "serving two masters"); *In re WPMK, Inc.*, 42 B.R. 157, 163 (Bankr. D. Haw. 1984) (finding that applicant's acceptance of funds from the principal of and investor in the debtor created a conflict of interest, making it inappropriate for the applicant to continue representing debtor); *In re Rabex Amuru of North Carolina, Inc.*, 198 B.R. 892 (Bankr. M.D. N.C. 1996).

27.   A truly disinterested trustee has the mandate of maximizing the value of the estate for all constituencies as their interests may appear. *See Weintraub, supra* note 24, 471 U.S. at 352.

28.   *But see* 11 U.S.C. § 506(c), and discussion on Expenses of Preserving or Disposing of the Collateral, *infra.*

29.   The protection provided to the secured creditor for the use of its cash collateral is only what a court determines is necessary to provide adequate protection, and the remedy for a shortfall in adequate protection is a superpriority administrative claim. A DIP lender, on the other hand, is entitled to negotiate whatever terms it can from the debtor in order to provide the new financing, including a superpriority priming lien, current interest payments, and the debtor's consent to lifting of the automatic stay to permit automatic foreclosure of its collateral on default.

30.   Fed. R. Bankr. Proc. 1007.

31.   11 U.S.C. § 343; Bankruptcy Rules 2004, 7026—7037, 9014.

32.   11 U.S.C. §§ 1106(a)(1) and (7); 1107(a); Bankruptcy Rules 2015, 4002.

33.   11 U.S.C. § 1123(b)(3)(A). *See, e.g., Holywell Corp.* v. *Bank of New York*, 59 B.R. 340 (S.D. Fla. 1986) (plan provided for dismissal of lawsuit against plan proponent); *In re Cellular Info. Sys., Inc.*, 171 B.R. 926 (Bankr. S.D. N.Y. 1994) (creditor's plan could settle debtor's lender liability lawsuit against creditor); *In re BBL Group, Inc.*, 205 B.R. 625 (Bankr. N.D. Ala. 1996) (following *Cellular Info. Sys.*).

34.   11 U.S.C. §§ 506(a), 1111(b).

35.   11 U.S.C. § 506(a). A claim against the debtor that could be offset against an obligation owed by the creditor to the debtor is also a secured claim to the extent of such offset (i.e., to the extent it could reduce the creditor's obligation to the debtor).

36.   11 U.S.C. § 502(a).

37.   11 U.S.C. § 502(b).

38.   11 U.S.C. § 1111(a).

39.   Possible exceptions may include when the secured creditor wishes to avoid the jurisdiction of the bankruptcy court over counterclaims or to preserve its right to a jury trial. *See, e.g., In re PNP Holdings Corp.*, 184 B.R. 805 (B.A.P. 9th Cir. 1995) (filing proof of claim evidences consent to jurisdiction); *In re Schwinn Bicycle Co.*, 182 B.R. 526, 532 (Bankr. N.D. Ill. 1995) ("[B]y filing a proof of claim, a creditor submits to counterclaims being resolved by the bankruptcy court as core proceedings rather than having such claims be treated as noncore proceedings that can only be finally resolved by the district court."); *Langenkamp* v. *Culp*, 498 U.S. 42 (1990) (by filing a proof of claim, creditor waives right to jury trial for preference action); *Travellers Int'l AG.* v. *Robinson*, 982 F.2d 96, 98—100 (3d Cir. 1992) (filing proof of claim waives creditor's right to jury trial even when the creditor purported to expressly reserve its right to jury trial on the claim form), *cert. denied*, 507 U.S. 1051 (1993).

40.   *See* 11 U.S.C. § 502(b).

41.   *See United Sav. Ass'n of Tex.* v. *Timbers of Inwood Forest Assoc., Ltd., supra* note 6, 484 U.S. at 372 (noting that Bankruptcy Code § 506(b) permits postpetition interest to be paid out of the oversecured creditor's security cushion); *In re Delta Resources, Inc.*, 54 F.3d 722, 727 (11th Cir.) ("it seems beyond peradventure that a creditor's right to recover postpetition interest on its oversecured claim pursuant to [§ 506(b)] is virtually 'unqualified'"), *cert. denied*, 516 U.S. 980 (1995).

42.   The Code's best interests test, set out in § 1129(a)(7)(A)(ii), requires that for a plan to be confirmed, either each creditor in an impaired class of claims must receive treatment at least as favorable as it would receive in a liquidation under chapter 7, or the impaired class must vote unanimously to accept the plan. Under § 726(a), creditors are entitled to interest on their claims at the "legal rate" before any distribution is made to the debtor. By virtue of §§ 1129(a)(7) and 726(a), an unsecured impaired creditor should have a legal right to postpetition interest in a chapter 11 proceeding if the debtor is liquidation solvent. *See In re Rocky Mountain Refractories*, 208 B.R. 709, 714 (B.A.P. 10th Cir. 1997) (Code § 726(a)(5) "enacted to codify the 'solvent debtor rule'"); *In re Carter*, 220 B.R. 411, 414 (Bankr. D. N.M. 1998) (concluding that unsecured creditors of a solvent chapter 11 estate should receive postpetition interest on their claims because "an underlying policy of the Code, as evidenced by Section 726, is that a debtor should not receive a windfall at the expense of creditors in the event that there is a surplus after payment of claims"); *In re Boehm*, 202 B.R. 99, 101 (Bankr. N.D. Ill. 1996) (Code § 726(a)(5) "allows for postpetition interest when the debtor is solvent").

43.   *See, e.g., In re Gaines*, 178 B.R. 101, 106 (Bankr. W.D. Va. 1995) (holding, after balancing the relative equities, that an unsecured creditor was entitled to postpetition interest when the plan contemplated a liquidation of the debtors' assets and the value of those assets exceeded the total amount of claims: "Relevant authority and the balance of the equities establish that [the unsecured creditor] should receive postpetition interest on his claims before the Debtors are themselves permitted to receive any surplus from their bankruptcy estate. [Section 726(a)(5)] states that interest should be paid at the federal legal rate. Even though this is a chapter 11 case, a similar result is indicated.").

44.   11 U.S.C. § 506(b).

45.   *See, e.g., In re Terry L.P.*, 27 F.3d 241, 243 (7th Cir.) ("What emerges from the post-*Ron Pair* decisions is a presumption in favor of the contract rate subject to rebuttal based on equitable considerations."), *cert. denied*, 513 U.S. 948 (1994).

46.   *Id.; In re Laymon*, 958 F.2d 72, 75 (5th Cir. 1992) ("Accordingly, whether the 18% default rate, rather than the 10% pre-default rate, should apply in this case must be decided by examining the equities involved in this bankruptcy proceeding."); *In re Ace-Texas, Inc.*, 217 B.R. 719, 723 (Bankr. D. Del. 1998) ("To determine the proper interest rate, courts employ a presumption in favor of the contractual rate of interest subject to rebuttal based on the equitable considerations specific to each case."); *In re Vest Assocs.*, 217 B.R. 696 (Bankr. S.D. N.Y. 1998); *In re Johnson*, 184 B.R. 570, 573 (Bankr. D. Minn. 1995) ("[B]ankruptcy courts recognize a presumption in favor of the parties agreed interest rate subject to rebuttal based on equitable considerations."). *See also In re Bohling*, 222 B.R. 340, 342 (Bankr. D. Neb. 1998) ("[I]n determining whether to allow interest at the base contract rate

or the default rate, the trial court should consider the equities of the case."). A key factor that courts have considered when deciding whether to approve contractual default rates is whether the default rate under consideration truly compensates the creditor for losses and expenses associated with the defaulted loan or is, instead, really a disguised penalty. *See, e.g., In re Vest Assocs., supra,* 217 B.R. at 702 ("These [equitable] considerations generally hinge on the question of whether the default rate compensates the creditor for any loss resulting from nonpayment or is in fact a disguised penalty."); *In re Johnson, supra,* 184 B.R. at 573 ("[D]oes the default rate merely compensate the creditor for any loss resulting from the nonpayment of the principal at maturity, or is it a disguised penalty?").

47.   *United States* v. *Ron Pair Enters., Inc.,* 489 U.S. 235 (1989).

48.   *See* § 506(b); *United Sav. Ass'n of Tex.* v. *Timbers of Inwood Forest Assocs., Ltd., supra* note 6, 484 U.S. at 372 (§ 506(b) denies oversecured creditors postpetition interest to the extent that such interest, when added to the principal amount of the claim, will exceed the value of the collateral).

49.   *See, e.g., In re Maimone,* 41 B.R. 974, 983 (Bankr. D. N.J. 1984) (senior mortgagees are entitled to postpetition interest before junior mortgagees may collect principal from the same security).

50.   11 U.S.C. § 506(b). Here, too, claims secured by junior liens on the collateral are disregarded when calculating excess value. *See, e.g., In re Anderson,* 28 B.R. 231 (Bankr. N.D. Ga. 1983) (Code authorizes award of postpetition interest and costs of collection, including reasonable attorneys' fees, to priority oversecured creditors to the detriment of junior creditors secured by the same property); *In re Anderson,* 51 B.R. 397 (Bankr. D. Haw. 1985) (same).

51.   *See In re LHD Realty Corp.,* 726 F.2d 327, 330 (7th Cir. 1984) ("reasonable prepayment premiums are enforceable"); *In re 433 South Beverly Drive,* 117 B.R. 563, 568 (Bankr. C.D. Cal. 1990) ("Nothing in title 11 automatically invalidates a provision for a Prepayment Premium which is otherwise enforceable under applicable non-bankruptcy law."); *but see Continental Securities Corp.* v. *Shenandoah Nursing Home Partnership,* 193 B.R. 769 (W.D. Va.), *aff'd,* 104 F.3d 359 (4th Cir. 1996) (creditor not entitled to prepayment premium where underlying instrument prohibited prepayment but did not include provision specifying damages in event of prepayment).

52.   *See In re 268 Ltd.,* 789 F.2d 674, 678 (9th Cir. 1986) (portion of oversecured creditor's attorney's fee charge that was not payable as a reasonable § 506(b) assessment nevertheless could be asserted as a general unsecured claim under § 502); *see also In re Homestead Partners, Ltd.,* 200 B.R. 274, 276-78 (Bankr. N.D. Ga. 1996) (assuming that postpetition fees may be recouped on an unsecured basis; reviewing case law; *but see In re Sakowitz, Inc.,* 110 B.R. 268 (Bankr. S.D. Tex. 1989); *In re Saunders,* 130 B.R. 208 (Bankr. W.D. Va. 1991) (undersecured or unsecured creditor cannot recover contractual attorney's fees as unsecured claim). Note that the oversecured creditor is probably entitled to attorney's fees even if, under state law, such agreements are unenforceable. *See In re Schriock Constr., Inc.,* 104 F.3d 200 (8th Cir. 1997) (state law cannot bar a fee recovery under Section 506(b)); *Unsecured Creditors' Comm.* v. *Walter E. Heller & Co. Southeast, Inc.,* 768 F.2d 580 (4th Cir. 1985).

53.   *See, e.g., In re Beker Indus. Corp.,* 55 B.R. 945, 949 (Bankr. S.D. N.Y. 1985).

54.   *See In re Diversified Capital Corp.,* 89 B.R. 826 (Bankr. C.D. Cal. 1988); *but see In re Wekiva Dev. Corp.,* 22 B.R. 301 (Bankr. M.D. Fla. 1982) (implying that secured creditors may not be entitled to a committee, at least to extent interests *inter se* not identical).

55.   *See In re Diversified Capital Corp., supra* note 54 (court approved retention by a secured creditors' committee of secured creditors' attorneys); *but see In re Cumberland Farms, Inc.,* 142 B.R. 593 (Bankr. D. Mass. 1992) (denying request of official committee of secured creditors to employ professionals).

56.   *See* 11 U.S.C. § 1102; *In re Seascape Cruises, Ltd.,* 131 B.R. 241, 243 (Bankr. S.D. Fla. 1991) (§ 1102 does not preclude a creditor who holds both secured and unsecured claims from serving on a creditors' committee); *In re Walat Farms, Inc.,* 64 B.R. 65, 68–69 (Bankr. E.D. Mich. 1986) (undersecured creditors may serve on unsecured creditors' committee); *In re Markunes,* 86 B.R. 933, 936 (Bankr. S.D. Ohio 1988); *but see In re Glendale Woods Apts., Ltd.,* 25 B.R. 414, 415 (Bankr. D. Md. 1982) ("Moreover, even if [the creditor] is not fully secured, its interests may be in conflict with the other members of the Creditors' Committee."); *In re America West Airlines,* 142 B.R. 901 (Bankr. D.

Ariz. 1992) (United States trustee's removal of creditor who made postpetition loan to debtor and as a result received claim secured by substantially all of the debtor's assets from unsecured creditor's committee was not abuse of discretion).

57.   11 U.S.C. § 506(c).

58.   *See, e.g., In re Visual Indus., Inc.*, 57 F.3d 321, 324 (3d Cir. 1995) ("classic examples" of compensable expenditures include storage costs when the collateral was warehoused and auction costs incurred on the sale of the collateral).

59.   *See, e.g., In re Annett Ford, Inc.*, 64 B.R. 946, 947 (D. Neb. 1986) (noting that the secured creditor had agreed that the continued operation of the debtor's business was in its best interests and that "the various administrative expenses incurred as a result of the continued operation of the business did benefit [the secured creditor] and should be paid out of the liquidation fund"); *see also In re Lunan Family Restaurants Ltd. Partnership*, 192 B.R. 173, 179 (Bankr. N.D. Ill. 1996) ("Costs expended while keeping the Debtor running as a going concern may be charged to the secured creditor where maintaining the going-concern value actually and specifically benefited the secured creditor.") (allowing utilities, payroll, withholding and unemployment taxes, and health insurance claims to be charged against collateral).

60.   *See., e.g., In re Annett Ford, Inc.*, *supra* note 59 (consent to continue business is consent to have expenses deducted from collateral); *see also United States Internal Revenue Serv.* v. *Boatmen's First Nat'l Bank of Kansas City*, 5 F.3d 1157, 1160 (8th Cir. 1993) ("It is important that the creditors in both *Annett Ford* and the instant case agreed to the postpetition preservation of the debtor business with an eye toward a better return on the collateral.").

61.   *See, e.g., In re Cascade Hydraulics & Utility Serv., Inc.*, 815 F.2d 546, 549 (9th Cir. 1987) ("Implied consent is generally limited to instances in which the creditor caused the additional expense."); *In re Visual Indus., Inc., supra* note 58.

62.   *See, e.g., In re Cascade Hydraulics and Util. Serv., supra* note 61(administrative expenses or general costs of reorganization may not generally be charged against secured collateral, except where expenses were incurred primarily for the benefit of the secured creditor or when the secured creditor caused or consented to the expense, and to satisfy the benefit test, debtor must establish in quantifiable terms that it expended funds directly to protect and preserve the collateral); *In re Flagstaff Foodservice Corp. I*, 739 F.2d 73 (2d Cir. 1984); *In re Flagstaff Foodservice Corp. II*, 762 F.2d 10 (2d Cir. 1985); *In re Visual Indus., Inc., supra* note 58; *In re K & L Lakeland, Inc.*, 128 F.3d 203 (4th Cir. 1997); *In re Delta Towers, Ltd.*, 924 F.2d 74 (5th Cir. 1991).

63.   11 U.S.C. § 552(a).

64.   *See, e.g., In re Texas Tri-Collar, Inc.*, 29 B.R. 724 (Bankr. W.D. La. 1983).

65.   11 U.S.C. § 552(b)(1).

66.   *In re Patio & Porch Systems, Inc.*, 194 B.R. 569 (Bankr. D. Md. 1996) (payments that contractor received after filing for chapter 11 relief, on contracts to which contractor entered prepetition, qualified as proceeds of creditor's prepetition security interest in contractor's accounts receivable, to the extent that such payments remained identifiable, accordingly, creditor's security interest continued in such identifiable payments); *In re Aerosmith Denton Corp.*, 36 B.R. 116 (Bankr. N.D. Tex. 1983) (Code continues claim of secured creditor to proceeds generated postpetition from collateral such as accounts receivable).

67.   *See, e.g., In re Bumper Sales, Inc.*, 907 F.2d 1430, 1437 (4th Cir. 1990). The issue of what constitutes "proceeds, product, offspring, rents or profits" is complicated and beyond the scope of this chapter. It is worth noting, however, that even if a security agreement does not explicitly include a lien on proceeds, such a lien may exist as a matter of state law because § 9-203(3) of the Uniform Commercial Code (UCC) provides that unless a security agreement provides otherwise, it automatically gives the secured party the rights to proceeds provided by Section 9-306 of the UCC.

68.   11 U.S.C. § 552(b)(2).

69.   Examples of subtraction cases include *In re Kalian*, 169 B.R. 503 (Bankr. D.R.I. 1994); *In re IPC Atlanta Ltd. Partnership*, 142 B.R. 547 (Bankr. N.D. Ga. 1992); *In re Oaks Partners, Ltd.*, 135 B.R. 440 (Bankr. N.D. Ga. 1991) and *Confederation Life Ins. Co.* v. *Beau Rivage Ltd.*, 126 B.R. 632 (N.D. Ga. 1991).

70.   Examples of addition cases include *In re Union Meeting Partners*, 178 B.R. 664, 676–677 (Bankr. E.D. Pa. 1995) (holding that the rents received by the secured creditor postpetition should not be credited against the secured portion of its claim, but instead should be deducted from its unsecured deficiency claim); *In re Columbia Office Assocs. L.P.*, 175 B.R. 199 (Bankr. D. Md. 1994); *In re Bloomingdale Partners*, 155 B.R. 961 (Bankr. N.D. Ill. 1993); *n re Birdneck Apartment Assocs., II, L.P.*, 156 B.R. 499 (Bankr. E.D. Va. 1993); *In re Vermont Inv. Ltd. Partnership*, 142 B.R. 571 (Bankr. D.D.C. 1992); *In re Landing Assocs., Ltd.*, 122 B.R. 288 (Bankr. W.D. Tex. 1990); and *In re Flagler-at-First Assocs., Ltd.*, 114 B.R. 297 (Bankr. S.D. Fla. 1990). *See also In re Cason*, 190 B.R. 917 (Bankr. N.D. Ala. 1995) (applying addition approach for purposes of determining a creditor's right to adequate protection).

71.   §§ 552(b)(1) and 552(b)(2).

72.   § 552(b). *See* 124 Cong. Rec. H11097-98 (1978). *See, e.g., In re Airport Inn Assocs., Ltd.*, 132 B.R. 951, 959 (Bankr. D. Colo. 1990) (discussing but declining to apply equity exception of § 552(b)); *In re Granda*, 144 B.R. 697, 698 (Bankr. W.D. Pa. 1992) (contract had no intrinsic value on petition date that lien could attach to postpetition; although security interest in accounts receivable had been perfected prepetition, all of the work on the contracts had been performed postpetition).

73.   § 506(a). A partially secured creditor may elect to have its entire claim treated as a secured claim, except in certain circumstances. For a discussion of this "election," *see infra* in this chapter, Secured Creditor's 1111(b) Election.

74.   § 506(a). *See Associates Commercial Corp.* v. *Rash*, 117 S. Ct. 1879 (1997).

75.   *See* S. Rep. No. 95-989, 95th Cong., 2d Sess. 68 (1978).

76.   *See* §§ 1126(c) and 1129(b)(2), eliminating unanimous consent requirement of pre-Code practice. *Cf. In re 203 N. LaSalle Street Partnership*, 126 F.3d 955, 975 (7th Cir. 1997) (Kanne, J., dissenting) ("In effect, Section 1129(b)(2)(B) of the Code gives the creditors—not the court—the right to decide whether to waive the absolute priority rule.") (*quoting In re A.V.B.I., Inc.*, 143 B.R. 738, 744 (Bankr. C.D. Cal. 1992)), *cert. granted*, 118 S. Ct. 1674 (1998); *In re Coltex Loop Central Three Partners, L.P.*, 138 F.3d 39, 44 (2d Cir. 1998) (quoting *LaSalle* dissent); *Kham & Nate's Shoes No. 2, Inc.* v. *First Bank of Whiting, supra* note 18.

77.   References throughout this chapter to the trustee should be considered also as references to the debtor in possession, as appropriate. If a trustee has not been appointed by the court (for "cause" or in the interests of the creditors, the equityholders, and the estate) under § 1104, then the debtor in possession has, generally, the rights, powers, and duties of a trustee. § 1107(a).

78.   11 U.S.C. § 544(a) (l)–(3).

79.   *See, e.g., In re Ryan*, 851 F.2d 502 (1st Cir. 1988) (applying Vermont state law).

80.   *Id.*

81.   *See* discussion *infra* on postpetition perfection of liens at note 143 and accompanying text.

82.   11 U.S.C. § 544(a). However, if there are facts that would put all creditors on "constructive" notice of a lien under applicable state law, even if improperly perfected, the lien may be enforceable against the trustee. *See In re Probasco*, 839 F.2d 1352 (9th Cir. 1988).

83.   11 U.S.C. § 544(b).

84.   11 U.S.C. § 547(b). For a general discussion of the law of preferences, *see* Countryman, *The Concept of a Voidable Preference in Bankruptcy*, 38 Vand. L. Rev. 713 (1985).

85.   *See In re Powerline Oil Co.*, 59 F.3d 969, 972 (9th Cir. 1995) (prepetition payments to fully secured creditor generally will not be considered preferential because creditor would not receive more than in chapter 7 liquidation); *In re Fitzgerald.* 49 B.R. 62, 65 (Bankr. D. Mass. 1985).

86.   11 U.S.C. § 547(c).

87.   *See Union Bank* v. *Wolas*, 502 U.S. 151 (1991); *see also In re Finn*, 909 F.2d 903 (6th Cir. 1990) (finding that payments in respect of long-term consumer debt which is incurred as part of a "normal financial relation" and which is not an "unusual action" taken during the "slide into bankruptcy" can qualify for the ordinary course of business exception); *In re Milwaukee Cheese Wisconsin, Inc.*, 112 F.3d 845, 848 (7th Cir. 1997).

88.   *See, e.g., In re Roblin Indus., Inc.*, 78 F.3d 30, 42 (2d Cir. 1996) (payments made pursuant to debt restructuring agreements, even when debt is in default, do not always fail to be made according to ordinary business terms as a matter of law; the determination is a question of fact that depends on the nature of industry practice in a particular case); *In re Gull Air, Inc.*, 82 B.R. 1 (Bankr. D. Mass. 1988) (payments received under a restructuring agreement within 90 days of the debtor's filing of its petition were found to be outside of the ordinary course of business because the restructuring agreement was part of the settlement of litigation initiated by the creditor on the debtor's initial default); *In re Magic Circle Energy Corp.*, 64 B.R. 269, 273 (Bankr. W.D. Okla. 1986) (payments made within 90 days of the debtor's filing of its petition pursuant to a restructuring agreement were in the ordinary course of business; "[t]he mere restructuring of the payment terms does not alter the fact that the underlying debt was incurred under normal circumstances"); *In re Gilbertson*, 90 B.R. 1006 (Bankr. D. N.D. 1988) (debtor's prepetition payment to creditor, made within 90 days of petition filing, pursuant to a deferral agreement entered into in connection with a restructuring negotiated between debtor and creditor was a transfer in the ordinary course of business).

89.   11 U.S.C. §§ 547(a)(2) and (c)(1).

90.   11 U.S.C. § 547(a)(2).

91.   *Id.*

92.   *See, e.g., In re Air Conditioning Inc. of Stuart*, 845 F.2d 293 (11th Cir. 1988) (forbearance from exercising preexisting rights does not constitute new value); *In re Energy Coop. Inc.*, 832 F.2d 997 (7th Cir. 1987); *In re Dempster*, 59 B.R. 453, 459 (Bankr. M.D. Ga. 1984) (no new value given by creditor by renewing notes where those notes were secured by the same collateral that secured the notes they replaced, and no new funds were advanced); *In re Spada*, 903 F.2d 971 (3rd Cir. 1990) (new value was granted to the debtor only to the extent of the value of the reduction in interest rate and the interest-only payment provision and, accordingly, any value given by the debtor to the creditor which exceeded the amount of that new value would not qualify for the new value exception); *In re Jet Florida Sys., Inc.*, 861 F.2d 1555, 1558-59 (11th Cir. 1988) ("[s]ection 547(c)(1) protects transfers only 'to the extent' the transfer was a contemporaneous exchange for new value"; a creditor seeking the protection of § 547(c)(1) must prove with specificity the new value given to the debtor); *Drabkin v. A. I. Credit Corp.*, 800 F.2d 1153 (D.C. Cir. 1986) (creditor's release of a security interest may constitute new value, even if transfer is not made to debtor, but rather for debtor's benefit to a third party); *cf. In re Buffalo Auto Glass*, 187 B.R. 451 (Bankr. W.D. N.Y. 1995) (where forbearance is alleged to constitute new value, actual value to debtor of forbearance in money or money's worth must be established by transferee).

93.   *See, e.g., Coral Petroleum, Inc. v. Banque Paribas-London*, 797 F.2d 1351 (5th Cir. 1986); *In re Bohlen Enter., Ltd.*, 859 F.2d 561 (8th Cir. 1988); *In re Kelton Motors*, 97 F.3d 22 (2d Cir. 1996); *In re Grabill Corp.*, 135 B.R. 101, 110 (Bankr. N.D. Ill. 1991); *In re Safe-T-Brake of South Florida, Inc.*, 162 B.R. 359 (Bankr. S.D. Fla. 1993).

94.   11 U.S.C. § 547(f).

95.   11 U.S.C. § 101(30).

96.   11 U.S.C. §101(30). The term *affiliate* is defined in § 101(2).

97.   *See In re Wescorp, Inc.*, 148 B.R. 161, 163–164 (Bankr. D. Conn. 1992) ("Bona fide, reasonable financial controls imposed on the debtor during an arms-length transaction which leaves managerial control with the debtor will not make the lender an insider"); *In re Cavalier Homes of Georgia*, 102 B.R. 878, 883–884 (Bankr. M.D. Ga. 1989) (bank was not an insider where no showing that it "exercised any managerial control over debtor"); *In re Huizar*, 71 B.R. 826 (Bankr. W.D. Tex. 1987); *In re Octagon Roofing*, 124 B.R. 522 (Bankr. N.D. Ill. 1991).

98.   11 U.S.C. § 551. Any liens avoided as preferences are preserved for the benefit of the estate. This provision prevents junior lienors from improving their position at the expense of the estate when a senior lien is avoided.

99.   *See* 11 U.S.C. §§ 548(a) and 550(a).

100.   *See* 11 U.S.C. §§ 548(a)(1) and (a)(2); *see also* UFTA §§ 4 and 5, 7A U.L.A. 643, 652–653, 657 (1985).

101. 11 U.S.C. § 548(d)(2); UFTA § 3, 7A U.L.A. 643, 650 (1985).

102. *See In re Anand,* 210 B.R. 456, 459 (Bankr. N.D. Ill. 1997) ("as a matter of law, collateralizing an antecedent debt cannot constitute less than reasonably equivalent value regardless of the value of the collateral").

103. 11 U.S.C. § 548(c); *see also* UFTA § 8, 7A U.L.A. 643, 662–663 (1985). *See* § 550(b) for exculpatory provisions under the Code for secondary transferees.

104. 11 U.S.C. § 544(b).

105. UFTA § 9, 7A U.L.A. 643, 665. Note that the statute of limitations for actions brought pursuant to UFTA § 5(b), dealing with certain transfers to insiders, is one year. For a comparison of the provisions of the Code, UFCA and UFTA *see* 5 *Collier on Bankruptcy* ¶ 548.LH [4] at 548-92–100 (Lawrence P. King, Ed. 15th Ed. Rev. 1998).

106. UFCA §§ 3, 4–6, 7A U.L.A. 427, 448–449, 474–475, 504, 507 (1985).

107. UFCA § 7; 7A U.L.A. 427, 509 (1985).

108. UFCA § 9(1); 7A U.L.A. 427, 577 (1985).

109. UFCA § 9(2); 7A U.L.A. 427, 578 (1985).

110. § 548(a)(2); UFTA §§ 4(a)(2), 5(a), 8(a), 7A U.L.A. 643, 652–653, 657, 662 (1985); UFCA § 3, 7A U.L.A. 427, 448–449 (1985). For a discussion of the requirements of "fair consideration," *see generally* 5 *Collier on Bankruptcy* ¶ 548.05[1][c] at 548-39–42 (Lawrence P. King, Ed. 15th Ed. Rev. 1998).

111. *See United States* v. *Gleneagles Inv. Co., Inc.,* 565 F. Supp. 556, 581 (M.D. Pa. 1983), *aff'd,* 803 F.2d 1288 (3rd Cir. 1986), *cert. denied,* 483 U.S. 1005 (1987); *Wieboldt Stores, Inc.* v. *Schottenstein,* 94 B.R. 488 (N.D. Ill. 1988); *In re O'Day Corp.,* 126 B.R. 370 (Bankr. D. Mass. 1991); *see also Kupetz* v. *Wolf,* 845 F.2d 842 (9th Cir. 1988); *Lippi* v. *City Bank,* 955 F.2d 599 (9th Cir. 1992); *Moody* v. *Security Pacific Bus. Credit, Inc.,* 971 F.2d 1056 (3d. Cir. 1992). *See generally* Robert J. White, *Leveraged Buyouts and Fraudulent Conveyance Laws Under the Bankruptcy Code—Like Oil and Water, They Just Don't Mix,* 1991 Ann. Surv. Am. L. 357 (1992).

112. Although lenders in leveraged buyout transactions are usually attacked on the ground of constructive fraud, it is also possible for them to be sued on the basis of intentional or actual fraud. *See, e.g., Gleneagles, supra* note 111, 803 F.2d at 1304-05.

113. *See, e.g., Gleneagles, supra* note 111; *Wieboldt Stores, Inc.* v. *Schottenstein, supra* note 111; *In re O'Day Corp., supra* note 111.

114. *Id.; see also Crowthers McCall Pattern, Inc.* v. *Lewis,* 129 B.R. 992, 997–998 (S.D. N.Y. 1991) (refusing to dismiss fraudulent transfers complaint).

115. *See Wieboldt Stores, Inc.* v. *Schottenstein, supra* note 111, 94 B.R. at 505; *but cf. In re Anderson Indus., Inc.,* 55 B.R. 922, 927 (Bankr. W.D. Mich. 1985). Note that some other or additional consideration can be provided to the target as part of the transaction that may constitute fair or reasonably equivalent value. *See, e.g., Mellon Bank* v. *Metro Communications, Inc.,* 945 F.2d 635, 646 (3d Cir. 1991) (in evaluating whether reasonably equivalent value has been given to the debtor under § 548, indirect benefits may also be considered).

116. *See, e.g., Moody* v. *Security Pacific Business Credit, Inc., supra* note 111, 971 F.2d at 1073–1075 (court applied a reasonable foreseeability standard, examining pretransaction projections, in determining that failed leveraged buyout did not create fraudulent transfer liability).

117. 11 U.S.C. § 510(c).

118. *See In re Mobile Steel Co., supra* note 12; *see also United States* v. *Noland, supra* note 12; *United States* v. *Reorganized CF&I Fabricators of Utah, Inc., supra* note 12.

119. *See In re Clark Pipe and Supply Co., Inc.,* 893 F.2d 693 (5th Cir. 1990) (enforcement of rights under loan agreement is not inequitable conduct justifying subordination).

120. *See In re 80 Nassau Assocs.* 169 B.R. 832, 839–840 (Bankr. S.D. N.Y. 1994); *In re Badger Freightways, Inc.,* 106 B.R. 971, 976 (Bankr. N.D. Ill. 1989) (in chapter 11, noninsider creditors are permitted to act strategically to protect their interests to the potential detriment of similarly situated claimants); *cf. In re Lifschultz Fast Freight,* 132 F.3d 339, 345 (7th Cir. 1997) ("undercapitalization is not in itself inequitable conduct" and alone is not sufficient grounds for equitable subordination).

121.   *See In re Mobile Steel Co., supra* note 12, 563 F.2d at 701 ("a claim or claims should be sub-ordinated only to the extent necessary to offset the harm which the bankrupt and its creditors suffered on account of the inequitable conduct.").

122.   11 U.S.C. § 510(a).

123.   *See In re Ionosphere Clubs, Inc.*, 134 B.R. 528, 535 (Bankr. S.D. N.Y. 1991) (applying rule of explicitness; providing sample language for indenture); *but compare In re Southeast Banking Corp.*, 156 F.3d 1114, 1124 (11th Cir. 1998) (concluding that § 510(a) abrogated the rule of explicitness). *See also In re Envirodyne Indus., Inc.*, No. 93 B 310, 1993 WL 566565, at *36 (Bankr. N.D. Ill. Dec. 20, 1993).

124.   *See Louisville Joint Stock Land Bank v. Radford*, 295 U.S. 555 (1935) (the bankruptcy power of Congress is subject to the Fifth Amendment).

125.   11 U.S.C. § 362(d)(l); *see* subsection, Automatic Stay, *infra.*

126.   11 U.S.C. § 363(e); *see* subsection, Obtaining Credit, *infra.*

127.   11 U.S.C. § 364(d)(1)(B); *see* subsection, Obtaining Credit, *infra.*

128.   11 U.S.C. § 361.

129.   *Id.*

130.   11 U.S.C. § 507(b).

131.   *United Sav. Ass'n of Tex.* v. *Timbers of Inwood Forest Assoc., Ltd., supra* note 6.

132.   *Id.* at 371.

133.   *House Report, supra* note 2, at 340.

134.   Section 541(a)(1). Insurance policies, for example, have been determined to be property of the estate, *see, e.g., MacArthur Co.* v. *Johns-Manville Corp.*, 837 F.2d 89 (2d Cir.), *cert. denied*, 488 U.S. 868 (1988); *In re Minoco Group of Cos.*, 799 F.2d 517 (9th Cir. 1986), as have servicing rights. *See In re Adana Mortgage Bankers, Inc.*, 12 B.R. 989, 1003 (Bankr. N.D. Ga. 1980), *vacated by, In re Adana Mortgage Bankers, Inc.*, 687 F.2d 344 (11th Cir. 1982).

135.   28 U.S.C. §1334(d).

136.   *See, e.g., In re McLean Indus.*, 74 B.R. 589, 601 (Bankr. S.D. N.Y. 1987) (automatic stay applies extraterritorially; foreclosure proceedings on ships in Singapore and Hong Kong come within the scope of § 362(a)).

137.   11 U.S.C. §§ 304(a) and (b). *See, e.g., Haarhuis* v. *Kunnan Enter., Ltd.*, 223 B.R. 252 (D. D.C. 1998) (affirming bankruptcy court's enjoining of pending breach of contract action under § 304).

138.   11 U.S.C. §§ 362(b)(1), (b)(4), and (b)(5).

139.   11 U.S.C. § 362(b)(12).

140.   11 U.S.C. § 1110.

141.   *See* 11 U.S.C. §§ 362(b)(3), 546(b), and 547(e)(2)(A).

142.   *See, e.g., In re Yobe Elec., Inc.*, 728 F.2d 207 (3d Cir. 1984) (filing of mechanic's lien not stayed; perfection relates back).

143.   Under the Uniform Commercial Code, as enacted in most states, a lender providing purchase money that perfects its purchase money security interest within the stated time after the debtor takes possession of the goods has a perfected security interest as of the date the security interest attached. UCC 9-301(2). Giving postpetition notice of this perfection (and filing the requisite Form UCC-1) will not violate the stay. *See House Report, supra* note 2, at 371; *see also In re WWG Indus., Inc.*, 772 F.2d 810 (11th Cir. 1985).

144.   *See, generally,* 11 U.S.C. § 105; *but see Norwest Bank Worthington* v. *Ahlers*, 485 U.S. 197, 206 (1988) ("whatever equitable powers remain in the bankruptcy courts must and can only be exercised within the confines of the Bankruptcy Code.").

145.   *See, e.g., In re A.H. Robbins Co., Inc.*, 788 F.2d 994 (4th Cir.), *cert. denied*, 479 U.S. 876 (1986); *In re Johns-Manville*, 26 B.R. 420, *modified*, 33 B.R. 254 (Bankr. S.D. N.Y. 1983), *aff'd in part*, 40 B.R. 219 (S.D. N.Y. 1984); *In re Eagle Pitcher Indus., Inc.*, 963 F.2d 855 (6th Cir. 1992); *In re Lazarus Burman Assocs.*, 161 B.R. 891 (Bankr. E.D. N.Y. 1993).

146. *See Willis* v. *Celotex Corp.*, 978 F.2d 146, 148 n. 3 (4th Cir. 1992) (letter of credit and its proceeds are not part of the estate). *But see In re Twist Cap., Inc.*, 1 B.R. 284 (Bankr. M.D. Fla. 1979) (court stayed drawing under the letter of credit reasoning that the letter of credit was property of the estate). Subsequent cases have rejected the holding in *Twist Cap. See, e.g., In re Compton Corp.*, 831 F.2d 586, 589-90 (5th Cir. 1987) (noting that *Twist Cap* "has been roundly criticized and otherwise ignored by courts and commentators alike"); *In re Zenith Lab., Inc.*, 104 B.R. 667 (Bankr. D. N.J. 1989).

147. 11 U.S.C. § 362(c).

148. *Id.*; *House Report, supra* note 2, at 343.

149. 11 U.S.C. § 362(d).

150. For purposes of determining whether there is an equity cushion, junior liens are disregarded. *See, e.g., In re Mellor*, 734 F.2d 1396, 1400 n. 2 (9th Cir. 1984); *In re Indian Palms Assocs., Ltd.*, 61 F.3d 197, 207 (3rd Cir. 1995).

151. *See In re Dunes Casino Hotel*, 69 B.R. 784, 794 (Bankr. D. N.J. 1986) ("The existence of equity above the secured party's interest which provides an 'equity cushion' to the secured party may, in a given case, provide adequate protection."); *In re Snowshoe Co., Inc.*, 789 F.2d 1085, 1090 (4th Cir. 1986) (observing that "some courts have found that the existence of an equity cushion is sufficient to demonstrate adequate protection while others have held that such a cushion is part of the bargained for consideration and cannot in itself protect the secured creditor"); *but see c.f. In re Swedeland Dev. Group, Inc.*, 16 F.3d 552, 566 n.17 (3d Cir. 1994) (en banc) (suggesting that secured creditor whose lien is to be primed must be supplied with replacement collateral or other new value in some form; "We do not. . . imply. . . . that a creditor no matter how great its security can be adequately protected without receiving additional collateral or guarantees"); *In re WRB West Assocs. Joint Venture*, 106 B.R. 215, 220 (Bankr. D. Mont. 1989) (equity cushion of 40% provided adequate protection, however, "the equity cushion itself. . . . must be protected against erosion by accruing interest, depreciation, or other changes."). Among courts that have found that an equity cushion may constitute adequate protection, most have found that the cushion must be substantial. *See, e.g., In re McKillips*, 81 B.R. 454, 458 (Bankr. N.D. Ill. 1987) (collecting cases and concluding that "[c]ase law has almost uniformly held that an equity cushion of 20% or more constitutes adequate protection," while it has "almost as uniformly held that an equity cushion under 11% is insufficient to constitute adequate protection."); *see also In re Atrium Dev. Co.*, 159 B.R. 464, 471 (Bankr. E.D. Va. 1993) (12% equity cushion falls "far short" of establishing that creditor is demonstrably oversecured); *In re C.B.G. Ltd.*, 150 B.R. 570, 572 (Bankr. M.D. Pa. 1992) (14% equity cushion did not constitute adequate protection); *In re Mediterranean Assocs., L.P.*, No. CIV. A. 93-MC-304, 1993 WL 541671, at *2 (E.D. Pa. Dec. 29, 1993) (bankruptcy court did not abuse its discretion in granting relief from stay on finding that creditor was not adequately protected by "meager 6% equity cushion").

152. *See In re Delta Resources, Inc.*, *supra* note 41, 54 F.3d at 730 (holding that under Code Section 362, "an oversecured creditor's interest in property which must be adequately protected encompasses the decline in the value of the collateral only, rather than perpetuating the ratio of the collateral to the debt.").

153. 11 U.S.C. § 362(d)(2). To determine whether the debtor has equity in the collateral under Section 362(d)(2), courts generally include junior liens. *See In re Indian Palms Assocs., Ltd.*, *supra* note 150, 61 F.3d. at 206 ("The classic test for determining equity under Section 362(d) focuses on a comparison between the total liens against the property and the property's current value."). *But see In re Palmer River Realty, Inc.*, 26 B.R. 138, 140 (Bankr. D. R.I. 1983) (calculating equity cushion without including junior lien, where junior lienholder expressed desire to support reorganization attempt).

154. *United Sav. Ass'n of Tex.* v. *Timbers of Inwood Forest Assoc., Ltd.*, *supra* note 6 at 375–376 (emphasis in original). *See, e.g., In re Swedeland Dev. Group, Inc.*, *supra* note 151, 16 F.3d at 567–568 (§ 362(d)(2) stay relief ordered).

155. 11 U.S.C. § 362(e).

156. *Id.*

157. 11 U.S.C. § 362(f).

158.   Bankruptcy Rule 4001(a)(3).

159.   11 U.S.C. § 362(g).

160.   *House Report, supra* note 2, at 344.

161.   *See Grella* v. *Salem Five Cent Sav. Bank*, 42 F.3d 26 (1st Cir. 1994) (order granting relief from automatic stay did not bar chapter 7 trustees subsequent preference counterclaim against creditor); *D-1 Enter., Inc.* v. *Commercial State Bank*, 864 F.2d 36 (5th Cir. 1989); *but cf. In re Pappas*, 55 B.R. 658, 660–661 (Bankr. D. Mass. 1985) (counterclaims that go to the validity of the secured creditor's lien may appropriately be considered, though not adjudicated, during a hearing on a motion seeking to lift the stay).

162.   11 U.S.C. § 363(c)(1).

163.   11 U.S.C. § 102(a).

164.   11 U.S.C. § 363(b).

165.   11 U.S.C. § 363(c)(2).

166.   11 U.S.C. § 363(a).

167.   11 U.S.C. § 363(c)(4).

168.   11 U.S.C. § 363(f).

169.   11 U.S.C. § 363(f)(3). The proper interpretation of "the aggregate value of all liens" is the subject of conflict among courts. *Compare In re Becker Indus. Corp.*, 63 B.R. 474, 476 (Bankr. S.D. N.Y. 1986) (value of liens means actual economic value of the lien as determined pursuant to Section 506(a), *i.e.*, the value of the collateral); *In re Collins*, 180 B.R. 447 (Bankr. E.D. Va. 1995) and *In re Milford Group, Inc.*, 150 B.R. 904 (Bankr. M.D. Pa. 1992) *with In re Terrance Chalet Apartments, Ltd.*, 159 B.R. 821, 825–826 (N.D. Ill. 1993) (sales price must exceed face amount of all liens; § 363(f) protects the amount of the secured debt, not the actual economic value of the lien) and *In re Perroncello*, 170 B.R. 189 (Bankr. D. Mass. 1994).

170.   *See In re James*, 203 B.R. 449, 453 (Bankr. W.D. Mo. 1997) (by failing to object to sale, creditor implicitly consented to sale for purposes of satisfying § 363(f)(2)); *In re Elliot*, 94 B.R. 343 (E.D. Pa. 1988).

171.   11 U.S.C. § 363(e).

172.   *See House Report, supra* note 2, at 345: "Most often, adequate protection in connection with a sale free and clear of other interests will be to have those interests attach to the proceeds of the sale." *See also In re Collins, supra* note 169 (commonly accepted method for adequately protecting secured creditor when sale is authorized under § 363(f) is to order liens to attach to sale proceeds).

173.   *Compare In re Equity Management Sys.*, 149 B.R. 120 (Bankr. S.D. Iowa 1993) (replacement lien on leases and proceeds of leases to extent of normal payments constituted adequate protection as required for lease and eventual sale of collateral in the ordinary course of business) *with In re Magnus*, 50 B.R. 241 (Bankr. D. N.D. 1985) (offer to replace first mortgage on farmland with lien on two used silos was not indubitable equivalent of creditor's security interest and did not provide creditor with adequate protection so as to permit debtor to sell the land and use the proceeds). *See also* cases discussing indubitable equivalent standard *infra* at notes 220–223 and accompanying text.

174.   11 U.S.C. § 363(k).

175.   11 U.S.C. § 364(d); *see, e.g., In re Swedeland Dev. Group, Inc., supra* note 151. *See also* cases cited *supra* at notes 124–132 and accompanying text for a discussion of the requirements of adequate protection.

176.   11 U.S.C. §1128(a).

177.   11 U.S.C. § 1126(f).

178.   11 U.S.C. § 1124.

179.   11 U.S.C. § 1124(1). *See In re Union Meeting Partners*, 160 B.R. 757, 771 (Bankr. E.D. Pa. 1993) ("'[I]mpairment' is a term of art and includes virtually any alteration of a claimant's rights."); *In re Barrington Oaks Gen. Partnership*, 15 B.R. 952 (Bankr. D. Utah 1981) (any alteration of rights constitutes impairment). Further, a creditor may be impaired even if its contractual rights are not altered if the debtor is left in a condition that increases the risk of default. *Id.* at 966 (changing identity

of obligor, irrespective of whether due on sale clause is breached, changes the risk to the creditor that obligor will not be able to perform; thus, creditor is impaired).

180.   *See In re Barrington Oaks Gen. Partnership, supra* note 179. Adopting a literal interpretation of § 1124, some courts have noted that enhanced treatment can constitute impairment. *See, e.g., In re L & J Anaheim Assocs.*, 995 F.2d 940, 942–943 (9th Cir. 1993); *see also In re Atlanta-Stewart Partners*, 193 B.R. 79, 82 (Bankr. N.D. Ga. 1996) (holding that "a class of creditors which will receive payment in full on the effective date of the plan is impaired within the meaning of the Bankruptcy Code."). Several others have found "the barest imaginable degree of impairment" sufficient. *In re Duval Manor Assocs.*, 191 B.R. 622, 627 (Bankr. E.D. Pa. 1996). In contrast, numerous courts have held that acceptance by an "artificially" impaired class will not satisfy the confirmation requirement that at least one impaired class has accepted the plan. *See* § 1129(a)(10); *In re Windsor on the River Assocs., Ltd.*, 7 F.3d 127 (8th Cir. 1993); *In re Fur Creations by Varriale, Ltd.*, 188 B.R. 754, 760 (Bankr. S.D. N.Y. 1995) (requiring a showing that the proposed impairment is necessary for economic or other justifiable reasons and not just to achieve a cram down).

181.   11 U.S.C. § 1124(2). Leaving a claim unimpaired by curing defaults in respect of that claim under the exception provided by § 1124(2) does not impair a creditor's claim, even though it may entail altering a contractual acceleration clause. *See In re Taddeo*, 685 F.2d 24, 28-29 (2d Cir. 1982); *In re Madison Hotel Assocs.*, 749 F.2d 410 (7th Cir. 1984) (§ 1124(2) permits the plan to reinstate the original maturity of a claim or interest as it existed before the default without impairing such claim or interest); *see also In re Entz-White Lumber & Supply, Inc.*, 850 F.2d 1338 (9th Cir. 1988) (plan may cure all defaults without impairing creditor's claim; such defaults include, but are not limited to, defaults resulting in acceleration); *but see In re Liberty Warehouse Assocs. Ltd. Partnership*, 220 B.R. 546, 549 (Bankr. S.D. N.Y. 1998) (rejecting, in part, *Entz-White* by interpreting § 1124(2) to apply where a debtor seeks to cure a default under an accelerated obligation and reinstate its original terms, but not where the underlying obligation has matured by its own terms).

182.   11 U.S.C. §§ 1124(2) (A)-(D).

183.   *See, e.g., In re Orlando Tennis World Dev. Co.*, 34 B.R. 558, 560 (Bankr. M.D. Fla. 1983); *In re Arlington Village Partners, Ltd.*, 66 B.R. 308, 316–317 (Bankr. S.D. Ohio 1986).

184.   *Compare In re Orlando Tennis World Dev. Co., supra* note 183, at 560–561; *In re Entz-White Lumber & Supply, Inc., supra* note 181; *In re Southeast Co.*, 868 F.2d 335 (9th Cir. 1989); *In re Udhus*, 218 B.R. 513 (B.A.P. 9th Cir. 1998); *In re Johnson*, 184 B.R. 570 (Bankr. D. Minn. 1995) *with In re Liberty Warehouse Assocs. Ltd. Partnership, supra* note 181, at 549 (rejecting, in part. *Entz-White* and *Johnson* and holding § 1124(2) to apply where a debtor seeks to cure a default under an accelerated obligation and reinstate its original terms, but not where the underlying obligation has matured by its own terms; debtor could not "cure" default of loan that matured prepetition by its own terms and thus creditors were allowed postpetition interest at default rate); *In re Ace-Texas, Inc., supra* note 46 (same); *In re Route One West Windsor Ltd. Partnership*, 225 B.R. 76 (Bankr. D. N.J. 1998) (same).

185.   11 U.S.C. § 1129(a)(7)(A)(i).

186.   11 U.S.C. § 1129(a)(7). § 1129(a)(7) provides that the holder of an impaired claim or interest must either accept the plan or the plan must provide that it will receive or retain under on account of such claim or interest, property of a value, as of the effective date of the plan, that is not less than the amount that such holder would so receive or retain if the debtor were liquidated under chapter 7 on such date.

187.   11 U.S.C. § 1126(g).

188.   11 U.S.C. § 1126(c).

189.   11 U.S.C. § 1126(d).

190.   11 U.S.C. § 1126(e); *see In re Figter Ltd.*, 118 F.3d 635 (9th Cir.), *cert. denied*, 118 S. Ct. 561 (1997). It is also worth noting that it is very important for creditors who oppose a plan to vote to reject that plan. Although it has been widely criticized, the Tenth Circuit has found that a creditor who fails to vote on a plan can have its inaction deemed to constitute an acceptance. *See In re Ruti-Sweetwater, Inc.*, 836 F.2d 1263 (10th Cir. 1988). Other courts have disagreed. *See In re Friese*, 103 B.R. 90, 92 (Bankr. S.D. N.Y. 1989) (disagreeing with *In re Ruti-Sweetwater, supra*, and finding "where

the class fails to vote, it should not be deemed to accept the plan" but the plan may nevertheless be subject to confirmation under the cram-down provisions); *In re M. Long Arabians*, 103 B.R. 211, 215 (B.A.P. 9th Cir. 1989) (declining to follow *In re Ruti-Sweetwater, supra,* "to the extent it holds that a creditor is 'deemed' to have accepted the plan."); *In re Higgins Slacks Co.* 178 B.R. 853 (Bankr. N.D. Ala. 1995).

191.   11 U.S.C. § 1122(a).

192.   11 U.S.C. §1123(a)(4).

193.   *See In re Gillette Assoc., Ltd.*, 101 B.R. 866, 872 (Bankr. N.D. Ohio 1989) ("The focus of classification is the legal character of the claim as it relates to the assets of the debtor.").

194.   *See, e.g., FGH Realty Credit Corp.* v. *Newark Airport/Hotel Limited Partnership*, 155 B.R. 93, 99 (D. N.J. 1993) ("Secured claims, however, are not substantially similar to unsecured claims."); *In re Sullivan*, 26 B.R. 677 (Bankr. W.D. N.Y. 1982).

195.   *See, e.g., In re Commercial Western Fin. Corp.*, 761 F.2d 1329, 1338 (9th Cir. 1985); *In re Bugg*, 172 B.R. 781, 784 (E.D. Pa. 1994) ("Courts have consistently held as a matter of law that secured creditors on different pieces of property are not similar" for classification purposes); *In re Sullivan, supra* note 194 at 678. *But see In re Palisades-on-the-Desplaines*, 89 F.2d 214 (7th Cir. 1937) (finding under the Act that claims may be classified together where the different properties are in the same location, were purchased at approximately the same time, and therefore are worth approximately the same amount).

196.   *See In re Richard Buick, Inc.*, 126 B.R. 840, 853 (Bankr. E.D. Pa. 1991) ("many courts have concluded that secured creditors may not be classified together when they have liens in different property, or possess liens of different priority in the same property, since their respective legal rights are not substantially similar."); *In re Holthoff*, 58 B.R. 216 (Bankr. E.D. Ark. 1985); *In re Martin's Point, Ltd. Partnership*, 12 B.R. 721, 727 (Bankr. N.D. Ga. 1981) (claims secured by the same real property and being equal in priority to each other were properly classified together).

197.   *See, e.g., In re U.S. Truck Co., Inc.*, 800 F.2d 581 (6th Cir. 1986); *In re Greystone III Joint Venture*, 948 F.2d 134, *republished*, 995 F.2d 1274 (5th Cir. 1991).

198.   §1122; *In re U.S. Truck Co, Inc.*, *supra* note 197, 800 F.2d at 585.

199.   *See In re U.S. Truck Co.*, *supra* note 197, 800 F.2d at 586 ("there must be some limit on the debtor's ability to classify creditors" in order to manipulate the voting process).

200.   *See In re Greystone III Joint Venture supra* note 197, 948 F.2d at 139 (stating the "one clear rule" that "thou shall not classify similar claims differently in order to gerrymander an affirmative vote on a reorganization plan"); *In re Lumber Exch. Bldg. Ltd. Partnership*, 968 F.2d 647, 649 (8th Cir. 1992) (a debtor may classify substantially similar claims differently for reasons independent of securing the vote of an impaired assenting class of claims) (citing *Greystone*); *John Hancock Mutual Life Ins. Co.* v. *Route 37 Bus. Park Assocs.*, 987 F.2d 154, 158 (3rd Cir. 1993); *In re Barakat*, 99 F.3d 1520, 1526 (9th Cir. 1996) ("We agree with the principles enunciated in the *Greystone III* line of cases, that is, absent legitimate business or economic justification, it is impermissible for Debtor to classify LICV's deficiency claim separately from general unsecured claims"), *cert. denied*, 117 S. Ct. 1312 (1997).

201.   The right to vote the unsecured portion of its claim along with the other unsecured claims is an important protection granted to the undersecured creditor by the Code. Often, this unsecured "deficiency" claim will be the most significant unsecured claim in the case, allowing the undersecured creditor to control the vote of the unsecured class in order to protect itself or extract concessions from other unsecured creditors in the plan negotiation process.

202.   *See* cases cited *supra* at note 200; *compare with In re U.S. Truck Co.*, *supra* note 197, 800 F.2d at 587 (allowing separate classification of union's claims because its interests differed substantially from those of the other impaired creditors); *In re Chateaugay Corp.*, 89 F.3d 942, 951 (2d Cir. 1996) ("[A]s LTV had a legitimate business reason—promoting harmonious labor relations—to categorize separately the claims of the unpaid workers and the paid workers (and those claiming derivatively through them), the plan's classification arrangement is a proper one.").

203.   *See In re Woodbrook Assocs.*, 19 F.3d 312, 319 (7th Cir. 1994); *In re City of Colorado Springs Spring Creek Gen. Improvement Dist.* 187 B.R. 683, 689 (Bankr. D. Colo. 1995); *In re Crosscreek*

Apartments, Ltd., 213 B.R. 521, 533 (Bankr. E.D. Tenn. 1997); *In re ZRM-Oklahoma Partnership*, 156 B.R. 67 (Bankr. W.D. Okla. 1993); *In re SM 104 Ltd.*, 160 B.R. 202, 218-221 (Bankr. S.D. Fla. 1993); *In re Baldwin Park Towne Ctr. Ltd.*, 171 B.R. 374, 377 (Bankr. C.D. Cal. 1994).

204.   *See, e.g., In re City of Colorado Springs Spring Creek Gen. Improvement Dist., supra* note 203, 187 B.R. at 689 ("Issues of gerrymandering can and should be addressed as part of the 'unfair discrimination' analysis of § 1129(b) . . . . Gerrymandering or disparate treatment of classes of similar claims falls squarely within the concept of unfair discrimination."); *In re Crosscreek Apartments, Ltd., supra* note 203, 213 B.R. at 538 (court, after rejecting objection based on improper classification, sustained creditor's objection to confirmation based on unfair discrimination where plan separately classified secured creditor's deficiency claim and accorded it significantly worse treatment than other unsecured claims); *In re Baldwin Park Towne Ctr. Ltd., supra* note 203, 171 B.R. at 378; *In re Aztec Co.*, 107 B.R. 585 (Bankr. M.D. Tenn. 1989) (plan could not be confirmed because it discriminated unfairly against dissenting unsecured deficiency claim).

205.   11 U.S.C. § 1129(a).

206.   *See, e.g., In re Briscoe Enter., Ltd., II*, 994 F.2d 1160, 1163-1165 (5th Cir.), *cert. denied*, 114 S. Ct. 550 (1993); *Corestates Bank, N.A.* v. *United Chem. Tech.*, 202 B.R. 33, 45 (E.D. Pa. 1996) (following *Briscoe*).

207.   11 U.S.C. § 1129(a)(8).

208.   11 U.S.C. § 1129(a)(7)(A)(ii).

209.   11 U.S.C. § 1129(a)(7) requires a hypothetical comparison against what a creditor would receive "if the debtor were liquidated under chapter 7" of the Code. *See, e.g., In re Voluntary Purchasing Groups, Inc.*, 222 B.R. 105 (Bankr. E.D. Tex. 1998); *In re Sierra-Cal*, 210 B.R. 168, 172 (Bankr. E.D. Cal. 1997) (best interests analysis requires comparison to hypothetical chapter 7 liquidation, which "contemplates valuation according to the depressed prices that one typically receives in distress sales.").

210.   11 U.S.C. § 1129(a)(8).

211.   11 U.S.C. § 1129(b)(l).

212.   11 U.S.C. § 1129(a)(10).

213.   *See* Kenneth N. Klee, *All You Ever Wanted to Know about Cram Down under the New Bankruptcy Code*, 53 Am. Bank. L.J. 133, 142 (1979).

214.   *See* cases cited *supra* at note 204 and accompanying discussion.

215.   It is worth noting that, with respect to a class of unsecured claims, the fair and equitable standard set forth in Section 1129(b)(2)(B) of the Code requires that (i) the plan provide that the holders of such claims receive or retain on account of such claims property of a value, as of the effective date of the plan, equal to the allowed amount of such claims or (ii) no holder of an interest junior to the claims of such class may receive or retain under the plan any property on account of such junior claim or interest. *See also* cases cited *supra* at note 76, discussing fair and equitable in the context of cram down of the unsecured portion of an undersecured creditor's claim.

216.   11 U.S.C. § 1129(b)(2)(A)(i).

217.   In accordance with Section 363(k) of the Code, and as discussed *supra* at notes 168-169.

218.   11 U.S.C. § 1129(b)(2)(A)(ii).

219.   11 U.S.C. § 1129(b)(2)(A)(iii).

220.   *In re Murel Holding Corp.,* 75 F.2d 941 (2d Cir. 1935).

221.   *See* 124 Cong. Rec. H 11,1103 (Sept. 28, 1978); S 17,420 (Oct. 6, 1978) ("Abandonment of the collateral to the creditor would clearly satisfy indubitable equivalence, as would a lien on similar collateral."). Since the ultimate right of a secured creditor is to obtain its collateral, abandonment of the collateral to the secured creditor in satisfaction of the secured portion of its claims ordinarily should meet the indubitable equivalence standard. *In re Sandy Ridge Dev. Corp.*, 881 F.2d 1346, 1350 (5th Cir. 1989) (since the value of a secured claim is equal to the value of the collateral and since "common sense tells us that property is the indubitable equivalent of itself," a plan which provides that a secured creditor will receive its collateral on account of the secured

portion of its claim satisfies the "indubitable equivalent" requirement); *In re Park Forest Dev. Corp.*, 197 B.R. 388, 396 (Bankr. N.D. Ga. 1996); *but see In re Arnold & Baker Farms*, 85 F.3d 1415 (9th Cir. 1996) (finding that an insufficient basis existed to conclude that abandonment of *only a portion* of the collateral to the secured creditor met the indubitable equivalence standard), *cert. denied*, 117 S. Ct. 681 (1997). It is also worth noting that, if the proponent of a plan uses abandonment to satisfy § 1129(b), the members of the affected class have a right to a determination of the value of their collateral pursuant to § 506(a) as of the date of abandonment. The purpose of the valuation would be to determine the allowed amount of their unsecured claims. In order to determine the unsecured portion of its claims, any party in interest may request the court to determine the value of the collateral and to allow the class to vote its deficiency claims as provisionally allowed. *See* Bankruptcy Rule 3012.

222.   124 Cong. Rec. H 11,103 (Sept. 28, 1978); S 17,420 (Oct. 6, 1978).

223.   *Compare In re Sun Country Dev., Inc.*, 764 F.2d 406 (5th Cir. 1985) (affirming bankruptcy court's finding of indubitable equivalence where plan had substituted 21 notes secured by 21 lots for a single first lien on a 200-acre lot over the objection of the secured creditor that the present value of the notes was only 50% of its present lien and barely exceeded the amount of the debt) and *In re San Felipe @ Voss, Ltd.*, 115 B.R. 526 (S.D. Tex. 1990) (affirming confirmation of a plan that substituted cash, stock, and certain guarantees for a first priority lien on an office building complex) *with In re Sparks*, 171 B.R. 860 (Bankr. N.D. Ill. 1994) (cram down of debtor's plan refused and § 362(d)(2) relief from stay granted because debtor's future conversion of apartments to condominiums would place impermissible additional risk on creditor secured by apartments); *id.* at 866 (new collateral not "indubitable equivalent" if new collateral "is so much riskier than the original collateral that there is a substantially greater likelihood that the secured creditor will not be paid") and *In re Sunflower Racing, Inc.*, 219 B.R. 587, 601–602 (Bankr. D. Kan. 1998) (no "indubitable equivalent" for cram down in plan's proposal to provide lender future letter of credit on terms unknown to either lender or court). Some additional cases considering the question of what constitutes the indubitable equivalent of a secured creditor's claim include: *In re Hoff*, 54 B.R. 746, 753 (Bankr. D. N.D. 1985) (replacement lien on after-acquired livestock and crops grown is not the "indubitable equivalent" of lien on livestock and crops presently existing, since just one crop failure would leave the secured creditor's interest unprotected); *In re Keller*, 157 B.R. 680 (Bankr. E.D. Wash. 1993) (substitution of a commercial annuity contract in exchange for partial release of security interest in certain property may satisfy indubitable equivalent standard); *In re Future Energy Corp.*, 83 B.R. 470 (Bankr. S.D. Ohio 1988).

224.   *See In re Briscoe Enter., Ltd. II, supra* note 206, 994 F.2d at 1168.

225.   *See, e.g., In re MCorp. Fin., Inc.*, 137 B.R. 219, 235 (Bankr. S.D. Tex. 1992); Kenneth N. Klee, *Cram Down II*, 64 Am. Bankr. L. J. 229 (1989).

226.   *House Report, supra* note 2, at 414.

227.   As a general matter, courts have held that, in conducting valuations as part of confirmation proceedings, courts should use conservative standards of valuation in order to protect the interests of senior creditors. *See In re Evans Prod. Co.*, 65 B.R. 870, 876 (S.D. Fla. 1986) (rejecting equity holders' argument that a "more flexible" valuation standard should have been applied by the bankruptcy court to yield a higher valuation; stating that "the senior creditors' interest must be protected"); *In re Envirodyne Indus., Inc.*, Nos. 93 B 310–319, 1993 WL 566565, at *37 (Bankr. N.D. Ill. Dec. 20, 1993) ("When determining the value of securities distributed on confirmation, a court should use a conservative, "meticulous regard" standard to protect the rights of senior creditors"), *citing Consolidated Rock Products* v. *DuBois*, 312 U.S. 510 (1941).

228.   11 U.S.C. § 506(a) provides: "An allowed claim of a creditor secured by a lien on property in which the estate has an interest, or that is subject to setoff under Section 553 of this title, is a secured claim to the extent of the value of such creditor's interest in the estate's interest in such property, or to the extent of the amount subject to setoff, as the case may be, and is an unsecured claim to the extent that the value of such creditor's interest or the amount so subject to setoff is less than the amount of such allowed claim. Such value shall be determined in light of the purpose of the valuation and of the proposed disposition or use of such property, and in conjunction with any hearing on such disposition or use or on a plan affecting such creditor's interest."

229. This discretion, however, the Supreme Court has made clear does not allow a court to disregard the dictates of § 506(a). *See Associates Commercial Corp.* v. *Rash, supra* note 74, 117 S. Ct. at 1886 n. 5 ("As our reading of § 506(a) makes plain, we also reject a ruleless approach [to valuing the collateral] allowing use of different valuation standards based on the facts and circumstances of individual cases").

230. *House Report, supra* note 2, at 356.

231. The legislative history to § 506(a) so states: "[A] determination of what portion of an allowed claim is secured and what portion is unsecured is binding only for the purpose for which the determination is made. Thus determinations for purposes of adequate protection [are] not binding for purposes of 'cram down' on confirmation in a case under chapter 11."124 Cong. Rec. H. 11095 (Sept. 28, 1978); S. 17,411 (Oct. 6, 1978).

232. *See, e.g., In re Addison Properties Ltd. Partnership* 185 B.R. 766 (Bankr. E.D. Ill. 1995); *In re Moreau*, 135 B.R. 209, 212 (N.D. N.Y. 1992); *In the Matter of Atlanta Southern Bus. Park Ltd.*, 173 B.R. 444, 450 (Bankr. N.D. Ga. 1994); *In re Melgar Enter., Inc.*, 151 B.R. 34, 39 (Bankr. E.D. N.Y. 1993); *In re Seip*, 116 B.R. 709 (Bankr. D. Neb. 1990). *But see In re T-H New Orleans Ltd. Partnership*, 188 B.R. 799 (E.D. La. 1995), *aff'd*, 116 F.3d 790 (5th Cir. 1997) (holding that petition date valuation fixes valuation for all purposes in bankruptcy case, including confirmation); *In re Wood*, 190 B.R. 788 (Bankr. M.D. Pa. 1996) (date of filing; application of multifactor test); *In re Johnson*, 165 B.R. 524, 528-9 (S.D. Ga. 1994) (valuing collateral for purposes of cram down in chapter 13 case as of the date of filing); *In re Beard*, 108 B.R. 322 (Bankr. N.D. Ala. 1989) (date of filing).

233. *Rash, supra* note 74, 117 S. Ct. at 1882.

234. *Rash, supra* note 74, 117 S. Ct at 1884.

235. *See* cases cited *supra* at notes 221-223.

236. *See, e.g., In re T-H New Orleans Ltd. Partnership*, 116 F.3d 790 (5th Cir. 1997) (declining to establish one particular formula for determining cram down interest rate); *In re SM 104, supra* note 203.

237. *See In re Valenti*, 105 F.3d 55, 64 (2d Cir. 1997), *abrogated on other grounds by Assocs. Commercial Corp.* v. *Rash*, 117 S. Ct. 1879 (1997); *cf. In re Milham*, 141 F.3d 420 (2d Cir.), *cert. denied*, 119 S. Ct. 169 (1998) (oversecured creditor not entitled to its contract rate of interest postconfirmation if that rate will enable it to receive more than the present value of its claim as of the effective date of the plan).

238. *See, generally, 7 Collier on Bankruptcy* ¶ 1129.05 [2] [a] [ii] at 1129–1131 and 1129.06[1][c] at 1129–1146 (Lawrence P. King, Ed. 15th Ed. Rev. 1998).

239. 11 U.S.C. § 1111(b)(2).

240. 11 U.S.C. §§ 506(a) and 1111(b)(1)(A).

241. 11 U.S.C. §§ 1111(b)(1)(A)(i) and 1111(b)(2). The other situation in which the nonrecourse creditor's claim will not be recourse is when its collateral is sold under § 363 or is to be sold pursuant to the plan. For reasons discussed in the text, *infra*, the recourse creditor is also not permitted to make the election in these situations.

242. *See* 124 Cong. Rec. 32,406–32,407 (1978).

243. 11 U.S.C. § 1111(b)(1)(A).

244. Bankruptcy Rule 3014.

245. *Id.*

246. *See In re Keller*, 47 B.R. 725 (Bankr. N.D. Iowa 1985); *see, e.g., In re Bloomingdale Partners*, 155 B.R. 961, 971 (Bankr. N.D. Ill. 1993); *In re IPC Atlanta Ltd. Partnership*, 142 B.R. 547, 553–554 (Bankr. N.D. Ga. 1992).

247. 11 U.S.C. §1111(b)(1)(B).

8

Representing the Unsecured Creditors' Committee in Insolvency Restructurings

David S. Kurtz
Jeffrey W. Linstrom
Timothy R. Pohl

Skadden, Arps, Slate, Meagher & Flom LLP

INTRODUCTION

Whether in the context of an out-of-court restructuring, a chapter 11 case, or situations combining both, the unsecured creditors' committee operates as the essential counterpoint on behalf of unsecured creditors in the reorganization of the troubled enterprise. Under the Bankruptcy Code,[1] the unsecured creditors' committee acts as the statutory representative of the unsecured creditor body. In contrast, the unsecured creditors' committee in the out-of-court restructuring is a creature of expediency. Its role, however, is no less significant.

The fundamental objective of the unsecured creditors' committee is to protect the interests of unsecured creditors. In its most classic role, the unsecured creditors' committee will serve as the primary negotiating constituency for the unsecured creditors in developing a restructuring plan with the debtor. In reality, the committee's responsibilities frequently are much broader. Insolvency restructurings rarely are binary endeavors between the debtor and the unsecured creditors. Far more often, the successful restructuring requires that a consensus be forged among a constellation of interests consisting of secured debtholders, subordinated creditors, equityholders, insurance providers, and unions, among others. How alliances among these disparate groups ultimately

The authors wish to acknowledge the able assistance of Mark A. Cody in the preparation of this chapter.

are constructed often becomes critical to the outcome. Therefore, in addition, to its responsibilities vis-à-vis the debtor, the committee must protect the unsecured creditors from other constituencies who often are competing with the unsecured creditors for a greater share of a limited pool of assets available to fund recoveries.

In many instances, however, the most important contribution of the committee has nothing to do with protecting the unsecured creditors in relation to competing interests. Frequently, the unsecured creditors' committee becomes the instrument for developing consensus among the unsecured creditors themselves, and providing leadership to the unsecured creditors in general. It is the unusual situation indeed in which the unsecured creditors will not have disparate views as to the appropriate course of action to be taken in the case. These differences stem from a multiplicity of factors ranging from the nature of the committee members' claims, the status of their business relationship and future prospects with the debtor, to sheer differences in the personalities of their representatives. In the absence of the committee, it would be virtually impossible to reconcile these competing views in any rational manner. The first responsibility of the creditors' committee, therefore, is to mediate among the competing factions of its own constituency.

While the appointment of an unsecured creditors' committee is mandatory under the Bankruptcy Code, like a jury, there are few, if any, rules that govern its decision making once its membership is selected. In many respects, therefore, the committee becomes what its members choose it to be. There are wide variances in the approaches adopted by committees to their task. For example, some committees evidence a strong desire to become intimately involved in the operation of debtors' businesses, whereas other committees are content to concentrate only on the financial issues. There are committees who conduct their business with a high level of formality and others with complete informality. Some committees take a litigious approach while others are quite conciliatory. What is clear is that the creditors' committee represents a fascinating object of study.

This chapter will take a practical approach to the exploration of the creditors' committee in both the out-of-court and the chapter 11 reorganization. It is, therefore, intended to be useful to lawyers, financial professionals, and others associated with the restructuring process.

FORMATION OF CREDITORS' COMMITTEES

Out-of-Court Restructurings

Restructurings often begin with a triggering event. The event can be a financial covenant default, a payment default on a public debt instrument, announcement of a failed "saving" transaction (e.g., a merger), discovery of fraud or accounting irregularities, or a host of other possibilities. If the subject company has unsecured debt in the form of bank loans, publicly issued debentures, privately placed notes, or other forms of debt held by sophisticated institutional creditors, the triggering event frequently is followed by efforts of these creditors to organize and often to form "ad-hoc" or "unofficial" creditors' committees. Creditors support the formation of committees so as to provide the creditors with leadership, organization, and a unified voice throughout the restructuring. Debtors, if they are well represented or savvy, should and often do support the formation of an unofficial creditors' committee to provide them with an organized creditor representative with which to develop the restructuring plan. The formation of a creditors' committee or committees, which are sometimes denominated "steering committees," is a vital initial step in the development of an out-of-court restructuring process.

The committee formation process will vary with each out-of-court restructuring. Depending on the capital structure of the debtor, more than one committee may be formed. As an example, banks extending revolving or term facilities and insurance companies holding privately placed debt often establish separate committees. This is the case even where their respective debt obligations are of equal priority. Similarly, holders of unsecured public debentures and banks usually form separate committees in workouts. The formation of multiple committees in such circumstances is sometimes driven more by institutional adversity than economic or legal necessity.

From an economic or legal perspective, multiple committees are not obviously necessary where the debt is *pari passu* and the restructuring requires conversion of existing debt to equity or a combination of new debt and equity. In such situations, the type of debt held and its maturity date or interest rate may well become irrelevant. In a classic equity-for-debt swap, the holder of such bank debt or debentures each will receive the same common stock or debt/equity combination at the culmination of the restructuring, based on their pro rata share of outstanding total unsecured debt. Therefore, a holder of such bank debt may in appropriate circumstances be able to provide adequate representation of the insurance companies in negotiating the restructuring and vice versa.

However, at the infancy of the restructuring, it is difficult to see clearly to the end result. Creditors are likely to begin any restructuring focused more on their differences (rates of default interest, differing maturity dates, existence of makewhole payment obligations) than their similarities. Multiple committees acting as representatives of different creditor constituencies are, in the out-of-court restructuring, not uncommon. As a restructuring progresses and these initial differences become less important, or as different debt instruments trade hands to the same purchasers, multiple committees may merge or form a super committee to complete the restructuring process.

Multiple committees are to be expected when a debtor has a capital structure consisting of senior and subordinated unsecured debt. Senior and subordinated creditors' interests in a restructuring often are adverse. Senior creditors may look for a quick fix to the debtor's problems that pays senior debt obligations in full. On the other hand, subordinated creditors normally can be expected to pursue a strategy that gives the debtor sufficient opportunity to restructure its business, thereby enhancing enterprise value for the benefit of junior constituencies. In a debt-for-equity swap, senior creditors invariably will argue for a low enterprise valuation, thereby maximizing their percentage ownership of the restructured entity. Subordinated creditors will argue the exact opposite. The existence of these inherent adverse interests almost always results in the formation of separate committees for the senior and subordinated unsecured debt holders in an out-of-court restructuring.

Once creditors coalesce into one or more groups and begin formation of a single or multiple committees, selection of the membership of the committee becomes an issue. There is no right answer as to how many members should be appointed to a creditors' committee. The answer will vary with each restructuring, turning largely on how many creditors are interested in serving. Typically, committees in out-of-court restructurings consist of seven members or less. This is a manageable number that permits quorums to be achieved on short notice. Committees with more than approximately seven members can become unruly and difficult to keep organized and productive in a fast-paced restructuring in which meetings must be called with very short notice.

Who should serve on the out-of-court committee? Once again, there is no right answer. Typically, creditors follow an unwritten rule that "size matters." The largest holders of the unsecured debt usually are given the opportunity to fill the membership slots, if they so choose. The unwritten rule is premised on the theory that those creditors with the largest exposure have the greatest incentive to maximize their recovery, making them the best advocates for the unsecured creditors. The rule also stems from the practical issue of commitment of resources. Service on a creditors' committee can be a very time-consuming task. At certain periods of the restructuring, such as the initial phase where the parties are developing an expertise as to the debtor's circumstances and the issues that will drive the restructuring, the task can be all-consuming for the members of the committee. The creditors with the largest claims are likely to be more willing to devote the time and energy required by service on the committee than are creditors with smaller exposure.

Of course, the unwritten rule is not always followed. While the largest creditors usually are given the opportunity to serve, they do not always do so. Many factors can lead to the establishment of an out-of-court committee that contains members that do not hold claims larger than other creditors not serving on the committee. Increasingly, unsecured debt of all types in an out-of-court restructuring trade from original par holders of the debt to institutions whose business is investing and trading in distressed debt securities. Many of these secondary purchasers have a policy or practice of not serving on creditors' committees. The policy or practice stems in part from a concern that service on a creditors' committee, which undoubtedly will require the members to review confidential, nonpublic information, could affect the ability of these holders to continue purchasing or selling the debt or equity securities of the debtor. The result of this policy or practice is that more frequently in large out-of-court restructurings, several of the largest holders of unsecured debt may choose not to serve on the creditors' committee so they do not become restricted from future trading. This opens the door for holders of smaller amounts of debt to serve on committees where they otherwise would not have had the opportunity to do so.

Other factors also result in the unwritten rule of "size matters" from not being followed in establishing out-of-court committees. Creditors often recognize that the absolute size of the exposure to an institution is not a fair measure of the importance of the workout to the institution. For example, the agent for a syndicated credit facility may not have retained a sufficient amount of the loan to qualify as one of the seven largest creditors of the debtor. However, given the institutional importance of the matter to the creditor as agent and the unique responsibilities of an agent under the loan documents, the agent is likely to serve on the creditors' committee. Similarly, the relative size of a claim to a creditor, given its other investments, may make the workout extremely important to that creditor. For example, $50 million exposure to one of the world's largest financial institutions will not be as important as a $25 million exposure to a hedge fund with several hundred millions in investments. Creditors often voluntarily recognize that the matter may be extremely important on a relative basis to a fellow creditor and allow that creditor to serve on the committee.

In an out-of-court restructuring, who selects the members of the committee? The creditors themselves select their committee representatives through open dialogue at group meetings, backroom discussions, debate, arm-twisting, negotiating, and occasionally voting. It is the unusual situation in which trade creditors participate in the out-of-court restructuring. This is because the continuing support of trade creditors through ongoing shipments of goods and/or raw materials is essential to the debtor's operations. Creditors that are interested in serving on the committee are advised to make that interest known immediately to fellow creditors. A creditor on the cusp of being on the committee as one of the qualifying largest creditors and interested in serving is well advised to solicit support from fellow creditors. Similarly, creditors who hold claims that are smaller than the seven largest and are interested in serving for a unique reason (e.g., the exposure is a relatively large one for the creditor) should also begin soliciting support from fellow creditors and alert them to their unique situations.

Chapter 11 Cases

The General Process of Appointment and Eligibility Issues. The formation of an official creditors' committee in a chapter 11 case is a very different process than in an out-of-court restructuring. First, the process is governed by statute, not by unwritten rules.[2] Second, the power of selection is vested in the United States trustee rather than creditors themselves.[3] Third, the process is subject to challenge and is judicially reviewable.

Section 1102 of the Bankruptcy Code governs the formation of a creditors' committee in a chapter 11 case. Specifically, Section 1102(a)(1) provides:

> Except as provided in paragraph (3), as soon as practicable after the order for relief under chapter 11 of this title, the United States trustee shall appoint a committee of creditors holding unsecured claims and may appoint

additional committees of creditors or of equity security holders as the United States trustee deems appropriate.

Section 1102(a)(1), mandates the appointment by the U.S. trustee of a creditors' committee in all chapter 11 cases with one exception. The one exception is set forth in Section 1102(a)(3):

On request of a party-in-interest in a case in which the debtor is a small business and for cause, the court may order that a committee of creditors not be appointed.

A *small business* is defined by Section 101(51C) of the Bankruptcy Code as a business whose total noncontingent secured and unsecured debts do not exceed $2 million. The small business exception was added to Section 1102 in 1994 as part of the Bankruptcy Reform Act of 1994.[4] The exception recognizes that in cases in which the amount at stake is relatively small, it is frequently difficult to find creditors willing to make the commitment required for committee service. In addition, the attendant cost in fees and expenses may not be justifiable in such small cases.

Section 1102(a)(1) identifies entities eligible to serve on a creditors' committee as "creditors holding unsecured claims." Two of these four words are defined in the Bankruptcy Code: creditor[5] and claim[s].[6] Creditor is defined to include any entity that has a prepetition claim against the debtor.[7] "Claim" is defined broadly and includes contingent, unliquidated, and disputed claims.[8]

Because of the broad definition of claim in the Bankruptcy Code, eligibility to serve on a creditors' committee may extend beyond traditional notions. For example, is a landlord eligible to be appointed to the creditors' committee in the debtor's case in which that debtor, a retailer, is current on all of its rent obligations at the time of filing? Yes, because landlords hold contingent claims against the debtor under their leases. These contingent claims include a possible claim for breach should the debtor choose to reject any of the leases under Section 365 of the Bankruptcy Code.[9] In addition, entities asserting claims against a debtor that are disputed in their entirety may, interestingly, also serve on the committee.[10] Therefore, creditors' committees can consist of parties beyond trade creditors and holders of funded debt. Even certain governmental units are statutorily eligible to serve on creditors' committees.

The words *holding* and *unsecured* in Section 1102(a)(1), while not defined, have well-accepted meanings in the context of Section 1102. Holding requires the creditor to presently own the claim. If the creditor sells its claim against the debtor, then it will no longer presently own the claim and is no longer qualified under Section 1102 to serve on the creditors' committee. With the increasing frequency of such claims trading, the membership of creditors' committees often changes in chapter 11 cases.

Finally, unsecured obviously means that the creditors' claim must not be fully secured by a lien on any collateral owned by the debtor. Creditors with fully secured claims are thought to have their own unique interests to protect in a chapter 11 case given their collateral positions and may not serve on the unsecured creditors' committee.[11] Section 506(a) of the Bankruptcy Code divides a claim of a creditor holding a lien on property of a debtor into two types of claims if the value of the collateral is less than the outstanding debt: a secured claim up to the value of the collateral and an unsecured claim for the balance of the debt. Is a secured creditor holding an unsecured deficiency claim eligible to serve on a creditors' committee? Technically, yes, but the practical answer varies.[12] U.S. trustees typically are unwilling to place an undersecured creditor on an unsecured creditors' committee unless the collateralized segment of the claim represents only a small percentage of the total debt, on the theory that the partially secured creditor may be unsuitable to serve as the fiduciary representative of unsecured creditors.

Section 1102(a)(1) sets forth the statutory eligibility for service on a creditors' committee. Section 1102(b)(1) establishes a framework for choosing who should be appointed from among those who are eligible. Section 1102(b)(1) provides:

> A committee of creditors appointed under subsection (a) of this section shall ordinarily consist of the persons, willing to serve, that hold the seven largest claims against the debtor of the kinds represented on such committee. . . .

The legislative history underlying Section 1102(b)(1) and case law recognize that the guidelines for appointment therein are precatory and not mandatory.[13] At least four categories of creditors have been the subject of dispute as to their eligibility to serve on chapter 11 creditors' committees, labor unions, indenture trustees, competitors of debtors, and claims purchasers.

Are labor unions technically "creditors" of a debtor? Certainly, their employee members meet the definition, but unions usually will not. Without being actual creditors of a debtor, can unions serve on creditors' committees? Recognizing that unions often play a crucial role in chapter 11 cases, U.S. trustees and courts have appointed labor unions to creditors' committees.[14] Unions represent the debtor's current employees and retirees that, in the aggregate, sometimes represent the largest unsecured claims against the debtor's estate.[15] Thus, the failure to appoint certain unions to the committee in such cases would leave unrepresented those interests that might be critical to the development of a successful plan of reorganization.[16]

Indenture trustees are similar to labor unions in that they serve as agents or representatives of creditors of a debtor.[17] The general practice is that indenture trustees are appointed to creditors' committees in cases involving public debentures.[18]

Debtors and creditors alike have disputed the propriety of including a debtor's competitors as members of the creditors' committee in a chapter 11 case. As a member of the creditors' committee, the competitor could gain access to trade secrets or other confidential trade-related information that it might well use to its advantage against the debtor. In addition, because of the very nature of a competitor's relationship to the debtor, the interests of the competitor/creditor are quite different from those of the other unsecured creditors.[19] Consequently, certain courts have disqualified competitors of the debtor from serving on the creditors' committee.[20] Despite these concerns, however, other courts have reached the opposite conclusion and permitted the debtor's competitors to serve.[21]

Can creditors whose claims have been purchased at a discount to face value sit on a creditors' committee? There is no distinction in the Bankruptcy Code between an "original" creditor and secondary purchaser of debt. Therefore, claims purchasers are eligible to serve on the creditors' committee under the language of the statute. Nevertheless, U.S. trustees in certain regions have not been eager to appoint claims purchasers to committees. This grows out of concern that the claims purchasers, motivated as they are by a desire to profit on a debt investment purchased at a discount, may not be suitable to represent in a fiduciary capacity the interests of the general unsecured creditor constituency in obtaining the fullest possible recovery for their class members. Occasionally, where claims purchasers have not been placed on the committee or where large amounts of debt trading have occurred after the committee was selected, the voting members of the committee will wish to involve in committee deliberations such debt purchasers that are likely to hold a significant amount of the unsecured claims against the debtor when it is time to solicit votes on a plan of reorganization. Since the committee determines its own method of self-governance, one practical option is for the committee to invite key secondary investors to serve on the committee in a nonvoting *ex officio* position. Since many committees make decisions by consensus, the nonvoting status of secondary purchasers may be treated by committees largely as irrelevant. The official committee members may well welcome the opportunity to involve a member of the distressed investing community into the midst of the committee process.

Formation Mechanics.   When a debtor files its chapter 11 case, it is required by Federal Rule of Bankruptcy Procedure 1007(d) to file a "List of Creditors Holding 20 Largest Unsecured Claims."[22] The official form for the "Top Twenty List," as it is called, provides that insiders[23] should be excluded as well as secured creditors unless their deficiency claims (i.e., their claims after subtracting from their debt the value of the collateral securing such debt) place them among the top twenty largest unsecured creditors. The Top Twenty List is used by the U.S. trustee to appoint the creditors' committee. The general practice of U.S. trustee offices is to distribute to the creditors identified on the Top Twenty List a written form on which the creditors can indicate whether they are interested in serving on the creditors' committee. In large cases, the U.S. trustee's office usually will call an organizational meeting of the top twenty unsecured creditors within the first two weeks of the case. At that meeting, the U.S. trustee will hear input from creditors and then appoint the creditors' committee.

A host of factors affects the U.S. trustee's decision in selecting creditors to serve on a creditors' committee. While Section 1102(b)(1) provides that "ordinarily" a creditors' committee should consist of creditors holding the seven largest unsecured claims, U.S. trustees by no means blindly follow the statute. First, in large cases, U.S. trustees often appoint committees having more than seven members. Second, U.S. trustees usually will attempt to achieve diversity among the committee members that reflects the composition of the unsecured creditor constituency.

Assume, for example, that a retail debtor's Top Twenty List identifies as the largest top unsecured creditors: six banks under a revolving credit facility, five insurance companies holding privately placed notes, five holders of publicly issued bonds, and four trade creditors. The top seven of these twenty include four banks, two insurance companies, one debenture holder, and none of the trade creditors. Under these facts, it would be rare that the U.S. trustee would appoint a committee consisting of the top seven unsecured creditors. More likely, the U.S. trustee will conclude that the committee should consist of representatives of all of the major creditor consistencies that are involved in the case. Accordingly, the U.S. trustee will weigh the relative amounts of bank debt, note debt, debenture debt, and trade debt in constituting the committee. A committee consisting of two banks, one insurance company, one debenture holder, two trade creditors, and one landlord would not be a surprising result. The U.S. trustee is left with wide discretion to choose a committee that he or she believes will adequately represent all unsecured creditors in the case.

In contrast to committees formed in out-of-court restructurings, in chapter 11 cases hybrid committees consisting of multiple constituencies of unsecured debt are the norm rather than the exception. It is the unusual case in which multiple unsecured creditors' committees are formed, and, when done, one of two circumstances typically is found to exist. First, if the debtor filed its chapter 11 case along with other related entities, such as wholly owned subsidiaries, the U.S. trustee may appoint a creditors' committee for the parent and a separate one for one or more of its affiliates.[24] This is more likely to happen where separate debtors operate distinct businesses with segregated assets and liabilities in significant amounts.

Second, multiple creditors' committees are sometimes formed by U.S. trustees for a single debtor where the capital structure consists of senior and junior unsecured debt. The U.S. trustee may conclude that the primary creditors' committee should consist of senior debt and an additional committee should be appointed to adequately represent the interests of subordinated holders. Section 1102(a)(1) expressly provides the U.S. trustee with the authority to appoint one or more additional committees of unsecured creditors for a single debtor.[25] The case law is clear, however, that the U.S. trustee in such circumstances has no obligation to appoint a "junior" committee and may, and frequently does, place subordinated debtholders on a committee with senior creditors.[26]

Appointment of a Prepetition Committee as the Postpetition Committee. Assume the debtor files a chapter 11 case after a year of out-of-court restructuring efforts with a plan of reorganization negotiated and agreed to by an unofficial committee of unsecured creditors. The purpose of the bankruptcy is to effectuate the negotiated settlement. Both the debtor and the unsecured creditors will desire that the unofficial committee become the official committee in the chapter 11 case to ensure continuity with respect to the prepetition negotiations. Section 1102(b)(1) expressly provides for this result so long as the committee "was fairly chosen and is representative of the different kinds of claims to be represented." Therefore, if the U.S. trustee believes the prepetition committee meets this test, he or she has the statutory authority to adopt the prepetition committee as the unsecured creditors' committee in the bankruptcy case.

What is the test for determining whether the committee (a) was "fairly chosen" and (b) is "representative of the different kinds of claims to be represented in the case"? Federal Rule of Bankruptcy Procedure 2007 (b) provides a litmus test for determining whether a prepetition committee was "fairly chosen" that, as a practical matter, no committee formed in an out-of-court restructuring will ever meet. The test requires that the committee was chosen by recorded vote at a meeting of the 100 largest unsecured creditors called after five days' written notice. This level of formality rarely, if ever, happens in the selection of the out-of-court committee. Fortunately, the advisory committee notes and commentators agree that this test is a permissive one and does not serve to automatically disqualify a committee not formed in accordance with the rule.[27]

Judicial Review of Appointment of Creditors' Committees. In out-of-court restructurings, creditors that are not successful in being appointed to an unofficial committee have no recourse for judicial review. In chapter 11 cases, the bankruptcy court maintains a level of discretion in reviewing the U.S. trustee's decision making in selecting the creditors' committee. Can the bankruptcy court disband the committee appointed by the U.S. trustee? Can the bankruptcy court order the U.S. trustee to appoint a specific creditor or type of creditor to an existing creditors' committee? Or is the bankruptcy court limited in its authority only to order the U.S. trustee to appoint an additional committee, leaving the existing committee in place? Courts are split on these issues.

In 1986, Congress amended the Bankruptcy Code by deleting Section 1102(c), which had provided that a bankruptcy court could change the membership or size of a committee.[28] The only remedy specifically left in the statute for bankruptcy courts to alter the committee structure established by the U.S. trustee is to "order the appointment of additional committees of creditors. . . . The United States trustee shall appoint any such committee."[29] Certain courts have held that the plain language of Section 1102(a)(2) combined with the deletion of Section 1102(c) in 1986 and its accompanying legislative history preclude the bankruptcy court from changing the membership or reconstituting a creditors' committee,[30] and limit its authority to the appointment of additional committees. Other courts take a diametrically opposed view and hold that the appointment of a creditors' committee is subject to *de novo* review by a bankruptcy court.[31]

There is also a line of cases setting forth a middle ground. These cases hold that a bankruptcy court can review the appointment of a creditors' committee by the U.S. trustee and can order the U.S. trustee to change the membership of the committee, but to do so, the court must find that the U.S. trustee abused his or her discretion in appointing the committee.[32] Under this approach, a court will not substitute its own judgment for that of the U.S. trustee in determining who should serve on a committee. Rather, the court may change the composition of the committee only if it first determines that the U.S. trustee acted arbitrarily and capriciously or whether relevant factors that should have been considered were not taken into account.[33]

In order for a court applying this standard to find that the appointment or failure to appoint a particular creditor to serve on a committee was arbitrary or capricious, the court must determine that the decision was based on an unsound legal conclusion, the evidence on the record shows that no rational party could have rendered such a decision, or the decision is "otherwise patently unreasonable, arbitrary or fanciful."[34] If the party opposing the committee appointment determination of the U.S. trustee is unable to show that the decision lacked a rational basis, then it will not prevail.[35] Application of this standard by a court ensures that a U.S. trustee does not have unreviewable authority over the composition of the committee in a chapter 11 case.[36] Nevertheless, establishing that the U.S. trustee acted arbitrarily or capriciously is no easy task for the objecting creditor. The party challenging the composition of a committee must provide strong evidence to persuade the court that the U.S. trustee's decision was devoid of logic or legal basis.

Those courts have determined that a court has the power to review the composition of the committee appointed by the U.S. trustee. These courts rely upon the authority granted to the court by Bankruptcy Rule 2020. Bankruptcy Rule 2020 permits a court to review the U.S. trustee's actions or failure to act. In addition, Section 105 of the Bankruptcy Code arguably provides a court with further ammunition in justifying any review of the U.S. trustee's committee member choices. Section 105(a) of the Bankruptcy Code provides bankruptcy courts with powers to "issue any order, process, or judgment that is necessary or appropriate to carry out the provisions of" chapter 11.

The ability of a party-in-interest to obtain relief from the bankruptcy court with respect to the U.S. trustee's appointment of a creditors' committee will turn in part on which line of cases the bankruptcy court follows. If the bankruptcy court follows the line of cases holding the courts cannot change membership of committees, then the only available remedy would be the appointment of an additional committee. Such relief will be granted only in unusual circumstances. "In recognition of the Bankruptcy Code scheme that the reconciliation of differing interests of creditors within a single committee is the norm, and that the appointment of a separate committee is an extraordinary remedy, . . . courts have been reluctant to appoint additional committees."[37]

If the bankruptcy court permits the remedy of adding members, then the outcome of a challenge to the U.S. trustee's decision may well depend on the standard of review adopted by the bankruptcy court. If the standard of review is *de novo*, then the party need only convince the court that the right decision is for the movant to be placed on the committee.[38] If the standard of review is abuse of discretion, then the movant must convince the court that the U.S. trustee acted without reason in leaving the creditor off the committee.[39]

A familiar battleground over the appointment of creditors' committees, both at the U.S. trustee level and before the bankruptcy court, is the attempt by subordinated creditors to obtain their own committee. Junior creditors will argue that a creditors' committee dominated by senior creditors cannot adequately represent the interests of junior creditors, given the typically adverse nature of their relationship. Courts have been reluctant to order the appointment of such committees because of intercreditor conflicts. "[C]ommittees often contain creditors having a variety of viewpoints. Conflicts are not unusual in reorganization and in most cases can be expected among creditors who are acting to protect their separate business interests. . . . The inclusion of such groups within one committee may facilitate the consensual resolution of the conflicting priorities among the holders of unsecured claims, and thereby facilitate the negotiation of a consensual plan."[40] Other courts have indicated that it is exactly these types of intercreditor conflicts that can require appointment of a separate committee. "Thus the chief concern of adequacy of representation is whether it appears that different classes of debt . . . may be treated differently under a plan and need representation through appointment of additional committees."[41] These decisions on appointment of additional committees are not consistent and the result will depend largely on the philosophical predilections of the U.S. trustee or court making the determination.

Unofficial Committees in Chapter 11.   Finally, a group of creditors has the right to form an unofficial creditors' committee in a chapter 11 case. Bankruptcy Rule 2019 governs situations involving such ad hoc committees. Rule 2019 requires that any unofficial committee file a verified statement setting forth the names and addresses of each committee member, the nature and amount of each such member's claim, the names of the entities that arranged the committee's formation, and the date that any committee member's claims were purchased and at what price. Interestingly, Rule 2019 requires disclosure of information, such as when a claim is purchased and at what price, not required to be disclosed by a member of a committee appointed pursuant to Section 1102 of the Bankruptcy Code.

In the event that an unofficial committee does not comply with the disclosure requirements described above, Rule 2019 provides that upon notice of a party-in-interest, or *sua sponte*, the court may refuse to allow an unofficial committee to be heard or intervene in the case. Any relief previously given to or provided by an unofficial committee may be invalidated if the disclosure requirements summarized above are determined not to have been satisfied.

Retention of Professionals by Creditors' Committees

To perform their intended functions, creditors' committees will require the services of professionals. A creditors' committee will require legal advice for the myriad of issues to be faced in the restructuring or chapter 11 case. A creditors' committee often requires the additional services of financial advisors to advise on the debtor's performance and strategic options available to creditors, such as the sale of all or a segment of the debtor's business. These financial advisors usually are accounting firms, boutique restructuring advisory firms or investment banking firms, and the creditors' committee must conclude which is best suited for the restructuring at hand. Some situations will call for a combination of more than one such firm.

Normally, in an out-of-court restructuring, as in chapter 11, the debtor will agree to bear the cost of the creditors' committee professionals. In a chapter 11 case, the fees and expenses of the creditors' committee professionals are always borne by the estate.[42] In a chapter 11 case, retention of professionals such as lawyers and accountants is expressly authorized by Section 1103 of the Bankruptcy Code. Section 1103(a) provides:

> At a scheduled meeting of a committee appointed under Section 1102 of this title, at which a majority of the members of such committee are present, and with the court's approval, such committee may select and authorize the employment by such committee of one or more attorneys, accountants, or other agents, to represent or perform services for such committee.

Section 1103(a) requires that bankruptcy court approval of the creditors' committee's retention of professionals is required. Court approval is obtained by the filing of retention applications by each professional for the creditors' committee. Rule 2014 of the Bankruptcy Rules sets forth a list of informational requirements that must be included in such retention application. While parties in interest and the U.S. trustee can object to these retention applications, in out-of-court restructurings there is little opportunity for other parties to interfere with the choice of professionals made by committees.

Sections 328 and 1103 of the Bankruptcy Code govern compensation and retention of professionals by creditors' committees. Section 1103(b) provides that an attorney or accountant may be employed so long as they do not "represent any other entity having an adverse interest in connection with the case." For example, counsel to the committee could not also represent a shareholder of the debtor in the chapter 11 case. Can counsel to the committee also represent creditors of the debtor that do not serve on the creditors' committee? The answer will depend on several factors. Section 1103(b) eschews an absolute rule, specifically providing that representation of one or more creditors of the same class as represented by the committee shall not *per se* constitute the representation of an adverse interest.

However, even if the creditor client is of the same class represented by the committee, counsel must consider whether there are circumstances unique to the creditor's claim or status that could create a conflict with the interests of the unsecured creditors generally. Perhaps the creditor received a fraudulent conveyance or preferential transfer potentially recoverable for the benefit of the estate under Section 550 of the Bankruptcy Code. Or the creditor may have a unique interest in seeing the case turn out a certain way that may or may not be in the best interests of unsecured creditors. For example, the creditor could be a major supplier of the debtor who will favor a reorganization over a liquidation even though liquidation could benefit the general creditor constituency. Obviously, no such representation should be taken on without prior consultation with the committee and disclosure to the bankruptcy court, as required under Bankruptcy Rule 2014(a).

Section 328 of the Bankruptcy Code addresses compensation of professionals retained by the committees and, in what most practitioners believe is a drafting anomaly, sets up a stricter compensation standard than the "no adverse interest" retention standard of Section 1103. Section 328(c) provides in relevant part:

> The court may deny allowance of compensation for services and reimbursement of expenses of a professional person employed under Section 1103 of this title if, at any time during such professional person's employment under Section 1103 of this title, such professional person is not a *disinterested person*, or represents or holds an interest adverse to the interest of the estate with respect to the matter on which such professional person is employed (emphasis added).

The term *disinterested person*, is defined in Section 101(14) of the Bankruptcy Code.[43] The inclusion of the disinterested person standard in Section 328 notwithstanding its omission from Section 1103 creates the statutorily unusual result that professionals retained by creditors' committees may be retained without meeting the disinterested person standard, but possibly not compensated under Section 328 unless they meet the requirement. Retention without compensation is not appealing to most professionals. Therefore, professionals retained by creditors' committees should make sure they qualify as disinterested persons under Section 101(14) of the Bankruptcy Code.

In determining whether a professional retained in a chapter 11 case fits within the definition of "disinterested person," courts scrutinize whether any relationships present a conflict that impacts a professional's "loyalty and confidentiality."[44] Although the term *adverse interest* is not defined by the Bankruptcy Code, courts have interpreted it as meaning "any interest or relationship, however slight, 'that would even faintly color the independence and impartial attitude required by the Code and Bankruptcy Rules.'"[45] This general definition of adverse interest tends to encompass economic interests such that if a professional represented the committee in light of an adverse interest, its ability to provide the committee with undivided loyalty would somehow be impaired.[46]

In *In re Marvel Entertainment Group, Inc.*,[47] the Third Circuit discussed in great detail the disinterested person requirement. In *Marvel*, the U.S. trustee appointed John Gibbons of Gibbons, Del Deo, Dolan, Griffinger & Vecchione as chapter 11 trustee. Gibbons then filed a motion to retain Gibbons Del Deo as counsel to the chapter 11 trustee. In its retention application, Gibbons Del Deo disclosed that it had represented Chase Manhattan Bank, a creditor in the bankruptcy, in a matter totally unrelated to the bankruptcy, and that it had since terminated its representation of Chase entirely. Despite the fact that Gibbons Del Deo no longer represented Chase and that Gibbons, a named partner, had already been selected to serve as chapter 11 trustee, the District Court disqualified Gibbons Del Deo because its former "representation of Chase taints the image of objectivity that the trustee and his counsel should possess."[48]

On appeal, the Court of Appeals for the Third Circuit reversed the district court and remanded with the direction that the court grant the employment application of Gibbons Del Deo.[49] In so holding, the Third Circuit determined that the district court had applied an improper legal standard in evaluating Gibbons Del Deo's retention application.[50] In reversing the district court, the Third Circuit stated that a professional can only be disqualified if it has an actual or potential conflict of interest, which it ruled Gibbons Del Deo did not.[51] "Therefore, the district court erred when it held that it could disqualify as disinterested any person who 'in the slightest degree might have some interest or relationship that would even faintly color the independence and impartial attitude required by the Code and the Bankruptcy Rules.'"[52]

Governance Issues for Creditors' Committees

Chapter 11 creditors' committees begin operating at the initial formation meeting called by the U.S. trustee. At that meeting, one of the first steps towards organization and governance is taken: the selection of a chairperson. Typically, the chairperson is the creditor with the largest claim willing to serve. The existence, however, of different types of creditors on the committee may yield a different result. For example, if the committee consists of banks and trade creditors, neither the banks nor trade creditors may be comfortable with one or the other type of creditor serving as chairperson. The compromise may be the selection of the largest bank creditor and the largest trade creditor as co-chairpersons.

The next task to organize the committee and determine how it will be governed will fall on counsel selected by the committee. Counsel usually will be asked to prepare bylaws for the committee that will serve as the constitutive document determining how the committee will operate and be governed. The bylaws should cover the eight topics discussed below and any others unique to the case:

1. Representatives of creditors. The U.S. trustee appoints institutions to the creditors' committee, not individuals. Bylaws should designate for each institutional member the individual representative of the institution who will be active on the committee on behalf of that creditor. The bylaws should also provide for each institution to designate alternate individuals to participate in committee deliberations when the primary individual is not available.
2. Resignation of creditors. The bylaws should anticipate that creditors may resign from the committee during the case. The bylaws should establish a procedure for resignation (e.g., automatic if a claim is sold, otherwise on written notice to chairperson) and a process for the committee to recommend a replacement creditor to the U.S. trustee. Some bylaws also contain a provision establishing circumstances under which it might be appropriate to remove a committee member. These provisions typically establish a litany of factors establishing "cause" for removal and require a two-thirds

vote for recommendation of the committee to the U.S. trustee to remove a member.[53]

3. Powers of chairperson. The bylaws should provide the unique powers and duties of the chairperson. These typically consist of the power to call meetings and act for the committee as to routine matters (e.g., asset sales below a specified dollar amount).

4. Governance of meetings. The bylaws should establish how meetings can be called, procedures for emergency meetings called on short notice, the quorum necessary to conduct meetings, actions that can be taken without meetings, ability to meet in person or by phone, and voting standards and procedures for meetings. Typically, committees operate on a "one-member, one-vote" rule with a majority vote required to take action. Supermajority votes usually are required for extraordinary action such as recommendation to remove a member. Special circumstances of a case or the makeup of a committee may require tailored voting procedures. For example, trade creditors may require that the committee take no action on reclamation issues without the affirmative vote of two trade creditors. Counsel should solicit input from the committee to determine if such special voting procedures are required in a case.

5. Conflicts of interest. The bylaws should require each member to disclose to the committee any potential conflict of interest it may have on a particular issue. The bylaws should provide for a procedure to determine if the potential conflict rises to the level of an actual conflict requiring that member of the committee to be recused from participating in deliberations on the matter.

6. Confidentiality. The bylaws should contain a provision restraining members from disclosing confidential information received as a member of the committee. The bylaws should also provide that a member of the committee cannot disclose attorney–client privileged information or work product or waive the attorney–client privilege of the committee.

7. Communications with nonmember creditors. The bylaws should establish a procedure by which the committee and/or individual members can communicate with nonmember creditors.

8. Subcommittees. If the committee desires to establish subcommittees, the bylaws should provide how the subcommittees will be formed, what their powers will be, and how they will meet and take action, as well as procedures for keeping the full committee informed of their actions.

The bylaws should be considered carefully by the committee to make sure they address any issues specific to the case.

The frequency and length of creditors' committee meetings will be determined by the demands of the chapter 11 case. Most committees try to meet telephonically on a regular basis, with in-person meetings reserved for important events or for meetings that the debtor will attend. These meetings usually are organized by the chairperson and cover an agenda previously identified to the members. Professionals often are asked to make reports to the committee at the meetings on the progress of matters they are working on for the committee.

Creditors experienced at serving on committees recognize that the use of subcommittees can dramatically improve the efficiency of the committee in whole. Certain tasks of the committee either do not require all members to be involved or cannot support the involvement of all members, such as monitoring the flow of routine motions filed in the case. In many cases, committees will establish a small plan negotiating team or plan subcommittee to conduct face-to-face negotiations on a plan of reorganization with the debtor and other significant parties-in-interest. Negotiations between the full committee and these other parties-in-interest, augmented by their full complement of professionals, is unruly and often counterproductive. By reducing the number of cooks in the kitchen, progress can be made quicker on reaching a consensual plan. Of course, the primary task of a creditors' committee is negotiating a plan of reorganization. The full committee will want to have established a general framework for its plan negotiating team or subcommittee to ensure that negotiations proceed toward a plan acceptable to the full committee.

PRIMARY FUNCTIONS OF UNSECURED CREDITORS' COMMITTEES

Functions Applicable in Out-of-Court Workouts and Chapter 11 Cases

In either an out-of-court workout or a chapter 11 case, the committee's primary function in the restructuring process is to maximize the recovery for the constituency it represents. In many respects, a committee's activities are substantially similar both out of court and in bankruptcy.

Fiduciary Duties.   In chapter 11 cases, committees serve as fiduciaries for the constituency they represent.[54] As a result, in chapter 11 cases, creditors not on the committee can take comfort that they are being adequately represented in the negotiating process. A committee member's fiduciary duties are those of care, loyalty, and obedience to the committee's constituency.[55] These fiduciary duties extend only to members of the class of creditors that the committee represents.[56]

To encourage participation on the creditors' committee, courts have crafted certain rights of qualified immunity for committee members.[57] Although a member of a creditors' committee clearly should be held accountable for a willful breach of its fiduciary duty to its constituency, committee members should be accorded protection for actions taken in good faith and in furtherance of committee business.[58] Thus, the general trend is to offer committee members a qualified immunity to any liability for actions taken during the proper performance of its duties.[59] Generally, this immunity "must be limited to actions taken within the scope of the committee's authority as conferred by statute or the court and may not extend to 'willful misconduct' of the committee or its members."[60]

In an out-of-court workout, whether a committee functions as a legal fiduciary for other creditors is less clear. Unlike a chapter 11 committee, a committee in an out-of-court workout has not been appointed by the United States trustee or any other government agency, nor has it been formed as a result of a statutory mandate. There is, nevertheless, a small body of case law that suggests that in the out-of-court workout the committee's fiduciary duties essentially parallel those of a chapter 11 committee.[61] A committee in an out-of-court workout may take certain steps to minimize the prospects that it will be deemed to have acted in a fiduciary capacity. Many committees will explicitly disclaim any fiduciary obligations. In addition, because committee composition in an out-of-court proceeding is determined privately by the creditors themselves, a committee may limit its members to a single type of creditor (e.g., public debtholders), minimizing the prospects of having to compromise intercreditor issues among the members of the committee. In any event, a creditor considering serving on a committee, in court or out, should be prepared to accept the responsibility of a fiduciary, even if that creditor intends to pursue its own interests individually in the case.[62]

Operational, Financial, and Legal Investigation.   Both because of the fiduciary nature of the committee and to enable the committee to advocate effectively on behalf of unsecured creditors, a committee must ensure that it becomes fully knowledgeable about the debtor's operational and financial affairs. In large or complex cases, this typically requires substantial due diligence, both financial and legal.

Financial due diligence usually begins immediately, as a committee must assess a debtor's financial and operational status quickly. Both in court and out, a committee likely will rely heavily on the advice of financial advisors to form a view as to whether a restructuring or liquidation is likely to provide a better outcome for creditors. At some point in the proceeding, unless the answer is clear on the surface, the committee's financial advisors usually will prepare an analysis and estimate of creditor recoveries if the debtor were liquidated in the most efficient manner practicable. Of course, any such analysis is premised on numerous assumptions, and thus the liquidation baseline begins with an inherent element of uncertainty and risk. That uncertainty is greater or smaller depending on the composition of the debtor's assets.

Even early in the case, differences among committee members may become apparent. For example, vendors may be willing to consider that an ancillary benefit of restructuring compared to liquidation (ancillary to the derivation of maximum return on existing debts) is having a customer to sell to in the future. Landlords may prefer not to lose the debtor as a tenant. Conversely, other creditors may prefer a quick liquidation and payout rather than taking the risks inherent in being repaid with securities to be issued by a reorganized debtor. Again, a well-advised committee will strive to balance those competing interests rather than allowing creditor fragmentation to stall the restructuring process.

A committee's attorneys also will be required to advise the committee quickly on numerous issues that arise early in the restructuring process. In a chapter 11 case, the debtor will have filed the petition commencing the case along with numerous motions seeking bankruptcy court relief that the debtor believes is critical to its survival and prospects for a successful turnaround. These motions will involve matters such as proposed financing, proposed payroll and employment compensation relief, and matters affecting the manner in which a case may be managed. A committee will rely heavily on its counsel to advise it as to the propriety, wisdom, and necessity of these requests.

In addition, throughout the restructuring process, the committee will continue to monitor the debtor's affairs. A principal part of the committee's job is to be in a position to form its own independent judgments regarding how a debtor's business is being managed and a debtor's restructuring and business initiatives. In fact, the committee may challenge the propriety or wisdom of company activities or initiatives, or lack thereof, that would otherwise be within the sole purview of the debtor's board of directors and senior officers. Because any nonordinary course decision by a debtor requires bankruptcy court approval,[63] the committee will have an opportunity to influence matters normally within the exclusive province of a debtor's management.

In the face of resistance by a debtor to a committee's efforts to complete a thorough investigation of a debtor's financial and legal affairs, a committee has certain options available to it. In an out-of-court workout, creditors facing an uncooperative debtor may refuse to engage in negotiations and instead commence litigation to enforce their claims. If certain statutory requirements are met, creditors can file an involuntary petition for chapter 11 relief against a debtor.[64] The undesirability of these actions is usually enough to garner sufficient due diligence cooperation from the debtor.

In a chapter 11 case, a committee gains the benefit of statutory authority giving it the explicit legal right to obtain information about a debtor's affairs. That right is extremely broad. Section 1103(c)(2) of the Bankruptcy Code authorizes a committee to investigate any matter related to the case or formulation of a plan.[65] Moreover, a committee may initiate an examination of the debtor or any other person or entity pursuant to Bankruptcy Rule 2004.[66] The scope of a Rule 2004 examination is far reaching, having even been characterized as encompassing a "fishing expedition."[67]

Management Issues.   In some cases, a committee will have doubts as to the ability or willingness of a debtor's board or management to act in a manner consistent with the best interests of creditors. Once a debtor enters the vicinity of insolvency, the primary fiduciary duties of the board of directors are to creditors.[68] Nevertheless, board members often consist of equityholders, or their representatives, or, possibly, potential targets in connection with causes of action that may belong to the debtor. These circumstances sometimes cast doubt on a board's ability to act objectively for the benefit of creditors. In both out-of-court and chapter 11 settings, however, there are few remedies for a committee to implement management or board changes during the pendency of the restructuring.

In an out-of-court workout, a committee's ability to impose management or board changes essentially is a matter of leverage. By refusing to engage in negotiations, terminating discretionary funding, or threatening to commence litigation to enforce creditor claims, creditors may, for example, convince a board of directors to replace a chief executive officer who has lost the confidence of creditors. In some cases, a committee may be successful in convincing a debtor to reconstitute its board or to make management changes, such as retaining capable turnaround financial professionals to work with management, as part of an overall package that provides the debtor with the concessions it seeks from creditors to enable the debtor to avoid having to file for chapter 11 protection.

A committee's ability to impose board or management changes is not much greater in chapter 11. One of the anomalies of chapter 11 is that it continues control over the debtor in the prepetition board of directors and management.[69] Other than seeking appointment of a trustee, the Bankruptcy Code provides no direct statutory assistance to a committee seeking management or board change during the course of a case. Nevertheless, a committee may negotiate for board or management changes to be implemented during a case and depending on circumstances, a committee may be successful in doing so. For example, in *In re Trans World Airlines*,[70] at the insistence of the committee as part of a larger package of significant agreements, during the pendency of the case, the debtor's entire board of directors resigned and was replaced by two "responsible officers"—one selected by the debtor's labor unions and one selected by certain members of the committee. Of course, the entire topic of board and management change is extremely sensitive, as no debtor is likely to respond favorably to an implication that it cannot or will not fulfill its fiduciary obligations.

Development of a Restructuring Game Plan.   All committee functions are predicates to, or tangents of, a committee's central function: development and negotiation of a restructuring plan that maximizes value for creditors. Simply put, all roads lead to the main task of identifying a restructuring goal, developing a strategy for attempting to achieve that goal, and then attempting to implement that strategy.

In this central task, many difficult issues must be faced by a committee, all of which are fact specific. What are the company's long-term prospects? On what assumptions are they based, and are those assumptions reasonable? What currency for repayment is potentially available based on a debtor's potential resources and capital structure alternatives—cash, debt, or equity—and in what amounts? How can the debtor increase its value and thus potential recoveries? Are operational changes required, and if so, does implementing them in chapter 11 provide benefits that cannot be obtained out of court? Can value be created through third-party transactions such as a merger with another entity? What is an appropriate time frame for the process? Is debtor's value deteriorating, and if so, by how much, and how can such deterioration be reversed? Is management composition an issue? Are there specific facts, such as potential liabilities of insiders, that can be a source of either value creation or leverage in negotiations?

Although the answers to these questions are dependent entirely on the unique facts of each case, they are fundamental considerations for a committee in every case. The answers will lead a committee to both establishing its restructuring goal and formulating its strategy for how to obtain it. While achieving consensus with the debtor and other constituencies through cooperative negotiations is surely the preferred outcome, committees often are forced to utilize, or at least threaten to consider utilizing their rights and powers, both in court and out, to achieve the desired outcome.

Functions Specific to Chapter 11 Cases

A committee attains certain rights and powers in a chapter 11 case that do not exist in an out-of-court workout. Section 1103 of the Bankruptcy Code sets forth the committee's principal statutory rights in a chapter 11 case, augmented by certain other Bankruptcy Code sections.[71] Section 1103 authorizes a committee to employ professionals such as attorneys and financial advisors,[72] consult with the debtor in the administration of the case, participate in the creation of a reorganization plan, request appointment of a trustee or examiner, and perform any other services that are in the interests of the committee's constituency.[73]

Although the right to operate the business remains with the debtor or trustee,[74] the breadth of the powers granted to the committee allow the committee to closely scrutinize the debtor's activities and, if necessary, make its views known to, or request relief from, the bankruptcy court.[75] Moreover, as discussed below, in some circumstances, such as when a debtor cannot or will not do so, a committee may perform certain of a debtor's functions on behalf of the estate.

Committee as a Party-in-Interest and Case Administrator.   Section 1109(b) of the Bankruptcy Code renders the committee a party-in-interest in the case. That means a committee may "raise and may appear and be heard on any issue" in the case.[76] Also, Section 1103(c)(1) of the Bankruptcy Code authorizes the committee to consult with the debtor concerning the administration of the chapter 11 case.[77] Accordingly, a committee may raise any matter affecting creditor rights or the administration of a case with the debtor and the court. Augmenting these rights as a practical matter is the requirement that a chapter 11 debtor obtain court approval of all nonordinary course transactions.[78] As a result, such transactions cannot be consummated without the committee being given an opportunity to consider the debtor's request, formulate its own views, and state them to the court.[79] A committee will request that a debtor consult with it before even seeking court approval on key matters in the case, and any debtor that hopes to form a cooperative working relationship with the committee will be well advised to do so.

A debtor is afforded the benefit of the sound business judgment standard when making decisions relating to the operation of its business throughout the duration of its chapter 11 case.[80] When exercising its authority, for example, to sell assets of the estate other than in the ordinary course of business under Section 363(b) of the Bankruptcy Code, or to reject an executory contract or unexpired lease of nonresidential real property under Section 365 of the Bankruptcy Code, in the face of objection, a court will defer to the sound business judgment of the debtor in rendering its decision.[81] Therefore, although the committee can appear and be heard in court, the views of the creditors' committee usually will not be accorded equal weight by the bankruptcy court, unless the committee can demonstrate circumstances establishing that the debtor should not be entitled to the benefits of the business judgment rule.[82]

In sum, a committee in chapter 11 monitors all aspects of the administration of the case. In order to monitor a case effectively, a committee will usually request periodic reports from the debtor on current and planned operations. The committee may even be more aggressive, making material recommendations to the debtor on key business initiatives and opportunities. Not surprisingly, many debtors resist these activities. The level of resistance varies with each case and at different times within a case, as well as with the unique personality of each debtor and the nature of advice it receives from its professionals.

Negotiation of a Reorganization Plan.   In a chapter 11 case, a debtor's restructuring proposal must be formalized in a plan of reorganization. To be implemented, that plan must satisfy various procedural and substantive requirements, culminating with a vote by creditors and court approval.[83] The committee's most important role in a chapter 11 case is to negotiate with the debtor and other constituencies regarding the proposed treatment of creditors in the plan.[84] A committee does not, however, actually vote to accept or reject a plan, but offers a recommendation to the unsecured creditor body. Fundamentally, all committee rights and powers exist to enable the committee to be in a position to negotiate a plan.[85] The ability to hire professionals, to investigate a debtor's financial affairs, to monitor case administration, to challenge the debtor in court, and, if necessary, to take affirmative action to preserve or create value, are all tied, directly or indirectly, to the plan process. Without these powers, a committee would not be able to have an educated, informed view as to what might or might not be fair, possible, or desirable with respect to restructuring alternatives. Without the power to challenge the debtor's business decisions, or to commence adversary proceedings, a committee would have no ability to guard against unnecessary depletion of value or missed opportunity to augment value.

Particularly in large cases, negotiation regarding a chapter 11 plan often will begin only after the debtor presents its long-term business plan to the committee. The business plan will contain long-term operating and financial projections, based on numerous assumptions, and forms the basis for valuation assumptions and calculations that ultimately drive the allocation of a debtor's value among creditors under the plan of reorganization. A committee, in turn, will review that business plan and the reasonableness of its assumptions.

In the absence of reaching agreement on a plan with the debtor, a committee has a number of options available to it under the Bankruptcy Code, which are discussed below. The existence of these remedies, and the potential that they will be invoked by the committee, frequently establishes the balance necessary in negotiations with the debtor to achieve a consensual resolution of the case.

Appointment of a Trustee.   Section 1103(c)(4) of the Bankruptcy Code allows a committee to seek the appointment of a trustee or examiner for the estate.[86]

Section 1104 of the Bankruptcy Code sets forth the standards for appointment of a trustee. A court shall order the appointment of a trustee:

> (1) for cause, including fraud, dishonesty, incompetence, or gross mismanagement of the affairs of the debtor by current management, either before or after the commencement of the case, or similar cause, but not including the number of holders of securities of the debtor or the amount of assets or liabilities of the debtor or (2) if such appointment is in the interests of creditors, any equity security holders, and other interests of the estate, without regard to the number of holders of securities of the debtor or the amount of assets or liabilities of the debtor. [87]

Seeking appointment of a trustee is firing the heaviest artillery.[88] A trustee replaces a debtor's current management and has the power to operate the business. Appointment of a trustee terminates a debtor's exclusive right to file a reorganization plan.[89] The party moving for appointment of a trustee must prove the need for a trustee by clear and convincing evidence.[90] Not surprisingly, courts generally are reluctant to appoint a trustee.[91]

Historically, requests for appointment of a trustee were predicated on allegations of the types of "cause" delineated explicitly in Section 1104(a). Recent cases, however, most notably *Marvel*,[92] have potentially expanded the notion of what can constitute "cause" within the purview of Section 1104(a). In *Marvel*, after extensive litigation culminating in a change in control of the debtor's board of directors during the chapter 11 case, the debtor's negotiations with other creditor groups broke down completely. Substantial acrimony among the parties made the prospects for resolving issues dim. Upon the motion for appointment of a trustee by Marvel's institutional lenders, the district court, which had withdrawn the reference of the case from the bankruptcy court, determined that the debtors and creditors were "unable to resolve conflicts" with creditors, and on the basis of this acrimony, appointed a trustee. The Third Circuit, relying heavily on a similar recent ruling by the Fifth Circuit Court of Appeals,[93] affirmed.

Because the list of factors that can constitute "cause" explicitly set forth in Section 1104(a) is not exclusive, the *Marvel* decision does not technically constitute a change in the law. However, the case does provide and illuminate with new clarity the possibility that, at least in some circumstances, a sustained negotiating impasse between a debtor and creditors alone can constitute grounds for appointment of a trustee. Undoubtedly concerned about an overly broad interpretation of its ruling, the Third Circuit was careful, however, to identify a number of facts specific to the *Marvel* case as important to its ruling. In *Marvel*, the debtor in possession had been taken over by a large but deeply subordinated creditor. As such, the creditor was placed in the awkward position of being a fiduciary for creditors whose interests were clearly adverse to its own.[94] While the court concluded that these unusual circumstances were sufficient to justify the appointment of a trustee, the court was careful to point out that its ruling cannot be read as leading to a per se rule requiring appointment of a trustee in every case in which there are conflicts or acrimony between the debtor and creditors.[95] In fact, the court noted correctly that inherent conflicts of interest exist in virtually every case, and cautioned that appointment of a trustee based on allegations of conflict and acrimony must be confined to a case-by-case analysis and should be granted only when parties move from seeking to resolve the healthy conflicts that always exist and begin working at cross-purposes.[96] A clear track record of failure by a debtor to demonstrate an ability to resolve conflicts, and thus the absence of any reasonable likelihood of any cooperation between the parties in the near future, was central to the court's decision.[97]

In sum, even after *Marvel*, the appointment of a trustee is likely to be obtained only under rare circumstances. Other than when atypical facts exist, appointment of a trustee is properly viewed as disruptive to the reorganization process and the operation of the debtor's business. If the request is made by a committee and is not granted, the committee's working relationship with the debtors, and its credibility with the court, may well be irreparably damaged. Accordingly, while the threat that a committee could seek appointment of a trustee always lurks in the background, absent unusual circumstances, it may not be a source of significant leverage in plan negotiations.

Appointment of an Examiner.   Short of seeking appointment of a trustee, a committee may seek appointment of an examiner.[98] Section 1104(c) of the Bankruptcy Code sets forth the standards for an examiner's appointment.

> If the court does not order the appointment of a trustee . . . on request of a party-in-interest . . . the court shall order the appointment of an examiner to conduct such an investigation of the debtor as is appropriate, including an investigation of any allegations of fraud, dishonesty, incompetence, misconduct, mismanagement, or irregularity in the management of the affairs of the debtor of or by current or former management of the debtor, if (1) such appointment is in the interests of creditors, any equity security holders, and other interests of the estate; or (2) the debtor's fixed, liquidated, unsecured debts, other than debts for goods, services, or taxes, or owing to an insider, exceed $5,000,000.[99]

An examiner's role is not as all-encompassing as that of a trustee. An examiner's role is usually limited to investigation of a debtor's actions and financial condition,[100] but may be extended to assisting in plan negotiations.[101] A court also may authorize an examiner to commence legal action on behalf of the debtor's estate.[102] As with appointment of a trustee, however, but to a lesser degree, injecting a new third party into the process carries the inherent risk that delay and additional cost will result, as well as the risk of a decrease in control of the process by the key parties in interest.

Exclusivity.   Section 1121 of the Bankruptcy Code grants a debtor the exclusive right for 120 days to file a reorganization plan.[103] That period can either be lengthened or shortened for cause on motion of a party-in-interest, such as a committee.[104] Although the Bankruptcy Code does not define cause, in determining whether cause exists for an extension or reduction of a debtor's exclusive periods, courts have relied on a variety of factors, each of which by itself may justify extending or reducing the period of exclusivity. These factors include: (a) the size and complexity of the case, (b) the debtor's progress in resolving issues facing the estate, and (c) the possibility that an extension of time will harm the creditors.[105]

Perhaps the most frequently utilized tool of leverage in plan negotiations is the threat by a committee to oppose a debtor's requests to extend exclusivity or to affirmatively seek its termination. Debtors typically view the exclusive right to file a plan as synonymous with control over the case, which almost no debtor is prepared to sacrifice. Accordingly, a debtor usually will attempt to establish a cooperative working relationship with a committee in the case administration and plan process to guard against the possibility that a committee eventually will be successful in terminating exclusivity and filing its own plan of reorganization.

As a practical matter, a threat by a committee to prosecute its own reorganization plan may prove to be a hollow one. In the face of resistance by a debtor, it may be difficult for a committee to obtain enough information to prepare an adequate disclosure statement, which is a prerequisite to pursuing confirmation of a reorganization plan.[106] It also may be difficult for a committee to prosecute its own plan in the face of debtor resistance and at the same time maintain the debtor's necessary business relationships with vendors and customers. It may be difficult for a committee to overcome allegiances formed between a debtor and secured creditors with respect to plan treatment. As a result, while there have been cases in which committees have successfully terminated a debtor's exclusive right to file a plan and filed its own plan, such cases are not the norm.

In large cases, extensions of the debtor's exclusive period for a year or more are common due to the size and complexity of such cases.[107] While a committee is unlikely to convince a court to allow a debtor's exclusive period to end early in a case barring unusual factual circumstances, a committee may, however, use early exclusivity extension requests by a debtor as an opportunity to map out for the court the committee's view of how a case should proceed. For example, a committee may view a case as largely a financial restructuring, or, to the extent operational improvements are needed, a committee may believe that they can be implemented more cost effectively outside of chapter 11. In such circumstances, a committee is likely to push for a fast process, appropriately viewing time as money. A committee may alert the court that its willingness to consent to early exclusivity extensions is premised on certain understandings of how a case will be conducted.

It also is important for a committee to keep in mind that terminating exclusivity in the face of broken-down negotiations with a debtor is not always risk free. For example, termination of exclusivity may allow a secured creditor or an individual holder of claims, which may or may not be a committee member, to file its own plan. In some cases, committees have been successful in convincing a court to expand the exclusive right to file a plan to include only the committee and no other party, while other courts have rejected this view.[108]

Prosecution of Estate Actions. In many cases, a chapter 11 estate will possess statutory causes of action under the Bankruptcy Code, as well as state law causes of action preserved for the estate by the Bankruptcy Code.[109] Fraudulent conveyance, preference, and breach of fiduciary duty claims are typical examples. In the first instance, the debtor is the proper party to commence such actions on behalf of the estate. In certain circumstances, however, active participation in estate litigation by a committee may be appropriate or necessary.

In some circumstances, although a debtor has initiated an adversary proceeding, a committee may desire to take an active role in that litigation to ensure that the interests of creditors are being fully protected. Pursuant to Section 1109(b) of the Bankruptcy Code, the creditors' committee "may raise and may appear and be heard on any issue in a case under this chapter."[110] Yet to be definitively decided is whether the committee has an absolute right to intervene in an adversary proceeding brought by the debtor. Some courts have held that the committee has an absolute right to intervene in any adversary proceeding commenced by the debtor.[111] Other courts hold that the right to intervene is not absolute, but, rather, that a committee had such a right only if it had standing under Federal Rule of Civil Procedure 24.[112] Courts requiring standing under the Federal Rules of Civil Procedure look to see "whether the intervention will unduly delay or prejudice the adjudication of the rights of the original parties."[113] Under such cases, a creditors' committee will be permitted to intervene in an adversary proceeding brought by the debtor when such intervention will not unnecessarily disrupt the proceeding to the detriment of the original parties to the action.

In certain situations, a committee may decide that it is necessary for it to commence litigation on behalf of the debtor's estate. For example, a debtor may be unable to prosecute effectively certain causes of action because the estate's claim is against the very board members or officers or controlling shareholders that are in charge of the debtors in possession.[114] Accordingly, in these circumstances, the committee may be the only impartial or most qualified entity to evaluate and commence the cause of action on behalf of the estate.[115]

In cases in which a committee seeks to prosecute such claims on behalf of the estate, the committee usually must demonstrate to the court that (a) a colorable claim exists, (b) the committee has demanded that the estate pursue it, and (c) the debtor has unjustifiably refused to do so.[116] The third of the three criteria is often the most difficult to satisfy. A court must determine the factors that dissuaded the debtor from bringing the action. In so doing, the court then will be able to evaluate the creditors' committee's assertions that the failure on the part of the debtor to bring a cause of action was indeed unjustified.

When determining whether to permit a committee to assert a claim on behalf of a debtor's estate, a court will look to a number of factors before granting the committee the authority to assert a claim. In so doing, "courts consider whether there are conflicts of interest that exist between the debtor and the defendant, whether the creditor's interests are protected despite the debtor's refusal to bring the action, whether pursuing the action will benefit the estate, and whether appointing a trustee would be more beneficial to the estate than letting the creditors' committee bring the action."[117] Prior to authorizing the committee to bring the cause of action on behalf of the estate, the court will determine whether the debtor's estate and the creditors would be better served by (1) compelling the debtor to bring the action, (2) appointing a trustee to replace the debtor in possession or (3) granting the committee's request to assert the cause of action on behalf of the estate.

NOTES

1.   11 U.S.C. §§ 101–1330 (1994).

2.   11 U.S.C. § 1102.

3.   The U.S. trustee, who serves under the general supervision of the U.S. Attorney General, is charged with overseeing the proper administration of cases filed under the Bankruptcy Code. *See* 28 U.S.C. §§ 581–589(a).

4.   Pub. L. No. 103-394, 108 Stat. 4106 (1994).

5.   11 U.S.C. § 101(10).

6.   *Id.* at § 101(5).

7.   *Id.* at § 101(10).

8.   *Id.* at § 101(5).

9.   Rejection of a lease gives rise to a prepetition claim for breach pursuant to 11 U.S.C. § 502(g).

10.   *See In re Barney's, Inc.*, 197 B.R. 431, 440 (Bankr. S.D. N.Y. 1996) ("Relying on the unambiguous language of the Bankruptcy Code, courts have permitted creditors holding disputed claims to sit on statutory committees."); *In re Laclede Cab Co.*, 145 B.R. 308, 309 (Bankr. E.D. Mo. 1992) (determining that disputed nature of claim is not grounds to exclude an entity with a claim against a debtor from service on a creditors' committee); *In re Richmond Tank Car Co.*, 93 B.R. 504, 506 (Bankr. S.D. Tex. 1988) (same).

11.   *See* 7 *Collier on Bankruptcy* ¶ 1102.02 [2][a][vii] at 1102-13 (Lawrence P. King, ed., 15th ed. 1993) ("There is no doubt that a creditor holding only a secured claim should not be entitled to serve on an unsecured creditor's committee. The Creditor will be in a separate class under the plan and will have interests adverse to general unsecured creditors.").

12.   *See In re Walat Farms, Inc.*, 64 B.R. 65, 68-69 (Bankr. E.D. Mich. 1986) (holding that "a secured creditor whose claim exceeds the value of its collateral and holds, in part, an unsecured claim, may be appointed to the unsecured creditors' committee under § 1102."). *See also In re Seaescape Cruises, Ltd.*, 131 B.R. 241, 243 (Bankr. S.D. Fla. 1991) ("[S]ection 1102 does not preclude a creditor who holds both secured and unsecured claims from serving on the Committee.").

13.   *See* H.R. Rep. No. 595, 95th Cong., 1st Sess. 401 (1977), *reprinted in* 1978 U.S.C.C.A.N. 5963, 6357 ("Subsection (b) [of § 1102] contains precatory language directing the court to appoint the persons holding the seven largest claims against the debtor of the kinds represented on a creditors' committee, or the members of a prepetition committee organized by creditors before the order for relief under chapter 11."). *See also Collier on Bankruptcy, supra* note 11, ¶ 1102.02[2][b] at 1102-14-15 n. 23 ("The language suggesting the seven largest [creditors] shall serve is precatory and not binding on the United States trustee.") (citing *In re Drexel Burnham Lambert Group, Inc.*, 118 B.R. 209 (Bankr. S.D. N.Y. 1990)); *In re Featherworks Corp.*, 25 B.R. 634 (Bankr. E.D. N.Y. 1982), *aff'd*, 36 B.R. 460 (E.D. N.Y. 1984).

14.   *See In re Altair Airlines, Inc.*, 727 F.2d 88 (3d Cir. 1984); *In re Barney's, Inc.*, *supra* note 10, 197 B.R. at 431; *In re Plabell Rubber Products*, 140 B.R. 179 (Bankr. N.D. Ohio 1992); *In re Northeast Dairy Co-op Federation, Inc.*, 59 B.R. 531 (Bankr. N.D. N.Y. 1986); *In re Enduro Stainless, Inc.*, 59 B.R. 603 (Bankr. N.D. Ohio 1986); *In re Schatz Fed. Bearings Col, Inc.*, 5 B.R. 543 (Bankr. S.D. N.Y. 1980).

15.   *See In re Altair Airlines, Inc.*, *supra* note 14, 727 F.2d at 91 (claims held by members of union represented the second largest unsecured claim against the debtor's estate); *In re Plabell Rubber Products*, *supra* note 14, 140 B.R. at 181 (in holding that the union's interests were not adequately represented, the court noted that "the union . . . is listed as one of the creditors holding the 20 largest unsecured claims. In fact, Debtor lists the union as a creditor with the sixth highest unsecured claim.").

16.   *See In re Northeast Dairy Co-op Federation, Inc.*, *supra* note 14, 59 B.R. at 534 (in holding that the union is entitled to representation on the committee, the Court noted that "The Committee is not representative as presently established, for interests critical to the formulation of a successful plan are unrepresented.").

17.   *See In re Value Merchants, Inc.*, 202 B.R. 280 (E.D. Wisc. 1996); *In re McLean Indus., Inc.*, 70 B.R. 852, 855 (Bankr. S.D. N.Y. 1987); *In re Charter Co.*, 42 B.R. 251, 254 (Bankr. M.D. Fla. 1984).

18.   *See, e.g., In re Value Merchants, Inc.*, *supra* note 17, 202 B.R. at 280. The court in *Value Merchants, Inc.* held that there is no per se rule in favor of or against the appointment of an indenture trustee to a creditors' committee, and that the decision should be made on a case-by-case basis. In determining under the facts of this case that the indenture trustees should serve on the creditors' committee and that the United States trustee had acted arbitrarily and capriciously in excluding them, the court relied on the fact that "there are no holders willing to serve on a committee, their claim volume is very large relative to other creditors, and the beneficial holders are scattered far and wide." The court concluded further that "the indenture trustees were and are likely to be the bondholders' only voice in the VMI reorganization process, militating in favor of their presence on the committee." *Id.* at 288–289.

19.   *See generally*, Kenneth N. Klee and K. John Shaffer, "Creditors' Committees Under Chapter 11 of the Bankruptcy Code," CA 46 ALI-ABA 133, 158–159 (1995); *Collier on Bankruptcy*, *supra* note 11, ¶ 1102.02[2][a][v] at 1102-11–12.

20.   *See In re Wilson Foods Corp., et al.*, 31 B.R. 272, 272 (Bankr. W.D. Okla. 1983) (holding that significant competitor of debtor could not serve on creditors' committee due to conflicting interests and divided loyalties inherent in role as competitor and in service to creditors' committee). *See also In re Manufacturing & Sales Co.*, 51 B.R. 178, 179 (Bankr. S.D. Ohio 1985) (court disqualified law firm from representation of creditors' committee because law firm currently represented debtor's former general manager who was now employed by competition).

21.   *See In re Map International, Inc.*, 105 B.R. 5, 6 (Bankr. E.D. Pa 1989) ("It is well established that the mere fact of competitor status is insufficient to disqualify a creditor from serving on the creditors' committee. Rather, the party seeking to exclude a creditor bears the burden of proving that the creditor's appointment will be detrimental to the debtor's reorganization efforts."); *In re Plant Specialties, Inc.*, 59 B.R. 1, 1 (Bankr. W.D. La. 1986) (in holding that "[t]he mere fact that a creditor is a competitor will not alone bar his appointment to the creditors' committee" court noted that a competitor's knowledge of the debtor's business could actually be very beneficial to the debtor's reorganization efforts).

22.   Official Form No. 4 of Official Bankruptcy Forms.

23.   *Insider* is defined in § 101(31) of the Bankruptcy Code.

24.   For example, in the chapter 11 cases of Federated Department Stores and Allied Stores Corporation, and Value Merchants, Inc. and Everything's A Dollar, Inc., creditors' committees for both entities were established.

25.   11 U.S.C. § 1102(a)(1) ("[T]he United States trustee . . . may appoint additional committees of creditors or of equity security holders as the United States trustee deems appropriate.").

26.   *See In re Hills Stores Co.*, 137 B.R. 4, 6–7 (Bankr. S.D. N.Y. 1992). *See also In re Dow Corning Corporation*, 194 B.R. 121 (Bankr. E.D. Mich. 1996), *rev'd on other grounds*, 212 B.R. 258 (E.D. Mich. 1997); *In re ORFA Corporation of Philadelphia*, 121 B.R. 294 (Bankr. E.D. Pa. 1990); *In re Sharon Steel Corp.*, 100 B.R. 767 (Bankr. W.D. Pa. 1989); *In re Public Service Co. of New Hampshire*, 89 B.R. 1014 (Bankr. D. N.H. 1988).

27.   Advisory Committee Note, Federal Rule of Bankruptcy Procedure 2007(b). *See also Collier on Bankruptcy*, *supra* note 11, ¶ 1102.02[3][a][ii] at 1102–18 ("At most, Bankruptcy Rule 2007(b) provides nonbinding guidance to the United States trustee and the court in analyzing the procedures used to create a prepetition committee.").

28.   11 U.S.C. § 1102(c) (1985).

29.   11 U.S.C. § 1102(a)(2) (1994).

30.   *See, e.g., In re Dow Corning Corp.*, 212 B.R. 258 (E.D. Mich 1997); *In re Wheeler Technology, Inc.*, 139 B.R. 235, 239 (B.A.P. 9th Cir. 1992); *In re Hills Stores Co.*, 137 B.R. 4, 8 (Bankr. S.D. N.Y. 1992); *In re Drexel Burnham Lambert Group, Inc.*, 118 B.R. 209, 210–211 (Bankr. S.D. N.Y. 1990); *see also Collier on Bankruptcy*, *supra* note 11, ¶ 1102.07[2] at 1102–32 ("The lack of express authority to alter committee membership, combined with deletion of Section 1102(c), renders the court unable to overturn a decision by the United States trustee with respect to committee membership.").

31.   *See, e.g., Sharon Steel*, 100 B.R. 767, 785-86 (Bankr. W.D. Pa. 1989); *In re Public Service Co. of New Hampshire*, 89 B.R. 1014, 1021 (Bankr. D. N.H. 1988); *In re Texaco*, 79 B.R. 560 (Bankr. S.D. N.Y. 1987).

32.   *See, e.g., In re Lykes Bros. Steamship Co., Inc.*, 200 B.R. 933 (M.D. Fla. 1996); *In re Barney's, Inc.*, *supra* note 10. 197 B.R. at 31; *In re America West Airlines*, 142 B.R. 901 (Bankr. D. Ariz. 1992); *In re Columbia Gas Sys., Inc.*, 133 B.R. 174 (Bankr. D. Del. 1991). *See also In re Mercury Finance Company*, 224 B.R. 380, 383 (Bankr. N.D. Ill. 1998) ("This Court concludes that as a matter of law, it does hold . . . that the actions of the U.S. Trustee with respect to the formation of [a] committee are subject to judicial review.").

33.   *See In re Barney's, Inc.*, *supra* note 10, 197 B.R. at 431, 439 (holding that the court has authority to review actions of the United States trustee to ensure that "the trustee has not acted arbitrarily or capriciously, or otherwise abused its discretion, in appointing a committee.").

34.   *Id. See also In re Lykes Bros. Steamship Co., Inc.*, *supra* note 32, 200 B.R. at 933, 940 (holding that a court can review composition of a committee to determine whether U.S. trustee acted arbitrarily or capriciously); *In re Columbia Gas System, Inc.*, 133 B.R. 174, 176 (Bankr. D. Del. 1991) (court held that it had the authority to review the U.S. trustee's refusal to include a certain creditor on the committee under an abuse of discretion standard, and could order appropriate relief).

35.   *In re Barney's , Inc.*, *supra* note 10, 197 B.R. at 431, 441.

36.   *See In re Lykes Bros. Steamship Co., Inc.*, *supra* note 32, 200 B.R. at 933, 940 ("The Court finds that Congress did not intend that the Trustee would have unbridled discretion over the appointment of creditor committees.").

37.   *In re Sharon Steel Corp.*, *supra* note 26, 100 B.R. at 767, 778.

38.   *Id.* at 786.

39.   *In re Barney's, Inc.*, *supra* note 10, 197 B.R. at 431, 439.

40.   *In re Hills Store Co.*, *supra* note 26, 137 B.R. at 4, 6–7.

41.   *In re The Drexel Burnham Lambert Group, Inc.*, *supra* note 30, 118 B.R. at 209, 212.

42.   *See* 11 U.S.C. § 328.

43.   Section 101(14) of the Bankruptcy Code provides as follows:

"disinterested person" means person that —
      (A) is not a creditor, an equity security holder, or an insider;
      (B) is not and was not an investment banker for any outstanding security of the debtor;
      (C) has not been, within three years before the date of the filing of the petition, an investment banker for a security of the debtor, or an attorney for such an investment banker in connection with the offer, sale or issuance of a security of the debtor;

(D) is not and was not, within two years before the date of filing of the petition a director, officer or employee of the debtor or of an investment banker specified in subparagraph (B) or (C) of this paragraph; and

(E) does not have an interest materially adverse to the interest of the estate or of any class of creditors or equity security holders, by reason of any direct or indirect relationship to, connection with, or interest in, the debtor or an investment banker specified in subparagraph (B) or (C) of this paragraph, or for any other reason;

44. *See In re Granite Partners, L.P.*, 219 B.R. 22, 33 (Bankr. S.D. N.Y. 1998); *In re Leslie Fay Companies, Inc.*, 175 B.R. 525, 532 (Bankr. S.D. N.Y. 1994).

45. *In re Granite Partners, L.P., supra* note 44, 219 B.R. at 33 (quoting *In re Roberts*, 46 B.R. 815, 828 n. 26 (Bankr. D. Utah 1985)). *See also In re Martin*, 817 F.2d 175, 181 (1st Cir. 1987) (in a discussion of the definition of a disinterested person, the court noted that "'a 'disinterested' person should be divested of any scintilla of personal interest which might be reflected in his decision concerning estate matters.'") (internal citations omitted); *In re Leslie Fay Companies, Inc., supra* note 44, 175 B.R. at 533 ("[I]f it is plausible that the representation of another interest may cause the debtor's attorneys to act any differently than they would without that other representation, then they have a conflict and an interest adverse to the estate.").

46. *See Collier on Bankruptcy, supra* note 11, ¶ 1103.04[2][a] at 1103-18-19. *See also In re Granite Partners, supra* note 44, 219 B.R. at 36; *In re Leslie Fay Companies, Inc., supra* note 44, 175 B.R. at 533.

47. 140 F.3d 463 (3d Cir. 1998).

48. *In re Marvel Entertainment Group, Inc.*, 1998 WL 181084 (D. Del. 1998), *rev'd*, 140 F.3d 463 (3d Cir. 1998).

49. *Id.* at 478.

50. *Id.* at 477 ("Section 327(a) presents a per se bar to the appointment of a law firm with an actual conflict, and gives the district court wide discretion in deciding whether to approve the appointment of a law firm with a potential conflict.") (internal citation omitted).

51. *Id.* at 476.

52. *Id.* at 477. In rendering its decision, the Third Circuit noted further that: "[Gibbons Del Deo] has never represented Chase on a matter related to this bankruptcy and severed all attorney-client relations with Chase in anticipation of its selection as trustee's counsel. If we were to uphold the district court's order under these circumstances, it is with utmost difficulty that we could imagine how a law firm with any prior relationship to a secured creditor could ever serve as trustee's counsel. Such a result would be tantamount to a per se rule. . . ."

53. A committee that desires to remove a creditor from the committee can obtain such relief from the U.S. trustee. *See In re America West Airlines*, 142 B.R. 901, 902 (Bankr. D. Ariz. 1992) ("The Court finds and concludes on this record that the U.S. Trustee has the authority to appoint as well as remove members to official committees.") In the event the U.S. trustee refuses to honor the request of the committee, the committee can arguably seek leave of the court to review the U.S. trustee's decision to determine "whether the U.S. Trustee has abused [its] authority [and] acted arbitrarily and capriciously." *See also In re First RepublicBank Corporation*, 95 B.R. 58, 61 (Bankr. N.D. Tex. 1988) ("Accordingly, the United States trustee would act arbitrarily and capriciously if he refused to remove a committee member who held a conflict of interest that amounted to a breach of the fiduciary duty that the creditor owed to the creditors represented by the committee."); *In re the Charter Company*, 44 B.R. 256 (Bankr. M.D. Fla. 1984); *In re Penn-Dixie Industries, Inc.*, 9 B.R. 941 (Bankr. S.D. N.Y. 1981). *But see In re Wheeler Technology, Inc.*, 139 B.R. 235, 239 (B.A.P. 9th Cir. 1992) (court found that ability to appoint and remove members of a creditors' committee belonged exclusively to U.S. trustee). For discussion of the court's authority to review decisions of U.S. trustee, *see supra* notes 28–36 and accompanying text.

54. *In re SPM Manufacturing Corp.*, 984 F.2d 1305, 1315 (1st Cir. 1993); *In re Granite Partners, L.P., supra* note 44, 210 B.R. at 508, 516; *In re Map Int'l, Inc.*, 105 B.R. 5, 6 (Bankr. E.D. Pa. 1989); *In re National Equipment & Mold Corp.*, 33 B.R. 574 (Bankr. N.D. Ohio 1983).

55.   *In re ABC Automatic Products Corp.*, 210 B.R. 437, 441 (Bankr. E.D. Pa. 1997); *In re Mesta Machine Co.*, 67 B.R. 151, 159 (Bankr. W.D. Pa. 1986); *In re Johns-Manville Corp.*, 26 B.R. 919, 925 (Bankr. S.D. N.Y. 1983). *Collier on Bankruptcy, supra* note 11, ¶ 1103.05[2] at ¶ 1103-30-32.

56.   *In re SPM Manufacturing Corp.*, 984 F.2d 1305, 1315 (1st cir. 1993); *Locks v. United States Trustee*, 157 B.R. 89 (W.D. Pa. 1993); *In Re ABC Automatic Products Corp.*, 210 B.R. 437 (Bankr. E.D. Pa. 1997); *In re Caldor, Inc.*, 193 B.R. 165 (Bankr. S.D. N.Y. 1996); *In re Drexel Burnham Lambert Group, Inc.*, *supra* note 30, 138 B.R. at 717, *aff'd on other grounds*, 140 B.R. 347 (S.D. N.Y. 1992); *In re FirstRepublicBank Corp.*, *supra* note 53, 95 B.R. at 58.

57.   *Id.*

58.   *See Collier on Bankruptcy, supra* note 11, ¶ 1103.05[4] at 1103-32-33.

59.   *See Pan Am Corp. v. Delta Airlines, Inc.*, 175 B.R. 438, 514 (S.D. N.Y. 1994) ("The Creditors' Committee in the Pan Am case enjoyed a qualified immunity, as a matter of law. In order to overcome the Creditors' Committee's qualified immunity and hold the Committee liable for alleged wrongdoing, Delta was required to prove that the Committee engaged in 'willful misconduct' or 'ultra vires activity.'"). *See also Luedke v. Delta Airlines, Inc.*, 159 B.R. 385 (S.D. N.Y. 1993); *In re Drexel Burnham Lambert Group, Inc.*, *supra* note 30, 138 B.R. at 717, *aff'd on other grounds*, 140 B.R. 347 (S.D. N.Y. 1992).

60.   *Luedke v. Delta Airlines, Inc.*, *supra* note 59, 159 B.R. at 385, 392–393.

61.   *See, e.g., N. Y. Credit Men's Adjustment Bureau, Inc. v. Lubin*, 95 A.D. 2d 736 (1983) (noting that chairman of unofficial creditors' committee has fiduciary duties to creditors), *but cf. In re Drexel Burnham Lambert Group, Inc.*, 123 B.R. 702, 712 (noting that the FDIC and RTC, as members of a committee that was neither an official nor unofficial committee in the debtor's bankruptcy case, do not have fiduciary duties). *See also Woods v. City National Bank and Trust Co. of Chicago*, 312 U.S. 262, 268 (1941) (finding that "[p]rotective committees . . . are fiduciaries" in reliance on *Bullard v. City of Cisco*, 290 U.S. 179 (1933), a case involving a bondholders' protective committee formed pursuant to an agreement among the bondholders to pursue an out-of-court restructuring).

62.   For example, in *In re Tucker Freightlines*, 62 B.R. 213 (Bankr. W.D. Mich. 1986), the court held a committee member liable for damages resulting from false and misleading statements made in correspondence to other creditors.

63.   11 U.S.C. § 363(b).

64.   Section 303(b) and (c) of the Bankruptcy Code set forth the requirements for the commencement of an involuntary case. This section provides:

> (b) An involuntary case against a person is commenced by the filing with the bankruptcy court of a petition under chapter 7 or 11 of this title—
> (1) by three or more entities, each of which is either a holder of a claim against such person that is not contingent as to liability or the subject of a bona fide dispute, or an indenture trustee representing such a holder, if such claims aggregate at least $10,000 more than the value of any lien on property of the debtor securing such claims held by the holders of such claims;
> (2) if there are fewer than 12 such holders, excluding any employee or insider of such person and any transferee of a transfer that is voidable under Section 544, 545, 547, 548, 549, or 724(a) of this title, by one or more of such holders that hold in the aggregate at least $10,000 of such claims;
> (3) if such person is a partnership—
> (A) by fewer than all of the general partners in such partnership; or
> (B) if relief has been ordered under this title with respect to all of the general partners in such partnership, by a general partner in such partnership, the trustee of such a general partner, or a holder of a claim against such partnership; or
> (4) by a foreign representative of the estate in a foreign proceeding concerning such person.
> (c) After the filing of a petition under this section but before the case is dismissed or relief is ordered, a creditor holding an unsecured claim that is not contingent, other than a creditor

filing under subsection (b) of this section, may join in the petition with the same effect as if such joining creditor were a petitioning creditor under subsection (b) of this section.

65.   11 U.S.C. § 1103(c)(2).

66.   Fed. R. Bankr. Proc. 2004.

67.   *See In re Wilcher*, 56 B.R. 428 (Bankr. N.D. Ill. 1985). *See also In re The Bennett Funding Group, Inc.*, 203 B.R. 24, 28 (Bankr. N.D. N.Y. 1996) ("The scope of [the Rule 2004] examination is admittedly 'unfettered and broad.' . . . The purpose of such a broad discovery tool is to assist the trustee in revealing the nature and extent of the estate, and to discover assets of the debtor which may have been intentionally or unintentionally concealed."); *In re Valley Forge Plaza Assoc.*, 109 B.R. 669, 674 (Bankr. E.D. Pa. 1990) ("The scope of a R2004 examination is even broader than that of discovery permitted under the [Federal Rules of Civil Procedure], which themselves contemplated broad, easy access to discovery.").

68.   *See, e.g., In re Healthco International, Inc.*, 208 B.R. 288, 300 (Bankr. D. Mass. 1997) ("When a transaction renders a corporation insolvent, or brings it to the brink of insolvency, the rights of creditors become paramount."). *See also Pepper v. Litton*, 308 U.S. 295 (1939); *Clarkson Co. Ltd.* v. *Shaheen*, 660 F.2d 506 (2d Cir. 1981), *cert. denied*, 455 U.S. 990 (1982); *In re Buckhead America Corp.*, 178 B.R. 956 (D. Del. 1994). *See also Geyer v. Ingersoll Publications Company*, 621 A.2d 784, 790 (Del. Ch. 1992) (holding that under Delaware law "fiduciary duties to creditors arise when one is able to establish the fact of insolvency."). The court in *Ingersoll* determined that insolvency in fact (*i.e.*, when a corporation's liabilities exceed assets or when a corporation is unable to satisfy debts as they come due) rather than when insolvency proceedings commence is determinative. *Id.* at 787. This holding set the standard under Delaware for determining the point at which a director's fiduciary duty shifts from the corporation's shareholders to its creditors. The *Ingersoll* holding also clarified the uncertainty surrounding this issue that the court in *Credit Lyonnais Bank Nedeland, N.V.* v. *Pathe Communications Corporation*, 1991 WL 277613 (Del. Ch. Dec. 30, 1991), propagated in determining that a director owes a fiduciary duty to a corporation's creditors when the corporation is in the "vicinity of insolvency." *Id.* at * 34 n. 55.

69.   *See* 11 U.S.C. §§ 1107(a) and 1108. Section 1107(a) of the Bankruptcy Code gives a debtor in possession all of the powers and the ability to perform all of the duties of a chapter 11 trustee. One such power of a chapter 11 trustee granted by § 1108 of the Bankruptcy Code is the ability to operate the debtor's business.

70.   *In re Trans World Airlines*, Case no. 92-115(HSB) (D. Del. 1992).

71.   *See* 11 U.S.C. § 1103. *See, e.g., In re Structurelite Plastics Corp.*, 91 B.R. 813, 819 (Bankr. S.D. Ohio 1988); *In re Finley, Kumble, et al.*, 85 B.R. 13, 17 (Bankr. S.D. N.Y. 1988); *In re UNR Indus.*, 30 B.R. 609, 612 (Bankr. N.D. Ill. 1983).

72.   11 U.S.C. § 1103(a).

73.   *Id.* at § 1103(c).

74.   *See id.* at §§ 1107 and 1108. *See In re Johns-Manville Corp.*, 801 F.2d 60, 62 (2d Cir. 1986); *In re Structurelite Plastics Corp., supra* note 71, 91 B.R. at 813, 819.

75.   *In re Lifschultz Fast Freight, Inc.*, 140 B.R. 482, 488–489 (Bankr. N.D. Ill. 1992); *In re AKF Foods, Inc.*, 36 B.R. 288, 289 (Bankr. E.D. N.Y. 1984); *Collier on Bankruptcy, supra* note 11, ¶ 1103.05[1][c] at 1103-23.

76.   11 U.S.C. § 1109(b).

77.   11 U.S.C. § 1103(c)(1).

78.   11 U.S.C. § 363.

79.   *See In re Structurelite Plastics Corp., supra* note 71, *91B.R.* at *813, 819 In re McLean Industries, Inc.*, 70 B.R. 852, 680 (Bankr. S.D. N.Y. 1987) ("[The] committee is also to be given notice of, and is expected to respond to, various requests . . . includ[ing] highly significant matters on which committee position is crucial, such as sales of property out of the ordinary course of business, post-petition financing agreements, and settlements.") (internal citations omitted).

80.   *See, e.g.*, *NLRB v. Bildisco & Bildisco*, 465 U.S. 513, 523 (1984) (noting that business judgment standard governs the debtor's decision to reject executory contracts); *In re Structurelite Plastics Corp.*, 86 B.R. 922, 925 n. 4 (Bankr. S.D. Ohio 1988) (same); *In re FCS, Inc.*, 60 B.R. 405, 411 (Bankr. E.D. N.C. 1986) (same).

81.   *See In re After Six, Incorporated*, 154 B.R. 876, 881 (Bankr. E.D. Pa. 1993) ("[Section] 363(b) allows only the trustee and, in the absence of a trustee in a Chapter 11 case, a debtor in possession ('DIP') . . . to sell a debtor's assets other than in the ordinary course of business. Thus, deference to a DIP's decision as to a successful bidder of its assets is appropriate, and that decision may be honored unless it is proven that the DIP abused that discretion."); *In re Constant Care Community Health Center, Inc.*, 99 B.R. 697, 702 (Bankr. D. Md. 1989) ("In determining whether to permit a debtor to reject an executory contract, the Court defers to the debtor's sound business judgment.").

82.   *See In re Gateway Apparel, Inc.*, 210 B.R. 567, 570 (Bankr. E.D. Mo. 1997) (court denied debtor's motion to assume unexpired lease of nonresidential real property because assumption "would not be a good business judgment."); *In re Ron Matusalem & Matusa of Florida, Inc.*, 158 B.R. 514, 522 (Bankr. S.D. Fla. 1993) ("The court determines that the Debtor has failed to demonstrate good business judgment or even mediocre business judgment. There is no economic benefit to the estate and its unsecured creditors from a rejection of [the] franchise agreement . . . ."). *See also In re Health Science Products, Inc.*, 191 B.R. 895, 909 n.15 (Bankr. N.D. Ala. 1995) ("When evaluating a request by a trustee or debtor in possession to assume or reject an executory contract or unexpired lease, most courts apply the 'business judgment rule' and approve the decision unless there is bad faith or a gross abuse of discretion.") (citing *Lubrizol Enters., Inc. v. Richmond Metal Finishers, Inc.*, 756 F.2d 1043 (4th Cir. 1985)).

83.   11 U.S.C. §§ 1122, 1123, 1125, 1126, 1128, 1129.

84.   H.R. Rep. No. 95-595, 95th Cong. 1st Sess. 401 (1977), *reprinted in* 1978 U.S.C.C.A.N. 5963; *In re Wire Cloth Products, Inc.*, 130 B.R. 798, 812 (Bankr. N.D. Ill. 1991) ("Participating in formulation of a plan and advising the Court of the Committee's determinations with respect to any plan formulated are among the most important functions of a Creditors' Committee and its counsel.").

85.   *See In re Johns-Manville Corp.*, *supra* note 74, 801 F.2d at 60, 62; *In re Structurelite Plastics Corp.*, *supra* note 71, 91 B.R. at 813, 819 ("[c]learly the most important aspect of a committee's functions is to negotiate the terms of a plan of reorganization.").

86.   11 U.S.C. § 1103(c)(4); § 1104(a) also provides a committee with the authority to seek the appointment of a trustee because the committee is clearly a "party-in-interest" that can make such a request.

87.   11 U.S.C. § 1104(a).

88.   *See Collier on Bankruptcy*, *supra* note 11, ¶ 1103.05[1][e] at 1103-27 ("Obtaining appointment of a trustee is a serious matter and a committee should not seek one unless it is formerly convinced that management of the debtor is dishonest or incapable of taking the steps necessary to obtain confirmation of a plan.").

89.   11 U.S.C. § 1121(c)(1).

90.   *In re Sharon Steel Corp.*, 871 F.2d 1217, 1226 (3d Cir. 1989).

91.   *Id.* at 1225 ("it is settled that appointment of a trustee should be the exception, rather than the rule.").

92.   *In re Marvel Entertainment Group, Inc.*, *supra* note 47, 140 F.3d at 463. *See supra* notes 47–52 and accompanying text for a discussion of *Marvel* in connection with the application of the disinterested person standard to the retention of professionals in a chapter 11 case.

93.   *In re Cajun Elec. Power Corp., Inc.*, 74 F.3d 599, 600 (5th Cir. 1996) (adopting on rehearing the opinion of dissent in 69 F.3d at 751), *cert. denied*, 117 S.Ct. 51 (1996).

94.   *In re Marvel Entertainment Group, Inc.*, *supra* note 47, 140 F.3d at 473.

95.   *Id.*

96.   *Id.* at 472–473 (citing *In re Cajun Electric Power Corp., Inc.*, *supra* note 93, 74 F.3d at 599.

97.   *Id.* at 473. The court determined that its reasoning supported appointment of a trustee either for "cause" under 11 U.S.C. § 1104(a)(1) or under the more flexible discretionary standard of 11 U.S.C. § 1104(a)(2). *Id.* at 474–475.

98.   11 U.S.C. § 1104(c). § 1103(c)(4) expressly authorizes a committee to request the appointment of an examiner.

99.   11 U.S.C. § 1104(c).

100.   *In re Gilman Serus, Inc.*, 46 B.R. 322 (Bankr D. Mass. 1985).

101.   *In re International Distrib. Centers, Inc.*, 74 B.R. 221 (S.D. N.Y. 1987).

102.   *In re Carnegie Int'l Corp.*, 51 B.R. 252 (Bankr. S.D. Ind. 1984).

103.   11 U.S.C. § 1121(b) ("Except as otherwise provided in this section, only the debtor may file a plan until after 120 days after the date of the order for relief under this chapter.").

104.   11 U.S.C. § 1121(d). § 1121(d) provides that:

"(d) On request of a party-in-interest made within the respective periods specified in subsections (b) and (c) of this section and after notice and a hearing, the court may for cause reduce or increase the 120-day period or the 180-day period referred to in this section."

105.   *See, e.g., In re Gibson & Cushman Dredging Corp.* 101 B.R. 405, 409–410 (E.D. N.Y. 1989); *In re Traverse Dev. Co. Ltd. Partnership*, 147 B.R. 418, 420 (Bankr. W.D. Mich. 1992); *In re General Bearing Corp.*, 136 B.R. 361, 367 (Bankr. S.D. N.Y. 1992).

106.   11 U.S.C. § 1125.

107.   *See, e.g., In re Edison Brothers Stores*, Case No. 95-1354 (PJW) (Bankr. D. Del. Aug. 21, 1997) (extending the exclusive periods for 21 months); *In re Perkins*, 71 B.R. 294, 296 (W.D. Tenn. 1987) (exclusive periods extended for more than 22 months); *In re Phar-Mor Inc.*, Case No. 92-41599 (Bankr. N.D. Ohio Sept. 21, 1994) (exclusive periods extended for more than two years); *In re Federated Dep't Stores, Inc.* Case No. 1-90-00130 (Bankr. S.D. Ohio Aug. 27, 1991) (exclusivity retained by the debtors for almost two years); *In re Trans World Airlines, Inc.*, Case No. 92-115 (HSB) (Bankr. D. Del. May 6, 1993) (exclusivity retained by the debtor for approximately 16 months); *In re R.H. Macy & Co.*, Case No. 92 B 40477 (BRL) (Bankr. S.D. N.Y. Feb. 22, 1994) (debtor retained exclusivity for two and one-half years); and *In re Caldor, Inc.*, Case No. 95 B 44080 (JLG) (Bankr. S.D. N.Y. July 30, 1996) (exclusive period extended for 17 months).

108.   *See In re Express One International, Inc.*, 194 B.R. 98, 100 (Bankr. E.D. Tex. 1996) ("The Bankruptcy Code provides debtors a limited period to propose a plan of reorganization and obtain acceptance without fear of competition. During the first 120 days of the Chapter 11 case, only the debtor-in-possession may file a plan of reorganization."); *In re Mother Hubbard, Inc.*, 152 B.R. 189, 195 (Bankr. W.D. Mich. 1993) ("The purpose of § 1121 is twofold. First, it allows the debtor a reasonable time to obtain confirmation of a plan without the threat of a competing plan. Second, it ensures creditors will not endure unreasonable delay after a debtor files chapter 11."); *In re National Safe Center, Inc.*, 54 B.R. 239, 240 (Bankr. D. Haw. 1985) ("Section 1121(b) of the Bankruptcy Code expressly states that only the debtor, and no one else, may file a plan of reorganization within the 120 days after the date of the order for relief.").

109.   *See* 11 U.S.C. § 544.

110.   11 U.S.C. § 1109(b). § 1109(b) provides that "A party interest, including the debtor, the trustee, a creditors' committee, an equity security holders' committee, a creditor, an equity security holder, or any indenture trustee, may raise and may appear and be heard on any issue in a case under this chapter."

111.   *See In re Marin Motor Oil, Inc.*, 689 F.2d 445 (3d Cir. 1982), *cert. denied*, 459 U.S. 1206 (1983).

112.   *See Fuel Oil Supply and Terminaling v. Gulf Oil Corp.*, 762 F.2d 1283 (5th Cir. 1985); *In re George Rodman, Inc.*, 33 B.R. 348 (Bankr. W.D. Okla. 1983) (holding that right to intervene not absolute but permissive).

113.   Fed. R. Civ. Proc. 24(b).

114.   *See In re Louisiana World Exposition, Inc.*, 832 F.2d 1391, 1397-98 (5th Cir. 1987) ("As we review the record, it seems plain that [the debtor] would not have sought the relief the Committee seeks, even if the Committee had filed a formal request. The Committee did ask [the debtor] to bring an action for malfeasance against its directors and officers. [The debtor] refused, apparently being unable to act because of the conflict of interest presented to its decision makers . . . .").

115.   *See, generally, Collier on Bankruptcy, supra* note 11, ¶ 1103.05[6] at 1103-35–36.

116.   *See, e.g., Starzynski v. Sequoia Forest Industries*, 72 F.3d 816, 821 (10th Cir. 1995) ("[U]nder 11 U.S.C. § 1109(b)(1993), a creditors' committee or even an individual creditor may, with leave of the bankruptcy court, initiate avoidance and other actions when the debtor-in-possession has failed to do so."); *Louisiana World Exposition v. Federal Ins. Co.*, 858 F.2d 233, 247 (5th Cir. 1988); *In re V. Savino Oil & Heating Co.*, 91 B.R. 655 (Bankr. E.D. N.Y. 1988); *In re Nicolet, Inc.*, 80 B.R. 733 (Bankr. E.D. Pa. 1987); *In re STN Enter.*, 779 F.2d 901 (2nd Cir. 1985).

117.   *Collier on Bankruptcy, supra* note 11, ¶ 1103.05[6][a] at 1103-36.1.

9

Lender Services:
Let the Lender Beware!

Robert S. Paul and Kris Coghlan

PricewaterhouseCoopers LLP

INTRODUCTION

In working with troubled companies, as a consultant to a creditor, we often encounter lenders who are surprised by some of the business and accounting practices of their borrowers. Lenders often learn the hard way that they have not equipped themselves with sufficient information to effectively manage the relationship with their borrowers when things get tough. Thus, lenders may find themselves scrambling to verify facts, gather data, and understand business practices before they can make critical credit management decisions.

The degree to which lenders are surprised by a borrower differs depending on the safeguards they employ in the due diligence process. For example:

- *Asset-based lenders* generally perform extensive analyses at the borrower's corporate and operating locations, so they typically know a great deal about the borrower's accounting and operating practices. At the first sign of operating weaknesses, lenders will increase the frequency and depth of on-site analyses.
- *Subordinated lenders* rarely perform the level of analysis that an asset-based lender would employ. At the first sign of operating weaknesses, the subordinated lender is constrained for information and must rely on the borrower and borrower's counsel for information.

Granted, all lenders cannot always operate like asset-based lenders, staging expensive and time-consuming field exams. However, we have found that those lenders who mandate on-site due diligence of specific aspects of a prospective borrower's accounting and business practices best position themselves for more

191

intelligent credit decisions throughout the lending cycle. This is especially true if credit quality deteriorates and a restructuring or workout is necessary.

This chapter discusses some of the best due diligence practices performed today. For example, financial and strategic buyers typically perform excellent business plan evaluations; asset-based lenders are knowledgeable about working capital assets and liabilities; real estate investors perform sophisticated analyses of real estate investment trusts (REITS) and funds. We are increasingly being asked to help clients understand these assets and issues as well as a business' non–brick and mortar assets, such as brand value. Following are observations regarding selected due diligence areas of inquiry that should be considered by lenders in their evaluation of either new deals or restructuring existing credits.

BUSINESS PLAN EVALUATION

Business plans and related financial projections are often critical elements in making lending decisions and in structuring financial relationships. The purpose of a business plan evaluation is threefold:

- *To help assess management's leadership ability.* The absence of a thoughtful business plan and regular planning processes reflect poorly on management. In short, the less inclusive the business plan is, the higher the risk.
- *To highlight internal accountability and responsibility deficiencies.* Reviewing a company's management is a sensitive yet critical aspect in analyzing a business plan. Lenders must understand corporate leaders—their roles and effectiveness, as well as their strengths and weaknesses. Understanding other factors is equally important: whether corporate lines of responsibility are ambiguous, how duties are delegated, and whether morale or other factors will affect continuing operations. In addition, knowledge of management's qualifications and track record can provide a lender with insight into the company's future performance.
- *To assess the plan's feasibility.* A potential borrower will maximize the appearance of its financial position in order to secure the best financing. Business plans, therefore, tend to be optimistic. The value of a plan depends on the quality of its information and the validity of underlying assumptions. The best plans present facts objectively, without exaggerated or biased views of reality. While a well-prepared business plan also is a highly effective marketing tool, it must be credible to be useful. Credibility reflects management's competence and should be closely examined by lenders.

With all these issues, the question now becomes: *How do lenders validate a business plan before using it to gain insight into a potential client?* In order to assess risks and opportunities associated with financing, a lender must have a complete, quantitative, and specific business plan. This business plan assessment process can help structure more meaningful bank covenants, downgrade risk, and maximize return value.

There is no standard process in evaluating a business plan. Analyses depend on the lender's policies and the uniqueness of the potential borrower. The various levels of analysis include:

- *Financial accounting analysis.* Assess whether financial statements represent actual performance and whether future projections are reasonable.
- *Operational analysis.* Examine revenue and cost structure to assess current and prospective levels of operational efficiency. Evaluate prospective expenses, review supplier contracts, and examine key customer relationships. Identify opportunities to reduce costs and bolster efficiency.
- *Cash flow forecasting.* Analyze projections using historical performance, industry expectations, and strategic plans.
- *Competitive, product line, and industry analyses.* Examine pricing strategies, competitive advantages, market share, industry trends, and risk. Review management's plan for taking on the competition and decide whether cash flow projections adequately address possible competitor actions.
- *Other analyses.* Review employee compensation and benefits, including insurance. Examine management information systems. Assess potential environmental liabilities. Perform business and asset appraisals for collateral financing and insurance.

Cash Flow Analysis

Cash flow analysis is critical to a company's survival as well as to any lending decision. A thorough analysis will identify sensitive periods of cash flow, and will allow lenders to tailor debt payments accordingly. In order to effectively analyze cash flow, lenders must determine what drives it.

- *Sources and uses of cash.* Cash primarily comes from financing (i.e., revolving loans, commercial paper sales), operations (customer payments), and investments. Payments, in part, are determined by operational requirements, storage costs, financing costs, and repayment of debt. The various ways a company manages cash can alter its net cash position. For instance, if a business consistently pays suppliers before collecting from its customers, it could suffer liquidity constraints. Ordering inventory before it is needed (inventory buildup) can also lead to a shortage of cash.
- *Drivers of cash flow.* Lenders must understand what affects cash flow. Some factors include required capital investment, cost structure, cash reserves, growth expectations, exchange rate fluctuations, and market demand.

Assessment of Industry and Competitive Risk

All business activities face hazards, depending on the industry, competition, and political and economic situations in countries in which the prospective borrower has operations or customers. The prospective lender must assess whether a company's strategy addresses the external environment and internal circumstances.

When management demonstrates a sound knowledge of industry and competitive conditions as well as its own internal operations, they instill confidence in their business plan. Investors and lenders look for executives who can establish a strategic vision, set objectives, and craft a viable strategy. Without effective insight, managers may pursue a plan that does not build a competitive advantage nor boost company performance.

Industries differ in their economic characteristics, structure, competitive situations, and outlook. Therefore, a good analysis should begin with an economic overview of the industry. Factors to consider include:

- Market segment and size
- Market growth rate and where the industry is positioned in the growth cycle
- Degree of industry profitability
- Scope of competition (local, regional, national, or international)
- Number of rivals and their size (Does the industry consist of many small companies, or is it dominated by a few large ones?)
- Whether competing products and services are differentiated or commodities
- Number of suppliers and their size
- Ease and expense of entry and exit
- Capital requirements
- Pace of technological change
- Whether high rates of capacity utilization are crucial to achieving efficiency

Economics and competition suggest much about the nature of an industry, but cannot help predict how an environment will change. It is therefore important to identify and consider the effect of factors that bring on change. The most common industry driving forces include:

- *Changes in the long-term industry growth rate.* Increases or decreases in industry growth alter the balance between supply and demand, intensity of competition, and facility of entry and exit. A jump in long-term demand can attract new entrants and encourage established firms to grow. A shrinking market can cause some companies to leave and induce remaining firms to retrench to a smaller production base and close inefficient plants.
- *Changes in buyers and how a product is used.* Shifts in buyer composition and new uses for a product may force companies to change the way they offer credit, technical assistance, and maintenance and repair, and can also alter the distribution network (e.g., a different mix of dealers and retail outlets). This factor could prompt producers to broaden or narrow product lines, increase or decrease capital requirements, and change sales and promotion approaches.

- *Product innovation.* Technology and creativity can expand product differentiation among sellers, broaden an industry's customer base, and rejuvenate industry growth.
- *Technological change.* Innovation can allow an industry to produce new and/or better products more efficiently. Technological developments also can bring about changes in capital requirements, minimum plant sizes, vertical integration benefits, and learning/experience curve effects.
- *Marketing innovation.* When firms successfully introduce new ways to market products, they can alter rivals' competitive positions and thus force strategy revisions.
- *Entry or exit of major firms.* The arrival of foreign firms into a market once dominated by domestic companies generally shakes up competitive conditions. Likewise, when a domestic firm from another industry tries to enter the field (either by acquisition or by launching its own venture), its resources generally introduce competition. Exit of major firms similarly affects competitive structure.
- *Diffusion of technical know-how.* As technology spreads, firms that exclusively possessed the know-how see their expertise erode. In recent years, technology transfer nationally and internationally has helped drive globalization of markets and competition.
- *Increasing global competition.* Industries move toward globalization for several reasons. A national firm, for example, may launch an aggressive long-term strategy to win a global market position. Demand for the industry's product may show up in new countries. Trade barriers may drop. Cheap foreign labor may lead a company to produce labor-intensive goods in low-wage countries. A company may realize it can achieve economies of scale if it expands overseas rather than just selling at home. Globalization becomes a more significant issue in industries in which natural resources are located only in select countries, inexpensive localized production is an overriding consideration, and at least one company is pushing to gain a competitive position in as many countries as possible.
- *Changes in cost and efficiency.* Building large market share becomes especially important in industries in which new economies of scale are emerging or a strong learning curve allows more experienced firms to undercut rivals. Likewise, sharply rising costs for a key input (like raw materials or labor) can cause a scramble to line up reliable supplies at affordable prices or to find less expensive substitutes. The balance of competition can shift with changes in cost or efficiency.
- *Regulatory forces and government policy change.* New laws often force significant changes in industry practices. Deregulation has been a major force in the airline, natural gas, banking, and telecommunications industries.
- *Risk.* Emerging industries are characterized by an unproven cost structure, uncertainty over potential market size, the cost and time necessary to surmount technological problems, and questions regarding the best way to get products to buyers.

WORKING CAPITAL ASSETS AND LIABILITIES

With most companies, lenders may get excellent insight by analyzing working capital accounts. The historical performance of receivables and inventory is rich with information including returns, billing practices, product quality, credit quality, revenue recognition practices, and value. Payables management and performance provide insight into vendor relationships, materials management, and liquidity. Inventory and accounts receivable typically are the primary assets used as loan collateral.

Accounts Receivable

The asset-based lending community has designed and implemented specific programs and techniques to evaluate accounts receivable. While analyses are often similar for different industries, specific companies merit special considerations. Key areas include:

- *Credit and collection policies.* Analyze the underwriting process for new customers and periodically update information on existing clients. Are credit limits in place, and how are they determined? What are the collection processes through the various stages of delinquency? What is the extent of management subjectivity in any of the control processes?
- *Receivable statistics.* Analyze aggregate and customer-level aging trends. Examine turnover and dilution experience, including seasonality and underlying business practices. Evaluate return and allowance trends as a percentage of sales, and understand underlying causes of unusual fluctuations.
- *Concentrations and terms of sale.* Analyze portfolio concentrations, including customer, industry, and geographic factors. Determine different terms of sale offered and the underlying reason for any unusual terms.
- *Ineligible receivables.* Identify receivables that may not be easily collectable. Types and quantity of ineligible receivables, even in a non-asset-based transaction, can provide the lender with insight into company practices
- *Billing practices.* Analyze practices. Does the company bill and record revenues at times other than shipment (such as bill-and-hold transactions)? With which customers?

Accounts Receivable Statistics.   Companies rarely perform more detailed analyses of accounts receivable statistics other than receivables agings. They do so only when they have some form of receivables-based financing such as a securitization or an asset-based loan. Preparing an analysis is relatively straightforward, involving a monthly roll-forward of the accounts receivable over some period greater than 12 months. The roll-forward should disclose all components of receivables, including new invoices, cash collections, and non-cash credits and debits.

The statistical analysis is derived from data gathered in the roll-forward. Dilution is the extent of noncash credit activity in the receivables base. Turnover assesses the relationship between cash collection, outstanding receivables, and terms of sale. Further analysis of credit activity, such as returns and allowances, is possible given the degree of credit memo reporting detail available. Credit and rebill activity could represent a red flag for billing and or shipping problems.

Concentrations and Terms of Sale.   Terms of sale should be considered within the context of industry standards. Any significant variance warrants follow-up. For example, why would a company offer 90-day sale terms when its competitors offer 30-day terms? Terms of sale may vary seasonally or from customer to customer. A customer with a troublesome payment history, for example, may have cash-on-delivery terms, and may not actually represent a dependable long-term source of revenue; the lender should know this.

Lenders also should pay attention to significant concentrations. A company reliant on relatively few customers, foreign relationships, or industry representations can present unique credit risks.

Ineligible Receivables.   Ineligible receivables may be difficult to collect. Types and quantity of these receivables, even in a non–asset-based transaction, can provide lenders with insights about the company. Examples of ineligible receivables:

- *Past due/delinquent.* Receivables longer than 90 days or so past due. Large overdue balances might indicate credit quality or product quality issues.
- *Credit balances in the past due categories.* Old credit balances might indicate poor accounting controls, high returns, and product quality issues.
- *Cross-aging.* Customers with significant past due balances could indicate credit quality issues as well as general risk control concerns.
- *Contra accounts.* When a company buys products from a vendor and sells to the same merchant, an accounts receivable and an accounts payable ledger entry are created. Such balances are ineligible because they represent offsets against accounts receivable where no cash would be exchanged.
- *Miscellaneous charges.* This category includes charges such as freight, finance charges, and sales tax, which are considered pass-through charges.
- *Advertising, promotion, and volume allowance.* Allowances are considered dilutive, and it is important in due diligence to identify such potentially dilutive items.

Collection of Receivables—In Good Times and Bad.   As with all industries and businesses, cash flow—and thus prompt collection of receivables—is critical. Working capital improves when the time between billing and payment is reduced.

The first step to timely collection of receivables is capturing payments and related billing information. This can be accomplished via various collection methods, the most widely used being the lockbox. Lockboxes minimize the timing float and allow for greater control over cash collections, especially when a credit is becoming troubled.

A well-oiled credit and collections department has access to payment information and aging reports, and encourages prompt payment of invoices and responds quickly to customers' billing questions.

Inventory

Validating the cost and quantity of inventory is a critical part of the loan proposal process. Often, inventory may be altered for financial statement purposes. Examples include inflated values and quantities, items billed in advance of shipping dates, and the nondisclosure of obsolete inventory, slow-moving inventory, and liens.

As with receivables, the asset-based lending community has designed and implemented programs and techniques for inventory. While the types of analyses are applicable in many industries, specific companies may require special consideration. Some key areas include:

- Inventory valuation
- Inventory statistics
- Physical inventory observation
- Ineligible inventory
- Inventory liquidation

Inventory Valuation.   In analyzing inventory, it is important to consider the type of costing system:

- Whether standard costs are in use
- How under- and over-absorbed costs are allocated to inventory
- How standard costs are updated in cost of goods sold
- The effects of interim and year-end results
- Which costs are included in overhead
- How costs are distributed
- The treatment of intercompany profit and its effect on statistics

In a typical audit, an accountant tries to verify the quantity of goods in inventory and their proper valuation. Accordingly, a lender must understand and test the company's costing and valuation methodology. Cost valuation is tested by examining sales invoices, bills, and other supporting documents. Comparing reported inventory costs to vendor invoices will help identify inconsistencies if the sample size is statistically significant. When verifying inventory valuation, take care to consider these precautions:

- *Actual cost.* This should include all cost incurred to bring the item to production. Such costs may include shipping, storage, and miscellaneous charges. Lenders should understand how costs are calculated because capitalized costs may be unrecoverable in a liquidation scenario.

- *Standard cost.* Standard costs are determined at the beginning of the year based on last year's costs and adjustments for price variances. It is important to understand whether the company capitalizes or expenses the price variances and whether they are abnormal. Abnormal variances may signal problems with the company's cost accounting system.

Inventory Statistics. The following data provide a good beginning to understanding inventory valuation issues:

- Trends in inventory levels and seasonal fluctuations
- Stratification by fast-moving, slow-moving, excess, and obsolete inventory
- Inventory turnover by product line, line of business, division, or subsidiary
- Trends in customer service levels, stock-outs, substitutes, and back orders
- Product returns

Physical Inventory Observation. Actual observation of the physical inventory, in addition to statistical sampling to test the accuracy of the inventory records to actual goods, will help validate the quantity reported. In addition to the physical count, it is equally important to observe the condition and accessibility of the inventory. Conversely, it is important to examine items that were either scrapped or failed quality control inspection. For example, if the inventory is typically stacked in a manner in which the goods are being damaged, then the value of the inventory may be overstated. ABC Laboratories engaged in a practice of stacking boxes of caps for aerosol cans too high, and many of these caps would get damaged. This practice had a detrimental impact on their production runs, because the inventory records did not accurately reflect the "actual" quantity available for production.

Ineligible Inventory. Ineligible inventory displays certain characteristics that place some uncertainty on the ability to sell the inventory within a reasonable time frame. The types and quantity of ineligible inventory, even in a non–asset-based transaction, can provide the lender with insights into some of the practices of the company. For example, inventory that is slow moving, obsolete, consigned, in transit, or at outside locations are typically considered ineligible for advance purposes. Following are examples of ineligible receivables:

- *Raw materials.* Proprietary raw materials are usually ineligible for advance purposes since the items most likely have limited application outside the company, and the pool of potential buyers may be limited. Commodity like raw materials, on the other hand, have widespread application outside the company and an extensive pool of potential buyers, and therefore would be considered eligible.
- *Work-in-process.* Work-in-process inventory typically requires additional time and costs to convert the inventory to finished goods, and is therefore ineligible for advance purposes.

- *Slow-moving and obsolete inventory.* Slow-moving and obsolete inventory are ineligible for advance purposes because the items may have limited or no value. The cost of liquidating the items may exceed the estimated salvage value.
- *Consigned inventory.* Consigned inventory is ineligible for advance purposes. Although the inventory may be located on the company's premises and included in its perpetual inventory system, title does not transfer until it is purchased by the company. For example, ABC Laboratories fills aerosol cans on behalf of Clean-All, a manufacturer of household cleaners. Because the cleaners contain proprietary formulas, a preblend mix is sent to the company. Although the mix is included in the perpetual system for tracking purposes, title does not transfer until the company purchases the formula from Clean-All to fill an order.
- *Inventory in transit or at outside locations.* Inventory that is either in transit or at an outside location is ineligible for advance purposes. Because the inventory is in the custody of a third party, it may be difficult to repossess in the event of a liquidation. Consequently, inventory stored at warehousing facilities that are leased and items that have been sent to subcontractors for additional services may be considered ineligible.

The criteria described above provide an overview of whether inventory should be considered eligible for advance purposes, but are by no means exhaustive. The lender must evaluate other critical business issues, such as industry trends, historical performance, competitors, and the customer base.

Although determining the value of the inventory available for advance purposes is somewhat subjective, one cannot rely solely on financial statements to assess the value of the collateral. It is essential to understand both the classification and nature of the inventory. In addition, conducting physical inventory counts, testing the cost and valuation methodology, and examining the company's records and books will help the lender determine the actual value of the assets available for advance purposes, and assist the lender in determining whether the collateral is sufficient to cover the loan.

Accounts Payable

Detailed analysis of accounts payable can provide much information about how the company orders materials and manages its vendors, the level of reliance on any one group of vendors over any other group, and management's control of its payables. Analysis of payables should consider the following:

- Payable aging and turnover trends will provide insight into the company's payable management program. Any analysis of payables should consider and include the existence of book overdrafts, held checks, and payable accruals. Results should consider the payment terms offered by the company's suppliers.

- Widespread usage of letters of credit may indicate some concern for the credit quality of the company.
- Comparisons of payable and purchasing concentrations could indicate a vendor management program being used by the company or differing payment terms for certain vendors (i.e., Are there multiple sources of supply for key raw materials?).
- Has the company negotiated any special supply arrangements and terms with any of its vendors?

INTANGIBLES—WHAT ARE THEY WORTH?

According to a study of the Standard & Poor's (S&P) 500 performed by PricewaterhouseCoopers, intangible asset value of the S&P 500 has nearly tripled over the past five years, while the book value of these companies has risen by just 40%. Intangible assets are a significant and growing part of the value of U.S. companies. As the U.S. economy becomes increasingly driven by services, technology, and information, lenders are more frequently using a company's intellectual property (one category of "intangibles") as collateral for extending credit.

In certain situations, asset-based lenders and cash flow lenders have become less distinct from one another as asset-based lenders include advances against intangibles or rely on intangible values as a significant factor in the lending decision. Some believe that these lenders are becoming increasingly aggressive as to the types of deals they are financing, while others suggest that they are simply smarter because they recognize the significant value of intangible assets previously ignored. In most companies, there is significant value to intangibles; however, it is essential that a lender understand intangible value and how it changes in a distressed situation.

Intangibles Defined

Intangible assets can be broadly identified as "intellectual property" and "other intangibles". Intellectual property includes patents, trademarks, trade names, trade dress, copyrights, and trade secrets. Other intangibles can include business processes, customer lists, supplier agreements, and know-how (labor skills, distributor relationships, facility locations) to name a few.

Intellectual property, unlike other intangible assets, is protected by law and treaty which provides certain rights, limitations, proscriptions, and remedies. For example, enforcement provisions enable an intellectual property holder to stop unauthorized users from using its intellectual property, and provide economic remedies when unauthorized usage is declared. Since intellectual property is afforded this protection, a company can enjoy the benefits of reduced production costs, premium pricing, and/or increased market share resulting from the various advantages over competition that intellectual property rights afford.

Specific types of intellectual property include:

- *Patents.* Include products and services with rights of ownership. Patents have different classifications and, depending on the classification, have different patent lives as defined by law.
- *Trademarks.* Include words, logos, brand names, symbols, or combinations thereof, and are used by companies to distinguish their products from competitors.
- *Copyrights.* Consist of original works by an author that are reproduced or communicated in some tangible medium. Copyrights protect the form of expression of an idea, but not the idea itself. Examples include sound recordings, literary works, and computer software programs.
- *Trade secrets.* Any proprietary confidential device, pattern, formula, or knowledge of a business that enables it to gain a competitive advantage over others that do not know how to use it. An example is the formula for Coke.

Basis of Valuation of Intangibles—A Cursory Review

There are many reasons for valuing intangibles, including damage assessment in intellectual property litigation, purchase price allocation in mergers and acquisitions, transfer pricing, determination for a sale or purchase offer price, or financing purposes.

Various methods are used to value intangibles, and the resulting "price" of an asset depends on the basis of valuation. Two concepts are commonly applied in intangible valuation: (1) *value in use* and (2) *value in exchange*. *Value in use* is the intangible asset's going-concern value, or fair market value. Fair market value is defined as the price at which property would change hands between a willing buyer and a willing seller, when the former is not under any compulsion to buy, and the latter is not under any compulsion to sell, and both parties have reasonable knowledge of relevant facts. *Value in exchange* represents the intangible asset's value in an orderly or forced liquidation, and will almost always result in a lower value for (and quick disposition of) the asset. A secured lender will most likely want to use an intellectual property's liquidation value for loan advance purposes.

Factors Impacting Intangible Asset Value in Distressed Companies

Much has been written about intangible valuation methods and approaches, and the actual methods employed will not be discussed here. Instead, we will put forward a framework for lenders to begin thinking about the factors that impact intangible value in distressed situations.

Ultimately, the "salability" or affirmation of rights (e.g., value of rights) is enhanced as the risk of integrating elements into a commercially successful product is reduced. The impact of various factors on intellectual property value discussed herein have a number of underlying assumptions. These include the assumptions that all other factors are static, that the various factors are not interrelated, and that equal practical application is given for an intellectual property asset. In reality, of course, these factors are dynamic and interrelated, and the factors identified in this chapter are only a subset of those relevant to intangible value and retention of that value in distress.

The value of most intangible assets decline as a company becomes distressed or troubled. However, we suggest that broadly speaking, the degree to which an intangible asset value declines in distressed companies is dependent on three key factors (among others):

- The type of intangible (i.e., whether it is an intellectual property or other intangible asset. Also, within intellectual property, whether it is a patent, trademark, copyright, or trade secret.)
- The diversity and richness of the rights (sublicensing allowances, exclusivity provisions, remaining years to expiration, etc.)
- The industry (industry size, nature of competition, future prospects, international implications, technological change in the industry, product life cycle, etc.)

Types of Intangible Assets

There is a pecking order to value retention of intangible assets as a company becomes distressed. That is, the degree to which an intangible asset holds its value is dependent in part on its type. Generally, we assert that the priority is as follows:

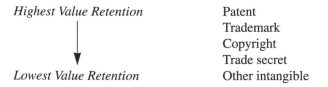

Highest Value Retention	Patent
	Trademark
	Copyright
	Trade secret
Lowest Value Retention	Other intangible

We suggest this pecking order theory because different types of intangibles are valued differently, because they are afforded different types of rights, responsibilities, and limitations. Depending on the type of intangible, its value may be more or less dependent on the general reputation of a company, its performance, and the quality of its products and management. A basic example of this is a comparison between a utility patent with 20 years of remaining life, covering a critical component of a product versus a trade secret involving the speeds and feeds for manufacturing the component. The point is that the latter's value is not as significant to the commercial success of the product.

However, when making a comparison between a utility patent with 20 years of remaining life covering a critical component and that of a trade secret or "know-how," one needs to consider the following: the net realizable value of a trade secret and "know-how" is dependent on the owner's continued investment and maintenance of the subject matter's confidentiality and protection, whereas the value of a patent is not as dependent on the owner's fulfillment of those responsibilities.

Diversity and Richness of Intellectual Property Rights

The diversity and richness of intellectual property rights may also impact the degree to which the value of the intangible asset declines in distressed companies. A few factors to consider include the following:

- *Exclusivity versus nonexclusivity.* Exclusivity significantly increases the value of these rights because it reduces, if not eliminates, competitors who cannot reap the advantages provided by the intellectual property.
- *Sublicensing allowance.* Generally, being able to generate revenues by transferring rights to others will increase the value of rights to the intellectual property. As a company becomes distressed, the company sublicensing provision enables it to retain more value because of its broader distribution rights and market responsiveness.
- *Grant-backs, pooling, and other collaborative forms.* This arrangement will increase value by passing on "leasehold improvements" developed by one licensee back to the licensor (grant-back) who can then distribute those improvements to other licensees (pooling) in a nonexclusive license agreement. In short, grant-backs, pooling, and other collaborative forms free the intellectual property from being dependent on the existence of the original owner of the intellectual property. An example of this is a licensor of software who has a number of licensees, and an arrangement in which any enhancements made by the licensee are reverted back to the licensor.

Industry Intangible Value

Value is impacted by dynamics and factors specific to an industry in which a company operates. The degree to which an intangible value declines is influenced by the industry within which the company operates. From an industry perspective, the following factors play a role in impacting intangible value and changes in this value on company distress.

- *Degree of technical change in the industry.* This factor directly impacts the economic life of the intellectual property or other intangible; in fact, the greater the pace of technical change, the shorter the economic life of any intangible. A distressed company in an industry of significant technical change will experience greater reductions in intellectual property value than a distressed company in an industry of little technical change, because the technology may become obsolete. However, when looking at value and value changes, care must be taken to assess whether the "old" technology offers a building block that is a necessary adjunct to newer technologies in an industry. That is, to use these newer technologies effectively, a company must obtain product rights for the old, foundational technology. In this case, although it may be obsolete, the foundation technology's value decline is mitigated because it serves as a blocking technology. An example is in the computer technology industry. Certain patented technology in the area of redundant array of information disks (RAID) may be foundational to ex-

ploiting new technologies for faster processes, and hence be a blocking technology. Another example of foundational technology is the pull-down menu system integrated into Windows-based applications.
- *Market size, demand, future prospects.* The size of the market, market demand, and future prospects are directly linked to maximizing intellectual property value. Shrinking markets, elastic demand, or poor industry outlook will ultimately decrease intellectual property value. A distressed company in an industry in which demand is declining, or demand is elastic, will suffer reduced value of its intellectual property because the applicable sales available to collect royalties is reduced. An example of this can be found in the cigarette manufacturing industry.
- *Industry practices.* Different industries have different norms regarding cross-licensing and standard setting. Cross-licensing practices will boost the value of intellectual property.

In summary, in most companies there is significant value to intangibles, and given the changing economy to one of services and technology, intangible value is becoming an increasingly larger percentage of a business's value. However, it is essential that a lender understand the complexities involved in estimating value, especially as it mutates in a distressed situation. Understanding the nature or type of intangible being assessed, the diversity and richness of rights associated with the intangible, and considering how the intangible value is impacted by factors and dynamics specific to the industry in which the company operates are all critical to assessing how intangible value changes on distress.

INTERNAL CONTROL ENVIRONMENT

The purpose of the internal control environment evaluation is to gain comfort that the proper controls and processes that support stated asset values are in place and functioning optimally to ensure existence, valuation, measurability, ownership, and identification of any related liabilities on a periodic basis.

The Control Environment

Integrated Control—Integrated Framework, authored by Coopers & Lybrand LLP, outlines control activities that can be classified by their specific control objectives. The following are examples of certain control activities, such as ensuring completeness and accuracy of data processing, which are performed by personnel at various levels throughout an organization:

- *Top level reviews.* Top level reviews are performed to determine actual company performance as measured against such benchmarks as forecasting, budgeting, and so forth. Major initiatives, such as marketing thrusts, improved production processes, and cost containment programs, are tracked and evaluated to measure the extent to which targets are being reached.

- *Direct functional or activity management.* Performance reports are reviewed by management, whose functional responsibility specifically includes reviewing output. Managers review these reports in order to verify information, identify trends, and ultimately compare the information to company targets and economic statistics.
- *Information processing.* Numerous data integrity controls are performed to check for completeness, accuracy, and authorization of transactions. Data entered into a system are subject to edit checks (or matching to approved control files). Typically, clerical personnel act on any exceptions discovered that require follow-up. New system development, as well as updates to existing systems, are controlled. Access to data, files, and programs is restricted.
- *Physical controls.* Inventories, equipment, securities, cash, and other assets should be physically secured, resulting in a control mechanism that compares periodic counts to amounts shown on control records.
- *Performance indicators.* The relation of different sets of data to one another, and the resulting analyses and corrective action that transpires, serve as control activities. The percentage of returned merchandise to total orders, for example, is a typical performance indicator. The investigation of performance indicators ensures that management is aware of, and taking action on, any unexpected trends or results.
- *Segregation of duties.* Duties are divided among employees to reduce the risk of inappropriate behavior or erroneous processing. For instance, responsibilities for authorizing transactions, recording them, and handling the related asset are typically divided among employees.

Critical business cycles, such as inventory and accounts receivable, have many control components to consider. PricewaterhouseCoopers' current *Record of Application Controls,* a template used by audit professionals to help assess the overall integrity of a client's control environment, identifies issues that need to be addressed when performing an assessment of a company's internal control structure:

- What is the basis for the release of raw materials into production, and how are they approved?
- What is the basis for transfers from production to finished goods, and how are they approved?
- What ensures that finished goods are released based on actual shipping orders?
- How are adjustments to perpetual inventory records authorized?
- What ensures that all requisitions for materials and component parts are input for processing?
- What ensures that all movements of goods during production are recorded and input for processing?
- What ensures that all shipments of finished goods are input for processing?

These are only a few of the many questions that need to be effectively answered when performing a thorough evaluation of a company's control environment of inventory. They provide insight into the thought processes that need to be initiated in order for a truly effective control assessment to take place.

Case Study

An example of a critical inventory control breakdown occurred at Company X in the early 1990s. At one time, Company X was a leading retailer in the fabrics and crafts industry. Due to slowed growth, increasing competition, and declining profit margins, industry leaders shifted focus to mass merchandising by converting smaller stores into larger superstores. Between 1990 and 1994, Company X increased its distribution from 300 stores to over 500 superstores. However, its information technology and the resulting quality of its managerial accounting data lagged far behind the industry leader, Company Y.

An analysis revealed that Company X's inventory turnover averaged only 1.3 times a year between 1990 and 1994. Company Y averaged over 3 times per year during the same time period. Company Y's inventory turnover was superior due in large part to its aggressive inventory management system. Company Y had computerized its point of sale and invested in inventory management systems, whereas Company X often performed manual inventory counts to keep track of its goods, resulting in outdated data and inconsistent count quality. As a result, Company X's management of its inventory spun out of control, which was in part responsible for the company's ultimate demise.

Systems Integration

Systems integration is also a critical component of an effective control environment. Company Z was a public mechanical and electrical construction contracting conglomerate in the early 1990s that filed for bankruptcy. The company was marred by many problems, predominant among them was an inefficient financial reporting system. After numerous acquisitions that were never integrated into the parent company, Company Z was left with a management and systems nightmare, including inconsistencies in reported data and a slow, clumsy reporting structure.

The overall flexibility of accounting systems is critical to lenders. The lender needs comfort regarding a company's flexibility in generating useful and reliable accounting reports, such as asset concentration, stratifying receivables, aging reports, past due reports, delinquency trends, roll-forwards, and dilution.

Besides systems integration issues, the lender must be very sensitive to other computer-related issues, including:

- Year 2000 issues:
  - Has the company performed a Y2K risk analysis and documented it in writing?
  - Does the company have specific contractual requirements or obligations to customers or business partners, and can the company's systems address Y2K issues?

- If the company uses vendor-supplied packaged software or a service bureau, have Y2K issues been discussed with each vendor and service bureau under contract?
- What area(s) of the company's operations can potentially be impacted by Y2K problems?
- Has the company developed any written contingency plans to ensure that there will be an uninterrupted supply of goods and/or services to it and its customers?
- Data backup/storage issues:
  - Are backup procedures appropriate for both data and programs?
  - Are backups stored in a secure location?
  - What ensures that backup and recovery procedures will work when required?
- Disaster recovery issues:
  - How has management assessed, and do they continually assess, the impact that a loss of information technology would have on key business functions?
  - How does management ensure that the business continuity plans are in place, current, and adequately documented?
- Hardware/software issues:
  - What ensures that the package is appropriate for the computer hardware and operating environment?
  - Is the package selected well known and widely used?
  - Is customization of the package appropriately controlled?
  - How mature are the accounting system and control procedures used by the organization?
  - Is the current infrastructure capable of future requirements? What are the company's capital expenditure plans?

Internal Audit

The primary role of internal auditors in an organization is to directly test and examine the company's internal control structure and make recommendations for improvements. The Institute of Internal Auditors specify that the focus of internal auditing should encompass the examination and evaluation of the adequacy and effectiveness of the organization's system of internal control and the quality of performance in carrying out assigned responsibilities.[1]

Typically, asset-based lenders are allowed access to the results of a company's internal audit testing, which gives the lender an opportunity to review the testing strategy and results. Internal audit testing is typically comprehensive in its coverage of business processes, including more difficult areas such as accounts receivable and inventory.

The Institute of Internal Auditors standards also outline the internal auditors' responsibilities and their relationship relative to the tasks that they are assigned. Perhaps most importantly, these standards provide that internal auditors should have sufficient independence from the areas that they are auditing.

Internal auditors can maintain objectivity only when they are not placed in situations of deferring their opinions regarding their activities to others. In order to maintain the internal auditors' effectiveness and value to the organization, there must be an appropriate reporting structure in place. Internal auditors should have ultimate accountability to only the board of directors or the audit committee and should have overall authority to follow up on any important findings and recommendations.

An internal audit department that is not functioning properly is a profound structural weakness that the lender should view as a red flag. For example, a company whose internal audit function reports to the chief financial officer (CFO), or whose compensation is correlated to some degree with the company's financial results, may have a conflict of interest which should be investigated by the lender. PricewaterhouseCoopers personnel witnessed this very situation in the aforementioned Company Z, in which the internal audit division reported to the CFO, who was the brother of the controller. Management compensation was driven on the basis of company accounting earnings, creating a rather unscrupulous situation in which upper management began focusing on manipulating accounting earnings, rather than managing cash flow. Ultimately, the reporting relationships coupled with management's compensation drivers undermined the effectiveness and value of the internal audit department.

Testing of a Control Environment

Many elements of a control environment should be investigated or tested by the lender in order to gauge the overall effectiveness of the control environment as it pertains to the assets in question. The following outlines some areas of focus for a lender performing lending due diligence.

Typically, in asset-based lending due diligence, the lender must ensure that the company is reconciling its cash, accounts receivable, accounts payable, and inventory, if applicable. This reconciliation should be prepared periodically, preferably on a monthly or more frequent basis. An appropriate segregation of duties should be established, wherein the preparation of the reconciliation is subjected to at least one level of independent review. A reconciliation ensures the overall integrity of financial data by documenting that any material adjustments to the financial records of a company are made known and are accurately reflected in the borrowing base calculation.

For example, a lender's review of the inventory reconciliations of the aforementioned Company X may have noticed consistently large write-downs of inventory, which would have been at least partially attributable to Company X's lack of adequate controls.

Another critical area a lender should focus on are computer controls as they relate to who has access to the company's data records. Only authorized personnel should have access to inventory records, including standing data. Areas of concern to the lender include whether the data is secure, how easily an individual can make changes to the data, and whether the computer system's integrity can be compromised.

The credit process is another area on which the lender should focus. The credit process is critical to the underlying quality of the assets involved in the transaction. The credit process may include credit analyses of potential customers, tiered authorization levels, monitoring of credit quality, and internal compliance with credit standards.

Overall, the lender should be cognizant of the various elements of a company's control environment, the interwoven relationships the control mechanisms have on the overall integrity of the analyzed data, and the underlying quality of the asset or liability subjected to scrutiny.

External Auditors and Access to Audit Workpapers

The external audit report should reflect that the audited financial statements are not materially distorted according to generally accepted accounting principles (GAAP). This opinion should supply the lender with some comfort. However, specific asset balances may still be in error, even though they may not be large enough to cause the overall financial statements to be materially misstated. The primary function of the audited financial statements for the lender is limited to providing assurance that the company is a going concern. The audited financial statements provide less value in assessing the carrying values of assets against which the lender is funding.

The external auditor's work papers often provide a source of insight for the lender. Through discussions with the auditor and possibly gaining access to auditor work papers, the lender can determine the types of analysis the auditors used to gain confidence over that particular audit area. Auditor work papers may, for example, identify major variances in the assets being analyzed. For example, analysis of the audited financial statements of a large auto parts manufacturer who is securitizing the accounts receivable of a troubled division, may not reveal problems. However, through extensive discussions with the audit firm and through access to the audit work papers, the lender has greater opportunity to identify what, if any, receivable problems exist and how extensive the problems are. To gain access to auditor work papers, the lender must obtain a letter of understanding between the audit firm and the company and provide an indemnification letter to the audit firm providing access. These legalities often deter lenders from soliciting the auditor work papers because the process can be troublesome due to time and cost constraints.

An additional source of information related to external auditors is the management letter, a report that auditors issue along with the audited financial statements. This report focuses on operational and financial reporting issues identified by the external auditors, such as segregation of duties, supervisory and review processes, reconciliations, the budgeting/forecasting cycle, the revenue cycle, and the credit cycle. The management letter will provide insight to the lender in assessing the overall control environment of its prospective borrower.

REAL ESTATE—ASSET OR LIABILITY?

During the 1970s and 1980s, real estate was a relatively low-risk, prestigious investment. Transactions were often driven by the tax savings the investor would receive from the project, rather than the profit it would generate. Projects were financed using very aggressive loan-to-value ratios to maximize the tax benefits. In the mid-1980s, the U.S. enjoyed considerable economic growth. At the same time, commercial real estate development continued at a rapid pace. This pace caused supply to exceed demand. This condition was further exacerbated by the 1986 tax law changes, as well as the slowdown in economic growth in the late 1980s and the recession in the early 1990s. With the recession of the 1990s came the largest real estate crash since the Great Depression of the 1930s.

With the 1990s came a new emphasis on cash-on-cash returns, low or no leverage, and shorter-term investment horizons. The most popular way to invest in real estate now is through individual ownership, REITs, and real estate partnerships. Particularly with the re-emergence of the REIT, real estate investment has changed from an individual asset purchase to an investment in an operating company that acquires and manages real estate. Additionally, the public REIT vehicles provide the marketplace with detailed information not previously available to investors investing in private limited partnerships during the 1980s.

What Is the Value of the Real Estate?

Monitoring and assessing the value of a real estate asset is essential to initial underwriting as well as maintenance of a facility. Valuing an asset or portfolio of assets can take many forms, from full narrative appraisals to desktop analyses utilizing discounted cash flows or available comparable sale transactions. The ultimate scope of the valuation work should be a function of the current need by the user of the information. However, if a transaction is being considered, a thorough analysis of the property should be performed. This would include an analysis of the physical condition of the property, financial operations (if income producing), market demographics, competition, comparable sale transactions, capital availability, and so forth. Availability of this information provides a much clearer picture for decision-making purposes.

Understanding the Structure of the Real Estate Investment

Understanding the structure of a real estate investment is key to developing financing vehicles and collateral protection. The structure of the transaction includes equity and debt considerations. Specifically, the type of ownership and the potential exposure to other claims has a bearing on the ultimate financing a lender will consider.

Real estate owner–operators have historically owned real estate through partnerships, with each partnership having its own unique debt and equity components. The early 1990s saw an explosion of REITs whose emergence has shifted the ownership of real estate from the private sector to the public sector. Each type of ownership creates its own opportunities and difficulties.

Real estate owned privately and held in partnerships allows a lender to focus on the specific collateral support. This provides a greater comfort level when assessing potential downside scenarios given the usually secured position lenders take with real estate. The potential third-party influence on the collateral, which may come from the general partners' credit issues in other investments, is minimized. Barring this influence, the lender can exert a fair amount of control over the collateral in the event of nonpayment and/or default. Because this structure usually involves privately held real estate, the availability of information is of concern to the lender. Even when the facility is paying currently, credit should be continually evaluated to allow for proactive measures in the case of ensuing problems. Specifically, red flags to watch for are either market influences or borrower influences or a combination of both.

Given that real estate is a cyclical business, information concerning market dynamics is available and should be evaluated regularly to monitor issues relevant to the industry. Considerations such as significant new construction, low or negative net absorption of vacant space, out-migration of businesses from a particular market, and changes in the availability of capital should be closely monitored. Trigger issues like these indicate the potential of a downward cycle and will impact most if not all real estate owner–operators.

By looking at borrowers' profiles and their various investment needs, one may be able to identify other trends that signal trouble for lenders. For example, aggressive expansion plans (new construction or acquisitions) require considerable cash needs in either total dollars or multiple projects. Historically, many borrowers have accessed cash from various partnership investments through loans between the individual partnerships, which could lead to potential cash flow problems. Obtaining partnership financial statements on some periodic basis (quarterly, semiannually) will assist in identifying potential cash flow problems with the borrower.

Public REIT vehicles have changed the rules somewhat. On the positive side, information concerning this type of borrower is plentiful and available at least quarterly. The market has dictated that loan-to-value (loan-to-market capitalization) be managed at historically lower levels, therefore reducing the risks associated with highly leveraged assets. The market has also forced management to think more like public corporations and less like real estate entrepreneurs, which appears to have had a positive impact on the quality of management. However, there are some downside issues to consider. Borrowers are moving toward unsecured versus secured facilities, new acquisitions are financed through lines of credit (at times 100% of the purchase price), and access to the capital markets could impact efficient management of the balance sheet. The same red flags mentioned above apply here also. In particular, the availability of capital is critical to the success of the public REIT. Without it, borrowers will have difficulty competing in the marketplace, which will have a direct impact on their long-term viability. Understanding Wall Street's view of the borrower is critical to proactive management of loan facilities.

Corporate Real Estate

Corporate users of real estate have other issues to consider. Generally, they control real estate to allow them to execute their core business (retail, high-tech, manufacturing, etc.). These users will both own and lease real estate based on their individual philosophy of controlling real estate. Understanding this is critical to the lender, because cash flow problems create a potential bankruptcy scenario. Owned assets are available to satisfy claims of numerous parties but are subject to individual financing transactions incurred at the time of acquisition or development. Leases create different issues. Value may exist in the borrower's leased portfolio, through a spread existing between the current contract rent and the current market rent. This value, however, may be mitigated by lease language allowing the landlord to recapture the space on certain events (i.e., change in ownership, closing of a store, etc.) Many of the red flags discussed earlier apply to corporate users and should be followed closely to allow the lender to be as proactive as possible.

Real Estate Case Study

The following case study is an example of a real estate investment company forced into bankruptcy and the warning signs that were ignored. We will look into why the real estate problem occurred and key issues the lenders should have known.

> The XYZ Realty Inc. was an owner–operator of various types of real estate throughout the world. It was a privately held company that acquired and held its real estate investments in various tiered partnerships, thus creating a confusing web of ownership interests. XYZ not only acquired income-producing assets but also developed properties for its own account. The use of leverage to finance projects, the typical financing choice during the 1980s, was used extensively by XYZ.
>
> During the late 1980s and early 1990s, the market dynamics indicated certain red flags to the lender community. The ambitious 1980s produced significant new construction in all property types and locations. Demand for this new construction lagged, creating increased levels of vacant space. Additionally, the United States was in a recession. Many companies were reducing their costs through layoffs and jettisoning real estate that was not critical to their operations. This action compounded the vacancy rates created by the new construction. Overlay the fact that many projects were financed using high leverage ratios, and what ensued was one of the most horrific real estate markets ever.
>
> XYZ's use of leverage produced very high risk/reward scenarios. As long as the market was strong and properties leased and cash flowed, re-

turns to XYZ were superior. However, the recession and oversupply of space caused many projects to incur significant vacancy, creating negative cash flow for XYZ. Compounding the issue was the need for XYZ to finance development projects with the expected cash flow from income-producing projects. In its attempt to stay afloat and continue funding debt service, construction projects, and other expenses, XYZ continued to finance its operations through its existing lending sources. Both secured and unsecured vehicles were obtained from numerous institutions. The partnership-to-partnership loan game was in full swing. Effectively, XYZ was attempting to buy time by using lender dollars to wait out the storm. When the lender financing ran out, XYZ had no choice but to file for bankruptcy.

All the red flags flew in this situation. Understandably, debt financing persisted during this time when it probably should have been curtailed. The lenders working with the borrower to salvage the facility and the relationship resulted in continuing and more significant losses.

As the real estate market of the 1980s taught us many lessons, the advent of the public REIT vehicle during the 1990s has created many new opportunities as well as some new issues. However, one thing remains constant: Market conditions impact both the short and long-term viability of a real estate project. Quality owner–operators and corporate users will manage their business, taking into account downturns in the economy. By implementing a watchdog approach, problem issues can be anticipated, mitigated, and resolved through timely action.

REFERENCES

Aron Levko and Glenn Karlov, Valuing Intangible Assets Key to Your Bottom Line, *Corporate Legal Times*, Coopers & Lybrand LLP, 1993.

Estate Tax Regs., § 20.2031-1 (b); Rev. Rul. 59-60, 1959-1 C.B. 237.

NOTES

1. *Codification of Standards for the Professional Practice of Internal Auditing*, The Institute of Internal Auditors, Inc., Altamonte Springs, FL, IIA, 1989.

10

Financing Alternatives for Troubled Companies

William C. Repko

The Chase Manhattan Bank, N.A.

INTRODUCTION

In this chapter, we will consider some of the financing options available to companies whose ongoing operations are now, or could be, threatened by a liquidity or operating crisis, including voluntary, consensual negotiated debt restructurings and refinancings, as well as those implemented under the protection of the Bankruptcy Code.

THE TROUBLED COMPANY SCENARIO

The factors underlying financing crisis are numerous and, more often than not, occur in conjunction. *Situational* causes include unexpected, unplanned, and unfavorable changes in the competitive or economic environment; management's inability to execute on its business plan or to absorb acquisitions; massive or continuing systems failure; the threat of litigation or the effect of an adverse judgment; and fraud.

At the same time, even a fundamentally strong company, one with productive assets, clear market opportunities, and a sound business plan, can be imperiled by poor balance sheet design and management.

Heavy debt burden, overreliance on short-term or high coupon financing, liens against assets, too narrow a funding base, or waiting for a more favorable debt issuance market—all characteristic of or resulting in a "bad" balance sheet—can limit severely a company's operating flexibility and capacity to withstand industry and economic cycles.

In the face of these difficulties and adding to them, vendor support may well weaken; sales or revenues may start to erode, payments slow, and employee morale decline dangerously.

Whether the underlying causes are situational, structural, or both, the company faces an unacceptable and escalating level of uncertainty. The objective, then, of any financial restructuring is threefold:

- To create liquidity and promote flexibility
- To restore confidence in the company and its direction and prospects
- To maintain the company's ability to operate while a new financial structure is put in place

This last objective is, of course, the most important. The speed and credibility with which management acts will have a direct bearing on the success of any restructuring.

Therefore, management must move as quickly as possible to understand the root causes of its financial difficulties, communicate those problems to the relevant constituencies, and develop a turnaround strategy that will support the company's capital structure. In the absence of a strategy that will rapidly restore market confidence in the existing capital structure, financial restructuring must be executed. This may take the form of extending debt maturities through a revised private solution (a new bank loan) or the replacement of private debt with longer-term securities accessed through the capital markets.

More often than not, however, a turnaround plan will reveal that the business cannot support its current capital structure, or the confidence of the market will not entertain a complete restructuring. In that case, the financial restructuring is not completely voluntary. One definition of restructuring that is particularly apt is when a corporation's funding sources either are no longer available to it (no further access to the commercial paper market, for example, or a company is downgraded by rating agencies so that it cannot roll over its bonds) or the credit facilities it is currently using were not designed for the purpose now being used. In such cases, a restructuring is required to redesign the funding sources while management either turns around the business or the market returns to its previously held view.

VOLUNTARY, NEGOTIATED REFINANCINGS AND RESTRUCTURINGS

The common denominator of out-of-court restructurings and those that require a filing under chapter 11 of the Bankruptcy Code is a fundamental change in the way a company funds its operations. In some cases, management anticipates these changes and undertakes a refinancing. In 1991, the management of Chrysler Financial recognized that an extended recession, upcoming bank maturities, and noninvestment-grade ratings precluded the kind of debt issuance that would have relieved pressure on Chrysler Financial's banks. Importantly, Chrysler had instituted a massive organizational change that would lead, in only several years, to its being recognized as the low-cost producer with a new product slate that would ultimately include the Jeep Grand Cherokee, the "LH" cars, and the Viper sports car. The solution to the refinancing problem, in addition to Chrysler management's description of the organizational changes and new product development plan, was a bank financing that gave each lender the confidence that even in the highly unlikely event of a bankruptcy, these loans would retain sufficient asset coverage to remain fully secured. Even if Chrysler's business plan did not come to pass and the company's access to the capital markets was not restored prior to maturity of the bank lines, the structure of the bank facilities provided sufficient comfort. The combination of the correct financing structure and a superbly competent management resulted in the 100% lender support that was necessary for success.

Key considerations involving this type of financial restructuring must include (1) a comprehensive operational review of the business, including its problems, management's solutions to those problems, how long the solution will take, how much it will cost, and identified risk factors; (2) the creation of a financing vehicle that will provide appropriate protection to a lender's perceived risk as well as adequate compensation to ensure that the risk is suitably distributed (for example, in the Sunbeam debacle of mid-1998, it was entirely unworkable for so much exposure to be concentrated in the underwriters); and (3) complete and open communication so that management and its creditors understand the parameters of the restructuring, including sufficient flexibility to allow for the inherent uncertainties in any undertaking of this sort.

At other times, circumstances prevent even an aware management from executing a refinancing outside of bankruptcy. In 1994, Bradlees, Inc. was well into an attempt to reposition its merchandise offerings to differentiate itself in an overcrowded retail environment. Bradlees' management, aware of its difficult task, knew that vendor and factor support were critical to its success and undertook an effective communication strategy to ensure that these constituencies were aware of the company's progress.

However, in the face of increased competition, declining margins, and decreasing sales, the necessary level of support was withdrawn. Perhaps the easiest way in which a retailer can determine the erosion of its financing is to gauge its merchandise deliveries. With vendors eager to reduce exposure, shipments will be promised in return for paydowns on previous invoices, a technique as old as the W.T. Grant bankruptcy. Any sizable retailer schedules deliveries at its distribution centers to avoid unnecessary waiting time for the vendors' trucks and unworkable congestion within its logistics framework. The week prior to Bradlees' filing its petition under chapter 11, 30% of previously scheduled confirmed deliveries were not made. Management recognized this signal and immediately began to arrange postpetition financing. Within five days, the preparations were complete and Bradlees filed for bankruptcy.

Importantly, merchandise disruptions were minimized, the company avoided the problems of stretching vendors' exposures, and sufficient liquidity was clearly available for postbankruptcy operations. One result was that out-of-stock problems, which did increase over normal, were minimized, and the company was able to achieve a high percentage of accounts payable support. Although markets were rattled by the swiftness of the filing, prompt action preserved the enterprise value that would have been otherwise squandered.

DUE DILIGENCE

A financing constructed for an out-of-court restructuring must be specifically tailored and priced for the circumstances. The company and its lead lender(s) must understand all the parameters involving the company and the financing markets. In the normal course of events and for highly creditworthy borrowers, financings can be arranged with selective disclosure. With a restructuring company, the ability to communicate the problem and a financing and operating solution is a prerequisite to any refinancing.

As an obvious point, perhaps, the company must have a franchise in order to be restructured. Simply put, it must produce a product or service that the market wants or needs at an affordable, appropriate, and competitive price that will generate sufficient enterprise value that will support the volume of business needed to sustain operations. With large companies, the financing must create a capital structure that will not only support the ongoing operation of the company but will eventually allow the company to return to the capital markets.

The development of this financing structure outside of the safe harbor (for a lender) of chapter 11 can be a time-consuming task. In several situations (such as the 1992 Chrysler Financial refinancing or the 1993 syndication of approximately $25 billion for General Motors and its worldwide subsidiaries), the timing has been from initial steps to as long as eight months to complete the refinancing. A financing that does not involve the replacement of an existing arrangement, in whole or in part, or which does not involve a syndicate of financial institutions, can obviously be accomplished in far less time, perhaps even in days.

Our strategy is first to collect the facts, because any refinancing effort must begin with an explicit understanding of the company's current corporate and financial structure and its operations. This process of due diligence consists of a detailed analysis of the following six areas:

1. *General information and background.* An organizational/structural chart of the company and its subsidiaries (where appropriate) to identify borrowers and the operating and financial interrelationships among them; the nature and location of assets; ownership and capitalization structure.
2. *Business plan and forecasts.* For a manufacturer, for example, this would include a description of production units; production capability, utilization, and operational efficiency; terms of supply contracts for materials; major market segments in terms of size, market share (penetration), and competitors; sales results by product/line over the past three years and projected sales; new product pipeline; pricing policies

and pricing history; and marketing methods and efficiency. Also included would be management's view of the economic circumstances under which it operates.

3. *Industry/competition.* A review of the industry in which the company competes, including historic performance, cycles, and aberrations to those cycles; competitors and their market position; the company's own competitive advantages and disadvantages, as well as a broad-based forecast for the industry itself.

4. *Sources and uses of financing.* Issues to be addressed include the overall liquidity characteristics, cash requirements, and required spending needs. Receivables should be identified by category and operating subsidiary. Separately, there should be a review of intercompany transactions, as well as an analysis of liquidity needs, portfolio maturities, and capitalization.

   Liquidity is perhaps the most important single factor during the due diligence phase of the transaction. The lender should understand all the factors that could affect liquidity and not underestimate the complexity of something as simple as cash. All businesses have a minimum level of cash below which they cannot operate. For example, a retailer's balance sheet cash will include amounts in the store necessary for making change. A multinational company may have cash at its subsidiaries all over the globe, backstopping local debt, minimum cash till amounts, and so on. In some cases, the cash is available but cannot be repatriated without paying taxes, some of which can be prohibitively expensive. Cash that serves these purposes does not contribute to liquidity.

   Another aspect of liquidity involves the basic inflows and outflows of cash. This analysis can start with questions that are quite basic. In our due diligence at one major retailer, for example, management discussed its efforts at identifying the checkwriters, that is, those areas or individuals who were authorized to make payments to third parties. The list can be quite extensive: reimbursement of expense accounts, vendor payments, payroll, taxes, acquisition of office supplies, capital equipment, or real estate. Vigilant as it was, management was surprised by the potential amount of cash that was disbursed without direct control of the treasury. In an environment of cash shortage, central control becomes a critical operating goal.

5. *Prospective financial information.* Earnings projections, cash and working capital budgets and requirements.

6. *Debt profile.* Short- and long-term loans outstanding. Review of all debt instruments' terms and conditions, assets pledged, and repayment status; schedule of debt maturities by subsidiary and contingent liabilities.

With the information assembled, the financing can be structured. The parameters to be addressed are size of aggregate funding requirements; diversity of funding sources (e.g., off-balance-sheet financing, asset-backed transactions); pricing; terms; collateral, if appropriate; and execution. If the transaction involves a loan syndication, even if it is a restructuring of an existing transaction, the execution must be carefully considered.

REFINANCING/RESTRUCTURING UNDER THE PROTECTION
OF CHAPTER 11 OF THE BANKRUPTCY CODE

It is not always possible or advantageous for a company to attempt a financial restructuring without filing for protection to reorganize under chapter 11 of the U.S. Bankruptcy Code.

Under chapter 11, the company—now called the debtor-in-possession (DIP)—remains in possession of its assets, and the law normally allows the company to operate under the court's protection and then reorganize, all while minimizing disruption to society at large.

The framers of the Bankruptcy Code knew, of course, that an entity in bankruptcy is not a business that is easily financed. Section 364 of the Code provides an elegant, yet simple, mechanism that recognizes the varying risk profile of a DIP. Sections 364(c) and (d) are the most relevant for DIP financing generally. A debtor, previously authorized by the bankruptcy court to operate its business, may obtain unsecured credit in the ordinary course as an administrative expense. If the debtor cannot obtain unsecured credit, the court may authorize it to grant the financing a priority over all administrative expenses as well as prepetition unsecured claims. This is commonly referred to as a superpriority claim and in circumstances in which the prepetition creditors are unsecured is our preferred method of granting postpetition credit to a chapter 11 debtor.

A DIP financing using a superpriority claim does not require significant structural differences when compared to a credit facility outside of the chapter 11 environment. The automatic stay prevents prepetition creditors from taking action to collect their debts and the debtor is precluded (under most circumstances) from paying interest or principal, so liabilities to be compromised under a plan or reorganization can be viewed as "equity" for purposes of postpetition financial analysis.

These facilities are normally extended for periods between one and two years, initially. Although substantial pressure from a debtor and its advisors is applied to extend credit on terms that are beyond a two-year time frame, the lender must recognize that the mere fact of filing a chapter 11 petition does not end a company's problems. In many cases, a new set of problems will result from the filing, adding to the complexity of the turnaround and the level of uncertainty facing a company that has just filed a chapter 11 petition.

An interesting example of unforeseen and unusual circumstances arose in the initial stages of the Caldor, Inc., bankruptcy. Prior to the filing, Caldor was using a nonlender banking organization's cash management system. The basic purpose of this sort of system is to slow down the clearing of checks (and thereby retain cash for as long as possible) by using a remote branch of the bank as the checking account. In Caldor's case, management of the Connecticut-based company wrote payments to vendors using checks drawn on a bank branch in Juneau, Alaska. In the weeks before the filing, vendors became increasingly nervous and, of course, sought paydowns on their existing outstanding bills before agreeing to ship new product. Management in fact wrote vendors checks in return for new shipments. Unfortunately, a large number of vendors were caught by bounced checks after they had shipped new merchandise and had their exposure to Caldor increased inadvertently. Because the cash management bank was outside the lender group, the account was unfunded the day after Caldor defaulted under its credit facilities and was unable to access the facilities and fund the disbursement account.

The vendors, naturally, were enraged and for months refused to grant Caldor normal postpetition trade terms. Caldor, in turn, did not have the sort of liquidity it had built into its business plan and suffered increased interest expense because borrowings under the DIP loan were significantly higher as a result of having to pay cash on delivery for most of its merchandise requirements. Ultimately, this situation was never favorably resolved, and Caldor languished without the kind of vendor support it deserved even after new management had been retained.

As alluded to above, postpetition liquidity is one of the most important factors when considering the amount of a DIP financing. It is at the onset of its chapter 11 case that management has the strongest hand in acquiring a DIP loan adequately sized for its needs. Our advice has always been to seek a financing that will not only fund the business as it has been funded in the past, but to add an amount that will cover a downside scenario. Our experience in the months following a chapter 11 filing have occasionally seemed to be an out-of-body experience. From unusual events to completely implausible ones (e.g., Marvel Entertainment, which was originally going to be a six-month "prepack"), management must be aware that it is always possible to downsize a financing, but it can be difficult or impossible to increase one. A financing appropriately sized for normal circumstances, with a cushion for the unlikely and unforecastable events that will certainly occur, will in most circumstances create sufficient confidence that vendors will return to providing a measure of trade credit. The proper result of an appropriately sized DIP facility and a management that has communicated well with its vendors is a facility that remains virtually unused. Postpetition unsecured creditors, operating with an administrative claim, provide trade credit; the working capital cycle is relatively undisturbed by the bankruptcy, with the end result of increasing enterprise value for the prepetition creditors, including the claims of the vendors.

In circumstances in which the debtor has pledged assets to secure its prepetition indebtedness, the DIP lender must adopt a higher standard to protect the postpetition facility. If nonproductive assets (those that are not converted into cash in the normal course of the debtor's business, e.g., stock of subsidiaries, intellectual property, and the like) serve as collateral, the DIP lender can look to assets that are converted into cash for protection and can either take these assets as collateral or lend unsecured on a superpriority claim basis.

If, however, the productive assets (e.g., inventory and accounts receivable) are pledged as collateral to the prepetition indebtedness, the DIP lender has a more difficult task. Section 364(d) of the Bankruptcy Code provides that existing lienholders may be primed or effectively subordinated to the new DIP facility. For this to gain approval of the bankruptcy court, the debtor must prove that the existing lienholders are "adequately protected" such that the existing lienholders are not harmed by the subordination of their existing first liens. There are several theories concerning what constitutes adequate protection, but it is my belief that this remains more of a legal argument than a corporate finance solution. It is difficult to imagine a DIP lender's gaining bankruptcy court approval to subordinate first liens over the objections of the lienholders without considerable time and effort being expended in the litigation of the merits of the priming and the adequacy of the protection. In most circumstances, the debtor and its creditors recognize that the disruption that would occur would destroy enterprise value to the detriment of the case as a whole and some compromise is reached.

In the situation we encountered in the bankruptcy of Rockefeller Center Properties, the debtor, which had mortgaged the Rockefeller Center real estate property in New York City, sought a modest DIP facility to build out floors in the buildings in preparation for new tenants. The new tenants were signing rental agreements for extended periods at less than forecast but still profitable rates, and required certain work to be performed on their floors prior to occupancy. In a highly negotiated structure, the DIP loan was not objected to, even though there was little argument among the parties that the mortgage exceeded the value of the real estate. Moreover, even though Rockefeller Center was a complex corporation, it was, in effect, a single property. Thus, it was impossible to justify a DIP loan on the basis that there was sufficient additional collateral and that the prepetition mortgage holders were going to be adequately protected after subordination of the mortgage debt to the new DIP facility. Instead, the parties reached a compromise, the basis of which was that the proceeds of the DIP loan were being used to fund property upgrades to allow for new tenants at increased rents and, therefore, the value of the property was being preserved rather than depreciating.

Another situation that involved secured debt was the Caldor, Inc., bankruptcy. When Caldor filed bankruptcy, its prepetition debt included a $250 million revolving credit agreement and a $225 million term loan, both of which were secured on a pro rata basis by inventory. At the time of the filing, the term loan, of course, was fully drawn and the revolving credit was substantially drawn as Caldor was nearing the peak borrowing period in anticipation of the holiday season. A new $250 million DIP facility was arranged to provide for working capital that primed the liens on inventory held by the existing banks. After consultation with the syndicate for whom we acted as agent, the transaction that was proposed (to which the lenders being primed consented) had a number of important features: (1) additional liens on virtually all other assets were granted to the DIP lenders, with junior liens granted to the prepetition syndicate members; (2) interest at the prepetition contract rate (versus the default rate) was paid currently; and (3) the prepetition revolving credit had its defaults waived and was made available to the debtor as an effective addition to the new $250 million DIP facility. The latter point, which is deserving of some further description, became known as the *roll-up*. Our view was that subjecting the prepetition revolving credit to compromise under a plan of reorganization would not result in any substantial monetary benefit to the estate because it was clear to us (and the debtor) that the facility was fully secured at the time of filing and the liens were free of defects. Treating the revolver as a normal prepetition liability would have allowed inventory to be sold, converted to cash, used to buy new inventory, and so on. The debtor would have had the liquidity provided by the cash, but would have incurred a negative arbitrage on what it could earn on the invested cash (which we assumed to be the A1/P1 commercial paper rate) and the contractual default rate (approximately London Interbank Offered Rate [LIBOR] plus 3.0%). This difference at the time was estimated to save the debtor $25 million over a two-year bankruptcy.

The alternative was to allow the working capital cycle to work, with cash generated by retail sale of inventory used to pay down the prepetition revolver as long as the lenders agreed to readvance amounts paid down as an additional $250 million DIP facility senior to all other creditors except the new $250 million "Tranche A" DIP facility. The debtor thus was able to retain $500 million of postpetition liquidity and avoided the approximately $25 million of unnecessary expense due to the negative arbitrage between its default rate and the potential interest income from the cash investment.

In this case, substantial adequate protection was granted in the form of additional collateral, current interest paid in cash, and postpetition status afforded the prepetition revolving credit. Our view at the time was that moving the R/C (revolving credit) to this status could actually help junior creditors in a reorganization since it was unlikely that either of Tranche A or B would be compromised in any way.

CREDIT CONSIDERATIONS

Generally, the credit considerations that predominate in the analysis of a chapter 11 financing remain remarkably similar to those considered for other companies.

The first issue is *viability*. It is important to make a determination on whether or not the company has the ability to function as a chapter 11 debtor for a reasonable period of time and to reorganize around a franchise.

Although *positive operating cash flow* is an important indicator of the ability to move into and through reorganization and suggests that the company's core business is sound and able to withstand the potentially dramatic effect on operations of filing for protection under chapter 11, it is not a prerequisite as a credit matter. In the absence of cash flow, the DIP lender must make a conscious decision to fund the losses. In doing so, it is implicit that the lender believe that the core business can be reorganized in a timely manner, including whether lenders will consent to a reorganization at the values possible or vote for liquidation. In the latter case, the DIP lenders' second way out will require assets sufficient to cover the projected outstandings.

The determination of whether sufficient assets exist must be based on a worst case scenario. Highly liquid assets such as inventory and consumer receivables are preferred to assets like real estate or equipment. Seasonal inventory or slow-paying receivables, such as car loans, would be viewed differently than general merchandise or credit cards, which pay in a timely fashion and have a short maturity.

The borrowing base constructed as a result of this analysis evaluates the level and quality of free assets on a liquidation basis and establishes an advance rate at a discount to this value. To determine liquidation values, outside specialists are often used, particularly where assets are unique, but even in the case of a retailer's inventory.

Failure to accurately value the assets that back the financing is always a risk. For this reason, the cushion should be substantial enough to accommodate a wide margin for error. Similarly, failure to continuously monitor the supporting assets could threaten the credit. Because DIP financings are usually based on current assets, the lender must review the company's control and monitoring systems at the outset.

During the course of the financing, the lender must rely on the company's ability to report inventory and receivables accurately. Accordingly, it is important to have confidence in systems that track inventory levels and aging, outstanding orders, the tracking of outstandings, past due accounts, and overall credit quality of receivables.

It is common to repeat an audit of the company's systems and current assets during the term of the facility.

Although unanticipated, it is always possible that the bankruptcy could ultimately turn into a chapter 11 liquidation. Since the DIP lender's priority remains superior to all other unsecured creditors, the DIP lender, though disappointed, should be relatively indifferent to such an outcome. This assumes, of course, that the liquidation value of the assets is adequately projected.

Finally, the most tangible risk (at least for the lender) is that of timing. Debtor-in-possession financings usually have an initial term of 12 to 24 months, with the intent of matching the business cycles of the debtor. In reality, however, the DIP lender is in for the duration of the chapter 11. This is readily accepted as long as things are going well; and less readily, of course, when things are going badly.

If the DIP lender decides that its position is in jeopardy and declares the financing in default, its recourse is through the court, which theoretically could delay the liquidation of assets to a point where the value is less than the amount of the loan. The only recourse to this highly undesirable result is constant vigilance and a covenant structure that will afford the DIP lender the opportunity to exit the credit before values have been dissipated.

11

Valuation of Companies within Workout and Turnaround Situations

Thomas J. Millon, Jr. and Shannon P. Pratt

Willamette Management Associates

INTRODUCTION

Even though the economic climate in the United States has remained somewhat robust over the past few years, there remain a significant number of business enterprises suffering from some form of economic and financial distress. This article will examine how the principles of business valuation apply to firms involved in either a turnaround or workout situation

THE INITIAL STEPS OF THE VALUATION PROCESS

Before we discuss some of the more technical aspects of the basic approaches to business valuation, it may be worthwhile to highlight some of the basic elements of the valuation process. These aspects of the assignment must be communicated and agreed to by all parties, and then carefully documented at the very outset of the project:

- The purpose and objective of the appraisal
- The standard, or definition, of value (i.e., fair market value, investment value, etc.)
- The premise of value (i.e., liquidation basis versus going-concern basis)
- The specific business interest to be appraised (i.e., equity, total invested capital, total assets, etc.)
- Stating the appropriate valuation or "as of" date

After properly considering each of the above items, the valuation analyst begins to consider the quantity and quality of data that is both relevant to the subject firm as well as generally available for the purpose of conducting the assignment. These data may be either financial or operational in nature. Additionally, these data may be historical or prospective.

Some of the data gathering will occur during the valuation expert's due diligence activities. It is useful, if not crucial, to get an overview of the subject firm at an early meeting with member(s) of the management team. This will give the analyst a sense of what information will be relevant and what data can be collected early.

The type of data required for valuing a closely held firm can generally be grouped into five categories:

1. Data regarding the subject firm
2. Relevant economic and investment data, including data an interest rates and required rates of return on various securities relative to their risk
3. Guideline transactional data
4. Other relevant information, such as data for use in quantifying any valuation discounts and/or premiums
5. Relevant industry data, for comparative analysis purposes

If time allows, the valuation analyst will request financial statements and other readily available information before visiting the subject company. Documents of this type may provide the analyst with information to prepare questions and develop discussion, which will maximize the productivity of that initial meeting with the management team.

THE THREE BASIC BUSINESS VALUATION APPROACHES

Once the scope of the available data has been measured, the business valuation consultant must select from the various valuation methods. While there are a vast number of individual methods and procedures used by practitioners and other interested parties to estimate the value of a business, each method and procedure can be categorized into one of the three general analytical approaches: The income approach, the market approach, and the asset-based or cost approach.

Income Approaches

Under the various applications of the income approach, the going-concern value of the subject business interest is based on the present worth of the economic income or cash flows that the business is anticipated to generate.

Within the broad category of income approaches, there are two general groups of valuation methods used in valuing a business: discounted net cash flow methods and direct capitalization methods.

Discounted Net Cash Flow Methods.   In applying valuation models that fall under the category of discounted cash flow methods, the business valuation analyst uses projected annual flows of some appropriate form of economic income for a number of discrete future time periods. Typically, the number of discrete projection periods is between three and five years beyond the "as of" date of the assignment.

The projected periodic levels of economic income or cash flow are discounted using a present value discount rate that reflects the appropriate rates of return to the stakeholders in the subject business for their investments in the business. These required rates of return reflect both the time value of money and the risk commensurate with holding a security interest in the subject firm. At the conclusion of the discrete projection period, a residual value of the business is estimated and discounted to the as of date.

In developing the discounted net cash flow model, there are several common measures of economic income that are relevant. As the name of the method itself suggests, net cash flow is the measure of economic income recommended by most financial analysts. Net cash flow is defined as the level of after-tax income, plus the level of all noncash expenses (such as depreciation, amortization, etc.), minus the level of cash requirements needed to fund working capital and capital expenditures.

Although net income is an economic variable that is more commonly recognized by people who observe its use in presentations for financial reporting purposes, net cash flow remains the measurement of economic income preferred by a majority of corporate finance professionals. This preference reflects the underlying objective of the discounted net cash flow method, which is to compute the amount of cash generated by the business that is available for discretionary distribution to investors. At best, the accounting concept of net income is only a proxy for this concept of economic income.

The discounted net cash flow method was once considered to be of such a subjective nature that it was often dismissed by many valuation professionals. However, recent trends point toward a much greater degree of acceptance. This increased adaptation and recognition is largely due to a wider dissemination of the method among valuation practitioners in reference sources. Even the courts have recognized the appropriateness of the discounted net cash flow method, as the Delaware Chancery Court characterized it as "increasingly, the method of choice in this court."[1]

The other major component of the discounted net cash flow method is the discount rate used to present value future economic income. Risk represents the relative uncertainty of realizing the expected level of economic income, with respect to both magnitude and timing, over the expected time horizon of the investment.

While the quantification of this concept of relative uncertainty appears especially subjective, several methods have been developed that provide the valuation professional with guidance in estimating this critical variable. A wide body of recognized empirical research is available to quantify the risk-versus-return tradeoffs on the investment securities that collectively represent the components of the distressed firm's capital structure. These required rates of return translate into the present value discount rate used within the discounted net cash flow model.

Direct Capitalization.   The other income approach category, the direct capitalization method, involves the identification and measurement of the normalized level of economic income that is anticipated during the first period beyond the valuation date. The normalized level of that next period's economic income is then capitalized at, or divided by, an appropriate investment rate of return. As is the case with the present value discount rate, this rate of return reflects not only the time value of money and the relative riskiness of an investment in the firm but also an expected annual growth rate in economic income over the remaining life of the business enterprise. This rate of return, including considerations for growth, is referred to as the capitalization rate.

Several attributes of the distressed firm affect the selection of the key input variables in both of these income methods as well as the interpretation of their results.

First among these attributes is the type of stakeholder or stakeholders to whom the prospective economic income is distributable. Economic income can be measured on either a debt-free or an after-debt basis. The consequences of this selection influence the estimation of the appropriate discount and capitalization rates.

Second, income approaches are typically conducted on an after-tax basis, which impacts the estimated value of the appropriate capitalization and discount rates.

Third, the actual or optimal capital structure of the enterprise impacts the relative weighting of the alternative investment rates of return that comprise the discount and capitalization rates.

Using either of these two general categories under the income approach, the value of the business entity's capital is the present value of the prospective economic income over the expected remaining life of the firm.

The income approach methods obviously involve many elements of professional judgment. The analyst's preparation of financial projections, or his or her review of the financial projections prepared by the management of the subject company, entails considerable efforts. The analysis of revenues, expenses, investment requirements, and the like must all be examined within the context of not only the entity's historical performance but also the going-forward environment. Despite this necessary degree of rigor, there are many advantages to pursuing an indication of value through one or more applications of an income approach.

Market Approaches

The valuation methods that fall under the market approach category also take many different forms. Collectively, these market approach methods and procedures represent the most commonly used and recognizable set of valuation models. The underlying principle of the market approach is that arm's-length market transactions entail market multiples that can be applied to the subject business.

One of the more obvious ways to distinguish among the wide array of market-based methods is to take note of the nature of the market from which the valuation multiples or ratios develop. At least two very distinct and different markets exist. The first is the widely discussed market for shares of common stock in publicly traded companies. The other distinct market is the merger and acquisition marketplace for business enterprises in their entirety.

Guideline Publicly Traded Company Methods.   To carry out the guideline publicly traded company method, a number of independent procedures must be carefully carried out.

Utilizing any variation of the guideline publicly traded company method, the valuation consultant first analyzes the financial statements and accounting practices of the subject entity. This normally involves the analysis of the profitability of the company over some finite historical time period.

Next, comparability criteria are established for the purpose of selecting comparable or guideline companies that are engaged in business activities that are similar to those of the subject company, and which can then be used to select valuation multiples that are appropriate for the subject business. These criteria may include the specific operating economic activities of each firm, as well as its size or the breadth of its customer base, and so forth. The ideal guideline publicly traded security would reflect a risk-versus-potential return profile that can be compared to the same profile of the subject entity.

After establishing effective selection criteria, the analyst searches through any number of comprehensive databases for companies issuing securities that are traded in an active market, such as the New York Stock Exchange or the National Association of Security Dealers Automated Quotation System (NASDAQ), in order to identify the set of appropriate guideline companies. One of the more obvious criteria used to assess whether a publicly traded company could serve as a guideline company is the industry in which each operates. Standard Industry Classification (SIC) codes serve as a convenient starting point to make those comparisons. In many cases, especially those involving subject companies that are closely held, publicly traded companies tend to be much larger and more diversified than the subject entities, with respect to the types of products and services offered as well as the scope and diversity of their respective customer bases. Despite the inability to find a perfect, or near perfect match, the method retains its validity even if the comparable companies selected as guideline companies are only generally similar.

Once the set of guideline companies are selected, the valuation consultant analyzes their historical financial statements and accounting policies of each guideline company in the same way he or she did for the subject company in order to ensure a consistency of presentation. Part of this process involves making similar adjustments to the historical data for any nonrecurring or extraordinary items that may represent aberrant or nonoperating events.

Next, the analyst combines the financial data of each guideline publicly traded company with the price of its publicly traded securities to compute an array of market ratios or multiples. These multiples represent the evidence that can be applied to the fundamental data of the subject in order to estimate its value on an as-if publicly traded basis. Each market multiple or market ratio expresses the market value of the public company's securities as a multiple of some piece of fundamental financial data.

The market value of the public company's securities represents the numerator of its market multiple. These securities can be defined so as to include either the market value of the guideline company's equity or the market value of the guideline company's total invested capital, which includes its total equity plus total interest-bearing debt.

The denominator of each market multiple can literally be any relevant item of financial data, such as earnings, cash flow, book value, and so forth. These fundamental data can be measured over the most recent period, such as the latest 12 months, or over some extended historical time period, such as average value over the past five years. Additionally, and this may be more appropriate under workout and turnaround situations, one can compute market multiples based on expected values of a fundamental variable, such as projected net income.

After computing the market multiples for each of the selected publicly traded guideline companies, the consultant analyzes these multiples compared to those of the other guideline publicly traded companies in order to reconcile or explain the differences and similarities among them. Usually, although certainly not in all cases, differences among the market multiples of publicly traded companies can be correlated with differences in their growth rates, their rate of profitability, or their mere size. Ultimately, the factors that explain differences among the market multiples of publicly traded companies operating in the same industry boil down to differences among their respective prospects for generating future profits or cash flows. Securities analysts and investors alike constantly seek out companies that are "priced" differently from its underlying intrinsic values. Undervalued companies receive buy recommendations, whereas overvalued securities receive sell recommendations.

Once he or she sufficiently understands the market pricing within the array of selected guideline publicly traded companies, the analyst then selects the market multiples that are appropriate to the subject company. The selected multiples will reflect the differences between the size, profitability, and growth of the subject company in comparison to the same attributes of the publicly traded companies.

Usually, the multiples are selected so that they are consistent with the pricing among the entire group of guideline companies. Conceptually, the market value of the subject company as implied by the selected multiples should not upset the overall risk-versus-expected return profile of the entire market basket of securities, which now includes not only the guideline publicly traded companies but also the subject closely held company.

Guideline Merged and Acquired Company Methods.   The mechanics of the guideline merged and acquired company method are generally identical to the procedures outlined under the guideline publicly traded company method. The essential difference between these two guideline company methods is the nature of the marketplaces.

In the merger and acquisition marketplace, the sold or target companies are either acquired or merged into another company, the purchaser. In this market, the transaction involves the purchase or transfer of the control of the target company.

In contrast, the guideline publicly traded company method utilizes pricing evidence from market transactions involving the exchange of security interests that do not include elements of corporate control. The shares of stock exchanged in any single stock market transaction involve a relatively insignificant number in comparison to the total number of shares outstanding.

As outlined earlier, the consultant seeks out companies that are in a line of business similar to that of the subject company. If the acquiring entity is a publicly traded company, and if the acquisition is material, then it will be required to disclose the terms of the transaction as well as the recent historical financial statements of the acquired company. In such a case, the valuation consultant will be able to calculate a similar variety of market multiples as are developed within the publicly traded company approach.

There is now also a database providing detailed information on privately held company transactions, Pratt's Stats, published by Business Valuation Resources, in Portland, Oregon. Data are collected from members of the International Business Brokers Association, sponsor of the database, as well as from other sources.

Asset-Based Approaches

One common thread among the methods described so far is that they all revolve around the subject company's potential to generate income or cash flow. From a financial analyst's perspective, these methods involve data derived from the entities' statement of operating performance, or profit and loss statement.

Asset approaches focus on the subject company's statement of financial position or balance sheet. The underlying notion of the asset approach is that the value of the ownership interest is the difference between the value of the assets less the value of the appropriate liabilities.

There are two primary examples of asset approach methods: the adjusted net asset (or asset accumulation) method and the excess earnings method.

Asset Accumulation Method.   Under the asset accumulation method, the value of the subject entity is estimated as the fair market value of all the firm's assets less the fair market value of all its (appropriate) liabilities. This method follows the accounting identity that an entity's total assets must equal its total liabilities and equities. The asset accumulation method involves the preparation of a valuation-based, fair market value balance sheets, rather than the historical cost-based format.

This involves a detailed analysis of each asset and liability category as of the valuation date in order to estimate what the possible difference between each item's historical cost, or book value basis, and its fair market value.

The total assets of a business entity typically can be grouped into several categories: financial assets, tangible personal property, tangible real estate, and intangible assets.

For the most part, a business's financial assets (as well as its current liabilities) are already stated on a near-to-cash basis, since by definition these assets are expected to be converted into cash as part of the normal course of business operations within one year. These types of financial assets include cash, accounts receivable, and prepaid expenses.

The book value of an entity's tangible real and personal property rarely corresponds to the market values. Tangible personal property, including items such as machinery and equipment, furniture and fixtures, data processing equipment, and so on, tend to depreciate in terms of their value within the business. However, real estate–based assets, such as owned and leased land and buildings, tend to appreciate in value.

Of greatest importance is the fact that most companies possess a significant body of identifiable intangible assets, each of which has a value separate from the value of any other asset of the firm. These intangible assets are normally not included in generally accepted accounting principles (GAAP)-based financial statements. As part of the due diligence effort, the analyst investigates the nature of the firm's intangible assets, so that they can be discretely identified and valued for inclusion on the fair market value balance sheet.

The value of each intangible itself lends itself to one or more appropriate valuation methods. In some cases, the valuation methods used to value an intangible asset may also require that the asset's remaining economic life be estimated. In these cases, the value of an intangible asset depends on its remaining economic life.

After this detailed analysis, the difference between the accumulated fair market value of the firm's total assets and the fair market value of its liabilities represents the fair market value of the firm's equity. This residual value, which in effect represents what is available to equityholders after accounting for the market value of the entity's underlying assets and liabilities, is comparable to the net book value of the firm.

In a potential workout or turnaround situation, the analyst will usually consider the net asset value on a liquidation basis, rather than a going-concern basis. The workout is generally considered practical if the discounted or capitalized cash flow value exceeds the liquidation value.

Excess Earnings Method.   The excess earnings method is the more commonly applied version of an asset-based method. This is undoubtedly due to its relative simplicity in comparison to the asset accumulation method outlined earlier. Originally, the excess earnings method was promulgated by the U.S. Treasury Department for the purpose of computing the value of goodwill associated with distilleries and breweries that were impacted by Prohibition. One consequence of this method's simplicity is the wide number of disagreements on the details of its actual application.

In general terms, the first step of the excess earnings method is to estimate the net tangible asset value of the subject company. Next, the analyst calculates the required amount of annual economic income that the company must earn in order to earn a satisfactory rate of return in comparison to the previously estimated value of net tangible assets.

Next, the required amount of annual economic income is compared to the actual level of economic income. If the actual level exceeds the required level, the difference is interpreted as the firm's excess earnings, which are attributable to the unidentified intangible assets that were not included in the original estimate of net tangible assets.

This flow of excess earnings is then capitalized in order to estimate the value of those underlying unidentified intangible assets that are theoretically providing the subject company with its volume of excess economic income

The estimated value of the subject company's intangible assets is then added to the historical cost-based value of the firm's net book value in order to adjust this net book value to a fair market value basis.

The excess earnings method is itself somewhat of a hybrid method. It involves the capitalization of a component of the subject company's earnings, an income approach method, in combination with an adjustment to the balance sheet.

Special Characteristics of Workouts and Turnarounds

For the purpose of this discussion, distressed companies are defined as those unable to achieve a sufficient or reasonable level of income relative to the value of their underlying assets.

In a workout situation, the firm is in the midst of reorganization, such as that required under chapter 11 of the Bankruptcy Code. In this case, even though the firm may still be generating some overall level of positive cash flow, it is obligated to pay out too much of this cash flow to suppliers, lenders, or other investors in or claimants of the firm. In this case, the firm is under financial distress and, therefore, must change the terms of some or all of its financial relationships. Creditors or stockholders force the company to alter its capital structure, so that additional capital can be infused into (or existing capital is not called out of) the business.

Firms undergoing turnarounds are faced with more fundamental core business problems. Turnaround firms struggle along, generating inadequate revenues and/or income, earning less than a normal rate of return. In the long run, fundamental operational changes must be implemented in order prolong the life of the enterprise. This may involve either changing the mix of products or services offered, or bringing in a new management team, or both. Senior members of the new management team will undoubtedly require incentives through the issuance of stock options or stock appreciation rights or convertible securities.

Fairness Opinions and Solvency Analyses

When the distressed firm restructures or reorganizes its capital structure, or issues additional securities, the services of a valuation professional are required.

These services typically lead to the rendering of either a fairness opinion or a solvency opinion in connection with the securities transaction.

A fairness opinion is typically a short letter issued by the advisor, stating that a proposed transaction is fair or adequate from a financial perspective of the interested shareholders. Boards of directors obtain fairness opinions primarily to satisfy their fiduciary obligation to ensure that selling shareholders receive a fair price for their securities. The independent financial adviser's scrutiny of the proposed transaction also provides the directors with some degree of assurance regarding the overall soundness of the deal. Additionally, corporate directors may seek fairness opinions to assist shareholders in assessing whether or not to approve a proposed transaction.

Solvency opinions summarize the analysis of the distressed firm's capacity to satisfy its post-transaction obligations. There are three standards used to assess solvency:

1. Does the fair market value of the firm's assets, including any intangible assets that are traditionally not recorded on the GAAP balance sheet, exceed the fair market value of the firm's liabilities?
2. Does the firm have adequate capital to conduct business operations?
3. Will the firm have sufficient cash flows to support its ongoing operations as well its financial obligations?

Valuation science plays an essential role in analyzing the status of a distressed company. As a distressed company assembles the pieces to implement a turnaround plan, or introduces different securities into its capital structure in a workout situation, value can be transferred, created, or destroyed.

The relative riskiness associated with the distressed firm's generation of income and cash flow must also be reassessed in line with the new strategic direction. The estimation of the intrinsic value of the business enterprise on a going-concern basis is approached with this in mind.

Valuation of Firms Involved in a Workout Situation

As previously mentioned, a firm undergoing a workout is in the midst of a financial reorganization or capital restructuring. This reorganization occurs in connection with a confrontation between the firm and its stakeholders regarding the distribution of cash flows.

Estimating the value of the securities of a firm in a workout situation is carried out on a market value of invested capital (MVIC) basis. A firm's MVIC is made up of its interest-bearing debt plus all of its various forms of equity.

The MVIC of a workout company is based on its prospective operating and financing plans, which are provided by the firm's management, to demonstrate that, on a going-forward basis, the firm is unlikely to default in the future on its debt securities. Using information embedded in these projections, the valuation analyst estimates the overall value of the firm's MVIC. Once this value is established, the analyst allocates total MVIC to its components.

The addition of new capital and subsequent restructuring of the firm's capital structure alters the nature and value of securities held by its present, or "prerestructuring," stakeholders. As part of the analysis, the valuation expert may be called on to estimate the value of each component of the subject firm's capital structure. An immediate question of interest is what portion of MVIC is allocated to the senior securities.

Generally speaking, the restructuring of a firm's capital structure constitutes a new contract, whereby the terms of the existing capital structure are replaced with a new agreement, thereby changing the relative values of various stakeholders' holdings. These changes in the terms and conditions of the capital structure are all subject to a valuation analysis.

In most workout situations, current debtholders end up holding less attractive securities after the implementation of the workout plan. By definition, the senior position demanded by new creditors places existing creditors into less senior positions.

The debt securities existing before the workout are now likely to take on the characteristics of junk bonds after the restructuring is complete. Any new debt securities issued to "old" creditor groups carry higher coupon rates, which reflects the potentially higher compensation commensurate with greater risk. Even though higher coupon rates represent a more attractive feature, these securities may end up being no-pay or deferred-pay debt instruments. The terms of the new bond indentures or loan agreements, as negotiated by the new lenders, tend to be especially restrictive. This implies that the existing creditors, despite holding higher coupon rate securities, may not receive current interest payments until the troubled firm makes significant financial progress.

In light of the prospects for no current payments, junior security holders attempt to negotiate not only higher stated interest payments, or as a tradeoff, some form of equity attachments to their subordinated debt securities. These potential equity attachments include preferred stock, which can have various dividend payment rates and terms. Preferred dividends can be either cumulative or noncumulative. Preferred stock dividend payments can be paid in either cash or in-kind, that is, in the form of additional shares of the same class of preferred stock.

These alternative features, or more accurately, the differences among the features of the debt securities within the newly restructured capital structure, depends on how many types of postrestructuring capital holders are in place.

Finally, once the various classes of long-term debt and preferred stockholders are allocated value, the remaining, unallocated portion of the firm's invested capital reverts to the common stockholders. Common shareholders almost always retain very little, if any, equity.

As mentioned above, the basis for the overall value of the subject firm in a workout situation will be the operating and financing projections prepared by management. These projections should not be confined to prospective profit and loss, or income statements, but should also include integrated projected balance sheets and cash flow statements. The valuation analyst needs to test the reasonableness of management's projections, by comparing them to industry average data. If necessary, the consultant will adjust management's financial and operating projections to bring them more in line with these industry standards. Another important aspect of this reasonableness check is to identify the financial and operating strengths and weaknesses of the subject firm, again in comparison to industry averages.

Based on this overall assessment of the viability of the firm's projections, the business valuation involves estimating the appropriate present value discount rate. Appropriate market multiples are also selected and applied to prospective financial data as part of a guideline company method.

Bankruptcy judges tend to look at valuation methods involving the capitalization of cash flow or income projected for the first year of the projection period. More junior security holders, however, have a longer time horizon and therefore tend to look at the assumptions and implications of the discounted net cash flow method.

Valuation of Firms within a Turnaround Situation

In comparison to a workout situation, unpaid creditors in a turnaround situation do not necessarily force a company into action. The firm in a turnaround situation is typically struggling along in its traditional line of business, earning less than a normal rate of return on its assets. At some point the firm's ownership or management realizes that continuing with the status quo business strategy will not be viable over the long run. If the ownership solely holds this opinion, management changes may be required. Senior members of the new management team will undoubtedly require incentives through the issuance of stock options or stock appreciation rights or convertible securities.

Since the turnaround company is headed in a new strategic and operational direction, the financial projections of the firm play a prominent role in the valuation exercise.

As was the case for the valuation of a firm in a workout situation, considerable effort will be required to review the assumptions. This task is likely to be conducted by an independent valuation firm. All stakeholders have their biases, which requires the presence of an independent party to evaluate the reasonableness of the projected financial and operational financial statements, thereby minimizing the likelihood that minor disagreements among capital providers prevent the deal from going forward to completion.

The supervisory firm needs to put together sufficient documentation with respect to its opinions regarding the source and reasonableness of the assumptions making up the plan.

In a turnaround situation, stock options are almost always a necessary management incentive. This will require the involvement of the valuation expert on a more continual basis, as the value of those options must be periodically updated.

As is the case for workouts, the discounted net cash flow plays a prominent role in estimating the MVIC of the turnaround company. Therefore, the valuation analysts must consistently review management projections to minimize the possibility that financial projections are not being developed for the devious purpose of inflating the value of management's stock options.

In connection with the guideline company market methods, the analyst may have to go higher up along the income statement of the turnaround firm to identify meaningful data that can be applied to market multiples.

Besides confining the search for guideline companies to those in the same SIC code, it may still be applicable to look for comparable companies operating outside the subject's industry that are also in turnaround situations, or perhaps perform the same economic function as the subject.

Asset-based methods are, practically speaking, relevant only in liquidation settings. However, professional standards require the valuation expert to address whether the liquidation value of a firm exceeds its value on a going-concern basis. This same question is in the mind of every investor in a distressed company.

NOTE

1. *Charles L. Grimes* v. *Vitalink Communications Corporation,* No. 12334, 1997 WL 538676 (Del. Chancery Court, August 28, 1997).

12

Market Dynamics and Investment Performance of Distressed and Defaulted Debt Securities

Edward I. Altman*

New York University

INTRODUCTION

The market for investing in distressed and defaulted debt is continuing to receive a great deal of attention despite the shrinkage in the supply of new securities in the last few years and the recent (1997–1998) poor return performance to investors. This is primarily due to the expected growth in the supply of new distressed and defaulted public and private debt paper, the perception that prices are now at attractive levels, and the documented relatively low correlation of returns with the more traditional debt and equity markets. This chapter reviews some of the important attributes of this unique investment vehicle and updates our analysis of the risk and return performance of defaulted debt.

Distressed securities can be defined narrowly as those publicly held and traded debt and equity securities of firms that have defaulted on their debt obligations and/or have filed for protection under chapter 11 of the U.S. Bankruptcy Code. A more comprehensive definition would include those publicly held debt securities selling at sufficiently discounted prices so as to be yielding,

*Professor Altman is the Max L. Heine Professor of Finance, Vice Director, NYU Salomon Center, Leonard N. Stern School of Business. The author acknowledges the research assistance of M. Christian Saxman and Luis Beltran. Edward I. Altman, New York University, Salomon Center, 44 West 4th Street, Suite 9-61, New York, NY 10012. Tel: 212 998-0709, Fax: 212 995-4220; E-mail: ealtman@stern.nyu.edu

should they not default, a significant premium over comparable-duration U.S. Treasury bonds. For this segment, I have chosen a premium of a minimum of 10% over comparable U.S.Treasuries. With interest rates falling as much as they have by mid-1998, this definition would currently include bonds yielding at least 15.0%.

Finally, distressed securities can include those bank loans and other privately placed debt of the same or similar entities with rather acute operating and/or financial problems. With the continued growth in the volume of distressed bank loans that now trade rather frequently, investors are increasingly aware of the potential price movements of these heretofore illiquid securities. Recent estimates, from professionals, of the annual volume of distressed bank loan trading in the United States is in the $10 to $15 billion range. Indeed, trading is apparently sufficient to have spawned several brokers who specialize in distressed bank debt, and most large securities firms have analysts and sales and trading personnel dedicated to this market and investors.

SUPPLY OF DISTRESSED SECURITIES

In my prior works on the distressed and defaulted debt market,[1,2] estimates of the size of the market were as high as $300 billion (face value) and $200 billion (market value) at the start of 1990. Since that date, the size of the market has diminished consistently. This data is shown in Exhibit 12.1 and includes public and private debt estimates. The private debt total was estimated by applying a multiplier of as high as three times the public debt in 1990 and as low as 1.85-to-one in 1992. Both of these estimates are based on empirical observations of a large number of bankrupt firms' balance sheets. I will use an estimate of 2.4 to 1, approximately the midpoint between the two prior estimates for estimates in 1995 and 1998.

As of June 30, 1995, I estimated that the *public* defaulted and distressed markets had face values of $16.5 billion and $13.3 billion respectively (Exhibit 12.1). Using the aforementioned multiplier of 2.4 for private debt, the private totals are $39.6 billion (defaulted) and $31.9 billion (distressed). We are quite confident that, on average, defaulted public debt, which is a mixture of senior and subordinated securities, sells for about 50% of face value and public distressed debt for about 60% of face value. Private defaulted debt, which is predominantly senior in priority, is estimated to sell at 60% of face value and private distressed debt at 75% of face value. Hence, the June 1995 estimate of total public and private, defaulted and distressed debt was about $100 billion (face) and $64 billion (market). These figures include only domestic, U.S. debt.

It appears that the 1998 totals are somewhat lower due to the benign credit cycle in the United States for the years 1993 through 1997, when default rates on public high-yield bonds averaged less than 2% each year (Exhibit 12.2).[3] The supply of public, domestic defaulted bonds was about $10 billion as of mid-1998, and our best estimate of distressed public debt is about $13 billion. At the same time, we have noticed an increase in distressed securities in 1998.

Exhibit 12.1 Estimated Face and Market Values of Defaulted and Distressed Debt (1990–1998) ($Billions)

	January 31, 1990		August 31, 1992		August 31, 1993		June 30, 1995		August 31, 1998	
	Face Value	Market Value	Face Value	Market Value	Face Value	Market Value	Face Value	Market Value	Face Value	Market Value
Public Debt:										
Defaulted	$ 25.0	$ 11.4	$ 42.6	$ 20.5	$ 31.5	$ 15.8	$ 16.5	$ 8.3	$ 10.0	$ 5.0
Distressed	50.0	33.0	28.4	16.5	15.6	9.4	13.3	8.0	13.0	7.8
Total Public	**75.0**	**44.4**	**71.0**	**37.0**	**47.1**	**25.1**	**29.8**	**16.3**	**23.0**	**12.8**
Private Debt:										
Defaulted	75.0[1]	46.8	78.8[2]	47.3	75.6[3]	43.4	39.6[3]	23.8	23.0[3]	16.8[4]
Distressed	150.0	112.5	52.5[2]	39.4	37.4[3]	28.1	31.9[3]	23.9	31.2[3]	25.0[5]
Total Private	**225.0**	**159.3**	**131.4**	**86.7**	**113.0**	**71.5**	**71.5**	**47.7**	**54.2**	**41.8**
Total Public & Private	**$300.0**	**$203.7**	**$202.4**	**$123.7**	**$160.1**	**$96.6**	**$101.3**	**$ 64.0**	**$ 77.2**	**$ 54.6**

[1] Assumes 3-to-1 ratio of private to public debt.
[2] Assumes 1.85-to-1 ratio of private to public debt.
[3] Assumes 2.4-to-1 ratio of private to public debt.
[4] Assumes 70% of face value.
[5] Assumes 80% of face value.

Source: E. Altman and B. Simon (1996) and updates, e.g., "Yield-to-Worst Rankings," Merrill Lynch & Company, monthly.

Exhibit 12.2   Historical Default Rates—Straight Bonds Only, Excluding Defaulted Issues from Par Value Outstanding 1971–1997 ($ million)

Year	Par Value Outstanding[a]	Par Value Defaults	Default Rates (%)
1997	$335,400	$4,200	1.25
1996	$271,000	$3,336	1.23
1995	$240,000	$4,551	1.90
1994	$235,000	$3,418	1.45
1993	$206,907	$2,287	1.11
1992	$163,000	$5,545	3.40
1991	$183,600	$18,862	10.27
1990	$181,000	$18,354	10.14
1989	$189,258	$8,110	4.29
1988	$148,187	$3,944	2.66
1987	$129,557	$7,486	5.78
1986	$90,243	$3,156	3.50
1985	$58,088	$992	1.71
1984	$40,939	$344	0.84
1983	$27,492	$301	1.09
1982	$18,109	$577	3.19
1981	$17,115	$27	0.16
1980	$14,935	$224	1.50
1979	$10,356	$20	0.19
1978	$8,946	$119	1.33
1977	$8,157	$381	4.67
1976	$7,735	$30	0.39
1975	$7,471	$204	2.73
1974	$10,894	$123	1.13
1973	$7,824	$49	0.63
1972	$6,928	$193	2.79
1971	$6,602	$82	1.24

			Standard Deviation (%)
Arithmetic Average Default Rate	1971–1997	2.61	2.55
	1977–1997	2.94	2.77
	1978–1997	3.54	3.26
Weighted Average Default Rate[b]	1971–1997	3.31	3.05
	1977–1997	3.35	3.06
	1978–1997	3.51	3.26
Median Annual Default Rate	1971–1997	1.50	

[a]As of midyear, except for Q1–Q2 1998, which is as of 12/31/97.
[b]Weighted by par value of amount outstanding for each year.

The resulting total of defaulted and distressed public bonds and private debt as of August 1998 was about $77 billion (face value) and $55 billion (market value). The latter is impacted by recent estimates that bank loan defaults sell at about 70% of face value.[4] Distressed debt is therefore higher, at 80% of face value. The private component (e.g., bank loans) is definitely lower than it was in 1995. The flight-to-quality problems of August 1998, however, have resulted in a marked decrease in prices of all bank debt, especially in the distressed sector. With the tremendous growth in syndicated bank loans from 1996 to 1998 (midyear), the potential supply of distressed private debt has definitely increased.

In summary, the 1998 totals of distressed and defaulted debt in the United States is probably $77 billion (face value). If we include international debt, especially Asian loans and securities, this number is dramatically higher, because in the first six months of 1998 alone, over $2.5 billion of non-U.S., rated, public debt defaulted (see Moody's tabulations of domestic and international debt[5]).

FUTURE SUPPLY OF DISTRESSED DEBT

A critical question for the distressed security investor, sometimes called a *vulture*, is the likely supply of new defaulted and distressed paper (i.e., the expected raw material for possible future investments). A reasonable method would be to extrapolate default totals based on the amount of new issuance in the recent past and the relationship between new issuance, segregated by original bond credit ratings, and expected defaults of these new issues. A method for doing just this is the mortality rate approach, first developed in the late 1980s[6] and updated each year. (For a discussion of formal default prediction models as well as a proposed method based on macroeconomic conditions and the existing credit and aged profile of the high-yield debt market, see Johnson and Fridson.[7]) Estimates, based on new issuance from 1971 to 1996 and defaults through 1997, are given in Exhibit 12.3.

Based on new issuance by bond rating from 1987 to 1996 and the mortality rate data in Exhibit 12.3, I estimate that new default totals will be approximately $36.4 billion over the next three years (Exhibit 12.4). Due to the high proportion of senior bonds issued in the high-yield debt market since 1990—about 65% of the total new issuance—the expected average price at default is about 45% of par value. This implies a market value estimate of about $18.2 billion of new defaults over the period 1998 to 2000. These public defaults will probably be accompanied by new private defaulted debt face value totals of about $87 billion. This is based on a 2.4 to 1.0 ratio of private to public. The resulting expected total of public and private defaulted debt at face value is therefore approximately $124 billion (face value) and $79 billion (market value). Incidentally, although these numbers look quite large, the resulting implied default rate in the U.S. high-yield debt market is approximately 2.4% per year—still below the historical annual weighted average of 3.3% (Exhibit 12.2).

Exhibit 12.3   Mortality Rates by Original Rating—All Rated Corporate Bonds[a] (1971–1997)

| | | Years after issuance | | | | | | | | | |
		1	2	3	4	5	6	7	8	9	10
AAA	Yearly	0.00%	0.00%	0.00%	0.00%	0.06%	0.00%	0.00%	0.00%	0.00%	0.00%
	Cumulative	0.00%	0.00%	0.00%	0.00%	0.06%	0.06%	0.06%	0.06%	0.06%	0.06%
AA	Yearly	0.00%	0.00%	0.43%	0.24%	0.00%	0.00%	0.01%	0.00%	0.04%	0.03%
	Cumulative	0.00%	0.00%	0.43%	0.67%	0.67%	0.67%	0.67%	0.67%	0.71%	0.74%
A	Yearly	0.00%	0.00%	0.04%	0.12%	0.06%	0.13%	0.06%	0.15%	0.10%	0.00%
	Cumulative	0.00%	0.00%	0.04%	0.15%	0.22%	0.34%	0.40%	0.54%	0.64%	0.64%
BBB	Yearly	0.03%	0.29%	0.36%	0.67%	0.31%	0.45%	0.19%	0.09%	0.08%	0.37%
	Cumulative	0.03%	0.31%	0.67%	1.34%	1.64%	2.09%	2.27%	2.36%	2.43%	2.80%
BB	Yearly	0.37%	0.72%	2.94%	1.94%	2.63%	1.09%	2.65%	0.26%	1.69%	3.39%
	Cumulative	0.37%	1.08%	3.99%	5.85%	8.32%	9.32%	11.72%	11.95%	13.44%	16.37%
B	Yearly	1.47%	3.76%	6.89%	6.05%	5.89%	5.95%	4.12%	1.88%	1.72%	1.30%
	Cumulative	1.47%	5.18%	11.72%	17.06%	21.95%	26.59%	29.62%	30.94%	32.13%	33.01%
CCC	Yearly	2.28%	13.56%	13.25%	9.19%	2.96%	9.69%	1.00%	5.50%	0.00%	3.71%
	Cumulative	2.28%	15.53%	26.72%	33.46%	35.42%	41.68%	42.27%	45.44%	45.44%	47.46%

[a]Rated by S & P at issuance. Based on 647 issues.

Exhibit 12.4   Expected Supply of New Defaulted Debt (United States Only, 1998–2000)

Debt Type	Defaulted Debt Par Value ($ Billion)	Defaulted Debt Market Value ($ Billion)
Public Straight Debt	$36.42	$18.21
Private Senior Debt[a]	$87.42	$61.19
Total	$123.84	$79.41

[a]Assumes private/public ratio of 2.4; market value at default at 0.60 of face value.

DISTRESSED SECURITIES INVESTOR PROFILE

Despite the fact that some distressed investors have abandoned the market in the last few years as the supply of new defaulted debt has diminished, there still exists an impressive number of investors who specialize in this rather unique asset class. The primary vehicle for investing is a limited partnership, whereby a particular distressed-asset investment manager raises funds from financial institutions and wealthy individuals. Also, increasingly we observe institutions putting together a distressed or restructuring fund in order to place money with a small number of distressed securities managers who have different styles and preferences (e.g., active vs. passive investors).

The overwhelming majority of these investors specialize in debt securities with between 85 and 100% of their assets in distressed debt. In many cases, however, the original debt purchase will evolve into an equity interest via either a distressed exchange issue or bankruptcy reorganization. Most vultures have become more active in particular situations as well as continuing to operate under the traditional passive investment strategy. "Active" investing implies purchasing sufficient amounts of bonds in a particular debt class either to help formulate the restructuring plan or to be capable of blocking a proposed plan of reorganization that is unattractive to them.

Despite these variations of investment strategies, the formula for successful investing continues to require a set of fundamental valuation and technical skills complemented by a patient and disciplined approach to asset management. Skillful negotiation talent will prove particularly rewarding in some of the more contentious restructuring battles,[8] (See Gilson[9] for an overview of the market.)

Because there is a premium put on specialized talents and backgrounds and the need to attract capital by performing exceptionally well, I have found that investors require relatively high minimum annual rates of returns in the 20 to 25% range. The risky and illiquid nature of this market make such required returns necessary. As we will show, however, the average performance in this market over the last 11 years, although good, has been considerably below the 20 to 25% per year range. The remainder of this chapter reports on the performance of defaulted bonds in the 1987 through 1998 period. While it still debatable to refer to distressed and defaulted debt securities as an asset class or market,[10] especially in view to its diminished size in 1998, we are confident that investment attention in defaulted securities will not only continue but will increase in both supply and demand in the near-term future as well as the long run. In the final analysis, there will always be a market for the buying and selling of securities of problem firms that afford opportunities for considerable price appreciation greater than more typical corporate debt securities, provided that the firms' problems are addressed successfully, and where the current prices may be overly discounted due to the temporary distressed condition of the issuers.

MONITORING PERFORMANCE

In order to monitor the performance of defaulted debt securities, a measure called the Altman-NYU Salomon Center Index of Defaulted Debt Securities (A-NYU Index) was developed.[11] The publicly traded bonds of companies that have defaulted on their interest and/or principal payments comprise the Index. In almost all cases, the companies are operating at various stages of the chapter 11 bankruptcy-reorganization process—from just after default up to when the bankrupt firm either emerges from chapter 11, is liquidated, or the default is "cured" or resolved through an exchange. The index includes issues of all seniorities, from senior-secured to junior-unsecured debt. A study by Altman and Eberhart assesses the performance of defaulted debt from the time of original issuance through default and to emergence from bankruptcy.[12] That study finds that both the seniority of the issue and convertibility (or lack thereof) into common stock are extremely important determinations of the performance of defaulted debt for specific periods (i.e., from issuance to emergence). Note that the Index does not include convertible issues.

The size of the Index has varied over time in terms of the number of securities and their book and market values. The Index starts in December 1986 = 100 with 30 different securities. The number of issues has been as high as 231 in 1992 and as of December 31, 1997 included 37 issues (33 companies) with a face value of $5.9 billion and a market value of $2.7 billion. The 1997 totals are considerably reduced from the high point in 1992. These changes in the size of the Index reflect trends in the number of defaults and bankruptcy filings versus those firms and securities that have emerged from the chapter 11 process. The trend toward a reduced size of the Index appears to have reversed in 1998 with defaults ($3.7 billion, 26 issues) in the first six months, almost doubling the number in the comparable period of 1997. For a variety of reasons, I expect the number of issues to rise in the next several years. The Index is calculated based on the market values of the component securities on a monthly basis. Hence, larger issues weigh more heavily on the performance of the Index than do smaller ones. Except in rare cases, none of the securities are making interest payments while in default and the performance is strictly based on price changes. Price values are derived from a number of dealer quotes. We use either the end-of-month transaction price or the mean of the bid-ask spread when no transaction takes place.

Due to the relatively long historical record of the A-NYU Index, its relatively large and comprehensive nature, and its objective sources and maintenance, the Index is considered one of the most, if not *the* most, authoritative performance benchmarks for distressed investor money managers and for market observers and other investors. Moody's unveiled their bankrupt bond index in June 1998, and Salomon Smith Barney also publishes a bankrupt bond index.

In addition to our defaulted bond index, we also maintain an index of defaulted bank loans; this index was started in December 1995 = 100. A combined bond and bank loan index is also available.

1997 AND 1998 PERFORMANCE OF DEFAULTED BONDS

1997 Performance

The Altman-NYU Salomon Center Index had a relatively poor year's performance in 1997, falling by 1.578%, the first negative year since 1990 (Exhibit 12.5). The overall performance of defaulted debt securities was considerably less than the total return of the Standard & Poor's (S&P) Common Stock Index (+34.43%, assuming reinvestment of dividends) in 1997, and also below the Merrill Lynch High-Yield Bond Master Index (+12.73%). In general, most risky fixed income securities did well in 1997 as spreads narrowed throughout the year. The longer duration, 10-year U.S. government securities also performed well, reversing their poor 1996 performance. Defaulted securities, however, are not very sensitive to interest rate changes except as they affect the future earning power of the firm after it emerges (if it does) from reorganization.

1998 Performance

Through the first seven months of 1998, the defaulted bond index performed quite well, registering a total return of 5.10%. Similar results were achieved by our private bank loan index. The financial crisis in August changed everything. The carnage in the world's financial markets impacted all risky securities' performance and did not exclude defaulted and distressed debt. Indeed, our public bond index declined by an incredible 18.25% in one month, resulting in the worst single month's performance in the history of our index (the previous worst month was -8.92% in October 1987). Hence, the year-to-date performance was -13.15% as of August 31, 1998 (Exhibit 12.5). A similar decline in August was suffered by common stocks (-14.46%), indicating a high correlation in August between defaulted debt and stocks (see discussion page 000).

The near-term outlook for risky debt remained quite uncertain as the world's economic and financial problems were still prominent. Further shocks (from Russia, for example), political paralysis, and the lack of liquidity were perhaps not completely discounted in prices. Still, the eventual value of a distressed claim is, to a great extent, particular to the restructured company. Although the subsequent price of equities of emerged firms will certainly depend on the duration of the bankruptcy and market conditions upon the

Exhibit 12.5 Altman–NYU Salomon Center Defaulted Bond Index Comparison of Returns (1987–1997)

Year	Altman–NYU Salomon Center Defaulted Bond Index	S&P 500 Stock Index	Merrill Lynch High-Yield Master Index
1987	37.85%	5.26%	4.67%
1988	26.49%	16.61%	13.47%
1989	−22.78%	31.68%	4.23%
1990	−17.08%	−3.12%	−4.35%
1991	43.11%	30.48%	34.58%
1992	15.39%	7.62%	18.16%
1993	27.91%	10.08%	17.18%
1994	6.66%	1.32%	−1.16%
1995	11.26%	37.58%	19.91%
1996	10.21%	22.96%	11.06%
1997	−1.578%	34.359%	12.726%
1998 (8 mos.)	−13.149	−0.380%	0.569%
1987–1997 Arithmetic Average (Annual) Rate	12.49%	17.71%	11.86%
Standard Deviation	20.93%	14.41%	10.93%
1987–1997 Compounded Average (Annual) Rate	10.62%	16.91%	11.38%
1987–1997 Arithmetic Average (Monthly) Rate	0.91%	1.40%	0.91%
Standard Deviation	3.59%	4.21%	1.52%
1987–1997 Compounded Average (Monthly) Rate	0.84%	1.31%	0.90%

emergence from chapter 11, the main valuation ingredient is still the fundamental earning power of the firms' restructured assets and the distribution of new securities to the various old creditor classes and, in some cases, to the old equity. See our recent paper on the performance of equities of emerged companies.[13] In other words, investors should not be discouraged from continued investing in particular situations that appear attractive based on expected values and current prices.

ELEVEN-YEAR COMPARATIVE PERFORMANCE

In Exhibit 12.5 we observe the return on defaulted bonds as well as common stocks and high-yield bonds for the entire 11-year sample period 1987 through 1997. Note that both the arithmetic average (12.49% per year) and the geometric average (10.62% per year) for defaulted bonds are considerably less than the S&P 500 (17.71% and 16.91%, respectively) and about the same as the high-yield bond index (11.86% and 11.38%, respectively), for the same period. In five of the 11 years, defaulted bonds performed better than both of the other two indexes, while in five years it performed the worst. The standard deviation is largest for defaulted bonds. On a monthly basis, however, the volatility comparison (as measured by the standard deviation of return) is considerably different, with defaulted bond issues actually showing lower volatility (3.59%) than common stocks (4.21%) but considerably higher than high-yield "junk" bonds (1.52%). This latter comparison is understandable because high-yield bonds pay a fairly steady fixed interest each month, whereas defaulted bonds do not.

BANK LOAN INDEX

Our Altman-NYU Salomon Center Index of Defaulted Bank Loans is also a market-weighted index that started with 18 facilities (December 1995): and at the end of 1997 also had 18 (falling from 23 a year earlier). As of the end of 1997, the Index had a face value of $3.36 billion and $2.39 billion in market value—a market to face value of 0.71. This compares with a market-to-face value ratio of only 0.39 for our public bond index. The bank loan index entails only senior debt, much of which is secured; the bond index, discussed earlier, is a mix of senior and subordinated debt.

The performance of our bank loan index was also quite poor in 1997, rising by only 1.75%. The two-year defaulted bank loan return was 10.66%, considerably below the stock market's continued incredible performance and just below that of high-yield bonds.

DIVERSIFICATION ATTRIBUTES:
RISKY ASSET RETURNS CORRELATIONS

One of the less obvious potential strategies suggested by our analysis is to include defaulted debt in a larger portfolio of risky securities. Some pension funds have, in effect, taken this approach by allocating a small proportion of their total investments to distressed debt money managers. With a few exceptions, almost all portfolio managers involved in the distressed market have been specialists in the sector, rather than investors in distressed bonds within broader-based portfolios. Therefore, the avenue for diversification appears to be primarily through the use of different investment managers. There are some rare exceptions whereby a mutual fund combines investments in more traditional debt and equity securities with distressed securities (e.g., Mutual Shares Fund managed by Franklin Resources, Inc.).

Exhibit 12.6 demonstrates the most recent correlations between the Altman-NYU Index and two other risky asset classes: common stocks and high-yield

Exhibit 12.6 Correlation of Altman–NYU Salomon Center Index of Defaulted Securities with Other Speculative Securities Indexes 1987–1998 (August)

	Altman–NYU Salomon Center Index	S&P 500 Stock Index	Merrill Lynch High-Yield Master Index
Correlation of monthly returns:			
Altman–NYU Salomon Center Index	100.00%	35.04%	53.48%
S&P 500 Stock Index		100.00%	53.45%
Merrill Lynch High-Yield Master Index			100.00%

bonds. We see that the monthly return correlation is only 0.35 between risky defaulted debt and equities. Defaulted debtholders usually end up owning the equity of the emerged chapter 11 entity, unless they sell the debt just prior to emergence from restructuring; it is interesting to note the somewhat low correlation of returns between these two indexes. Furthermore, the quarterly correlations are even lower (0.26). The correlation between high-yield bonds and defaulted bonds is considerably higher, at about 0.53 (both monthly and quarterly). We believe this moderate correlation is partially a function of the operating performance of firms in general, the outlook for risky companies and the overall confidence in the market for risky debt. Although these correlations are fairly high, it is also clear that the defaulted debt index is more volatile in both good and bad years.

This is not surprising because high-yield debt has a base return equal to the interest payments received in each period while most defaulted debt trades "flat" (without interest receipts). In addition, there is a great deal of uncertainty about what the reorganization plan will specify and how each class of creditors will be treated—not to mention the possibility that the end result will be a liquidation. Finally, there are several critical event dates during a bankruptcy reorganization (i.e., bankruptcy filing, postdefault financing, filing of a reorganization plan and plan confirmation/liquidation), which can result in large swings in the price of debt issues.

We do observe that the relative volatility between defaulted debt and equity returns, when measured on a monthly basis, puts the former in a much more favorable light. This implies a greater degree of autocorrelation (strings of gains or losses), which can exacerbate annual return levels and volatility but not monthly return variability.

CORRELATIONS IN EXCEPTIONAL MONTHS

The correlations listed in Exhibit 12.6 are for the entire period 1987 through 1998 (August). Because we observed such a dramatic decline in both the defaulted debt and common stock markets in August 1998, we thought it instructive to analyze the correlation between these two asset classes, and also with high-yield bonds, when the stock market performs exceptionally well or poorly. We selected an arbitrary criterion of (5.0% monthly return as a definition of an exceptional month. Over the $11^1/_2$-year sample period, there were 25 months when the stock market's performance exceeded this ±5% criteria (Exhibit 12.7). Note that there are six observations in 1987 and 1997, none during the period 1992 throough 1995, and three so far in 1998. August 1998 standsout as the biggest one-month decline for all of our indexes except for the October 1987 stock market meltdown.

The correlations shown in Exhibit 12.7, for exceptional months, are all considerably higher than when measured over the entire $11^1/_2$-year period. For ex-

Exhibit 12.7   Exceptional[a] Monthly Performance Comparisons (1987–1998)

Month	Bank Loan Index	Market Weighted Bond Index	S&P 500 Stock Index	Merrill Lunch High Yield Master Index
1. Jan 87		9.802%	13.470%	2.828%
2 Jun 87		2.897%	5.050%	1.382%
3. Jul 87		5.503%	5.070%	0.544%
4. Oct 87		–8.916%	–21.540%	–2.672%
5. Nov 87		3.215%	–8.240%	2.529%
6. Dec–87		7.534%	7.610%	1.328%
7. Jan 89		–4.468%	7.320%	1.500%
8. Apr 89		2.056%	5.190%	0.295%
9. Jul 89		2.462%	9.030%	0.474%
10. Jan 90		12.909%	–6.710%	–1.954%
11. May 90		–1.234%	9.750%	1.806%
12. Aug 90		–3.026%	–9.040%	–3.830%
13. Nov 90		–2.691%	6.460%	0.850%
14. Feb 91		8.486%	7.150%	7.423%
15. Dec 91		13.530%	11.437%	1.162%
16. Sep 96	0.791%	2.107%	5.628%	2.146%
17. Jan 97	1.879%	–1.544%	6.248%	0.517%
18. Apr 97	–6.6 27%	–2.132%	5.970%	1.138%
19. May 97	–1.933%	0.109%	6.880%	2.150%
20. Jul 97	0.453%	–0.228%	7.957%	2.400%
21. Aug 97	1.190%	2.267%	–5.602%	–0.175%
22. Sep 97	2.406%	1.639%	5.477%	1.656%
23. Feb 98	–0.843%	1.960%	7.212%	0.413%
24. Mar 98	1.677%	0.819%	5.121%	0.862%
25. Aug 98	–6.265%	–18.254%	–14.458%	–4.315%

[a]Stock Market Increase or Decline by more than 5% in a month.
Sources: Altman–NYU Salomon Center's Defaulted Bond and Bank Loans Indexes, Standard & Poor's, and Merrill Lynch & Company.

ample, our defaulted bond index had a 0.59 correlation with the stock market compared to 0.35 for the entire period. The S&P 500 Stock Index correlation with high-yield bonds jumps from 0.53 to 0.68. This implies a type of contagion effect from the more liquid and larger stock market to "fixed" income securities that are also perceived as risky and quite a bit less liquid.

Despite the higher correlations during exceptional months, we also observe that in 9 of 25 months, the stock market and defaulted bond market moved in opposite directions. This is in contrast to the direction of the monthly correlations between the S&P 500 and high-yield debt when in only two instances was the sign of the monthly return different. In the case of negative exceptional stock market months, however (five instances), only once did the defaulted bond market increase (August 1997).

NOTES

1.   E.I. Altman, The Altman/Foothill Report on Investing in Distressed Securities: The Anatomy of Defaulted Debt and Equities, April 1990; and "The Market for Distressed Securities and Bank Loans, October, Foothill Corporation, Los Angeles.

2.   E.I. Altman, and B. Simon, The Investment Performance of Defaulted Bonds for 1995 and 1986-1995, Special Report, NYU Salomon Center, January.

3.   E.I. Altman and V. Kishore, "The NYU Salomon Center Report on Defaults and Returns on High Yield Bonds: Analysis Through 1997," Leonard N. Stern School of Business, NYU, Special Report, January.

4.   *Moody's Bankrupt Bond Index,* Special Comment, New York, Moody's Investors Service, April 1998.

5.   *Moody's Bankrupt Loan Recoveries*, Special Comment, New York, Moody's Investors Service, June 1998.

6.   E.I. Altman, Measuring Corporate Bond Mortality and Performance" *Journal of Finance*, 45, 1989, pp. 909-922.

7.   Jonsson and M. Fridson (1995): Forecasting Default Rates on High Yield Bonds, *Journal of Fixed Income*, pp. 69-77, June 1995.

8.   Swank, T. and T. Root (1995): "Bonds in Default: Is Patience a Virtue?" Journal of Fixed Income, 5, June, pp. 26-31.

9.   Gilson, S. (1995): "Investing in Distressed Securities: A Market Survey," Financial Analysts Journal, November/December 1995, pp. 8-27.

10.   F. Reilly, E. Altman, and D. Wright, Including Defaulted Bonds in the Capital Market's Asset Spectrum, *Financial Management Association*, October 16, 1998 (Chicago), argues that defaulted securities are indeed a bona-fide asset class.

11.   This index is maintained and published on a monthly basis at the NYU Salomon Center of the Leonard N. Stern School of Business and is available via the Center.

12.   E.I. Altman, and A. Eberhart, Do Seniority Provisions Protect Bondholders' Investments? *Journal of Portfolio Management*, 20, pp. 67-75, Summer,1994. An updated study by Standard & Poor's was published in *Ratings Performance 1997: Stability and Transition*, "Recoveries on Defaulted Bonds Tied to Seniority Rankings," by Leo Brand, S&P, New York, August 1998.

13.   A. Eberhart, E. Altman, and R. Aggarwal, "The Performance of Equities of Firms Emerging from Chapter 11," NYU Salomon Center Working Paper #S-97-4, and *Journal of Finance*, forthcoming 1999.

REFERENCES

E.I. Altman, *Distressed Securities*, Chicago, Probus Publishing, 1991.

——— Defaulted Bonds: Supply, Demand and Investment Performance, 1982-1992, *Financial Analysts Journal*, 44, pp. 55-60,May/June 1993.

——— *Corporate Financial Distress and Bankruptcy*, 2nd ed. New York, John Wiley & Sons, 1993.

B. Branch and H. Ray, *Bankruptcy Investing*, Chicago, Dearborn Press, 1992.

H. Rosenberg, *Vulture Investors*, New York, HarperCollins Publishers, 1992.

D. Ward and G. Griepentrog, Risk and Return in Defaulted Bonds, *Financial Analysts Journal*, 49, pp. 61–65, May-June 1993.

13

International Restructuring: Overcoming Cross-Border Hurdles in South America

*Deborah M. Smith, PricewaterhouseCoopers LLP and
Jeffrey A. Sell, Chase Manhattan Bank, N.A.*

INTRODUCTION

As the economic world gets smaller, businesses and their operations have no boundaries. Markets do not recognize borders on a map. There is money to be made and lost globally. Stakeholders are investing in businesses that have operations in more than one country. Today, even the smallest of business operations is affected by cross-border situations, whether its supplier of raw materials is located in another country or a subsidiary of that business is located on another continent. The complications of business transactions grow because of different sovereign laws and regulations, economics, governments, financial markets, and cultures. Assets of a business are often located in several different countries, as are the business' creditors and investors. Businesses have intercompany transactions with and investments in cross-border related entities. The central challenge for troubled businesses is how they restructure themselves in an international environment in which stakeholders in different countries with various interests and agendas are forced to overcome international barriers in order to reach a solution without common laws or structures. Presently, there is no road map on how to restructure in a cross-border situation. Every deal is different, and ground is being broken with each new restructuring that is consummated.

No matter what the stakeholder's position—an equity investor, lender, or trade creditor—the same issues arise and the same questions are asked. How do I collect my debt or investment in a company that has operations or assets in foreign countries? Can I collect on my overseas collateral? What are the bankruptcy and lien laws in the various jurisdictions? Do I have standing in a foreign proceeding, and what is my priority? What are the foreign creditors' claims? Am I going to be able to make my collection decisions based on economics or will the legal structure control the process? In situations of dual filings, which country's laws prevail? How do multiple jurisdictions interact? Are the provisions of the United States Bankruptcy Code recognized in Latin American countries?

International restructuring complications include country economics, government, financial markets, reporting, and cultural differences. A key to operating in cross-border troubled company situations is understanding the differences in each country's laws and regulations regarding restructurings, workouts, insolvency, and bankruptcy, as well as agreements of cooperation and reciprocity between courts in various countries. The options available for a restructuring in Latin America vary depending on the legal structures of individual countries. Each option results in its own timeline and costs. Most Latin American countries have provisions for out-of-court restructurings or prenegotiated judicial reorganizations, but these provisions vary greatly. Historically, in Latin America, a nonjudicial reorganization has had a higher probability of a successful restructuring and a shorter timeline than a judicial reorganization. Some countries have forced liquidation rules in their statutes triggered by the financial or economic results of the business. Some have provisions for receivers or trustees, and some do not. Some countries have governmental agencies with oversight responsibilities of the troubled company's operations and/or the judicial process. In certain Latin American countries, such as Mexico, the directors and officers of the company filing bankruptcy may be subject to criminal prosecution. Even the terms used in a restructuring or reorganization can have different meanings in different countries. For example, in Argentina, Brazil, Chile, Mexico, and Venezuela, the use of the term *bankruptcy* means the liquidation of the debtor and has no association with a chapter 11–type reorganization proceeding. Some countries have provisions in their laws to recognize certain foreign proceedings of another country if there is reciprocity shown to their country, whereas others do not. Restructuring becomes even more complicated when there are different related companies incorporated in different countries, each with its own set of stakeholders, and the companies have intercompany debt, receivables, cross guarantees, or the asset of one company is the other company. There is significant uncertainty as to rights, authority, and roles of each party in different countries and how and if a stakeholder's standing will be recognized.

The issues and challenges raised by the lack of a uniform bankruptcy law or procedures are not new and have been reviewed and addressed over time by many professionals dealing in cross-border situations. The notion of uniform insolvency legislation across all jurisdictions is not a practical one even if there is a common goal to rescue a core business, save employees' jobs, and compensate creditors and other stakeholders justly, or to liquidate the entity to pay creditors. For a multinational restructuring to be successful, a set of basic procedures must be negotiated among all interested parties whether through an out-of-court restructuring agreement or a judicial process. Presently, cross-border insolvency court cases are handled using informal protocols among the courts through judicial cooperation. The uncertainty of not knowing how a multinational judicial reorganization will be handled makes it difficult to consider the pros and cons of filing a case in proceedings versus an out-of-court restructuring.

Case law in Latin America surrounding restructurings, reorganizations, and bankruptcy is not well developed or universal in application, thus resulting in a high degree of uncertainty when trying to predict the outcome of a troubled company. For this reason, most international restructurings of commercially viable companies tend to be accomplished through consensual agreement among the parties outside the court environment to preserve value and maximize the recovery to the stakeholders. In pursuit of consensual agreement, stakeholders return to the basic fundamentals of restructuring by:

- Identifying the business' problems
- Assessing the business' financial position and viability
- Stabilizing its operations
- Assessing its financial, operational, and strategic options
- Determining the true cash flows of the business using forecasts on a line of business basis with good underlying assumptions
- Developing a business plan to maximize value and produce the best economic result
- Understanding the strengths and weaknesses of different claims
- Negotiating for a consensual agreement

Whether in a cross-border or a domestic restructuring, the methods to finding the solutions are the same. There is a business in distress that has issues causing the problems that need to be identified and addressed. The stakeholders go back to the basic fundamentals of restructuring to develop the best business solution. The goal of all stakeholders is to maximize their recovery. If it is possible to reach a consensual solution and avoid having to deal with local courts and judges, the home court advantage factors, and the uncertainty that surrounds the judicial process, a consensual deal will maximize the recovery of the stakeholders.

This chapter discusses the issues surrounding cross-border insolvency in Latin America, the initiatives taken by countries in addressing cross-border situations, and some of the general procedures of insolvency in selected Latin American countries. The purpose of this chapter is to inform the reader about the general cross-border restructuring environment. It is not meant to be a legal outline of insolvency law and should not be used for that purpose.

UNITED NATIONS COMMISSION ON INTERNATIONAL TRADE LAW MODEL LAW ON CROSS-BORDER INSOLVENCY

The United Nations Commission on International Trade Law (UNCITRAL) adopted a cross-border insolvency model law in May 1997 at its thirtieth session. The preamble of the law states:

The purpose of this Law is to provide effective mechanisms for dealing with cases of cross-border insolvency so as to promote the objectives of: (a) cooperation between the courts and other competent authorities of this State and foreign States involved in cases of cross-border insolvency; (b) greater legal certainty for trade and investment; (c) fair and efficient administration of cross-border insolvencies that protects the interests of all creditors and other interested persons, including the debtor; (d) protection and maximization of the value of the debtor's assets; and (e) facilitation of the rescue of financially troubled businesses, thereby protecting investment and preserving employment."[1]

Although the UNCITRAL model law has not yet been adopted by any country and addresses only insolvency cases, it represents a significant step in international cooperation in cross-border restructuring situations. If adopted by the member nations of the United Nations Commission, the model law would give some certainty of the authority and roles that will be recognized in a cross-border situation that are presently undefined. By taking some of the uncertainty out of the process, the model law could help build reliance and confidence in cross-border negotiations and restructurings. The model law addresses procedures for issues such as access of foreign representatives and creditors to courts in the state, recognition of a foreign proceeding and relief, cooperation with foreign courts and foreign representatives, and coordination of concurrent proceedings.[2] The model law is presently before the United States Congress for consideration. Argentina, Brazil, Chile, Ecuador, Mexico, and Uruguay are among the 36 members of the United Nations Commission; however, to date, none have enacted the model law. Even if the Model Law is enacted in Latin American countries, restructuring professionals would still have to look to the laws and regulations of the countries as they relate to nonjudicial or judicial reorganizations in that country. The UNCITRAL Model Law on Cross-Border Insolvency appears at the end of this chapter as an appendix.

UNITED STATES BANKRUPTCY CODE
RECOGNITION OF FOREIGN PROCEEDINGS

The United States Bankruptcy Code does allow for recognition of foreign proceedings under Section 304, Cases Ancillary to Foreign Proceedings. A foreign representative, defined as "duly selected trustee, administrator, or other representative of an estate in a foreign proceeding,"[3] can commence a case ancillary to a foreign proceeding by filing a petition with the bankruptcy court. There are various types of relief the court can grant to a foreign representative under this section. In making relief determinations, the court is "guided by what will best assure an economical and expeditious administration of such estate, consistent with—

- just treatment of all holders of claims against or interests in such estate;

- protection of claim holders in the United States against prejudice and inconvenience in the processing of claims in such foreign proceedings;
- prevention of preferential or fraudulent dispositions of property of such estate;
- distribution of proceeds of such estate substantially in accordance with the order prescribed by [the Bankruptcy Code];
- comity; and
- if appropriate, the provision of an opportunity for a fresh start for the individual that such foreign proceeding concerns."[4]

The relief the court can grant to a foreign representative under Section 304 of the Code is varied and is limited only to what the Court determines to be "appropriate relief."[5] The Code specifically provides for the court to enjoin the commencement or continuation of any action against a debtor with respect to property involved in foreign proceedings, to enforce any judgment against the debtor with respect to property, to create or enforce a lien against the property, or to turn over the property or proceeds from the property to the foreign representative.

Section 305 of the Bankruptcy Code allows a foreign representative to seek dismissal or suspension of a case from the court if there is a foreign proceeding pending. The court is required to give notice, hold a hearing, and consider the factors of Section 304(c) outlined above in determining if such a dismissal or suspension is warranted.[6]

The U.S. system does recognize foreign representatives' interests and fosters cooperation between the U.S. court and foreign courts. The court has leeway in how it handles foreign requests and negotiates protocol with foreign representatives. Given the flexibility the Bankruptcy Code allows the courts, the "appropriate relief" granted is varied and in some instance has yielded conflicting results. This process becomes very complex when there are proceedings brought in several different countries and requires interaction of several states. The reciprocity from the foreign body depends on the Latin American country, its laws, and the foreign decision maker.

LATIN AMERICAN INITIATIVES TOWARD REGULATION OF CROSS-BORDER INSOLVENCIES

In 1993, the Secretariat of the United Nations Commission on International Trade Law outlined the following existing Latin American initiatives toward regulation of cross-border insolvencies as part of a note on the possible future work the Commission might like to consider related to the international aspects of bankruptcy. There have been three instances in Latin America in which initiatives have been taken toward regulation of cross-border insolvencies within Latin American countries. They are the Convention on Private International Law, Havana 1928 (Bustamante Code), and the 1889 and 1940 Montevideo Treaties on Commercial International Law (Montevideo Treaties).

Fifteen Latin American states have adopted the Bustamante Code. It provides that:

> [T]he debtor's civil or commercial domicile is the link required for juris-diction to open insolvency proceedings. If the debtor has one domicile, only insolvency proceedings in the State of domicile are allowed; if the debtor has a commercial domicile in more than one State, proceedings can be opened in each of those States. Provisions are included on: recognition in other contracting States of bankruptcy and composition orders; recognition of the powers of a bankruptcy administrator appointed in a foreign contracting State; recognition of foreign decisions setting aside or modify-ing transactions that were concluded within a specific period prior to the insolvency declaration and that prejudice the debtor's creditors.[7]

The Montevideo Treaty of 1889 provides rules for liquidations and governs the relations between Argentina, Bolivia, Colombia, and Peru. The relations be-tween Argentina, Uruguay, and Paraguay are governed by the Montevideo Treaty of 1940, which also provides guidance for compositions, suspensions of payments, and other corresponding proceedings provided for in the contracting states. The Montevideo Treaties do not provide uniform insolvency legislation among contracting states but rather unify numerous rules of Private International Insolvency Law.[8]

> Both Treaties refer to the debtor's commercial domicile as the required link for jurisdiction to open insolvency proceedings. If the debtor has a commercial domicile in other States, proceedings can be opened in each of those States. Under the scheme of the Treaties, the authority of bankruptcy administrators, as determined by the laws of the State where the insol-vency proceedings were opened, is recognized in all contracting States. Provisional measures can be enforced over property located in other States, and courts in those other States are to publicize the opening of the proceedings and the taking of the provisional measures. Provision is also made for local creditors in those States to petition for separate involuntary proceedings to be carried out in accordance with the law of the State where they are opened. Creditors can rely on security interests, in both immov-able or movable property, before the court where the property is located, as long as those security interests were established before the opening of the insolvency proceedings.[9]

Argentina

In the third quarter of 1995, the Argentine National Congress passed the Argen-tine Bankruptcy Law 24,522 (ABL 24,522), which was approved by the execu-tive branch of the Republic of Argentina in December 1995, modifying the previous Argentine insolvency laws. ABL 24,522 applies to both legal entities and individuals. It also applies to businesses with government ownership. There are some exceptions to the application of ABL 24,522 relating to financial institutions and insurance companies, and there are some differences related to pension funds, mutual companies, and public utilities.

There is uncertainty as to how some issues will be resolved under the Argentine Bankruptcy Law. There are numerous cross-border insolvency issues that are not addressed in Argentine law; other issues that are specifically addressed by the law are subject to interpretation. There have been few cross-border judicial proceedings in Argentina. Some cross-border issues are addressed in the Argentine law and have been applied by the courts, which gives some predictability to the outcome of those issues. However, Argentine law does not require judgments binding precedents for future cases.[10]

Argentine law provides for an out-of-court restructuring or agreement and judicial proceedings. There are two judicial proceedings: *Concurso Preventivo*, which is the reorganization of an insolvent debtor, and *Quiebra*, which is the liquidation of a debtor (bankruptcy).

Out-of-Court Restructuring. There is a provision in ABL 24,522 that allows a debtor and some or all of its creditors to reach a restructuring agreement to prevent the bankruptcy of a company. Once an agreement is negotiated, notice in the newspapers is required to allow parties-in-interest the ability to challenge the agreement. Although this is an out-of-court restructuring, the agreement is presented for approval by a judge in order to legitimize the workout. The judge determines whether the agreement meets certain basic provisions and holds a brief proceeding. Court-approved restructurings are binding to the creditors who were parties to the agreement and cannot be challenged by pre-existing or future creditors of the debtor even if the debtor converts to Concurso Preventivo or Quiebra.

There have been partial or complete debt restructuring agreements in Argentina that have not gone through the court approval process. This raises the question as to whether the above process is required in all instances of restructuring and whether the validity and enforceability of a nonjudicial workout without the court's blessing can be challenged.

Concurso Preventivo—Reorganization Proceedings. Although creditors can force a debtor's hand to file for Concurso Preventivo by threatening the initiation of Quiebra, only an insolvent debtor can commence the filing of a petition for a reorganization of a company. Under Argentine law, insolvency means being in a "state of cessation of payments," defined as the inability to regularly pay debts as they come due. The debtor must also provide proof to the court of its probable ability to reorganize to qualify for Concurso Preventivo. As part of the petition, the debtor is required to file several corporate, financial, and other reports and documents, some of which require certification by an accountant. The preparation of these documents can be costly and time consuming. The judge can deny reorganization if the documents are not filed at the time of the petition. The court has five days from the written petition to decide whether reorganization will be allowed.

Historically, Argentine courts have been very hard on debtors and very strict when deciding whether the conditions exist to allow a debtor to reorganize. If a judge denies a debtor's petition for reorganization, the debtor will not be able to stop a creditor's petition for bankruptcy for one year.[11] In a reorganization, the debtor remains in control of the company and its assets; however, the court appoints an individual (sindico) to supervise the debtor's activities. The judge also appoints a creditors' committee (comités de acreedores) consisting of the three largest creditors. The creditors' committee has an oversight and advisory role.

The debtor is required to get approval from the court, after giving prior notice to the sindico and the creditors' committee, for any activities that are outside of the normal course of business or would be considered material transactions. Argentine law has restrictions related to the transfer of assets or the payment of antecedent debt. If the debtor does not follow the requirements and enters into a transaction that would adversely affect the prepetition creditors, the debtor's estate could be placed under the control of the sindico.

Creditors are stayed from further proceedings against the debtor once a judge opens a reorganization proceeding, and bankruptcy (Quiebra) cannot be filed against the debtor. Interest on unsecured debt ceases to accrue. Secured debt, such as mortgages and pledges, are delayed only until the secured lender brings execution proceedings in the relevant court, with notice to the bankruptcy judge. Secured lenders can enforce both conventional and punitive interest until date of payment. If the judge believes that the secured asset is needed for the fundamental operation of the business, he can stay the action against the asset for a 90-day period.

The sindico writes to the creditors from the creditor list filed by the debtor at the time of petition, notifies them of the reorganization proceeding, and reports certain debtor summary information. He also notifies them of the bar date and address where creditors need to file their claims. The creditors, including foreign creditors, must file evidence of their claims (including the amount, type of claim, [secured or unsecured], and its origin) with the sindico who reviews the claims and reconciles them with the debtor's books and records. The sindico reports its recommendations as to acceptance or rejection of the claims to the court. Within 10 days of the sindico's recommendation as to the claims, the court rules on the admissible claims.

Within 10 days of the court's ruling on admissible claims, the debtor submits its plan to classify its creditors into groups to the court, the sindico, and the creditors. Creditors are grouped based on their like nature. Argentine law requires at least three creditor classifications: secured creditors, unsecured creditors, and unsecured labor creditors. The creditor classes are subject to court approval. Once the court approves the creditor classes, a new creditors' committee is appointed by the court to consist of at least the largest creditor of each creditor class. The debtor then has a 30-day exclusivity period to propose and negotiate a reorganization agreement with each creditor class. The court can extend the exclusivity time period up to an additional 30 days, for a total not to exceed 60 days.

The reorganization proposals negotiated with each creditor class may be different and can take many forms, including discounting of amount, refinancing of terms, paying in assets, paying in various debt or equity securities, capitalizing of debt, combining of any these payment methods, or any other solutions agreed to by the parties-in-interest. Each creditor within a class is required to have the same treatment. In order to reorganize, a company is required to obtain the approval of its proposal by the majority of each creditor class and two thirds of the unsecured debts. An information hearing is held five days prior to the end of the debtor's exclusivity period. The debtor is required to submit the reorganization proposal in writing to the court. If the proposal has received the required votes, the court will approve the reorganization. The judge does not have the power to reject a plan approved by the creditors. If the creditors do not approve the proposal, the company is subject to the business rescue procedure or will be converted to liquidation.

If the debtor is unable to reach agreement with its creditors during the exclusivity period, the Argentine law has a provision referred to as the salvage or business rescue procedure that allows the court to place the business up for sale in order to salvage it as a going concern. The salvage procedure allows for creditors and/or third parties to present a plan to the creditors to purchase the business. If the proposed plan meets the requirements of the law and receives the majority vote of the creditors (and in some instances, if there is proven "equity," that of the shareholders), the judge will approve the plan. The plan proposers will then become the owners of the company and will have rescued the company from liquidation procedures.

Quiebra—Liquidation Proceedings. An Argentine debtor can end up in Quiebra in one of three ways: an unsuccessful reorganization, the filing of a petition by a creditor, or the filing of a petition by the debtor itself. It should also be noted that under Argentine law, if a company reports a shareholder's deficit in its annual financial statements under generally accepted accounting principles, the company is placed in a state of liquidation unless the shareholders agree to recapitalize the company. More often than not, liquidation proceedings in Argentina are initiated by a creditor. Any creditor, no matter what the amount owed to it by the debtor, can file a petition against the debtor. The creditor is required to present evidence that a debt is owed to it and that the debtor has not paid its debt as it became due. The debtor has five days from the notification of a petition filed by a creditor to prove that it is not in a state of cessation of payment or the judge can declare the debtor bankrupt.

In Quiebra, management loses control of the company and is replaced by a sindico, whose job is to protect and liquidate the assets of the company to pay the creditors of the debtor under the oversight of the court. Usually, the court orders the company's operations shut down, the assets of the company seized, and the books and records obtained. At the time bankruptcy is declared, all claims and actions against the debtor are stayed. Notice of the bankruptcy is given in the newspapers and legal journals. Creditors are required to file evidence of their claims. A creditors' committee may be formed to monitor the liquidation process. The sindico sells the assets of the business in an orderly manner. The sale can take different forms, from selling the company as a whole to the sale of its parts. The proceeds from the sale are paid to the creditors from a distribution plan, in order of priority set by law, which was filed with the court by the sindico, agreed to by the creditors, and approved by the court. The priority of creditors under Argentine law is complex, but generally priority is given to secured claims and the estate's administrative claims over other claimants.

There are claw-back provisions in Argentine law. The suspect or preference period cannot be longer than two years prior to the declaration of bankruptcy and is considered the time period from which the company was unable to make payments as they were due through the day it was declared bankrupt. If certain conditions are met and preferential treatment to a party is determined, the assets transferred are recoverable to the estate.

Argentine Cross-Border Factors. Argentine insolvency laws pertain to debtors that are domiciled in Argentina. The Argentine courts do not have jurisdiction over foreign debtors except to the extent that they have assets located in Argentina and the credit owed is payable in Argentina. The Argentine court's jurisdiction would then bear on only those assets.

Orders of attachment or staying of actions of a foreign court may be enforced in Argentina if all the requirements of the Argentine law are met and if reorganization or bankruptcy proceedings have not been initiated in Argentina. A creditor of a foreign reorganization or bankruptcy proceeding has grounds to petition a proceeding in Argentina if the creditor has amounts payable to it in Argentina.

Under Argentine insolvency law, when there is both an Argentine and a foreign bankruptcy proceeding, a foreign unsecured creditor of the Argentine bankruptcy is paid from Argentine assets only if reciprocity of similar treatment to an Argentine creditor in the foreign country is proven to exist and only after all the local creditors are compensated. A *foreign creditor* is defined as a creditor whose debt is not payable in Argentina. Under this definition, a resident of another country could be considered a local creditor if the debt owed that creditor is payable in Argentina. For example, if a global bank lent money to an Argentine company with the debt payments payable to the local Argentine bank branch, that global bank would be considered a local creditor. If the same global bank structured the loan payable to its New York bank branch, then the bank would be classified as a foreign creditor. Secured creditors are not required to meet the rule of reciprocity.

If the foreign unsecured creditor does not belong to a foreign proceeding, reciprocity still has to be proven to obtain standing in an Argentine bankruptcy; however, there is no subordination of the foreign creditor, and creditors are paid *pari passu* with local creditors. Foreign creditors (e.g., those who do not have credits payable in Argentina) cannot request the opening of liquidation proceedings in Argentina.

In an Argentine reorganization proceeding, reciprocity has to be shown for a foreign unsecured creditor to have standing. However, the local rule of priority does not apply to reorganization. Once a foreign creditor is given standing in a reorganization, he is treated *pari passu* with the local creditors.

Brazil

Brazilian law provides for three types of proceedings available to a financially troubled Brazilian entity: insolvency, bankruptcy, and Concordata. Insolvency and bankruptcy proceedings in general are liquidation proceedings and are governed either by the Brazilian Code of Civil Procedure or the Bankruptcy Law 7661 of June 21, 1945, as modified by law 4,983 of May 18, 1966, depending on the nature of the entity's operations. If the entity is not engaged in a trade or business, is an individual debtor, and the value of its assets is less than its debts owed, it is a candidate for insolvency and falls under the Civil Code procedures. However, if the entity is engaged in a trade or business and has not made payment of certain proven debts as they came due, it is a candidate for bankruptcy and falls under the Bankruptcy Law. The third type of proceeding, Concordata, is a court-supervised reorganization that applies only to unsecured creditors with some similarities to the U. S. chapter 11 bankruptcy process. To file for Concordata, the entity has to be engaged in a trade or business; however, financial institutions, airlines, insurance companies, and cooperatives are not allowed to file Concordata. There are two types of Concordata: preventive and suspensive.

Brazil does not have a local culture of out-of-court restructurings or workouts of insolvent companies. However, in some major cases, financial institutions have taken the lead to negotiate an out-of-court agreement between the company and its creditors. These out-of-court restructurings are likely to become more frequent, as recovery to creditors in a Brazilian judicial proceeding is not high.

Concordata—Reorganization Proceedings.   Concordata is a judicial process in which a company is granted the right to continue to operate its business under the oversight of a trustee (comissario) and, through an agreement, can pay its debts to its unsecured creditors over a period not to exceed two years. An entity engaged in a trade or business, which is temporarily unable to pay its debts as they come due, can find moratorium from bankruptcy by filing Concordata proceedings, if the entity meets the following criteria:

- The entity has registered or filed the books and documents necessary for the regular operation of its business with the commercial registry
- The entity has not failed to apply for bankruptcy protection within the decreed period
- The entity has not been convicted for any bankruptcy offense, robbery, fraud, contraband, or other similar crime
- The entity has not petitioned for Concordata in the last five years or failed to comply with the terms of an earlier Concordata

The intent of a Concordata proceeding is to allow a viable business to restructure, survive, and continue to operate and contribute to the Brazilian economy. A creditor is not allowed to petition for Concordata—only the entity can file such a petition. The sole judicial action a general creditor can take against an insolvent Brazilian company is to petition for bankruptcy (liquidation).

When an entity believes, and can substantiate to a judge, that it has the ability to rehabilitate and survive, in practice, it will file for Concordata before any bankruptcy proceedings are initiated. If at any time the entity does not comply with the requirements of the Concordata, it can be converted into a bankruptcy and liquidated. During the larger case workout negotiations among creditors and companies, the threat of petitioning for bankruptcy by the creditor or the filing of Concordata by the company becomes a negotiating tactic to try and bring the other party into agreement. Under the Brazilian law, in Concordata, the agreement to pay one's debts to its creditors is not to exceed two years from the court petition date. In reality, the judges can extend the period and have been known to allow the proceedings to drag on. Historically in Brazil, the returns to parties-in-interest tend to have been faster and greater in amount in a nonjudicial proceeding than in a judicial one.

Preventive Concordata.   The most common Concordata is preventive, in which a company applies to the court for this moratorium prior to a declaration of bankruptcy. To qualify for preventive Concordata, the entity must fulfill certain criteria, including the operation of its business in the normal course for more than two years without consideration of Concordata; the ownership of assets valued at more than one-half the amount of its unsecured liabilities; not in bankruptcy; if formerly in bankruptcy, the discharge of its liabilities has occurred; and the nonexistence of documents protesting for failure to pay. As part of the petition, the debtor must either offer to pay its creditors at least 50% of their claims on sight or offer to pay 60%, 75%, 90%, or 100% of their claims within 6, 12, 18, or 24 months, respectively. If the offer is made for an 18-or-24-month period, 40% of the claims must be paid in the first year.

If the court determines that the requirements for Concordata are met, it will grant the petition without hearing from the creditors. Concordata binds all general creditors, domestic and foreign. Once the petition is granted, all suits and actions against the debtor by the unsecured creditors are stayed. The stay does not affect secured creditors. The debtor maintains control over its assets and operations of its business with the oversight of a court-appointed trustee selected from the list of creditors. Management cannot, however, grant guarantees or dispose of real property without prior permission of the court.

When the debtor has paid its creditors in accordance with the agreement and all the obligations under the Concordata are met, the court declares the debtor's liabilities extinguished, and the court's ruling is publicly noticed.

Suspensive Concordata.   If a bankruptcy has already commenced and the debtor can offer to meet the payments to its creditors as required under suspensive Concordata, the debtor can petition the bankruptcy court to suspend the bankruptcy and grant a suspensive Concordata to the debtor. If the request is granted, the debtor may be able to forgo liquidation and continue to operate. To accomplish this goal, the debtor is required to (1) offer to pay its unsecured creditors at least 35% of their claims on sight or (2) offer to pay them 50% of their claims within a maximum of two years, of which 40% of the 50% must be paid in the first year. Suspensive Concordata is similar to preventive Concordata in procedure once the petition is granted.

Bankruptcy—Liquidation Proceedings. Under Brazilian law, *bankruptcy* is defined as an entity's not paying its proven obligations as they come due without a legal justification for not doing so. In general, a company's bankruptcy means loss of management control, the acceleration of its debts, sale of its assets to pay the debts, and the liquidation of the company. Both the debtor and its creditor have the right to petition the court to place an entity into bankruptcy. The filing of a bankruptcy petition by the debtor is a legal requirement, not an option, if the entity meets the above definition, although there is no mention in the law of criminal liability for its failure to do so. In order for a creditor to file the petition, it must hold an unpaid, matured, proven debt. In reality, the creditors initiate most bankruptcies in Brazil. The debtor can contest the filing of a petition by another party by mounting a defense within 24 hours. The debtor also has the option of avoiding bankruptcy by depositing the claim amount within 24 hours without having to discuss the merits of the claim.

Upon the declaration of bankruptcy, the judge appoints a sindico (trustee) from the major creditors who are residents in its jurisdiction. Management loses control of the business and can be investigated for criminal liability for a bankruptcy offense. All claims and actions against the debtor are stayed. Public notice of the bankruptcy is given in the *Commercial Registry* and in the newspapers. Creditors are required to file their claims within 20 days of the notice. The formation of a creditors' committee is not usual in Brazil; however, the creditors have the rights to oversee the administration of the estate, review books and records, and participate in proceedings. The sindico manages, protects, and liquidates the assets of the company to pay the creditors of the debtor under the supervision of the court. The court makes all final decisions. The creditors are paid by the priority set out in the law as follows: on-the-job accident claims, employee and labor, tax claims, secured claims, claims with special privilege on certain assets, claims with general privilege, and unsecured claims. During a bankruptcy proceeding, interest on debts is limited to 12% per year and will be paid only if funds from liquidation are available after the payment of principal (except in the case of secured claims in which interest will be paid up to the value of the collateral). Under the Brazilian Bankruptcy Law, the court should terminate the bankruptcy proceedings within two years. In practice, this limit has been greatly exceeded.

Brazilian Cross-Border Factors. The Brazilian Bankruptcy Law pertains to debtors that are domiciled in Brazil. The courts in Brazil do not necessarily recognize the orders of a foreign court. The Brazilian Bankruptcy Laws govern bankruptcy in Brazil. Foreign representatives of bankrupt estates are required to obtain local Brazilian counsel to represent them on all claims of those estates.

Foreign creditors are treated *pari passu* with Brazilian creditors in the debtor's asset distribution under both Concordata and bankruptcy proceedings. Foreign creditors, like all creditors, are required to file their claims in a bankruptcy within the 20-day filing period. Foreign currency claims are converted into local currency at the exchange rate on the date that the Concordata was ordered or the date of the bankruptcy decree. All foreign-language documents are required to be officially translated for filing with the Brazilian court.

CONCLUSION

In addition to the legal and regulatory differences, there are many other country-specific differences that affect a business operating and restructuring in a cross-border environment. Some of the differences are cultural: the times of the day people work and the hours in a workweek, the settling of priorities, the acceptable pay wage, the motivation of people, the social benefits and related payment structures, and the ethical standards practiced in business. The cross-border restructuring options available to a troubled company are also affected by the structure of each country's government, the amount of control each government exercises over business and monetary systems, the interactions of governments with each other, and the stability of each government. Other issues that can affect a cross-border restructuring include the quality of each country's investment markets, the regulatory oversight bodies in each country, and the various generally accepted financial reporting and accounting practices in different countries.

As companies become increasingly global in scope, as international financial markets continue to interact, as the Internet and communications technologies expand, and as continents unite through monetary union, we will operate in an increasingly global economy. Economic incentives will continue to spur more cross-border financial relationships, resulting in the further erosion of barriers to international restructuring procedures. As cross-border restructurings become more prevalent, new procedures and precedents for international cooperation will be created, and operating in this emerging cross-border restructuring landscape will become more commonplace.

NOTES

1. The United Nations Commission on International Trade Law, *UNCITRAL Model Law on Cross-Border Insolvencies*, May 1997.

2. *Id.*

3. 11 U.S.C., § 101 (24).

4. 11 U.S.C., § 304 (c).

5. 11 U.S.C., § 304 (b) (3).

6. 11 U.S.C., § 305(a) (b).

7. United Nations Commission on International Trade Law, *Possible Future Work, Cross-Border Insolvency, Note by the Secretariat, Addendum*, twenty-sixth session, Vienna, July 5–23, 1993.

8. *Id.*

9. *Id.*

10. Adolfo A.N. Rouillon, "Rules of International Private Law, Priorities on Insolvency and the Competing Rights of Foreign and Domestic Creditors, Under the New Argentine Bankruptcy Law No. 24,522 Argentina, March 23–26, 1997.

11. *Id.*

BIBLIOGRAPHY

Argentine Bankruptcy Law 24,522.

Brazilian Bankruptcy Law 7661 and Law 4983.

Dobson, Juan M. "Argentina's Troubled Debtors and Its Top Creditors." Paper presented at INSOL: International 5th World Congress, New Orleans, LA, March 23–26, 1997.

Felsberg, Thomas Benes. "Reorganizations, Insolvency and Bankruptcy in Brazil." September 1997. Online newsletter www.felsberg.com.br/new0997reorganization.htm.

Gitlin, Richard A. and Rona Mears, eds. *International Loan Workouts and Bankruptcies.* Butterworth Legal Publishers, 1989.

KPMG. *International Insolvency Procedures.* London, Great Britain, Blackstone Press Limited, 1997.

Marval, O'Farrell & Mairal. "Doing Business in Argentina." August 1997. Online article, www.hg.org/guide–argentina.htm.

Montevideo Treaty of 1889. Commercial International Law Treaty.

Montevideo Treaty of 1940. Commercial International Law Treaty.

Mori, Celso Cintra. "Risk Management in Brazil: Due Diligence, Creditors' Rights and New Investment Issues." unpublished article from the law firm of Pinheiro–Neto Advogados, Brazil, January 1997.

Rouillon, Adolfo A. N. "Rules of International Private Law, Priorities on Insolvency and the Competing Rights of Foreign and Domestic Creditors, Under the New Argentine Bankruptcy Law No. 24,522." Argentina, March 23–26, 1997.

The United Nations Commission on International Trade Law. "Cross-Border Insolvency, note by the Secretariat, Report on UNCITRAL–INSOL Colloquium on Cross-Border Insolvency." Twenty-seventh Session, New York, May 31–June 17, 1994.

The United Nations Commission on International Trade Law. "Possible Future Work, Cross-Border Insolvency, note by the Secretariat, Addendum." Twenty-sixth Session, Vienna, July 5-23, 1993.

The United Nations Commission on International Trade Law. "UNCITRAL Model Law on Cross-Border Insolvencies." May 1997.

The United States Bankruptcy Code, Title 11.

APPENDIX

UNCITRAL Model Law on Cross-Border Insolvency

PREAMBLE

The purpose of this Law is to provide effective mechanisms for dealing with cases of cross-border insolvency so as to promote the objectives of:

(a) cooperation between the courts and other competent authorities of this State and foreign States involved in cases of cross-border insolvency;

(b) greater legal certainty for trade and investment;

(c) fair and efficient administration of cross-border insolvencies that protects the interests of all creditors and other interested persons, including the debtor;

(d) protection and maximization of the value of the debtor's assets; and

(e) facilitation of the rescue of financially troubled businesses, thereby protecting investment and preserving employment.

CHAPTER I. GENERAL PROVISIONS

Article 1. Scope of Application

(1) This Law applies where:

(f) assistance is sought in this State by a foreign court or a foreign representative in connection with a foreign proceeding; or

(g) assistance is sought in a foreign State in connection with a proceeding under [identify laws of the enacting State relating to insolvency]; or

(h) a foreign proceeding and a proceeding under [identify laws of the enacting State relating to insolvency] in respect of the same debtor are taking place concurrently; or

(i) creditors or other interested persons in a foreign State have an interest in requesting the commencement of, or participating in, a proceeding under [identify laws of the enacting State relating to insolvency].

(2) This Law does not apply to a proceeding concerning [designate any types of entities, such as banks or insurance companies, that are subject to a special insolvency regime in this State and that this State wishes to exclude from this Law].

Article 2. Definitions

For the purposes of this Law:

(j) "foreign proceeding" means a collective judicial or administrative proceeding in a foreign State, including an interim proceeding, pursuant to a law relating to insolvency in which proceeding the assets and affairs of the debtor are subject to control or supervision by a foreign court, for the purpose of reorganization or liquidation;

(k) "foreign main proceeding" means a foreign proceeding taking place in the State where the debtor has the centre of its main interests;

(l) "foreign non-main proceeding" means a foreign proceeding, other than a foreign main proceeding, taking place in a State where the debtor has an establishment within the meaning of subparagraph (f) of this article;

(m) "foreign representative" means a person or body, including one appointed on an interim basis, authorized in a foreign proceeding to administer the reorganization or the liquidation of the debtor's assets or affairs or to act as a representative of the foreign proceeding;

(n) "foreign court" means a judicial or other authority competent to control or supervise a foreign proceeding;

(o) "establishment" means any place of operations where the debtor carries out a non-transitory economic activity with human means and goods or services.

Article 3. International Obligations of This State

To the extent that this Law conflicts with an obligation of this State arising out of any treaty or other form of agreement to which it is a party with one or more other States, the requirements of the treaty or agreement prevail.

Article 4. [Competent Court or Authority]*

The functions referred to in this Law relating to recognition of foreign proceedings and cooperation with foreign courts shall be performed by [specify the court, courts, authority or authorities competent to perform those functions in the enacting State].

*A State where certain functions relating to insolvency proceedings have been conferred upon government-appointed officials or bodies might wish to include in article 4 or elsewhere in chapter I the following provision:

Nothing in this Law affects the provisions in force in this State governing the authority of [insert the title of the government-appointed person or body].

Article 5. Authorization of [insert the title of the person or body administering a reorganization or liquidation under the law of the enacting State] to Act in a Foreign State

A [insert the title of the person or body administering a reorganization or liquidation under the law of the enacting State] is authorized to act in a foreign State on behalf of a proceeding under [identify laws of the enacting State relating to insolvency], as permitted by the applicable foreign law.

Article 6. Public Policy Exception

Nothing in this Law prevents the court from refusing to take an action governed by this Law if the action would be manifestly contrary to the public policy of this State.

Article 7. Additional Assistance under Other Laws

Nothing in this Law limits the power of a court or a [insert the title of the person or body administering a reorganization or liquidation under the law of the enacting State] to provide additional assistance to a foreign representative under other laws of this State.

Article 8. Interpretation

In the interpretation of this Law, regard is to be had to its international origin and to the need to promote uniformity in its application and the observance of good faith.

CHAPTER II. ACCESS OF FOREIGN REPRESENTATIVES AND CREDITORS TO COURTS IN THIS STATE

Article 9. Right of Direct Access

A foreign representative is entitled to apply directly to a court in this State.

Article 10. Limited Jurisdiction

The sole fact that an application pursuant to this Law is made to a court in this State by a foreign representative does not subject the foreign representative or the foreign assets and affairs of the debtor to the jurisdiction of the courts of this State for any purpose other than the application.

Article 11. Application by a Foreign Representative to Commence a Proceeding under [identify laws of the enacting State relating to insolvency]

A foreign representative is entitled to apply to commence a proceeding under [identify laws of the enacting State relating to insolvency] if the conditions for commencing such a proceeding are otherwise met.

Article 12. Participation of a Foreign Representative in a Proceeding under [identify laws of the enacting State relating to insolvency]

Upon recognition of a foreign proceeding, the foreign representative is entitled to participate in a proceeding regarding the debtor under [identify laws of the enacting State relating to insolvency].

Article 13. Access of Foreign Creditors to a Proceeding under [identify laws of the enacting State relating to insolvency]

(1) Subject to paragraph (2) of this article, foreign creditors have the same rights regarding the commencement of, and participation in, a proceeding under [identify laws of the enacting State relating to insolvency] as creditors in this State.

(2) Paragraph (1) of this article does not affect the ranking of claims in a proceeding under [identify laws of the enacting State relating to insolvency], except that the claims of foreign creditors shall not be ranked lower than [identify the class of general non-preference claims, while providing that a foreign claim is to be ranked lower than the general non-preference claims if an equivalent local claim (e.g., claim for a penalty or deferred-payment claim) has a rank lower than the general non-preference claims].*

Article 14. Notification to Foreign Creditors of a Proceeding under [identify laws of the enacting State relating to insolvency]

(1) Whenever under [identify laws of the enacting State relating to insolvency] notification is to be given to creditors in this State, such notification shall also be given to the known creditors that do not have addresses in this State. The court may order that appropriate steps be taken with a view to notifying any creditor whose address is not yet known.

(2) Such notification shall be made to the foreign creditors individually, unless the court considers that, under the circumstances, some other form of notification would be more appropriate. No letters rogatory or other, similar formality is required.

(3) When a notification of commencement of a proceeding is to be given to foreign creditors, the notification shall:

(a) indicate a reasonable time period for filing claims and specify the place for their filing;

---

*The enacting State may wish to consider the following alternative wording to replace article 13(2):

(2)   Paragraph (1) of this article does not affect the ranking of claims in a proceeding under [identify laws of the enacting State relating to insolvency] or the exclusion of foreign tax and social security claims from such a proceeding. Nevertheless, the claims of foreign creditors other than those concerning tax and social security obligations shall not be ranked lower than [identify the class of general non-preference claims, while providing that a foreign claim is to be ranked lower than the general non-preference claims if an equivalent local claim (e.g. claim for a penalty or deferred-payment claim) has a rank lower than the general non-preference claims].

(b) indicate whether secured creditors need to file their secured claims; and

(c) contain any other information required to be included in such a notification to creditors pursuant to the law of this State and the orders of the court.

CHAPTER III. RECOGNITION OF A
FOREIGN PROCEEDING AND RELIEF

Article 15. Application for Recognition of a Foreign Proceeding

(1) A foreign representative may apply to the court for recognition of the foreign proceeding in which the foreign representative has been appointed.

(2) An application for recognition shall be accompanied by:

(a) a certified copy of the decision commencing the foreign proceeding and appointing the foreign representative; or

(b) a certificate from the foreign court affirming the existence of the foreign proceeding and of the appointment of the foreign representative; or

(c) in the absence of evidence referred to in subparagraphs (a) and (b), any other evidence acceptable to the court of the existence of the foreign proceeding and of the appointment of the foreign representative.

(3) An application for recognition shall also be accompanied by a statement identifying all foreign proceedings in respect of the debtor that are known to the foreign representative.

(4) The court may require a translation of documents supplied in support of the application for recognition into an official language of this State.

Article 16. Presumptions Concerning Recognition

(1) If the decision or certificate referred to in article 15(2) indicates that the foreign proceeding is a proceeding within the meaning of article 2(a) and that the foreign representative is a person or body within the meaning of article 2(d), the court is entitled to so presume.

(2) The court is entitled to presume that documents submitted in support of the application for recognition are authentic, whether or not they have been legalized.

(3) In the absence of proof to the contrary, the debtor's registered office, or habitual residence in the case of an individual, is presumed to be the centre of the debtor's main interests.

Article 17. Decision to Recognize a Foreign Proceeding

(1) Subject to article 6, a foreign proceeding shall be recognized if:

(a) the foreign proceeding is a proceeding within the meaning of article 2(a);

(b) the foreign representative applying for recognition is a person or body within the meaning of article 2(d);

(c) the application meets the requirements of article 15(2); and

(d) the application has been submitted to the court referred to in article 4.

(2) The foreign proceeding shall be recognized:

(a) as a foreign main proceeding if it is taking place in the State where the debtor has the centre of its main interests; or

(b) as a foreign non-main proceeding if the debtor has an establishment within the meaning of article 2(f) in the foreign State.

(3) An application for recognition of a foreign proceeding shall be decided upon at the earliest possible time.

(4) The provisions of articles 15, 16, 17 and 18 do not prevent modification or termination of recognition if it is shown that the grounds for granting it were fully or partially lacking or have ceased to exist.

Article 18. Subsequent Information

From the time of filing the application for recognition of the foreign proceeding, the foreign representative shall inform the court promptly of:

(a) any substantial change in the status of the recognized foreign proceeding or the status of the foreign representative's appointment; and

(b) any other foreign proceeding regarding the same debtor that becomes known to the foreign representative.

Article 19. Relief That May Be Granted upon Application for Recognition of a Foreign Proceeding

(1) From the time of filing an application for recognition until the application is decided upon, the court may, at the request of the foreign representative, where relief is urgently needed to protect the assets of the debtor or the interests of the creditors, grant relief of a provisional nature, including:

(a) staying execution against the debtor's assets;

(b) entrusting the administration or realization of all or part of the debtor's assets located in this State to the foreign representative or another person designated by the court, in order to protect and preserve the value of assets that, by their nature or because of other circumstances, are perishable, susceptible to devaluation or otherwise in jeopardy;

(c) any relief mentioned in article 21(1)(c), (d) and (g).

(2) [Insert provisions (or refer to provisions in force in the enacting State) relating to notice.]

(3) Unless extended under article 21(1)(f), the relief granted under this article terminates when the application for recognition is decided upon.

(4) The court may refuse to grant relief under this article if such relief would interfere with the administration of a foreign main proceeding.

Article 20. Effects of Recognition of a Foreign Main Proceeding

(1) Upon recognition of a foreign proceeding that is a foreign main proceeding,

(a) commencement or continuation of individual actions or individual proceedings concerning the debtor's assets, rights, obligations or liabilities is stayed;

(b) execution against the debtor's assets is stayed; and

(c) the right to transfer, encumber or otherwise dispose of any assets of the debtor is suspended.

(2) The scope, and the modification or termination, of the stay and suspension referred to in paragraph (1) of this article are subject to [refer to any provisions of law of the enacting State relating to insolvency that apply to exceptions, limitations, modifications or termination in respect of the stay and suspension referred to in paragraph (1) of this article].

(3) Paragraph (1)(a) of this article does not affect the right to commence individual actions or proceedings to the extent necessary to preserve a claim against the debtor.

(4) Paragraph (1) of this article does not affect the right to request the commencement of a proceeding under [identify laws of the enacting State relating to insolvency] or the right to file claims in such a proceeding.

Article 21. Relief That May Be Granted upon Recognition of a Foreign Proceeding

(1) Upon recognition of a foreign proceeding, whether main or non-main, where necessary to protect the assets of the debtor or the interests of the creditors, the court may, at the request of the foreign representative, grant any appropriate relief, including:

(a) staying the commencement or continuation of individual actions or individual proceedings concerning the debtor's assets, rights, obligations or liabilities, to the extent they have not been stayed under article 20(1)(a);

(b) staying execution against the debtor's assets to the extent it has not been stayed under article 20(1)(b);

(c) suspending the right to transfer, encumber or otherwise dispose of any assets of the debtor to the extent this right has not been suspended under article 20(1)(c);

(d) providing for the examination of witnesses, the taking of evidence or the delivery of information concerning the debtor's assets, affairs, rights, obligations or liabilities;

(e) entrusting the administration or realization of all or part of the debtor's assets located in this State to the foreign representative or another person designated by the court;

(f) extending relief granted under article 19(1);

(g) granting any additional relief that may be available to [insert the title of a person or body administering a reorganization or liquidation under the law of the enacting State] under the laws of this State.

(2) Upon recognition of a foreign proceeding, whether main or non-main, the court may, at the request of the foreign representative, entrust the distribution of all or part of the debtor's assets located in this State to the foreign rep-

resentative or another person designated by the court, provided that the court is satisfied that the interests of creditors in this State are adequately protected.

(3) In granting relief under this article to a representative of a foreign non-main proceeding, the court must be satisfied that the relief relates to assets that, under the law of this State, should be administered in the foreign non-main proceeding or concerns information required in that proceeding.

Article 22. Protection of Creditors and Other Interested Persons

(1) In granting or denying relief under article 19 or 21, or in modifying or terminating relief under paragraph (3) of this article, the court must be satisfied that the interests of the creditors and other interested persons, including the debtor, are adequately protected.

(2) The court may subject relief granted under article 19 or 21 to conditions it considers appropriate.

(3) The court may, at the request of the foreign representative or a person affected by relief granted under article 19 or 21, or at its own motion, modify or terminate such relief.

Article 23. Actions to Avoid Acts Detrimental to Creditors

(1) Upon recognition of a foreign proceeding, the foreign representative has standing to initiate [refer to the types of actions to avoid or otherwise render ineffective acts detrimental to creditors that are available in this State to a person or body administering a reorganization or liquidation].

(2) When the foreign proceeding is a foreign non-main proceeding, the court must be satisfied that the action relates to assets that, under the law of this State, should be administered in the foreign non-main proceeding.

Article 24. Intervention by a Foreign Representative in Proceedings in This State

Upon recognition of a foreign proceeding, the foreign representative may, provided the requirements of the law of this State are met, intervene in any proceedings in which the debtor is a party.

CHAPTER IV. COOPERATION WITH FOREIGN COURTS AND FOREIGN REPRESENTATIVES

Article 25. Cooperation and Direct Communication between a Court of This State and Foreign Courts or Foreign Representatives

(1) In matters referred to in article 1, the court shall cooperate to the maximum extent possible with foreign courts or foreign representatives, either directly or through a [insert the title of a person or body administering a reorganization or liquidation under the law of the enacting State].

(2) The court is entitled to communicate directly with, or to request information or assistance directly from, foreign courts or foreign representatives.

Article 26. Cooperation and Direct Communication between the [insert the title of a person or body administering a reorganization or liquidation under the law of the enacting State] and Foreign Courts or Foreign Representatives

(1) In matters referred to in article 1, a [insert the title of a person or body administering a reorganization or liquidation under the law of the enacting State] shall, in the exercise of its functions and subject to the supervision of the court, cooperate to the maximum extent possible with foreign courts or foreign representatives.

(2) The [insert the title of a person or body administering a reorganization or liquidation under the law of the enacting State] is entitled, in the exercise of its functions and subject to the supervision of the court, to communicate directly with foreign courts or foreign representatives.

Article 27. Forms of Cooperation

Cooperation referred to in articles 25 and 26 may be implemented by any appropriate means, including:

(a) appointment of a person or body to act at the direction of the court;

(b) communication of information by any means considered appropriate by the court;

(c) coordination of the administration and supervision of the debtor's assets and affairs;

(d) approval or implementation by courts of agreements concerning the coordination of proceedings;

(e) coordination of concurrent proceedings regarding the same debtor;

(f) [the enacting State may wish to list additional forms or examples of cooperation].

CHAPTER V. CONCURRENT PROCEEDINGS

Article 28. Commencement of a Proceeding under [identify laws of the enacting State relating to insolvency] after Recognition of a Foreign Main Proceeding

After recognition of a foreign main proceeding, a proceeding under [identify laws of the enacting State relating to insolvency] may be commenced only if the debtor has assets in this State; the effects of that proceeding shall be restricted to the assets of the debtor that are located in this State and, to the extent necessary to implement cooperation and coordination under articles 25, 26 and 27, to other assets of the debtor that, under the law of this State, should be administered in that proceeding.

Article 29. Coordination of a Proceeding under [identify laws of the enacting State relating to insolvency] and a Foreign Proceeding

Where a foreign proceeding and a proceeding under [identify laws of the enacting State relating to insolvency] are taking place concurrently regarding the same debtor, the court shall seek cooperation and coordination under articles 25, 26 and 27, and the following shall apply:

(a) when the proceeding in this State is taking place at the time the application for recognition of the foreign proceeding is filed,

(i) any relief granted under article 19 or 21 must be consistent with the proceeding in this State; and

(ii) if the foreign proceeding is recognized in this State as a foreign main proceeding, article 20 does not apply;

(b) when the proceeding in this State commences after recognition, or after the filing of the application for recognition, of the foreign proceeding,

(i) any relief in effect under article 19 or 21 shall be reviewed by the court and shall be modified or terminated if inconsistent with the proceeding in this State; and

(ii) if the foreign proceeding is a foreign main proceeding, the stay and suspension referred to in article 20(1) shall be modified or terminated pursuant to article 20(2) if inconsistent with the proceeding in this State;

(c) in granting, extending or modifying relief granted to a representative of a foreign non-main proceeding, the court must be satisfied that the relief relates to assets that, under the law of this State, should be administered in the foreign non-main proceeding or concerns information required in that proceeding.

Article 30. Coordination of More Than One Foreign Proceeding

In matters referred to in article 1, in respect of more than one foreign proceeding regarding the same debtor, the court shall seek cooperation and coordination under articles 25, 26 and 27, and the following shall apply:

(a) any relief granted under article 19 or 21 to a representative of a foreign non-main proceeding after recognition of a foreign main proceeding must be consistent with the foreign main proceeding;

(b) if a foreign main proceeding is recognized after recognition, or after the filing of an application for recognition, of a foreign non-main proceeding, any relief in effect under article 19 or 21 shall be reviewed by the court and shall be modified or terminated if inconsistent with the foreign main proceeding;

(c) if, after recognition of a foreign non-main proceeding, another foreign non-main proceeding is recognized, the court shall grant, modify or terminate relief for the purpose of facilitating coordination of the proceedings.

Article 31. Presumption of Insolvency Based on Recognition of a Foreign Main Proceeding

In the absence of evidence to the contrary, recognition of a foreign main proceeding is, for the purpose of commencing a proceeding under [identify laws of the enacting State relating to insolvency], proof that the debtor is insolvent.

Article 32. Rule of Payment in Concurrent Proceedings

Without prejudice to secured claims or rights in rem, a creditor who has received part payment in respect of its claim in a proceeding pursuant to a law relating to insolvency in a foreign State may not receive a payment for the same claim in a proceeding under [identify laws of the enacting State relating to insolvency] regarding the same debtor, so long as the payment to the other creditors of the same class is proportionately less than the payment the creditor has already received.

14

Asian Markets*

M. Freddie Reiss

PricewaterhouseCoopers LLP

INTRODUCTION

This chapter is devoted to providing an overview concerning the recent Asian crisis and an understanding of the reforms and restructurings underway. All of the Asian economies have experienced substantially slower economic growth, if not recession through 1998. These economies were reporting declines in quarterly gross domestic product (GDP) and significant instances of bankruptcies and business failures. The International Monetary Fund (IMF) had provided funding to prevent the collapse of economies in Thailand, South Korea, and Indonesia. Many articles have been written about the cause of the Asian economic malaise, but the only way to get a better understanding is to recognize some of the economic background to seven key countries in the region.

Without discussing each of the countries individually, one could easily accept broad-sweeping generalizations as to the region and its recent status. It would be better not to think of the problems of Asia, but rather the problems within each country and how reforms and recovery are under way. Therefore, this chapter will discuss briefly the economic background of Japan, South Korea, Hong Kong, Thailand, Singapore, Malaysia, and Indonesia. However, it is fair to say that today most of these countries are affected by the massive borrowings used to fuel their growth and, in particular, their export-focused economies. Once foreign lenders to Thailand realized that some of their borrowers could not repay debt, a much more careful scrutiny of all borrowers and a slowdown in funding for some of these borrowers brought the much bigger problems to light. This caused a liquidity crunch, which began the process of business failures. It quickly became apparent to major lenders that many major companies throughout the region had debt levels that

*Note to the reader: This chapter describes the early days of the Asian crisis and reflects how markets can change rapidly and dramatically. The chapter was written during the first quarter of 1999 and reflects facts and projections known at that time.

were not sustainable. As consumer confidence dropped, demand for products also contracted, further exacerbating the problem. Quickly, the domino impact was evident as lenders were carefully re-evaluating all major commitments. To further complicate this process, it became very evident that the legal and financial systems in place in many countries were not designed to cope with problems as widespread as the recent economic crises. Local business and social practices to deal with the problem have created tensions and unrest.

Finally, it has become clear that much improved transparency is required so that financial statements allow for complete understandings of the underlying enterprises, especially the debt and capital structure. With the recent crisis, an understanding of the legal, political, and cultural landscape in each country is very essential. Accordingly, the following information on the seven countries is important to gain an understanding of the Asian markets.

JAPAN

With one of the world's largest economies, a prosperous Japan is critical to the world's economic well-being. Unfortunately, it has yet to find the political strength to forcefully address and correct its structural problems. As a result, Japan remains mired in its seventh year of economic malaise and has been suffering through its deepest recession in 50 years. Importantly, Japan remains unable to provide the leadership and the markets necessary to help pull the rest of Asia out of the region-wide economic crisis, as the United States was able to do for Mexico in 1994 and 1995. Recently, however, financial deregulation has begun, and there is a growing recognition that Japanese banks may require a more forceful approach to clean up their balance sheets. The debate for significant banking reform has again reached parliament. Currently, there are few distressed asset sales actually coming to market, nor are there restructuring opportunities, although vulture funds are circling anxiously.

Japan recently announced that in the second quarter 1998, GDP contracted to a 3.3% annualized rate. Almost every sector of the economy looks gloomy. Corporate profits are down. The one bright spot is that the trade surplus, rising 50% annually, is due to imports collapsing faster than exports. The increase in exports to America and to Europe is not being offset by the loss of the Asian markets. Domestic consumption has been steadily dropping over the last year and a half. Consumer confidence is low, and unemployment, at 4.3% in June, is at a postwar high. Japan's official unemployment also understates the unemployment rate in comparison to U.S. figures. Housing starts dropped 11% during the second quarter of 1998. The property market remains shattered. Business investment and capital spending are depressed, with machine orders down 22% in the second quarter of 1998.

Japanese firms are going bankrupt at a record, albeit slow, pace. Bankruptcies rose for the twentieth straight month in August 1998. In 1997, corporate failures led to 14 trillion yen in bankruptcy debts. Many of the bankruptcies are the result of companies losing access to banking services as banks continue to cut lending. Even with eye-popping low interest rates, there remains a severe credit crunch as banks are unwilling to lend to consumers or businesses.

Toa Steel Company, with debt estimated at 260 billion yen (approximately $1.89 billion when filed), is the largest failure of a Japanese manufacturer since World War II. Toa failed under the burden of overcapacity in the steel industry, weak demand, and stiff competition from manufacturers in Korea. NKK Corp, Japan's second largest steelmaker and Toa's largest shareholder, will roll up most of Toa's assets and employees into a new company. The rollup will do little to reduce the production glut that is affecting the whole industry. Luckily for Toa, both Toa and NKK are members of the Fuyo group of companies (keiretsu). Firms without keiretsu affiliations will fail outright. Keiretsu are increasingly taking on the role of creditors in the Japanese economy, as Japanese banks are not able to or are unwilling to lend. In the ultimate role reversal, Japanese banks are now even borrowing from their keiretsu to remain solvent.

Other high-profile bankruptcies include Mita Industrial Company, and Okuara & Company. Okuara, a trading company with liabilities of 252.8 billion yen ($1.9 billion), has been the second biggest failure of 1998. Mita, a maker of photocopiers, fax machines, and laser printers, filed for bankruptcy in August 1998, with a total of 200 billion yen in liabilities. The Mita case has raised questions about the solvency of Japan's apparently stable manufacturers.

The Nikkei Stock Index is down over 60% from its peak in 1989, and in September 1998 was trading at levels not seen since 1996. The yen has also been in a slow devaluation since hitting a high of 79.75Y/US$ in 1995; the exchange rate as of September 1, 1998 stood around 136Y/US$. Capital is flooding out of Japan, avoiding the low rates of return and declining stock market; estimates are that $83.46 billion left Japan in the first half of 1998. On September 9, 1998, the Bank of Japan reduced the target rate for overnight loans between banks to 0.25% from 0.50%. This was the first rate cut in three years, because the Bank of Japan has become increasingly concerned about tight liquidity and a deflationary spiral. The Japanese government's half-hearted attempts to stimulate the economy have been failures. The latest, a 16.65 trillion yen economic stimulus package with 10 trillion yen in active public spending and temporary tax rebates, has been more than offset by drops in wages and job opportunities.

The finance industry remains the biggest obstacle to recovery. The size of the bad loan problem is unclear, but some have estimated its size to be as large as US$1 trillion, with US$620 billion having already been disclosed. The Japanese prime bank system, in which lead banks guarantee the loans to companies made by smaller, affiliated banks, masks the true exposure of banks' loan portfolios, and potentially raises the risk of financial collapse. These smaller banks face no credit risk and undertake no due diligence. Japanese banks' capital positions continue to deteriorate with the declining stock market. Since Japanese banks are allowed to hold stock as capital reserves, and hold quite large amounts, every market decline further tightens liquidity. As banks try to sell their stock positions, this problem gets worse. The property market remains moribund, as property used for collateral remains in the hands of deadbeat borrowers who have no incentive to make improvements or sell underwater assets. Banks are reluctant to foreclose and thereby recognize the actual loss. Until this process begins, the property market will remain illiquid. As banks' capital erodes, banks are forced to further reduce lending, tightening credit, and continuing this vicious cycle. Keiretsu in many cases are now financially supporting their banks. Banks' balance sheets need to be cleaned up, and the property market must be allowed to clear at market prices, in order for the Japanese economy to recover.

Two separate entities have been created to alleviate the situation. The Resolution and Collection Bank (RCB) is a government agency charged with trying to recoup losses from failed banks. It therefore deals with only the six banks and 32 credit cooperatives that have collapsed. Unfortunately, this represents only a fraction of the problem. Additionally, the RCB's power is quite limited and virtually impotent in comparison to America's version, the Resolution Trust Corporation (RTC). The RCB cannot close institutions, confiscate property, or sell property used as collateral for loans. It is allowed to sell property only when the debtor agrees to sell the property. On average, it takes the RCB up to two to three years to resolve each problem loan. By the end of fiscal year 1998 (May 31), the RCB had raised only $612 million from the sales of bad loans.

The Cooperative Credit Purchasing Company (CCP) has been created by the financial institutions to buy and dispose of their worst loans. From 1993 to March 1998, the CCP purchased 11,030 loans, with a total face value of 14.9 trillion yen, for 5.76 trillion yen. To date, it has recovered a total of 1.28 trillion yen. This has allowed the banks to clear the bad debts off their balance sheets. However, the financial institutions remain responsible for the losses suffered. Therefore, the financial institutions do not want the CCP to dispose of the loans. The CCP will resume purchasing loans in September, after stopping in March to concentrate on the disposal of properties used as collateral.

The government has also created the Financial Supervisory Agency (FSA), which is currently inspecting banks to ensure that they are solvent, whether the banks have assessed their loans properly, and are covered against their estimated losses. The Financial Crises Stabilization Committee is then empowered to decide when public funds can be used to aid individual banks. Currently, there is a 13 trillion yen ($98.6 billion) fund available for shoring up banks' capital, and the FSA will determine which bank qualifies for the money. Ideally, these monies will be used to help capitalize solvent banks and clean up their balance sheets, rather than going to supporting insolvent banks. Parliament is currently debating financial reform measures introduced by Prime Minister Keizo Obuchi to further expedite the disposal of banks' bad loans. The Liberal Democratic Party (LDP) of the Prime Minister, traditionally the party of big business and banking, has introduced measures that will basically rescue shareholders with public money. The opposition is naturally opposed to this plan, and would rather see an institution more like the RTC created and allowed to operate unencumbered. The resolution and enactment of substantial legislation is critical to the economy's recovery.

The Long Term Credit Bank of Japan Ltd. (LTCB) is the flashpoint in these developments. The LTCB is one of three long-term lenders that helped to fund Japan's postwar economic miracle. It therefore has a lot of friends in high places. The government has co-opted Sumitomo Trust & Banking Company, a smaller and healthier bank, to merge with LTCB. Sumitomo, however, is insisting that the government must remove LTCB's bad loans before the merger proceeds. The

LDP would like to help its old friends and rescue the bank with taxpayer money, under the FSA plan, which is not sitting well with most of the citizens. The resolution of the LTCB case is a highly charged debate, and will go a long way in determining who ultimately pays the cost of the reform.

One of the most important changes to result from Japan's economic recession has been the "Big Bang" series of financial reforms. Begun by former Prime Minister Ryutaro Hahimoto in 1997, and scheduled to be finished by 2001, Japan's Big Bang will introduce more market forces and transparency to the financial sector, and allow banks, brokerages, and insurance companies to compete on each other's turf. More importantly, it will free up an estimated 1,200 trillion yen ($8.6 trillion) in household assets that previously had been limited to low-yielding savings accounts. Already restrictions have been removed on casualty insurance premiums, which can now be set freely; foreign exchange trading, as companies and individuals are allowed to open overseas banking accounts; brokerage commissions (fixed rates have been eliminated); and mutual funds (banks are now allowed to sell them). Many Japanese financial giants have announced plans to merge and sell new products. For example, Bank of Tokyo-Mitsubishi Ltd., Mitsubishi Trust and Banking Corporation, Tokio Marine and Fire Insurance Company, and Meiji Life Insurance Company, will invest in a joint venture which will rate and market mutual fund packages. Additionally, restrictions on foreign investment have been loosened, and many foreign financial institutions have formed alliances with Japanese institutions. Among these include the joint venture between Travelers' Solomon unit and Nikko to form an investment bank; the alliance between Chase Manhattan and Daiwa Bank to sell yen-investment funds, with Chase managing the money that is collected from Japanese investors by Daiwa; Fidelity Investments selling its mutual funds through Asahi Bank branches, and Merrill Lynch's acquisition of Yamaichi Securities.

The bankruptcy system resembles a hybrid of the U.S. and the U.K. models: primarily a liquidation, with no receiver. As in the United Kingdom, the reorganization provision removes management, and shareholders get wiped out. The process involves the compulsory administration, collection, and realization of a debtor's assets and the fair allotment of them to the creditors by the court administrators, in the event of the debtor's insolvency. In September 1998, the Justice Ministry proposed that the corporate reconstruction law be changed to become easier for financially troubled small companies to seek court arbitration with creditors and negotiate terms of loan payments.

The major banks have been selling part of their troubled loan portfolios to foreign investors. Many of these transactions include loans collateralized with real estate. The few major transactions to date are at very substantial haircuts to par (i.e., 10 cents) and are motivated by the tax system, which does not provide any tax relief until an asset is disposed and all economic interest terminated.

As capital under the reform programs is infused into banks, one would expect a significantly increased activity of loan/asset sales by banks. There is a high level of foreign investor interest in these loan sales, especially at the current pricing.

KOREA

The recent collapse of the Chaebol, and the Korean economy along with it, has been astounding. The expansionist policies pursued by the Korean government using the Chaebol as the engine, train, and caboose for economic growth had succeeded in turning Korea into the eleventh largest economy in the world. This is especially remarkable considering that the Korean War had left the country completely decimated in 1953. The Chaebol, a conglomerate with many autonomous units with interlocking financial structures, dominated every aspect of Korean life. The Chaebol's heavy reliance on debt and a symbiotic relationship with banks would be exposed, however, when overinvestment and excess capacity would severely depress world prices and make their debt loads unsustainable. As the Chaebols and Korea begin to pick up the pieces, many opportunities for bankruptcy and financial restructuring abound.

The 30 major Chaebols operating in Korea had their fingers into everything, with the five biggest Chaebols (Hyundai, Samsung, Daewoo, LG, and SK) accounting for 30% of Korea's GDP prior to the economic crisis. These Chaebols were responsible for turning Korea into a world-class manufacturer in industries such as memory chips, shipbuilding, chemicals, and electronics, where, until recently, Korea had no significant global presence. To build these world-class factories, the Chaebols took on enormous debt loads. The Chaebols benefited from the nationalized commercial banks which, during a 20-year period beginning in the 1960s and ending in the early 1980s, channeled funds to these favored companies. It is estimated that the top five Chaebols have an average debt-to-equity ratio of 393%, while the Hyundai Group's is the largest, at 565%. Total debt in Korea is estimated at over $600 billion. Much of this debt came from foreign banks, as the companies captured lower overseas interest rates. The total foreign debt load in Korea is estimated at over $150 billion. These debt loads proved to be unsustainable as lower world prices drove down profits and cash flow.

An excellent example of the Chaebol's industry building is with the dynamic random access memory (DRAM) chip industry. This industry, like many the Chaebols plunged into, required heavy investment and huge capacity to capture economies of scale. The Chaebols were successful in building plants producing competitive memory chips. The large Korean chip plants, however, have contributed to the market's excess capacity, resulting in the current glut of chips (DRAMs) and rock-bottom prices in the world market. This has forced Korean manufacturers to close down their shops for weeks at a time and to undergo a painful consolidation.

With such heavy debt loads, Korea became a natural target for currency speculators following the Thai baht devaluation. In fact, the Hanbo Steel failure, under $6 billion in debt, followed closely by the failure of Sammi Steel in early 1997, had already signaled that there might be a looming debt crisis. Beginning in September 1997, the won comes under forceful attack, depreciating from the 880 won/US$ level to a low of 1,633 won/US$ in February 1998. This depreciation of the currency further exacerbated the debt service problem, nearly causing a sovereign default, and sending the economy into a tailspin. Approximately 22,000 companies have gone bankrupt in 1998, combining for 100 trillion won in unrecoverable loans. Eight Chaebols have filed for protection or are insolvent. The stock market was down 70% from its 1994 peak. Exports have fallen by 13.7% in July 1998 compared to last July. Unemployment had reached 7.6% in July 1998, its highest level since 1966. Domestically, both demand and production have plunged. In fact, GDP contracted at a 6.6% annualized rate in the second quarter of 1998 compared to a positive 6.6% growth rate a year ago. In the first quarter of 1998, the economy contracted at a 3.9% annualized rate. The Ministry of Finance is forecasting the economy to shrink by over 5% for all of 1998.

The IMF had come to the Koreans' aid, providing a bailout package of loans and financial assistance of over $57 billion in December 1997. With this aid has come agreements to curb economic growth, to open markets, to increase transparency, and to allow troubled companies to go into bankruptcy. The Korean government has complied in raising the ceiling of foreign ownership in listed companies, and is reviewing companies for possible closure. This should prove interesting, as the government and the business community have always had a close and trusting relationship. Traditionally, big business has contributed heavily to political campaigns, forming the foundation for widespread collusion and corruption. An excellent example of this can be found in the Hanbo Group case, which received billions of dollars of loans as a result from its large donations to Kim Young-sam's 1992 presidential campaign. When Hanbo Steel collapsed, it set off a chain of business failures and uncovered the high degree of collusion within Korea.

The political situation, however, has recently seen a drastic change. The February 1998 presidential election of Kim Dae-jung marked a dramatic departure from past elections. Significant firsts included strict compliance of election laws, including campaign funding, and the utilization of mass media by the candidates. The lack of heavy corporate funding may be the beginning of greater transparency and less corruption in the Korean system. This election was a further victory for democracy, as it marks the first time in Korean history that the opposition will be brought into office through the vote. Political obstacles to economic reforms are still large. Parliament remains under the control of the former ruling party, and nationalistic tendencies will be an easy crutch when faced with difficult decisions. Mr. Kim is also viewed as being weak on economic issues and is pro labor. He is charismatic and will have to depend on his charisma to implement fundamental change.

To provide relief for the distressed financial system, authorities have established the Korean Asset Management Company (KAMCO). KAMCO currently holds approximately $35 billion in nonperforming loans from Korean banks, which it expects to dispose of through securitization. In 1998, the government closed 92 financial institutions, including five banks and 16 merchant banks.

The biggest challenge facing this industry remains the banks' lack of independence. The relationship that had developed over the 20-year nationalization period between the Chaebol and the banking sector discouraged any development of autonomous methods of risk assessment or credit evaluation. Even after most banks were returned to private ownership in the early 1980s, the government remained very influential in banking decisions. The government must encourage the banks to start acting autonomously.

Bank mergers are beginning as rationalization accelerates in this industry. The September 1998 announcement that Kookmin Bank and Korea Long Term Credit Bank had plans to merge was the third such announcement in the last two months. With assets of over 100.6 trillion won ($74.18 billion), and over 47 trillion won in loans and trust accounts in their combined portfolio, this merger will create Korea's largest bank in terms of loan portfolio. The largest bank in terms of asset size will be the newly merged Commercial Bank of Korea and Hanil Bank. The government is likely to offer financial assistance in these mergers. Not only does the government want to encourage further consolidation in this industry, but it also wants to prevent a repeat of the labor unrest and disruption to the banking system caused when the government shut down five small banks in June 1998. The financial assistance is likely to include tax breaks, the purchase of some bad loans, and potentially equity stakes. The government has earmarked 50 trillion won to write off bad loans held by financial institutions as part of this program.

The Korean government also announced plans to establish a $1.16 billion investment fund to provide liquidity to small and medium-sized companies. Rothschild Inc., State Street Corporation, Scudder Emerging Markets Inc., and Templeton Investment Trust will manage the money in four separate funds. The companies won the managing rights through a bidding competition open only to foreign firms. The funds will be allocated through both debt and equity to Korean companies, excluding the top five business groups, and with only 50% available for businesses ranked 6 through 64 on the list of Korea's largest companies. The funds will be listed on the Korean stock market to attract more capital.

Consolidation is accelerating in other industries as well, as the Chaebols have moved to combine groups in similar industries. Dubbed "Big Deals" in the Korean media, the mergers will hopefully deal with the excess manufacturing capacity that exists in Korea today. Five Chaebols have agreed to merge companies in seven industries, including chemicals, energy, aerospace, and train manufacturing. Notably, Hyundai Electronic Industries and LG Semicon have agreed in principle to merge, creating the world's second largest memory chip maker in terms of sales, with over 16% of the DRAM market. This new company, however, is estimated to have a debt-to-equity ratio of 641%. These mergers make economic sense, however, only if management follows through on layoffs and capacity reduction, with the end goal of improving competitiveness. The government is considering providing financial assistance and tax breaks for these new companies.

The case of Kia Motors also presents an interesting test case in how Korea will deal with its highly indebted companies. Kia and affiliate Asia Motors Company collapsed in 1997 under $10 billion in debt, which exceeded assets by $3.6 billion. In September 1998, two government-sponsored auctions for the company were called off as potential bidders refused to assume the company's several billion in debt. Kia's creditors, having already agreed to write off $2.1 billion of debt, will have to write off a more substantial amount of debt in order to entice a buyer. The Ford Motor Company, currently Kia's largest shareholder, with 17% ownership combined with Mazda Motor Corporation, has expressed an interest in buying Kia at the right debt level. Alternatives, such as creditors moving part of the debt onto a new company before selling off good assets, are being considered. The viability of the Korean car industry, currently operating at only 40% capacity, is also highly questionable.

With Korean companies going bankrupt at a rate of over 2,500 a month, the bankruptcy system needs be updated to keep pace. The present system includes three different statutes that address insolvency and reorganization, including the Corporate Reorganization Act (CRA), the Composition Act, and the Bankruptcy Act. There are presently only four bankruptcy judges, and the insolvency process can take up to 20 years. The system is seen as overly complex and ineffectual. However, in late September 1998, the Korean government announced plans to change the bankruptcy laws in order to speed up restructuring. First, the time required to decide whether a company will be placed under court supervision will be reduced to one month from the current three to five months. Second, the approval time of restructuring plans is to be reduced to under a year.

Further reforms are planned. The IMF has agreed to increase the size of the fiscal deficit to 4% from 1.7% of GDP, to be financed through a bond sale, which will allow the government to continue to offer incentives for rationalization of its industries. The government bond sale may, however, crowd out the ability of the private sector to raise capital in the marketplace. Other financial reforms include putting into place bank recapitalization plans, consolidating the three financial reform bodies, and giving the central bank more autonomy. A new labor bill is in the works, which would allow for layoffs and flexible work hours. Tax reform is also under way. The government plans on cutting income tax on the transfer of property and the consumption tax on durable goods. A value-added tax on tobacco products is being considered, while loopholes in the personal and corporate tax code will be closed.

Recently a Financial Supervisory Commission (FSC) was formed to review the domestic banking system and more specifically the ability of the banks to recover loans to Chaebols. In June 1998, the FSC issued a "death list", identifying 55 heavily indebted, small companies to be closed. One project recently funded by the IMF provides for a due diligence review of all Chaebols identified as number 6 through 64 in size to determine their ability to repay their debts and to select nonviable companies in order to be liquidated. The top five Chaebols have already been developing their own business plans to address the same issue. Hopefully, these reviews when completed in the next few months will allow for greater restructuring activity and negotiations.

Next year, the government intends to consider privatization of certain key industries, which should raise capital for other reform measures.

HONG KONG

Hong Kong has been a relative island of stability during the ongoing Asian crisis. While the Hong Kong economy endures a painful recession, mainly as a result of defending its currency peg with high interest rates, the authorities have not been forced to devalue the Hong Kong dollar as of this writing. In doing so, the island has avoided the massive bankruptcies and dislocations that its neighbors are suffering through. Yet Hong Kong has produced one of the highest-profile bankruptcy cases that has emerged from the Asian crises, Peregrine Inc., thus proving that this freewheeling capitalist center was not immune to the Asian flu and provides its own unique restructuring opportunities.

Hong Kong enjoyed years of uninterrupted economic growth. The former British colony took advantage of the Crown's hands-off policy and low tax environment to become the financial and trade center of Asia. With its origins in the opium trade, Hong Kong has always been a trading city, and remains a central transshipment point today for goods heading both east and west. The financial center of today arose to meet the capital needs that resulted from these trading activities. Today, most of the world's major banks have a presence here, while many manage their entire Asian network from the island. Hong Kong also plays a major role in the economic activity in China. Prior to the recent loosening of restrictions in the People's Republic of China, all capital and goods entering or leaving China came through Hong Kong. It remains the starting point today for most mainland investment and business.

The property market, with land being a scarce commodity on this small island, plays a large role in the economy. Prior to the crises, land values were among the world's highest. The local stock market traditionally has also been quite lively, giving speculators another avenue besides the property market in which to invest. With all of this economic activity, living standards rose to become among the highest in the world, with per capita GDP of approximately $25,000. The backbone to this growth over the last 15 years has been the currency peg: the Hong Kong dollar is pegged to the U.S. dollar at HK$7.80 to US$1. This peg is backed with the massive $96.5 billion treasure chest of reserves that the central bank has amassed.

Hong Kong's defining moment for the future came in July 1997, when the British formally returned Hong Kong to the Chinese. The transition was smooth, and there have been few complaints about the first post-transition government led by Chief Executive Tung Chee-hwa. Beijing has kept its word, and generally kept out of Hong Kong's political and economic business, although there appears to be a greater incidence of voluntary self-censorship and curtailment of political extremes.

With the ongoing Asia crises, Hong Kong's currency peg and the will of the Hong Kong monetary authorities naturally came under attack from currency speculators. Furthermore, the looming threat of a possible devaluation of the Yuan by the Chinese government, with its accompanying dire consequences for Hong Kong, further fueled the fire of those out to break the Hong Kong peg. With huge selling of Hong Kong dollars came big increases in the local interest rates, the automatic adjustment made to keep the peg in place. The higher interest rates depressed property values, created a credit crunch, and hurt corporate profits. As a result, property prices were off 50% in the last 13 months, while the Hang Seng Stock Index is down 33% from its July 1997 peak. Unemployment is also rising. With this loss in wealth and tight credit, consumer demand has also declined. Additionally, tourism has greatly slowed, as other Asian visitors cut back on their travels. The retail sector has suffered as a result, with three of the island's biggest department stores having already closed. Real GDP contracted at an annualized rate of 5.0% in the second quarter of 1998, following a 2.8% decline in the first quarter. Hong Kong is in its worst recession in 30 years.

Hong Kong's financial system has withstood this storm in relatively good shape, with the exception of Peregrine. The banking system has proved resilient and is practicing sound policies. The local banks do have region-wide exposure, however, with heavy exposure to mainland China. Therefore, profits are down, but banks are not becoming insolvent. Peregrine is the exception. The largest Asian-owned investment bank, it collapsed as a result of its heavy exposure to Indonesia and Indonesia swap contracts.

The Hong Kong Monetary Authority (HKMA) has been taking on more functions of a typical central bank, and other government institutions have been performing well under the pressure of a crisis. During August 1998, however, the HKMA, in its efforts to defend the currency peg, spent roughly $12.5 billion buying stocks in the Hong Kong market over a two-week period. The HKMA also announced that it would ensure that banks have enough cash to withstand the liquidity crunches arising from attacks on the currency.

Hong Kong's legal system, based on common law, is of very high standard and is a legitimate means of dispute resolution. Hong Kong's bankruptcy system, the Companies Act, is based on British bankruptcy laws. Creditors drive the bankruptcy process. In general, there is a judicial proceeding governed by statute, whereby possession of property is taken for benefit of creditors. Hong Kong does not have a chapter 11 equivalent or U.K.-style administration. Thus, the debtor company is at the mercy of its creditors, who can liquidate the company at any time. In practice, this does not happen much—creditors forcing debtors into liquidation—unless all out-of-court workout measures have failed. Accordingly, all troubled company situations in HK are run like classic U.S.-style workouts, with the banks/bondholders pushing for information from the debtor and the debtor trying to both come up with a new investor or new lenders. There is no formal stay period, unless the banks sign a formal standstill agreement. About one half of large workouts have a formal standstill agreement and the other half have informal standstills—nothing in writing but no one does anything to upset the process like trying to attach unencumbered assets. The system works well, except many commentators urge for the adoption of a formal stay period to constrain the immense power of the creditors. New corporate rescue laws are awaiting Hong Kong's legislative council approval, which hopefully will be given sometime next year. The new laws are based on U.K. and Australian insolvency laws, and will provide for both a stay period and administrators to sort things out. There will be no debtor-in-possession concept.

All major successful restructurings are done out of court and typically end up with a reorganization plan that all creditors accept. This is all done out of court with shareholder approval. Typically, the banks and other major financial creditors will take haircuts, get debt for equity, and so on, and the trade creditors will get paid in full over time. If such a restructure cannot be agreed upon, the company will be put into liquidation by a disgruntled bank.

Big Five accounting firms currently work on leading workouts, including undertaking viability studies of the underlying business, formulating restructuring proposals, searching for new investors, completing due diligence, and sales of assets. What is unique about workouts in Hong Kong is that typically there will be only one Big Five firm for each workout, and that firm plays two roles—both as an independent reporting accountant to the creditors and as the company's financial advisor. In essence, this means that the firm gives its independent assessment of the true financial position and, based on this information, brokers a deal that is fair and equitable among all the parties involved. While financial reporting is sophisticated, the banking sector does not share information freely with each other. This still allows debtors more time before creditors realize the total borrowings of the company and the need to start a workout.

Hong Kong's future outlook appears bright. It has consolidated its position as Asia's leading financial center along with Singapore, as Malaysia's and Thailand's aspirations die off. However, recent government interventions could hurt the island's reputation and attraction as an unregulated and free market. This will have repercussions on China's ability to raise private equity and capital. Furthermore, when the HKMA sells its stock position, there will be a potential for a huge selloff. China is Hong Kong's Achilles' heel. Can the mainland economy survive the crisis without devaluing the yuan? Shanghai's financial system is weak; can it hang on? State enterprise reform is ongoing; will they be able to raise private equity in these difficult times? Finally, as interest rates keep rising to hold the peg, more corporate bankruptcies are occurring. At what point will the level of bankruptcy cause a change in policy?

THAILAND

With real GDP growth rates averaging over 8% per year between 1982 and 1996, it is not surprising that Thailand's economic performance produced inflated asset values and easy credit terms. The good times, it appeared, were going to roll forever. Unfortunately, reality kicked a huge hole in the party's bubble. When domestic economic fundamentals faltered and exposed a highly leveraged private sector economy, investors began to flee the country and sell the baht. The government initiated a costly and ultimately losing defense of the currency, including pushing overnight interest rates as high as 1,000% per annum to punish speculators. The baht's flotation in July 1997 triggered a region-wide examination of economic fundamentals, resulting in the Asian economic crises. Thailand now appears to be on the right path. A new government has implemented a program of structural reforms that should clean up and strengthen the financial system, improve the bankruptcy process, privatize more state enterprises, and further liberalize the economy. This economic restructuring will leave Thailand more competitive and ready for renewed economic growth.

Thailand's structural problems first became visible through its trade and current account balance. Export growth had been slowing, suffering from a lack of price competitiveness due to two important changes. First, labor-intensive industries in Thailand could no longer compete against China, Vietnam, and Indonesia, as the Thai labor force had become relatively too expensive during the boom years. Second, the baht became overvalued as the U.S. dollar, to which the baht's value was closely tied, had appreciated significantly against most currencies. Imports, with capital equipment accounting for close to 50% of total imports in 1996, continued to grow strongly. The trade deficit, totaling $11 million in 1997, and the current account deficit, accounting for 8% of GDP in 1996, were therefore significant weaknesses in the economy.

To attract the capital inflows necessary to finance this ongoing current account deficit, and to cool inflation resulting from rapid lending growth, domestic interest rates were kept high. With the baht's value stable under the close management of the Bank of Thailand, there was no apparent currency risk, and short-term foreign capital flowed into the financial system. Many local companies were able to avoid the high borrowing costs at home by going offshore to capture lower interest rates. The Thai corporate sector owes approximately $65 million to foreign banks. Close to $20 billion of this total is owed to Japanese banks, which were heavy lenders to Thai affiliates of Japanese firms. The government sector owes an additional $20 million to foreign creditors. Property developers and finance companies were quick to take advantage of this liquidity. By 1997, there were approximately 91 finance companies lending for cars, homes, and stock market investment. Risky real estate projects by first-time developers were popping up everywhere. Pet projects of the well connected were common. Inflation increased as the short-term money kept entering the system. The local consumer price index varied between the 5% and 8% range from 1995 to 1996.

Overdevelopment and the lack of quality product depressed the property market. Finance companies, with heavy stock market exposure through margin lending, were in trouble. These factors, together with slower export growth, hurt corporate profits. The Stock Exchange of Thailand, which peaked in January 1994 at 1,754 points, began to decline. Nonperforming loans were growing, although different reporting standards masked the full extent of the problem. Insolvent finance companies and growing worries over the ailing stock and property markets, together with political uncertainty, aggravated flows out of the baht. Somprasong Land, a home developer, missed a payment on its foreign debt in February 1997, followed closely by the failure of the country's largest finance company, Finance One, in May 1997. Defense of the currency proved futile, even though the Bank of Thailand spent close to half of its $40 billion in reserves defending the currency. On July 2, 1997, the baht was floated, quickly falling from 25 baht/US$ to 50 baht/US$.

The IMF arrived on the scene with a $17.2 billion rescue program but could not prevent the economy or government from collapsing. Real GDP for

1998 is expected to contract by 7%. The devaluation further increased the interest payment burden. Current estimates for nonperforming loans using a delinquency definition of three months are as high as 40% of the 4,622 billion baht of outstanding domestic loans. Approximately 4,000 companies closed during the first five months of 1998. The freefall of the Stock Exchange of Thailand, now trading near the 200 level, has devastated the capital position of listed companies.

Today, the country, with a new but familiar and experienced government, is on the road to recovery. The economy is showing signs of life, as exports have clearly benefited from the massive devaluation. Export growth has increased by 50% in baht terms in the first six months of 1998 over 1997, and the Thai current account surplus is $1500 million U.S. in 1998. Interest rates are easing, as liquidity has improved. The new Prime Minister Chaun Leekpai and his reputable economic and finance team, pursuing national priorities with increased transparency, have begun the process of restructuring the economy.

The establishment of the Financial Restructuring Authority (FRA) as an asset resolution vehicle has effectively accelerated the cleanup of the finance sector. The Financial Restructuring Authority closed 56 finance companies in December 1997 and split the firms' assets up into good and bad categories as part of the liquidation process. The good assets were rolled up into the Radtanasin Bank, a new government-sponsored bank. The bad assets are being auctioned off, with the proceeds going to the creditors of the closed firms. Already, two auctions have been completed. The first auction, consisting of a package of car loans, was sold for 48% of book value at 25 billion baht. General Electric Capital Corporation bought 85% of the loans. The second auction consisted of a package of 17,474 home loans with a face value of 11.5 billion baht ($282 million), and was bought for 50% of face by Lehman Brothers Holdings Inc. The next auction, packages of 20,000 commercial loans with a face value of 460 billion baht, is currently scheduled for December 2, 1998. This is to be the least attractive of the auctions, because most of the loans have property as collateral. This presents difficulties due to the new, untested bankruptcy law, no foreclosure law as of yet, and restrictions on foreign ownership of land. With this auction, 90% of the assets will have been disposed of, with the remaining assets to be liquidated by the end of the year. Another government agency, the Asset Management Corporation, created to be the bidder of last resort to keep asset prices from falling too far, has been inactive in the auctions.

The government also passed a series of comprehensive financial sector restructuring bills on August 14, 1998. Included in the act are steps to accelerate consolidation of banks and finance companies; encouragement of private investment in the banking system; funds to be provided for the recapitalization of remaining finance companies, with appropriate safeguards and linked to progress in debt restructuring; and a framework for the development of private asset management companies. The Corporate Debt Restructuring Advisory Committee has also been formed to promote market-based debt restructuring, which included the elimination of tax disincentives for restructuring. The "Bangkok approach," worked out by the IMF and foreign and domestics banks, provides a framework for debt conflict resolution without going to court so that viable businesses may continue. The government has also brought criminal charges of loan fraud against high executives at two of the largest finance companies to be shut down. One of these executives, Narongchai Akrasanee, was the former commerce minister.

Thailand's bankruptcy codes have also undergone improvements. In March 1998, the government passed a law introducing a new proceeding allowing for financial rehabilitation of insolvent companies under court supervision much like a chapter 11. The code states that if one creditor wins a lawsuit in bankruptcy court, the entire company will be classified as bankrupt. There still lacks, however, recourse to sue for the borrower's personal assets, allowing for shell dummy corporations. The whole society has taken the cue from the initial cases and is beginning to overcome the cultural bias for compromise without conflict. Civil lawsuits involving debt rose 41% during the first four months of the year. Without a foreclosure law, however, there remains little incentive for debtors to pay. The legal system, as a whole, is still seen as Byzantine and corrupt, and needs to be modernized.

The case of Alphatec Electronics Pcl. (ATEC) provides an early example of the new law. Alphatec, once Thailand's largest memory chip assembler that owes $330 million (55% denominated in foreign currency) to dozens of banks and suppliers, filed for protection under the new law after a creditor group of 50 led by five banks sued. In June, the court put ATEC into receivership, and PricewaterhouseCoopers LLP had been hired to recharge the firm along with management and creditors. The creditors were to file a debt payment schedule within a month to the auditor, and a rehabilitation program within 90 days. Last July, PricewaterhouseCoopers was brought in as a new auditor, and found three years of falsified financial statements. Fictional loans, made to companies and people associated with the founder and biggest shareholder of ATEC, were recorded as assets and not detected by former auditor KMPG Peat Marwick. These accounting "discrepancies" totaled at least 8 billion baht ($307 million at exchange rates then).

In August 1998, a motion for receivership by five creditors against Thai Modern Plastic Industry Pcl., which had a total of $43 million of foreign debt outstanding at the end of 1997, was approved by Thai civil court. Unfortunately, a big blow to the new law occurred with one of the first rulings of court in September 1998. Creditors of the Hotel Nikko Mahanakorn, which had not paid its debts for two years, lost their bankruptcy suit when the court supervised restructuring was not approved. The court, using book valuations instead of market valuations, ruled that the company was not on the verge of bankruptcy and still solvent. This was a big victory for the large shareholder that has fought restructuring at every turn.

Bangkok Land (BLAND), which developed the single largest residential project in Thailand on the outskirts of Bangkok, will also provide another interesting case study in the new bankruptcy process. Due to Thailand's four-year property slump resulting from overbuilding and high interest rates, BLAND lost 17.7 billion baht in 1997, compared with a profit of 7 million baht the prior year. Most of the 30 high-rise buildings in its single project are vacant, with only 30,000 residents, compared to the original plans of 500,000. In March 1998, BLAND missed a coupon payment on its 400 million Swiss franc seven-year convertible bond due in 2001 and was declared in default. Bangkok Land also has a $150 million convertible Eurobond outstanding, with a put option in October 1998. With such large foreign currency payments, BLAND's profitability is being driven by fluctuations in the currency exchange rate. The issuer and the trustee will put forth a restructuring plan and hope that bondholders will approve.

Planned reforms should further improve the process. A law providing for foreclosure is set to be passed in October 1998. The Alien Business Law, restricting foreign participation in certain industries, is to be revamped into the more liberal Foreign Investment Law. The Land Code and the Condominium Act are to be loosened to allow for more foreign ownership rights. The leasing provisions of the Civil and Commercial Code will be amended to extend the period for foreigners. Finally, a recently announced Master Plan for State Enterprise Reform will accelerate the privatization strategy for selected industries such as energy, water, transport, and telecommunications.

Thailand remains vulnerable economically to regional developments and instability, especially the prospect of a competitive devaluation of the yuan by the Chinese government. However, the relatively stable political environment and improved transparency should be attractive for foreign investors in the near future.

The speed of recovery may be highly dependent on the foreign banks who have begun using steering committees and hiring financial advisors to determine the ability of borrowers to repay debt. Pressure to improve financial reporting and disclosures will encourage workout solutions as an alternative to bankruptcy. More cooperation between domestic and foreign lenders will become essential as borrowers redo their business plans and determine their cash flows available for debt.

SINGAPORE

Singapore's star has never shone brighter. Although many may find fault with Singapore's draconian laws, transparency and accountability have carried the day. As a direct result of the government's years of prudent economic management, Singapore will likely squeeze out economic growth this year, even as the tempest continues to blow all of its neighbors down. While there will be noticeable effects on Singapore's economy from the crisis, both the private and public sector have been able to withstand the shocks. Now, Singapore finds itself in the position of being able to take advantage of the many opportunities presenting themselves throughout the region.

Singapore's development into an economic power began by the utilization of its location on the sea route between East Asia and Europe to turn into Southeast Asia's busiest port. By becoming a regional trade hub, maintaining current account and budget surpluses, implementing a compulsory employee retirement savings plan in which citizens contribute 20% of their income, and investing heavily in infrastructure and telecommunications, Singapore's per capita GDP (precrisis) had risen to over $30,000. The electronics industry accounts for over 46% of GDP and over 71% of total exports. Finance has also become an important cog in the economy, contributing 25% of GDP. Singapore is the world's fourth largest currency trading center, with daily volumes of approximately $135 billion. Many international financial institutions maintain their Asian headquarters here. Singapore's reputation as the regional financial capital soared during this crisis, following the black eye it had received from the Barings/Nick Leeson scandal in February 1995. Although this remarkable growth may have come at the expense of personal liberties, few of the 3.5 million citizens are complaining today.

Today, the Singapore economy is slowing, suffering from the economic collapse of its neighbors. Forecasts for real GDP growth in 1998, range from 0.5 to 1.5%, down from 7.8% in 1997. Recession, however, is forecast for 1999, with unemployment expected to reach 7%. The economic collapse in the region has greatly reduced demand for Singapore-made products. The real estate industry has felt the pain of higher interest rates necessary to protect the currency. Property sales are down 43% from 1997, with home prices having fallen as much as 30% since 1996. In September 1998, the government announced that Singapore banks' domestic bad loans totaled $3.12 billion. While the ratio of non-performing loans to total loans is relatively low, local bank exposure to Indonesia is troublesome. Even as interest rates are lowered, fears of the coming recession will keep consumers from borrowing. However, this will ease the interest burden for the highly geared property companies. In this environment, corporate profits are down sharply; the Strait Times Index is down 60% since July 1997. The Singapore dollar has depreciated by 19% since July 1997.

The regional crisis has focused the authorities' attention on the need for further improvements in the finance industry. Planned changes include further development of the asset management industry, greater transparency in the banking industry, and increased liberalization throughout the financial industry, including more services and products. The government's goal in fostering competition and improving efficiencies is to build a world-class financial center.

Singapore's future challenges lie in becoming more globally competitive, rather than regionally competitive. Additionally, it must learn how to take a stronger leadership and higher visibility role in the Association of South East Asian Nations (ASEAN), without fearing backlash from its non-Chinese neighbors.

Singapore's legal system is based on the common-law judicial system. It is of a very high standard, and not subject to overt political influence or corruption. The bankruptcy code is based on the U.K./Commonwealth model as opposed to the U.S. model. Creditor rights takes precedence over debtor in possession, and the appointment of provisional liquidators is common. It is a system in which accountants are typically the lead professional in bankruptcy matters.

When a company is unable to meets its debts, its creditors have the right to take over the management of the company via the appointment of a judicial

manager (or administrator), liquidator, or receiver. Recoveries from the realization of assets are usually used to pay creditors first in the following order of
priority:

1. Secured creditors
2. Costs of petitioning the company
3. Executors' costs
4. Preferential creditors
5. Unsecured creditors

The type of appointment is determined as follows:

- When a company is hopelessly insolvent, a liquidator is normally appointed to wind up the company.
- When there is hope that a company or part of it may be viable and res-
  cuable, normally a receiver or judicial manager is appointed to rehabilitate
  the company.
- When the appointment of a receiver or judicial manager may be detrimental
  to the company's businesses, a voluntary scheme of arrangement (S.210)
  may be the best option.

Section 210 of the Companies Act allows for a scheme of arrangement to be
put in place, provided that 75% value and 51% in number of creditors attending
and voting at the meeting approve such a scheme.

Accounting firms are hired primarily through financial institutions based in
Singapore, government authorities, and regulators.

In conclusion, although Singapore is likely to fare better than most of its
neighbors in Asia, it nevertheless cannot avoid the tidal wave sweeping throughout Asia. In fact, its very strength, including its current stability, will put it at risk
in competing with other countries as price deflation and currency devaluations
will affect Singapore's exports and ultimately its trade activities.

We have already seen a significant slow-down in imports of luxury products,
and bankruptcies are beginning to increase in many sectors. The professional
service sector of this economy will be very busy in dealing with troubled companies. Foreign investment and international bank policies will be key factors in
determining the timetable for recovery.

MALAYSIA

Prime Minister Dr. Mahathir Mohamed, the man who is largely responsible for
guiding Malaysia to economic glory, is also the man whose words consistently
hammer away at business confidence. In the beginning of the Asian crisis, Dr.
Mahathir blamed a conspiracy of American and Jewish interests for Asia's economic problems. Without his xenophobic tirades, Malaysia may have been able
to quietly restructure its weak financial sector and avoid serious macroeconomic
dislocations. Now, with Malaysia suffering through its first recession in 13 years,

Dr. Mahathir has made matters worse in the eyes of the international financial community by imposing a series of currency and capital controls in an attempt to curb currency speculation. Even so, Malaysia's financial and property sector will continue to consolidate and provide some interesting restructuring opportunities in the near future.

Between 1990 and 1997, Malaysia averaged real GDP growth of over 8%. With a population of only 20 million, this economic expansion was achieved mainly through an export-led strategy, as well as through exploitation of natural resources like rubber. The government's heavy investment in infrastructure and telecommunications, excellent public services, and low business costs, turned Malaysia into a world-class manufacturing base. Many foreign companies took advantage of these benefits and turned Malaysia into their Asian base for high-end manufacturing and assembly. The weak link became the financial sector, which became overbanked during these good times. Prior to the crisis, Malaysia had 31 banks and 46 finance companies, which quickly became overexposed to the property and stock markets.

This weakness was bound to be exposed when Malaysia's neighbor, Thailand, devalued the baht. Speculators, figuring the country's debt levels would be unsustainable, sold out of, or attacked, the ringgit, whose value was closely managed around a basket of currencies of its largest trading partners. This is when Dr. Mahathir's ill-timed comments did heavy damage, increasing capital flight. To defend the currency and reduce capital flight, interest rates were raised, which in turn suffocated property and finance companies, sending the economy into a recession. For the second quarter of 1998, the economy contracted at a 6.8% annualized rate, while in the first quarter GDP fell by a 2.8% annualized rate. Over the last year, the ringgit has lost over 30% of its value, and over 60% of its precrisis value; in June 1997, the ringgit traded at 2.5/US$, and now trades in the 4.2/US$ range. The Malaysian Stock Index has also plummeted by over 69% since July 1997 after trading near its all time high in February 1998. Nonperforming loans are increasing, and banks are not lending. With liquidity tight, no working capital is available, preventing viable businesses from operating and dampening hopes for an export-led recovery. While the excellent infrastructure remains, with an eased labor market and lower than ever business costs, foreign direct investment has also dried up.

The level of problems is nowhere near that of its neighbors. Therefore, Malaysia has not been reduced to going to the IMF for a bailout loan. Structural reforms, however, are necessary. The government has accelerated the process of consolidating banks and finance companies, in part to rationalize the industry and in part to prepare for increased foreign competition. Connections, the scourge of Asia, are presenting obstacles to this process. As the government has elevated the priority of this merger program, well-connected firms believe that they now have leverage to hold out for better terms. Additionally, there appears to be a strong bias toward well-connected Malay firms at the expense of bigger, well-run Chinese firms in the announced program. The announced government program would create six large finance groups through mergers, each to be headed by a government-appointed (well-connected) anchor firm. As an incentive for the finance companies to play along, the government has announced that it will not rescue any firm that fails to merge. Bank mergers are also being encouraged; however, procrastination is occurring in the same manner as above.

Critically, Malaysia may have taken a huge step backward when it implemented capital restrictions in September 1998. A few academics are beginning to examine limited restrictions on short-term capital flows as a success factor in avoiding the market meltdowns that have plagued emerging markets. For example, Chile, which taxes short-term capital inflows, has successfully withstood the pressures on emerging currencies. However, controls often target the wrong place and encourage black markets and cheating. It appears that Malaysia missed the mark with its restrictions, and may fail in its goals of minimizing short-term capital flows, reducing interest rates, bringing back foreign investment, increasing liquidity, and allowing the economy to take a breather to begin recovery. Its controls include fixing the ringgit at 3.8/US$; preventing investors from converting ringgit earned on sales of securities for more than a year; and central bank approval of all ringgit transactions by nonresidents. The firing of Finance Minister Anwar Ibrahim, historically the free market white knight against Dr. Mahathir's nationalistic tendencies, and the resignation of central bank chief Ahmad Mohd Dodd dealt another blow to international confidence. Altogether, these moves are more likely to discourage foreign investment, fuel inflation, and create a black market for the currency without helping the economy to recover.

The Malaysian legal system is based on the British legal system and the principles of common law. The Malaysian Bankruptcy Code, incorporated in the Companies Act of 1965, is fundamentally drawn from the U.K. Companies Law of 1948. Creditor rights are quite well defined. This system, while having survived at least one major recession in the mid-1980s, is seen as not being adequate, however, to deal with the present crisis, which is much more pervasive and affects many more public companies. Expected improvements include judicial management legislation, which borrows practices from the United Kingdom, Australia, and Singapore. Plans also include the creation of an asset management company to take up nonperforming loans from banks for rehabilitation or restructuring, and the formation of a debt restructuring committee by the central bank to encourage informal restructuring and workouts. Currently, there has been a clear increase in the volume of executory work, including receiverships and liquidations. A great deal of debt restructuring and workouts are happening. The Big Five accounting firms are involved in the full range of executory work as well as larger restructurings involving significant public groups. Related to these are asset sales, mergers and acquisitions, and sale mandates as well as acquisition mandates from foreign buyers.

Future opportunities include plans on liberalizing the financial sector for foreign investment. Recently, the Malaysian government hired Solomon Smith Barney to advise on ways to raise funds to be used to help the banking sector, as the government was just forced to shelve plans for a $2 billion sovereign issue. Malaysia's ratings are close to junk.

INDONESIA

Indonesia could be considered the country undergoing the most difficult adjustments as a result of the Asian contagion. Following a decade of real GDP growth averaging 7%, the floor has given way, and the country stands on the brink of a complete meltdown. The crisis forcefully displaced General Suharto, who had served 30 years as an all-powerful president, and who had recently been elected in March 1998 to serve his seventh consecutive five-year term. The crisis painfully revealed the shortcomings of this country's economic success, built on a foundation of nepotism, patronage, and corruption. The aftermath will provide countless bankruptcy and restructuring opportunities, as soon as the macroeconomic situation stabilizes, and structural and legal reforms take hold.

With a population of 207 million people, Indonesia has one of the largest markets in the world. This market size, and cheap available labor base, proved very attractive for foreign direct investment during the previous 20 years, and was the foundation for the 7% average annual GDP growth between 1985 and 1995. This expansion was not distributed evenly, however, and the small Chinese minority controlled a large percentage of the wealth. The Muslims, who make up 87% of the population, were left behind. This disparity created severe ethnic tensions between the Chinese and the Muslims, and was the flash point in the social unrest that eventually brought down General Suharto. Additionally, the first family of General Suharto benefited greatly from their positions of power, and were behind the large corporate conglomerates through which most foreign investment had to pass. Corruption was rampant. As long as the economy continued to grow rapidly, however, no opposition party or effective opposition leader could mount any type of challenge to the General's leadership. Finally, the military, whose leaders also took part in the economic expansion, fully supported General Suharto and played a major role in maintaining his power.

This comfortable arrangement began to unravel in 1997 following the devaluation of the Thai baht. Investors began to examine Indonesia more closely, and saw a country with an overbanked financial industry and corporations with huge debt loads. By 1997, there were approximately 215 local banks operating in Indonesia, with rapid lending growth and lax underwriting. Estimates of local debt levels are in the trillions of rupiah. The attractive lending rates offshore, often at 9 to 10% versus the 18 to 20% at home, induced corporations to borrow abroad, usually through foreign banks. With a system of managed exchange rates, currency risk was thought to have disappeared, and a case of "moral hazard" was at play. Much of the foreign currency debt was therefore unhedged, even though local revenue streams were paying the foreign currency interest payments. It is estimated that the foreign debt level in Indonesia totals $133 billion, with as much as $80 billion in the private sector.

When Thailand fell, Indonesia was quick to follow. Speculators powerfully attacked the rupiah, forcing the Indonesian government to abolish the system of managed rates in August 1997. The rupiah, which had been at 2,500 rupiah/US$, quickly fell to 17,000 rupiah/US$ by January 1998. With the ensuing inflation, food shortages, hoarding, unemployment, drought, and lack of business confidence, social unrest quickly arose. General Suharto resigned and appointed cabinet member B.J. Habibie to replace him. Mr. Habibie has been characterized as an economic nationalist, and lacks credibility in many Indonesian and international eyes to end corruption, as his family enriched itself during the Suharto reign. The IMF did arrive early in the crisis with a plan for a $43 billion rescue program of loans and other financial assistance. The government's half steps and backtracking on structural reforms, including seriously considering the adoption of a currency board, has delayed the complete dispersal of funds and has further shaken international confidence in the country, exacerbating the economic situation.

In the middle of this depression, Indonesian corporations have been unable to increase their local revenue streams. This fact, together with the severe depreciation of the rupiah, left corporations unable to service their foreign currency–denominated debt. As a result, many Indonesian companies have gone into default; some estimates have the corporate default rate at 50%. There has been a near cessation on all scheduled bank debt payments, both local and foreign. Incredibly, the government has spoken of the entire corporate sector being entitled to a pause in debt service payments. Additionally, the Jakarta Stock Index has toppled, with the overall stock market capitalization having declined to $10 billion from $65 billion. Almost all listed companies are technically insolvent. International trade is at a standstill. Liquidity has completely dried up. Interest rates on the central bank's (Bank Indonesia) paper are currently around 70%. Debt defaults and bankruptcies are more pervasive here than anywhere else in Asia.

Understandably, the Indonesian financial sector has collapsed. Approximately 50 banks, and 70% of all bank assets, are now under the official supervision of the Indonesian Bank Restructuring Agency (IBRA). The IBRA, established in January 1998 as part of the IMF reforms, has been charged with taking over insolvent banks, cleaning out their bad debts, and seeking new buyers for the assets. Additionally, the IBRA has been charged with recovering the nearly $12 billion in government loans pumped into the banking system last year in an attempt to rescue the banking system. In typical Indonesian fashion, the bankers swiftly turned around and lent the 141.6 trillion rupiah (US$12 billion) to shareholders. The IBRA has given a highly anticipated deadline of September 21 to the tycoons in charge of the banks to repay the loans or face the consequences. The three largest of the failed banks, and among the top 5 before the crisis, owe a combined 50 trillion Rupiah. Additionally, there is a criminal probe investigating additional banking violations and corruption by the Indonesian attorney general. These investigations are being watched carefully to see if Indonesia is serious about changing the way it traditionally operates.

Other mandated IMF reforms are also running into problems. Dismantling of the powerful monopolies has proved difficult to implement. The plywood monopoly has resurfaced. BULOG, the state logistics agency, has not allowed market forces to determine the supply of basic staples for fear that the resulting high prices could trigger further social unrest. It is unclear whether government subsidies and major infrastructure projects have been canceled. The government announced plans to relax limits on foreign ownership, and to introduce measures to induce the remaining 150 banks into mergers.

The IMF has also pushed Indonesia to reform its bankruptcy proceedings. Prior to the IMF agreements, the Indonesian bankruptcy law was based on Dutch code and dated back to 1906. This law was conceptually similar to the U.S. Bankruptcy Code and provided for two types of proceedings: bankruptcy or liquidation and a corporate reorganization. In reality, however, the process was never used. No recovery system was in place, and there were no powers available to creditors to recover assets. Instead, the powers of persuasion were relied on, and often debtors who did not feel like paying back their debts got away with it. Amendments to the code were passed in April 1998; however, only two substantial changes were made. First, the process is to be expedited through a new bankruptcy court. Second, the rights and influence of creditors have been strengthened. The new bankruptcy court opened for business on September 1. The new court has 16 judges and five administrators, and provides the first legal means for creditors to extract payments. Only four cases, however, have been filed as of September 9, 1998. The first case involves the contractors for PT Karabha Digya, a golf course developer, suing for 15 billion rupiah ($1.5 million) for services rendered, and will be heard shortly. The restructuring process has also been brought to life, with numerous steering committees being formed. The necessary financial restructurings have been put on hold, however, until the macro and currency environment stabilizes. A problem unique to Indonesia's restructuring process is the high level of investment in failed companies by top government officials, and the potential for harmful influence over the process that they represent. This problem is unique to Indonesia and will not affect the restructuring process in either Korea or Thailand.

There have been attempts by the government, companies, and creditors to devise debt repayment frameworks based on a subsidized exchange rate. These plans have not been used because of their expensive costs, as creditors who use the mechanism will be lent rupiah to buy dollars at a rate floating 550 basis points above Indonesia's annual inflation rate. More recently, the IMF and the government have created the Jakarta initiative, a set of general principles that hopefully will lead to an acceleration of settlements between bankers and creditors. The framework encourages creditors to agree to a standstill and to provide working capital, while encouraging debtors to be forthright about their financial condition. It is doubtful that such a framework will do much until the currency and economy stabilize.

Activity by accountants and financial advisors has been mainly due diligence for financial institutions. Until some stability in the rupiah is established, foreign investment will not be a factor. Restructuring work for borrowers will not be significant in the near term.

Although there are a substantial number of Bank syndicates, they do not have a tradition of working together. A change in this culture and the activities of the wealthy families who control many conglomerates will determine whether recovery will be a long-term process. Because there is a shortage of trained workout people at both the banks and the accounting firms in Jakarta, a significant infusion of expatriate talent is necessary. Given the current social unrest, the need to have language skills and the description of Indonesia as a hardship posting will further affect the progress of fixing the country's economic woes.

CONCLUSION

The crisis in Asia will take years to remedy, and those expecting quick fix solutions will have to accept that they are not likely to work. First, an improvement in capital allocation must occur so that today's liquidity crisis or credit crunch is alleviated. This will follow the current consolidation of financial institutions and in part will work only when borrower and lender discipline is achieved on feasible projects.

In addition, economic policies that deal with global overcapacity must be developed. There is probably no doubt that easy money funded too much expansion of manufacturing capacity. To some degree, such development moved from country to country in search of low-cost production. This has caused great competition within Asian economies, and each country's attempt to export its way out of crisis results in new instability on a country-by-country basis.

Hopefully, global policies and practices with significantly improved disclosures and communication will eventually stabilize these markets. In the short term, the best advice is to have a local presence to assist in knowing what is happening and, in the case of bankers, who your customer is. To those in the restructuring advisory business, your skills are in great demand, and the opportunities are seemingly endless.

15

The Accountant's Role in the Workout Environment— Beyond "Bean Counting"

DeLain E. Gray

PricewaterhouseCoopers LLP

THE CHANGING ROLE OF THE ACCOUNTANT

The last two decades have seen extensive changes in the role of an accountant (turnaround accountant, workout accountant) in bankruptcy, corporate turnarounds, and workout situations. Throughout the early 1980s, accountants typically became involved in a workout situation when an audit client was distressed. The services provided to troubled clients traditionally involved specialized accounting and tax expertise needed in a financial restructuring. This limited and narrow role expanded greatly throughout the 1980s and 1990s, as restructurings and bankruptcies became larger and more complex and parties-in-interest came to rely on and require the multidimensional and often global skill sets that large accounting firms were able to provide.

All parties involved in the restructuring process have demanded an ever-increasing specialization in insolvency and operational consulting as well as relevant industry experience and expertise. Accountants have broken down the traditional walls governing the services of turnaround professionals by acquiring many skills previously provided by lawyers, investment bankers, and management consultants. Moreover, in a significant break from past perceptions, accountants are now increasingly relied on as the company's/creditors' primary financial advisor; professionals who are best positioned to analyze, critique, and rehabilitate a company's operational, cash flow, and capital structure issues. In fact, many accountants are now assuming interim management roles; not just as

I would like to thank my colleagues, Mark Edson, Andrew Hinkelman, and Rebekah Bill, for assisting me in the preparation of this chapter.

chief financial officers (CFOs), but often as chief executive and/or chief operating officers in troubled companies.

As a result, many accountants and boutique turnaround firms have begun to concentrate solely on corporate restructurings in and outside of the bankruptcy forum. This growing market represents a challenging opportunity for accountants to work with a diverse cross-section of companies of various sizes and industries.

No one knows for sure whether the coming years will see an increase in the number of businesses seeking relief under the Bankruptcy Code, but many experts point to several indicators when predicting a continued increase in financial restructurings and bankruptcy filings. The recent downturn of various international economies has caused many multinational and domestic companies to miss earning projections. From Asia to Russia, currency fluctuations and devaluations, bank failures, falling property values, and highly visible bankruptcies have caused economic tension throughout the world. Additionally, the recent record levels of high-yield bond offerings during the mid-1990s coupled with the increased competitive lending environment during this time frame suggests that there will be an increased demand for the corporate restructuring accountant in the near future.

Many U.S. market analysts also point to the Year 2000 compliance problem as another potential source of economic instability, and it is believed that many companies have made limited progress in addressing the problem. Companies that have not fully prepared for the Y2K issues may find themselves facing operational nightmares and large shareholder lawsuits, leading to financial distress and ultimately a noticeable increase in workouts and potential bankruptcy filings.

The role of accountants as financial advisors and reorganization consultants will continue to expand for parties-in-interest in workouts and bankruptcy situations in the coming decades. Increased specialization, global resources, credentialed industry experience, and the ability to quickly focus those resources on a constituency's behalf will be the driving factors that continue to push accountants into a myriad of restructuring roles for their clients. This chapter will outline some of the roles accountants have assumed in the global bankruptcy and workout arena.

DEBTOR SERVICES

Early Stages of a Financial Restructuring

The early stages of a troubled company engagement are critical for all turnaround professionals, including accountants. For many reasons, management has often delayed making the decision to employ restructuring professionals until the situation has become critical. Early engagement planning is extremely important in shaping the direction and strategy of a workout, especially if the debtor is unfamiliar with the restructuring or bankruptcy process. Accountants can help the debtor clearly define and communicate its financial position and strategy to key employees, creditors, and vendors in an effort to strengthen support and cooperation throughout the ranks. Distressed management can often be overwhelmed by the company's situation and may avoid making difficult and time-driven decisions. Experienced accountants in workout situations can help the debtor recognize what immediate decisions must be made and analyses completed to ensure the company's survival.

An important part of the initial planning with management is providing the debtor with the specific financial and strategic analyses necessary to decide which path of restructuring would be more effective: an out-of-court restructuring, bankruptcy filing, or liquidation. Sometimes, even the idea of bankruptcy can frighten and paralyze corporate executives. They dread the negative publicity, expense, potential downsizing, detailed reports required in bankruptcy, and the general public scrutiny of their financial troubles. Often, management views bankruptcy as the ultimate failure as opposed to a widely accepted strategic business tool that can provide a business the time required to make changes for correcting and revitalizing the entity. Through timely financial and operational analyses, advisors can assist management in understanding the options available under the Bankruptcy Code as well as an out-of-court workout. These analyses help management objectively choose the path of restructuring best suited for their company's particular financial and operational situation. The best option today may not be the best option as the workout progresses; accordingly, ongoing analyses and review must be part of the strategy and process of the turnaround accountant.

Prepackaged Bankruptcy Filings

Since the early 1990s, prepackaged bankruptcies have become commonplace in the world of corporate restructuring. A prepackaged bankruptcy occurs when a debtor solicits the creditors' approval for its plan of reorganization before actually filing for bankruptcy relief. By obtaining the approval of its reorganization plan before filing its bankruptcy petition, a debtor can often have its plan confirmed by the courts within a few months of filing, saving the distressed company considerable time and financial resources. Prepackaged bankruptcy filings under chapter 11 have represented approximately 11% of public filings of the past few years.[1] However, prepackaged bankruptcies may not be a viable alternative in all situations, particularly if the underlying reason for the financial distress emanates from management or operational issues.

One of the foremost benefits of a prepackaged bankruptcy is the time and expense it saves a debtor, principally by eliminating the costly process of reaching creditor consensus within the judicial bankruptcy system. A typical chapter 11 filing can be a long and involved process, with the debtor remaining in bankruptcy an average of 16 months.[2] An experienced accountant can provide an added level of credibility to the process, assist in the communication of information, and foster the shuttle diplomacy between constituents necessary to effectively develop a prepackaged plan.

A separate chapter of this book is devoted to outlining and describing the advantages of both an out-of-court workout and a bankruptcy turnaround. The following section highlights and discusses services representative of those provided by accountants to debtors in workout and bankruptcy situations, as well as general operational restructuring services provided.

Out-of-Court Restructuring Services

Cost/Benefit Analysis of Out-of-Court Workout versus Bankruptcy Filing. A distressed company should continuously analyze the advantages and disadvantages of a bankruptcy petition and negotiation of an out-of-court restructuring. All actions pursued during a turnaround should be dependent on this dual analysis. Even if the results of this analysis point toward an out-of-court restructuring, a debtor's accountants must stress the importance of and include prebankruptcy planning during all stages of the restructuring. Management is often not receptive to this advice and may be reluctant to consider the possibility of a bankruptcy filing. Experienced workout accountants know that out-of-court restructurings often deteriorate and that if a company is forced to file for protection under the Bankruptcy Code, the success or failure of its ultimate reorganization will in part depend on the adequacy of prebankruptcy contingency planning efforts. Prebankruptcy planning can include such areas as cash and operations management, financing, legal planning with counsel, the handling of public relations, and the optimum time and information required to file for court relief.

Improve Relationships with Key Lenders, Vendors, and Other Parties-in-Interest. Just as the success of a bankruptcy turnaround is dependent on pre-bankruptcy planning, the success of an out-of-court restructuring is largely dependent on maintaining and improving relationships and obtaining consensus from key lenders, creditors, and other parties-in-interest. Often, the company has already lost credibility due to missed commitments and projections, and distressed management has not fully disclosed the severity of the company's situation to lenders or vendors. These parties can easily become frustrated and unwilling to cooperate with the debtor if relations are not maintained. A turnaround accountant often acts as a respected and credible independent party and can provide a critical role in developing and structuring alternatives acceptable to all parties. A workout can be successful only if these parties are willing to participate in and agree to a workout plan. Creditors will be more likely to agree to a proposed plan if they are approached early with credible financial information, showing management's recognition of their company's challenges and a willingness to solve them.

Analyze Alternative Financing Options. Negotiations toward a financial restructuring are commonly started when the debtor realizes it will be unable to meet its future financial obligations. When an accountant is first retained, they may realize that the current lender is either reluctant or no longer willing to work with the debtor. A turnaround accountant can be instrumental in securing a new credit facility and lenders willing to work with the debtor through its troubled period. Accountants quickly break down and analyze potential loan facilities, helping the debtor understand the costs/benefits of each proposal. The experience of workout accountants allow the debtor to quickly secure the most beneficial financing package, which will allow the company to function on a daily basis while preparing for long-term viability.

Strengthen Cash Position of Distressed Company.   A debtor must be persistent in strengthening its cash position during all stages of a turnaround, especially at the beginning of a financial restructuring. A strong cash position will allow for more routine day-to-day operations for essential employees and key vendors. The ability to generate positive cash flow and meet projections will also be a strong influence on the debtor's ability to negotiate with its lenders, key vendors, and all other parties-in-interest. An accountant's financial wherewithal and experience in working with distressed companies is critical to the identification and implementation of cash flow enhancement measures, such as cutting unnecessary overhead spending, restructuring vendor payments, or temporarily shutting down production facilities. The conservation of cash is a large hurdle for a distressed company, but is essential to any successful turnaround and significantly increases the restructuring options available to a distressed company and improves the possibility of a smooth and successful reorganization.

Develop Short- and Long-Term Action Plans.   The conservation of cash is one of many short-term action plans developed by a debtor and its accountant. Immediately after a workout accountant is retained, he or she works closely with management to outline short- and long-term action plans. The state of the company's finances and operations dictate the structure and content of these plans. Short-term plans should concentrate immediately on stabilizing the company so that management has enough time to engage in discussions with its lenders and/or major creditors. Once short-term stabilization is accomplished, accountants will often take on a greater role in developing and carrying out long-term action plans that go beyond what initially was sufficient for the company to survive. These long-term strategies focus on the future viability of the company and often change as an accountant helps management understand the profitability of various products and lines of business. Whether short- or long-term, the action plans decided on by management need to be concise and identify the employees who will be responsible for seeing the plan through to completion.

Bankruptcy Restructuring Services

Prepare Bankruptcy Schedules and Reports.   Upon filing for court relief, a debtor is legally required to produce many complex reports and schedules for the bankruptcy court. Among the initial court-required reports are supporting schedules and a statement of financial affairs, which are initially required when any corporate debtor files under chapter 11.

The supporting bankruptcy schedules require sworn statements regarding the debtor's assets, liabilities, operations, and other obligations as of the date of filing. The statement of financial affairs consists of 21 detailed questions about the debtor's property and conduct. It provides a starting point from which creditors may investigate the debtor's finances and business conduct prior to the bankruptcy filing. These schedules, along with monthly required operating reports, can consume the valuable time of many key employees. A workout accountant's experience working within the bankruptcy environment can prove essential to streamlining the preparation of many required reports. This allows management more time to concentrate on managing business on a day-to-day basis and dealing with other operational issues as they arise as opposed to allocating their time to "bankruptcy" issues.

Obtain Debtor-in-Possession Financing.   Throughout any turnaround situation, adequate liquidity is vital. As soon as accountants are retained, they should work closely with the company to gain an understanding of the debtor's cash management system. In a chapter 11 reorganization, one of the primary goals of both the debtor and creditors is to secure or maintain adequate liquidity to operate the business. This is frequently obtained through debtor-in-possession (DIP) financing with either the existing lender or a new financing institution.

DIP financing is a term used to describe the postpetition lending of money to a debtor. Once a debtor is able to secure a DIP loan, the bankruptcy court must approve it. The DIP loan is typically provided priority status over all other claims against the debtor's bankrupt estate. Lending institutions are attracted to these loans because they will be treated as the senior creditors throughout the bankruptcy process. The bankruptcy court has allowed for this superpriority status, because otherwise it would be almost impossible for a bankrupt debtor to obtain the necessary liquidity to continue operations.

The objectivity and assurance of a workout accountant can be instrumental in finding a lending institution willing to work with the debtor through its reorganization. Accountants normally get involved in the preparation of the detailed financial projections and collateral audit reviews required by the potential DIP lender, as well as analyzing the requirements and covenants of potential DIP facilities, and helping the debtor negotiate the best financing alternative. Debtor-in-possession loans often have strict covenants and reporting requirements, but obtaining a DIP facility quickly ensures that the company has adequate short-term financing, allowing management the necessary time to address and develop the long-term exit strategy.

Employee Severance and Retention Issues.   Frequently, one of the most valuable resources a company has is its employee workforce. This valuable asset is at extreme risk in the early stages of a bankruptcy, and its preservation and management is generally one of the most important steps a debtor must make to ensure its immediate survival and lay the foundation for a successful reorganization. Competitors and other companies may utilize the instability and uncertainty of a reorganization to recruit the debtor's key employees. Many employees will be focused on seeking new employment, wondering "what will happen to me," and accordingly the focus and productivity of the workforce is diverted from the company's issues at a very critical time. It is usually essential that some mechanism or incentive program be instituted to assure key employees and management that they will be fairly treated and should remain with the debtor. If employees leave and must be replaced, the cost and effort to recruit and compensate new employees in a troubled or bankrupt situation may be much higher than that of a properly structured retention plan.

Seasoned turnaround accountants in bankruptcy and troubled situations recognize this need and can structure an employee retention plan that will result in increased stability in the workforce and preserve this vital asset of the organization. There is not a standard employee retention plan that can be used for all situations, rather the individual retention issues faced by the company and the creditor views and perceptions surrounding management must be incorporated into any retention plan. Some of the key issues that must be considered in developing an employee retention plan are as follows:

- *Identify key employees.* The accountant should work with the debtor to identify the managers and employees that are critical to the company. Many times, employees can be grouped by level or other attribute, with different incentive programs provided for each group. Certain positions may be significantly more at risk for attrition (e.g., information systems, sales personnel, etc.) due to demand and market forces, and, accordingly, different treatment may be required to retain these groups.
- *Develop incentive structure.* Many times, the needed incentives are not as much cash based as stability based. Reorganizations are very stressful on a workforce, and employees need to know how they will be treated throughout the reorganization. Stability-based retention incentives may include stipulated severance payments in the event employees' jobs are eliminated or the reorganization is unsuccessful. This may, in many cases, result in no cash cost to the debtor if jobs are retained, but provides for employee stability throughout the restructuring. Alternatively, it may be necessary to provide incentives that are more financially lucrative to key employees if the labor market is very tight and employees can easily find better opportunities. Various performance or length of employment-based incentives may be used in structuring a plan that incentivizes individuals to remain with the debtor through the reorganization and promotes a maximized recovery to the estate and parties-in-interest. Additionally, adequate assurance must be provided that the necessary cash will be available for payout to those employees covered by the plan.
- *Assess creditor perceptions and issues.* As part of developing a retention plan, creditor input should be solicited. Typically, any payment to employees or management theoretically reduces cash otherwise available to the creditors. Creditors may have perceptions regarding the need to retain certain management, cost of the incentive plan, or nature of incentive structure. These issues should be resolved to the greatest extent possible before

any plan is presented to the court for approval. Accountants provide the necessary guidance in educating the creditors as to why the retention plan is in their best interests and in negotiating a balanced retention plan that is acceptable to all parties.

- *Existing severance policy.* Because employee reductions in force are frequently part of the restructuring process, the issue of severance of employees arises and must be dealt with. Most employers have some form of severance policy or individual agreements in place prior to a reorganization, which is a starting point for postpetition treatment. Generally, court approval must be obtained to pay severance, and the debtor often looks to an accountant for assistance in quantifying various proposals and their impact on the estate for alternative employee configurations. Often, the message that is sent to employees remaining via the treatment of those severed can have significant impact on the attrition and retention of the debtor's remaining workforce. An experienced accountant can assist in negotiating with creditors and communicating with employees and management, thereby minimizing these risks.
- *Communication to employees.* Once a plan has been developed and approved by the court, the nature of the plan should be expeditiously communicated to the relevant members of the workforce. Depending on the circumstances and timing, the debtor may find it beneficial in quelling employee unrest for some form of interim communication regarding the development of a retention plan to be communicated even before the specifics are finalized and approved.

Employee severance and retention plans can be a vital tool in maintaining a productive and focused employee workforce. If structured properly, the plan should maximize the recovery to the estate and increase the probability of a smooth and successful reorganization, benefiting all parties-in-interest.

Provide Insolvency Accounting and Tax Expertise.   Throughout a bankruptcy filing and reorganization, a debtor's accountants and financial advisors are usually required to provide the company with the traditional accounting and tax analyses specific to a bankruptcy. A debtor's internal finance team is often unfamiliar with the provisions of the Internal Revenue Code, which address the accounting and tax treatment of debtors in bankruptcy. Turnaround accountants are well versed in both accounting and tax issues specific to bankruptcy, such as fresh-start accounting, certain treatments of cancellation of debt (COD) income, and net operating loss (NOL) carry-forwards. This bankruptcy expertise can help mitigate the effects of bankruptcy on a debtor's internal financial team by making the financial process more efficient and less time consuming.

Development and Negotiation of the Plan of Reorganization.   The end game of a chapter 11 filing is the development, negotiation, and confirmation of a debtor's plan of reorganization, culminating in its emergence from bankruptcy. Workout accountants work closely with management and bankruptcy counsel in the creation of a reorganization plan. The bankruptcy court gives exclusive rights to a debtor to file a plan within 120 days of filing for bankruptcy. Once a plan is filed, it is thoroughly reviewed by all parties-in-interest and requires both creditor and court approval. If a debtor fails to file a plan of reorganization within 120 days or fails to receive an extension, any creditor or party-in-interest may file a competing plan and seek its confirmation with the bankruptcy court. Unlike many parts of the bankruptcy process, the Code provides few rules and regulations regarding the components of a plan of reorganization.

The accountant plays a primary role, with counsel, in negotiating an acceptable plan of reorganization with the various parties-in-interest. The development of a well-documented and achievable plan is critical in finalizing a plan acceptable to other parties-in-interest. Accountants provide the necessary resources to develop the financial models, test sensitivity of various assumptions, determine liquidity needs, develop debt capacity constraints, and assist the debtor in the formulation of reorganization value and an optimal capital structure. Accountants also provide critical guidance to the debtor in anticipating creditor issues and formulating acceptable solutions with interaction and negotiation with the creditors and their financial advisors.

Preparation of Liquidation Analysis. As part of the plan development, and often earlier in the case, the debtor's accountant is often expected to create or analyze the liquidation value of the enterprise. This is typically performed on an asset class basis, and a range of potential recoveries is determined based on various sale and liquidation assumptions. These analyses may play a critical role throughout the case and should be disseminated with care and should be prepared with consideration as to their potential purpose throughout the case. They may have impact on such issues as creditor-secured status, adequate protection, DIP financing, plan confirmation, and other various valuation and collateral issues.

Claims Reconciliation/Management. Another major role of a debtor's accountant is that of claims reconciliation and claims management. Especially in a large bankruptcy proceeding, numerous creditors will file claims against a debtor's estate. An accountant is often retained to reconcile these claims filed in court with the claims currently in the debtor's financial records. An accountant helps the debtor in two crucial ways: developing a flexible computer database to quickly process and sort claims and offering specific bankruptcy expertise in dealing with claims filed against the estate.

The Bankruptcy Code has many rules and regulations dealing with how and when creditors can file claims against a bankrupt estate. Accountants must be familiar with these specific time restrictions placed on a creditor's filing or amending a claim as well as a debtor's objecting to these claims. This expertise is crucial in helping a debtor deal only with valid claims filed within the court's specific time restrictions.

Operational Restructuring Services

In addition to these specific financial services provided to a debtor in bankruptcy, workout accountants have expanded their role to include overall operational improvement skills. The barriers governing the roles of various turnaround professionals have vanished as accountants (as financial advisors) have increased the depth of services and specialization they are providing to clients. Accountants serving as financial advisors for distressed companies are now providing the services previously provided by boutique and operational consultants. Some of those operational services are highlighted and discussed below.

The primary goal in a reorganization is to restructure the company into an economically viable enterprise. Frequently, financial deleveraging by itself is not sufficient to accomplish this goal, and changes in the operating environment of the company must be explored. In many cases, the fundamental underlying causes of a company's problems are operational in nature. These problems may arise due to internal performance and management issues, or failure to anticipate external market and industry changes. The first step in correcting operational issues is to identify the underlying cause of the problem. Often, a troubled company is facing so many issues and exhibiting such a plethora of problems, that the primary goal of the accountant will be one of problem identification and prioritization of the most critical issues. Accountants have expanded the industry-specific and specialized resources within their firms, and they should be looked to as objective facilitators to work within the organization. They can provide leadership in diagnosing problems, identifying areas of underperformance, developing strategies for improvement of performance, and assisting management in implementing the solutions. Although the specific areas of operational improvement are as diverse as the industries and individual situations involved in reorganizations, there are some common areas in which the accountant can assist.

- *Cost realignment services.* Troubled companies need an immediate improvement in performance, and a reduction of unnecessary, duplicative, or overly high cost structure can quickly improve cash flow. The accountant's ability to efficiently analyze the company's performance and cost structure and determine where underperformance exists is critical. A company's cost structure can be benchmarked to industry standards and competitors' performance to determine areas for further investigation. Financial trend analyses should also be considered to determine the timing, nature, and extent of cost inefficiencies. Once immediate cost reduction areas are identified, further analysis by the accountant may include interviews with management and operational personnel to identify causes of cost inefficiencies and possible solutions. Some of the services provided as part of a cost realignment review include the following:
  - Review and analyze the cash management system to focus on areas of liquidity improvement.
  - Perform a walk-through of the company's facilities and operations to assess other possible cost-saving procedures such as departmental and divi-

sional consolidation, facility utilization modifications, activity realignment, or personnel reductions.

– Analyze selected general ledger expense accounts–related documentation and review with management to determine other areas of costs and expenses that could be reduced or eliminated.

• *Asset redeployment.* Accountants often provide an evaluation of the company's assets to identify potentially underutilized assets that can result in opportunities for improved return on investment. By analyzing the current utilization of assets and systematically benchmarking existing performance against prior company performance, industry averages, competitors, and alternative uses, possible areas for improvement may surface. Based on these analyses, the accountant can assist management in developing and implementing a plan to redeploy selected assets. As part of this redeployment plan, the accountant can provide assistance in quantifying the potential costs to redeploy and the anticipated improved return.

• *Inventory rationalization.* In many organizations, inventory is the largest asset owned by the company. Significant opportunities for performance and liquidity improvement can be found if this asset can be reduced or better managed. The accountant can review for optimum inventory mix, appropriate level of Stock Keeping Units (SKUs), and efficient distribution system and production planning capabilities. If a significant amount of working capital is tied up in excess slow-moving or obsolete inventory, plans can be developed with management to liquidate this inventory, thus increasing cash flow.

• *Strategic assessment.* The purpose of a strategic assessment is to analyze the business of the company and determine its core strengths. Based on the identification of these strengths, the accountant can help management in developing a plan to maximize these strengths and focus the necessary company resources toward that plan. An early assessment of this nature is critical to developing a business plan and understanding and managing the primary factors which are driving the business. The strategic assessment should incorporate the organizational aspects of the company including its people and culture, existing processes and systems, technology, and organizational structure. Areas that could be addressed as part of a strategic assessment and development of a plan to maximize core strengths areas follows:

– Analyses of company's current operations

– Assessment of the company's market position and trends within the relevant industry. This could include a forward-looking analysis of industry trends, their impact on the company, and opportunities for improvement.

• *Analyses of strengths, weaknesses, opportunities, and threats.* After analysis of the company, its market, competitors, industry trends, and so on, the accountant can evaluate the strengths and weaknesses of the company. Furthermore, the opportunities and threats to the organization, both internal and external, should be highlighted to assist management.

The end result of the strategic assessment should be a clearly defined plan focusing the core strengths of the business for maximum improvement and the steps and timing to implement the plan.

- *Industry best practices.* Due to the increased industry specialization within the accounting firms, the accountant can identify the practices and methods used by top performers within the industry. This can provide the company with bases to compare selected performance and determine whether their practices should be modified or improved. This could involve areas such as production planning and sourcing, manufacturing processes, marketing, or distribution.

Corporate Finance and Transaction Support

One area of specialization in which accountants and their firms are providing an increased role is the disposition or purchase of distressed assets. These assets may include surplus or nonperforming assets, going-concern production facilities or operating units, or the entire business. Workout accountants involved with troubled companies requiring the disposition of assets can play a pivotal role in coordinating the overall process to maximize the return to the estate and parties-in-interest.

When an underperforming company is going through a restructuring, either out-of-court or under the protection of chapter 11 of the Bankruptcy Code, the workout accountant can add significant value to the process. Management focus and efforts can be directed back to daily operations of the core business, when transaction specialists are involved in the sale process to effectively and efficiently package the assets to maximize recovery and bring increased credibility and objectivity to the negotiation phase of the deal. Accountants play a key role in targeting potential buyers and analyzing the specifics of their sales packages. These accountants can leverage their industry knowledge, merger and acquisition experience, and thorough knowledge of the Bankruptcy Code to help management develop a strategy and process to maximize the value of these assets. The following are typical areas in which a workout accountant may assist a company in the sale of selected assets:

Preparation of an Offering Memorandum.   The process begins with an analysis of the bus .ness and to gain an understanding of the company's products and markets, history, management, and employees. Within this phase, the workout accountant will analyze the value of the assets to be sold, develop an appropriate selling strategy, and provide recommendations on the appropriate transaction structure. In order to effectively market the assets, the debtor's accountants will draft a "teaser" and eventually a formal offering memorandum. The marketing of the assets occurs generally to parties referred to as strategic or financial buyers. Strategic buyers are entities that are currently operating in the same business or one that complements the assets being sold. These buyers are in the market to enhance their current position either by expanding market share and/or increasing efficiency of operations through economies of scale. Unlike strategic buyers, financial buyers are purchasing the assets of a distressed company principally for financial purposes or stand-alone return on investment.

The contents of the offering memorandum can include, but are not limited to, the following:

- Executive summary
- Key investment considerations
- Business overview
  - History and company overview
  - Industry overview
  - Brands and products
  - Competition
  - Sales and marketing
  - Management information systems and logistics
  - Trademarks and intellectual property
  - Facilities and equipment
  - Organization and management
  - Legal, environmental, and regulatory
- Historical and projected financial information

Managing War Room and Due Diligence Process. In a workout environment that requires the disposition of assets, one of the accountant's primary responsibilities is managing the war room and due diligence process. The war room is a secured location, normally on-site at the company, which contains all the necessary documents to properly educate the purchaser about the assets or businesses being sold, such as historical financial data, detailed listing of all assets and liabilities (including on and off balance sheet), key operational statistics, and industry/competitor information. The due diligence process gives the potential purchaser the opportunity to gain in-depth knowledge of the assets for sale. Management of the process is critical to the seller because most of their internal data is open for review, often by competitors. The accountant must treat this process with extraordinary care in order to maintain the confidentiality and integrity of the company's internal information. Prior to commencing this process, the accountant should screen all potential purchasers to ascertain whether they have adequate financial backing to consummate a transaction. Assuming the potential purchaser has the financial wherewithal to consummate a deal, a confidentiality agreement should be signed prior to any dissemination of data or visiting the war room.

Upon receiving a signed confidentiality agreement and any deposits, the potential buyer will begin to have access to confidential information. The workout accountant should be on-site at all times to monitor progress, provide requested data, and answer any questions regarding the assets. Additionally, the accountant can assist management by controlling access, ensuring that consistent information is conveyed to all interested parties, and assisting in the development of presentations to potential buyers.

Managing the Negotiation and Transaction Closing Process. Managing the negotiation process and eventually closing the transaction can be a difficult and tedious process, especially if the company is operating under court protection. If the company has filed for bankruptcy, the accountant and debtor's management have additional fiduciary responsibilities to all the parties-in-interest compared to an out-of-court disposition. When a company has filed for bankruptcy protection, the court generally must approve all dispositions of assets, other than ordinary-course transactions. Additionally, creditors have an opportunity to object to any proposed transaction. Creditors can object for numerous reasons; however, the most common objection is based on the proposed transaction price, deal structure, or an attempt to extract additional leverage. Prior to liquidating or selling assets, the debtor should seek court approval for the proposed transaction. During this hearing, the court may entertain additional offers to obtain the highest value for the assets being held. This inherent control that resides with the court and creditors increases the complexity of negotiating with a buyer of the debtors assets.

Once the auction or bidding period is closed, it is imperative to quickly determine the winning party. The workout accountant will assist in summarizing and evaluating each offer to determine the highest return to the seller and all other parties-in-interest.

CREDITOR SERVICES

The use of accountants by creditor constituencies in a troubled credit situation has become commonplace both in and outside of a bankruptcy setting. This role is no longer that of a generalist, as creditors demand increasing specialization and specifically relevant industry experience. The use of professionals by creditors can, in many cases, be the most effective and efficient mechanism for creditors to obtain crucial, timely, and objective advice regarding their options and the related strategic implications of pursuing a particular course of action. It is important for creditor groups to have advisors specifically representing their interests in distressed situations due to the critical, and often time-sensitive, decisions and issues that must be dealt with and the divergent views and interests of various parties. Accountants can provide a critical and valuable role to creditor constituencies throughout all stages of a troubled credit situation. The following section of the chapter will explore some of the various situations in which creditors can effectively utilize accountants and the diverse roles accountants can play in the bankruptcy and workout environments.

Early Involvement Can Avoid Later Problems

Perhaps the most proactive approach in which accountants can assist creditors involves the retention of accountants prior to the actual extension of credit and assistance in the prelending due diligence process. In many instances, lenders are extending credit as a result of new or changing situations such as to a borrower they are unfamiliar with in terms of management, a new industry to the borrower or the lender, or the borrower may be experiencing a "sea change" in capital structure (e.g., new entity startup, acquisition financing, etc.). An accountant can serve various roles in performing and assisting a lender in evaluating the borrower and the associated lending risks.

- *Collateral Review.* If the loan is to be asset based, the accountant is often expected to provide an objective assessment of collateral value and quality. This could include analyses of receivable aging, dilution, credit concentration, collection procedures, control over cash, and other review of credit and collection procedures and controls to assess potential credit and collection risks. Inventory collateral quality issues are another key area that can be reviewed. Valuation assistance in determining asset values under varying sale or liquidation scenarios is also a valuable prelending service, which can assist the lender in evaluating collateral positions before extending financing to a potentially troubled situation.
- *Businessman's Review.* In many instances, the decision to lend is primarily based on more than the underlying collateral values, and an evaluation of the underlying economics and viability of the business is in order. This can be a key decision point in the lending process and in many cases a troubled credit situation could have been avoided altogether if a more thorough understanding of the business, management, and related projections and assumptions had been obtained. An accountant can provide valuable objective insight into the business issues surrounding a lending situation. Some of the issues that may be relevant include the following:
  - What is the overall business strategy of the enterprise? What is the perceived ability of management to execute the proposed strategy? Does the management team have the necessary experience and track record within their industry?
  - Does the business plan and related projections have adequate conservatism to be achievable in light of current and anticipated economic and industry trends?
  - What are the key "driver" assumptions in the business plan and are they realistic? How do they compare to historical industry and company performance?
  - Does the company have adequate working capital and liquidity for the projected revenue levels that have been forecast?
  - What changes are occurring within the borrower's industry, and how has the borrower recognized and dealt with these issues?

The above areas represent two principal services that can be used by creditors on a prelending basis. Once credit has been extended, similar periodic analyses may be valuable in maintaining and monitoring credit quality.

Identification of the Warning Signals of Credit Problems

Early recognition of potential credit problems and effecting the appropriate creditor actions can be critical to maximizing recoveries and improving the strength and performance of a troubled company. Typically, the first signal a creditor receives concerning problems arises well in advance of a missed payment or default under a loan covenant.

Accountants can assist lenders and creditors in identifying and diagnosing the key warning signals of a potentially troubled credit. In many cases, these can occur precipitously with little advance warning to a lender, but in most cases, the signs and indicators of a potential problem may exhibit themselves for some time before a crisis point is reached. Although no single indicator portends disaster, a combination or sustained trend can point to serious issues for creditors. These warning signs exhibited by the company may include, but are not limited to, the following:

- Liquidity issues—lack of cash or inadequate borrowing availability
- Deviation in performance from the industry or key competitors
- Rapidly aging receivables and payables
- Buildup of inventory—working capital quality may deteriorate rapidly if goods are seasonal, eclipsed by technology improvements, or subject to very thin margins
- Recent entry into new business, new product areas, or lack of focused business strategy
- Attrition of key management members
- Delay in releasing financial results
- Deteriorating margins or significant loss in market share

Accountants may be requested by creditors to assist in evaluating trends and identifying warning signals even before a default or missed payment exists. These services may include discussions with management, desktop review, and benchmarking of financial and operational information provided by the company, or actual site visits to the company. This analysis would typically be performed through a series of on-site interviews with management and on-site assessment of the company's operations, and is not designed to counsel management, but rather to provide critical and objective insight to the creditor into the underlying problems that the business is facing. The accountant can provide the lender a candid assessment of the situation and analyze various alternative courses of action. The creditor then evaluates the best alternatives, such as advancing additional funds, modifying debt instruments, waiving covenant defaults, or pursuing its existing rights and remedies. In many cases, this may be the point at which the lender suggests to management that certain corrective actions must be taken, additional collateral provided, or outside turnaround managers retained for the loan position to be maintained.

Timely Assessment of the Advantages of a Workout versus Bankruptcy from the Creditor's Perspective

Often, financially challenged debtors will seek creditor concessions in an out-of-court restructuring as opposed to a judicial or bankruptcy setting. This can be a positive step, if the company has correctly diagnosed its problems and is executing the necessary corrective actions with a reasonably high probability of success. Creditors must evaluate the potential outcome to them under various alternatives, such as a nonjudicial workout and bankruptcy environment, in order to adequately assess their willingness to participate in an out-of-court restructuring. A creditor must be able to assess the long-term viability of the enterprise and the depth of corrective action being taken, and ascertain whether the resultant outcome for them in a workout is as favorable as would be received in a judicial bankruptcy setting. The accountant should also assist the creditors in analyzing the recovery to various constituencies if the company were liquidated. (Liquidation analyses were previously discussed in the Debtor's Services section of this chapter.)

As these broad assessments are made, the creditor must also address some of the more specific issues pertaining to the workout and respond to the debtor requests being made. A creditor's accountant can provide guidance for requesting information, analyzing information received, and determining whether creditors are receiving full and timely access to requested information. It is imperative that the information be deemed reliable in order to properly evaluate the financial position of the debtor and determine the necessary restructuring options available and impact on the creditors.

Often, one of the paramount concerns of a creditor is whether it is being treated fairly as compared to other creditor constituencies. This concern can often be addressed through open communication facilitated via the formation of ad hoc creditor committees. The accountant, in conjunction with counsel, can assist in the development, formation, and ongoing operation of these committees. In many cases, the debtor will agree to pay the cost of professionals for the creditors in an out-of-court restructuring. Some of the areas of committee interest that may be orchestrated by the accountant include analyses of information regarding the debtor, review of restructuring proposals presented by the debtor, monitoring of collateral position, assisting creditors in negotiations, and developing alternative restructuring plans. The accountant can effectively act as the committees' eyes and ears in monitoring debtor operations and evaluating progress made by the debtor in diagnosing and correcting problems. The use of a committee with adequate leadership can function to alleviate creditor concern that all parties-in-interest are receiving fair and equitable treatment under any restructuring proposal.

Negotiating the Pitfalls of a Workout from the Creditors' Perspective

In a workout environment there are certain factors that increase the probability of a successful workout. The creditors and their accountant should evaluate these factors as the restructuring develops. Some of the key factors include, but are not limited to, the following:

- *Management's ability and wherewithal to take the necessary corrective action.* The creditors must be comfortable with the competence of the management team and its ability to execute the necessary cost-reduction measures, operational improvements, and other aspects of the plan. If this comfort level does not exist, then the creditor group should critically assess their willingness to move forward with a restructuring plan until the deficiencies are rectified.

- *Viability of the core business.* The core business of the debtor must have the capacity to be a self-sustaining economic entity, or the restructuring process will be ultimately rendered futile. Viability may be hampered by rapid technological changes with which the debtor cannot keep pace, industry consolidation resulting in an inability to effectively compete, or loss of margin/market share to low-cost production capabilities as competitors shift operations offshore. Regardless of the cause, the creditors and their professionals must carefully evaluate the ongoing viability of the entity.

- *Adequate liquidity.* A key component in the execution of any business plan will rest with the ability to gain access to adequate working capital. The current and projected liquidity of the debtor should be carefully reviewed by the creditors. This should include careful analysis of the debtor's projected working capital components, with consideration given to seasonality and market forces. The borrowing capacity and cash requirements of the debtor based on the proposed capital structure must be assessed throughout the projection period to determine whether an adequate liquidity cushion exists. The development of a sensitivity model to analyze the impact of various changes in the debtor's projection assumptions is often developed by the creditors' accountants.

- *Constructive working relationship between the company and its creditors.* By the time a workout is initiated, typically a significant amount of history between the debtor and creditors exists. Based on the circumstances, it can be a fairly acrimonious or highly fatigued relationship. If the circumstances are such that the parties cannot trust each other or work in a mutually constructive manner to improve the condition of the debtor and the relative position of the creditors, then an out-of-court workout may not be the most effective forum.

If the factors noted above cannot be positively addressed or reconciled by the creditor and its advisors, the opportunities for a successful out-of-court restructuring are severely limited, and a bankruptcy filing with the requisite structure and judicial oversight may be more effective.

Creditors Providing New Funds Outside of Bankruptcy.   Frequently, creditors are faced with a debtor request for additional funds or to expand credit terms to assist a potentially troubled and illiquid debtor prior to any initiation of a workout or bankruptcy filing. The creditors should proceed carefully at this juncture and ensure that they are not unnecessarily exposing themselves to additional recovery risk in the event of a bankruptcy filing by the debtor. An accountant can play a principal role in assessing the underlying cause for the liquidity problems and ascertaining the overall financial health of the enterprise. If the creditor and accountant can become satisfied that the additional credit is fixing the problem and not postponing the inevitable, then the extension of credit may be justified. Some examples of the risks for which the creditors should be aware include the following:

- *Potential improvement in lien position postpetition.* In many cases, a lender or creditor may improve their recovery by withholding the extension of additional credit or advancement of funds until after the company has filed for bankruptcy relief. If it is the belief of the creditors that a filing is probable or will be required to correct the debtor's problems and that the probability of a successful workout is unacceptably low, the risk of advancing funds prepetition is imprudent. A superpriority or administrative claim status could be obtained for funds advanced postpetition, which enhances the creditors' chances of recovery. Once again, the timely objective analysis of the debtor's financial condition and prospects for rehabilitation play a key role in creditor decision making. The creditors' accountant can play a leadership role in assessing the viability and prospects for rehabilitation of the debtor and advise the creditors as to areas of potential risk and exposure.
- *Preference exposure.* Trade and other creditors should proceed cautiously in modifying trade terms outside of the prior ordinary course if it is anticipated that a bankruptcy filing is imminently forthcoming. Section 547 of the Bankruptcy Code provides for recovery of preferences, which includes the transfer of any property of the debtor to or for the benefit of a creditor, for or on account of antecedent debt made by the debtor within 90 days before the filing of a bankruptcy petition, when the effect of the payment or transfer is to enable the creditor to receive a greater recovery than it would receive if the debtor were liquidated. Creditors providing funding should also consider their preference exposure and any preference exceptions they may have relative to new value or funds provided. Accountants, in conjunction with counsel, can assist creditors in assessing this risk and responding appropriately with collection and credit procedures.

Although it would be the desire of the creditors that the debtor has produced the best possible plan to correct operational deficiencies, eliminate excess cash outflows, and provide for the fair and equitable treatment of all constituencies, such is rarely the case. The creditors in most instances will be best served by taking a proactive role in analyzing and carefully evaluating any plans proposed or requests made by the debtor.

Creditor Assistance Postpetition.   The period immediately subsequent to the filing of a bankruptcy petition is critical for all parties-in-interest. There are numerous issues that arise consistently in most cases that are unique to the bankruptcy process. This section will explore some of these issues from the perspective of the creditors and the utilization of accountants throughout the process.

Preservation of Debtor Liquidity.   Cash is always one of the first and foremost issues in bankruptcy. The debtor will typically be seeking court approval to use cash collateral as receivables and inventories are converted to cash in the ordinary course of business. In order to obtain court approval, an interim budget of intended cash sources and uses is prepared by the debtor. The creditor's accountant plays a key role in reviewing the adequacy of the budget and assisting the creditors and counsel in negotiating a cash collateral agreement that provides adequate controls and covenants over the use of cash to protect the creditors, while still providing the debtor the flexibility to operate the business to protect the presumed going-concern value of the enterprise. It should be quickly determined that no diminution of estate value is occurring without the creditors' knowledge. Accordingly, the cash collateral budget may require weekly monitoring by the creditors' accountant to ensure that funds are being received and disbursed pursuant to the budget and court order. The creditors, particularly the secured lender, will want to monitor the value of the underlying collateral to ensure that their position has not eroded since the petition date.

Adequate Protection Issues.   Creditors with a security interest in an asset become concerned if the value of the collateral is subject to diminution in value during the pendency of the case. Accountants frequently act on behalf of the creditors in monitoring the value of their collateral held by the debtor in a bankruptcy filing. If a creditor believes that the value of its underlying collateral is decreasing, it may petition the court for adequate protection. Although practices vary by courts, a secured creditor may also be allowed an equity cushion in determining adequate protection. Accountants provide tremendous value to a creditor in valuing the relevant collateral at historical and projected future points in time to determine whether a diminution in collateral value has occurred or is anticipated to occur. The collateral may also require valuation and analyses under several different assumptions such as forced liquidation, orderly liquidation, or going-concern bases. The relevant basis of valuation will be determined by the specific circumstances of the matter at hand and ultimately by the court.

If it is determined that the creditor is entitled to adequate protection, due to a decline in the value of the creditor's collateral, Section 361 of the Bankruptcy Code provides that the court may grant adequate protection to the creditor in the following three ways:

1. *Cash payments to the creditor.* The debtor may be required to make a cash payment or periodic cash payments to the creditor for diminution in collateral value.
2. *Additional or replacement lien.* The debtor may provide additional liens in collateral to cover any decrease in the creditor's interest in the property value.
3. *Indubitable equivalent.* The debtor may provide substitute collateral, which will result in the equivalent of the debtor's interest in the collateral.

The accountant can provide valuable assistance in monitoring creditors' collateral values for diminution, assisting in adequate protection negotiations with the debtor, and providing testimony in related court hearings.

Evaluation of Debtor-in-Possession Financing Proposals. After a debtor files for bankruptcy protection, it will frequently obtain postpetition financing or DIP financing. The creditors must evaluate whether the debtor is receiving a fair financing proposal due to the fact that the DIP lender will usually be given a superpriority claim status and will typically encumber assets that may have been available to the creditors. An accountant can assist the creditors in determining the effective cost of the financing and assessing the reasonableness of the cost and covenant constraints. The analyses should be based on current market conditions, the individual circumstances of the case, and financing terms from other potential lenders. Often, the creditors and their accountant will provide the debtor with assistance in negotiating with the lender to improve the overall financing package. Creditors often seek accountants' advice on evaluating a DIP financing, including the following aspects:

- Assess the level of DIP financing required by the debtor based on debtor projections, including seasonal peaks.
- Evaluate the reasonableness of covenants, advance rates, and financing fees imposed by the DIP lender.
- Assist in negotiating with the lenders and the debtor to improve the overall financing package and fee structure.
- Locate potential DIP lenders who may be willing to provide more favorable financing alternatives to the debtor.

Debtor-in-possession financing is a critical step in the reorganization process. The use of experienced workout accountants in proactively participating in the process will enable a smooth financing transaction and should result in improved terms and conditions for the debtor, thereby improving the chances of a successful reorganization and the ultimate recovery to the creditors.

Investigate the Issues and Causes Underlying the Filing. It is important for the creditors to have a clear understanding of what caused the company to end up in bankruptcy. Although on the surface the answer may appear obvious, the underlying causes and solutions are often not so clear. The accountants can quickly assess the situation and determine the underlying causes of the filing and business failure. Typically, this involves interaction with both the debtor and its financial advisors in analyzing the operations, management, and financial structure of the organization. An early and accurate assessment is critical in determining the direction of the case for the creditors. For example, an early assessment that the company should be sold or liquidated would be critical if the debtor was pursuing a course of rehabilitation.

Plan Negotiation and Strategic Considerations. One of the key areas in which the accountants can provide assistance to the creditors is in the phase of plan development and negotiation. The plan of reorganization is based on the debtor's projections for the performance of the reorganized entity. It is primarily from these projections that the reorganization value of the entity is determined. The accountant can help the creditors determine the obtainability of the projections and the reasonableness of the underlying assumptions. This, in many cases, may involve the development of an alternate projection model to test the sensitivity of the debtor's assumptions under different operating scenarios.

In addition, accountants can provide the creditors the necessary analyses to challenge aspects of the plan they deem unrealistic or speculative. After the creditors have vetted the debtor's plan, workout accountants often perform a valuation of the business to determine a reasonable reorganization value for the entity. The determination of this value among the parties-in-interest is critical in determining the distribution to each creditor class. The accountant can also play a crucial role at this point in evaluating the optimal capital structure of the entity and its debt capacity based on the projections of operating performance. The accountant provides significant input in the negotiations regarding the composition and terms of the currency of return (e.g. cash, debt, stock, etc.) provided to the creditor classes. The creditors' accountant may also evaluate the feasibility of any proposed plan to determine that adequate cash flow and liquidity exists to service the proposed debt. Additionally, the accountant may review the debtor's liquidation analyses and assess the reasonableness of the underlying assumptions in order to ensure that any proposed plan is truly providing the creditors as much as they would receive were the company liquidated.

The creditors' accountant can provide many services to the creditor constituency through the various stages of a troubled company situation both in and out of bankruptcy. The timely and effective use of accountants in analyzing operations, interacting with the management and the other constituencies, negotiating with various parties-in-interest, and providing advice and judgment to the creditors will speed the transition from a troubled entity to a reorganized entity and should result in a maximized return to the creditor constituency.

COURT-APPOINTED SERVICES

With an increase in large national and international companies filing bankruptcy, the court system has relied heavily on the services of workout accountants. These services have ranged from analyzing complex transactions to being appointed as liquidating trustees. This section of the chapter will address the accountant's role as trustee, examiner, and various other court-appointed positions.

Accountants Serving as Court-Appointed Trustee or Financial Advisor to Trustee

Accountants are frequently appointed as a trustee in either a chapter 7 or 11 case. In most chapter 7 cases, the U.S trustee will appoint an interim trustee at about the time the order for relief is filed. The interim trustee's responsibility is to liquidate the assets of the business. However, in a chapter 11 case, a trustee is not normally retained unless specifically requested by a party-in-interest. Section 1104 of the Bankruptcy Code provides that the courts may, on the request of an interested party, order the appointment of a trustee for cause, including fraud, dishonesty, incompetence, or gross mismanagement by current management or the debtor, or if the courts believe it is in the best interest of all parties-in-interest. At this time, the trustee assumes primary responsibility for managing the enterprise. The following are examples of tasks performed by an accountant who is acting as a court-appointed trustee, or advisor to the trustee:

- Managing and directing all functions of the day-to-day operations
- Developing and implementing operating enhancement programs
- Analyzing and summarizing all available assets to pay claims, including tax refunds, preferences, and litigation claims
- Valuing and liquidating assets to maximize returns to creditors
- Distributing funds to creditors upon liquidation of the estate's assets
- Developing a plan of reorganization and disclosure statement
- Investigating related party transactions and preferences

The accountant serving as court-appointed trustee or as financial advisor to the trustee is subject to the restrictions imposed by the Bankruptcy Code. At all times throughout the case, the trustee or advisor to the trustee must maintain a position of disinterestedness.

Accountants Serving as Court-Appointed Examiner or Financial Advisor to Examiner

Under Section 1104 of the Bankruptcy Code, creditors or any party-in-interest may request the appointment of an examiner to investigate the actions of the debtor. Examiners are accountants, attorneys, or business professionals who have expertise in the relevant subject. The duties of the examiner under Section 1106(a)(1) of the Bankruptcy Code are to "investigate the acts, conduct, assets, liabilities, and financial condition of the debtor, the operation of the debtor's business and the desirability of the continuance of such business, and any matter relevant to the case or to the formulation of a plan." Additionally, the examiner has the responsibility, according to Section 1106, to "file a statement of any investigation to the court, including any fact ascertained pertaining to fraud, dishonesty, incompetence, misconduct, mismanagement, or irregularity in the management of the affairs of the debtor, or to a cause of action available to the estate."

INTERIM MANAGEMENT SERVICES

Companies may experience significant changes in their operating environment due to internal growth, acquisition, financial instability, and lack of liquidity or any other significant event. Current management may not have the experience, resources, or the time to effectively manage this change. The retention of an experienced interim manager by the company can be a valuable tool in moving the company beyond the crisis. Accounting firms are well situated to provide these services, having hired and developed seasoned managers from industry to serve in these roles. Accounting firms have the resources to provide executives with particular industry and crisis management experience to fill the key interim management roles required.

The role of an interim manager is to stabilize a distressed situation, provide leadership in managing the necessary change, and ultimately increase shareholder value. An interim manager should institute the programs necessary within the organization to produce targeted and measurable results. Typically, an interim manager is supported by the resources of a large firm and can provide focused, experienced on-point resources on an as-needed basis. These transitional needs could include areas such as supporting an overburdened accounting department, assisting the management information systems department with implementation issues, proactively implementing manufacturing changes, or designing marketing initiatives. The interim manager can serve in a focused manner, working shoulder-to-shoulder with senior management or can serve in the broader leadership role of chief executive officer or chief operating officer. The following are specific examples of entities experiencing change in which an interim manager could provide assistance.

- *Turnaround restructuring.* As a company is going through a turnaround, management is often required to make hard and unpleasant decisions in order to achieve the organizational changes necessary for a successful restructuring. Interim managers play an important role in assisting management in analyzing and making those difficult decisions that will lead to a successful turnaround. Interim managers will work with management in negotiating with secured lenders or trade creditors, and develop and implement action plans to reestablish customer trust and employee loyalty.
- *High-growth situations.* Companies experiencing fast growth frequently lack the experienced executive(s) to manage the needed change in operations and financial management. Establishing formalized structures and controls can mean the difference between profitability and negative cash flows. In addition, an independent opinion on defining needed capabilities and skill sets allows a better alignment of responsibilities and duties in developing a new organizational structure.
- *Loss of a key executive.* The loss of key executives can be devastating to the operations of a business. Immediately after the departure of an executive, the internal infrastructure of the company can deteriorate quickly, affecting all facets of the business. The external perception of the company can quickly change from stable to being perceived as troubled. Locating and recruiting the right permanent executive can take significant time; therefore, companies rely on interim managers to assist in managing the day-to-day operations and providing the correct message internally and externally.

- *Business interruption.* Interim managers are often retained to help management when an event occurs that causes an interruption to the ongoing business, such as a plant closing, fire, or new product line or facility. Interim managers can focus on the disruptive situation and implement the needed changes to the business while management continues to operate the day-to-day aspects of the company.
- *Postacquisition trauma.* The transition period following an acquisition or merger can be extremely disruptive, damaging productivity and profitability of the combined companies. An interim manager can provide management with the necessary leadership and focus to manage through this traumatic period. Additionally, an interim manager can provide his or her expertise in monitoring and guiding the combined enterprise toward achieving its strategic objectives while allowing management to continue its focus on the ongoing core business.

CONCLUSION

The past decade has seen broad changes within the roles played by accountants in a workout environment. As bankruptcies and troubled situations have become more complex and global in scope, the skills and resources of many accountants and their firms have expanded to meet the needs of the marketplace. Accountants and their firms now are providing skills and resources previously reserved for operational consultants, investment bankers, valuation experts, turnaround managers, and industry specialists. Accountants have become vital as change agents in the turnaround and restructuring process due to the diversity of business experience they bring to the table. As future changes and issues arise in the global restructuring area, accountants will be providing the needed service to meet the challenges of their clients into the next millennium.

NOTES

1. Christopher M. McHugh, *The 1998 Bankruptcy Yearbook and Almanac*, 8th ed. pp. 143–144. New Generation Research, Boston, MA, 1998.

2. *Id.*, p. 70.

16

Dealing with Employee Issues in a Bankruptcy Situation

*Robert J. Rosenberg and David S. Heller**

Latham & Watkins

INTRODUCTION

While there are many issues that a company in bankruptcy (debtor) must address regarding its workforce, there are several areas of particular importance. Union contracts, employee benefit plans, plant closures and layoffs, and retention issues can each be critical issues for the financially distressed company. The first two sections of this chapter discuss the treatment of collective bargaining agreements and retiree benefits in bankruptcy. The third section addresses the serious consequences that may arise when layoffs occur and the Workers Adjustment and Retraining Act is implicated. A discussion of the various issues that can arise as debtors work to retain key employees and preserve morale follows. The chapter closes with a brief discussion of the relatively narrow but important issue raised by covenants not to compete in the bankruptcy context.

COLLECTIVE BARGAINING AGREEMENT ISSUES IN BANKRUPTCY

To the extent a debtor determines to seek concessions from its labor force, or is encouraged or required to do so by other constituents, the existence of a collective bargaining agreement will dramatically affect how and whether any concessions can be arranged. Efforts to modify or reject collective bargaining agreements in a chapter 11 reorganization are governed by Section 1113 of the Bankruptcy Code.[1] Section 1113 of the Code provides important protections for

*The authors gratefully acknowledge the invaluable contribution of Martin C. Attea, a 1998 summer associate at Latham & Watkins and a law student at the University of Pennsylvania Law School.

employees covered by collective bargaining agreements. These protections prevent the debtor from making unilateral changes to the agreement without satisfying the procedural and substantive requirements of Section 1113.

HISTORY OF SECTION 1113

The current state of bankruptcy law as it relates to a debtor's modification of a collective bargaining agreement can only be understood in light of the Supreme Court's decision in *NLRB* v. *Bildisco & Bildisco*.[2] The *Bildisco* decision precipitated the enactment of Section 1113. Prior to *Bildisco*, the circuit courts were split as to whether a debtor could unilaterally reject a collective bargaining agreement. The disagreement reflected differing views of how to resolve the natural tension that existed between bankruptcy and labor law. A debtor could seek to reject burdensome contracts under Section 365 of the Code merely by satisfying the "business judgment" test. Under Section 365, a contract can be rejected or eliminated if it makes business sense for the debtor to do so. However, the National Labor Relations Act (NLRA), which deals with the broader issue of collective bargaining in all sectors and contexts, prohibits unilateral modification or termination of collective bargaining agreements by an employer.[3] Prior to *Bildisco* and the enactment of Section 1113, bankruptcy courts presented with debtors seeking to reject collective bargaining agreements were forced to reconcile this tension.

Under applicable bankruptcy law, it has been argued that the filing of a chapter 11 petition creates a new legal entity, even though, as a practical matter, the "employer" does not change. Generally, a "successor" employer is not bound by a collective bargaining agreement entered into by previous management.[4] Determining that a debtor was, as a legal matter, like a successor employer, some courts held that a debtor could reject a collective bargaining agreement without offending the provisions of the NLRA.[5] Nonetheless, the question remained: Must the rejection of a collective bargaining agreement under Section 365 satisfy *only* the business judgment rule governing the rejection of other executory contracts or, giving due regard to national labor policy, a more stringent standard? Generally, it was agreed that some deference should be shown to labor policy,[6] but the battle lines were drawn over how much deference need be shown. One line of cases held that rejection was appropriate only when necessary to prevent a debtor from going into liquidation.[7] Another line of cases permitted rejection when the collective bargaining agreement burdened the estate and the balance of equities favored rejection.[8] Not surprisingly, the latter standard was preferred by debtors, the former by labor. In *Bildisco*, the Supreme Court set out to resolve the split.

Bildisco presented a relatively typical collective bargaining agreement rejection scenario. On April 14, 1980, Bildisco filed for relief under chapter 11. At the time of the filing, Bildisco was bound by a collective bargaining agreement, set to expire on April 30, 1982, with the International Brotherhood of Teamsters, Chauffeurs, Warehousemen, and Helpers of America (Teamsters). Bildisco had breached the contract in January 1980 by failing to pay benefits and to remit union dues, and did so again, postbankruptcy, in May 1980, by refusing to pay wage increases required by the collective bargaining agreement.

In response, the Teamsters filed an unfair labor practice charge with the National Labor Relations Board (NLRB). As *Bildisco* had failed to pay benefits and to remit dues to the Teamsters, the Board ruled in favor of the Teamsters. It found that Bildisco had committed an unfair labor practice "by unilaterally changing the terms of the collective bargaining agreement and by refusing to negotiate with the union."[9] Bildisco was ordered to cure its breach of the collective bargaining agreement. The NLRB petitioned the Third Circuit Court of Appeals to enforce its order.

Meanwhile, Bildisco sought, and the bankruptcy court granted, rejection of the collective bargaining agreement. The Teamsters appealed the bankruptcy court's decision. The Court of Appeals consolidated the Teamsters appeal and the NLRB's petition for enforcement. The Third Circuit ruled that a chapter 11 debtor could unilaterally modify or reject a collective bargaining agreement without committing an unfair labor practice. In doing so, it adopted the debtor-friendly "balance of the equities" standard for rejection of a collective bargaining agreement.

Given the split among the circuits, the Supreme Court took the case for review and affirmed the decision of the Third Circuit Court of Appeals. In reaching its decision, the Supreme Court made several findings. First, collective bargaining agreements were, indeed, executory contracts subject to Section 365 of the bankruptcy code. However, a collective bargaining agreement could not be treated as an ordinary executory contract. Instead, the court adopted a special standard for rejection requiring a showing "that the collective bargaining agreement burdens the estate, and that after careful scrutiny, the equities balance in favor of rejecting the labor contract."[10] Second, the court held that before a bankruptcy court may authorize rejection, the court must be persuaded that the debtor made voluntary efforts to negotiate a reasonable modification of the agreement with the union.[11] Finally, the court held that a debtor's unilateral breach of a collective bargaining agreement without bankruptcy court approval did not, in and of itself, constitute an unfair labor practice. The court justified its holding by stating that "from the filing of a petition in bankruptcy until formal acceptance, the collective bargaining agreement is not an enforceable contract within the meaning of the NLRA."[12] The Supreme Court kept collective bargaining agreements within the realm of Section 365, while increasing the degree of difficulty for rejection.

CONGRESS'S RESPONSE TO *BILDISCO*: SECTION 1113 OF THE BANKRUPTCY CODE

The decision in *Bildisco* proved an unpopular one, particularly, and not surprisingly, with organized labor. Congress reacted with unusual speed. On the very day the Supreme Court decided *Bildisco*, Congressman Rodino introduced a bill to overturn the decision. Within the year, Congress enacted Section 1113 of the Bankruptcy Code. By enacting Section 1113, Congress accomplished two goals. First, it stopped employers, like Bildisco, who otherwise enjoyed the benefits of bankruptcy, from making unilateral changes to collective bargaining agreements in bankruptcy. Second, it imposed a statutory framework requiring that bankruptcy judges refrain from approving the rejection of a collective bargaining agreement without first giving appropriate—and some would argue undue—consideration to national labor policy. Labor hailed its passage as a victory; however, the celebration may have been premature. As applied, Section 1113 did not repudiate *Bildisco*. Rather, it adopted, modified, and reversed parts of *Bildisco*.

Section 1113 adopted the "balance of the equities" language from *Bildisco*.[13] The ruling in *Bildisco* had already required a debtor to make voluntary efforts to negotiate a reasonable modification of the collective bargaining agreement with the union, but the statute codified Bildisco's mandate in favor of negotiation by requiring that: (1) the debtor submit a proposal to the union[14]; (2) the debtor make available to the union the information on which the proposal is based[15]; and (3) the debtor meet and confer with the union in good faith.[16]

Section 1113 modified *Bildisco* by requiring that rejection be denied unless the union refused the proposal "without good cause"[17] and that any modification be "necessary" to permit reorganization.[18] Section 1113 overturned *Bildisco* by forbidding the unilateral termination or alteration of a collective bargaining agreement unless Section 1113's requirements were met.[19]

Like many sections of the Code, Section 1113 provides an impetus for negotiation and compromise. The subjective discretion reserved to the court as to what constitutes "good cause" or is "necessary" undoubtedly was intended to, and, in practice does, promote negotiation; there can be no assurance of *how* a court will resolve these subjective judgments. In sum, Section 1113 eliminated the more lenient rejection standard of Section 365 and imposed a statutory framework of negotiation and compromise more consistent with that which governs the treatment of collective bargaining agreements outside of bankruptcy.

Procedural Aspects of Section 1113

The debtor's modification proposal must be made to the union after the case is commenced, but before the debtor makes an application to the court seeking rejection of the collective bargaining agreement.[20] Once the debtor files the application, the court is to hold a hearing within 14 days, but may postpone the start of the hearing by an additional seven days.[21] Further extension of the commencement of the hearing is only possible if both sides agree to the extension. The court is to rule on the application within 30 days of the hearing's commencement. An extension on the 30 days is possible, provided both parties agree to the extension. Failing an extension, after 30 days without a ruling, the debtor may make a temporary unilateral modification or termination of the collective bargaining agreement pending the court's eventual disposition.

Requests For Interim Relief under Section 1113

Occasionally, a debtor's cash flow situation is so desperate that it cannot afford to await the satisfaction of Section 1113's procedural requirements. In such cases, the debtor may petition the court for interim relief.[22] Section 1113(e) requires that the interim modifications be "essential to the continuation of the debtor's business" or necessary "to avoid irreparable damage to the estate."[23] Provided the debtor meets this standard, the requested changes, or those changes the court finds appropriate, will be made. The changes are temporary, and are subject to the court's final disposition. The debtor must proceed to meet all the requirements of Section 1113 as if no relief had been granted.[24] Clearly, if such interim relief is granted, the debtor will have favorable momentum in any further negotiations with the union as a preliminary finding that necessary concessions by labor will have been made.

The Elements of Section 1113

In determining whether a debtor may reject a collective bargaining agreement under Section 1113, the majority of courts apply the nine-part test first articulated in *In re American Provision Co*.[25] The-nine part test requires that, before the court approves rejection:

1. The debtor makes a proposal to the union to modify the agreement
2. The proposal be based on the most complete and reliable information available
3. The proposed modifications be necessary to permit reorganization
4. The modifications ensure that the creditors, debtor, and affected parties are treated fairly and equitably
5. The debtor provide to the union such relevant information as is necessary to evaluate the proposal
6. The debtor meet at reasonable times with the union between the making of the proposal and the time of the rejection hearing
7. The debtor negotiate with the union in good faith at these meetings
8. The union refuse to accept the debtor's proposal without good cause
9. The balance of equities clearly favor rejection of the agreement

Meeting The Section 1113 Requirements

The *American Provision* standards require the debtor to make the first move in negotiations with the union. As in any negotiation, the first proposal need not be the last. However, ultimately, the debtor must put the proposal it wants the court to evaluate in making its findings, on the table.

As a practical matter, the second element (complete information) and the fifth element (information necessary to evaluate the proposal) are treated together. These requirements should not, and seldom do, pose a problem for the debtor. If the debtor is concerned about the sensitivity of the information it is providing, the debtor may seek a protective order from the court.[26]

Predictably, the third element (modifications necessary) has been the most lit-igated and has attracted the most academic attention. There is a general consen-sus that this element is often determinative in a court's decision to grant or deny rejection.[27] The Third Circuit has ruled that only the barest modification "essen-tial" to stave off liquidation is "necessary."[28] The Second Circuit has directly criticized this view, and held that a modification is "necessary" if it is required to ensure that the debtor will emerge successfully from bankruptcy. This issue has not been settled by the Supreme Court. However, the view set out by the Second Circuit in *Truck Driver's Local 807* v. *Carey Transp., Inc.,* has garnered the most support.[29]

In *Carey*, the union rejected the proposed modification of its contract because the debtor sought changes designed to get it to better than operating break-even. The union argued that any concessions greater than those required for *Carey* to get to break-even were not "necessary" as defined by the Third Circuit. The court responded by stating that in its view "it [is] impossible to weigh necessity with-out looking into the debtor's ultimate future and estimating what the debtor needs to attain financial health."[30] Thus, the *Carey* standard is more favorable to a debtor and its other constituents as it allows for modifications greater than those necessary to stave off liquidation, and instead focuses more on what is nec-essary to a "successful" reorganization.

The fourth element (fair and equitable treatment) can also promote an inter-esting give and take. Often, unions will argue that "fair and equitable" requires that cuts in union salaries be proportionately matched by concessions from other groups, such as management, unsecured creditors, and nonunion workers.[31] Al-though it is unlikely that a court could establish or would require a precise and proportionate "sharing of the pain," the "fair and equitable" test does seem to re-quire that the debtor and its nonunion creditors sacrifice as well—union employ-ees will not be expected to bear an unfair burden. As a practical matter, a reorganization disproportionately based on cuts by the rank and file may be doomed to failure for reasons having little to do with legal niceties in any event.

In response to proposed cuts, unions will often seek a so-called "snap-back" provision.[32] A snap-back provision is designed to restore union salaries to pre-modification levels when and if the debtor reaches certain agreed-upon perfor-mance criteria. Such a provision generally is eminently fair and should be acceptable to all constituents as it allows participation by employees for "bet-ter or worse" and is quite similar to the so-called "hope notes" or contingent future profit participations that unsecured creditors often take as part of a plan of reorganization.

Courts should, and do, treat the sixth element (meeting at reasonable times with the union), and the seventh element (negotiating in good faith), as one. To establish that it met these combined tests, the debtor is well advised to meet fre-quently with the union. Courts tend to look to the frequency of meetings as an important indication of good-faith bargaining and satisfaction of the "reasonable times" requirement.[33] One empirical study noted that data strongly supported the notion that "[t]he more bargaining that fails to produce a settlement, the more likely that rejection will be granted."[34] The study's author speculated that "if the parties engage in good-faith negotiations, but are unable to arrive at a mutually acceptable solution, the bankruptcy court will 'reward' the debtor for having at least engaged in the effort."[35]

Good-faith negotiations do take place at reasonable times and with reasonable frequency. Frequency cannot, however, in and of itself, substitute for quality. Parties to the negotiation who are confident the record will support their claim that they negotiated in good faith should have bargaining sessions recorded, transcribed, or routinely summarized, as disputes as to what transpired at such sessions will inevitably arise. Because management often does quite well in bankruptcy and their motives and agendas may be suspect, a debtor is well advised to employ independent consultants to validate the information it provides and otherwise facilitate and support the debtor's proposals and negotiating positions.[36]

The eighth requirement (rejection of the proposal to be with good cause), must be viewed in the context of the third requirement (necessity of modifications). In order to establish that the union rejected a proposal without "good cause," a debtor must presumably establish that the proposal is "necessary." A debtor's success in satisfying the ninth element (balance of equities) depends on the debtor's success (or lack thereof) in establishing the other factors. As such, as a practical matter, the ninth factor has little independent significance.

Damages and Priority Of Claims Arising From Section 1113 Rejection

There has been a substantial amount of academic speculation over whether the rejection of a collective bargaining agreement gives rise to a claim for damages. To date, only one case, *In re Blue Diamond Coal Company*, has directly addressed the issue.[37] In *Blue Diamond*, the court ruled that when Congress passed Section 1113, it removed collective bargaining agreements from Section 365 and that,[38] by extension, this resulted in their removal from Section 502(g), which provides that a damage claim arises as a result of a rejection pursuant to Section 365.[39] Prior to the enactment of Section 1113, the rejection of a collective bargaining agreement under Section 365 clearly gave rise to a prepetition claim for damages under Section 502. However, if Section 1113 made Section 365, and therefore Section 502, inapplicable to collective bargaining agreements, then, ironically, absent an express provision in Section 1113, a union would have no recourse for damages arising from rejection under Section 1113—a section designed, in most part, to benefit labor. As Section 1113 contains no provision stating that rejection gives rise to a claim, the *Blue Diamond* court held that no claim for damages could arise from a Section 1113 rejection. The court justified this result by noting that "if rejection is truly necessary, then allowing a claim for damages . . . would necessarily assure the failure of the reorganization."[40]

Legal commentators have heavily criticized the *Blue Diamond* decision.[41] Critics accurately point out that union workers under this ruling are worse off under Section 1113 than they were under *Bildisco*. Moreover, while it is possible that, as the *Blue Diamond* court noted, a damage claim arising from a "necessary" rejection would be so large as to materially affect the prospects of a successful reorganization, this result does not necessarily follow.[42] Allowing a claim for damages merely dilutes the value available for unsecured and other creditors. There is a material and real distinction between the burdens of a collective bargaining agreement, with its various implications for cash flow, corporate profits, and flexibility, and the allowance of an unsecured claim. *Blue Diamond* will likely remain an isolated decision, and it is expected that claims arising from Section 1113 rejection will be recognized.[43]

PRIORITY STATUS FOR DAMAGES FOR THE BREACH OF AN "UNASSUMED, UNREJECTED" COLLECTIVE BARGAINING AGREEMENT

Occasionally, a debtor will neither reject nor assume a collective bargaining agreement prior to plan confirmation. When a debtor under these circumstances fails to fulfill its obligations under the collective bargaining agreement, courts will allow a claim for damages. Substantial academic and judicial controversy, however, has arisen over the priority status, if any, to be afforded to the claim for damages in these circumstances. The general priority scheme in bankruptcy is set out in Section 507 of the Code. As noted, it does not expressly contemplate claims arising out of Section 1113. Section 1113(f) is, on its face, an "absolute" prohibition against the unilateral modification of collective bargaining agreements.[44] Some courts have opined that, therefore, Section 1113 and Section 507 conflict, and these courts disagree over which section governs. The circuit courts have split over the issue, and the Supreme Court has yet to resolve it.

The Second, Third, and, most recently, the Fourth Circuits have decided that the priority of claims arising under these circumstances is governed by Section 507(3), with resulting priority treatment as allowed unsecured claims subject to the well known $4,000 per employee cap.[45] However, the Sixth Circuit has determined that Section 1113(f)'s prohibition against unilateral termination or alteration of the collective bargaining agreement requires that no less than administrative expense priority be afforded to claims arising out of "breaches" of Section 1113. Any lower priority in effect enables the debtor to unilaterally modify or terminate its collective bargaining agreement without sufficient sanction. The courts following the Sixth Circuit's lead hold that Section 1113(f) preempts the priority scheme set out in Section 507. This line of cases holds that a breach of a collective bargaining agreement that has not been assumed or rejected in compliance with Section 1113 gives rise to a superpriority claim with administrative expense status.[46]

Debtors must be careful to avoid "inadvertent assumptions" of collective bargaining agreements as some courts have resolved the priority issue by holding that the failure to reject the collective bargaining agreement in accordance with Section 1113 results in its assumption.[47] Under this approach, any default under the "assumed" collective bargaining agreement is also given administrative priority status.[48] A debtor should initiate and complete the Section 1113 process as soon as it is clear a modification will be necessary.

Collective bargaining agreements and the priority claims that may arise in connection therewith will not go away if ignored.

THE CONSEQUENCES OF SECTION 1113 REJECTION OF THE COLLECTIVE BARGAINING AGREEMENT

If the debtor satisfies all of Section 1113's procedural and substantive requirements, the court will allow rejection of the collective bargaining agreement. The debtor will be liberated from its obligations under the rejected collective bargaining agreement. While a successful rejection marks the end of the Section 1113 process, it may also mark the beginning of a new round of negotiations between the debtor and the union to determine what the new terms and conditions of employment will be. Under the NLRA, the debtor has the statutory duty to negotiate a new collective bargaining agreement.[49] Furthermore, while the workers will no longer have the protection of Section 1113, they retain a union's ultimate weapon—the right to strike.[50]

RETIREE BENEFIT ISSUES IN BANKRUPTCY—SECTION 1114

While a collective bargaining agreement may create material ongoing and financial burden on a reorganizing debtor, a debtor's obligation to honor welfare benefits for retired employees can be equally burdensome. The ability of a debtor to free itself of obligations to pay such benefits can be of great importance to a debtor seeking to reorganize. These benefits typically include increasingly expensive medical and life insurance coverages. When such benefits are not covered by a collective bargaining agreement, and are therefore not subject to Section 1113, efforts to modify those benefits are governed by Section 1114.[51] Section 1114 prevents the unilateral modification or termination of retiree benefits by a debtor.

Section 1114 is patterned after Section 1113. Section 1113 governs the treatment of current workers, and Section 1114 governs retirees not otherwise covered by collective bargaining agreements. Section 1114 bears more than a superficial resemblance to Section 1113. The sections contain similar language, both govern the treatment of worker's claims in bankruptcy, and both owe their origins to similar events. Important differences do exist, however. Perhaps most significantly, Section 1114 expressly grants administrative priority status to certain claims arising under it. This section describes the circumstances surrounding the adoption of Section 1114, details its provisions, and discusses the legal issues that arise under it in the bankruptcy context.

Section 1114: A Response to LTV

Like Section 1113, Section 1114 was hastily enacted by Congress in response to adverse public reaction to a bankruptcy case. In 1986, the LTV Corporation filed for chapter 11. Soon afterward, it announced the termination of health benefits for 78,000 retirees and their dependents. A public outcry ensued.[52] Within a month, the Senate held a hearing on the matter. Two days later, it passed a bill ordering LTV to reinstate its benefits. Simultaneously, LTV's workers threatened to strike. The combined pressure forced LTV to seek permission from the bankruptcy court to continue paying its retiree benefits. Eventually, LTV and the retirees reached a compromise that modified, but continued, the payment of benefits. However, the legislative wheels had been set in motion. Congress passed stop-gap legislation to address the issue. Two years later, the substance of the stop-gap legislation was passed as the Retiree Benefits Bankruptcy Protection Act of 1988. On July 16, 1988, President Reagan signed the Act into law. The Act contained Section 1114 and amended Section 1129.[53]

The Scope of 1114's Protection

Unlike Section 1113, Section 1114 applies to all retirees, union and nonunion alike. The scope of Section 1114 is limited to "retiree benefits," however.[54] The statute includes spouses and dependents of the retiree, and "retiree benefits" within the meaning of the statute encompasses sickness, accident, disability, and death benefits provided by the debtor to its retired employees.[55] Section 1114 is inapplicable to retirees with gross income in excess of $250,000 per year.[56] Pensions are *not* considered "retiree benefits" under Section 1114, and are not subject to Section 1114's provisions.[57] Section 1114 does not create greater rights than existed prebankruptcy. For example, in one case, the plan under which the benefits were being paid expired while the debtor was in chapter 11.[58] In another, the plan contained a termination provision that the debtor exercised while in chapter 11.[59] In both cases, the courts held that Section 1114 does not apply to create benefits outside the contractual obligations of the debtor.

Occasionally, a debtor files for chapter 11 with no intention of reorganizing. The debtor wishes to liquidate, but for a variety of reasons—some noble, some not—desires that the current management team, rather than a chapter 7 trustee, administer the liquidation. As Section 1114 explicitly requires that modification of retiree benefits be "necessary to permit reorganization," retirees faced with what would otherwise be a so-called liquidating chapter 11 case run the risk that benefits will be eliminated and enjoy no priority status in a chapter 7 case. The alternative is to negotiate acceptable treatment in the liquidating chapter 11 or to find a basis for extending the provisions of Section 1114 to the liquidating debtor.[60]

In the *Eastern Airlines* case,[61] Judge Lifland thoughtfully found a basis to reconcile the "reorganization" criteria of Section 1114, with the practical give and take present in that case and so many others.[62] Noting Senator Metzenbaum's view that "reorganizing companies may never unilaterally cut off retiree insurance benefits," as well as other aspects of the legislative history of Section 1114, Judge Lifland noted that "Congress did not contemplate that this legislation would impact debtors who were not in the process of reorganizing (i.e., not turning around)."[63] Moreover, he correctly observed that, where the debtor is liquidating its assets in chapter 11 (as opposed to, but in a manner similar to, chapter 7) the "debtor should not be compelled to continue paying benefits, in full, on a priority basis."[64] Accordingly, he ruled that as to Eastern, "necessary to permit the reorganization" must be interpreted to mean "necessary to accommodate confirmation of a chapter 11 plan."[65] The retirees were left with some leverage, as Eastern wanted to proceed in chapter 11 and therefore had to deal with the retiree claims. Eastern and the other constituents were in a position to argue that, if need be, the case would convert to a chapter 7 proceeding in which the retirees would merely be unsecured creditors.

The Retirees' Right to Representation under Section 1114

Section 1114 expressly provides a right of representation for retirees who may be affected by chapter 11 proceedings. While this benefit is of obvious value to nonunion workers, it might appear redundant for union retirees who are, presumably, ably represented by their union. However, it is hard to imagine a situation in which retirees would not want their own representative, as an inherent conflict usually exists between the interests of current union workers and union retirees; the more the retirees get, the less there is for all other constituents, including current workers.

The court may appoint a committee of nonunion retirees to represent the interests of all nonunion retirees upon the motion of any interested party.[66] The court will do this only where a debtor seeks to modify the retiree's benefits, or where the court otherwise "determines it is appropriate."[67] In determining whether to appoint a committee, the court will undoubtedly consider whether any other constituent can properly represent the interests of retirees, the amount in controversy with respect to such retirees, the ability of the estate to absorb the costs attendant to such committees (and its counsel), and the complexity of the issues raised by the class of retirees. While the court may appoint a committee, unless its interests are substantial, it may look less kindly on the appointment of, or compensation claims filed by, counsel for such committee.

While the union retirees' authorized representative is presumed to be the labor organization that is the signatory to the collective bargaining agreement,[68] union retirees are themselves entitled to separate representation if the labor organization elects not to represent the retirees,[69] or upon any party's motion, in which case the court may decide that separate representation is appropriate.[70] Again, this provision enables the court to alleviate any conflict-of-interest concerns that may arise from the varying interests of current workers and retirees.

The Modification Process of Section 1114

Section 1114 requires that a debtor "timely pay and . . . not modify any retiree benefits," except in compliance with Section 1114.[71] A debtor can avoid this mandate only by reaching a voluntary agreement with the retirees or by being granted a court-ordered modification. In either case, various requirements similar to those found in Section 1113 must be met. The debtor must make a modification proposal to the authorized representative of the retiree group that is based on complete and reliable information and contains only those modifications "necessary" to permit reorganization.[72] These "necessary" modifications must treat all parties "fairly and equitably."[73] The requested modification must be made by motion.[74] If the retirees' authorized representative rejects the debtor's proposal without good cause, the court may then, and only then, enter an order modifying the retirees' benefits.[75]

The modification hearing is to be held within 14 days of the debtor's motion.[76] The court, in its discretion, can extend this deadline by seven days. Further extensions can be obtained if the parties agree. Once the hearing is held, the court has 90 days to make a formal ruling.[77] The statute allows for extension, but only if the debtor and the authorized representative agree. If the court fails to issue a ruling on time, the debtor may effectuate the proposed modifications while awaiting the court's decision.

Little case law interpreting the substantive standards under Section 1114 exists, and that which does references the case law interpreting Section 1113. Section 1114, like Section 1113, fails to provide reliable guidance regarding what is meant by "necessary to permit reorganization." However, Section 1114's legislative history supports the adoption of the "necessary" standard set forth by the Third Circuit (necessary to avoid liquidation) and rejection of the more lenient standard adopted by the Second Circuit (necessary to a "successful reorganization).[78] As one court has observed, while retirees "arouse a special sense of compassion" and Section 1114 assumes they will receive enhanced treatment in chapter 11, like other constituents, however, they will still need to be prepared to negotiate to a resolution that is, in the end, fair and equitable.

Section 1114 and Interim Relief

Like Section 1113, Section 1114 allows a debtor to seek interim relief.[79] To dissuade any but the most desperate debtor from seeking such relief, however, the standard for relief is significantly more stringent than that required for final relief. The statutory language requires that the interim modification be "essential to the continuation of the debtor's business" or necessary "to avoid irreparable damage to the estate."[80] Provided the debtor meets the standard, the requested changes, or those changes the court finds more appropriate, will be made. The changes are merely temporary and are subject to final disposition under the Section 1114 process. The debtor must continue forward to satisfy all the requirements of Section 1114 as if no interim relief was granted.[81] The debtor's financial performance during the interim period may provide persuasive evidence as to whether relief is, in fact, necessary.

Priority Status of Section 1114 Claims

Unlike Section 1113, Section 1114 specifically addresses the status and priority suffered—or enjoyed, depending on the constituents' point of view—by retiree claimants with modified benefits. Retiree benefit claims under Section 1114 have the status of allowed administrative expenses under Section 503.[82] As a result, any qualifying benefits that come due before plan confirmation receive payment subject only to secured claims and other administrative claims with the same priority. Any lost benefits arising from a proper modification receive unsecured claim status.[83] For example, a debtor under Section 1114 must, in the first instance, pay 100% of the benefits owed to retirees. Say the debtor seeks and receives a 25% modification of the benefits. If the debtor continues to pay at the 75% level, no administrative claim arises. The retirees have a general unsecured claim for the remaining 25%. If the debtor fails to pay at the 75% level, the difference between the 75% level and the amount paid receives administrative expense priority.

MODIFYING THE MODIFICATION

Whether the relief is interim, consensual, or court-mandated, the authorized representative may seek to revisit cuts in benefits. If the authorized retiree representative determines that circumstances have changed such that the modifications are no longer "necessary" to the reorganization and should be abated, the authorized representative may petition the court "at any time."[84] In deciding whether to modify the modification, the court will determine whether the original modifications no longer satisfy the standards necessary for their enactment. By the same token, a debtor may seek additional modifications if circumstances change, and the original modifications are subsequently found inadequate to permit reorganization. There is no statutory limit on the number of motions for modification that may be made.

RETIREE BENEFITS AND PLAN CONFIRMATION: SECTION 1129

Congress amended Section 1129 of the Code, which contains the base requirements for confirmation, by adding provision (a)13 in the same bill enacting 1114.[85] Section 1129(a)13 locks in the result of the Section 1114 process by requiring the debtor to undertake, as part of its plan, to continue retiree benefits at the level determined to apply in the Section 1114 process.[86] As the plan must be feasible—"not likely to be followed by the liquidation, or the need for further financial reorganization, of the debtor"[87]—the debtor must demonstrate it can faithfully discharge its obligations to retirees as part of its feasibility proof at confirmation.

A WARNING ABOUT THE WORKERS
ADJUSTMENT AND RETRAINING ACT TIMING

This chapter does not review the history or detail the workings of the Workers Adjustment and Retraining Act (WARN).[88] There is ample literature on this subject.[89] "In essence, WARN requires that employers who fall within its parameters must provide 60-day prior notice to employees, unions, state dislocated worker agencies, and local governments of a 'plant closing' or 'mass layoff.'"[90] The employers who fall within the WARN Act:

[employ] 100 or more full-time employees, or which employ 100 or more part-time employees, who in the aggregate work at least 4,000 hours a week, exclusive of overtime hours. Nonprofit organizations are included in the definition of employer; but federal, state and local public service companies are not. If an employer has temporarily laid off employees but those employees are expected to be recalled, the laid off employees are included in the counting of employees.[91]

Two events trigger WARN: plant closings and mass layoffs. Plant closings "[include] (1) the permanent or temporary shutdown of a single site of employment or (2) a permanent or temporary shutdown of one or more facilities or operating units within a single site of employment, if the shutdown results in an employment loss of 50 or more full-time employees during any 30-day period."[92] A mass layoff "is defined as a reduction in the work force that results in an employment loss at any single site of at least 33 percent of all full-time employees, with a minimum number of 50 full-time employees. The 33 percent minimum requirement does not apply if 500 or more full-time employees will be affected by the layoff."[93] The material consequences arising from the timing of WARN processes in bankruptcy are briefly visited below.

A company subject to WARN must give 60 days' notice before terminating any employee. If the company fails to give the notice, the terminated employee will be entitled to back pay as defined by WARN. Depending on the timing of the termination, claims may receive varying priority status in bankruptcy. Consequently, in conducting its pre- and postbankruptcy planning, the debtor and its professionals must carefully consider not only the impact of WARN, but the timing of events giving rise to a WARN claim and the WARN notice.

THIRD-PRIORITY WAGE STATUS

In determining whether WARN damages were entitled to any priority status, courts first had to determine whether WARN damages were penalties or the more favored wages within the meaning of Section 507. In the first case to consider the issue, debtor had terminated employees within 90 days of bankruptcy. The terminated employees filed wage claims under WARN and requested that they receive Section 507(a)(3) ($4,000) wage priority. Seeking to avoid the Section 507(a)(3) priority, the trustee claimed that the damages were more akin to a statutory penalty and therefore not entitled to priority status. The court disagreed. It noted the specific use of the language "back pay" in the WARN Act.[94] It also analogized WARN damages to severance pay at termination in lieu of notice. As a result, the right to damages were earned upon termination[95] and "[t]he employees' claims arising under [WARN] are unsecured claims for wages earned within 90 days of the cessation of business by the debtor . . . and are entitled to priority status under 11 U.S.C. § 507(a)(3)."[96]

FIRST-PRIORITY ADMINISTRATIVE STATUS

Workers Adjustment and Retraining Act claims, however, can obtain even greater priority status. If the termination without notice occurs *after* the petition is filed, administrative expense priority results. This can have adverse effects on the reorganizing debtor. Not only will these claims be paid before all but secured creditors and other administrative claims with equal priority, they are not subject to the $4,000 per employee limitation.

In *In re Hanlin Group*,[97] the debtor terminated employees without notice *after* it filed for chapter 11. Under Sections 507(a)(1) and 503(b)(1)(a) of the Code, wages for services rendered after the commencement of the case are entitled to first-priority administrative expense status. The court noted the case law that treated WARN damages as back pay earned at termination. The court then determined that "[b]ecause the date of termination occurred postpetition, any back pay due for a WARN violation will be deemed as earned postpetition, and therefore in the nature of wages for services rendered after the commencement of the case entitled to administrative expense status."[98] The court further noted that, even if the WARN damages were not back pay, they would still be entitled to administrative expense status as losses caused by the continued operation of the debtor's business.[99]

A debtor must be sensitive to the timing issues inherent in WARN's requirements. While there may be extraordinary practical reasons for not commencing the WARN notice process prior to bankruptcy, generally, a putative debtor should make any WARN termination notices in advance of the filing date, or ideally, more than 90 days before filing.

RETENTION OF KEY EMPLOYEES IN BANKRUPTCY

It is certainly not uncommon for a debtor to seek and obtain pay cuts from the rank and file, as well as senior management. It is also not uncommon for a debtor to seek to provide bonus and incentive arrangements to its management and other employees in an effort to keep such management and employees in place pending a bankruptcy proceeding. The existence of a bankruptcy can adversely affect morale and employee loyalty across the ranks. There is ample anecdotal and other evidence for the proposition that bankruptcy may lead to the loss of key employees not willing to go "down with the sinking ship." Accordingly, it is not surprising that there is substantial precedent for the proposition that a debtor may take steps to sweeten compensation for employees it determines it must retain as it proceeds through a reorganization proceeding. Employee inducements can take several forms, including:

- Increased severance packages
- Stock options
- Continuation of group, medical, and life insurance benefits for negotiated periods

- Relocation expenses if a company liquidates
- Confirmation "bonuses"
- In the case of liquidations, bonuses paid on the amounts achieved in liquidations in which the employees participate

To the extent that the proposed implementation of a retention program for key employees is outside the ordinary course of business, court approval for the arrangement must be sought. Virtually every pleading filed in support of an increase in employee compensation will cite either the *America West* or *Interco* decisions.[100] In *America West*, the debtor sought authority to pay "success" bonuses to certain officers and employees. The debtor also proposed a \$9.5 million bonus fund to be divided among its employees, structured for \$1,000 cash payments. The bonuses were urged as tokens designed to serve as a morale booster to show all employees that their efforts and sacrifices had been appreciated. After conducting an interesting analysis of the purpose of the payments, and the evidence supporting the debtor's motions, the court found that such matters were within the debtor's business judgment. The court ruled that it is a "proper use of a debtor's business judgment to propose bonuses for employees who help propel the debtor successfully through the confirmation process." Citing *Interco*, the court noted that confirmation awards to senior executives are common and tend to be for very significant amounts. Having considered the record and history of the case, the court focused on whether the proposed bonuses were reasonable and fair under the circumstances. Finding that the proposed bonuses would aid in continuing the momentum the debtor had gained up to and through the confirmation process, the court found that the proposed success bonuses were reasonable and fair under the history of the case and a valid exercise of the debtor's business judgment.[101] Interestingly, the court had received approximately 700 *ex parte* letters from employees of the debtor. All but three of the letters objected to the success bonus for management.

Since *Interco* and *America West* were decided, executive salaries have made front page news and have come under increasing scrutiny both in and out of bankruptcy. Investors and creditors alike are challenging the rich compensation packages provided to executives who are viewed to be underperforming. The situation is exacerbated when a debtor seeks to enhance compensation to executives whom creditors believe "got us into this mess in the first place." As a practical matter, a debtor is well advised to proceed with special arrangements for its executives and other employees only after consultation with affected creditors and other constituencies in the bankruptcy case. The responses to the debtor's efforts will be driven by how the employees are perceived. We are familiar with several unreported examples of compensation packages that were abandoned after the vociferous objections of creditors surfaced.

Even if creditors support retention plans, there are other practical considerations that must be taken into account. The experience of *Pegasus Gold Corp.* is illustrative.[102] *Pegasus* proposed a severance and retention plan for its key employees. Notwithstanding that the proposal was supported by its largest creditor, the media, politicians, rank-and-file employees, and other parties strenuously opposed it. One media source that reviewed the company's plan touted the headline, "[M]ore than the company is bankrupt in this deal."[103] The U.S. trustee joined in the objection on the grounds that the retention bonuses were not performance based. The package was ultimately approved, but only after *Pegasus* decreased the total amount of the package and tied the awards to performance goals. Whether the inclusion of these requirements would have prevented the original uproar is impossible to determine. Without the changes, the plan might have still passed the business judgment standard. However, the *Pegasus* experience illustrates the importance of touching base with not only creditor constituents, but other interested parties before seeking to motivate management or other employees.

ENFORCEMENT OF COVENANTS NOT TO COMPETE IN BANKRUPTCY

Covenants not to compete are often used to restrict an individual's ability to terminate employment with one company and thereafter work for a competitor. As a general rule, reasonable covenants not to compete will be enforced by the courts through the issuance of injunctions or other specific remedies designed to prevent the offending conduct. As bankruptcy has lost its stigma, employees seeking to avoid restrictive covenants have opted into bankruptcy in an effort to reject what they argue are executory contracts not to compete.[104] Thus, while some courts wrestle with the issues raised by thousands of retirees who may not see their benefits or union contracts that may be disavowed in chapter 11, other courts are setting precedent with respect to the trials and tribulations of actresses seeking to reject contracts on soap operas in order to be free to accept more lucrative contracts performing on the "A Team."[105]

While the treatment of covenants not to compete in bankruptcy has been described by one author as "at best a tricky, and at worst an incoherent business," there are certain key principles that have emerged.[106] However, even these principles have yet to be applied on a consistent basis. Section 365 is the focal point against which the treatment of covenants not to compete is most often visited. Bankruptcy courts have come to differing conclusions as to whether noncompetition covenants can be avoided by debtors during and after bankruptcy. Courts that hold that rejected noncompetition covenants do not survive bankruptcy generally do so on the basis that, under Section 365, a contract must be assumed or rejected in its entirety. If a contract is rejected, then all of its elements, including any element preventing competition, are eliminated. Other courts either find that noncompetition covenants are not executory, or that rejection under the Code affects only monetary rights, or, more technically, that the nondebtor's equitable rights to enjoin competition do not constitute a claim that is dischargable in bankruptcy.

As the growing body of literature in this area makes clear,[107] there is much that can be said with respect to the analysis attendant to whether a noncompete agreement can be rejected in bankruptcy. In any event, unless the bankruptcy of the covenantor can be ruled out, the beneficiary of the covenant would be well advised to take the possible risk of rejection in bankruptcy into account when bargaining with respect to the covenant. The employer's best argument is that, in a truly well-constructed and necessary covenant not to compete, money damages are wholly inadequate, and therefore, no claim that is dischargable in bankruptcy exists. Subject to technical arguments, which are well beyond the scope of this chapter, it has become all too convenient for parties seeking to escape burdensome noncompete contracts to avail themselves of the benefits of Section 365, which clearly were intended for other purposes.

NOTES

1. *See* 11 U.S.C.A. § 1113 (West 1993).
2. *NLRB* v. *Bildisco & Bildisco*, 465 U.S. 513 (1984).
3. *See* 29 U.S.C.A. § 158(d) (West Supp. 1998).
4. *See* Daniel Keating, The Continuing Puzzle of Collective Bargaining Agreements in Bankruptcy, 35 W. & Mary L. Rev. 503, 508 (1994).
5. *See id.*
6. *See Bildisco* at 523–524.
7. *See id.* at 524–526.
8. *See id.* at 525–526.
9. *Id.* at 519.
10. *Id.* at 526.
11. *See id.* at 526.
12. *See id.* at 532.
13. *See* 11 U.S.C.A. § 1113(c)(3).
14. *See id.* § 1113(b)(1)(A).
15. *See id.* 1113(b)(1)(B).
16. *See id.*§ 1113(b)(2).
17. *See id.*§ 1113(c)(2).
18. *See id.*§ 1113(b)(1)(A).
19. *See id.*§ 1113(f).
20. *See id.*§ 1113(b)(1).
21. *See id.*§ 1113(d)(1).
22. *See id.*§ 1113(e).
23. *Id.*
24. *Id.*
25. *In re American Provision Co.*, 44 B.R. 907, 909 (Bankr. D. Minn. 1984).
26. *See* 11 U.S.C.A. § 1113(d)(3).
27. *See, e.g.*, Christopher D. Cameron, *How "Necessary" Became the Mother of Rejection: An Empirical Look at the Fate of Collective Bargaining Agreements on the Tenth Anniversary of Bankruptcy Code Section 1113*, 34 Santa Clara L. Rev. 841, 847 (1994); Anne J. McClain, *Bankruptcy Code Section 1113 and the Simple Rejection of Collective Bargaining Agreements: Labor Loses Again,* 80 Geo. L. J. 191 (1991).
28. *See Wheeling-Pittsburgh Steel* v. *United Steelworkers,* 791 F.2d 1074 (3d. Cir. 1986).
29. *See Truck Driver's Local 807* v. *Carey Transp., Inc.*, 816 F.2d 82 (2d Cir. 1987).

30.   *See Carey supra* note 29, at 89.

31.   *See* Daniel Keating, *The Continuing Puzzle of Collective Bargaining Agreements in Bankruptcy*, 35 W. & Mary L. Rev. 503, 514 (1994).

32.   *See* Daniel Keating, *The Continuing Puzzle of Collective Bargaining Agreements in Bankruptcy*, 35 W. & Mary L. Rev. 503, 515 (1994).

33.   Christopher D. Cameron, *supra* note 27, at 841.

34.   *See id.* at 847.

35.   *Id.*

36.   *In re K & B Mounting*, 50 B.R. 460 (Bankr. N.D. Ind. 1985).

37.   *In re Blue Diamond Coal Company*, 147 B.R. 720 (Bankr. E.D. Tenn. 1992), *aff'd*, 160 B.R. 574 (E.D. Tenn. 1993).

38.   *See* 11 U.S.C.A. § 365 (West Supp. 1998).

39.   *See* 11 U.S.C.A. § 502(g) (West 1993).

40.   *Blue Diamond, supra* note 37, 160 B.R. at 576.

41.   *See, e.g.,* Michael St. Patrick Baxter, *Is There a Claim for Damages From the Rejection of a Collective-Bargaining Agreement Under Section 1113 of the Bankruptcy Code?*, 12 Bankr. Dev. J. 703, 717 (1996).

42.   Several cases have strongly implied that a damage claim would arise from rejection under § 1113, but no express rulings to this effect have issued. *See, e.g., Adventure Resources, Inc.* v. *Holland*, 137 F.3d 786, 1998 U.S. App. LEXIS 3880, *30 n. 17 (4th Cir. 1998) ("If the contract is instead rejected, the resulting damages (including any prepetition breach) constitute general, unsecured claims against the estate.").

43.   *See, e.g.*, Michael St. Patrick Baxter, *supra* note 41, at 703, 732–733.

44.   *See* 11 U.S.C.A. § 1113(f).

45.   *See Adventure Resources, Inc.* 1998 U.S. App. LEXIS 3880, *21–23; *In re Ionosphere Clubs, Inc.*, 22 F.3d 403, 408 (2d. Cir. 1994); *In re Roth American, Inc.*, 975 F.2d 949, 956 (3d Cir. 1992); *In re Unimet Corp.*, 842 F.2d 879, 884 (6th Cir. 1988).

46.   The use of the term *superpriority* by these courts and in the attendant commentary is somewhat misleading, as it seems to suggest something greater than administrative expense priority.

47.   *See Adventure Resources, Inc., supra* note 45 at *29–31.

48.   *Id.*

49.   *See Bildisco supra* note 2, at 534.

50.   This right is possibly limited by § 362, the automatic stay. If the union sought to use the strike as leverage to recover prepetition claims rather than better working conditions, the automatic stay may apply. *See* Daniel Keating, *supra* note 31, at 503, 523.

51.   *See* 11 U.S.C.A. § 1114 (West 1993).

52.   *See* Daniel Keating, Good Intention, Bad Economics: Retiree Insurance Benefits in Bankruptcy, 43 Vand. L. Rev. 161, 162 (1990) (stating that Congress was "prompted by tragic stories of LTV retirees and their spouses who were forced to postpone critical medical treatment" enacted legislation that would eventually be codified as § 1114).

53.   *See* 11 U.S.C.A. § 1114.

54.   *See* 11 U.S.C.A. § 1114(e)(1).

55.   *See id.* § 1114(a).

56.   *See id.* § 1114(l).

57.   Pension plans, ERISA, and the PBGC have received extensive treatment elsewhere. *See, e.g.*, Daniel Keating, Chapter 11's New Ten-Ton Monster: The PBGC and Bankruptcy, 77 Minn. L. Rev. 803 (1993); John F. Horstmann III and S. Fain Hackney, Other Considerations in Dealing with a Troubled Company, Workouts & Turnarounds 302, 321–327 (Dominic DiNapoli et al., eds., 1991).

58. *See In re Chateaugay Corp.*, 945 F.2d 1205 (2d Cir. 1991).

59. *See In re Doskocil Companies Inc.*, 130 Bankr. 870 (Bankr. D. Kan. 1991). *See also In re Ames Department Stores, Inc.*, 76 F. 3d 66 (2d Cir. 1996).

60. *See In re Ionosphere Clubs, Inc.*, 134 B.R. 515 (Bankr. S.D. N.Y. 1991). See also *In re Garfinckels, Inc.*, 124 B.R. 3 (Bankr. D.C. 1991).

61. *In re Eastern Airlines*, case nos. 89B 10448 (BRL) and 89B 10449 (BRL).

62. *See In re Ionosphere Clubs, Inc. supra* note 60.

63. *Id.* at 522–523.

64. *Id.* at 523.

65. *Id.* at 524.

66. *See* 11 U.S.C.A. § 1114(d).

67. *Id.*

68. *See* § 11 U.S.C.A. § 1114(c)(1).

69. *See id.* § 1114(c)(1)(A).

70. *See id.* 1114(c)(1)(B).

71. *Id.* § 1114(e).

72. *See id.* § 1114(f)(1)(A).

73. *See id.*

74. *See id.* § 1114(e)(1)(A).

75. *See id.* § 1114(g).

76. *See id,* § 1114(k)(1).

77. *See id.* § 1114(k)(2).

78. See *supra* notes 25–27 and accompanying text.

79. *See* 11 U.S.C.A. § 1113(e).

80. *Id.* § 1114(h)(1).

81. *See id.* § 1114(h)(3).

82. *See* 11 U.S.C. 1114(e)(2).

83. *See* Daniel Keating, Bankruptcy Code § 1114: Congress' Empty Response to the Retiree Plight, 67 Am. Bankr. L. J. 17 (1993).

84. 11 U.S.C.A § 1114(f)

85. *See* 11 U.S.C.A. § 1129(a)(13) (West 1993).

86. *See id.*

87. *Id.* 1129(a)(11).

88. 29 U.S.C.A. § 2101 et seq. (West Supp. 1998).

89. *See, e.g.*, John F. Horstmann III & S. Fain Hackney, *supra* note 57.

90. *Id.* at 322.

91. *Id.*

92. *Id.*

93. *Id.*

94. See *In re Cargo* 138 Bankr. 923, 926 (Bankr. N.D. Iowa 1992).

95. *See id.* at 927.

96. *Id.* at 928.

97. *In re Hanlin Group*, 176 Bankr. 329 (Bankr. N.J. 1995).

98. *Id.* at 334.

99. *See id.*

100. *In re America West Airlines, Inc.*, 171 B.R. 674 (D. Ariz. 1994); *In re Interco, Inc.*, 128 B.R. 229 (Bankr. E.D. Mo. 1991).

101.   *See In re America West Airlines, Inc. supra* note 99, at 677.

102.   *See In re Pegasus Gold Corp.*, BK-N-98-30088, (Bankr. D. Nev. 1998).

103.   *See* Jim Fisher, More Than the Company Is Bankrupt in This Deal, Lewiston Morning Tribune, May 2, 1998, at 10A.

104.   *See In re Carrere*, 64 B.R. 156 (Bankr. C.D. Cal. 1986).

105.   *Id.*

106.   Jeffrey C. Sharer, Comment, Noncompetition Agreements in Bankruptcy: Covenants (Maybe) Not to Compete, 62 U. Chi. L. Rev. 1549 (1995).

107.   *See id.*; Jonathan H. Moss, Claim and Opinion: Has Bankruptcy Forgotten the Restrictive Covenant? A Disturbing Trend for Franchise Systems, 10 Bankr. Dev. J. 237 (1994).

17

Financial Aspects of Bankruptcy Disputes

Harvey R. Kelly and Daniel V. Dooley

PricewaterhouseCoopers LLP

INTRODUCTION

Disputes are an inevitability in today's complex business environment. Nowhere is this more evident than during a bankruptcy proceeding. The bankruptcy process often results in controversial substantial financial losses to debtors, shareholders, and creditors. In an attempt to ensure that the bankruptcy process equitably considers the interests of parties, the United States Bankruptcy Code, Title 11, United States Code, and the Federal Rules of Bankruptcy Procedure (Bankruptcy Rules) provide a framework for resolution of disputes that may arise during a bankruptcy proceeding. Bankruptcy litigation procedurally falls into two main categories: (1) adversary proceedings, which are initiated by the filing of a complaint; and (2) contested matters, which begin with the filing of a motion.

Part VII of the Bankruptcy Rules defines disputes considered to be adversary proceedings and establishes rules related to the proceedings. The breadth of disputes that can arise in bankruptcy is evident by the definition of *adversary proceeding* which includes proceedings[1]:

- To recover money or property
- To determine the validity, priority, or extent of a lien or other interest in property
- To obtain approval for the sale of both the interest of the estate and of a co-owner in property
- To object to or revoke a discharge
- To revoke an order of confirmation of a chapter 11, 12, or 13 plan of reorganization
- To determine the dischargeability of a debt

- To obtain an injunction or other equitable relief
- To subordinate any allowed claim or interest, except when subordination is provided in a chapter 9, 11, 12, or 13 plan of reorganization
- To obtain a declaratory judgment relating to any of the foregoing
- To determine a claim or cause of action removed pursuant to 28 U.S.C. Section 1452.[2]

In addition to adversary proceedings covered by Part VII of the Bankruptcy Rules, other disputes, referred to as *contested matters*, arise in which at least two opposing parties seek relief. The types of potential contested matters are numerous. Contested matters that arise with some frequency in bankruptcy cases include objections to confirmation of a plan of reorganization; objections to a claim; objections to the use of credit; objections to a disclosure statement; relief from automatic stay; use of cash collateral; avoidance of a lien; assumption, rejection, or assignment of executory contracts; objections to a compromise or settlement proposed by a trustee; and objections to the proposed use, sale, or lease of property of the estate.[3]

A critical element to resolving many of the disputes that arise in a bankruptcy case involves fact finding with respect to disputed financial issues. Consequently, the outcome of such disputes often revolves around the resolution of financial disputes.

A complete analysis of the applicable law and all disputed financial issues arising in bankruptcy cases is beyond the scope of this chapter. Rather, we have selected some of the more prevalent bankruptcy proceeding disputes involving financial issues. In the next section of this chapter, we provide a general overview of selected provisions of the Bankruptcy Code and the related disputes that can arise. Later in the chapter we will explore litigation consulting and forensic accounting considerations relevant to such financial issues.

SELECTED BANKRUPTCY DISPUTES INVOLVING FINANCIAL ISSUES

Preferences and Fraudulent Conveyances

Equitable treatment of similarly situated creditors and other parties-in-interest represents a fundamental principle underlying the Bankruptcy Code. Ensuring equitable treatment often involves analyzing the debtor's transactions shortly prior to the filing for bankruptcy protection to ensure that value was not depleted from the debtor's estate in favor of one party at the expense of another. As one author described:

> A cornerstone of the bankruptcy structure is the principle that equal treatment for those similarly situated must be achieved. It would be highly inequitable to disregard what transpires prior to the filing of the bankruptcy petition; to do so would encourage a race among creditors, engender favoritism by the debtor, and result in inequality of distribution.[4]

The Bankruptcy Code includes Sections 547 and 548 dealing with preferential transfers (i.e., preferences) and fraudulent transfers and obligations (i.e., fraudulent conveyances). In brief, preferences and fraudulent conveyances represent transactions that result in value of the debtor's estate being transferred to one party to the detriment of another. The Code provides that demonstrable preferences and fraudulent conveyances are avoidable (i.e., reversible). For example, prior payments or transfers of money, property, or other assets[5] made by the debtor adjudicated to be preferences or fraudulent conveyances may be recovered by the estate for use in settling claims of all creditors in accordance with the plan of reorganization.

Allegations with respect to preferences and fraudulent transfers often involve major transactions. Parties can be required by the court to repay large sums of money to a bankrupt estate so that the funds can benefit other parties. Not surprisingly, therefore, allegations that transactions constitute preferential or fraudulent transfers are often vigorously disputed.

Preferences.   Preferences represent prepetition transfers by a debtor that result in one or more creditors' obtaining economic benefit at the expense of other creditors. The Bankruptcy Code establishes five required elements for a transfer of a debtor's property to be considered an avoidable preference. Unlike fraudulent conveyances, discussed below, intentional or constructive fraud is not a required element of a preference. To avoid a preferential transfer, it must be demonstrated that the transfer was:

- To or for the benefit of a creditor
- For or on account of an antecedent debt owed by the debtor before such transfer was made
- Made while the debtor was insolvent
- Made within 90 days before the date of the bankruptcy petition (or within one year if the creditor was an insider)
- A transaction that enabled the creditor to receive more than it would receive if: (1) the case were a chapter 7 liquidation case; (2) the transfer had not been made; and (3) the creditor received payment for such debt pursuant to the rules of a chapter 7 proceeding.[6]

It should be noted that other circumstances may result in the transfer's not being avoidable. The Bankruptcy Code provides that certain transfers meeting the above criteria are not avoidable.[7] The avoidance exceptions provided for in the Code primarily attempt to consider other factors relevant to equitable treatment of creditors (e.g., transfer resulted in new value to the debtor, ordinary course of business transfers, etc.).

Litigation involving avoidance of preferences is an adversary proceeding. As will be discussed more fully later in this chapter, forensic accounting analysis plays a vital role in identifying and proving whether the transactions represented avoidable transfers. Forensic accountants play an important role in, among other matters: (1) identifying prepetition transactions that represent possible preferential transfers; (2) evaluating whether the debtor was insolvent; and (3) analyzing the creditor's hypothetical recovery in a chapter 7 liquidation scenario.

Fraudulent Conveyances.   The bankruptcy laws also provide protection to debtors and creditors by allowing for avoidance of fraudulent transfers. Under the Bankruptcy Code, a transfer can be deemed to be either actual or constructive fraud. In order to establish that a transfer constituted actual fraud under the Code, one must establish that a transfer of an interest of the debtor in property occurred within one year before the date of the filing of the petition and that the debtor:

> . . . made such transfer or incurred such obligation with actual intent to hinder, delay, or defraud any entity to which the debtor was or became, on or after the date that such transfer was made or such obligation was incurred, indebted.[8]

Thus, avoidance of a fraudulent conveyance under the actual fraud provisions of the Code requires one to establish parties' intent, which can frequently be difficult to prove. Fraudulent conveyance actions are more commonly brought based on a constructive fraud theory. In order to avoid a fraudulent conveyance under the constructive fraud provisions of the Bankruptcy Code,[9] one must establish, in an adversary proceeding, that in connection with such transfer the debtor:

- Received less than a reasonably equivalent value in exchange for such transfer or obligation; and
- (a) was insolvent on the date that such transfer was made or such obligation was incurred, or became insolvent as a result of such transfer or obligation;
- (b) was engaged in business or a transaction, or was about to engage in business or a transaction, for which any property remaining with the debtor was an unreasonably small capital; or
- (c) intended to incur, or believed that the debtor would incur, debts that would be beyond the debtor's ability to pay as such debts matured.[10]

Analysis of potential fraudulent conveyances may be undertaken by, *inter alia*: a trustee, receiver, examiner,[11] official committee(s), or creditor(s). Such analysis enables one to: (1) identify transactions potentially avoidable; (2) assess whether the debtor received less than reasonably equivalent value; (3) determine whether, and at what point, the debtor became insolvent; (4) evaluate whether the debtor had unreasonably small capital; and (5) address the debtor's ability to pay debts as they became due. A more detailed review of related forensic accounting analysis appears later in this chapter.

Use of Cash Collateral and Debtor-in-Possession Financing

In order to conduct their business, debtors often seek to use cash collateral[12] in daily operations. The Code requires debtors to gain creditor or court approval prior to using cash collateral.[13] The Code further requires that the affected creditor is entitled to "adequate protection" when a court authorizes the use of cash collateral.[14] A debtor is unlikely to get unconditional approval of a creditor to use cash collateral on which the creditor has a lien. However, the ability to use cash collateral generally is crucial to the debtor's efforts to conduct daily business. This tension between debtors' needs to use as much cash collateral as possible and creditors' interests in allowing debtors as little cash collateral as possible (or its use with the most adequate protection possible) sets the stage for disputes. Consequently, court intervention is often required to resolve such disputes between the debtor and the affected creditor.

Similarly, companies filing for protection under chapter 11 of the Bankruptcy Code typically seek to obtain new credit to operate while in bankruptcy. Although estates are authorized by the Code to obtain unsecured credit,[15] a reorganizing debtor often requires credit beyond that which it can obtain on an unsecured basis, even though the Code allows the unsecured creditor's claim for such new credit to be treated as an "administrative priority claim." Consequently, the Code provides a mechanism to allow debtors to obtain additional secured credit,[16] generally referred to as debtor-in-possession (DIP) financing. In certain instances, debtors seek to obtain DIP financing which will be secured by a senior or equal lien on property of the estate that is already subject to a lien. The Code allows for such DIP financing only if:

- The debtor is unable to obtain such credit otherwise
- There is "adequate protection" of the interest of the holder of the lien on the property of the estate on which such senior or equal lien is proposed to be granted.[17]

The consequence of such secured DIP financing to other creditors is subordination or dilution of their claims, notwithstanding the DIP lender's infusion of new money into the estate. Thus, creditors' acquiescence or acceptance of such consequences may turn on the terms of adequate security (e.g., is the DIP lender being oversecured) or on the use of the new money. Put another way, creditors must evaluate whether DIP financing will be throwing good money after bad, after which creditors find themselves worse off than before.

Litigation over cash collateral issues represent contested matters involving a debtor's motion for authority to use cash collateral or a creditor's motion to prevent or otherwise restrict its use. A common point of dispute between the existing creditor (holding the lien) and the debtor seeking to use a creditor's security either through use of cash collateral or incurrence of DIP financing with additional liens revolves around the requirement that the lienholder be adequately protected. Resolution of these disputes involves complex financial analysis, since the concept of adequate protection hinges on projections as to future cash flows of the debtor and the value of the debtor's assets. This in turn implicates projection of the future financial condition of the estate.

Use of cash collateral and DIP financing issues can be hotly contested and have far-reaching consequences. Cash and access to credit are like oxygen to estates;

and debtors will fight for their lives if their air supply is threatened. In the absence of an ability to use cash collateral and/or obtain DIP financing, a chapter 11 debtor may be forced to convert the case to a chapter 7 liquidation proceeding. Complicating this situation is the fact that debtors' needs to use cash collateral or access DIP financing come early in the bankruptcy process—when creditor mistrust of debtors can be high, when the path to reorganization is long, and when the future is unclear. Clarity of decisions about use of cash collateral and DIP financing requires the ability to develop and understand prospective financial information. Such prospective financial information lies at the heart of disputes in this area.

Conversion to Chapter 7

The conversion of a chapter 11 reorganization case to a chapter 7 liquidation case can occur as the result of a debtor's voluntary conversion or as the result of a court ruling upon the request of a party-in-interest or the U.S. trustee or bankruptcy administrator. The Bankruptcy Code delineates various bases upon which a court can convert a case to a chapter 7 liquidation.[18] One such basis for conversion is "continuing loss to or diminution of the estate and absence of a reasonable likelihood of rehabilitation."[19]

Not surprisingly, contested matter motions to convert cases from a reorganization to a liquidation are frequently disputed, especially when the debtor prefers to reorganize. In particular, parties typically express widely disparate views on the "reasonable likelihood of a rehabilitation." The issue often involves evaluating the question as to whether creditors' interests are better served by liquidating the estate's assets or by taking a chance on the future. Disputes in this area center most often on prospective financial information that forecasts future economic events. Fully addressing this issue requires projecting and interpreting the debtor's future operations and cash flows.

Claims

A bankruptcy case must consider and dispose of all claims against the debtor's estate. The Bankruptcy Code defines claim as: (1) a right to payment whether such right is reduced to judgment, liquidated, unliquidated, fixed, contingent, matured, unmatured, disputed, undisputed, legal, equitable, secured, or unsecured; or (2) a right to an equitable remedy for breach of performance if such breach gives rise to a right to payment, whether such right to an equitable remedy is reduced to judgment, fixed, contingent, matured, unmatured, disputed, undisputed, secured, or unsecured.[20]

Thus, the Code leaves no doubt that all types of contingent or unliquidated claims must be dealt with in the bankruptcy process. Indeed, the existence of contingent and unliquidated claims has caused debtors to resort to filing for protection under the Bankruptcy Code. Nowhere is this more true than in debtors subject to mass tort claims. Widely publicized bankruptcy cases involving mass tort claims related to product liability issues with asbestos, breast implants, medical devices, and so forth, evidence the important role the bankruptcy process plays in resolving such claims. The National Bankruptcy Review Commission, established by Congress to review the U.S. bankruptcy system, acknowledged the importance and complexity of dealing with such matters in the bankruptcy laws:

> Massive tort or contract liabilities can have an enormous impact on otherwise viable enterprises that are vital to the American economy ... The bankruptcy system offers a structured system to manage multiple liabilities and has provided a forum for companies with massive liabilities to attempt to do so ... A company may not be able to preserve its going concern value and its work force if it is not able to deal collectively and definitively with all actions arising out of a certain activity.[21]

Mass tort claims are necessarily complex and involve issues such as the unique circumstances of the alleged tortious act, cognizability of future claims, projections that may advance far into the future, and estimates of damages, which may depend on a number of complex exogenous factors.

Mass tort claims are certainly not the only claims that are subject to dispute. Examples of other common disputed contingent claims include: claims asserted in other types of litigation proceedings; federal, state, and local government tax claims; pension claims (including those of the Pension Benefit Guaranty Corporation); and environmental cleanup claims.

Contingent claims are particularly contentious and can have a major impact on a bankruptcy case. As one author noted:

> In [some] cases, the magnitude or priority of disputed claims is so large that the uncertainty retards the entire plan negotiation process. In these cases, the disputed claims must be resolved for the case to proceed....Claims filed with the bankruptcy court, in the absence of an estimation procedure are litigated as fiercely as all other civil claims brought in the federal courts.[22]

Some claims are not fixed in dollar amount and, by their nature, may not be fixed for a lengthy period of time. Therefore, the Code requires the court to estimate, for purpose of allowance of claims, any contingent or unliquidated claim, the fixing or liquidation of which would unduly delay the administration of the case.[23] This estimation process can significantly influence particular parties' rights and recoveries in a bankruptcy case, and therefore such estimates are frequently the subject of much dispute.

Plan Confirmation

The ultimate objective of a chapter 11 bankruptcy case is the development and confirmation of a plan of reorganization. There are a number of requirements that a plan must meet in order to be approved by the court.[24] Two prerequisites for plan confirmation that often result in contested matter disputes involving financial issues are plan feasibility and the "best interests" test.

A party-in-interest can object to a debtor's plan of reorganization on the grounds that the plan fails the feasibility test. The feasibility test refers to the Bankruptcy Code's requirement that confirmation of the plan of reorganization is not likely to be followed by the liquidation, or the need for further financial reorganization of the debtor or any successor to the debtor under the plan, unless such liquidation or reorganization is proposed in the plan.[25] Disputes over feasibility typically center on differing financial projections with respect to the debtor's future cash flows if the plan is confirmed. Factors considered in evaluating the issue of feasibility include: (1) adequacy of the reorganized debtor's capital; (2) the earning capacity of the reorganized debtor; (3) general economic conditions; and (4) the probability of management's continuation.[26]

In addition to the requirement for plan feasibility, to be confirmable a plan must be in the best interests of the creditors. The best interests test refers to meeting the following requirement of the Bankruptcy Code with respect to each holder of a claim or interest in an impaired class of claims or interests: (1) each holder must have accepted the plan; or (2) each holder will receive or retain under the plan on account of such claim or interest property of a value, as of the effective date of the plan, that is not less than the amount that such holder would receive or retain if the debtor were liquidated under chapter 7 of the Code on the confirmation date.[27]

The later criteria implicates comparisons of two projected results: what a claim holder will get under the plan of reorganization; and what a claimholder would get under a hypothetical liquidation.

Determinations of whether a plan meets the best interests test typically involve fairly complex financial valuations of returns to creditors under both a going-concern (as a reorganized debtor) and liquidation basis, turning upon competing views of an estate's prospective financial condition and financial capacity to fulfill the promises made under its plan of reorganization.

If proposed plans called for payments to creditors only in cash, there would be no questions concerning what a claimholder might get under a plan. Unfortunately, few plans so propose. Instead, most plans propose repayments over time, payments in new debt, or exchanges of debt for new equity. These "payments" may be subject to much uncertainty (and dispute) surrounding the future of an estate.

LITIGATION CONSULTING AND
FORENSIC ACCOUNTING IN BANKRUPTCY

Insolvency

As described earlier in this chapter, insolvency is requisite to a claim of preference under Section 547 of the Bankruptcy Code and fraudulent conveyance under Section 548 of the Code as well as under the Uniform Fradulent Transfer Act (UFTA). The definition of insolvency is the starting point for its proof; it is that the assets of an entity are exceeded by the liabilities, at a fair valuation. Added to the basic definition are two other conditions—that the subject conveyance itself leaves the entity with an unreasonably small capital (i.e., inadequate working capital) or that the entity was operating near bankruptcy. These conditions are not necessary, but may be sufficient to establish insolvency. Establishing the date of insolvency is an essential element to resolving whether potential preferences and fraudulent conveyances are avoidable under Section 548 of the Code.[28]

Proving that an entity's assets are exceeded by its liabilities at a fair valuation is a step-by-step process in 12 parts, as follows:

1. Establish an *ambit of insolvency*, usually within one year of the bankruptcy filing date.[29]
2. Identify any questionable transactions falling within the ambit.[30]
3. Obtain a statement of financial condition (i.e., balance sheet) of the entity as of the date(s) of the identified transactions, or at the closest previous reporting date (e.g., quarter- or year-end).
4. Adjust the balance sheet for any *intervening transactions*, between the reporting date and the date(s) of the subject transactions.
5. Select the basis of valuation—usually either *going concern or quitting concern*—depending on the circumstances and assumed financial condition of the entity.
6. Project *prospective financial information* (e.g., forward-looking results of operations or cash flows) for the entity, and as appropriate to the assets or liabilities to be valued, to be used in determining the *business enterprise value* of the entity and the net *present value* of any specific assets.
7. Determine appropriate *discount rate(s)*, based on analysis of comparable entities, asset yields, debt costs, or capital costs.
8. Assign to each asset and liability element (e.g., asset classification), or to specific asset balance(s) where appropriate, a valuation method.
9. Obtain appropriate market value (i.e., fair market value) information, such as comparable sales data, asset impairment statistics, and costs of disposition.
10. Estimate the entity's assets, at their fair value, using the applicable valuation methods (e.g., market value, net present value, etc.).
11. Determine the value of the entity's liabilities, adjusting, as appropriate, certain obligations, such as leases, deferred revenue, and deferred tax liabilities.
12. Determine the overall business enterprise value of the entity.

This 12-step program produces two complementary measures of insolvency (or solvency): the *balance sheet test* and a *business enterprise valuation* (BEV); the latter is used as a proof of the former. The results of the two valuations should be comparable and consistent. Where both valuations demonstrate insolvency, there should be sufficient competent evidence to establish the condition. Where both valuations demonstrate solvency, the inapposite condition is supported by the evidence. Where one test demonstrates solvency and the other test demonstrates insolvency, there may be no clearly dispositive conclusion. In this case, additional evidence may need to be considered. Such additional evidence may consist of a determination of whether the level of working capital was reasonable for the entity, or whether there were other indicia of probable bankruptcy (e.g., inability to pay upcoming debts, illiquidity, material contingencies).

Insolvency Ambit.   For purposes of this writing, the time span of the ambit of insolvency is assumed to be one year; depending on applicable state law and the particular circumstances of the entity, this period may be longer. Usually, the time span is marked off from the date of bankruptcy filing, at which date the entity is presumed to be insolvent,[31] to the shorter of one year back or the date(s) of the subject transactions in question. Unless such transactions fall on a month-, quarter-, or year-end, an entity's books typically will not have been closed, and compilation of a balance sheet as of intraperiod dates will be difficult, if not impossible. Therefore, the insolvency test date usually is set at the closest period end prior to the subject transaction(s). Under the concept of *retrojection*, if insolvency is established as of this prior date, then an entity is presumed to be insolvent at all intervening dates up to the bankruptcy filing date. Practically, the most reliable (and accessible) period-end financial information will be found at quarter- or year-ends.

An *events line* (or timeline) should be established for at least the 12 months preceding the selected insolvency test date, and from that date to the date of bankruptcy filing. An investigation should be made of the financial and economic events, results of operations, financial transactions, and exogenous factors affecting the entity during this period. Key events should be established on the events line for further analysis in connection with the insolvency tests. In addition, financial statements of the entity should be obtained, if available, for at least the three years preceding the bankruptcy filing date.[32]

Operating statistics (e.g., sales or revenue, gross margins, earnings and profits (or losses), net working capital, net worth) then should be superimposed on the events line. The result should be a graphic depiction of the entity's financial condition, critical financial and economic events and transactions, and financial capacity during the time leading up to its bankruptcy filing. Picture hospital readouts like electroencephalograms and electrocardiograms. The purpose is similar, namely, to depict the financial health and business life-threatening events of the entity during this critical time period.

Financial Accounting Information for Insolvency Analysis.   A balance sheet test[33] requires, as its starting point, a balance sheet! This may seem evident, but *what kind* of balance sheet? Year-end, quarter-end, audited, unaudited, historical cost-basis, fair value? Understanding the differences, characteristics, and limitations of these very different financial statements is essential to conducting a proper balance sheet test.

All corporations registered with the Securities and Exchange Commission (SEC) are required to report annual results of operations on Form 10-K and quarterly results of operations on Form 10-Q. The annual results of operations for such corporations include four basic financial statements: balance sheet, statement of operations (or profit and loss), statement of cash flows, and statement of changes in equity and retained earning. These basic financial statements, along with notes thereto, constitute an entity's *financial statements*, and for SEC registrants, annual financial statements must be audited. Quarterly financial statements are presented in a more condensed form, and their footnotes may be more limited. Quarterly financial statements need not be (and usually are not) audited; however, they may be reviewed[34] by independent auditors.

Companies and other business entities (e.g., partnerships, joint ventures, sole proprietorships) not registered with the SEC may not need (and may not obtain) audited or reviewed financial statements. Financial statements for these entities may not conform, in every material respect, to generally accepted accounting principles (GAAP). For example, not all four of the basic financial statements may be prepared, or the notes to the financial statements may be less extensive or omitted entirely, or the statements may be prepared on the *cash basis* and omit accrued assets and liabilities (e.g., accounts receivable and accrued liabilities). In many circumstances, the only reliable financial statements may be those prepared as the entity's income tax return filings. Such financial information would be on a *tax basis* of accounting, which differs from both a cash basis and GAAP. However, companies and other entities not registered with the SEC also may obtain audits or reviews of their financial statements for other purposes, such as: obtaining bank loans or complying with loan covenants; complying with partnership articles, contractual terms, or supplier agreements; or complying with regulatory or legal requirements. Even if unaudited or unreviewed, financial statements may be compiled by independent accountants.[35] Financial statements that are not audited, reviewed, or compiled by independent auditors, still may comport with GAAP or another established basis of accounting in all material respects. However, the reliability and usefulness of such financial statements will not be attested to by independent auditors, and such statements' overall quality will depend solely on the management's internal accounting controls, accounting competence, objectivity, and integrity.

Financial statements prepared at interim periods (e.g., month- or quarter-end) may omit necessary accruals of assets or liabilities, and may need adjustments to be comparable to financial statements prepared at year-end. All financial statements require many estimates and the application of management judgment in measuring revenue, costs and expenses, earnings and profits, and the carrying value of assets and liabilities. Some of these estimates and judgments include: allowances for doubtful accounts receivable; allowances for customer returns; reserves for inventory impairments (associated with obsolete or slow moving goods, or to reflect write-down of goods to the lower-of-cost-or-market); impairment of long-lived assets[36]; or accruals of obligations in connection with commitments or contingencies, taxes, employee or postemployment benefits, retirement benefits, leases, and so on. All financial statements are subject to changes in estimates resulting from future information which may be more accurate than the information available at the date the financial statements are prepared. Some financial statements also may contain material errors or irregularities due to misapplication of GAAP, failure to consider or misuse of facts known or knowable at the reporting date, or arithmetic error. No matter what financial information is to be used for a balance sheet test, it should first be conformed to GAAP and adjusted to correct any accounting errors or irregularities. Why GAAP? The Bankruptcy Code does not specify an accounting basis, it merely requires a fair valuation of an entity's assets and liabilities. In fact, various bankruptcy case law take exception to GAAP as the arbiter of value.[37] However, as a starting point for the development of any fair valuation, GAAP is essential. By its very definition, GAAP is generally accepted—not only in the United States, but also throughout most developed countries and world economies. For companies registered with the SEC, GAAP is required by law.[38] GAAP reflects the fundamentals of bankruptcy in respect of the accrual of all assets and all liabilities of an entity (as opposed to cash basis, modified cash basis, or tax basis of accounting). GAAP is presumed to be the accounting method used in the ordinary course of business. Also, GAAP can represent a commonly agreed-upon point of reference from which to make all necessary fair valuation adjustments. GAAP reflects historical cost. Conversion from historical cost to fair value only requires adjustment, upward or downward, of GAAP accounting elements and balances, to reflect current fair value or fair market value. In fact, in everyday use, GAAP requires many of these market value adjustments, for going concerns, to accounts such as: accounts receivable, marketable securities, inventory, long-lived assets, accrued liabilities, commitments and contingencies, and long-term obligations. In today's state of GAAP for going concerns, most assets already should be adjusted *downward* to reflect fair value, market value, or net realizable value when these are less than historical cost or amortized historical cost. Likewise, for going concerns, most liabilities already should be stated at their fair value under GAAP. Some adjustments still will be needed—to refine valuation estimates, correct errors, and account for certain special situations, and to reflect *upward* valuations of assets, where current fair value or fair market value exceeds historical cost or amortized historical cost. Regardless, GAAP is the best place to begin the revaluation process.

Intervening Transactions: Between the Dates of the Selected Financial Information and the Balance Sheet Test.   Unless the closest reported financial information is as of the balance sheet test date, the balance sheet information used must be "rolled forward" (or "rolled back")[39] to the balance sheet test date. This process may require no adjustment, but it might require substantial adjustment to take into account material intervening transactions. The simplest examples of such transactions are purchases and sales of assets between the two dates. Other examples include: income or loss; changes in estimates for reserves and allowances; resolution of contingencies; repayments of debts, additional borrowings, or the incurring of other obligations; payment of dividends or other changes in capital; or any conveyance of assets from the entity. Ultimately, financial information used for the balance sheet test should reflect all assets owned by the entity and all liabilities owed by the entity at the test date, including a proper cutoff of all accruals such as sales and receivables, purchases and accounts payable, payroll and employee obligations, taxes, postemployment and retirement obligations, and other long-term obligations.

Basis of Valuation: Going Concern or Quitting Concern?   Unless there is persuasive evidence to the contrary, solvency analysis should assume a going-concern basis for valuing an entity.[40] A fair valuation of assets and liabilities assumes that value may be realized in the ordinary course. The ordinary course does not presume forced sale or fire sale of such assets. The valuation difference between going-concern and quitting-concern bases can be profound. On a going-concern basis, accounts receivable should be worth their net realizable cost, after allowance for doubtful accounts (i.e., uncollectible receivables) and ordinary costs of collection. On a quitting-concern basis, any sale of receivables to a third party (e.g., factor) must assume not only transaction costs, but also substantial discounting for third-party risk and to provide a profit to the buyer. Likewise, on a quitting-concern basis, long-lived assets should be worth their productive, in-use value, established by amortized replacement cost, or by a discounted cash flow method (or income approach) such as set forth in Statement of Financial Accounting Standards (SFAS) No. 121, "Impairment of Long-Lived Assets."[41] On a quitting-concern basis, assets such as plant may be worth no more than the underlying land value, *after* reduction for transaction costs, buyer's risk (e.g., environmental liabilities, real or potential), and forced sale discounting. Similarly, marketable securities intended to be held to maturity on a going-concern basis may be subjected to significant downward market adjustment, if assumed to be held for sale under a quitting-concern concept. Absent compelling evidence that liquidation was imminent or foreseeable, as of the balance sheet test date, going concern should be the assumed valuation basis.

Balance Sheet Test Valuation Methodologies and Practice.   The objective is a fair valuation, the paths to reach this objective will depend on the asset or liability being valued. The individual valuation methods may include face amount, estimated net realizable value, comparison to ready market values for comparable assets, estimated fair market value or replacement cost, income approach (or its variant, discounted cash flow analysis), and market transaction approach. Essentially, the balance sheet test is a form of net asset approach, a valuation technique in which the value of an entity is based on the value of its underlying assets and liabilities, including the value of any future claims against the entity. An approximation of the business enterprise value or fair market value of the equity can be calculated by subtracting the aggregate fair market value of the liabilities from the aggregate fair market value of the assets. Fair market value is defined as the price at which a property would change hands between a willing buyer and a willing seller, neither being under compulsion to act, and both having reasonable knowledge of relevant facts.[42] The following are various commonly occurring types of assets and liabilities, by accounting classification, with comment on applicable valuation method and practice.

Cash.   Cash is an asset comprising monies or monetary equivalents in the form of currency, balances in bank and other depository accounts, and investments in near-cash equivalents, such as certificates of deposit, money market certificates, and certain short-term government securities (e.g., treasury bills). Cash is fair valued at its face amount in U.S. dollars, or converted to U.S. dollars at the exchange rate in effect on the balance sheet test date for any foreign currency. In practice, a problem with the value of cash may be its ownership. Obviously, cash balances must be reduced for outstanding checks (and conversely increased for deposits in transit). But cash on an entity's books also may be the property of others. For example, cash accounts may include customer deposits, funds held in escrow, or accounts under joint custody.

Marketable Securities.   Marketable securities may be stocks, bonds, government securities, or more specialized financial instruments, such as derivatives. Most marketable securities have two values: current market value and nominal value. In the case of common stocks, the nominal value typically is not relevant; rather, the market value should represent fair value. However, in the case of bonds, government securities, convertible debentures, and certain preferred stock, the nominal value (i.e., the redemption value of the instrument) may be the fair value of the security. If a debtor is able to "hold to maturity" such securities, fair value may be the *higher* of market or adjusted nominal value.[43] If, on the other hand, marketable securities are "held for sale" or must be reclassified as held for sale, owing to a need to liquidate, then fair value may be current market value (i.e., marked to market.)

Accounts Receivable.   Accounts receivable refers to both trade accounts and notes receivable from customers arising from sales of goods and services. In the ordinary course, accounts receivable are reduced to cash, except for uncollectible accounts (i.e., bad debts, doubtful accounts, receivable charge-offs). Bad debts may occur because of customer bankruptcy or other inability to pay. Doubtful accounts constitute the aggregate of accounts for which the likelihood of some loss due to uncollectibility is deemed "probable" and the amount of such loss is "estimable."[44] Other adjustments to receivables may include charge-offs due to customer returns and allowances or because customers have taken discounts on payment. Under GAAP, net receivables—that is, the gross balance of receivables, less allowances for doubtful accounts, customer returns, and other credits—should equal net realizable value of such receivables. However, if in the ordinary course, the entity factors its receivables, then a factoring discount also may be appropriate to calculate net realizable value. For receivables expected to be repaid over periods longer than customary trade terms (e.g., one year), a discount for the time value of money may be appropriate.

Inventory.   Inventory is divided into three parts: raw materials, work-in-process, and finished goods. Raw materials are valued at the higher of replacement cost or allocated manufacturing value, unless the raw materials are deemed surplus, overstocked, or obsolete, in which case such raw materials may require valuation at current market. Work-in-process represents partially completed goods, which, if completed, is assumed sold in the ordinary course. Valuation of work-in-process starts with a determination of "market," just as for any "lower-of-cost-or-market" adjustment of finished goods. Next, the state of completion (based on input measures such as labor or materials or output measures, such as physical percentage complete) is estimated, and the cost of materials and labor required to reach completion is deducted, along with any profit thereon. The result is the fair value of work-in-process, assuming that such work will be completed and the goods sold at current market value exceeding estimated finished cost.[45] Finished goods traditionally are valued at "lower-of-cost-or-market." This convention does not reflect profit presumably recognized on sale, because the selling event has not yet occurred. If such profit is critical to the measurement of insolvency (or solvency), it may need to be taken into consideration.[46]

Prepaid and Other Deferred Current Assets.   These include payments in advance of the receipt of goods or services (e.g., utility deposits, prepaid rents, prepaid insurance premiums). For a going concern, such payments are assumed to be realizable in due course as the goods or services are received; hence, their value is cost. Exceptions to this valuation practice relate to certain deferred current assets for which accounting rules require that historical cost be recorded, but to which no separate market value obtains. One example is a premium paid on securities. If the securities are held to maturity, their value remains adjusted nominal value, which should account for the interest value inherent in any premium (or discount). If the securities are held for sale, then their market value governs, regardless of any premium paid (or their amortized cost). Another example is deferred costs, such as start-up costs or preoperating costs, or certain capitalized interest costs reflected as amortizable assets under GAAP, but representing no current or future separately identifiable fair value, fair market value, or realizable value.

Plant, Property, and Equipment.   Plant, property, and equipment comprises land, real estate held for development or sale or rent; plants and other manufacturing facilities; offices; warehouses and distribution facilities; machinery and equipment; furnishings and fixtures; certain other long-lived productive assets, such as mines, wells, pipelines, transportation assets (e.g., ships, aircraft, rolling stock, cars and trucks, rails and roadway), and property rights (e.g., mineral rights, water rights, grazing rights, landing "slots"); and assets under capital leases. In certain circumstances, property under operating lease may have inherent value due to favorable lease clauses (e.g., the right to sublease, where the market value of such sublease exceeds the underlying lease cost). Certain assets, such as oil or gas wells, mineral rights, mines, vessels, or aircraft may require specialized valuation approaches combining engineering, survey, and financial valuation techniques. However, the most common elements of *fixed assets* are plant, property, and equipment. Valuation approaches typically are: market comparable, income (or discounted cash flow), and replacement cost.

Market comparability may be established by reference to published resale

values for similar items, such as machinery and equipment, furnishings and fixtures, or even aircraft. Market values can be obtained by comparing the subject
property (e.g., commercial real estate, hotel, plant, office building, or land) to
similar properties recently sold, and developing a consensus value. Particularly
for plant and property, such valuations should be performed by, or in consultation with, professional appraisers and valuators.

For a going concern, the *income approach* should be performed to value all
productive plant, property, and equipment, as the alternative valuation to the
market comparable approach. By definition, the market comparable approach assumes that a property's highest and best use is established in a sales transaction,
which may be true for individual properties, real estate investments, and so forth.
However, productive assets operated in concert in a business enterprise may be
worth more together than sold apart. Certainly, the rational management decision
for a going concern is *not* to sell productive assets for market values lower than
their income approach value, left in place, assuming that such income approach
value is positive.

The income approach, or discounted cash flow analysis, entails calculating
the present value of future "distributable earnings," produced by the subject enterprise, properties, or individual assets. The theory is predicated on accepted financial and valuation practice that future results of operations can be forecast
within reason, and an appropriate rate of return can be determined. Under the income approach: (1) annual cash flows from the business, property or asset(s) are
estimated for a specific future period (e.g., five or ten years); (2) future cash
flows are reduced to their present value at an appropriate discount rate; (3) a
residual value as of the end of the projection period is computed, using an appropriate capitalization rate; (4) the residual value is reduced to its present value at
the selected discount rate; and, (5) the two present values are combined to derive
a fair value of the business, property, or asset(s). Cash flows may require adjustment, to arrive at distributable earnings, before discounting to present value.
Such adjustment may be required to produce cash flows that do not impair the
rate of growth (or decline) assumed in the projection model, and that do not impair (or overprovide) working capital necessary for the normal level of business
operation assumed in the projection model.

Discount and capitalization rates used in the income approach, or discounted
cash flow analysis, are subject to professional judgment, some reasonable degree
of acceptable variation for similar properties, and limitations relating to underlying data. The data used to derive such rates usually are derived from analysis of
investment yields for comparable businesses, properties, or asset(s). The quality
of such data will depend on (1) availability and sufficiency, (2) comparability,
and (3) reasonableness of interpretation. The projected cash flows modeled for
the income approach also are subject to professional judgment, degree of predictive accuracy of the forecast model, and reasonableness of underlying assumptions (e.g., rate of earnings growth or decline, inflation rate, gross margin, tax
rate). Absent strong evidence supporting any assumption(s) of significant operating changes, past performance (i.e., historical operating results and statistics)
should reconcile reasonably to estimated future performance.

Other Long-Term Assets.   Other long-term assets may include deferred charges, amortizable over more than one year, or identifiable intangible assets, such as intellectual property, or unidentified intangibles, such as *goodwill.* Deferred charges require analysis to determine whether such accounting assets represent any separate, realizable future value to the entity. Intellectual property may represent *substantial* fair value, not reflected in the historical cost recorded for such assets. In part, this is because GAAP requires that most research and development costs be expensed as incurred. Discounted cash flow analysis of assumed royalty streams, or estimated income associated with such intellectual property, should be done to calculate appropriate fair valuation adjustments. Even for distressed entities, goodwill may have value, and such value can be determined for the balance sheet test. Using the income approach, applied to the business as a whole, total enterprise fair value can be computed. From this value, the values of all identifiable tangible and intangible assets are deducted. The remainder, if positive, represents the value of goodwill.

Current Liabilities.   Trade payables, payroll and other accrued liabilities, current income tax liabilities, and other current obligations of the entity comprise current liabilities. In the main, these obligations should be shown at their face amounts for the balance sheet test.

Long-Term Debt.   Long-term debt includes notes payable, bonds and debentures, and mortgages. For the balance sheet test, these obligations usually are reflected at their carrying values as of the test date.

Lease Obligations.   Lease obligations may include long-term capital leases recorded in an entity's GAAP financial statements, as well as commitments relating to operating leases. Under GAAP, operating leases are not reflected as liabilities; rather, their future lease payments are reflected as an expense when they come due. In the ordinary course, for a going concern, the effect of operating leases should be taken into account only in predicting future cash flows for any income approach valuation associated with such leased property. An exception may be where the entity plans to abandon the leased property by sublease or straight rejection, in which an obligation (or asset, in the case of a favorable sublease) may obtain and should be calculated. For long-term capital lease obligations, the terms and imputed interest rate used for GAAP purposes should be reanalyzed to compute the remaining lease obligation, using a reasonable currently imputed interest rate, and reflecting the entity's most recent plans regarding future terms of such leases.

Income Tax Liabilities.   Under GAAP, income tax liabilities may reflect deferred tax liabilities (or deferred tax assets) arising from the timing of recognition of differences between income and expense reported for tax purposes and reported in GAAP financial statements. Any such future deferred tax items should be reanalyzed in light of the entity's most recent tax position and estimated taxable income (or loss) as of the balance sheet test date. Previous tax payments, available for tax refunds, should be computed in the case where estimated future results of operations indicate creation of tax loss carry-backs (which may give rise to tax refunds receivable). Also, the entity's effective tax rate should be computed for use in (1) estimating tax cash out- or inflows for any income approach valuations, (2) computing the amount of any estimated tax refunds from tax loss carry-backs, and (3) estimating tax liability (or benefit) in respect of fair valuation gains (or losses).

Other Long-Term Obligations.   Other long-term obligations may include pension plan(s) liabilities, postemployment or other postretirement benefit obligations (e.g., medical, job retraining, disability), workers' compensation or other self-insured reserves, legal liabilities on account of legal judgments or litigation contingencies deemed probable and estimable, or unfavorable purchase commitments reduced to probable and estimable future obligations. Pension plans and postemployment or postretirement benefit obligations usually are recorded based on actuarial analysis. Such actuarial analysis may not reflect all current actuarial gains (or losses) of such plans due to changes in assumed rates of inflation or imputed interest, or costs of benefits, or fair market value of plan assets, or assumed growth of plan assets value. Fair valuation of pension- and employee benefit–related obligations should be based on reanalysis of all key actuarial and cost assumptions used in previously computing such obligations, as of the balance sheet test date. Likewise, insurance reserves for self-insured portions of workers' compensation, property and casualty loss, environmental claims, and so forth should be reanalyzed, as of the balance sheet test date, using most recent, reasonable, actuarial assumptions (e.g., imputed interest rate, incurred but not reported loss factors, inflation rates, cost of claims). Other forms of deferred compensation or employment benefits need to be analyzed, first, to determine whether the amounts due represent true liabilities to be included in the balance sheet test. For example, deferred stock plans, in which future payments are to be made just in stock of the entity, may represent only future increases in equity, not liabilities. Under GAAP, such stock-based compensation plans may be recorded as some amount of obligation, yet for the balance sheet test any such future obligation may be in the nature of an equity interest, as opposed to a liability claim.

Legal judgments should be divided between those currently due and payable, and those structured to be paid over long-term periods of time. The former are reflected at their current amounts due and owing. The latter should be reduced to their present value, using the legal interest rate to be paid thereon and an imputed discount rate applied to the computed structured payments of judgment principal and interest.

Unfavorable purchase commitments may represent overpurchases of raw materials, unfavorable supply or service contracts, or other contractual obligations estimated to give rise to future losses and liabilities (in the form of either payments or performance obligations). Any resultant liabilities should be computed based on analysis of the terms of such commitments (e.g., contracts, purchase orders) and a comparison of estimated cash inflows (including any assumed resale, at estimated market prices of overcommitted goods) and estimated cash outflows due under the specific commitments.

Contingencies.   Contingencies may include potential legal liabilities, disputed claims, or any other potential increase of liability or impairment of an asset dependent on the outcome of one or more future events. Certain contingencies, relating to allowances for doubtful accounts, reserves for customer returns and allowances, warranty reserves, and other reserves and allowances, are addressed in the computation of fair value of the asset or liability to which such reserves and allowances pertain. After these contingency items, the most commonly occurring contingencies relate to potential legal liabilities. Under GAAP, the standard for recording liability is similar to the standard applied in the *Xonics* case,[47] that is: liability equals likelihood of loss (or settlement) multiplied by estimated amount of loss. However, under GAAP, no liability is deemed recognizable if the likelihood is judged to be less than *probable* (as opposed to *possible* or *remote*).[48] Bankruptcy case law imposes no such probability cutoff, although the legal concept of burden—"by a preponderance" or "clear and convincing"—may be equated to the range contemplated by the GAAP concept of probable.[49] Estimation of legal contingencies should include consultation with specialists, such as legal counsel.

Business Enterprise Valuation Method and Practice.   As a complement to the balance sheet test, the BEV method should produce a comparable result, thereby providing additional proof of the reasonableness of the fair valuation shown. Business enterprise valuation analysis starts with the basic methodology of the income approach, then subtracts from the indicated fair value of the entity's assets the total of the entity's liabilities, producing the indicated value of the entity's equity, at a fair valuation, or its enterprise value. Like the income approach, critical to a reasonable valuation is the reasonableness of underlying projections of distributable income, discount rates, and capitalization rates used. Working capital may need to be normalized (i.e., adjusted to reflect a proper amount of net working capital for the assumed level of business operations being modeled). Changes in future operations due to discontinued operations, assumed restructurings, or other significant business changes need to be carefully supported by objectively developed assumptions. Business enterprise valuation results may need to be compared to a market comparable valuation to evaluate the reasonableness of the assumptions and predictive modeling used in the BEV method.

Another benefit of the BEV method is that it also can demonstrate whether the entity is left with "an unreasonably small capital." If working capital has been normalized for the level of projected business operations used in computing BEV, and the BEV value is positive (i.e., the result is positive equity or net worth), capital should be deemed not to be unreasonably small.

Solvency Analysis.   The results of the balance sheet test and any other complementary analysis, such as BEV, should be considered in light of other information, including (1) events analysis, (2) the subject's questionable transactions, and (3) causes of the subsequent bankruptcy filing. Each solvency analysis will be different, and each will require careful analysis of the elements comprising an entity's assets and liabilities, the accounting applied thereto, and the competence and validity of the financial information used in the accounting process. Reasonable experts may reasonably disagree on underlying assumptions, and many assumptions will be used in a typical solvency analysis. Just a 1% change in discount rate, from say 12% to 11%, could be the difference between solvency and insolvency. Future projections of results of operations are inherently subject to estimates that may have ranges of reasonableness. Judgments as to comparable market values also may fall within ranges. Any reasonable solvency analysis must take into account these "ranges of reasonableness" and the inherent limitations that exist in all financial analyses involving judgments and estimates.

Transaction Analysis

Analysis of Transactions for Possible Fraudulent Conveyances.   Within the period in which a transaction may be deemed a fraudulent conveyance, business transactions should be divided between those that appear to be in the ordinary course and those that do not. Other-than-ordinary-course transactions may include disposal of discontinued operations; bulk sales; sale or factoring of receivables; sale of raw material inventory; sale of fixed assets; loans to officers, directors, or shareholders; liens granted to third parties against unencumbered or partially encumbered assets; debt refinancing or restructuring; or stock repurchases. Transaction analysis is done in three steps: (1) identification of questionable transactions; (2) development of accounting evidence; and (3) analysis of the transaction elements and resultant effects on the entity. Comparison then can be made of the value of assets conveyed (or liabilities assumed) to the value of consideration received, leading to a conclusion as to whether less than reasonably equivalent value may have been received in the transaction. Following are procedures designed to accomplish these three steps.

1. Identification of questionable transactions
   (a) Review of financial statements and notes thereto for disclosure of large or unusual transactions, issuance of new debt, significant asset sales, and so on
   (b) Fluctuation analysis, comparing individual account balances (e.g., receivables, plant, etc.) and identifying any material changes in amounts for the purpose of further investigation
   (c) Review of general ledger accounts for large or unusual entries, particularly profit and loss accounts classified for gain (or loss) on sales, other income (or loss), and fixed-asset and long-term liability accounts
   (d) Review of general journal entries, accountants' working papers or schedules, and tax returns and related tax working papers
   (e) Inquiry of management, particularly accounting officers
   (f) Review of transactions with identified "related parties"

2. Development of accounting evidence
   (a) Accumulation of accounting media (e.g., journal entries, general ledger accounts, invoices, bills of sale or sales receipts, contractual agreements, correspondence and memoranda, and working papers)
   (b) Confirmation of transactions by inquiry of counterparties, review of property transfer records or title transfers or lien records, review of Uniform Commercial Code filings, and so forth
   (c) Interview of management or employees
   (d) Physical inspection, survey, or appraisal
   (e) Accumulation of specialized information, as required, bearing on ownership, asset value, or asset condition, including legal opinions, engineering or other technical reports (e.g., reservoir engineering studies, mineral assays, aircraft or vessel surveys, adjuster reports), and valuation reports for specialized assets such as computer software, patents, trademarks, copyrights, trade secrets, trained labor force, rights-of-way, easements or usufructs, water rights, and so forth
3. Analysis of transaction elements and effects
   (a) Diagrammatic analysis of complex transactions
   (b) Analysis of cash flows
   (c) Tracing of proceeds and payments
   (d) Recalculation of gain or loss arising from transaction(s) based on historical costs and fair values of assets conveyed or liabilities assumed and consideration received

Analysis of Payments on Antecedent Debt for Possible Preference Items. For the preference period, payments should be identified through review of cash books, bank statements, disbursement journals, and general ledger accounts— particularly the entity's debt accounts. Some potential preferences may entail noncash transactions, such as transfer to a lender of other assets, such as receivables, equipment, land, and so forth in satisfaction of unsecured or undersecured debt. Payments on secured debt should be analyzed to determine that at the time of payment the value of collateral was equal to or exceeded the value of the debt. Restructurings of debt should be analyzed to determine if the extension of new credit or change in debt terms were commensurate with payments made or other value given to the lender (e.g., new collateral). Analysis of such transactions may require valuation of underlying collateral.

Financial Condition of Debtors

Bankruptcy Litigation Involving Financial Condition.   As discussed earlier in this chapter, litigation may arise over the feasibility or fairness of a plan of reorganization proposed by a debtor, or over whether DIP financing should be permitted by the bankruptcy court, or whether a bankruptcy reorganization under chapter 11 of the Bankruptcy Code should be converted to a straight liquidation under chapter 7 of the Code. All three circumstances have at least one common, critical element: the need for decision making based on predictive information, that is, prospective financial information. Putting new money into a bankrupt estate, to finance continued operation under bankruptcy protection, presumes that such continued operations will produce a future estate that yields more value to creditors than they would receive from immediate liquidation. Allowing an estate to continue to reorganize, instead of converting it from chapter 11 to chapter 7 and commencing its liquidation, again presumes that continued operations will not diminish the value of the estate and that on future reorganization, the value of the estate to its creditors will be greater than the value from immediate liquidation. Feasibility of any plan of reorganization is determined in part by: (1) the likelihood that reorganization will not lead to return to bankruptcy; (2) prediction of future financial condition sufficient to effect the repayments to creditors set forth in the plan; and (3) reasonable assurance that the reorganized debtor will be able to meet its administrative claims, tax liabilities, and other obligations falling due upon consummation of a plan. Key to bankruptcy court decisions regarding any of these matters is the reasonableness and credibility of evidence submitted in support of predictions about the future financial condition of a debtor. In the main, that evidence focuses on financial projections, or prospective financial information.

Litigation over Prospective Financial Information.   Few if any soothsayers, seers, or oracles are likely to qualify as experts in bankruptcy proceeds. This leaves the realm of prospective financial information to accountants, financiers, or economists. Prospective financial information is not ungoverned by rules; in fact, there is a substantial body of authoritative literature and professional guidance written on the subject. The American Institute of Certified Public Accountants (AICPA) provides one of the best sources, its "Guide for Prospective Financial Information." One form of professional attestation performed by independent accountants is that of providing examination, or review, opinions on projections or forecasts. The examination opinion includes specific assurance that key assumptions used in developing the projection or forecast are reasonable. It is precisely the reasonableness, or unreasonableness, of the assumptions used to predict the future financial condition of a debtor that forms the basis for most disputes in this area of bankruptcy.

No projection or forecast can be assured to be accurate. The best that can be expected is that prospective financial information is reasonably prepared, based on reasonable assumptions, and that the predicted outcome is more likely to occur than not. Evidence supporting (or disproving) one or more of these conditions forms the basis for most dispute resolutions involving predicted financial condition of a debtor.

Basic Theory of Prospective Financial Information.   Forecasts or projections of financial information should present such information in accordance with GAAP and on a reporting basis similar to that of historical financial information. Usually, this means that prospective financial information will be in the form of a statement of financial condition (or balance sheet) and a statement of operations (or profit and loss), accompanied by notes to these financial statements. The notes should include explanation of the basis of presentation, a description of accounting principles and policies used, and disclosure of all key assumptions underlying the forecast or projection. Forecasts should represent the most likely estimated outcome. Projections may reflect one or more possible outcomes depending on the use of alternative assumptions.

Historical results should be reconcilable to predicted future results. Past performance may not be a perfect predictor of future performance, but financial results generally do not vary that significantly from past trends except when due to specifically identifiable (and demonstrable) factors of change. In bankruptcy, such factors of change may include reduced costs of debt called for in a plan of reorganization, or the effects of downsizing, plant closings, labor concessions, and the like accomplished while under bankruptcy protection, or called for in the plan of reorganization. The reasonableness of assumptions involving significant change factors should be judged on a continuum. Obviously, changes already put in place by a debtor can be measured as to their effect on results of operation and financial condition, and such measurement can be compared to the assumed results in a forecast or projection with a reasonable degree of reliability. Likewise, changes assumed to occur in the near term can be assessed more reliably than changes assumed to be wrought years hence. The bane of most projections or forecasts are growth curves, substantial improvement in margins or reductions in expenses assumed to occur in the "out years." Such longer-range assumptions, if critical to the overall positive outcome of a forecast or projection, should be scrutinized with care.

Exogenous factors may have a significant effect on future operations and may need to be reduced to economic assumptions in a forecast or projection. Typical examples include industry growth, market share, rate of inflation, general economic growth, cost of funds, and tax rates. Development of assumptions regarding exogenous factors may be based on reference to readily available econometric data, macroeconomic forecasts, indices, or statistical sources. However, more complex influences of exogenous factors may require development by specialists, such as economists. In the case of assumptions dealing with market share or industry growth, the use of industry specialists may be required.

Forecast or projection models should be internally consistent, easily tested for computational accuracy, and able to be replicated with respect to their output results for a given set of inputs. The model used should describe the key elements of business operations of the business being modeled. That is, a financial institution model will be different from a manufacturing model, or from a service enterprise model. The right model should be chosen, or developed, for the industry and business subject to projection or forecast.

Common Areas of Dispute over Prospective Financial Information. *Sensitivity* is the degree or amount of change effected for model outputs by a change in model inputs. Where small changes in one or more inputs (i.e., assumptions) cause large changes in the model outputs (i.e., the forecast or projected financial condition or results of operations), then the forecast or projection may be highly sensitive. Conversely, when larger changes in inputs do not materially affect predicted outcomes, then the forecast or projection may be less sensitive. Forecasts or projections should be tested for sensitivity. High degrees of sensitivity, combined with assumptions based on insufficient historical support, may indicate overall unreasonableness of the projection or forecast. Alternatively, the degree of sensitivity may have weight as to the probability that the predicted outcome likely will occur.

Exogenous factors may be subject to a wide range of reasonably predictable outcomes. Some exogenous factors, such as near-term economic growth rates, inflation rates, and cost of funds, are more reliably tested by comparison to published economic data and statistics. Other exogenous factors, such as market share, may be reasonably estimated in the near term, based on published industry data, but may be subject to less predictable longer-term estimation. This may be because of competitor actions that cannot be known with any degree of certainty, such as mergers, new product introductions, or price cuts. Some exogenous factors may involve more predictive art than science. Examples of these less scientific factors are effects of new management, ability to retain key employees, future currency exchange rates, and technological change. Whenever exogenous factors form the basis of key assumptions in projections or forecasts, such factors should be tested for reasonableness, and, if necessary, subjected to scrutiny by an expert in the field.

Operating assumptions include sales units and rate of sales growth; sales price(s) and rate of price changes; gross margin; expenses, their relationship to sales, and their rate of change; tax rates; inventory turns and receivable collection rates; levels of capital investment; and other assumptions regarding cash flows. Assumptions used should be reconciled to historical results of operations, and significant variances should be challenged and investigated. Particular attention should be given to assumptions of rapid acceleration in sales growth or prices and to predicted declines in gross margins or expenses as percentages of sales. Such ratios should be compared for reasonableness to industry data, or published financial statements of comparable companies. Likewise, other ratios, such as inventory turns, days' sales in receivables, and working capital, should be compared to industry and comparable businesses statistics.

Model accuracy may seem elementary, but it should be tested. Projection models are typically prepared using spreadsheet software programs. The calculation formulas and input data should be reviewed to ensure that the output is the result of a properly functioning model. Modeling errors that can occur include logical flaws in the underlying calculus, clerical errors in the model setup or input, and the failure to properly address stated assumptions.

Assumption errors and omissions can include miscalculation of assumption elements, misinterpretation of underlying data or statistics used in building assumptions, or failure to include key assumptions. Common examples of the latter include all payments due under the plan of reorganization; effects of foreign competition; differentials between rates of increase in product prices and increases in costs of labor or raw materials; sales returns and allowances, warranty reserves, and provision for doubtful accounts; capital expenditures and maintenance expense; and necessary increases in working capital commensurate with projected increases in levels of operation.

Investigations

In addition to fraudulent conveyances and preferences, investigations in bankruptcy may relate to disputed claims of creditors, claims asserted in connection with litigation, potential irregularities or illegal acts (e.g., bankruptcy fraud), or management of an estate by a debtor in possession. Where claims involve financial damages, assertions of financial irregularities, or matters of accounting, such investigation should be undertaken by counsel, using forensic accounting specialists and other specialists, as appropriate. The first objective of any claims investigation should be to ascertain the full inclusion of all lawful claims at the proper amount and the exclusion of all claims without merit.

Investigations may be undertaken by the debtor in possession, creditors appointed by the bankruptcy court to act in the debtor's stead, or an "examiner," again appointed by the bankruptcy court. Who conducts the investigation can depend on relative disinterestedness and objectivity, lack of potential conflict, and requisite resources and capabilities. Often, investigations are undertaken by special counsel, selected for their experience and expertise in the area of litigation implicated by such claims, assisted by litigation consultants and experts, as appropriate. Because the work product of investigations may be associated with ensuing litigation, it should be protected, wherever possible, by the qualified privilege of attorney work product. This means that consulting professionals should be retained, subject to bankruptcy court approval, by counsel, and that all work be undertaken at the request, on behalf of, and under the supervision of counsel.

Investigations may result in the production of written reports, expert opinions, or submission of facts found in their course. Therefore, decisions ought to be made early on concerning which information will be maintained as privileged and which information eventually may be disclosed. Also, the use to which investigative fact finding ultimately may be put must be considered at the outset. Findings based mainly on interviews and uncorroborated assertions of fact may be deemed inadmissible as hearsay in subsequent legal proceedings.[50] While most investigations will involve interviews taken of witnesses not under oath, and without official records made by court reporters, the interview process should be rigorous, well documented, and supported by corroborative evidence, wherever possible. For business claims, much corroborative evidence will be in the form of business books and records; accounting information; testimony of business executives, officers, or employees; and business-related documents. Well-conducted investigations will produce well-constructed proofs of the conclusions reached, supported by logical and persuasive accumulations of relevant evidence, organized in a manner to establish the validity or invalidity of the subject claim(s) under investigation.

Claims litigation in bankruptcy most often implicates matters requiring expertise in one or more of the business sciences. Consulting experts in forensic accounting, finance, economics, marketing, or management may be required to analyze facts and form expert opinions relating to matters in litigation, involved in claims settlements, or under investigation. Expert qualifications vary; however, certain required expertise will be discipline-specific, as in matters of accounting or audit or finance, while certain required expertise will be industry- or transaction-specific. Often, when the stakes are high and the areas are complex, multiple experts may be needed. Expertise and expert opinions should not be an end result. Rather, the expert should be an integral part of a fact-finding and analytical process designed to ascertain the truth concerning claims and matters in litigation. Expert opinions are then witness unto such truth. The expert must possess three attributes *sine qua non*—objectivity, integrity, and expertise. Credibility stems from knowledge of one's subject, quality of work performed and information used, preparedness, and objectivity in the expert's work and conclusions derived therefrom.

The nature and direction of investigations will depend on the type of claim or litigation matter. The specifics of investigations and consulting relating to general litigation are beyond the scope of this chapter. However, the following are some typical areas in which claims investigation or litigation consulting may be required.

- Loss of profits damage calculations and causation analysis
- Calculation of intellectual property damages arising from patent infringement or violation of copyright
- Calculation of damages from breach of contract
- Analysis of claims arising from lease rejections
- Forensic accounting investigations and consulting in respect of securities litigation
- Calculation of damages or costs associated with environmental liabilities
- Data "mining," management and analysis associated with product liability and other class-action matters
- Investigations into alleged accounting irregularities, bankruptcy fraud, or other possible illegal acts
- Investigation into administration of the estate in bankruptcy (e.g., regarding potential diminution of value, conflicts of interest, excessive professional fees, excessive management compensation, misuse of DIP financing proceeds)
- Data development, investigation, management, and analysis regarding claims, including identification of duplicate or time-barred claims, verification and validation of claims amounts, classification of claims, and assistance in supporting rejection of claims
- Assistance in estimating contingent claims

NOTES

1.   Certain disputes of the types described herein are covered by Bankruptcy Rules other than Part VII. *See* U.S.C.S. Bankruptcy R 7001 (1998).

2.   Federal district courts have original jurisdiction over all bankruptcy cases and, therefore, can withdraw, in whole or in part, any case or proceeding referred to the bankruptcy court for cause. *See* 28 U.S.C. §158 (1998). A party to a dispute can file a motion to remove certain claims or causes of action in civil actions to the district court where such action is pending, if the district court has jurisdiction of such proceedings under §1334 of the Code. Recent examples of bankruptcy cases in which significant legal proceedings were withdrawn from the bankruptcy court include *In re Phar-Mor, Inc. Securities Litigation*, 185 B.R. 497 (W.D. Pa. 1995) and *In re Drexel Burnham Lambert Group Inc.*, 960 F.2d 285 (2d Cir.1992).

3.   *See* Collier on bankruptcy §9014.01. Mathew Bender, 1999, NY, NY.

4.   Charles Segilson et al, The Code and the Bankruptcy Act, 42 N.Y.U. L. Rev. 292 (1967).

5.   Preferences and fraudulent conveyances are not limited to transfers of assets by the debtor to a third party. Other transfers that are subject to the preference and fraudulent conveyance laws include incurrence by the debtor of liabilities or liens on the debtor's assets.

6.   11 U.S.C. § 547(b)(1998).

7.   *Id.* §547(c).

8.   *Id.* § 548(a)(1).

9.   It should be noted that § 544 of the Bankruptcy Code provides that trustees may avoid certain transfers voidable under applicable state law, including the Uniform Fraudulent Transfer Act (UFTA). State laws and the UFTA contain certain provisions that differ from those addressed in this chapter. For example, state laws often contain statute of limitation periods beyond the one-year period covered by the Code.

10.   11 U.S.C. §548(a)(2) (1998).

11.   The Code authorizes the bankruptcy court to appoint an examiner to conduct investigations of the debtor, as appropriate, including investigations into any allegations of fraud, dishonesty, incompetence, misconduct, mismanagement, or irregularity in the management of the affairs of the debtor. *See* 11 U.S.C. §1104(c).

12.   Cash collateral represents cash and cash equivalents of the estate in which a third party has a lien or similar legal interest. The term also applies to the debtor's proceeds from the noncash collateral (e.g., sales of secured inventory, collections on secured receivables, etc.).

13.   11 U.S.C. § 363(c)(2)(1998).

14.   *Id.* § 361.

15.   *Id.* § 364(a), (b).

16.   *Id.* § 364(c).

17.   *Id.* § 364(d)(1)(1998).

18.   11 U.S.C. § 1112.

19.   *Id.* § 1112(b)(1).

20.   *Id.* § 101(5).

21.   National Bankruptcy Comm'n, *Bankruptcy: The Next Twenty Years*, p. 315 (1997).

22.   Martin J. Benenstock, *Bankruptcy Reorganization,* pp. 634, 635 (1987).

23.   11 U.S.C. § 502(c)(1)(1998).

24.   *Id.* § 1129(a)(1998).

25.   *Id.* § 1129(a)(11)(1998).

26.   *See In re Clarkson*, 767 F.2d 417 (8th Cir. 1985).

27.   11 U.S.C. § 1129(7)(A) (1998).

28.   The Bankruptcy Code limits the need to prove insolvency to avoid certain preference transfers by establishing a presumption of solvency of a debtor on and during the 90 days preceding the filing of a bankruptcy petition. *See* 11 U.S.C. § 547(f) (1998).

29.   Typically, the period established is back one year, or *retrojective.*

30.   Absent any questionable transactions, proving insolvency is moot; stop work.

31.   As insolvency is defined under 11 U.S.C. § 101(32) of the Bankruptcy Code.

32.   Quarterly financial information also should be obtained, if available; and, ideally, key financial information, such as sales or revenue, gross margin, and earnings and profits, should be obtained for at least five years. In practice, available information usually falls short of ideal, but the goal should be to establish a reliable history of operating trends and financial results of the entity, to be used as a reasonable basis for developing estimates of future results of operations (i.e., prospective financial information).

33.   The Code establishes a balance sheet insolvency standard for most debtors by defining insolvency as when the sum of the entity's debts is greater than the sum of the entity's applicable assets, at fair value. See 11 U.S.C. §101(32) (1998).

34.   Both an audit and a review are attestations by independent auditors; an audit reports on whether the financial statements *present fairly* financial information in accordance with GAAP, while a review is a more limited form of (i.e., negative assurance) opinion that reports on whether financial statements require any material modification to comport with GAAP. All financial statements comporting with GAAP must be reported on the basis of historical cost.

35.   A compilation is a form of attestation by an independent accountant that expresses no opinion on financial statements complying with GAAP, but that does provide assurance that the financial information was compiled in a manner that reflects one or more of the basic financial statements (e.g., balance sheet or statement of operations).

36.   The most common impairments of long-lived assets typically are depreciation or amortization; however, other impairments may require reserves due to loss of value, discontinued operations, or change in classification from "held to maturity" to "held for sale."

37.   See inter alia, In re Joshua Slocum, Ltd., 103 B.R. 610, 623 (E.D. Pa. 1989); In re Sierra Steel, Inc., 96 B.R. 275, 278 (Bankr. 9th Cir. 1989); In re Ohio Corrugating Co., 91 B.R. 430, 438 (N.D. Ohio 1988); In re McLean Industries, Inc., 132 B.R. 247, 258 (S.D. N.Y. 1991); In re Excello Press, Inc., 96 B.R. 840, 843 (Bankr. N.D. Ill. 1989).

38.   See S.E.C. Reg. S-X, Rule 4-01(a)(1): "Financial statements filed with the Commission which are not prepared in accordance with generally accepted accounting principles will be presumed to be misleading or inaccurate."

39.   Because of the concept of retrojection, this process typically will be a "roll-forward;" however, in certain circumstances, a "roll-back" may be more appropriate. For example, where the balance sheet test date is, say, June 29th, the quarter-end financial statements as of June 30th should be more reliable than the prior quarter-end, March 31.

40.   See inter alia, In re Vadnais Lumber Supply, Inc., 100 B.R. 127, 131 (Bankr. Ma. 1989), and In re Taxman Clothing Co., 905 F.2d. 166, 170 (7th Cir. 1990).

41.   See SFAS No. 121, ¶7: "An impairment loss . . . shall be measured as the amount by which the carrying amount of the asset exceeds the fair value of the asset."

42.   See James H. Zubin, Financial Valuation: Businesses and Business Interests 2.1[1] (1990). Under this definition, given a basis of going concern, debtor is assumed to make the rational choice not to sell, in the ordinary course, at market value less than the higher of amortized replacement cost or income approach value. By way of example, raw material needed in the manufacturing process of a debtor may have been bought for $100, be worth $105, if incorporated into finished goods reasonably assumed to be produced in the ordinary course, and have a resale value—as raw materials—of only $95 (due to transaction costs, temporary market conditions, etc.) The highest and best use of such raw materials is "as is" and its value should not be impaired artificially by an assumed market sale when the rational economic choice is to use the asset for its intended purpose, in the ordinary course of business. Likewise, an operating production facility may produce goods for sale at a reasonable gross profit margin of 30% (comparable to profitable competitors), may be efficiently utilized in the firm's production plans, and may be valued at $100 using a discounted cash flow analysis of reasonably projected future distributable earnings. Yet this same plant and equipment only may fetch $90 on the market, due to, inter alia: transaction costs, discounting for buyer risk, diseconomies of this plant on a "stand-alone" basis, etc. The rational decision for any seller, as a going concern, must be not to sell at market, because the inherent value of the plant and equipment, in its current use, is higher.

43. This assumes that the security is unimpaired by credit loss, with a reasonable yield to maturity, and is adjusted for inherent discount or premium. (That is to say, such securities should reflect the time value of money and investment risk; a "zero coupon" bond priced to yield $1000 at maturity, but paying no interest in the interim, would not be worth $1000 three years before maturity.)

44. See SFAS No. 5, "Accounting for Contingencies," ¶¶ 3, 8, and 22–23.

45. A more specialized form of work-in-process, requiring analysis, special accounting and, possibly, specialized valuation is inventory (and related receivables, deferred assets, or deferred revenue) associated with construction contracts and certain production contracts accounted for under the "percentage-of-completion" method. See American Institute of Certified Public Accountants Statement of Position 81-1, "Accounting for Construction-type and Certain Production-type Contracts."

46. Consider the fair valuation of other assets, such as land. The cost may be $100, yet the market value, assuming a sale that has not yet taken place, may be $1,000. A fair valuation reflects this inherent gain, by valuing the land at $1,000, even though the selling event has not occurred. On the other hand, inventory sales are regular events in due course, and short-term profit is not recognized in practice until the goods actually are sold.

47. *See In re Xonics Photochemical, Inc.*, 841 F.2d 198 (Bankr. 7th Cir. 1988), in which the court issued a detailed dictum on how to handle contingent liabilities, finding support for its proposed formula (face amount of liability x probability of occurrence = discounted amount) in " . . . proper accounting treatment under GAAP."

48. *See* SFAS No. 5, *supra.*, at ¶ 3.

49. *Id. See also* AICPA Emerging Issue Task Force ("EITF") Issue 93-5, Discussion Paper dated March 16, 1993, ¶ 26.

50. For example, in connection with the bankruptcy case of *In re Phar-Mor, Inc. Securities Litigation*, 185 B.R. 497 (W.D. Pa. 1995), the bankruptcy court appointed an examiner to conduct an examination into, among other matters, allegations of financial reporting fraud at the debtor prior to filing for bankruptcy protection. In connection with a related adversary proceeding, the court ruled the examiner's report to be inadmissable as evidence on the grounds that it contained hearsay and "lack[ed] a guarantee of trustworthiness." *See Monus* v. *Antonucci, et al.*, 1995 WL 469694 (Bankr. N.D. Ohio 1995).

18

Tax Planning in Corporate Reorganizations

Mitchel R. Aeder

PricewaterhouseCoopers LLP

INTRODUCTION

Tax advisors tend to have a shell-shocked look about them. The rules in their peculiar universe are voluminous, complex, and constantly changing, and their application to any particular set of facts seems never to be perfectly clear. They tend to talk mostly among themselves, in a private language punctuated with references to this or that ruling or doctrine, sending up a puff of smoke when they have solved the problem or reduced it to a "business issue."

This chapter attempts to demystify some of the principal federal income tax issues that particularly afflict troubled or bankrupt corporations. While some of the rules discussed herein also apply to partnerships and other business entities, the generally applicable tax law pertaining to partnerships creates its own complications and is beyond the scope of this chapter. It is written for non–tax professionals and, as such, much important detail (where, of course, the devil lurks) is omitted.[1] For many troubled or bankrupt companies, tax concerns are an afterthought—another big problem to deal with only after the really big problems are dealt with. Yet early intervention by tax advisors may help preserve flexibility in structuring a reorganization plan and in preparing the company for the postworkout era. It is hoped that this general overview of some of the tax rules that a troubled or bankrupt corporation is likely to encounter may help the managers of the troubled company identify potentially nettlesome issues and embolden them to seek professional assistance (or other therapy).

The author, a partner at PricewaterhouseCoopers LLP, gratefully acknowledges the assistance of his colleague, Michelle Wu, in the preparation of this article.

NET OPERATING LOSSES AND OTHER TAX ATTRIBUTES

While losing money typically is what causes a corporation to be troubled in the first place, tax losses often are among a troubled company's most valuable assets. In fact, some bankruptcy courts have exercised broad injunctive power to preclude actions (including trading of debt or equity interests in the debtor) by creditors or shareholders that might impair the value of a debtor's tax net operating losses (NOLs). Preserving tax attributes such as NOLs, or obtaining value therefrom, often is the paramount tax consideration in a corporate restructuring.

A corporation's NOLs generally may be carried back to offset taxable income in the taxpayer's two tax years immediately preceding the year of the loss, thereby creating a refund, and carried forward as a deduction against taxable income in the 20 tax years after the year of the loss. (For NOLs produced in tax years prior to 1998, the carryback period is three years and the carryforward period 15 years.) An NOL is first carried back to the earliest year to which it may be carried, with any excess carried to each subsequent year in which the corporation has positive income. However, the corporation may elect to waive the right to carryback an NOL. This election is often made if the NOL otherwise would be carried back to a period when the corporation was under different ownership.

The carryback and carryforward rules are designed to ameliorate (but not eliminate) the harsh consequences that otherwise would befall a company that does not have the foresight to make and lose money in the same tax year.

Example 1

Corporation C² has taxable income or NOL as follows:

Year	Income
1995	($1.2 million)
1996	$1.6 million
1997	$2.5 million
1998	$4.0 million
1999	($8.2 million)

C carries the 1995 NOL forward to 1996, reducing 1996 taxable income to $400,000. In 1999, C's business has a severe downturn, and C has an $8.2 million NOL, effectively eliminating all its previous tax earnings. Unless it elects otherwise, C may carryback $2.5 and $4.0 million of the 1999 NOL to 1997 and 1998, respectively, and receive a refund of the tax paid for those years (plus interest). But because 1996 is beyond the two-year carryback period, C cannot recover the tax paid in 1996. Instead, the remaining $1.7 million 1999 NOL may be carried forward and deducted against taxable income in 2000 through 2019.

For purposes of the alternative minimum tax (AMT), an NOL carryforward may not offset more than 90% of income (as specially computed under the AMT rules). As a result, in most cases, a corporation will be required to pay a tax of 2% (10% of income times the 20% AMT rate) even if it has a substantial NOL carryforward.

Although the focus of this chapter is on U.S. federal income tax, it is important to note that many states impose far more severe restrictions on the carryback and carryforward of NOLs, if they allow them at all. Therefore, although a large NOL may eliminate federal tax (other than AMT), there may be a significant state tax liability. For companies whose successful reorganization depends on the availability of NOLs, consideration of the potential cash flow consequences of the AMT and state taxes is essential.

Notwithstanding the general two-year carryback rule, to the extent the NOL results from a specified liability loss—generally, a deductible loss attributable to a product liability or a liability arising under federal or state law or from a tort in which the event causing the liability occurred at least three years before the year of the NOL—the NOL may be carried back 10 years. Thus, in Example 1, if the 1999 NOL were a specified liability loss, $400,000 million of the NOL could have been carried back to 1996, thereby increasing the refund. Some taxpayers have attempted to take broad views of what constitutes a liability arising under federal or state law for this purpose—including interest on federal income tax deficiencies and regular compliance with federal securities laws—as well as of the connectivity between the liability and an event that occurred three years earlier. These attempts have been aggressively and successfully challenged by the Internal Revenue Service (IRS). Under recently enacted legislation, effective for 1998 and beyond, specified liability losses are limited to deductions and losses arising from product liability, land reclamation, workers' compensation, environmental remediation, and other specified laws.

Unlike NOLs, capital losses can be deducted by a corporation only against capital gains and can be carried back three tax years and carried forward five tax years. More complicated rules apply to the carryforward and carryback of foreign tax credits and other tax credits.

As will become more apparent in the discussion of cancellation of debt income later in this chapter, a corporation's basis in its assets, which can affect depreciation and amortization deductions as well as the amount of income realized on sale, also is an important tax attribute.

One final, but often overlooked, procedural point regarding NOLs (and other tax attributes): The IRS has the right to audit, and potentially challenge, an NOL for the year in which it is actually offset against income, even if the deductions or losses resulting in the NOL were incurred much earlier.

Example 2

In Year 1, C reports a $55 million NOL based in large part on an aggressive interpretation of the tax law. C carries this NOL forward and deducts it in Year 8. Even if the IRS previously audited C's Year 1 return or the statute of limitations for Year 1 otherwise lapsed, the IRS would not be precluded from challenging the deductions that created the Year 1 NOL within the applicable statute of limitations (typically three years) for its Year 8 return.

Among other things, this demonstrates the importance of retaining comprehensive files detailing the factual and legal support for positions taken on NOL returns. In addition, a purchaser of an NOL corporation needs to take into account that the use of the NOL will be subject to IRS review, as well as to the limitations discussed immediately below.

LIMITATIONS ON THE USE OF TAX ATTRIBUTES

As seen above, NOLs and other tax attributes can be powerful assets. But they are valuable only if the corporation has income to offset within the carryforward period; otherwise, they expire unused. Consequently, there is a long tradition of profitable companies devising schemes to acquire NOLs generated by others, to reduce their own tax burden. Because the carryback and carryforward rules are primarily designed to address timing issues, there is an almost equally long tradition of Congress and the IRS attempting to ensure that losses incurred in a business be deductible only against income of that business. Thus, the tax law has several rules intended to prevent the trafficking in NOLs and to limit their use to those that "earned" them.

Ownership Changes of Loss Corporations: Section 382

Under Section 382 of the Internal Revenue Code of 1986 (the Tax Code), the ability of a loss corporation to deduct its NOLs generally is limited following an "ownership change" of the corporation. (Similar rules apply for capital losses and certain tax credits.) The regulations governing the NOL limitations under Section 382 are among the most intricate and complex in the tax law. Simply stated, the basic rule is as follows:

> Following a more-than-50% change in the ownership of a corporation (measured over a three-year period), the corporation's ability to deduct its pre-ownership change NOLs will be limited, annually, to an amount equal to the product of (1) the fair market value of the company's equity immediately prior to the ownership change and (2) the "Sec. 382 rate" published by the IRS for the month in which the ownership change occurs (5.02% for November 1998). Special rules may mitigate the limitation if the ownership change occurs while the corporation is in bankruptcy.

The potential impact of this rule can be demonstrated by a simple example.

Example 3

Corporation C, which is not in bankruptcy, has NOLs of $115 million. In November 1998, C experiences an ownership change. If C's equity value is $90 million immediately before the ownership change, Section 382 will permit C to deduct only about $4.5 million ($90 million times 5.02%) of its NOLs in each subsequent year until they expire under the regular carryforward rules. If

the full \$4.5 million is not used in any year (because the company has insuffi-
cient income), the excess may be carried forward to subsequent years.
Nonetheless, in this case, a significant portion of C's NOLs will expire unused because, even if all the NOLs are fresh, no more than \$90 million (\$4.5
million per year for 20 years) can be used.

Having stated the basic rule, it is now necessary to examine its component
parts.

What Is an Ownership Change?   In general, an ownership change occurs if,
during a three-year period, the ownership of stock of the corporation by "5%
shareholders" increases by more than 50 percentage points. It is irrelevant
whether the event causing the ownership change is a taxable or a tax-free transaction.

Example 4

At the beginning of Year 1, A owns 10% and B owns 12% of the stock of
C. In Year 2, B sells some shares, reducing B's interest to 4%. In Year 3, A
and B contribute additional funds to C, following which both A and B own
35% of C. Because A and B are 5% shareholders in Year 3 and their ownership increased by more than 50 percentage points from its lowest point
during the three-year period (i.e., A from 10% to 35% and B from 4% to
35%), C experiences an ownership change in Year 3.

For purposes of identifying a 50% stock ownership change, "stock" generally
includes any stock of the loss corporation other than straight, nonconvertible
preferred. Moreover, options, warrants, convertible debt, and the like also may
be treated as stock (i.e., considered as if they were exercised) if a principal purpose for the issuance, transfer, or structuring of the option (or similar right) is to
avoid, or ameliorate the impact of, an ownership change and, in addition: (1) the
holder of the option and related persons are in control of the loss corporation (or
would be on the exercise of the option) or (2) the option holder has attributes of
stock ownership, such as voting rights, prior to the time the option is actually exercised or (3) the option is designed to delay the occurrence of an ownership
change until income or gain is accelerated or realized. Compensatory options,
stock purchase agreements, rights of first refusal, and pledges of stock as part of
a security arrangement generally will not be treated as exercised and therefore
are not counted in the ownership change equation.

Example 5

On April 1, 1996, A exchanged a portion of its debt into 45% of the stock
of C. In 1998, A offered to exchange the remainder of its debt into an additional 15% of C. To avoid an ownership change, A instead received deep-
in-the-money warrants to acquire 20% of C stock on June 1, 1999 (more
than three years after its original purchase). As the largest shareholder, A

exerted significant influence over the management of C. In this situation, the issuance of the warrants could cause an ownership change.

Section 382 tests for ownership changes by reference only to 5% shareholders, so that even high-volume trading of a loss corporation's shares on a public market generally will not trigger an ownership change. Yet even the determination of who or what is a 5% shareholder can be complicated. Although special rules, definitions, exceptions, and presumptions abound, here are some operating principles:

- An individual who directly owns 5% or more of the loss corporation is a 5% shareholder.
- If the loss corporation is owned in whole or part by other entities, any owner of a higher-tier entity who indirectly owns 5% of the loss corporation is considered a 5% shareholder. Therefore, if a corporation transfers all of the stock of its subsidiary to a sister corporation that is wholly owned by the same individual, there is no ownership change of the subsidiary even though 100% of its shares changed hands, because the only 5% shareholder (the individual) indirectly owned all of the stock of the subsidiary before and after the transfer.
- All of the less-than-5% shareholders of the loss corporation are treated as if they were one conglomerate 5% shareholder, even if their actual aggregate ownership is less than 5%. Thus, if a closely held corporation issues more than 50% of its stock in an initial public offering (IPO), the public shareholders will be considered a 5% shareholder, thereby triggering an ownership change.
- All of the less-than-5% shareholders of a higher-tier entity are treated as if they were one *separate* conglomerate 5% shareholder, but only if their indirect aggregate ownership of the loss corporation is at least 5%.
- In certain circumstances (e.g., as a result of multiple public offerings or a non–pro rata redemption or a merger, whether these involve the loss corporation or a higher-tier entity), the conglomerate 5% shareholder group may be segregated into two or more distinct 5% shareholders.

Example 6

C is a widely held corporation with no 5% owners. Accordingly, all of its shareholders are treated as one 5% shareholder. C merges with X Co., also widely held, with the X Co. shareholders receiving 65% of stock of the combined entity. Even though the combined entity has no 5% owners, the former X Co. shareholders and the former C shareholders are segregated into two separate groups. Because the X Co. shareholders—treated as a single 5% shareholder—increased their ownership by more than 50 percentage points (from 0 to 65%), the merger causes an ownership change with respect to C (but not with respect to X Co.).

Keeping track of a corporation's 5% shareholders, and increases and decreases in their ownership, can be a full-time job, particularly in multitiered corporate groups in which there may be numerous classes of stock, foreign ownership, multiple public groups, valuation uncertainties, and the like. Nonetheless, the regulations impose on a loss corporation an affirmative duty of inquiry to determine this information. Our experience is that far too few NOL companies monitor changes in its "5% shareholders." A word to the wise: it is usually far easier to maintain this information on a current basis than to attempt to recreate it at a later date (such as when the structure of a reorganization plan depends on whether the company's NOLs already are subject to limitation under Section 382).

Calculating the Annual Limitation.   As previously noted, the annual limitation on the use of NOLs after an ownership change generally is determined by reference to the fair market value of the corporation and a rate published monthly by the IRS. The theory underlying the formula is that the original owners of the corporation could have caused the corporation to sell all its assets, pay all its liabilities, and invest the proceeds in long-term tax-exempt bonds; use of the NOLs to this minimal extent is thus inherent in the corporation and not particularly subject to abuse.

For this purpose, the value of the company generally is the value of its stock, including "straight" preferred stock and any options to acquire stock, immediately prior to the ownership change. (As noted below, the value may be computed immediately *after* the ownership change in certain bankruptcy restructurings.) Often, there will be objective indicia of value, as in a publicly traded company or where the ownership change is caused by an arm's-length purchase of stock. However, in other cases (e.g., a stock-for-debt restructuring of a privately held company), there may be no such indicia. In such cases, it may be prudent to commission a formal valuation study, particularly if the preservation of NOLs (subject to the Section 382 limitation) is important to the workout.

There are some additional rules relating to the computation of the postownership change annual limitation on the use of NOLs:

- *Continuity of business.* If the loss corporation fails to continue its business enterprise for at least two years after the ownership change, its annual limitation is zero (i.e., its NOLs evaporate), *retroactive to the date of the ownership change.* As a rule of thumb, this requires the continuation of at least one significant line of business or the use of at least one third of the corporation's historic business assets in a business.
- *Antistuffing.* In computing the value of the loss corporation, any capital contributions made to the company during the two years prior to the ownership change will be disregarded unless it can be demonstrated that the contributions were not made for the purpose of increasing the annual limitation.
- *Substantial nonbusiness assets.* If one third or more of the assets of the loss corporation are held for investment, the value of the corporation for Section 382 purposes will be reduced by the value of the investment assets (net of liabilities allocable to these assets).

- *Redemptions.* If the loss corporation redeems any of its stock in connection with an ownership change, the redemption will be taken into account in determining the corporation's Section 382 value. Similarly, if the corporation's equity value is reduced as a result of leverage incurred in connection with the ownership change transaction, the Section 382 value also will be reduced accordingly.
- *Built-in gains.* If, at the time of the ownership change, the corporation has a net unrealized built-in gain, that is, the fair market value of all of its assets exceeds their tax basis by at least 15% (or $10 million, if less), the corporation's annual limitation will be increased by gain realized on the disposition of any of these assets (up to the amount of the net built-in gain) during the five years following the ownership change. The notion is that it is proper to use the preownership change NOLs to offset these gains, which accrued economically prior to the change. Here, too, care should be taken to document the value of the assets to protect against a later IRS assertion that the gain ultimately realized was not built-in as of the ownership change date.
- *Income from debt cancellation.* Income arising from the cancellation of debt may in certain cases result in a reduction in the tax basis of the corporation's assets. That is the bad news. The good news is that the basis reduction may create or increase a built-in gain, thereby easing the Section 382 limitation on use of NOLs.
- *Year of ownership change.* The taxable year in which the ownership change occurs is divided into a prechange portion, in which income may be freely offset by NOL carryforwards, and a postchange portion, to which the Section 382 limitations apply. Income or loss for the year is allocated to the pre- and post-change portions on a ratable basis, unless the corporation elects to "close its books" as of the ownership change date.
- *Bankruptcy reorganizations.* If the ownership change occurs while the corporation is a debtor in a bankruptcy case—and the "special bankruptcy exception" described below does not apply—the value of the corporation is computed immediately *after* the ownership change, that is, taking into account any discharge of debt in the transaction. As can be easily seen, this rule may provide a significant tax benefit to reorganizing in bankruptcy rather than out-of-court. However, as cautioned above, establishing the fair market value of the company immediately on emergence from bankruptcy may be elusive.

Example 7

Pursuant to C's Chapter 11 reorganization plan, all of C's existing stock is canceled, and new stock is issued in full satisfaction of all of C's liabilities. For Section 382 purposes, C's annual limitation on the use of its NOLs is determined by reference to the value of its stock immediately after the reorganization (i.e., free of debt). Had C reorganized outside of bankruptcy, its annual limitation would have been zero because its stock had no value immediately prior to the reorganization.

Multiple Ownership Changes. If a loss corporation experiences successive ownership changes, the most restrictive annual limitation applies.

Example 8

C has $55 million of NOL carryforwards as of the end of 1994. C has an ownership change in January 1995 following the sale of all the outstanding shares of its only class of stock for $90 million. As a result, C may use $6.1 million ($90 million times 6.83%, the then applicable rate) of its pre-1995 NOLs annually. C's fortunes improve, and it is sold again in November 1998, this time for $160 million. Notwithstanding that the Section 382 limitation calculated for this second sale would be $8 million ($160 million times 5.02%), use of the pre-1995 NOLs would continue to be subject to the $6.1 million annual limitation that arose from the first ownership change.

Built-in Losses. As previously noted, the strictures of Section 382 are relaxed if a corporation has a net unrealized built-in gain, because this gain reflects income that accrued economically prior to the ownership change. The corollary is that if the corporation has a net unrealized built-in loss, the aggregate tax basis of its assets exceeds their fair market value by a threshold amount, any such net losses that are realized during the five-year period after the ownership change will be subject to the Section 382 annual limitation as if they were NOLs. Similarly, a "built-in" deduction item, such as depreciation, may be treated as a built-in loss.

It is unclear whether, or how, the built-in loss rules apply to contingent liabilities that become noncontingent during the five-year period.

Special Bankruptcy Exception. In the sea of darkness that is Section 382, there is a ray of light. Under certain circumstances, the Section 382 limitations described above will not apply to ownership changes that occur while the loss corporation is under the jurisdiction of a bankruptcy court. However, this special bankruptcy exception imposes its own restrictions on the company's NOLs, and the eligibility requirements exclude many chapter 11 debtors.

The special bankruptcy exception applies where, immediately after the ownership change, at least 50% of the stock of the corporation is owned by: (1) its existing shareholders, (2) creditors that held debt of the corporation for at least 18 months prior to the commencement of the bankruptcy case, or (3) creditors whose debt arose in the ordinary course of the debtor's business and has been held continuously by the same person. The theory behind the exception is that, like shareholders, long-term or ordinary-course creditors of a bankrupt company also participate in the economic losses giving rise to the NOLs and therefore earn the right to benefit therefrom.

Consequently, where there has been significant trading of the corporation's debt or bankruptcy claims, the corporation may not qualify for the exception. While a corporation generally has a duty of inquiry to determine whether its creditors have met the requisite holding periods (although the corporation generally is permitted to assume that creditors that end up with less than 5% of the stock have indeed met the holding period), the regulations permit the corporation to ignore certain transfers of debt. Some bankruptcy courts have enjoined the trading of claims in order to preserve the debtor's ability to qualify. However, many companies discover that by the time they first begin to consider the tax consequences of a reorganization plan, previous trading of claims has rendered the exception inapplicable.

If the special bankruptcy exception applies, the annual limitation previously described will not be applied to the corporation's NOLs. However, the gross amount of the NOLs will be reduced by interest paid or accrued during the three years prior to the ownership change on any debt that was converted into stock in the bankruptcy case. In addition, if the corporation undergoes a second ownership change within two years, it forfeits all of its remaining NOLs. Because of this, many companies that take advantage of the special bankruptcy exception attempt to impose legal or contractual restrictions on the transfer of their stock in order to prevent a subsequent ownership change.

Example 9

Pursuant to C's chapter 11 reorganization plan, all of its existing stock is cancelled, and all of its new stock is issued to the holders of its senior bank debt. Forty percent of the bank debt is held by a fund that purchased the debt during the pendency of the chapter 11 case. No other person owns 5% or more of the bank debt. C qualifies for the special bankruptcy exception. C's NOLs are reduced by any interest paid or accrued on the bank debt for the previous three years.

The IRS is particularly concerned about abuse of the special bankruptcy exception. Thus, for example, an option with respect to the loss corporation's stock is treated as exercised if its exercise would cause the corporation to fail to qualify for the exception. For example, this would preclude an outsider from funding a bankruptcy plan by acquiring 49% of the corporation's stock and obtaining an option to acquire additional stock from the historic creditors that received the other 51% under the plan.

A corporation may elect not to have the special bankruptcy exception apply. This election may be beneficial if, for example, the NOLs would be significantly reduced by the interest rule or if a subsequent ownership change is a distinct possibility. Where this election is made, the annual limitation is determined by reference to the corporation's equity value immediately *after* the ownership change. (See Example 7, on page 385).

Planning for Section 382.   As is evident from the above summary, Section 382 can have a significant impact on the success of a reorganization. In most workouts, the occurrence of an ownership change will be dictated by commercial considerations. Nonetheless, careful planning often can mitigate the impact of Section 382.

- *Know where you stand.* A loss corporation should keep track of changes in its stock ownership. Has an ownership change already occurred? How much additional stock can change hands without causing an ownership change? Delaying a restructuring may avert the impact of Section 382. In that regard, a bankruptcy court may be willing to enjoin transfers of a debtor's stock, where preservation of NOLs is important to the reorganization.
- *Plan for the realization of income.* Special rules apply to calculate the limitation on the use of NOLs during the year in which the ownership change occurs. Careful planning for the timing of asset sales, the accrual of deductible expenses, and other income and loss items may alleviate the impact of Section 382.
- *Consider the special bankruptcy exception.* As soon as practicable, a corporation in bankruptcy should assess whether it could qualify for, and benefit from, the special bankruptcy exception. Here, too, a bankruptcy court may be willing to restrict transfers of the corporation's debt to avoid exclusion from this rule.
- *Calculate built-in gains and losses.* The impact of Section 382 can be exacerbated or alleviated if the corporation has a net unrealized built-in loss or gain. An analysis of this amount (possibly including a valuation of the company's assets) as of the ownership change date is important to "lock in" the value/basis differential.

Acquisitions of Built-in Gains by Loss Corporations

Understanding that there is more than one way for income and losses to meet, Section 384 of the Tax Code is intended to prevent a company with NOLs or built-in losses from acquiring assets with built-in gains and marrying the acquired gains with the pre–existing losses. Section 384 applies where a corporation either (1) acquires, directly or indirectly, stock representing 80% or more of the vote and value of another corporation or (2) acquires the assets of another corporation in a tax-free reorganization, and either corporation (the "gain corporation") has a net unrealized built-in gain (defined in the same manner as for Section 382). In these circumstances, any of the net built-in gain that is recognized by the gain corporation during the five–year period after the acquisition may not be offset by preacquisition NOLs or net unrealized built-in loss of the other corporation or its affiliates. The Section 384 limitations do not apply where the gain and loss corporations were under common control (more than 50% common ownership) for the five-year period prior to the acquisition.

Example 10

C has $75 million of NOLs. B Corp.'s only significant assets are two office buildings, each with a tax basis of $10 million and a fair market value of $40 million. B Corp. merges into C in a tax-free reorganization. Even if there were valid nontax business reasons for the merger (e.g., C intended to use one of the buildings as its headquarters), if C sells the other building within five years after the merger for $60 million, it may not offset $30 million of the gain—the amount "built-in" as of the merger—with its pre-transaction NOLs.

Joining a Consolidated Group: Separate Return Limitation Year (SRLY) Limits

If a corporation with NOLs or built-in losses becomes a member of another corporate consolidated group, these losses may be used against such loss corporation's own future income (subject to Section 382 and any other applicable limitations) but generally may not offset the income of other members of the consolidated group.

Example 11

C, which has a $3 million NOL, is purchased by P Corp. Thereafter, P and C file a consolidated return. In the first year after the acquisition, P has $7 million of income and C has a $2 million loss. As a result of filing a consolidated return, P may offset its income with C's $2 million loss. However, the SRLY rules would prevent the use of C's $3 million NOL against P's income. On the other hand, if it was C that produced the $7 million of income, the NOL would be available, subject to Section 382.

These SRLY rules (pronounced "surly," which fairly describes the disposition of those who try to read them) can be harsher or more flexible than Section 382, depending on the circumstances. Thus, the SRLY rules may apply even in the absence of a significant ownership change (e.g., if a 79% subsidiary becomes an 80% subsidiary subject to consolidation). However, if the NOL corporation generates substantial future income, there is no annual limitation concept, and in some cases it may be possible to eliminate the SRLY taint through intercompany restructurings. The IRS recently announced that, in the interest of tax simplification, it is studying the advisability of replacing the current SRLY rules with a regime more closely modeled on Section 382.

Antiabuse Rule

The aforementioned rules designed to restrict trafficking in tax attributes typically apply mechanically, irrespective of tax motives. However, the IRS has another weapon reserved for those with evil intent. Under Section 269 of the Tax Code, the IRS may disallow the use of any tax benefit, including NOLs, by a person who acquires at least 50% of the vote or value of a corporation in which the principal purpose of the acquisition is tax avoidance through the use of the tax benefit. Tax benefits similarly may be disallowed following certain tax-free acquisitions with a tax avoidance motive. The IRS has asserted that this loss disallowance may apply to the acquisition by creditors of control of a corporation in a stock-for-debt exchange, particularly if the special bankruptcy exception to Section 382 is applied to the exchange.

Income from Cancellation of Debt

The act of borrowing money, in and of itself, is not a taxable event. But being relieved of the obligation to repay a debt in whole or part, generally does create taxable income to the extent the amount of the debt exceeds the cash and the fair market value of any property paid in satisfaction thereof. [3] Despite the evenhandedness of these principles, if a troubled company were required to pay tax currently on its cancellation of debt (COD) income, many debt restructurings would be imperiled by an immediate tax bill.

Section 108 of the Tax Code provides that COD income arising from the discharge of a debt that occurs while the debtor is in a title 11 bankruptcy case or is insolvent (to the extent of the insolvency) is excluded from the debtor's gross income.

But the piper eventually must be paid, so Section 108's exclusion from income does have a cost: The debtor generally is required to reduce its tax attributes by the amount that otherwise would constitute COD income, in the following order: (1) NOLs (including any NOL for the year of discharge), (2) general business credits, (3) minimum tax credits, (4) capital loss carryforwards, (5) tax basis in the debtor's assets, (6) passive activity loss or credit carryforwards, and (7) foreign tax credit carryforwards. Credits are reduced by 33.3 cents for each dollar of excluded COD income. Asset basis may not be reduced below an amount equal to the aggregate amount of the debtor's liabilities after the discharge.

Example 12

Pursuant to its confirmed chapter 11 reorganization plan, Corporation C, which has a $20 million NOL, pays $7 million cash and issues 5,000 shares of its common stock having a fair market value of $4.5 million to the holders of its subordinated debentures which have an adjusted issue price of $25 million. Under Section 108, C's NOLs will be reduced by $13.5 million ($25 million debt less payments of $11.5 million).[4]

Notwithstanding this general ordering rule, a company may elect to reduce the basis of its depreciable property first, prior to reducing NOLs. This election may be beneficial if, for example, the company largely owns slow-depreciating assets (e.g., real estate) that it does not plan to sell. In such a case, the company may want to sacrifice future depreciation deductions in favor of currently valuable NOLs. Of course, the decision of whether to make the election must take into account the effect, if any, of Section 382 on the use of the NOLs after the workout.

The reduction of tax attributes under Section 108 does not occur until *after* the calculation of the debtor's tax liability for the year of the debt discharge. Thus, it may be possible to defer, or eliminate, the attribute reduction. For example, delaying the debt discharge until shortly after the start of the tax year may postpone the Section 108 consequences for almost a year (during which year the company may be able to use NOLs that otherwise would have been reduced). Alternatively, if the corporation liquidates prior to the end of the tax year in which the discharge occurs, any otherwise unlimited NOLs carried into that year may be used against income generated in that year, including gains recognized on the disposition or distribution of assets; after the year ends, the corporation will have liquidated, so there will be no tax attributes to reduce.

In the case of corporations filing consolidated returns, the Section 108 reduction of tax attributes arguably occurs on a company-by-company basis. Thus, if one subsidiary in the group is discharged from debt but does not have a significant amount of NOLs or asset basis (or other tax attributes), calculated on a separate company basis, the tax impact of the debt discharge may be minimal even if the consolidated group as a whole has substantial NOLs. In this case, it may be prudent not to liquidate or merge this subsidiary with an affiliate as part of the restructuring. However, the IRS recently indicated that it may seek to apply Section 108 on a consolidated basis.

Any debt that would, if paid, result in a deduction does not create COD income (or attribute reduction) if settled at a discount. For example, forgiveness of interest which has not been deducted, or the discharge of a tort liability, should not result in COD income.

For purposes of Section 108, the acquisition of outstanding debt, directly or indirectly, by an affiliate of the debtor from a nonaffiliate generally will be treated as if the debtor settled the debt directly, and thus may result in COD income to the extent the amount paid for the debt is less than its adjusted issue price. The same rule applies if a nonaffiliate acquires the debt in anticipation of becoming affiliated with the debtor.

As a general matter, the cancellation of debt between a parent and a subsidiary will be treated as a contribution to capital or as a distribution to a shareholder, as the case may be. The consequences of the settlement of other intercompany debts will depend on the particular facts. However, no immediate adverse tax consequences should arise if both parties to the debt are members of the same consolidated tax group.

DEALING WITH THE DEBT: MODIFICATIONS AND COMPROMISES

Every troubled company workout or reorganization involves the rearrangement of the relationship between the debtor and some or all of its creditors. This may involve settling the debt for cash at a discount, altering the terms of the existing debt, exchanging a new debt instrument for the existing debt, converting the debt into stock or warrants of the debtor, issuing property in satisfaction of the debt (whether or not the property served to collateralize the debt), or some combination of the above. From a tax perspective, the creditor is likely to focus on the ability to recognize a loss (or, possibly, the need to recognize gain) on the transaction. Of course, if the creditor will retain an interest in the company after the workout, the creditor also will care about the tax consequences to the company and their effect on the value of his continuing interest.

Depending on the structure of its agreements with the creditors, the debtor may realize income for tax purposes, even if its liabilities are unchanged on its balance sheet. As seen in the preceding pages, whether income is realized and whether this income is COD income—implicating the favorable rules under Section 108 if the debtor is bankrupt or insolvent—may impact the debtor's NOLs and other tax attributes.[5]

Exchanging Property for Debt

The conveyance of property (other than debt or equity of the debtor) to a creditor, whether by deed, abandonment, or foreclosure, is treated as a taxable disposition of the property. The amount of COD income and gain or loss arising from the conveyance can vary significantly depending on the recourse or nonrecourse nature of the debt.

Nonrecourse Debt. When a debtor satisfies nonrecourse debt with the property securing the debt, the debtor is deemed to have sold the property to the creditor for the amount of the debt (including accrued interest), or its adjusted issue price. This holds true regardless of the fair market value of the property at the time of transfer. As a result, the debtor would recognize gain or loss measured by the difference between the adjusted issue price of the debt and its tax basis in the transferred property. No COD income would arise, even if the fair market value of the property is lower than the adjusted issue price of the debt. The gain or loss would be capital or ordinary corresponding to the nature of the property transferred.

Example 13

In 1996, C purchased equipment for its business for $20,000, consisting of $1,000 cash and a $19,000 nonrecourse note secured by the equipment. Insolvent by more than $4,000 in 1998, C transferred the equipment back to the seller in satisfaction of the note. At the time of the transfer, the fair market value of the equipment was $15,000, its tax basis was $12,000 (the $20,000 purchase price less $8,000 of accumulated tax depreciation), and the remaining principal balance on the note was $19,000. C will realize a gain of $7,000 ($19,000 minus $12,000) on the transfer, which will be included in the computation of C's 1998 taxable income.

Recourse Debt. If, instead, the debt is a recourse obligation and the debtor satisfies the debt with property securing it, the debtor is considered to have satisfied an amount of the debt equal to the fair market value of the property and been relieved of the balance of the debt. Thus, the debtor would recognize gain or loss measured by the difference between the fair market value of the property and its tax basis and, in addition, would have COD income to the extent the amount of the debt exceeds the fair market value of the property. This may yield a dramatically different result than the nonrecourse case because, as discussed earlier, if the debtor is insolvent or in bankruptcy, the COD income will be excluded from the debtor's gross income (but generally will reduce tax attributes).

Example 14

The facts are the same as in Example 13, except the note is a recourse obligation. C will realize a $3,000 gain on the transfer of the equipment ($15,000 fair market value less $12,000 basis). C also will have $4,000 of COD income which will not be included in 1998 income but will reduce NOLs or other tax attributes remaining after 1998.

If the creditor does not formally extinguish a recourse debt (and it is not discharged in a bankruptcy case), at least one court has held that no COD income arises even if it is unlikely that the balance of the debt ever will be collected. However, the validity of this result is questionable.

Modification of Existing Debt

In order to enable a troubled company to service its debt and meet its other obligations, a creditor may agree to alter one or more terms of the company's debt, for example, by deferring required payments of interests or principal, waiving restrictive covenants, providing for a reduced interest rate, extending the maturing of the debt, or reducing the principal amount of the debt. These alterations may be effected by substituting a new debt instrument with the revised terms for the existing debt or by amending the terms of the existing debt. (Similarly, the creditor could extend a new cash advance to the debtor, who would use the cash to satisfy the old debt. In certain instances this form, if respected, may change the tax consequences to the creditor.)

It is a fundamental principal of the tax law that gain or loss is realized whenever property is exchanged for other property differing materially either in kind or in extent. While it sometimes comes as a shock to the uninitiated, if the terms of a debt instrument are modified sufficiently, the amended debt instrument may be treated as a "new" debt for which the "old" debt has been exchanged, even in the absence of a physical exchange of instruments. An exchange will be deemed to occur if there has been a "significant modification" of the instrument. Such a deemed exchange may have dramatic tax consequences for both the issuer and the holder of the debt instrument: COD income for the debtor and gain or loss for the creditor. In addition, the "new" debt may be subject to any of the myriad tax rules that can apply on the issuance of a debt instrument, such as the original issue discount (OID) rules.

Regulations issued in 1996 define a *modification* as any alteration of a legal right or obligation of the issuer or a holder of a debt instrument, other than an alteration that occurs by operation of the original terms of the instrument. For example, an agreement by the parties to change the interest rate on a note is a modification. But a change in the interest rate resulting from a provision in the note providing for the rate to be reset annually based on a specified index is not considered a modification. However, certain alterations (e.g., change in obligor, change in recourse/nonrecourse status) will be considered modifications even if built into the original instrument. The exercise of an option contained in the original instrument is not a modification if the option is unilateral and does not result in the deferral or reduction of scheduled payments of principal or interest.

In general, whether the modification of a debt instrument is sufficiently "significant" to cause a deemed exchange depends on whether, based on all the facts and circumstances, the degree to which the parties' legal rights or obligations are altered is economically significant. However, certain modifications are considered significant per se. For example:

- A change in the yield of a debt instrument by the greater of 25 basis points or 5% of the yield of the unmodified debt is a significant modification.
- A change in the timing of payments is a significant modification if it results in a "material" deferral of scheduled payments, either by extending the final maturity date or by deferring payments due before maturity. Under a safe harbor, a deferral is not material if the deferred payments are unconditionally due no later than the end of the period that begins on the original due date of the first scheduled payment and extends for the lesser of five years or 50% of the original term of the debt.
- A modification is significant if there is a substitution of a new obligor (even if affiliated) on a recourse debt instrument unless, for example, the new obligor acquires substantially all the assets of the old obligor and there is no change in payment expectations.
- A change in the nature of a debt instrument from recourse to nonrecourse (or vice versa) generally is considered a significant modification.
- The addition, release, or substitution of collateral, a guarantee, or other form of credit enhancement on a nonrecourse note generally is a significant modification. A similar alteration of security on a recourse note is a significant modification if it results in a change in payment expectations.

Example 15

A debt instrument with a 10-year term provides for 10% interest, payable annually, and a $100,000 payment at maturity. At the end of the fifth year (after the annual interest payment), the parties reduce the amount payable at maturity to $80,000. The interest rate remains at 10%, but is payable on the reduced principal. Taking into account the lower annual interest payments and the reduced payment at maturity, the yield on the instrument after the modification is 4.3%. Because the yield changed by more than 25 basis points and 5% of the original yield, the revised terms of the debt constitute a significant modification.

The failure of a debtor to perform its obligations under a debt instrument is not itself a modification. Importantly, an agreement by a creditor to stay collection or temporarily waive an acceleration clause or similar default right is not a modification unless and until the forbearance remains in effect for a period that exceeds two years following the debtor's initial failure to perform and any additional period during which the parties conduct good-faith negotiations or the debtor is in bankruptcy.

If an exchange of old debt for new debt occurs (or is deemed to occur under the rules described above), the debtor will have COD income to the extent the issue price of the new debt is less than the adjusted issue price of the existing debt. The debtor also will need to be concerned with whether the new debt has OID and, if so, whether it is a "high-yield discount obligation" subject to limitations on the deductibility of interest under the applicable high-yield discount obligation (AHYDO) rules.

Whether the creditor will recognize gain or loss on the deemed debt exchange will depend on whether the exchange constitutes a tax-free recapitalization. The recapitalization rules will apply if both the old and new debt constitute "securities" for tax purposes. Although there is no hard-and-fast rule, a security includes a debt that reflects a meaningful interest in the debtor's business by virtue of being a long-term investment or by virtue of the impaired value of the company's equity and junior indebtedness.

If the exchange qualifies as a recapitalization, the creditor will not be allowed to recognize loss, but will recognize gain to the extent (1) it receives cash or property other than stock or securities of the debtor or (2) the extent the issue price of the new debt exceeds the adjusted issue price of the old debt. The creditor also will recognize income to the extent that the new debt received is attributable to accrued but unpaid interest on the old debt. If the exchange does not qualify as a recapitalization, the creditor will recognize gain or loss in an amount equal to the difference between issue price of the new debt and its adjusted basis in the old debt.

TAX-FREE G REORGANIZATIONS

Under the Tax Code, several types of corporate acquisitions, recapitalizations, and reorganizations may be accomplished wholly or partly tax free, provided that the form of the transaction comports with the requisite technical requirements. Tax-free acquisitions are referred to as "reorganizations" (and given original names: "A" reorganization, "B" reorganization, etc., based on the order in which they are listed in the statute) because the assets of the acquired company remain in corporate solution and some or all of the owners of the target company continue their ownership in the combined operation.

The standard reorganization types have little applicability to bankrupt companies because of, among other things, the requirement that existing shareholders maintain a significant interest. However, under the "G" reorganization rules, which apply only to corporations in bankruptcy cases, some of the requirements that apply to other reorganization forms are loosened.

The most common use of the G reorganization provisions involves the acquisition by a corporation of substantially all the assets of the bankrupt corporation in exchange for stock and securities of the acquiror.[6] At least 40% or so of the aggregate consideration received in the transaction by creditors and shareholders of the bankrupt corporation must consist of stock or securities of the acquiror, and at least one recipient of such stock or securities must have been a shareholder or "security" holder of the bankrupt entity. This "continuity" rule takes into account the consideration paid to the most senior class of creditors that receives stock or securities, and all classes equal or junior thereto. The acquiror must continue to operate a historic business of the bankrupt corporation or use a significant portion of its assets in a business. In an acquisitive G reorganization such as described in this paragraph, the bankrupt corporation generally must liquidate as part of the transaction.

In a G reorganization, the bankrupt corporation generally will not recognize gain or loss except, in certain cases, if the liabilities assumed by the acquiror exceed the tax basis in the acquired assets. The acquiror will inherit the bankrupt corporation's tax attributes, including NOLs and tax basis (subject to reduction for COD income). However, where tax avoidance motivates the transaction, the Section 269 antiabuse rule discussed earlier may apply to eviscerate the NOLs.

Any creditor that held a "security" in the bankrupt corporation and receives stock or securities in the G reorganization will not recognize a loss on the transaction but will recognize gain, if any, to the extent of any cash or non–stock-or-security property received.

OPERATING IN CHAPTER 11

As seen above, the Tax Code contains several liberal rules designed to facilitate the rehabilitation or reorganization of bankrupt corporations, including the exclusion of COD income from current taxation, the special bankruptcy exception to Section 382 (and the beneficial valuation rule where the exception does not apply), and the G reorganization provisions. In addition, certain tax-related provisions in the Bankruptcy Code may make a chapter 11 reorganization more palatable than an out-of-court workout: bankruptcy court jurisdiction over tax claims, prohibition against the imposition of certain transfer taxes on assets transferred pursuant to a confirmed chapter 11 plan, and restrictions on state and local tax on the cancellation of debt.

Aside from these special rules, the filing of a chapter 11 bankruptcy petition generally does not alter the routine tax obligations of a bankrupt corporation, except that payment of prepetition tax liabilities is prohibited, absent court approval, other than pursuant to a plan of reorganization. Nevertheless, the life of a tax director is rarely routine during a chapter 11 case, what with handling claims by taxing authorities and structuring a reorganization plan in light of Section 382 and other relevant rules.

Following is a brief discussion of two recurring issues that require attention before and during the bankruptcy period.

Trust Fund Taxes: Personal Liability

Under various federal, state, and local laws, corporate officers, directors, and other responsible persons may be held personally responsible under certain circumstances for the failure of the corporation to pay employment, withholding, sales, use, and other "trust fund" taxes. Because taxing authorities generally are prohibited from collecting prepetition taxes from a debtor corporation during the pendency of a chapter 11 case, but are not prohibited from collecting them from a corporate officer, it is of crucial importance to these responsible individuals that the corporation's liability for all such trust fund taxes be paid in full up to the time that a chapter 11 petition is filed. This can be a tricky proposition, such as in the case of a corporation with retail sales (and sales tax obligations) in numerous states. The threat of tax collection activity against a corporation's officers can be a severe distraction to the company's business operations and reorganization efforts.

Deductibility of Expenses

Chapter 11 tends to be an expensive experience, as outside advisors are necessary to assist with the legal process, claims resolution, creditors, and equityholders committees, developing and negotiating terms of the reorganization, disposing of assets, and the like. To add insult to injury, the IRS has been aggressive in asserting that many of these expenses are not currently deductible for tax purposes. The basis for the IRS position is that the Tax Code generally requires the capitalization of expenses whose benefit is intended to extend to future years. Thus, the IRS has argued that any expenses that would not have been incurred but for the bankruptcy should be treated as incurred for the purpose of facilitating the reorganization and long-term recovery of the company, and therefore are not deductible.

While the IRS position as thus articulated probably is extreme, the extent to which expenses are deductible undoubtedly depends on the particular facts and circumstances, as well as on the debtor's ability to support an allocation of the expenses to deductible items. It is clear that the continuing ordinary and necessary expenses of running the debtor's business are deductible, even during the bankruptcy period. It is equally clear that expenses directly related to the bankruptcy filing and the formulation of a confirmed reorganization plan are not deductible. The treatment of other bankruptcy-related expenses is less certain. It is thus crucially important that a debtor corporation require its attorneys, accountants, investment bankers, and consultants to allocate their fees with exactitude among the tasks performed and that the debtor reflect this allocation on its tax returns. Our recent experience has shown IRS auditors to be aggressive in disallowing any deduction that smacks of a general bankruptcy expense, but more flexible regarding an expense that would be deductible in a nonbankruptcy situation.

CONCLUSION

The tax issues that are faced by troubled and bankrupt corporations can be complex and frustrating; yet proper planning often can mitigate problems, or create opportunities. Early attention to tax issues can help facilitate the reorganization process and, in some cases, ensure its success.

NOTES

1. An excellent and comprehensive analysis of the technical issues touched on here can be found in Gordon D. Henderson and Stuart J.Goldring, *Failing and Failed Businesses* (New York: Panel Publishers, 1998).

2. Except as otherwise indicated, "C" in each example is a calendar-year domestic corporation that has not elected to be treated as an S corporation.

3. Actually, COD income is determined by reference to the "adjusted issue price" of the debt which, in the case of a debt instrument without original issue discount (OID) generally will be the face amount of the debt plus accrued interest.

4. The "stock-for-debt" exception to COD income for bankrupt corporations was, sadly, repealed in 1993.

5. The calculation of these consequences can be dramatically affected by the OID rules, a discussion of which is beyond the scope of this chapter.

6. A G reorganization also can take the form of a spin-off (divisive) or a triangular merger (acquisitive).

19

The Retail Industry—
Trends in the Next Century

Kevin Regan

PricewaterhouseCoopers LLP

INTRODUCTION

In 1960, the *New York Times* reported that there were 600 shopping centers in the United States and that, the newspaper said, was clearly enough. Today, according to *Shopping Center Today*, the monthly magazine of the International Council of Shopping Centers, there are approximately 44,000 shopping centers in North America. They registered about $1 trillion in sales in 1997 and employed more than 11% of the domestic workforce.

Looking at the industry from a real estate perspective, the current per capita retail space in America is close to $20 per square foot (Dallas leads the parade at $29 per square foot). The country that most closely resembles the United States in retail real estate investment is Great Britain, at $2.2 per square foot. What's wrong with this picture?

Since the end of World War II and up to the late 1980s, the dynamics of the American economy fostered the belief, so well portrayed in the movie *Field of Dreams*, " . . . If you build it, they (customers) will come." By the end of the 1980s, the consumers were spending everything and saving practically nothing during a flourishing economy. Marginal retailers were able to open more stores, often unprofitably, while facing stiffer competition from discount powerhouses such as Wal-Mart and Target and emerging category killers. These retailers were blinded by the fact that the prospect of retail sales growing appreciably faster than overall gross national product (GNP) could not continue much longer. The shopping frenzy had to come to an end.

During the early 1990s, an economic downturn showed signs supporting a bold 1990 prediction by *Management Horizon* that by the end of the 1990s half of today's retailers would not be in business. Despite a sustained economic boom, during the mid- to late 1990s, as evidenced by several years of stock market growth, most channels in general retailing have been struggling, as shoppers stopped going to stores in record numbers. This was evidenced by accelerated consolidations, bankruptcies, and constant reinvention by the survivors, which were often the high-performance leaders in their specialty. The single most important long-term factor driving bankruptcy today is the oversupply of real estate. Another of the primary causal factors is the fact that the ever-dynamic retailing industry has reached maturity.

THE RETAIL LIFE CYCLE

What is meant by an industry's reaching maturity? The answer requires that one understand the concept of a business life cycle. There are four major stages that make up the retailing life cycle, which is illustrated in Exhibit 19.1.

- *Introduction.* The first stage, which is also referred to as the "pioneering" stage, is embodied in the notion that a new way is being offered to satisfy a new or existing need. This is the stage embraced by the entrepreneur whose vision is limited only by what can be afforded in testing a new concept. Since new test concepts require relatively minimal capital, retailing is a familiar industry to the entrepreneur. However, just as it is easy to engage in a new retail concept, the success rate of startups is low, and the incubation period is typically demanding on the risk-taking visionary. The challenge of the retailer during this phase is to attempt to change the consumer's purchasing habits and attitudes.
- *Growth.* The second stage is characterized by market acceptance. Because retail concepts are easily replicated, successful new ideas are quickly

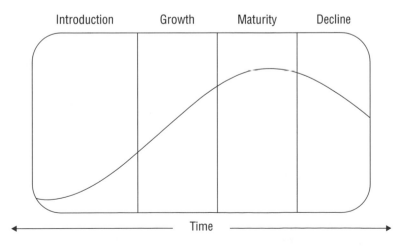

Exhibit 19.1   Retail Life Cycle

copied by "me-too"–type opportunists, often in noncompeting markets around the country. A somewhat recent example of this replication phenomenon was the rapid growth of the office products superstore concept. Within three years of Staples' first store launch, followed closely by Florida-based Office Depot, there were close to 15 office product superstore operations throughout the country. During this phase, a severe shakeout eventually follows near the end of the cycle, due to intense competition and eventual cannibalism. Ultimately, the strong firms, with strong brand loyalty, survive and move on to the next cyclical phase.

- *Maturation.* The third stage, also referred to as the saturation stage, is evidenced by stable sales volume for the given retail channel. In this phase, all segments of the market are reached and saturated. During this stage, sales rise during good economic times and fall when times are depressed. Retailers try to differentiate themselves by private label branding, item or category dominance, and proficient marketing and servicing at the store. Consolidation among the competitors often begins to take place during this stage. At maturity, an oligopolistic situation becomes common, where a handful of firms dominate the market, while economies of scale inhibit any newcomers. An example of this is the current dominance in mass merchandise retail by Wal-Mart, Kmart, and Target, which combined to record $171 billion in 1997 sales—approximately 70% of the discount retail channel. The survivors in this third stage have established their logistical channels, their general product assortments, and their servicing levels, while the customer has achieved a certain comfort level.

- *Decline.* The final stage is reflective of declining sales on a continual basis. The pace of the decline depends in part on the alternative retail channels offered to the customer. Nevertheless, any adverse conditions will only hasten the demise of the retail channel. The classic case of an obsolete channel of distribution is the old downtown variety store, with its rows of bargain tables featuring low-priced consumables, health and beauty aids, and crafts. The recent demise of Woolworth, McCrory's, and Ben Franklin stores points to ideas that outlived their original purpose, while Kmart judiciously reinvented itself from its Kresge variety store strategy to its more successful suburban discount store strategy.

THE RISE AND FALL OF THE DEPARTMENT STORES

An industry segment that has journeyed through the retailing life cycle and is currently in the declining stage of its life cycle is the department store segment. In fact, it took the department stores over 140 years to cycle through their four life stages, while new retail concepts may cycle through all four life cycle stages within 10 years.

A brief history of the department store industry illustrates the cycle vividly.

1840–1950s

The first American department store was most likely A.T. Stewart & Co., built of white marble, in New York City, around 1846. A popular landmark, known as the Marble Palace, drew visitors from around the world.

As the Industrial Revolution brought people to the cities after the Civil War, and mass production of quality merchandise resulted in affordable pricing, department stores such as Macy's and Wanamakers became the favored shopping emporiums. By the end of the nineteenth century, there were 1,000 department stores throughout American cities.

In 1929, several of the principals of the leading stores agreed to set up a holding company to help improve the efficiencies of their businesses. However, the holding company originally had no headquarters and no formal authority to run the different retailers. They named the holding company Federated Department Stores. Other ownership groups followed, including Allied Stores Corporation, Associated Dry Goods, and May Department Stores.

In 1945, Federated decided to centralize power under the direction of Fred Lazarus. Offices were established in Cincinnati, where central functions such as finance, mergers and acquisitions (M&A) strategy, and research were conducted. Acquisitions ensued, beginning with Foley's in Houston, followed by the Boston Store (Milwaukee), Sanger Harris (Dallas), Burdine's (Miami), and Goldsmith's (Memphis).

During the 1950s and 1960s, the department stores followed their customers to the suburbs. The branch store concept became the growth strategy, as land was plentiful. Shopping malls became the denouement, with department stores featured as low cost anchors, while the developers made their money by renting space to the specialty store operators.

However, while malls were being situated at highly trafficked suburban crossroads, convenient neighborhood strip centers, featuring local supermarkets, drugstores, and local specialty shops, were being developed as well.

1950–1960s

As the flight to the suburbs continued into the 1970s, the downtown department stores saw a deterioration in store traffic. At the same time, the growth of the generic credit card, the forerunners of Visa and Mastercard, affected the customer buying habits as well. Instead of being locked into a private-label credit arrangement with your favorite department store, the generic card opened the shopping alternative to the neighboring mall-based specialty stores, whose customers were often the younger generations, who did not want to shop where mom shopped. In short, the mall became a horizontal department store.

While department stores had grown to over 4,000 stores during the 1950s, their creativity led the way for the emerging discount store channel when they introduced their bargain basement stores, such as Filene's and Gimble's. This new format carried the department store's irregulars, overruns, and second-quality merchandise on bargain tables in their basements. The next generation of discount department store was exemplified most notably by the independent operator E.J. Korvettes, in the New York metropolitan market. They carried both hard goods and soft goods for the masses, in large, 100,000 square foot locations. Other regional discount stores began to start up in earnest around 1960, most notably in the Northeast, California, and even around Bentonville, Arkansas. These stores were self-service and offered first-quality branded hard goods at bargain prices.

1970s

During the 1970s, as the discounters became firmly entrenched in the suburbs, the department stores jumped on the bandwagon and began acquiring or starting divisions of their own. Associated had Caldor and Venture; Strawbridge and Clothier owned Clover; Federated started Gold Circle; and Dayton Hudson launched Target. There were others.

The evolution of mail order developed into a more formidable shopping alternative as well during the 1970s. Mail order dated back to the late nineteenth century, where both Sears and Montgomery Ward reached the rural populace, which was 70% of the domestic population, with an assortment of goods that small town shops could not carry. Throughout rural America, JCPenney, Sears, and Montgomery Ward followed suit with combination stores and order fulfillment centers in county seats. More recently, specialty apparel catalogs from Maine (L.L. Bean) to Washington state (Eddie Bauer) and specialty products from farm supplies to home health devices began to offer customers a convenient home shopping alternative. The development of overnight package delivery eventually spurred on cable TV shopping, the forerunner of E-commerce. As a result of this home shopping movement, the department stores also began to experiment with mail order catalogs.

1980s

As the 1980s arrived, even though department store chains, discounters, and specialty store groups continued to open as new malls were built throughout the country, the real excitement was taking place outside the malls. Category-dominant superstores like Toys "Я" Us, Home Depot, and Circuit City; closeout stores like TJ Maxx, Marshall's, and Ross Stores; and warehouse clubs like Price Club, Costco, and Sam's Club emerged and challenged the pre-eminence of the department and discount stores due to their varied appeal to the customer. These stores provided unprecedented selection and deep discount prices due to improved logistical efficiencies. Superstores grew to $550 billion in annual sales, or fully one third of the nation's retail revenues in 10 years flat.

Another example of a retail format that took shape during the mid-1980s to challenge the department store, and proliferated in the early 1990s was the outlet mall. Large enclosed and strip center malls were located a hundred or more miles away from major metropolitan areas, featuring up to 100 manufacturer's and retail brand name stores, selling department store overruns, irregulars, and the like at discount prices, along with local and fast food eateries that encouraged a full–day outing and shopping spree in the country.

Allied, Federated, and Macy's—a Surprising Combination

Growth in retail real estate continued at a frenzied pace, rising by 30% between 1986 and 1995, reaching 5.0 billion square feet. The department store segment was encountering a new dilemma, as consolidation became the watchword in the industry. In 1986, a new breed of investor appeared on the horizon. Easy access to high-yield debt, in the form of junk bonds, opened the retail acquisition and consolidation game to financiers and real estate developers. The investor with the greatest notoriety at the time was Canadian real estate developer Bob Campeau. In 1986, he successfully completed a hostile takeover of Allied Stores. At that same time, May Department Stores acquired Associated Dry Goods, and Macy's had gone private. However, the Allied strategy was different. Here, the acquirer's strategy was to sell off its noncore holdings while keeping a small number of cash flow–producing department store divisions. By the end of 1987, Campeau had sold off 16 of the 24 Allied divisions for $1 billion, while leaving a $3 billion company in sales, generating an earnings before interest, tax, depreciation, and amortization (EBITDA) of $373 million. Campeau's investment was $350 million. In short, it appeared to be a very successful deal. But Campeau did not stop there. In January 1988, he announced a tender offer for Federated. Joining him in the foray was Macy's, who agreed to purchase Federated's California businesses for $1 billion in order to eliminate some of the overlap with Allied Stores. Campeau also sold Foley's and Filene's to May Department stores for $1.5 billion to reduce its acquisition debt. Campeaus's strategy in this acquisition was to consolidate the back office functions of the consolidated Allied and Federated chains and to generate cost savings from the consolidation. This centralization strategy would have seemed reasonable if the economy had not started to stagger in 1989. In January 1990, Federated and Allied filed for bankruptcy. Macy's was soon to follow.

What became evident, in hindsight, was the notion that department stores were saddled with high operating leverage. High fixed costs, due to high maintenance costs, expensive service, and the high cost of regional buying, along with unsophisticated technology, translated into significant fluctuations in profitability given small changes in sales. To compound this structural problem, management added financial leverage to the equation, which together increased the risk of financial failure under any economic hiccup or downturn.

While it took two years for Federated to get back into business, by 1992 Macy's hit hard times. Already suffering from the heavy overhead and poor systems common in most chains, Macy's added complexity to its strategy by attempting to attract a new upscale customer. It was lured by the success of Nordstrom's and its newsworthy commissioned sales force. Macy's chairman thought their allure could be replicated. As a result, Macy's lost its focus on its core customer.

In the summer of 1992, Federated offered to acquire Macy's, while in bankruptcy, to help re-engineer their business. The offer was rejected. In December 1994, a second offer for $1 billion more succeeded in creating the largest department store chain in America. May Department stores fell to second place.

In 1995 the industry consolidation continued as Federated acquired Broadway stores, while May acquired Strawbridge and Clothier and Woodward and Lothrop and its Wanamaker subsidiary, who were in bankruptcy.

As recently as 1998, Dillard's acquired Merchantile, while Proffitt's, which had been acquiring small southeastern regional department stores over several years, added the revitalized, upscale Saks label to its stable.

The Industry Segment in Decline

These acquisitions, in general, were designed to increase sales and profitability by increasing buying power and reducing costs through centralized consolidation. Few developers are building new stores in this overstored society. Thus, to sustain growth and to protect markets from better competitors, the stronger chains are forced to buy the weaker chains.

However, while this consolidation has reduced the department store industry to a handful of chains, the preference of today's female shopper for women's apparel has shifted away from the department stores to the "Big 3" discounters, the off-price apparel stores like TJ Maxx and Ross Stores, the mall specialties, and the mail order catalog (see Exhibit 19.2). This trend away from department stores is the cause for this segment's slipping into the final stage of the life cycle.

Exhibit 19.2   Store Preferences for Women's Apparel
(Share of Female Shoppers Buying Women's Apparel Most Often at Store Type)

Store/Store Type	1996	1994	1992	Change 1992–1996
Traditional department stores	13.1%	15.7%	20.6%	−7.5 pp
Upscale department stores	2.5%	2.6%	3.4%	−1.0 pp
Popular price department stores	5.7%	5.9%	5.7%	0.0 pp
JCPenney	10.2%	9.3%	10.4%	−0.1 pp
Sears	4.9%	3.2%	4.0%	+0.9 pp
Kmart	7.3%	7.5%	6.9%	+0.4 pp
Target	3.7%	4.0%	1.9%	+1.8 pp
Wal-Mart	12.8%	11.9%	10.1%	+2.8 pp
Other discount department stores	2.9%	5.9%	6.5%	−3.6 pp
Mall apparel stores	7.8%	8.1%	7.7%	+0.2 pp
Non-mall apparel stores	6.5%	6.1%	5.6%	+0.9 pp
Factory outlet stores	2.6%	2.4%	1.5%	+1.1 pp
Off-price/one-price apparel stores	5.7%	6.4%	3.9%	+1.8 pp
Mail order catalogs	4.8%	4.0%	4.0%	+0.8 pp

Source: 1992, 1994, 1998 Consumer Database, Management Horizons. A Consulting Division of Price Waterhouse LLP.

The once popular allure of the department store has lost ground to changing consumer demands in a growing society where choice is constantly changing.

THE CHANGING AMERICAN DEMOGRAPHICS

Reflecting on the influence of today's customer in the retail environment, one needs to look back at the changing view of the shopping experience over the last 50 years. It was not until the post–World War II era that many Americans had discretionary income. There was a herd mentality during the 1950s and 1960s, when a homogeneous middle-class population moved to the suburbs, surrounded by green lawns, new cars, and home appliances. The new suburbanites were influenced by TV commercials, made by branded manufacturers who controlled the supply chain. Merchandise demand far exceeded supply during this period, so that merchandise was allocated to the retailers while the customer pursued the American dream. The customer was not well understood during that time, nor, for that matter, during the 1970s. Middle America was still growing, and product demand continued to exceed supply. Manufacturers faced new foreign competition, and product quality became a key issue propelling the importance of national brand merchandising. Due to the availability of low-cost debt, retail chains were growing rapidly, by staking their regional markets, due to the availability of low-cost debt. The retailers' focus was on convenience, by offering a wide breadth of merchandise, closer to home. Retailing had become a social event. If one had nothing to do, he or she went to the mall or the nearby discounter.

As time went on, retailers distinguished themselves by their weekly advertised promotions. This led to overcrowded stores, generally on weekends, slow checkouts due to poor store personnel scheduling, erratic service, and frequent out-of-stock conditions of the promoted items. This made the shopping experience more of a chore than a positive experience. During the 1970s, the rise in inflation caused a rise in the cost of living, which brought about the second family wage earner. The fickle middle class was shrinking. Consumers began to place a premium on their time and sought greater control over how it was being used. In short, average consumers were being pressured by time, with limited discretionary income, and were seeking to gain control over their daily life while living in the proverbial rat race.

Mass merchandise retailers' weekly promotional strategies often resulted in chronic out-of-stock conditions, thus conflicting with the customers' desire to control their busy lifestyle. Shopping became a frustrating experience. This opened the door for the successful "everyday low price" strategy that Wal-Mart offered to its customer base. It focused on being in stock. It passed its efficiencies on to its customers in lower prices. In short, it created value—differentiation, convenience, and dependability—for its customers. The 2 to 3% savings in advertising alone gave the customer value that its competition had difficulty matching. The juggernaut became unleashed.

During the 1970s, Wal-Mart grew under the leadership of the infamous Sam

Walton, who was known to fly his single-prop airplane, counting cars in church parking lots on weekends throughout the Southeast to decide where a new Wal-Mart could be located. By the early 1980s, this successful retailer developed over 100 criteria that were the basis for determining new real estate sites. The company included various demographic statistics in their evaluation. Like other more sophisticated retailers, they also began using psychographic market research at the zip code level. They understood that there was a systematic way of how people buy. They understood that people chose to live in neighborhoods where they found compatible lifestyles. Thus, communities with common characteristics and similar consumer behavior patterns could be merchandised with a more focused assortment. As a result, they were better than their mass merchandise competition in carrying desirable merchandise, at competitive prices, in a friendly, convenient, store format. The consumer voted in favor of this "hassle-free" formula by becoming a loyal, frequent shopping customer.

As the 1990s began, the shopping frenzy of the prior two decades subsided. Retailers began to see red ink on their quarterly financials. They responded by cutting prices in order to reinvigorate the shopping frenzy that made them profitable in the past. They wanted to return to the days of explosive growth, when customers just kept coming. Instead, they produced the "perpetual sale" strategy, which impacted margin, while the retailers' costly infrastructure stayed in place. This resulted in a death spiral for many marginal retailers that was not anticipated. The old reliable customer did not respond as expected. This forced retailers to cut costs, close stores, and increase their promotional activity, which further reduced margins, cut costs, closed stores, and so on.

Today, the discriminating customer has become the major focus for the marketing departments in this overstored retailing environment. Retailers are fighting to win back former customers who have gone to the competition by trying to understand their buying habits. Retailers compete for shoppers who have other uses of time and disposable income. The average consumer claims to have 30% less time to shop than just two years ago. Shopping has become boring. Consumers complain that there is too much sameness. The stores all look the same. Uniformity is what is selling. For example, there are 100 brands of bottled water on the market. What is the difference between the Gap jeans versus Levi's, Wrangler, Rider, Polo, Guess, Bongo, Sears, or Penney's private label, really, besides the label, without getting into a two-tiered brand marketing debate. The bottom line is that consumers are demanding change. The real estate developers have responded to this crisis by introducing entertainment into the new and refurbished malls, from movie theaters and ferris wheels, to ice rinks and miniature golf courses.

Besides consumer micromarketing issues centered on ethnic and special niches, retailers today are facing dramatic changes in demographic landscape in the near future. The core customer group of many retailers, households between the ages of 25 and 40, is set to shrink over the next five years. Going forward, demographic growth will be found in the younger segment between the ages of 15 and 24 and in households headed by the more mature 50-and-older age group.

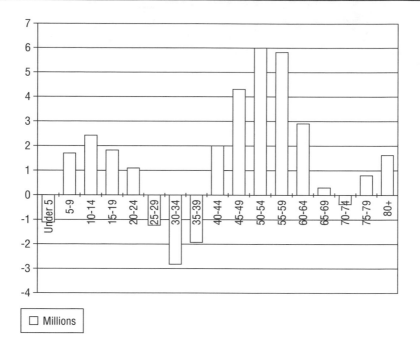

Exhibit 19.3   Projected Absolute Change in U.S. Population, 1995–2005

(See Exhibit 19.3.) Historically, personal expenditures for products peak between 25 and 40, as young adults leave home and begin their own families, thereby needing everything at once.

The growing baby boom segment is entering its peak earning years, which may be good news for retailers. On the other hand, this group has not saved for retirement. They also face other demands on income, including rising educational costs for their children and higher health care costs for themselves and for their parents, who are living into their eighties and longer. The youth wave that will show significant growth over the next several years are growing up in very different circumstances than their parents. They are more urban and more ethnically diverse, and experience a much higher level of poverty and crime. They are growing up in smaller families in which the incidence and aftereffects of divorce are substantially greater. This technologically savvy group will most likely put off independent living and marriage, due to the high costs of education and housing, which are key barriers to household formation. As a result, they have more discretionary income left for spending on items like apparel, entertainment, and food.

Thus, the shift in demographics toward both older and younger consumers may be favorable for certain retail channels. The challenge will be which of the approximately 250,000 retail stores operating in this country will be able to generate sufficient productivity to service the ever-changing demographics.

DIFFERENTIATION AND CONSOLIDATION AMONG RETAILERS

As a natural evolution of a mature industry, there has been an ever-increasing consolidation of retailers. This shifting concentration in most channels, from drugstore and supermarket to mass merchandising and specialty, has also seen the shifting of power away from the manufacturer. A decade ago, the top 100 U.S. retailers represented 30% of nonauto retail sales. Today, they are approaching 40%. With size comes power!

Not only are chains becoming bigger, they are becoming stronger. As the leaders have increased size through mergers, acquisitions, and organic expansion, they have successfully obliterated much of the easy, conventional competition and are increasingly facing off against one another. As a result of this phenomenon, the competitive ante has been raised dramatically, leading to a narrowing of the competitive edge of the industry leaders and a noticeable slowdown in profit growth. Even the giants have been forced to reinvent ways to produce more profitability. Besides the obvious cutting of overhead expenses, by reducing functional redundancies while improving efficiencies through re-engineering, the chains have sought other competitive advantages. Private-label merchandising of commodity products has been a popular strategy, as has service-intense businesses such as pharmacy, optical, and one-hour photo processing at supermarkets, discounters, and drugstores alike. Recently, the large drugstore chains have reverted back to neighborhoods with their stand-alone convenience superstores, with special features like the drive-through pharmacy window.

Another approach to a competitive advantage among the established leaders was to cultivate close alliances with key suppliers. An outgrowth of the popular movement in the 1980s toward the adoption of electronic data interchange (EDI) and quick response between retailers and suppliers, which essentially automated the purchase order and receiving processes, became the basis for companies like Wal-Mart and Procter & Gamble to truly develop a partnership. Today, the two companies share daily sales information at the store level, electronically, in order to improve on the flow of merchandise and optimize inventory levels. This data sharing lowers unnecessary costs for both parties, reduces non–value-added activities, and improves the supply chain efficiencies by means of automatic replenishment. Today, this partnering movement has spawned an overall reduction in inventory levels across the retail landscape. However, not all retailers are created equal.

Those retailers who can write large purchase orders are gaining in channel power and are able to dictate terms of their vendors. The manufacturers are being pressured to bear more of the cost of doing business, as retailers continue to strive to deliver value to their loyal customers. Examples of new demands on suppliers include longer payment terms, customized packaging, vendor-managed inventories, more responsibility for performance on the selling floor, and pay-on-scan. Some retailers are even demanding vendor-supplied custom fixturing.

The leading retailer has discovered that he is the gatekeeper. He can open and close the gate on suppliers that do not meet his demands, whether that is helping control inventory or training the sales staff. The same retailer can also serve the supplier as change agent, by testing new products and shaping consumer attitudes about the products in the stores. However, the large, successful retailers are also vehicles that could open up channels of distribution beyond the domestic market. Many suppliers today have their sights on global brand distribution and seek to increase market share outside the U.S. border.

THE MOVE TOWARD GLOBALIZATION

Today we live in a global economy. While North America generates 26% of the retail revenues out of the 70 countries in which large-scale retailers operate, comprising $7 trillion in 1997 sales, Asia and Northern Europe each have 24% of the global market share (see Exhibit 19.4). Although the United States has 9 of the top 25 retailers in the world, their foreign presence is minimal. As of 1997, JC Penney had the largest international presence by number of countries (12) out of these nine leading U.S. chains. During the same fiscal year, Wal-Mart generated 8% of its $111 billion in revenues overseas.

Faced with a saturated condition, the giant domestic retailers have two choices for sustained growth: either look beyond the current home markets and develop a global presence while testing new store formats domestically, or pursue a multitiered profit model by diversifying into manufacturing, exporting, restaurants, and so forth to leverage their product/distribution knowledge into new profit centers. The leaders are pursuing both avenues.

Like Toys "Я" Us, the Gap, Disney, and other specialty retailers that have ventured beyond the North American borders, the larger-format stores, such as Home Depot, have crossed the U.S. borders as well. While U.S. companies discover increasingly homogeneous global consumers, partly influenced by the end

Exhibit 19.4   World Retail Sales in MVI Regions (Excludes Auto and Restaurant)

Retail Sales in '97 Constant US$ (billions)

Continent	1994	1995	1996	1997	'94–97 CAGR	Share of Total
North America	$1,595	$1,660	$1,763	$1,817	4.4%	26%
Asia—developed	1,464	1,570	1,593	1,730	5.7%	24%
Northern Europe	1,549	1,600	1,579	1,662	2.4%	24%
Latin America	347	478	540	532	15.3%	8%
Southern Europe	355	386	558	495	11.7%	7%
Asia—developing	318	344	399	416	9.4%	6%
Eastern Europe	244	257	270	317	9.2%	4%
Middle East/Africa	81	90	97	95	5.3%	1%
Total	$5,954	$6,385	$6,801	$7,064	5.9%	100%

Note: This includes only the 70 countries where the top 200 retailers operate (about 50% of world population and 90% of GDP).

of communism, which in itself freed one third of the world population to join the dynamics of capitalistic consumption, the ease of transplanting successful U.S. retail formats has been disappointing. Fundamental issues involving managing locally versus globally are difficult concepts to navigate through. It is not good enough to have a broad assortment and the best pricing proposition if the local customs and affinities that generate the customer loyalties are not appreciated. American arrogance has adversely impacted at least one U.S. assault on Europe, where the lack of cross-border procedures and the lack of a global vocabulary has caused major setbacks in a European growth strategy.

U.S. retailers and suppliers alike are in the early stages of developing cross-border supply chains. They are both developing roadmaps to get into the international arena, and lining up alliances within the targeted borders. The specialty chains, in particular, with their flexible formats and superior brands, are making the more formidable market penetrations. However, even in the global arena, there is little that is new very long. As a result, as suppliers gain efficiencies in distribution and team up with their retail gatekeepers, the global retailers need to cultivate a local acceptance that affords them the opportunity to exploit their expertise, thereby becoming increasingly competitive overseas.

RETAILING AND TECHNOLOGY

The world is becoming a borderless marketplace, thanks in part to the meteoric growth of technology. Natural resource-based industrial societies are rapidly disappearing as brainpower industries rapidly emerge. The emergence of the Internet will have revolutionized the way that we view each other.

Technology is undergoing a paradigm change that is affecting most of society today, either at work or at home, through open networking architecture. There are still some stodgy retailers who are struggling with their obsolete, mainframed legacy systems and poorly documented COBOL programs, living in the past when the notion "location, location, location" was pre-eminent. Some retailers today, such as Woolworth (now Venator Group) and Montgomery Ward struggle to capture reliable, timely sales and inventory information because their former management teams failed to understand the importance of feeding information down to the key process managers who ran the day-to-day operations.

Retailers, in general, were slow to grasp the importance of owning historical item purchases and sale at the transactional level for years. Despite the fact that IBM, NCR, and various other technology suppliers had the equipment to allow their retail customers to manage their biggest investment—their inventory—most retailers did not see it. Instead, many retailers installed point of sale (POS) terminals in their stores during the 1970s and 1980s to improve employee productivity and save labor costs, while sales captured by department was a convenient by-product. When bar code scanning was introduced, the supermarket industry jumped on the technology in order to improve efficiencies in customer throughput and minimize the error in keying in item price and quantity. It was not until the mid-1990s that the supermarkets realized the missed opportunity that POS registers afforded in managing store inventories. The other mass retail channels, in general, were also very late and apprehensive in developing extensive informational systems for their companies. Their excuse was the lack of productivity improvement that these companies were able to measure by their investment. Instead, they felt that the capital would be better spent on new locations, since that was the basis for increasing sales growth. Management was forced to change its perception of technology in view of the fact that some of the competition viewed technology as a strategic advantage in managing inventories and targeting customers. Leading retailers began to embrace productivity enhancements through the use of technology. Their ability to improve efficiencies against their competitors spurred the rapid industry consolidation of the 1990s. Wal-Mart is a good example of a company that has been investing in new or improved systems, since the late 1970s, in order to better service their customers, while driving down their operating costs. It has piloted numerous technological tools in its store and logistical environments to improve inventory selection at the local level and optimize service by being in stock.

In retrospect, the mainframe phase of the computer revolution in retailing was a failure in that it produced a central command and control–type top-down environment in the 1970s and 1980s. The lack of research and development (R&D) spending to better manage inventories and supply critical information to decision makers was a myopic decision that has been costly to the old mainframe cultures that remain.

As retailers put workstations on the desks of their day-to-day decision makers and link them into networks so that employees and partners can share information, the opportunity to witness substantial productivity enhancements becomes more evident, and chances to reduce overhead become more apparent.

WELCOME TO THE INTERNET

Retailing has become a business of information and communication. What retailers did not fathom was the potential impact of putting computers in the hands of consumers that could be linked to a giant network. Due to the rapid technological advancement in society, and in particular the Internet, we are fast becoming a world without borders.

Shopping at home is not a new phenomenon, however. Catalogs, direct mail marketers, the Home Shopping Network, and QVC were all retail formats that enabled the customer to shop at home without leaving the living room. Telephone shopping was a primitive form of electronic commerce.

The Internet shopping mode may become the single most important new retail channel in history. It is becoming a genuine worldwide information and direct marketing system. It poses a serious future threat to certain segments of traditional brick-and-mortar retailers, especially certain specialty retailers that have saturated the country. Why the Internet? One reason is that home shopping is preferred by the time-constrained consumer whose rising frustration about time wasted in checkout lines is thwarted on the Internet. Internet shopping will become quick, clean, and painless—no long lines; 24-hour shopping, seven days a week. There are no annoying sales pitches, but a wealth of information on a wide selection of merchandise. There are no geographic constraints. The shopper enjoys privacy and anonymity. From a life-cycle perspective, despite all the current retail participants (34% of all retailers have a Web page and are selling or plan to sell in the next year), the Internet is in its infancy. The formula for success is still being invented. There is no limit to the number of sellers and the investment for an entrepreneur is significantly less than for a brick-and-mortar startup. Today, certain product lines are more prone to be shopped for over the Internet at this early stage. The trust factor, as it relates to the shopper, in terms of reliability of product, service, and security is still emerging. Computers, books, music, flowers, gifts, and travel are more common on-line selections at this stage. However, apparel, particularly the casual and commodity side of this category, should eventually succeed through this medium. Today, apparel is a major segment of the catalog industry, which, according to *Women's Wear Daily*, is projected to generate between $70 and $90 billion in volume by the year 2000. The argument that there is a need to touch and feel products in order to sell them is shortsighted and inane. It stands to reason that the successful catalogers, such as Land's End and L.L. Bean, should do well via the Internet, as long as their graphics compare favorably with the photo quality of their catalogs.

Few retail channels have currently derived the success formula for on-line selling. The grocery industry is struggling with the Internet because of the existing constraint of access to products. Web grocers, who sell dry goods, meats, produce, and the like, are locked into local markets, lack buying advantages, and are constrained by delivery systems and time frames. Their added value is limited to time savings for the busy household. This comparative advantage may not be a sufficient justification in the end. Internet pioneers, such as Peapod, are reformulating their current business plan to devise a price and service advantage by means of operating their own warehouses.

Size does not necessarily ensure success in this new arena either. For example, Wal-Mart is struggling to understand its customer base on the Internet versus its store customer. The average income of the customer on the Internet is $50,000 a year, which is higher than the typical Wal-Mart shopper's. Sears has found its cyberstore customer and its store-profiled customer to be similar. As one can imagine, any discrepancy between customer bases leads to conflicting marketing and pricing strategies.

Other philosophical issues that are discouraging retailers on the Internet relate to the loss of impulse purchases and the issue of pricing. Should the retailer price the same product differently on the cybershop compared to the store? Retailers may also find direct competition from their direct suppliers, who could use the Internet as another distribution channel. In short, there are countless issues that will continue to be addressed as cybershopping grows across all borders. In fact, as domestic retail sales remain in line with our 2 to 3% growth in annual gross domestic product (GDP), the Internet is a major potential source of incremental sales for domestic retailers who do not plan to open stores outside the U.S. border, but can generate sales worldwide. The cyber retailer is not necessarily limited by the notion that retailing is a "zero sum game."

FUTURE TRENDS IN RETAILING

The 1990s have not been kind to retailers. Signs continue to appear in storefront windows featuring "going out of business" sales or "liquidation" sales. As high-performance retailers continue to expand their market share and become immune to the business cycles, the rate of bankruptcy will rise among the ranks of all retailers. Fewer companies will control an ever-larger share of the business.

The survivors will have much in common: progressive management; a skilled sales force whose competencies are reinforced through effective training systems; close alliances with key suppliers; an efficient supply chain that replenishes with speed; information that is accessible at the point where decisions can be made to satisfy the customer; and a culture that embraces customer intimacy. Tomorrow's retailer must build a partnership with the customer. That is a customer mandate. Retailers will have to play by the customer's rules. Management's challenge is to build a customer-focused, learning-centered organization.

The customer will be faced with a proliferation of shopping alternatives. The Internet will begin to displace real estate. Shopping will occur less frequently at conventional outlets, lowering the value of the retail shelf. The focus will be on offering convenience, as time continues to be the customer's nemesis. The notion of convenience will take on a service dimension. In other words, the customer will not tolerate the age-long problems of out-of-stocks, slow checkouts, uncompromising return policies, dirty bathrooms, and deplorable floor help. In fact, a recent survey by Chicago consultant Frankel revealed that 10% of customers will shop elsewhere if they have one bad experience in a store.

Customers today have plenty of choices. Look at the retail alternatives, for example, if one were in need of refrigerated milk, butter, and eggs on the way home from work. One can go to the nearby supermarket, the convenience store attached to the gas station, the local Kmart, the corner super drugstore, or the cheaper, one-stop-shopping supercenter—what is comfortable for the consumer. The growing retail challenge is to create top-of-mind awareness in the consumer's mind, when a need exists. How will retailers manage the customer when products that were once unique can now be found in similar if not virtually identical versions almost anywhere? Today's progressive retailers are looking at customer loyalty programs and customer rewards programs to generate share of wallet and lifetime value metrics on their captured customer tracking systems. Some are also successfully developing premium brands, by using imagery, well-known personalities as spokespeople, and a variety of other strategies to generate a certain mystique around their logo. Although one can argue that any retailer can copy another store's design, product mix, promotional strategy, and customer service philosophy, what is not easily replicable is the unique combination of these attributes into a cultlike following that is enjoyed by a handful of retailers today such as the Gap, Wal-Mart, Home Depot, Victoria's Secret, and Neiman Marcus.

In summary, the retail landscape will continue to shrink as this overstored society finds a new level of tolerance for shopping. As customers see more of the same in different retail venues, the winners in this mature industry will be those retailers that manage their customers' expectations consistently and go out of their way to increase the customers' comfort level within their location, knowing that the alternative is the risk of joining a growing list of retailers that have outlived their usefulness.

20

A New Paradigm Emerges

Jack Barthell, Pat Leardo and Mitch M. Roschelle
PricewaterhouseCoopers LLP

Mercurial market conditions, by definition, precipitate dramatic and widely variant consequences. These cyclical certainties are overt: indeed, the characteristics of bull and bear markets, economic recession, depression, and general fluctuations defy oversight by even the most casual or reluctant observer.

However, market volatility also inspires a more insidious, yet nearly pervasive, psychological effect. Crippling economic downturns seem to drag along a sense of permanence. Protracted economic vigor is shockingly formidable in erasing bad memories. This myopia is natural; in the real estate landscape, it is quite easy to feel invincible on the peaks, and lost in the valleys.

Certainly, it should be noted that market cycles are not entirely repetitive: They do evolve, giving rise to new opportunities, new problems, and, occasionally, new solutions. But the inherently cyclical nature of the real estate market all but guarantees the emergence of patterns. Therefore, the past merits study.

In the early 1990s, the real estate industry seemed to have adopted a motto: "Make it to 1995, if you're going to survive." This statement quite aptly reflected the greatest real estate recession since the Great Depression of the 1930s. More specifically, the early 1990s' debacle was the result of massive overbuilding in the 1980s. Today, almost one half of the Class A office space in the United States was constructed after 1980. The resulting overbuilding was national in scope and was fueled by various factors, including the growing economy, job formation, aggressive lenders, available equity, foreign investment, developers' optimistic assumptions, and other driving factors for new real estate product types, as well as the builders and developers that were enthusiastic about their marketplaces and the never-ending opportunities for new projects.

The predominant source of debt and equity capital in the 1980s was from private sources. In retrospect, it seems that the inherent inefficiencies of the private markets were scarcely considered in the flourish of activity; indeed, they did not incorporate all of the readily available information about then-current real estate supply and demand, nor anticipated supply-and-demand factors, which offered a

416

foreshadowing of the coming bust. Not surprisingly, the boom-and-bust cycle of real estate did reoccur with devastating results. As a result, a new paradigm has emerged for the capital markets.

This nascent "real estate capital market paradigm," so to speak, is the growing influence of public debt-and-equity markets in contrast to predominantly heretofore private debt-and-equity markets. The new model has been characterized as restoring some much-needed discipline to the real estate markets. In fact, it was postulated that the new paradigm would be a panacea for the boom-and-bust, cyclical nature of U.S. real estate markets. We contend that this is not the case. Rather, the new paradigm creates and encompasses a set of variables that indeed must be incorporated in the financing of real estate projects. One need not look far for evidence: the current disequilibrium of commercial mortgage-backed securities, and the inability of real estate investment trusts to attract capital, underscores the evolution and inherent validity of this new framework.

A contextual recap is beneficial here. The 1990s have witnessed a period of striking growth in public debt-and-equity markets. The major form of public debt has been commercial mortgage-backed securities (CMBS), and the major form of public equity has been the real estate investment trust (REIT). The growth has been quite dramatic.

Specifically, in 1990, approximately $4.8 billion of new CMBS issues were sold to the marketplace. At that time, transactions of over $100 million were deemed large. By 1997, $44 billion of CMBS were issued in 105 transactions. Commercial mortgage-backed securities issuances of more than $1 billion had occurred.

Moreover, in the first nine months of 1998, $56.4 billion of CMBS were issued, more than twice the $25.8 billing issued in 1997. In September 1998 alone, a bad month for the CMBS market, volume was up 30% over 1997. (See Exhibit 20.1.)

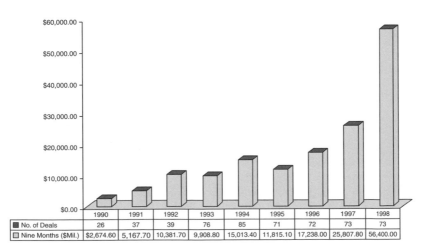

	1990	1991	1992	1993	1994	1995	1996	1997	1998
No. of Deals	26	37	39	76	85	71	72	73	73
Nine Months ($Mil.)	$2,674.60	5,167.70	10,381.70	9,908.80	15,013.40	11,815.10	17,238.00	25,807.80	56,400.00

Exhibit 20.1   New-Issue Three Quarters CMBS Volume (through September 30)
Source: Commercial Mortgage Alert, October 5, 1998.

A nine-month and full-year comparison provide a different and noteworthy perspective. Certainly, growth has been dramatic, and yet the realizability of 1998's full-year number is problematic because there has been a tremendous, unexpected change in the marketplace. To that end, a "credit crunch" on the debt side emerged beginning in late 1998. The strong economy helped this minor credit crunch. (See Exhibit 20.2.)

With respect to public real estate equity in REITs, the growth in year-end market capitalization of REITs has been equally dramatic. In 1990, there was less than $20 billion of market capitalization for REITs. There remain several plausible explanations for the decided reluctance. Public pension funds and other institutions were unsure whether REITs would be viable alternatives to owning equity real estate in their portfolio. It was believed that the REITs track the Russell 2000, a small-cap stock index, and therefore were more appropriate in plan sponsors' equity portfolios as part of the small-cap group. It was also believed there was not enough liquidity and that the growth of the market would not be such to provide adequate float. The forecast that the REIT market capitalization would exceed $100 billion by the year 2000, therefore, was greeted with skepticism.

The skepticism proved somewhat unwarranted. By year-end 1997, REIT market capitalization exceeded $150 billion. Exhibit 20.3 spotlights the rapid growth in year-end market capitalization of REITs.

This growth, however, has likewise been dramatically and unexpectedly undermined. At the beginning of 1998, many REITs were trading at between 1.2 and 1.3 times net asset value. The market was apparently providing value to the REIT stocks for management, going-concern value, and other factors. By midyear, this premium had dissipated. Most REITs were trading below net asset value. Similar to the public debt markets, the public equity markets took a turn for the worse.

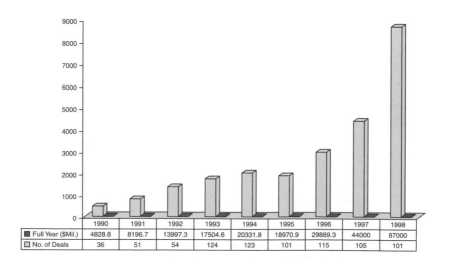

	1990	1991	1992	1993	1994	1995	1996	1997	1998
■ Full Year ($Mil.)	4828.8	8196.7	13997.3	17504.6	20331.8	18970.9	29889.3	44000	87000
□ No. of Deals	36	51	54	124	123	101	115	105	101

Exhibit 20.2   New-Issue CMBS Volume

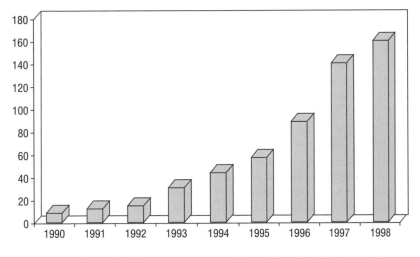

Exhibit 20.3   Real Estate Investment Trusts Year-End Capitalization
Source: NAREIT, March 31, 1998.

WHAT IS HAPPENING?

In December 1997, Bowen H. McCoy republished an adaptation of his article, "Commercial Real Estate Finance Trends," from the May 1997 issue of *Urban Land*. In the adaptation, "Real Estate Capital Markets: A New Paradigm,"[1] McCoy finds that "after surveying the state of the real estate capital markets, it is concluded that the trend toward public markets for real estate capital will continue. . . . This enhanced flow of information could fundamentally change the private nature of real estate finance." McCoy concludes that "over the next five years we will see many of the things we have seen in the past. On the margin, there will be too much capital flowing into real estate, primarily from commercial banks, Wall Street and pension funds. This will carry with it the continual threat of overbuilding in certain markets and locations. In my opinion, the new paradigm in real estate finance is not a dampening of the cyclical nature of the business, but the potential for a much broader and deeper marketplace for real estate capital driven by increased disclosure and information. . . . The millennium could prove to be a golden age for all of us associated with commercial real estate investment."

His comments are indicative of the conventional thinking regarding the new real estate capital market paradigm. Unfortunately, events in recent history have proved conventional thinking to be misguided. In fact, history is replete with examples of conventional thinking about capital markets, and its utter lack of predictive value. This reality now applies to the current real estate market.

A historical reference is surprisingly telling. A survey of capital markets over history indicates that the current status with respect to the U.S. CMBS and REIT markets for real estate debt and equity could indeed have been foreseen. In his 1852 book, Charles McKay, LLD, wrote about *Memoirs of Extraordinary*

Popular Delusions and the Madness of Crowds.[2] In this nineteenth century analysis, McKay points to example after example of mistakes made in what appeared, at the time, to be appropriate capital market conditions. A herd mentality led to a "blind side" in business decision making the size of which a fleet of Mack trucks could be driven through. For example, in the 1640s, "tulipomania" surged through Holland. A single tulip bulb was worth a small fortune. By 1636, tulip bulbs were effectively traded on the Stock Exchange of Amsterdam and the Exchange of London. The net result was not an efficient market mechanism but rather one of speculation and delusion.

In 1711, the South Sea Company was formed in England for the monopoly of trade to the Islands of the South Seas and South America. This capital market program, too, was one characterized by disequilibrium and negative results. Meanwhile, in 1719 through 1770, in France, John Law advanced his "Mississippi Scheme." Numerous companies were formed, including the Louisiana Company, the Mississippi Company, and the India Company. These companies' stock shares were backed by exclusive monopolies to a trade in the vast mineral and other wealth of the New World. It was postulated that "paper currency" such as stocks were highly desirable and could create great wealth. In fact, in France, the scheme led to a February 1720 edict that restricted coinage usage. Many fortunes were made, but ultimately lost, by trading in the shares of these companies. As Robert J. Shiller, author of *Market Volatility*, has said, "Anyone taken as an individual is tolerably sensible and reasonable; as a member of a crowd, he at once becomes a blockhead."[3]

WHAT IS THE MESSAGE?

What does this have to do with real estate? Even a cursory glance reveals that these statements capture, in their sentiments, our current status in the public capital markets. The CMBS market is chaotic. Many financial players rushed in, recognizing the opportunities that could be made in making loans, packaging them, and selling them to the secondary markets. Loans were underwritten at a given fixed or floating rate, packaged into tranches, and, at the appropriate time, packaged and sold to the secondary markets. As the market became more competitive, more loans were written at more competitive rates, and greater warehouse financing had to be undertaken by the issuer.

Recognizing the increasing "efficiency" of the market, it was anticipated that the normal relationships of the weighted average maturity and weighted average coupon (WAM/WAC) (shorter maturities have lower rates and longer maturities have higher rates) would prevail. Greater risks were taken by CMBS issuers in writing more and larger loans, holding these loans, and expanding warehouse borrowings. The new Financial Assets Securitization Investment Trust (FASIT) structure exacerbated the situation.

Unforeseen, of course, was the dramatic flight to quality that pervaded worldwide capital markets as a result of myriad, divergent factors, including the Asian financial crisis, the Russian devaluation of the ruble, and U.S. stock market volatility (all of which converged in mid-1998). This flight to quality affected all types of debt and equity instruments. Risk had not been appropriately measured and incorporated in CMBS pricing. As a result, many CMBS holdings could not be issued profitably. In fact, many were issued at a loss. The largest CMBS issuer, Capital America Partners, required a massive debt-and-equity infusion by its parent company. An interest rate drop, contrary to conventional thinking, put the CMBS warehouse portfolios "out of the money" and precluded issuance.

The REIT market did not fare much better. By mid-1998, concern mounted about the number of unsecured financings REITs were issuing to fund growth. Financial levitation became creative, with REITs issuing senior unsecured notes, medium-term notes, and new convertible preferred stock, in addition to bank lines. Further, discounted portfolios, such as those sold by the Resolution Trust Corporation and successors in interest, were not available. REITs became acquirers, using their shares as currency for the transactions. Overvalued shares could pay for overvalued pricing. The market reacted to such pricing in conjunction with leveraging up of REITs' balance sheets.

One major concern—that the REIT format was a transitory arbitrage of deleveraging real estate balance sheets to provide more attractive equity yields—was realized. The market lost its enthusiasm for REITs. New initial public offerings dried up. REITs began to trade at discounts to asset value. Many equity REITs lost more than 50% of their share market price.

The results were even more devastating for the mortgage REITs. The mortgage REITs had generally followed a strategy more aggressive than but similar to that of CMBS. Rather suddenly, they found themselves holding assets that were under water. Mortgage REITs have begun to file for bankruptcy as of this writing.

The preceding analysis gives us some insight and explanatory power in answering our question, "What's happening?" The "simple" reality is that we are in a real estate bust. This situation, of course, has nothing to do with basic real estate factors, supply and demand. Rather, it has to do with a host of external variables impacting a real estate market that has become dependent on public debt-and-equity capital. We are in a situation that is completely different, but nonetheless sets a precedent for the future. In short, the public debt-and-equity markets are effective, but they do have consequences that have not been anticipated.

WHAT DO WE DO NOW?

The renowned economist John Maynard Keynes said in his Great Theory in 1936, "We have to admit that our basis for estimating the yield 10 years hence of a railroad . . . of a building . . . amounts to little and sometimes to nothing."[4] While we may agree with Keynes with respect to operating companies such as railroads, we heartily disagree with regard to real estate.

Historically, we have been able to grapple with the inefficiencies caused by the private real estate capital market's boom-and-bust cycles. There are legal, regulatory, accounting, tax, and financial consequences to any distressed asset class, and particularly to real estate. We will look at real estate in the new paradigm as we have historically. However, we will look at it taking into account the broader asset advisory and capital market capabilities that are required to deal with these more complex public capital market issues. Strategic planning is now, more than ever, necessary in the real estate arena.

Fundamental to dealing with a hard asset class such as real estate is an understanding of the supply-and-demand economics at the property level in the marketplace. In times of this or any other crisis, the assets have to be examined under an orderly disposition strategy versus the forced liquidation value. The underlying income streams have to be looked at as stabilized asset values as opposed to current destabilized income flows. By matching up an orderly distribution with more stabilized income flows, maximum value can be realized. We apply this disciplined approach in these public market scenarios as well. We analyze and evaluate capital flows to assess public market pricing and liquidity in the short, intermediate, and long terms.

An interesting public capital markets analogy exists. A University of Chicago[5] study found that if the Orange County, California, portfolio had been held and disposed of in a more orderly basis, the county might not have suffered a loss in excess of a billion dollars and, in fact, may have profited. It is the "haste" to deal with the instant that creates or magnifies the potential loss. Just as "extraordinary popular delusions" may lead to the crisis, it is "the madness of crowds" that can lead to suffering a loss.

The new public real estate capital market paradigm is a given. It will continue to grow as do real estate markets themselves. This is but a cycle, and the first such dramatic cycle, in the public capital market finance of real estate. The cycle shows that a balance between public and private capital, both debt and equity, is fundamental to having "efficient" financing of real estate. While private capital, again both debt and equity, had been supplanted by the aggressive "efficient capital market" instruments, such instruments are now on the sidelines. Significant opportunities now exist for private capital to come in and arbitrage on the opportunities presented by the public capital markets' chaos. Private and public capital will assume dichotomous but complementary roles.

In the CMBS, those portfolios that are "under water" need to be repriced. They need to be disposed of. Private capital can purchase these portfolios at an appropriate risk-adjusted price. Due diligence is required to understand the nature and character of the assets, their WAC, their WAM, and their pricing. Portfolios must be analyzed and evaluated and cash flows need to be modeled.

It is well worth noting that there are significant opportunities for profit in the financial restructure. The mortgage REITs present similar opportunities. They have similar portfolio problems, and present not only the opportunity to pick up assets, but also to acquire the "entity value," if existent. They must, however, be studied from an accounting, tax, regulatory, legal, and financial standpoint. Significant resources need to be devoted on a "SWAT-team" basis to assess opportunities. Generally, there are dispositions that will occur rapidly, which will set the stage for market stability with respect to public debt in either CMBS or mortgage REIT formats.

For the public equity REITs, private capital infusions can provide engines for growth. In addition, private capital can look to "slicing and dicing" mixed-use or other REITs that do not rationalize the underlying assets. Further, private capital can potentially acquire entities at discounts to asset value as well as privatize other aspects of the company. Again, on a SWAT-team approach, the accounting, tax, regulatory, legal, and financial aspects of the company must be analyzed and evaluated. The orderly liquidation value and stabilized cash flows of the assets must be rationalized. It is in this manner that the size of the opportunity can best be gauged.

IS THERE A CONCLUSION?

Perhaps there is no conclusion. Nonetheless, some important insights can be derived from this exercise. The new paradigm is not the panacea for real estate's traditional boom-and-bust cycle. The efficient capital markets, like the private markets, will be subject to volatility. In fact, we postulate that public market debt-and-equity capital will potentially be more volatile than the historic supply-and-demand volatility that moves the real estate market. That is, colloquially speaking, the nature of the beast. This presents considerable opportunities for real estate owners, real estate operating companies, and developers who can harness the resources necessary to market time acquisition opportunities and "seize the moment." The public markets will always have a place in real estate finance, but a counterbalance of private market capital will have an equally substantial opportunity in real estate acquisition and development in normal as well as opportunistic times.

NOTES

1. Bowen H. McCoy, "Real Estate Capital Markets: A New Paradigm," *Urban Land*, vol. 56, no. 5, pp. 20-22.

2. Charles McKay, *Memoirs of Extraordinary Popular Delusions and the Madness of Crowds*, Office of the National Illustrated Library, London, England, 1852.

3. Robert J. Shiller, *Market Volatility*, MIT Press, Cambridge, MA, 1989.

4. John Maynard Keynes, *The General Theory of Employment, Interest, and Money*, Prometheus Books, 1936.

5. University of Chicago Study by Professor Merton Miller. Study commissioned by Merrill Lynch, 1996.

21

Merger and Acquisition Strategies for the Distressed Company

David R. Williams and Sudhin N. Roy

PricewaterhouseCoopers LLP

You are the president of a prestigious Fortune 500 company and have just completed the most critical board meeting in your impeccable 20-year career with the company and you find yourself staring out the tenth-floor window of your new corporate offices. You have dealt beautifully with significant problems in the past, but now you are at a complete loss on how to deal with the fact that your directors have mandated that you somehow resolve the company's current financial crisis while at the same time preserving shareholder value and interests. It's not that you haven't tried . . . You and your entire executive team and investment banking firm have spent three months preparing and presenting an in-depth strategic plan in an attempt to raise new equity capital. Unfortunately, the capital markets are not very interested in your new strategic plan. Your only option seems to be with an investor who is demanding significant and potentially detrimental equity terms, which could wipe out the current shareholders. To make matters worse, your current lenders are "tapped out" on their lines and will not even return your phone calls. Your chief financial officer is desperate for liquidity and is threatening to accept an offer from a competitor. Furthermore, your entire executive team is fatigued by the road shows and are becoming nervous about the viability of the company . . . but they still believe in you, as does the board.

There are no more free spin cards, mulligans, or get-out-of-jail-free cards. You are out of time and, potentially, options. What can you do?

For starters, don't jump. Unfortunately, this situation is not unusual and likely could have been avoided. The strategy used by the president required substantial resources devoted to a potential payoff that could have been significant; however, history would indicate his chances were slim at best. Raising capital in a distressed environment, in the form of equity or unsecured debt, is not a recommended merger and acquisition (M&A) solution, although it is pursued by most executive teams. It is human nature to use a strategy that worked in the past. Unfortunately, this is exactly the reason this strategy should not be followed. The operational and economic environment at a distressed company changes substantially from the time equity capital was previously raised. The recommended M&A solution requires a focus on core business units, the sale or liquidation of noncore assets, or the sale of the company, if necessary.

Basically, the president and executive team did not allow substantial time or resources to resolve their liquidity crisis. Two or even three months of liquidity is not adequate to implement basic reorganization strategies. This may sound intuitive, but factors leading to troubled situations do not occur overnight and should not be ignored. Early recognition of a problem by the president could have been paramount to the success of the remedial actions necessary to restore the company's short-term liquidity and, ultimately, its long-term health. If all had gone according to a plan we will discuss later in this chapter, the president may have realized the optimal value for the various constituents involved through an M&A solution. An M&A solution would not have been the only remedial direction or option available; however, it may keep one off the ledge.

The purpose of this chapter is to outline the conditions precedent to an M&A solution such as understanding some predominant symptoms or early warning signs of a distressed company, the benefits of early identification of a troubled situation, and the organization of the advisory team. We will then discuss various alternatives of accessing short-term liquidity, several longer-term strategic alternatives to maximizing value, and some of the methods of implementing the M&A solution. Finally, we will define and provide examples of certain M&A solutions considered effective.

For illustrative purposes, a fictitious subprime automotive financing company ("Second Chance Finance") is highlighted throughout this chapter to demonstrate how the alternate strategies could potentially succeed or, conversely, fail. To set the stage, an abbreviated background on the subprime automotive financing industry is necessary.

Second Chance Finance—Background

In the mid-1990s, the sub-prime automobile finance industry was a Wall Street darling. One hundred percent earnings growth rates were not uncommon as capital poured into the industry in the form of warehouse lines, asset securitizations, and bond/equity offerings. There was a euphoric atmosphere surrounding the industry. Not only was lending money to individuals with less than perfect credit histories the fastest growing segment in the consumer finance industry, it also had significantly higher margins than traditional consumer finance.

Many new enterprises formed in this environment, offering easy money. Within a three-year period, in excess of twenty subprime automobile finance

initial public offerings (IPOs) were issued. As the number of subprime automobile finance companies increased almost exponentially and Wall Street
pushed for continual earnings growth, competition for subprime auto loans
grew fierce. Credit quality started to deteriorate as firms were forced to
lower their credit standards to maintain loan volume. Losses started mounting and capital sources dried up.

Second Chance Finance (the Company) was not immune to these industry trends. The Company, which went public with much fanfare three years
earlier, was now facing some serious issues. Its common shares were trading at $0.50, off from a high of $15 just a year earlier. Market capitalization had decreased from $120 million to $4 million, and the Company's
10.25% senior unsecured bonds were trading at a distressed $0.60 on the
dollar. Finally, there was no availability under the warehouse line in the
near future due to a collapse in the securitization market. Faced with
shareholder pressure and the changing financial circumstances of the Company, the board of directors needed to assess its alternatives.

EARLY WARNING SIGNS

Many of the primary symptoms of a distressed company, when considered in
isolation, represent issues that every company may experience at one time or another during their business life cycle. However, the occurrence of a combination
of these factors, or the continual reoccurrence of one or more of these factors,
can force a company into a tailspin. Although these factors can have a very quick
and detrimental impact on the company, they usually do not occur overnight. As
such, it often may be difficult for management to identify the point at which the
company has become "distressed." Having the ability to identify the common
symptomatic characteristics of the distressed situation early in the process is critical to the success of remedial actions the company may elect. Some of the more
common symptoms of the distressed company include:

- Loss of market share
- Loss of top management personnel
- Frequent cash shortages
- Reduced availability of existing bank lines and unavailable additional liq-
  uidity
- Working capital stretched to capacity (current assets are being squeezed
  while current liabilities are being extended)
- Unfocused management
- Loss of key vendors

BENEFITS OF TAKING ACTION EARLY

The ability to identify the distressed situation early not only preserves the critical
value necessary to drive a successful turnaround/reorganization, but may maxi-

mize the residual value for shareholders in the event the company enters into a transaction. Unfortunately, management may not recognize the distressed situation, may be in denial, or may convince themselves that they can correct their course using internal resources. In these cases, the use of cash, time, employees, and lender and/or supplier relationships diverts critical resources to nonstrategic matters, usually resulting in a substantially depleted shareholder value.

Furthermore, early identification provides several benefits, including increased flexibility and options, the ability to maintain control of the process, and, in some cases, the necessary liquidity to continue operations without significant disruption. The following are some of the major benefits of early identification of the distressed situation:

- Additional time is available to evaluate the longer-term strategic alternatives.
- Higher intrinsic value of the company and/or the assets retain higher attractiveness for potential buyers or merger partners.
- Senior executives and board have time to "lock-up" key management personnel with contract and retention bonuses.
- There is an opportunity to obtain support from creditors for a restructuring plan while liquidity is available, thus facilitating an easier restructuring.
- There is adequate cash to sustain short-term operations (through cost reductions, monitoring all payments, and suspending interest, if necessary).

The recurring theme is the preservation of time and value—the time to implement the longer-term strategies and the value necessary to execute the strategies or to maximize return to shareholders.

Once the distressed environment has been identified by the executive or management team, a team of qualified and experienced individuals should quickly be organized to deal with the situation.

BUILDING THE ADVISORY TEAM

An integral part of any solution should include an advisory team organized to develop and implement short- and long-term strategies. The team should consist of key management people and external advisors who can assist with the development, measurement, and implementation of various strategic options. While key management individuals provide the expertise on the operations of the distressed company, outside advisors provide strategic insight in raising debt capital, buying/selling noncore assets, and gaining consensus among the various company stakeholders (creditors, shareholders, lenders, etc.).

Ideally, the advisors should include industry, corporate finance, legal, and restructuring experts. Working in concert with the management team, the industry experts can provide alternative strategies and insight not previously considered by management based on experience with other companies in the industry. The corporate finance specialist can focus on who is buying and selling in this market, assist in raising additional debt capital, restructure existing borrowings, and facilitate the various buy/sell transactions. Legal advisors can provide valuable insight and guidance in negotiating with stakeholders or completing a transaction. The goal of the restructuring expert is to focus on gaining consensus and cooperation among the creditors, lenders, bondholders, and shareholders, with the objective of optimizing the value in the new, reorganized entity for the various constituents.

Once the team has been assembled, one of its primary goals is gaining access to new liquidity sufficient to support the development of a long-term strategic plan.

ACCESSING LIQUIDITY

Even though management may have identified the symptoms early, gaining access to immediate liquidity is usually essential to implementing a longer-term plan. This is true in most cases because creditors typically tighten their control before management can react to the problem. There are various strategies available to procure the additional funds, at least in the short term. The amount of liquidity obtained should be sufficient to execute a transaction consistent with its long-term goals. Typically, these strategies take up to six months to execute. Therefore, the company should obtain liquidity which will last them through this period. Some of these strategies include raising new debt capital, working with the existing lenders, obtaining bridge financing, or selling noncore/excess assets.

New Debt and Equity Capital

Often, management's first inclination is to raise new capital in the form of additional unsecured debt and/or new equity. This may also be the recommendation of the company's current investment banker or director. While raising such capital clearly represents the most attractive solution, unfortunately, it is usually impossible to raise new equity for any company in a distressed situation. Furthermore, it is also unlikely that any unsecured debt could be obtained. The risk related to this option is substantial and customarily expensive. In addition, enlisting investment banks and the senior management required to "road show" the new debt/equity can be time and cash consuming. Pursuing this option may not only prove to be a futile exercise, but often produces no new liquidity while expending valuable, limited company cash and time.

> After raising capital through an initial public offering, a bond issue, and several asset-backed securitizations, Second Chance was no stranger to Wall Street. Instinctively, the Company returned to the street during its financial downturn to try and raise the additional capital it needed. However, its troubled financial situation made this transaction vastly different from its past offerings.

Second Chance's management, not understanding the likely outcome of its efforts, set out on a "road show" with its investment bankers, to 28 potential investors in 11 cities in 6 weeks. Countless hours, valuable resources, and considerable energy was spent pursuing a strategy that ultimately failed. More importantly, the operations of the business deteriorated greatly during that six-week period, primarily due to the lack of focus on operational matters by the traveling chief executive officer, president, and chief financial officer.

Thereafter, Second Chance's liquidity crunch continued to heighten. Furthermore, tensions continued to mount with the Company's bank group as management seemingly reneged on representations that they were going to raise the new capital.

There are other alternatives to procuring liquidity using the company's current resources and contacts, including, but not limited to, working with current banks to secure new funds or to temporarily delay interest payments, obtaining bridge financing from a third party, and/or selling noncore or excess assets. Choosing the appropriate alternative is company specific and depends largely on the resources available.

Working with Existing Banks

One option for the distressed company is to approach its current banks for additional funds. Depending on the relationship with the bank, the distressed company may be able to increase existing credit lines or procure new financing. Furthermore, the company may be able to temporarily suspend interest payments or extend the repayment of credit lines for 60 to 90 days. Often, this option produces little or no additional liquidity, as the relationship with the bank has already been strained due to late or missed repayments. In addition, the bank will most likely be unwilling to provide new financing based on the company's poor financial performance.

If the bank is willing to lend new funds, usually the terms are above market, the covenants are restrictive, and/or additional security is required through the encumbrance of company assets. These new encumbrances and restrictive loan covenants can be a burden in addition to reducing the company's flexibility to sell assets. Furthermore, the bank may require more frequent, supplemental reporting to monitor its risk. Accordingly, unless additional liquidity can be obtained at reasonable rates without restrictive convenants, this option may not represent the optimal alternative when seeking short-term liquidity.

Refinancings

In the event it is possible to raise the new funds, the loan capital will be based on the inherent value of the business. The value of the business will be measured in two forms, the liquidation value of the company's assets and the enterprise value of the company. The liquidation value represents the current sales prices of the company assets, which may represent market value (or often lower) due to the factors surrounding the sale of the assets. Enterprise value, in most cases, represents the discounted present value of the company's free cash flow from continued operations.

Asset-based lenders typically lend based on the liquidation value of the assets being identified as collateral. The liquidation value of the company's assets will be considered the primary source of repayment by the banks in the event the company's cash flows are insufficient to cover debt service requirements. The cost of this type of financing is typically less than other forms of financing.

Special-situation lenders will lend based on enterprise value; however, cost, covenant restrictions, and so forth make this type of capital unappealing to shareholders. Also, covenants associated with existing junior debt (bonds) may have limitations on total senior debt. In such instances, a waiver is necessary from the bondholders, or the new debt can only be incurred in a chapter 11 proceeding as debtor-in-possession (DIP) financing. Obtaining these waivers can be difficult because the individual bondholder groups must agree unanimously on the terms of the new debt. This financing is usually viewed as a bridge facility because it is expensive. It is to be paid off or refinanced typically within 12 months.

There are also inherent risks associated with encumbering additional assets. In exchange for new liquidity, the company opens itself up for increased scrutiny and restrictions by the bank, as well as reducing its ability for a feasible economic plan of reorganization under a chapter 11.

Obtaining Bridge Financing

An additional capital option is to seek bridge financing through or from third-party lenders, often referred to as *special situation lenders* or *vulture investors*. Vulture investors represent quasi-equity investors who often provide high-yield, interim financing to troubled businesses. These investors usually take investment positions in distressed companies by "cashing out" certain creditors. The most likely candidate for "cashing out" would be financial institutions that had loans outstanding at the time of the bankruptcy filing. Banks tend to prefer conservative investments and cannot hold long-term equity positions in distressed companies. The vulture investor will "buy" the creditor's position, usually at a discounted amount, and essentially assume the right to recover the creditor's position. This is becoming a very common strategy for the distressed company to obtain necessary liquidity.

These bridge financings are typically costly since the recoverability risk is high considering the distressed financial situation of the company. These loans are shorter in duration, usually 12 to 18 months, and typically have very high interest rates associated with them. The benefit to the company can be substantial because they now can maintain longer-term flexibility.

Noncore or Excess Assets as Liquidity Sources

As the financial situation deteriorates, the distressed company may also look to raise short-term liquidity through the sale of excess or noncore assets. Most companies have assets that can be sold individually or as a group.

The first step in this process is for the advisory team to identify the company's assets that are not essential to the company's core strategy. These are assets that may contribute to the overall profitability of the company but are not absolutely vital to the long-term viability of the company. Examples include excess warehouse, retail, production/office space, unused equipment, corporate luxuries, and divisions or subsidiaries with businesses that are unrelated to the core business strategy. Another consideration when choosing noncore assets to sell is the effect on loan covenants or restrictions. When considering this option, the team must quantify what pieces can be identified for sale without damaging the core profitability of the company.

Once the sellable, noncore assets are identified, the team must formulate a strategy for selling the assets. If valuing these assets is difficult, appraisals of the assets may be necessary. The financial advisor is skilled at identifying potential buyers and consummating the transaction. It is important for the distressed company to find qualified buyers that have the resources necessary to easily acquire the assets. Ideally, if the company has a substantial number of noncore assets, the option of selling these assets will create enough cash inflow providing the interim financing needed to fund the continued operations of the company during the development of a longer-term strategy.

In addition to the increased liquidity, the benefits of selling noncore assets include the ability to fine-tune the strategy and resources of the core business. Additionally, certain costs could be reduced by eliminating related overhead or administrative burdens. Noted risks of this type of strategy may include management's unintentional divesting of core assets in order to resolve a short-term liquidity crunch. Furthermore, the company may receive less value for the assets sold in the distressed environment if the time available to dispose is limited or a "fire sale" is perceived by the buyers.

Which strategy the advisory team selects depends on the relationship with the current banks, the ability to attract bridge financings, and the resources available. Once the distressed company has access to additional liquidity, the next step is to determine a longer-term strategic plan.

> Second Chance's liquidity had virtually been depleted. Unable to originate new loans, the Company had 26 loan originators sitting around with nothing to do. Management either had to reduce its loan origination staff, which would cause irreparable damage to the Company's value, or find additional funding.
>
> Management desperately pleaded with its bank to provide funds to buy them additional time to secure equity financing. The bank, looking to shore up its position in the event of bankruptcy, took the opportunity to lien up the Company's only remaining unencumbered asset, the residual interest in the Company's securitizations. Estimated to be worth approximately $21 million, the bank was willing to advance $5 million against these soft assets at rates 4 percentage points higher than their existing line of credit.
>
> Believing that they had no other alternatives, management agreed to the bank loan. The Company knew this was only a short-term fix designed to

buy it 60 days. At this time, management realized that the chances of an equity infusion were remote. Unclear as to its next plan of action, the Company hired advisors to help it assess its options quickly.

DEVELOPING THE LONG-TERM PLAN

Once the short-term liquidity crisis has been addressed and sufficient cash is in place to support current operations and pay key creditors, the advisory team can delve into the development of the longer-term strategic plan. The objective of this stage of planning is to develop a longer-term strategy that is feasible, from an implementation perspective, and maximizes shareholder value. It is important for the advisory team to understand the various alternatives available and how the market will perceive the actions taken by the team. Often, the perceptions of the market can impact the success of the long-term plan.

As discussed previously, often the first tendency of a distressed company is to attempt to raise capital through the issuance of new equity. This may be the case, especially at this juncture, because management was successful in securing the short-term funds necessary to maintain current operations. Often, it is perceived that this is the only option to finance the company's ultimate strategy, whether it is a turnaround, a restructuring plan, or a strategic bankruptcy.

Management may believe that the communication of a new and improved business plan will entice new or existing investors to infuse the distressed company with additional capital. Once again, however, due to the distressed nature of the business and the perceived investment risk involved, this is likely a futile pursuit. Unfortunately, valuable resources may be expended, to the ultimate detriment of the company and the shareholders if this strategy is followed.

From a market perspective, an unsuccessful attempt to raise new equity may be perceived by the market as a loss of investor confidence. When management is unable to drum up interest in the new equity, the market might conclude that the company has limited long-term feasibility. As a result, not only has management used their last spin card during this endeavor to raise equity, but future efforts may be adversely affected as well.

Fortunately, there are several strategies or combinations of strategies the troubled company can explore to support the longer-term plan. One strategy is to focus on the core business while procuring favorable financing through a recapitalization, which may include capital restructuring, and/or refinancing of the company's existing debt. Alternatively, the advisory team may want to investigate selling the company as a whole to a strategic buyer.

Recapitalization

In many instances, the benefits of a recapitalization include financial flexibility to support a longer-term plan. There are certain characteristics related to the operations and value of the company that the advisory team should consider in determining whether the distressed company is a candidate for a recapitalization.

Typically, a recapitalization addresses a capital structure imbalance. As such, the company's existing business structure, corporate structure, and management team do not need to be addressed.

A recapitalization can entail refinancing or restructuring the company's debt. Refinancing entails replacing the existing debt through the extension of new debt. Under this scenario, a new, larger loan procured through the existing or new lender/bondholder is used to satisfy the existing debt with additional funds available for use as working capital. Refinancings, typically, are established at prevailing market rates and terms. This is an attractive alternative as it is usually a quick, low-cost method of providing additional liquidity to the company.

Alternatively, capital restructuring involves renegotiating the terms and covenants of existing debt. This process usually begins with the advisory team's contacting the company's lender or bondholders in an effort to refinance or re-structure the company's debt. This may involve the deferment of interest and/or payments, extension of the loan term, reduction of the amount due, or some combination of the aforementioned. Under this scenario, the existing lender may be willing to work with the distressed company due to the risk that the company may ultimately default on the loan. If the troubled company ultimately seeks bankruptcy protection, the lender/bondholders may receive even less than if they had agreed on renegotiated terms. In concession for extending the terms, the lender may require additional liens, security interests in company assets, or eq-uity in the company.

As restructuring relates to bondholders, it may be difficult, if not impossible, to obtain unanimous consent by the many bondholders to restructure the bonds. If the team elects to facilitate the out-of-court alternative, the company may be unable to legally bind all the bondholders. In such situations, an in-court alterna-tive would have to be considered.

Working in tandem with the management on the advisory team, the corporate finance specialist can assist by working with the banks and/or bondholders to ei-ther restructure or refinance the debt, thereby gaining consensus among these constituents to support the company's strategy.

From a market perspective, refinancing debt is a mixed bag depending on the new terms of the refinanced obligation. If the new debt provides adequate liquid-ity and flexibility to carry out a turnaround plan, the markets will look at this transaction very favorably. If the terms are overly costly, restrictive, or do not provide the necessary liquidity, the markets may perceive these actions as a des-perate attempt to secure liquidity despite the consequences. The investment com-munity may lose confidence not only in management's ability to turn around the business, but may become more discouraged when it discovers that management has little or no support from its bank/bondholders.

Selling the Company

There are certain criteria that the advisory team should evaluate in determining whether the distressed company is a candidate to be sold. The primary criteria are as follows:

- Ability to access necessary capital on a "stand-alone" basis
- Ability to generate positive cash flow from operations
- Ability to maximize value on a stand-alone basis relative to amounts paid by potential buyers.

The sale can assume different forms, from a complete sale of the company to a liquidation of the assets, depending on valuations under various business profiles. Further, potential buyers could include strategic and financial investors. For the advisory team to evaluate which type of buyer it should be pursuing depends on various company characteristics and the interests of the constituents involved, including creditors, board of directors, and shareholders.

Selling the Company to a Strategic Buyer. Typically, strategic buyers have lower hurdle rates and take a longer-term view on their investment. This allows them to pay higher values relative to financial buyers. However, for strategic buyers to have an interest in the company or the assets being sold, there must be a strategic fit and long-term market positioning advantages. Some of the conditions under which sales to strategic buyers typically happen are as follows:

- Synergies exist for strategic buyers
- There is a lack of confidence in existing management
- Creditors have a strong reluctance to continue lending to the company
- The ability to restore profitability on a stand-alone basis is limited
- Assets/company have long-term value due to positioning within the industry

Given these characteristics, a strategic buyer may represent a feasible alternative to the distressed company. A corporate finance advisor can provide access to potential buyers around the world and assist with the sales transaction.

Selling the Company to a Financial Buyer. Financial buyers typically are buyers under circumstances in which strategic investors do not show interest in the company and its assets. They have a shorter-term outlook, with defined exit strategies, and have a higher hurdle rate for their investments. The characteristics that typically prevail in situations in which a company or its assets are sold to a financial buyer are as follows:

- Management strength
- Cash-flowing assets
- Depressed valuations
- Minimal synergistic value for strategic investors

Second Chance had 60 days of cash and few alternatives to choose from, especially as there was a remote chance of any equity infusion. Several key employees were gone, and resources were low. Market news was negative, and hopes of turning the Company around were gone. To compound the situation, shareholders had lost confidence in management and were looking for a way out.

With the assistance of the recently hired advisors, the management team assessed the eleventh-hour situation and determined that finding a strategic buyer was the best alternative for all involved. The ultimate buyer identified this opportunity to purchase the assets of Second Chance as a low-cost method of acquiring an automotive financing portfolio to expand its own line of products. Cash was paid for the loan portfolio and for the systems used to service the portfolio.

The management of Second Chance, with the assistance of the advisors, consummated the transaction and distributed the cash proceeds to the creditors. As a result, the creditors received only a portion of what they were owed, while the shareholders did not receive anything.

CONCLUSION

Financially distressed companies have several alternatives at their disposal that can be employed to assist in the emergence from its financial crisis. Frequently, if the situation is addressed early and the correct resources are in place to strategize a plan to secure short-term funds while developing a longer-term plan, a distressed company has an increased chance to regain its financial strength and in many cases, return to financial health. This approach not only assists in the preservation of value to support a longer-term plan, but also increases the return to the constituents involved.

There are several warning signs that a company should be able to identify to detect the often illusive, but impending financial difficulties on the horizon. Loss of market share, loss of top management personnel, frequent cash shortages, and loss of key vendors are several examples of these warning signs. Early identification provides increased flexibility with financing options as well as the preservation of precious time and company value to support a longer-term plan.

Once the crisis has been identified, a distressed company needs to quickly assemble a team consisting of current management, an industry expert, a corporate finance specialist, legal counsel, and a restructuring expert. Each of the respective professionals will bring unique skills to the company and allow for a smoother, more cost-effective turnaround by more quickly gaining access to new liquidity to support the development of a long-term strategic plan.

Once established, the advisory team should target short-term financing options to maintain its business operations while developing a longer-term strategic plan. The three primary methods through which a company can generate the liquidity it needs for short-term strategic plans are working with existing banks, obtaining bridge financing, and selling noncore or excess assets.

The first option, to work with existing banks, is beneficial to the company because a relationship already exists between the company and the bank. However, unless additional liquidity can be obtained at reasonable rates without restrictive covenants, this option may not represent the best alternative. The second option, obtaining bridge financing, is beneficial to the company because it allows for long-term flexibility; however, it is usually at the cost of higher interest rates. The third option, selling noncore or excess assets, can be a viable alternative, providing immediate liquidity while allowing the management to refocus resources back to the core business. One risk the company needs to avoid is selling core assets or violating loan covenants through the sale of noncore assets.

Once short-term financing is in place, the distressed company needs to evaluate and implement a longer-term M&A solution. It is imperative that management understands the various alternatives and how the market will perceive the company's actions, as such perceptions can affect the success of the long-term plan. One alternative is to pursue a recapitalization, which may include restructuring and/or refinancing the company's existing debt, while refocusing resources on the core business. Another option may include selling the company to a strategic or financial buyer. In determining which path to take, management needs to assess the various attributes that promote one alternative over another.

Capital restructuring or refinancing provides the additional financial flexibility to support a longer-term plan. Refinancing can be a quick, low-cost method of providing additional liquidity to the company, provided the bank is willing to work with the company. Capital restructurings may involve the renegotiation of terms and covenants of existing debt, including the deferment of interest payments, extension of the loan term, and reduction of the total amount due. When possible, these alternatives should be accomplished out of court, in order to minimize negative perceptions about the company, its reorganization plan, and the company's ability to achieve success under the plan.

Selling the company may be the recommendation of the advisory team. An M&A solution first requires that the team determine whether the company is, in fact, a suitable candidate to be sold. The sale of the company can take several different forms, including selling the company to a strategic buyer whose primary interest is the company's assets and/or product line. Conversely, the financial buyer is looking for a high-potential investment opportunity with little or no involvement in the day-to-day operations of the company. The corporate finance advisor can provide expertise in locating potential buyers and consummating the transaction.

You slowly back away from the ledge and decide to take action. You call your executive team into the boardroom and order coffee. You begin to describe your ideas, which are completely different than those strategized before by the investment bankers and the executive team. Discussions about your ideas of assembling an advisory team to raise short-term capital and develop a longer-term plan to maximize shareholder value begin to buzz around the room. You see nods . . . they're still behind you. Plans begin to take shape and phone calls are made.

Two hours later, you walk out of the boardroom looking forward to tomorrow. Best of all, you didn't even need the mulligan . . . maybe you'll even play a round of golf if all goes well.

Index